THE
PRUNE
B·O·O·K

THE PRUNE B·O·O·K

THE 60 TOUGHEST SCIENCE AND TECHNOLOGY JOBS IN WASHINGTON

JOHN H. TRATTNER
THE COUNCIL FOR EXCELLENCE IN GOVERNMENT

SPONSORED BY
THE CARNEGIE COMMISSION
ON SCIENCE, TECHNOLOGY, AND GOVERNMENT

Madison Books
Lanham•New York•London

Madison Books
4720 Boston Way
Lanham, Maryland 20706

3 Henrietta Street
London WC2E 8LU England

Distributed by National Book Network

The paper used in this publication meets the minimum requirements of American National Standard for Information Sciences—Permanence of Paper for Printed Library Materials, ANSI Z39.48–1984.♾™
Manufactured in the United States of America.

Library of Congress Cataloging-in-Publication Data

Trattner, John H.
The Prune Book : The 60 Toughest Science and
Technology jobs in Washington / John H. Trattner.
p.   cm.
1. Government executives—United States.
2. Executive departments—United States—
Officials and employees.   3. Administrative
agencies—United States—Officials and employees
4. Science and state—United States.
5. Technology and state—United States.   I. Title.
Q149.U5T73   1991
353.07' 4—dc20   91-35960 CIP

ISBN 0–8191–8419–5 (cloth, alk. paper)

British Cataloging in Publication Information Available

CONTENTS

FOREWORD

The United States government is the single largest user of science and technology in the world. It is the largest employer of scientists and engineers in the United States and probably the world. It is far and away the world's leading supporter of research and development in science, engineering, and medicine. The decisions the U.S. government must take that rely upon expertise in science and technology, and that affect the nation's scientific and technical enterprise, ultimately come together in the hands of a few score individuals serving in positions of great responsibility in the Executive Branch and the Congress. In this book the Council for Excellence in Government chronicles these jobs and the frustrations, challenges, opportunities, and satisfactions they offer.

When the Carnegie Commission on Science, Technology, and Government decided to sponsor the writing of this book, it had several purposes in mind. The book should increase the appreciation in all sectors of our society, the scientific community, and the general public of the importance and pervasiveness of science and technology in modern government. It should assist present and prospective incumbents of these positions to understand their obligations, relationships, and priorities. Of special import, it should help leaders in the White House and the Executive agencies who propose high-level appointments, and those in the Senate who approve them, to specify the kinds of individuals who may be most effective, and to act quickly and responsibly in filling positions.

The Carnegie Commission was established in 1988 by Carnegie Corporation of New York to help governmental institutions anticipate, weigh and take advantage of the unprecedented advances in science and technology that are transforming the world. Nothing could more vividly portray the transformation of government in the past few decades than the job descriptions in this book, which take us from launching missions in outer space to assuring the safety of the food we eat.

We are grateful to the book's author, John H. Trattner, of the Council for Excellence in Government, and to the president of the Council, Mark A. Abramson, for their initiative and diligence in preparing the book. On behalf of the Commission, a highly experienced review group including Rodney W. Nichols (chair), Norman R. Augustine, William O. Baker, Alan K. Campbell, Robert A. Frosch, John P. McTague, and Jesse H. Ausubel (study director) provided advice, assistance, and encouragement. David Z. Robinson, the Commission's executive director and a veteran of government science service, welcomed the initiative and oversaw the arrangements.

William T. Golden   Joshua Lederberg

Co-chairmen,
Carnegie Commission on Science, Technology, and Government

ACKNOWLEDGEMENTS

Several individuals and institutions contributed invaluably to this project.

Thanks and gratitude go first to the sponsor of the book, the Carnegie Commission on Science, Technology, and Government. In a breakthrough era for science and technology, the Commission believed the book would assist its task of helping strengthen the effectiveness of government's role. To that end, it provided generous support, steady encouragement--and a rewarding challenge.

The book owes an important debt to members of the Commission's review panel, which assessed the draft material with objective, wise and experienced eyes. This undertaking was admirably coordinated by Rodney Nichols, chairman of the group and a member of the Commission's advisory council, and Jesse Ausubel, the Commission's director of studies. Throughout the production of the book, both of them also supplied particularly helpful suggestions, ideas, comments, and guidance.

We are also grateful to The Upjohn Company for its financial contribution to the book, and to Mark Novitch, vice chairman of the company, for his steady and enthusiastic support.

More than 200 people--95 percent of those currently holding positions profiled in the book, plus scores of former occupants and others with informed views--set aside time from busy schedules to be interviewed. We are deeply thankful for their interest, and their ready willingness to share their knowledge, experience, insights and advice. These are the foundation materials of the book.

For the Council for Excellence in Government, president Mark Abramson played the important role in helping set the project in motion, and bolstered it thereafter in countless ways with his customary expertise, energy and skill. Council Chair Frank Weil, father of the *Prune* title and a founding architect of the *Prune* concept, continued the strong support that has marked his role from the beginning.

Monica Andres, associate editor for the project, handled one of its truly crucial and demanding tasks, conducting many dozens of interviews with spirit, sensitivity and intelligence. She was also an adept, eagle-eyed, reliable editor, a discerning sounding board and critic, and a productive researcher. Her work informed and enriched the book, and is warmly appreciated.

J.H.T.
September 1991

PART I

PART I

1

THE CHALLENGE
OF THE
APPOINTMENTS PROCESS

From Benjamin Franklin to Neil Armstrong to Everett Koop, capable and eminent scientists and technologists have served the U.S. government. They and the disciplines they work in represent today a special and inestimable resource not only for society in general, but for society's government.

Where it is government's responsibility to defend and repair, to alleviate and heal, and to find solutions, science and technology (S&T) provide substantial expertise and many of the most important tools. And in government's vital role within America's enormous S&T endeavor--activities that reach into every area of national life--it is scientists and technologists who help government understand and manage that role. It is a broad effort, one that helps meet the challenge both of human need, from AIDS to nutrition to earthquake prediction; and of economic development, as in advanced computing and superconductivity. To broaden national recognition of these truths is one of our major purposes here.

Those responsible for this book believe, further, that the country's continued well-being and progress, and perhaps its survival, depend substantially on strong federal management by qualified people. The American public chooses its presidents with the expectation that they will assemble teams able to carry out the policies on which they were elected. In doing that, presidents need the flexibility to weigh many factors. The professional competence to do a job is only one of these, and cannot alone govern appointments to high federal office. But the *Prune* concept asserts for competence an equal place among the other considerations that shape the choices. It argues that in giving competence full play--in finding the right match between individuals and jobs--the key lies in understanding the jobs themselves.

The present volume seeks to enlarge that understanding by

examining the most critical federal positions at the sub-cabinet level or equivalent through which administrations and the Congress attempt to steer their S&T policies and meet their S&T responsibilities. Statutory language and the uninformative boiler plate of standard federal job specifications offer little information about these positions. They provide few clues to the real dimensions of a job's responsibilities, the resources at its disposal, the contexts in which it functions, or the issues and problems it confronts. It is a gap which this book, like others in the series, is designed to fill. In doing so, we think it can also assist government in the necessary task of assessing the current structure and capabilities of the federal S&T endeavor and determining whether and how to redefine the mission and orientation of individual positions.

Every federal job in Washington is witness to the difficulties of making government run effectively in the late 20th century. Each has its share of workload, frustration and doubt. Few of those who accept senior executive or legislative appointment do not at some later point stop to wonder why on earth they did so. Yet the reasons are clear enough. These positions offer excitement, personal opportunity, change and challenge. Even with no guarantee of delivery on those promises, appointment to a high-level administration or congressional post continues to exert today the attraction that it has held from the beginning. It is an appeal to which motivated individuals of impressive learning, skill, and accomplishment--as well as spirit and imagination--continue to respond.

How long can the country rely on and benefit from this phenomenon? The answer is unclear, and the signs are not reassuring. A fine line exists between federal positions appealing enough to draw such people, and the same positions so hemmed in by professional and personal constraints that they lose their magnetism. For some time, and for a variety of reasons, the federal system has been moving close to that line; in a few instances it has already crossed it.

In the circumstances, there are a number of elements worth some reflection. What is the environment in which the staffing of the government's S&T establishment takes place? What are the points for biologists, physicists, aeronautical engineers or physicians to ponder in agreeing to serve in government? How difficult is it to gain appointment? What proportion of those jobs judged to need people with S&T training and experience are actually filled by such individuals? How long do scientists and technologists serving in appointive positions stay in their jobs? Why do they leave when they do? These and other questions go to the operational and substantive conditions that mold and drive the relationship between S&T professionals and government.

Appointments and Jobs: Pros and Cons

Certain facts of life, good and bad, affect every potential recruit to a senior appointive position. Especially in the executive branch, the negative side of this inventory is long and familiar. In a political system where presidents seek to satisfy a variety of perceived imperatives in staffing the upper levels of their administrations, competition for jobs is not only stiff; it is often not limited to individuals qualified by experience and training. Candidates offered nomination may wait months before hearing anything more. Those who do must also make it through complicated background checks and other kinds of scrutiny, as well as Senate confirmation hearings that can be onerous--or worse.

The survivors of these processes must then gear up for the further, tougher trials of the jobs themselves--long hours, many kinds of pressures including congressional oversight, and the difficulties inherent in running large bureaucracies. The pay is lower in many cases, the costs of living are higher, and burdensome conflict-of-interest rules abound. There is a perennial shortage of operating resources. It puts limits on the reach and imagination with which one can work and--because of barely competitive salaries--on the experience or quality of the colleagues and subordinates one can expect to work with.

Other disincentives to serve in government have perhaps greater relevance to scientists and engineers than to non-technical, non-scientific groups, as some who have studied the situation suggest (see, for example, *Presidentially Appointed Scientists and Engineers: Attracting the Best*, National Academy Press, Washington, D.C., 1991). For lawyers and business people, a tour of government service offers the distinct prize of an expanded circle of contacts. For S&T professionals, however, the decision to go into government for a few years might mean an irreversible career shift toward management and away from research and education.

Again, scientists and technologists considering federal appointment may be more sensitive than others to the value they see placed on their services: if it appears to be lacking, so may the appeal of the prospective job. Further, a physician managing the Public Health Service or a PhD scientist in charge of research at Energy Department may find it harder than a nonscientist to live with the rearranged priorities, routine compromises and other zigs and zags of federal life. And history has shown that ideology of whatever stripe, if pursued too zealously, can be an especially stifling drag on scientific work in government.

As for the White House appointments staff, a rip tide of conflicting currents swirls around their search for the "right" people to recruit. The recommendations they make are necessarily attuned to the personal proclivities and preferences of the president and the top-most White

House aides, and to the hard-edged but highly nuanced imperatives of gaining and using political power. Of the hundreds of sought-after positions they must fill, the great majority will be stocked with individuals who demonstrably share the administration's general political philosophy and direction, and who will reliably work to promote them. Some of those appointments will also represent recognition of political obligations and support.

Pressures also crowd the appointments process from countless outside sources: from political friends and supporters, from the Congress, and from cabinet officers and other powerful early appointees. They come from transition team members who have helped ease a new administration into office, and from campaign staff and other political outriders who usually number few scientists among them. They come from the authors of a tidal wave of unsolicited resumes, even though the nature of appointed positions makes them largely inaccessible to this kind of direct application. There is also the pressure of time, particularly during the short period of transition when many of the fundamental critical decisions are, or should be, made.

These are not the only circumstances that complicate the search for appropriate candidates or delay decisions on offering them appointment. Agency heads wage a traditional struggle with the White House to gain or retain influence in the appointments of their own lieutenants. On another front, as a number of people in senior federal S&T jobs observe, younger and mid-career professionals at or near their primes are those most attractive to government. But they are also at the stage when taking time out to serve in government is most disruptive to careers, families and personal budgets. And recruiters know in any case that agencies visibly struggling with fundamental and resistant problems, and consequently plagued with rapid turnover in important jobs, cannot easily attract or retain competent scientists, engineers or anyone else.

All such contrary conditions clearly act to dent or discourage interest among the S&T community in government service. They also go far in explaining why S&T personnel leave government service when they do. Still, despite the negatives, qualms and potential setbacks, scientists and engineers are drawn to government service for many of the oft-stated reasons that similarly motivate other professionals. To be sure, the realities of a job may differ from the personal hopes its occupant invests in it ahead of time. But the hopes, ambitions, and goals persist. What beckons is the chance to work on projects being pursued nowhere else; to operate in some cases at the frontier of scientific and technological progress; to be in on the approach to some of the toughest problems facing society; to learn, and to interact with a wider universe of colleagues; to wield some influence over events, make a difference, have an impact.

Other factors are also at work--the intercession of friends, or of former collaborators already in government; admiration for a particular current leader; the reputation of an institution or program. The examples of former flag-bearers, from Vannevar Bush to George Shultz, play their part. So do the promptings of public service as a duty. By reputation, influence, the nature of the work, and clout, certain agencies attract more powerfully than others.

Occupancy: Levels, Backgrounds, Tenures

About 100 high-level positions carry varying but significant responsibility for federal science and technology efforts and issues. Fifty-four of the 62 profiled here are executive branch posts, and most require presidential appointment and Senate confirmation. The other eight are positions in the legislative branch, their occupants selected by the heads of their organizations, by action of an oversight board, or by a congressional committee chairman. Many are "line" management and oversight jobs, charged with developing and defending budgets and responsible for how large amounts of money are spent. Most of them involve differing degrees of leadership and policy making; a few have a lot of both. Of the 54 executive branch jobs, six are at Executive Level II, eight at level III, 29 at level IV, and one at level V. Ten are posts in the Senior Executive Service or equivalent. (Executive levels are the five salary levels at the top of the federal job edifice to which presidential appointments are assigned.)

Over the last quarter century, time-in-office statistics show a steady decline for presidential appointees, from an average of nearly three years in the Johnson era to two years in the first Reagan term. By comparison, as shown in the table on the next page, a quick look at the collective figures for these 62 S&T jobs since 1969 indicates a considerably better performance--3.14 years. That does not include those who held positions on an "acting basis," usually for periods of a few months, while candidates were being sought, or cleared, or the advent of a new administration was being awaited. When these are cranked into the calculation the figure, at 2.59 years, is still better than the current average. If only the 54 executive branch jobs are considered, the averages are 3.07 and 2.50 years, respectively; and for the congressional jobs, 3.79 and 3.68 years. While generalizations are somewhat hazardous, turnover is usually higher in jobs or agencies with the busiest, most pressured agendas, constant public focus, or recently troubled pasts. Examples (in no particular order) are the Environmental Protection Agency (EPA), parts of the Energy Department, the Consumer Products Safety Commission, the Food and Drug Administration, and the Office of Management and Budget (OMB). Although better than the overall average tenure, these figures still highlight what the profiles in the book suggest: that the federal government has a serious problem in retaining S&T professionals long enough for them to get fully on top of their jobs. This damages the quality of the services they can deliver and, as the widespread phenomenon that it is, affects the general impact an administration can make. It takes a year, on average, for an appointee to become fully effective--and considerably more than that for government to get a reasonable return on the investment in them.

A mid-September 1991 snapshot of the occupancy situation showed that scientists or technologists held 41 of the 54 executive branch positions described here, and seven of the eight posts on the congressional side, or 77.4 percent of the total. Of the other 14, lawyers filled seven of the executive branch jobs, and one in the Congress; the remaining six jobs were occupied by individuals with training in international relations, history, business and other non-science disciplines, most at the graduate degree level.

Average Tenure in Years of 62 S&T Jobholders

	Executive Branch	Legislative Branch	Combined
Confirmed Occupants Only	3.07	3.79	3.14
Including Acting Occupants	2.50	3.68	2.59

Occupants of Jobs by Profession or Training

			Percent
Science and Technology (including social sciences)	41	7	77.4
Law	7	1	12.9
International Relations		1	1.6
History		1	1.6
Business	2		3.2
Other non-science	2		3.2

Should the proportion of these and other comparable jobs held by scientists and technologists be higher? A number of counter currents seem to flow here. Take two of the posts filled by lawyers, for example. The occupant of one of them came to it after several earlier years of similar work in the same organization but thinks much more substantial scientific training is necessary to do it well. The tenant of the other job believes an S&T background is not essential to it as long as technically expert assistance and counsel is ready to hand. But at least two predecessors in that position disagree. Unanimity does exist among those interviewed about these 62 jobs that certain of them require earned degrees at the PhD level or equivalent plus solid experience and reputation. For quite a few of the other positions, some kind of S&T education or background on a lesser scale is thought to be highly useful. But there is no pattern of insistence on this point, and many stress the equal or near-equal importance of political skills, management ability, and prior exposure to Washington.

Certainly, no established conventions or rules have emerged about how many bona fide S&T professionals should be placed in executive jobs, or the proportion of the total senior appointed work force they should represent. But on this question, agencies with large research and development missions, and those whose regulatory duties and other activities rely extensively on science and technology, need to make careful judgments, and share them with the administration's political chieftains. Failing to take aboard as much S&T expertise as necessary, or pushing it too low down the line, is bound to undercut an agency's mission. It can prevent an organization from dealing effectively, at eye level and on equal terms, with its S&T issues and problems, and with other entities in this and other governments. It can also hamper severely that essential dialogue which enables the specialized expert to educate the political leadership, bringing it to understand, then follow, the advice it is getting. Some may deem the notion of reserving a percentage of top S&T jobs for scientists and engineers impractical from various standpoints. Yet, if an administration respects the fact that some of these positions demand high-quality expertise applied at first hand, it comes to almost the same thing.

Improving the Picture

In its 1990 report, the National Commission on the Public Service, chaired by Paul Volcker, laid fresh emphasis on government's urgent need to reexamine and improve its ability to draw talented individuals to its ranks. One of the steps it suggested would create a permanent, independent advisory mechanism which, working with the White House and the budget and personnel management offices, would monitor the conditions and needs of the federal work force and make recommendations to the president and the Congress. Whatever may emerge from this recommendation, it and efforts to revise ethics rules should examine how change affects particular and important sub-populations among the federal work force. The S&T positions in this book constitute such a group. Perhaps an advisory body like that proposed by the Volcker commission should take a periodic look at them to determine, for example, what affects government's ability to recruit scientists and engineers, use them well, and retain them.

Beyond the obvious power of the purse, the actions and attitudes of the Congress have much to do with the health of science and technology in government. In its duty to examine and approve presidential nominees for these positions, for example, the Senate has a regularly recurring opportunity for much more than the cursory glance at credentials and qualifications that many candidates get. If they chose, senators could use confirmation hearings to augment greatly their insights into the positions in question and the agencies they serve. Legislators need to expand and update their understanding of what these jobs do, what their structural, operational and funding problems might be, and whether--in collaboration with the administration--the positions or their mandates need revision. It is in any event fortunate that a number of members of both houses, including but not limited to those on the science committees and subcommittees, demonstrate an informed and durable interest in the country's science and technology affairs. That is a basically positive circumstance for all concerned.

When it comes to the presence of women and minorities in the S&T talent pool--and in high-level S&T jobs in government--some dramatic correctives are necessary. The statistics over the past 20 years on the entry of women and members of minority groups into the science and engineering professions are "not terribly impressive," in the words of a senior National Science Foundation official. It's a situation clearly reflected in the positions this book discusses. Only five of the jobs selected for the book were held by women (the number subsequently rose to six). Minorities occupy only two.

Some of this country's most visible scientists and engineers work for the federal government. Officials like the president's science adviser, the chief of the space agency, and the surgeon general are role models. They stand for what has always been traditional American leadership, innovation and know-how in science and technology, but they also represent the present and the future of U.S. achievement in these fields. Who they are and what they accomplish can have important influence on two levels. They can affect career decisions taking shape in high schools and on college campuses, thereby helping to increase the pool of qualified young candidates over the long term. And they can play a decisive part in the decisions of their colleagues on the outside to take their own turns in government service. Those who occupy positions like the ones described herein should therefore be sensitive to their power and responsibility in this regard. By the same token, the president and the Congress should give greater weight to factors like these in thinking through the implications and consequences of whom they appoint.

Last but hardly least is the power inherent in political leadership to promote ideas and set examples. The presidency is the best, but not the only, high platform from which to call attention to programs or organizations and identify personally with them in ways that affirm their place in the scheme of things and elevate them in the public's interest and esteem. Thus did the president speak supportively and publicly to career civil servants in the first days of the present administration. A steady, visible belief in the institutions of government, regularly expressed by leaders of eminence and authority, is an important way to enhance their appeal as organizations to work for. By the same token, actions can speak louder than words. Competent professionals observing an administration's S&T policies and programs are more likely to support and work for what they perceive as logic, consistency, a sharp sense of priorities, and a vigorous insistence on results.

Thoughts for the Future

What will most change these jobs in the decade ahead? Surely, developments at the international level are near the top of the list. The apparent disappearance of the Soviet Union as a military and political (and perhaps an economic) entity will revise many department and agency missions in Washington. It is changing the calculations of defense, intelligence, arms control and foreign policy planners, among them the positions in those areas examined in this book. At the same time, with the lessons of the Persian Gulf war still sinking in, the agencies involved must also go on grappling with the real or potential challenges posed by regional conflict, which shows much less readiness to recede.

But the evolution in political and military relationships around the world increasingly shares center stage with the international community's deeply intertwined economic, environmental, and health concerns. Again, the ramifications are evident for S&T *Prune* positions everywhere along that spectrum. Operating styles will change as technically advanced countries increasingly acknowledge, for example, the special kind of interdependence that ties them together in large, complex, outer-edge S&T undertakings. Examples of these in the United States are the space station and deep-space exploration, the Earth Observing System, the human genome project, and the superconducting super collider.

These are colossally expensive projects. Other countries are participating in several of them. Debate may rage in this country over the relative merits of big versus little science and whether priorities are being misplaced. Assuming, however, that pursuit of the big ventures will continue, intelligent management of U.S. S&T partnerships with other countries--with a premium on shared research, shared costs and shared results--will grow ever more crucial. Or take U.S. medical and biomedical research, which remains the best in the world. Work on AIDS, Alzheimer's disease, and a hundred other advanced undertakings make this country what has been called "the world's greatest clinical laboratory," operating as much in the interest of populations around the globe as of those at home. This is both a substantial asset that benefits other kinds of U.S. relationships abroad, and a heavy responsibility.

Why entitle this a "Prune" book? Part of the answer lies with a congressional publication that appears near the end of every presidential election year. It lists several thousand executive branch positions that presidents fill by appointment. The information it provides about the jobs is scant, however--title, grade or salary, type of appointment and location, name of incumbent and expiration date, if any, of his or her appointment. Among those who use the book are people seeking federal appointment and interested in identifying potentially available positions. Its official title is *Policy and Supporting Positions*. In Washington, they call it the Plum Book.

By contrast, *Prune* books discuss the toughest of the high-level jobs in detail, supplying information and insights unavailable elsewhere. They emphasize the value of training and background in those appointed to the upper levels of government; and their content draws almost entirely on the views and comments of veterans of the jobs under discussion. In short, the books embody the idea of experience as a primary element in the business of filling federal positions with qualified people. Experience is what turns plums into prunes--and explains the title.

Published in 1988, the first Prune Book had considerable use among those involved in the crucial, intricate, difficult federal appointments process--at the White House, in the agencies, on Capitol Hill, in the press, and with the job holders themselves. While they are the audience for whom the book was primarily intended, it also found readership in some of the professional communities and in the general public.

While this second volume will have particular interest and utility for the science and technology communities in and outside of government, it is meant at the same time to serve, and instruct, the broader audience, with *Prune* objectives firmly in mind. To know the issues, problems and challenges that federal positions in science and technology involve, and what kinds of people they require, is to appreciate the measure of their difficulty. To understand the value they can contribute when qualified people perform well in them is to grasp their importance to the country.

2

APPROACH AND METHOD

Like the first *Prune Book* of 1988, this one focuses on descriptions of jobs, not on the performances of those who occupy them. It views responsibilities, programs and objectives as such, not in terms of how well or how badly they are actually handled.

Along with successes, every era in government records its share of the frailties, falterings or failures of people and systems. No informed or informative discussion of the management of government can ignore these facts of life; indeed, the book reflects them through the views and comments of those interviewed for it. But these volumes are something like the handbook for a new car that shows how the vehicle is supposed to operate, without accounting for the driving habits of its owner.

In no sense does this mean that good performance in these high-level appointive and congressional positions is not supremely important. Performance, however, begins with a thorough understanding of the jobs by all concerned, and with attracting and choosing experienced, competent people to manage them. That is the point of this book, and the view of those who sponsored and contributed to it.

Selecting Positions

The positions described in this volume are the most critical in the universe of senior executive and congressional jobs with significance for science and technology (S&T). Broadly specified for our purposes here, S&T encompasses the biological and behavioral sciences, computer science, the mathematical and physical sciences, geosciences, engineering in several disciplines, and the social sciences. (Economics, probably the most important social science for government, is represented by two positions in the book. A separate volume would be necessary to cover its full role.)

Identifying the universe of S&T posts was the first step in the process of choosing those the book would cover. One of the building blocks was an inventory of presidentially-appointed jobs listed by the Carnegie Commission on Science, Technology, and Government in its report, *Science & Technology and the President* (October 24, 1988). A number of other source materials was also used in developing a basic inventory that eventually contained more than 180 line and staff positions in the executive and legislative branches.

Using this broad list, representatives of the Carnegie Commission, sponsor of the project, assisted by the staff of the Council for Excellence in Government, did the work of choosing the jobs to be profiled. Two fundamental substantive considerations governed their work. First, jobs selected should be those in which the management of scientific and technical (S&T) programs, functions and staffs is either the primary responsibility on an operational or policy level, or is a major component of that responsibility. Second, each executive and legislative branch position chosen should satisfy certain criteria--established in the first *Prune* book--concerning its relative importance among all of the senior S&T positions under consideration. These measuring sticks are the nature and level of a job's responsibilities; the size and scope of its management duties, including budget and staff; its congressional and public visibility; and the consequences of failure to perform effectively in it. Although the position profiles do not in every case address each of these specifically, the criteria provided a uniform and consistent framework for judgment, one in which closely competing jobs could be compared and rank-ordered. Practical considerations--space, time, manageability of the published product--also necessarily figured in determining the number of positions to be covered.

The selection group chose 62 S&T positions for the book. These include eight posts representing the "science" committees of House and Senate and the four congressional support agencies. Of the total of 62, five are generically representative of several positions at the same level with identical or nearly identical assignments in other disciplinary areas of their organizations. Examples are the command, control, communications, intelligence, and information management positions within each of the military services, and the assistant director positions at the Office of Technology Assessment.

It is clear that many additional S&T positions and types of positions across the government need similar recognition. The chairs of several Senate and House committees and subcommittees with S&T responsibilities fall into this group, as do certain additional positions in the White House and executive office of the president. Among the latter are the chief of staff and the president's national security assistant, whose responsibilities have a substantial S&T content and whose deputies work in technology-oriented areas like arms control. Such categories of jobs can and should be the subject of planning for future *Prune* volumes.

As for cabinet positions, many of them are frequently in the public eye and the particulars of their missions and requirements are generally familiar. This, and the element of personal presidential choice involved in filling such positions, make detailed description of them here unnecessary. It should be noted at the same time that scientists, physicians and engineers come in for a share of cabinet posts, as currently seen at the Departments of Energy and Health and Human Services.

Information Sources

This book derives its principal authority from the experiences, views and wisdom of those who best know the jobs it discusses. They are the men and women who now hold the positions, those who have held them in the recent past, and other knowledgeable sources. Staff of the Council for Excellence in Government conducted personal interviews with an average of four individuals about each of the 62 positions in question. These were the incumbent of the post, two of its previous occupants, and an observer--a person whose present or previous close associations with the position provided informed insights from a different vantage point. We found helpful observers on congressional committee staffs, in think tanks and trade associations, in business and industry, and elsewhere in government.

In the interviews as in the writing of the book, objectivity and balance were abiding concerns. This meant recognizing that incumbents are prone to subjectivity, and their predecessors to selective memory gaps. For each position, whenever possible and practicable, it meant seeking to interview previous occupants representing a mix of administrations. Observers were often good sources of objectivity, but sometimes had special advocacies to be taken into account. In discussions with interviewees, the questions went to the mission of a job, its major responsibilities, its working context and close associates, the funds and work forces it manages, the issues it deals with, and the ordinary and extraordinary problems it encounters.

The interviews are the sole source of the scores of comments, inside and outside of quote marks, that the book attributes to those we talked with. In every case, our interviewees were given the opportunity to review, verify and authorize the material for use.

Additional Considerations

Each position profile in the book contains a biographic sketch of the incumbent, with the exception of one or two posts temporarily vacant at the time the book was completed. (Inclusion of the biographic data is meant to provide additional information, and does not imply any comment on the suitability or otherwise of the credentials for the position in question.) Except for one or two of the generically described positions, each profile also appends a list of all those who have held the job, and their present affiliations where known, since January 1969 or since the year in which the position was established if later than 1969. Inevitably, a few of these previous occupants proved impossible to locate.

Most of the executive branch jobs addressed here have an active relationship with the Congress. This normally involves a certain amount of formal testimony that is often, but not exclusively, tied to the budget cycle; a varying degree of informal dialogue with senators, representatives and personal and committee staff members; and the management of a considerable amount of correspondence and requests for information. Because this congressional dimension is common to most of the positions and is usually discussed in individual job profiles, it does not appear in each listing of their in-government relationships outside their own agencies.

Similarly, because many of the positions have duties that entail regular business with the Office of Management and Budget, the profiles do not specify the OMB each time among their close associations with other government entities and individuals. Further, the listings of close contacts outside the federal government are meant as indications only, not as complete catalogs of the many kinds of organizations and individuals that occupants of these jobs typically engage with in the external community.

In discussing budget aspects of the positions, most profiles provide fiscal year 1992 figures, sometimes comparing them with previous-year numbers to give some perspective on funding patterns. Readers should keep in mind that the 1992 figures are approximate. In most instances they reflect the budget authority requested in the 1992 presidential budget document, not the actual funding for that year since actual appropriation of funds for 1992 had not occurred at the time of the book's completion.

Matters like the rigors of the appointments process, conflict-of-interest and disclosure requirements and post-employment restrictions are prominent issues for present and prospective holders of all upper-level government positions, not just for scientists and engineers. Questions of ethics and the means to assure ethical behavior are important subjects for reflection that, however, extend beyond the objectives of this book.

Appointive and other federal positions change hands throughout the life of an administration or a Congress. In the executive branch, such comings and goings have a cyclical rhythm, and occur frequently at a point about two years into an administration. The preparation of this book spanned such a period; a number of current officeholders we interviewed left office before the book was completed. In some of these cases, we were able to interview the new occupants of the positions. In a very few others, this proved impractical because the newcomers arrived in their jobs too close to our publication deadline to have gained useful perspective on their new duties. Naturally the book does not take account of changes in incumbency that took place after it went to publication.

Finally, the book makes no claim for exhaustive coverage of each position's every circumstance, nor to have discussed every noteworthy issue, problem, and point of view involved. What these profiles do present are portraits with sufficient detail, history, depth, insight and authority to be continuingly useful to anyone wishing to know and understand them. As such, we think they constitute a constructive instrument of some value to the federal role in keeping American science and technology strong.

PART II

3

OFFICE OF SCIENCE AND TECHNOLOGY POLICY

ASSISTANT TO THE PRESIDENT FOR SCIENCE AND TECHNOLOGY AND DIRECTOR, OFFICE OF SCIENCE AND TECHNOLOGY POLICY

Level II - Presidential Appointment with Senate Confirmation

Major Responsibilities

- Provide the president with objective advice and perspective in policy formulation and budget development on all questions in which science and technology (S&T) are important elements. Prominent examples are technology development and economic competitiveness, the environment and health. Brief the chief executive on the science and technology aspects and implications of major national issues, and on significant developments in those fields.

- Monitor and evaluate federal government management of its science, engineering and technology responsibilities. Counsel and assist the effort to set priorities, broaden and coordinate the approach to projects and problems, raise the productivity of federally-funded research and development, and resolve conflict and overlap. Establish effective working relationships and communications with senior federal S&T executives.

- Articulate administration science and technology S&T policies and programs to the Congress, addressing and defending the need for appropriate resources. Speak for federal S&T policy to the national and international S&T communities and to the general public.

● Represent U.S. S&T objectives and policy to other governments and international organizations, seeking and negotiating cooperation and coordination arrangements where appropriate.

● Take a leading role in the process of identifying and recruiting federal S&T executives.

Necessary Training, Experience, Skills

Candidates for this position (widely referred to as the president's science adviser) must know and thoroughly understand what one of its former occupants calls the foundations of U.S. science and technology--industry, the universities and the national laboratories. The individual selected must have sufficient technical background to be entirely at home with one or more scientific or engineering disciplines, and offer the credibility that comes with an established record of accomplishment, preferably at the international level of renown. Does all this mean a trained, degreed scientist or engineer? It's extremely hard to argue otherwise, though another former science adviser suggests that an industrialist running a high-technology company might handle the job successfully. In addition, the occupant of this post must know Washington, including the Congress, and the techniques involved in communicating ideas and influencing decisions. Entrepreneurial talent, resourcefulness, and outreach skills are important. Finally, the science adviser must be someone with whom the president is personally comfortable.

Insight

In a real sense, the position of science adviser to the president today commands the heights of the federal government's science and technology (S&T) establishment. In the person of its occupant, the job stands as a symbol and advocate of continuing high-quality U.S. scientific and technological achievement. But it has not always, or even mostly, been that way.

Thoughts about such a post first surfaced after the second world war in the form of a proposal by former Atomic Energy Commission hand William T. Golden. He was acting at the request of President Truman, and the idea won a receptive White House response. But in creating the job and an accompanying consulting committee, Truman separated both from any primary reporting relationship to himself.

The Soviet launch of Sputnik was the event to which the science adviser's job, like certain other fixtures of the contemporary federal S&T scene, owes its real birth. Dwight Eisenhower brought MIT president James R. Killian Jr. into the White House in that autumn of 1957 as his special assistant for S&T and established a science advisory committee. "That group really had a remarkable amount of influence," recalls D. Allan Bromley, the Canadian-born Yale physics professor who has been the president's assistant for science and technology policy since 1989. "And one of reasons was that in those days there was practically no other S&T game in town." As time went on and administrations and circumstances changed, however, presidential interest in and use of scientific advice would wax and wane. For that and other reasons, the adviser position's usefulness, impact and reputation have followed a similar pattern.

By turns prominent and influential, underused or neglected, at one point banished from the White House altogether, the science adviser function today appears headed for another high. If the comments of a wide number of informed observers and government colleagues are any measure, the job is acquiring the kind of weight and regard it has not often known in the past 20 years. National Academy of Sciences president Frank Press held the science adviser's position in 1977-80, presiding among other activities over negotiation of the first U.S.-Chinese S&T agreement after normalization of relations between the two countries. To him the reemerging importance of the adviser's function is entirely in line with national and global realities. "Energy policy, the environment, controlling health costs, the nonproliferation of weapons, the level of the research and development budget, education and training of the technical work force, the competitiveness of American industry--all these things are very visible and very political, yet they have a strong technological basis to them," he says. "From that point of view alone, the role of scientific and technical professionals will increase with time, not decrease." And, says Golden (former president of the New York Academy of Sciences and now chairman of the American Museum of Natural History), "science, engineering and technology are increasingly playing a role in many fields which the public does not immediately recognize are intimately related to science as such."

To this Press adds the government's clear need for a "professional force" of scientists and engineers to manage many of its responsibilities, from the physicians and scientists who work at the National Institutes of Health to the engineers who run NASA. "If you think of every agency in government and its technical mission, the technical work force is of great significance," he asserts. There are also, he notes, the critical questions of whether scientists and technologists are going to be available in sufficient numbers and whether government service will be attractive to them--"very important in terms of the government performing its necessary mission."

For all these reasons, Press thinks the history of science adviser-type positions "begins now, in all countries and especially the advanced nations. They see the way the world is going. Whether it's the environment or how well their industries perform or what the industries of the future will be, I think they will increasingly recognize that the comparative advantage will come through technology." He therefore finds "good reason" for the 1989 elevation of the White House science adviser to the status of assistant to the president (a move recommended by the National Academy of Sciences, among others).

Bromley thus wears two hats. He has the responsibility for what he calls "science and technology for policy" as well as "policy for science and technology." The first of these means the contribution of S&T input-- information, analysis, recommendations--to the policy formation process "where S&T are generally not the dominant elements but are important elements." This includes, importantly, a reading on the reliability of the S&T components of a proposed policy, he says, since in the past "too many cases" have come to light of policy and laws based on "pretty shaky science and technology." The second half of the assistant's mandate-- providing policy for S&T--involves among other goals "keeping the S&T base strong" and "being aware of possible actions by the administration that might have a significant impact on S&T in the country--and that might not be appreciated" without his presence.

Under the second hat, as director of the Office of Science and Technology Policy (OSTP), Bromley identifies one main task as getting the maximum federal and federally-supported research and development effort per appropriated dollar. "The maximum amount, and the highest quality," he emphasizes. Another is to report to the Congress on the progress made and "what is required to make the right things happen." In pursuing these objectives, the budget process is a key OSTP instrument, and a public process with intense congressional and press attention. It is here that the science adviser's office as currently run has made perhaps its most recognized impact, reviving and strengthening the previously moribund Federal Coordinating Council for Science, Engineering and Technology (FCCSET) and--in collaboration with the Office of Management and Budget (OMB)--using it in shaping a new interagency budget approach to high-priority research and development areas.

This innovation is rooted in the creation of FCCSET in 1976 by the same legislation that established OSTP itself (and marked the beginning of the modern history of the science adviser's position). Bromley says one of his first goals was to understand "why the FCCSET structure hadn't been as effective as its creators had envisaged," since the times seemed to cry out for "real coordination and crosscutting activity" among agencies. He found two answers. First, the relationship between OSTP and OMB had degenerated into antagonism. Second, FCCSET was staffed at too low a level: "when the budget crunch came, the agencies they represented could disown agreements they had made in the council." Bromley repaired and broadened relations with OMB. As one step, the two offices agreed to work together throughout the development of upcoming fiscal year S&T budgets. That replaced the procedure in which OSTP saw the budget document only in its final form before it went to the Congress.

Next, FCCSET underwent dramatic overhaul. Its membership now consists of the secretaries or chief deputies of all but three of the 14 cabinet departments, and the heads of independent agencies with significant S&T in their mandates or missions. "That means," Bromley notes, "that when decisions are made by that group, they stick." Under the oversight of these top-level FCCSET members are permanent committees responsible for seven areas spanning the range of S&T issues. In turn, the committees have in some cases set up working groups. This new edition of FCCSET is designed to bridge what Bromley thinks is the biggest gap in the federal science and technical enterprise--the fact of many agencies working with differing views and approaches towards similar S&T goals without effective interagency communications. That is a strength in some ways, he acknowledges. But its price has been a lack of coherence--"nobody really understood what anybody else was doing, and we weren't getting the maximum impact in many areas per dollar spent."

In the new, corrective interagency approach to this problem, OSTP, FCCSET and OMB together select each year "a set of areas" to be targeted. The committees and their working groups then collect and analyze relevant budget and other data, and plan a single, coordinated program that integrates the work of all agencies involved. The coherence achieved in the first of these efforts in 1989--to assess the global climate change phenomenon--was visible in a very significant increase in the funding requested for the overall program compared to the resources the individual agencies could have otherwise expected. Under FCCSET's watchful guidance, sixteen agencies now coordinate the federal response to the challenge of global climate change. Through FCCSET their work goes to a working group of the Domestic Policy Council. From there, decision memoranda go forward to the president.

With FCCSET fixed and the new crosscutting strategy successfully tested, more such projects have followed. OSTP has applied the same formula and procedures to high-performance computing, mathematics and science education, human resources, materials science and biotechnology.

"Once we've done this in any given area in one year," says Bromley, "then that's the base on which we build for the next year." He thinks that, if he can make it work consistently, this will be the most important contribution he makes. At the same time, the FCCSET process, in his view, lacks one important ingredient: private-sector wisdom and counsel. "By law, every member is a government official. Marvelous ideas get generated, some of which are not terribly realistic, and we don't expose them to ground truths by running them by private sector people." To fill the gap, he got oval office agreement in 1989 to bring together the President's Council of Advisers on Science and Technology--PCAST--a "very distinguished" group of 12 academics, industrialists and administrators. It is part of his job, Bromley points out, to "make sure that PCAST and FCCSET mesh and cross-fertilize one another." He asserts that the chemistry has worked well between PCAST members and the president, with whom it meets directly, and with senior White House staff. The group, he says, "is listened to."

Bromley himself has access to the president whenever he needs it (the frequency varies), and operates in a broad, busy and heavily scheduled environment where the working day normally begins before 7. His activities routinely include a daily senior White House staff meeting, individual discussion with senior policy and budget officials in the West Wing/Executive Office orbit and in the departments and agencies, and meetings of the cabinet. He takes part in the deliberations of such groups as the economic and domestic policy councils, OMB, the Council of Economic Advisers, the Council on Competitiveness and the Space Council. There is also a newly widened working relationship between OSTP and the National Security Council on such matters as export controls and high-tech weapons that recalls the science office's primary concerns 35 years ago with air defense, space, and force postures.

But if this job currently enjoys influence and a growing reputation for imagination, energy and accomplishment, there are also plenty of problems and some setbacks. In pursuing projects like global climate change or strengthening U.S. economic competitiveness, for example, Bromley has had to negotiate some severe and well-publicized head winds generated within the White House itself. And the job of interagency coordination is no easy street, according to William R. Graham Jr., science adviser from 1986 to 1989. He supports the kind of coordination Bromley is now introducing, which "provides the best opportunities for economic and scientific progress from a government viewpoint without requiring one additional dollar." But, he observes, getting agencies to work together "is by no means a smooth road." When an agency really wants to pursue an issue in its own way and doesn't want to face the scrutiny of other agencies or of the president and his staff, "it tries basically to put a wall around the activity and pursue it behind that wall. They just quietly make it happen and then deliver a *fait accompli*." Sometimes this technique works, he says, and sometimes it produces "real trouble." In the latter category, the examples Graham cites from his own time are the troubled FSX fighter plane deal with Japan, and what he views as a premature and unbalanced agreement by the State Department at one stage of the international effort to reduce production of chlorofluorocarbons.

Further, says Bruce Smith, senior science policy scholar at the Brookings Institution, the science adviser is "pulled into too many things." At the same time, while "you can't be a budget examiner for the whole federal government, you want to play a role in the institutional processes or you miss one handle to influence." While operating within the president's policies, he says, the real problem is using discipline to "target a few things you can get done, devote energy in a focused way to make a difference. That's the problem of domestic policy generally, especially in an era of little money. There's never enough, so your constituencies beat up on you, think you're a traitor--you're not pushing hard enough, you're starting to talk priorities and that's bad: you're sounding like a bureaucrat." And unlike some other advisers, he adds, "the science adviser has no political base." On another front, a senior cabinet department official complains that "Bromley wants to have policy-level people at FCCSET committee and subcommittee meetings. We're finding that it's a tremendous demand on time." Eventually, he fears, agencies will begin delegating lower-level representatives to attend, and the impression will grow that these are meetings where decisions can't be taken. "Then," he says, "the process may deteriorate. It's a good system, it does provide coordination, and OMB loves it because in a sense it's doing part of their work. But there may be too many committees."

There are also two operational concerns that need mention. First, Graham warns, providing S&T advice to the president is not always a matter of assessing straightforward issues whose outlines and potential problems are readily visible. "No purely scientific or technical problems are ever raised in the White House for resolution," he says. "Nobody says that Joe thinks the speed of light is X, but Sam says it's Y, and we've got to settle it here in the cabinet meeting." Rather, "everything that comes up is a mixture of S&T, economics, diplomacy, national security, sometimes electoral politics, congressional relations, and on and on. It doesn't easily factor into separate pieces."

Second is the matter of the science adviser's dual status. When the Congress established OSTP in 1976 it included the requirement that the director's appointment be confirmed by the Senate. In the view of several observers, this may have weakened the position by comparison to its status at some earlier points. "It put the job in the executive office of the president, rather than in the White House," Press says. "And there's a difference." But he notes that President Bush, "to his credit, elevated the position and gave it a formal status within the White House staff and made Bromley an assistant to the president. It was rather unprecedented." But Senate confirmation also creates an enduring link between the job and the Congress, including the right of legislators to require testimony. It can interfere, some say, with relationships inside the White House. Currently, Bromley's is the only position at its level requiring Senate confirmation.

"When the Congress has some reason to want to know what the administration is up to, they know whom to come find," Bromley acknowledges. "And you do have some sessions before various congressional committees that are perhaps a little unpleasant. But on the other hand I rather enjoy interacting with Congress." He doesn't view his status as an impediment but as an opportunity, and says he has spent "a fair amount of time trying to rebuild the bridges" between his office and the Hill. In addition to testifying to the science and other committees, he talks informally to members and staffs in both Houses. Some portion of this dialogue addresses the OSTP budget, which stands at a requested $3.88 million in budget authority for fiscal 1992; in 1991, the estimated figure was $3.56 million, and the actual 1990 figure was $2.83 million.

The science adviser's staff has more than doubled from its 1989 level, and currently numbers about 40. "This office was set up as the office of science and technology policy," Bromley points out, "but traditionally it was the office of science policy." He thought it important to give additional emphasis to the "T" in the title. That is partly why "all four of the presidentially appointed, Senate confirmed associate directors of this office, provided for in the original 1976 legislation, are in place for the first time." Their areas of responsibility are physical sciences and engineering, life sciences, industrial technology, and international and policy affairs. Despite the statutory provision for these slots, some of them had remained unfilled before 1989. Among the factors limiting appointment to them in earlier administrations were the extensive time required by confirmation procedures, a general resistance within the executive office to Senate-confirmable individuals for reasons similar to those noted earlier, and the desire of some presidents for small staffs. Bromley made the filling of all four associate positions a condition of accepting his own appointment. "It was terribly important, for example, in the case of industrial technology," he says. "I also wanted to send a message that we were serious about this particular area."

Among the many other concerns the science adviser deals with, several projects and issues deserve brief discussion here.

● The debate about industrial policy. "We have a semantic problem here," says Bromley. There has never been any question that government should play a role in supporting basic research, and "government has accepted this right from the beginning." At times, people believed that pure research was the only area government should be involved in and that "everything else should go into the private sector." There were also, for example, the government's bail-outs of Lockheed and Chrysler, which was "far on the other side" of the issue; "that's what nowadays I would define as industrial policy," he continues. The current administration will not do that because it doesn't believe itself nearly as qualified as people in the private sector "to make the kind of decision as to who is going to survive in the market phase--in the purely competitive production or sales phase." But all this leaves a "very large gap" between basic research and the competitive stage. That is the precompetitive period ranging from "discovery of a basic scientific fact through its evolution into a commercial technology," an interval when Bromley believes a government role is appropriate.

- "Generic" technologies. The best example of that belief in action is OSTP's well-known advocacy of research and development of these technologies mostly in support of U.S. global competitiveness. In April 1991, OSTP announced a list of 22 such technologies developed from information prepared by industry, the universities and federal agencies. It had earlier begun setting up a critical technologies institute to cooperate with industry and guide government support for technologies on the list, but the institute is reported to be "on hold." In any case, it's clear that the generic technologies exercise is in part a way to mix public and private sector resources and effort under a rubric other than federal industrial policy.

Activity that reduces cost and risk and speeds up the development process for technologies in the precompetitive stage is crucial, Bromley says, and that's where government has a role. One way to achieve this is the funding of consortia such as Sematech, which gets $100 million a year from government and an equal amount from member industries to develop what Bromley calls "leapfrogging" technology into the future generation of semiconductors. Another way may be through advanced technology programs in manufacturing and research centers; so far the Department of Commerce has set up small pilot centers to test this idea (described elsewhere in this volume; see Under Secretary of Commerce for Technology; and Director, National Institute for Standards and Technology). A third is by transfer to the private sector of technology developed at government laboratories and through federal contracts.

● Attracting S&T talent to government. Money is not the major problem, in Bromley's view. It is, rather, burdensome and bureaucratic conflict of interest regulations that have allowed the impression to develop that people entering government service "are guilty of something, reversing the concept that a prospective appointee is innocent until proven guilty." This acts as a deterrent to people considering public sector jobs and is having "a significant impact on our ability to attract very good people." Current rules, he says, also make it impossible for scientists and technologists in mid-career to do a government tour because they require the total severing of connections with their parent organizations. "In mid-career, that would be totally crazy." Recruiting for federal S&T positions is thus reduced to young people who have no experience or people who have retired. The onerousness of the situation, Bromley adds, lies not in the rules themselves, but in how they are interpreted to protect administrations from possible embarrassment.

● Science and technology education. More than a dozen federal agencies working under FCCSET are involved in this area of the administration's general approach to the country's education problems.   Principal among them are the National Science Foundation and the Department of Education; and in his first meetings with their representatives, Bromley relates, "it turned out that apart from the two agency heads, none of those people had ever even met one another." The objectives of the FCCSET effort have been to establish budget information and guidelines, and develop a coherent interagency program in mathematics and science education at all levels. Such a program aims at contributing to the development of national standards (but not a national curriculum, Bromley emphasizes) for what students in various grades should know in the S&T area. "We can then measure their performance against those standards, which will tell us whether we are making progress and where we can improve."

Bromley sees three reasons why U.S. public education has fallen on hard times--a decrease in parental involvement in education at the K-12 levels, a failure to insist on high-quality teaching, and a lack of objective standards. He would like to decrease U.S. dependence on foreign graduate students who come here to study and remain to work, and increase the number of American students going on to graduate levels. Another problem he points to is the low rewards American society gives, compared with other countries, to the "supertechnicians" who keep production lines running and perform sophisticated tasks required in modern industry.

Should the science adviser be an advocate for particular projects or groups inside and outside the federal S&T enterprise, or a neutral arbiter? Views on this point vary. "If you're seen in White House discussions as the advocate of a constituency," Press answers, "that's quickly recognized and you're suddenly outside the loop. You have to be looked at as a member of the president's team." That doesn't mean, he says, that the science adviser shouldn't build networks into the government and nongovernment S&T communities to stay abreast of what is happening in order to do a better job. "You can make a case," Graham says, "that senior staff should merely present the options that the departments put together. I decided there wasn't enough S&T horsepower elsewhere on the White House staff to form sound recommendations on many of the issues, so I acted not only as a summarizer and consensus builder but also from time to time as an advocate." If the science adviser is perceived as a lobbyist for the S&T community, Bromley says, then effectiveness in the job "goes to zero." On the other hand, "I'm not supposed to be completely neutral. Take an area like high-performance computing, which I think is extraordinarily important, where we can make a major difference in this country's competitiveness or educational capabilities. If it's something I think is important, on the basis of my experience and background, then I say so. That's why I sit in on meetings with the president and the budget director and the agency heads. And if I think something isn't important, then I say that, too." But the overridingly vital necessity, he stresses, is that the rest of the presidential team recognize the science adviser as a fellow member of the team, with the president as the only constituent.

One way to look at the science adviser's function, suggests Graham, is as "a value-added kind of operation. It's not a line operation. It's more like the job of a chief scientist/engineer for a corporation in the sense that it is a staff function to the president." If it were to do nothing or disappear or ignore an area, government would not shut down. "The departments and agencies would simply proceed on their merry way, sometimes in cooperation with each other but each usually in total disregard for what the others are doing, until they ran into minor and sometimes major collisions."

"It doesn't run a big empire," Smith says, "but the science adviser has an important role in the budget plus the task any White House person has--to galvanize, use the bully pulpit, stimulate action within the departments." Although the job is a staff post, Press points out, "being there as an assistant to the president, able to comment and advise on S&T across the entire government, makes it a very powerful position."

"You have to create the structure as well as implement the programs," Graham says. Especially in the crucial coordinating responsibility, the job benefits from an ability "to see over the horizon. If you can understand issues before they become national issues, or crises, and lay the groundwork, line things up, get the coordinating body going, then you'll have control of the issue in the coordination sense." Global climate change and high-performance computing are examples of this, he says--issues where OSTP was ahead of the curve. In the last analysis, this is a position requiring "entrepreneurial spirit and initiative. You go out and create something almost out of nothing. In fact, that's part of the challenge and interest of the job."

Key Relationships

Within the White House and Executive Office of the President

Reports to: President

Works closely with:

Director, Office of Management and Budget
Assistant to the President, National Security Affairs
Assistant to the President, Economic and Domestic Policy
National Space Council
Cabinet Council on Competitiveness

Outside the White House

Members, Federal Coordinating Council for Science, Engineering and
Technology (most Cabinet secretaries, some heads of agencies)
Wide range of senior department and agency executives responsible for
managing all aspects of the federal role in science and technology,
including national laboratory directors
Officials of Congressional support agencies with responsibilities in, or
affected by, science and technology

Outside the Government

The global scientific and engineering communities, and national and
international scientific and engineering institutes, academies and boards;
academic science and engineering faculties; minister-level and other science
and technology policy officials of other governments; business and industry
executives and industrial laboratory managers; science policy groups; state
S&T officials

Profile of Current Assistant to the President for Science and Technology Policy

Name: D. Allan Bromley

Assumed Position: 1989

Career Summary: Physics faculty, Yale University, 1960-89, including Henry Ford II
Professor of Physics, and Chairman, Physics Department
Senior research officer, Chalk River Laboratory, Ontario, Canada,
1955-60
Assistant professor, physics, University of Rochester, 1952-55

Education: Queen's University, Ontario, Canada, BS, engineering (with highest
honors), 1948; MS, nuclear physics, 1950
University of Rochester, PhD, nuclear physics, 1952

Directors, Office of Science and Technology Policy Since 1969

Administration	Name and Years Served	Present Position
Bush	D. Allan Bromley 1990 - present	Incumbent
Reagan	William R. Graham Jr. 1986 - 1989	Chairman and CEO Xsirius Inc. Arlington, Va.
Reagan	John P. McTague (Acting) 1986	Vice President, Technical Affairs Ford Motor Co. Detroit, Mich.
Reagan	George A. Keyworth III 1981 - 1985	Distinguished Fellow Hudson Institute Indianapolis, Ind.
Carter	Frank Press 1977 - 1980	President National Academy of Sciences Washington, D.C.
Ford	H. Guyford Stever 1976	Commissioner Carnegie Commission on Science, Technology, and Government Washington, D.C.
Nixon	Edward E. David* 1972 - 1973	President Edward E. David Inc. Bedminster, N.J.

Nixon	Lee A. Dubridge*	President Emeritus
	1969 - 1970	California Institute of Technology
		Pasadena, Cal.

* Held position as Director, Office of Science and Technology

ASSOCIATE DIRECTOR
POLICY AND INTERNATIONAL AFFAIRS
OFFICE OF SCIENCE AND TECHNOLOGY POLICY

Level III - Presidential Appointment with Senate Confirmation

(Each of the four associate director positions in this office deals with its own subject areas, but all have similar objectives and responsibilities. The job described here represents all of them in a general way and, to some extent, the office's assistant director positions as well.)

Major Responsibilities

- Support the responsibility of the director of the office to provide the president with objective counsel on the science and technology (S&T) dimensions of administration policy across the board. Supervise the analysis and synthesis of broadly-sourced information and insights relevant to the issue at hand, and assist in the development of policy advice. Serve as overall coordinator for policy support efforts.

- Representing the director, take a central role in guiding the group of agencies working to improve U.S. science and mathematics education under the coordination of the Federal Coordinating Council for Science, Engineering and Technology. Function in a similar role for other such programs as may be assigned.

- Monitor U.S. plans, programs and actions in foreign policy and international affairs from an S&T perspective, focusing especially on increasing American trade competitiveness, protecting the domestic S&T base, and advancing U.S. foreign policy.

- In support of these duties, work with the leadership of the federal agencies involved and with other elements of executive office of the president. Maintain broad contacts within the U.S. scientific, technical and other communities.

Necessary Training, Experience, Skills

A science or engineering background richly and amply mixed with experience in Washington seems the best recipe for these positions. An associate director should have the technical competence to understand the issues and the language, gain and hold the respect of scientific and technical colleagues inside and outside government, and offer policy recommendations. A sound reputation within the S&T community is almost a requisite. So is political judgment and intuition; this may or may not derive from prior work in Washington, but must be in good working order. Associate directors must also be able and constant communicators.

Insight

Between them, OSTP's associate directors (ADs) divide the work of the office into individual areas of responsibility for science and technology enterprise within the federal government. At the same time, these positions collectively support the OSTP director's mandate as assistant to the president. And the "policy" half of this particular AD position therefore carries an oversight function for the office as a whole in OSTP's task of assisting that presidential advisory mission.

Wil Lepkowski, senior editor of *Chemical and Engineering News*, offers one view of this. The associate for policy and international affairs, he says, "has to know everything important out there that the director has to know, whether the director can politically present it or not. So it has an assignment scope that's fairly broad." While all of the associate and assistant directors (currently four of each) are involved in policy, this AD is "not restricted to any one portfolio," serves as a "nerve center for the rest of the OSTP staff," and "has to know what the others are doing."

The policy portfolio has other, more specific assignments. "The largest current item in that basket," says J. Thomas Ratchford, who has held this AD job since 1989, is math and science education. Those two subjects figure heavily in the education goals agreed on in 1989 by the president and state governors, he points out. One of the goals is U.S. world leadership in math and science education by the year 2000. As Ratchford notes, this has led to a decision to develop a crosscutting interagency program and budget for fiscal 1992 to try to point the country in that direction. The project is the third in a series of such multi-agency attempts to accelerate national progress--in more cost-effective fashion--in areas of science and technology where national progress is deemed to be urgent. They were launched in 1989 by OSTP director D. Allan Bromley under the newly-revived and strengthened Federal Coordinating Council for Science, Engineering and Technology (FCCSET). The first two projects concern global climate change and high-performance computing.

Ratchford, a solid-state physicist who came to OSTP from a leadership job at the American Association for the Advancement of Science, has direct OSTP responsibility for the math and science program. While this country, in his view, has "by far the best graduate science and math education system in the world" and at least a competitive undergraduate position, "we are doing abominably" at the kindergarten through twelfth grade levels. U.S. graduate schools attract talented, technically trained people from other countries, he observes, many of whom remain to work in this country; at the same time, U.S. high schools do manage to graduate enough qualified students into the system to keep U.S. scientific professions adequately staffed. That means, Ratchford says, that at least for the time being--an important qualifier--the problem of training adequate numbers of science and technology (S&T) professionals is not going to be as hard to solve as some have predicted. But meanwhile the K-12 general education problem is "much more complicated and is intertwined with what some call the need to reform our educational system as a whole. It is a tough nut to crack."

Another element of the policy component of his job is the area of social sciences. Unlike the National Science Foundation, which groups social and behavioral sciences in the same division, OSTP treats the social sciences--like economics, sociology, and political science--separately. The aim, says Ratchford, is to "provide a mechanism for viewing broad policy issues that relate to the ensemble of the social sciences," and also to develop ways to coordinate individual agency programs at an interagency level.

From 1986 to 1989, many of the international responsibilities of this position were those of Deborah Wince-Smith, who handled them as assistant director for international affairs and global competitiveness. Now an assistant secretary of commerce for technology policy, she describes the general thrust of her duties in this area as "promoting U.S. national goals in the S&T area in the international arena." More specifically, this meant helping to shape and coordinate policies aimed at improving the U.S. position in world trade, protecting national security interests, advancing foreign policy, and maintaining the domestic science and technology base. In the 1980s, she recalls, the realization grew that S&T policy exerted a "really important impact" on those four areas. "You saw more and more contentious issues debated within the bureaucracy" and raised to the White House level for attention, coordination and resolution. While the policy importance of these issues increased, agencies and departments were somewhat reluctant to submit what had been their isolated, largely uncoordinated ways of doing business in the international S&T area to closer interagency scrutiny at the top of the executive branch. "What was particularly challenging on any issue that reached the OSTP/White House level," Wince-Smith says, "was somehow to balance the various conflicting interests and come up with a position that was in the best overall interests of the country."

Another important question on OSTP's international agenda concerns the nature of the scores of S&T agreements the United States has concluded with other countries. In the past, Wince-Smith says, "the only two rationales for S&T cooperation with other countries were the impact on one's specific domestic program, and on foreign policy and/or foreign assistance. Nobody was concerned about the economic, commercial or national security implications." Foreign partners in these agreements, she asserts, "see this country as a huge potential gold mine for new knowledge and technology that they can obtain and utilize. They're not pursuing these agreements for foreign policy reasons, but rather because they see a direct relationship between access to U.S. science and technology and their economic development and prosperity." In her time, OSTP responded to this by "pushing the issue of linkage between international S&T and competitiveness, trade and economic concerns. We insisted on very strong and effective provisions" in the agreements for the protection and equitable division of intellectual property, as well as factoring in the economic and commercial implications for U.S. industry." There were "hundreds of different intellectual property agreements and no rhyme or reason for how intellectual property rights were handled."

It is therefore an appropriate role for OSTP, she thinks, to "step up and look at the generic issues as they cut across all of those agreements." The department of state "has the main oversight authority for the agreements per se," she says, "and the OSTP role is to provide policy guidance and general oversight. You have to distinguish between operational management responsibility and things the White House should have an interest in because they concern more than one agency and have real national implications."

The usefulness of OSTP's crosscutting role is also apparent in the comments of Nancy Maynard, a biologist who has served as the office's assistant director for the environment since 1989. Most of her time in that period has been absorbed in staffing the work of the global climate change working group of the White House Domestic Policy Council, and in liaison work in this and other areas with FCCSET's Committee on Earth and Environmental Sciences. "I think the primary value of OSTP is our role as the honest broker on S&T issues," she says. "We pull together the various positions on each issue as well as the supporting scientific and technological information, and then provide the forum for full and open discussion of all sides of the issue. Ultimately, based upon extensive discussion, agreement is reached on the most appropriate position or policy for that issue." Can this be described as consensus building? "Exactly," she replies.

Although the legislation that established the Office of Science and Technology Policy (OSTP) in 1976 gave it four associate director positions, some or all of them have remained unfilled for most of the office's history. There are two principal reasons. Individuals in positions where appointment requires Senate confirmation, as these do, can be called to testify to congressional committees--and, theoretically at least, to give legislators some access and insight into what might otherwise be unavailable to them under executive privilege. Second, some presidents and senior staff have viewed the number and rank of OSTP's associate director slots as disproportionate by contrast to other units in the White House and executive office of the president. Bromley, however, has filled all four associate director positions, making sure before he took his own job that he could do so. Beyond the areas addressed by Ratchford's job, they cover industrial technology, life sciences and physical sciences. The assistant director jobs focus on life sciences, physical sciences, and national security affairs, in addition to the environment responsibilities held by Maynard; the associates covering national security and environmental matters report directly to Bromley.

Ratchford and his colleagues have heavy schedules, but no individual budget duties and very few routine administrative matters to handle (although they can play a useful role in identifying candidates for senior S&T positions elsewhere in government). His job entails participation in meetings of some of the committees under FCCSET, and of certain of the formal and informal groupings under the Domestic Policy Council. He does some traveling overseas, but also sees "a very large traffic" of senior foreign science and technology officials in Washington. As a daily matter, he spends much of his time working with the 16 departments and agencies involved in the math and science education program (the major players are Education, Health and Human Services, Defense, the National Science Foundation and the National Aeronautics and Space Administration); and on the international side, with the department of state's geographic and international organization affairs bureaus and the Bureau for Oceans and International Environmental and Scientific Affairs. Of his work with State, Ratchford expresses the view that "we in the government and the country have not used our capacity for S&T as well as we should as a foreign policy tool. That requires strengthening State's abilities in the science area."

In Lepkowski's perception of OSTP, "if they're not objective and impartial, they're not doing their jobs in dealing with conflicts between agencies on issues like global warming." But he suggests that it's difficult to be objective on an issue that is still under debate, or on which opinion remains sharply divided, at the political levels higher in the White House. Ratchford supplies another wrinkle to this consideration. To be credible to the scientific community, he says, "you have to be perceived as not letting political considerations color your judgment." Further, scientists are at something of a disadvantage in the "starkly political environment. More than other professionals, a scientist or engineer is trained to find out why and how something works," and so is usually ready to give the factual answer "even if it defeats the basic policy position he or she happens to have taken. And that can often put you at a disadvantage" in operating in a political environment.

"Objectivity is a value-laden word," Lepkowski says. But he defines it as "providing all the information you can that will enable the policy makers to formulate the best option or group of options that in a practical sense will work."

Key Relationships

Within the Office

Reports to: Director

Works closely with:

Other Associate Directors
Assistant Directors

Outside the Office

Members and staff of the Domestic Policy Council, Economic Policy Council, National Security Council and Council of Economic Advisers
Senior officials of the Office of Management and Budget, the National Science Foundation and the U.S. Trade Representative; of the departments of State, Defense and Education; and of the National Aeronautics and Space Administration and the Central Intelligence Agency

Outside the Government

Professional science, engineering and technology associations and institutes; trade groups; research and political science organizations; academic S&T faculties; state and local education officials; S&T officials of other governments

Profile of Current Associate Director, Policy and International Affairs, OSTP

Name: J. Thomas Ratchford

Assumed Position: 1989

Career Summary: Associate executive officer, American Association for the Advancement of Science, 1977-89

Science consultant, House Science and Technology Committee, 1970-77

Physicist, Office of Scientific Research, U.S. Air Force, 1964-70

Assistant professor of physics, Washington and Lee University, 1961-64

Physicist, U.S. Naval Ordnance Laboratory, 1958-64

Research assistant, Union Carbide Metals, 1957

Education: Davidson College, BS (cum laude), 1957

University of Virginia, MA, 1959; PhD, 1961 (both in physics)

4

COUNCIL OF
ECONOMIC ADVISERS

CHAIRMAN

Level II - Presidential Appointment with Senate Confirmation

Major Responsibilities

- Provide the president with professional, realistic economic analysis and advice. Assist the chief executive in formulating national economic policies, and in developing and carrying out an economic program.

- Coordinate and consult closely in these responsibilities with other senior budget and economic policy officials within the president's executive office and across the executive branch. Take a leading part in drafting the president's important annual policy messages, including those on the economy, the budget, and the state of the union.

- Serve as a leading spokesman to the Congress for administration economic policy. Represent it also to international organizations and other governments, and to the public. Maintain productive relationships and communications with the corporate, banking, trade, research and other sectors that drive the national economy.

Necessary Training, Experience, Skills

Only well-trained and experienced PhD-level economists in the mainstream of the profession need apply. The chairman of the Council of Economic Advisers (CEA) should also be an established and respected practitioner who can move comfortably in the national and international economic communities. The chairman must be an individual who has, or can quickly win, the trust of the president, and political and personal compatibility in that respect is, of course, imperative. Professionally, the occupant of this job must have an appreciation, first, of how economic policy is made and where it fits in the broad sweep of decision making; and second, of Washington and the federal government. An ability to communicate skillfully, whether in the Congress, a media studio or on the speaker's platform, is greatly valuable.

Insight

"There is nothing I can think of that the chairman of the CEA can be said to be in charge of," reflects Charles Schultze, who held the job in 1977-80. "You're always working with other people." And that's just about right, he points out, because the key task here is to provide the president directly with "professional economic advice" either on purely economic questions or the economic aspects of other questions. "I stress the word professional," he adds. What's more, the advice must be "realistic, not ivory tower. The job is therefore different from, say, the role of an economist who happens to be secretary of the treasury or budget director." Schultze thinks every individual in the post must keep in mind that the position "is a channel directly to the president."

Similar comments are offered by Stuart E. Eizenstat, a Washington lawyer who was assistant to the president for domestic affairs and policy in 1977-81. The CEA chairman, in his view, should be "an objective, semi-academic advisor" who gives the president "cold, hard facts." There are "plenty of politicians around the White House," he notes, to try to ensure that an administration's economic actions respond to particular political needs or promises. What the president requires from the chairman is "solid, objective economic advice." That doesn't mean the chairman should not be politically experienced. "You want a worldly guy," Eizenstat says. How easy is it to hold one's self essentially harmless from the political process and yet function effectively--be taken seriously--in a basically political environment? "It's tricky," replies Murray L. Weidenbaum, chairman of the CEA in 1981-82. "Frankly, I think you take on a position like that to have some impact, to do some good, rather than to assure your longevity by your performance."

As a social science, economics enjoys at the CEA one of its most influential roles within the federal executive. The council works with other agencies of government to evaluate the state of the national economy and how it is evolving, and to develop a responsive economic policy that accords, to the extent possible, with the goals and philosophy of the administration in power, at the same time monitoring the integrity of government economic data and analyses. In doing so, says Michael J. Boskin, the Stanford University economics professor who has chaired the CEA since 1989, the council must cover a lot of ground--monetary, tax, regulatory and trade policy, and the federal budget among other areas-- and the various legislative proposals which shape and influence them. "It's sort of a full-service everything where the economy, broadly construed, is concerned," he remarks. To get this job done, there is usually some division of labor between the council's chair and its two other members. Boskin himself is especially interested in the relationship of technology to economic growth. If this were not the case, that topic might be the province of one of the other members. The international and environmental aspects of the council's work are other examples of this.

Much of Boskin's time goes into meetings, consultations and other kinds of steady interaction with the other key managers of economic decision making in the White House and the cabinet. These are the director of the Office of Management and Budget (OMB), the secretary of the treasury, the chief of staff, and the assistant to the president for economic and domestic policy. On a wide range of economics issues, the "troika"--Treasury, the CEA and OMB--is the prime mover in critical functions like formulating the economic outlook that underlies development of the budget. The chairman has regular contact with the assistant to the president for science and technology policy--"a very valuable resource," Boskin says--and with the director of the National Security Council. "We believe, and I think most economists do, that enhanced technology is one of the main sources of economic growth," he comments. In the national security sector, "issues in that area have a heavy economics component." Other contexts in which the chairman moves include daily White House staff meetings, cabinet meetings, and sessions of the Economic Policy Council and the Council on Competitiveness. The CEA chief also heads the Economic Policy Committee of the Paris-based Organization for Economic Cooperation and Development--by common consent, according to Schultze. This provides a formal channel to people who hold responsibilities in other countries similar to those of the chairman.

Beyond the White House, the chairman works with many federal agencies on specific issues. Boskin lists the departments of Commerce, Energy and State, the Environmental Protection Agency and the U.S. Trade Representative among these, but notes that "there are very few large agencies we don't have a major contact with." Most of them, he says, have some "quite good economists whom we rely on at times for levels of detail in areas that we couldn't possibly acquire because we haven't been administering the programs for years and years." The council is also a "well-situated" channel to "assist in explaining the president's decisions and overall philosophy, and for "making sure that people understand why it's important that what may be their particular view of things might have to be adjusted" to those decisions and views.

Weidenbaum thinks the chairman's work benefits from the mix of operating simultaneously at the White House and agency levels. "You interact with the cabinet departments, and you also function as part of the White House apparatus," he says. "It's nice having both sets of relationships because it gives you a tremendous amount of automatic entree into policy making and policy execution." And, of course, this job has the "special opportunity" provided by its relationship to the president. Boskin sees or communicates with the chief executive almost daily, depending on presidential and his own travel. He briefs the president on newly-released economic data, like those provided by the Bureau of Labor Statistics, the night before their public release. The chairman oversees the annual CEA economic report to the president, and has a major hand in the state of the union and budget messages to the Congress. These exercises usually require some hours-long planning and drafting sessions, Weidenbaum adds, where "you not only have access to the president at the meetings, but also as he walks into and out of them."

"Clearly," Schultze observes, "the importance of the job doesn't depend solely on whether or not its occupant has reasonably good rapport with the president. An awful lot of the work is done by working with other members of the administration before it gets to the president." In the end, however, "the only reason anyone pays any attention to the chairman of the CEA is because the president pays attention. You don't have any statutory powers to do anything."

As for contacts and connections with nongovernment people and institutions, Boskin tries to maintain "a two-way interchange, in which we have people in all the time" for consultation and discussion, and which also includes CEA participation in seminars and conferences. "We're very busy, we don't have a lot of time for it, but we want to keep up with what is going on in the academic profession and the think tanks," he says. Periodically, he also checks the views and expectations of corporate and Wall Street economists.

Time spent with the Congress in this job varies with the timetable of the federal budget process, but the chairman's exposure is broad. The House Appropriations Committee begins each budget cycle by inviting the joint testimony of the economic troika. In addition, the CEA chief testifies on the economic outlook to the House and Senate budget committees and presents the yearly economic report to the Joint Economic Committee (which was established simultaneously with the CEA by the Employment Act of 1946). Other congressional panels on the chairman's circuit are the Senate committees on Commerce, Science and Transportation; Finance; Labor and Human Relations; Foreign Relations; and Banking,

Housing and Urban Affairs (which conducts the chairman's confirmation proceedings). In the House, it's the committees on Ways and Means; Banking, Finance and Urban Affairs; Energy and Commerce; Science, Space and Technology; and Agriculture.

The CEA is staffed substantially by academic economists rotating in from the outside. About ten in number, selected and invited personally by the chairman and the other two members of the council, they come for a year on loan from their institutions. "You get continually refreshed," Schultze says. "Usually they're younger people, and you get to run through the latest professional thinking every year." Weidenbaum found them "a loyal group of professionals," a few of whom he asked to stay for a second year. Virtually the entire economic staff of the council is supplied in this way. The CEA's statisticians, who generate its economic data, are normally career federal professionals. Weidenbaum says he encountered no real problems in selecting each year's crop of outside economists, although there was "no shortage of suggestions from political sources" on whom to hire. "I responded always with great politeness," he advises, and "didn't take any of them."

Looking at the nature of the chairman's work, Schultze estimates that 70 percent of it "does not involve the grand, major questions of inflation, unemployment, or taxes, but rather day-by-day participation in hammering out policy on issues which have an economic content even though they are not all economic--welfare policy, energy policy, agricultural price supports, you name it."

Typically, this dialogue is not limited to the executive branch, and even less to the workings of pure economic science and theory. "Take a piece of agricultural legislation," Schultze says. "You start by drafting an administrative position, so you're jockeying back and forth between the secretary of agriculture and OMB. Plus the state department because there's an international angle." A recommendation to the president follows, and the decision goes to the Congress. On the Hill, Schultze says, it must follow the laborious route in both houses from subcommittee to full committee to the floor. Each such case "is a question of what should we give on, what should we negotiate on, what's important. At each stage, the secretary of agriculture is advising what points the administration can yield to avoid losing on the overall bill. You have to figure out whether that's bluffing. So you need to know a little about politics yourself."

It is extremely important for the chairman to have a voice in these exercises, Schultze continues. But "you never win or lose completely. Your whole point is to try to bring economic perspective to it. And it's not done in a vacuum. A lot of this job is negotiating and arguing and trying to influence people to get things done in an environment where not everybody agrees with you and you don't have any power."

Predictions about the issues that will face future CEA chairmen are not easy. "The economy," Boskin points out, "is always evolving. We can't think of it as a snapshot, but maybe as a mural moving along a screen" from which one tries to discern what the likely evolution and influences will be. "Some things are easy to predict--the dramatic changes other societies and our own are going through will affect their economies for some time. The forces of change through technology have enabled us to free up resources, for example in agriculture, that can be used elsewhere." But if these forces for change are not all easily anticipated, he says, "it means the job is never dull. Whether or not the economy is going well, there is always a veritable plethora of things to do. One of the things we have to do here is prioritize our time."

The true challenge in the job, Weidenbaum suggests, does not lie in "developing sensible economic policies. That's only the first step, the easy, fun part of it. The really difficult part is getting the political agreements, compromises, and understandings." While the CEA is properly a part of that process, he believes, "it's highly desirable that the chairman doesn't get caught in those political cross fires." Eizenstat sees the continuing challenge as two-fold. "First, to be the president's eyes and ears on the economy: where is it headed, and what's likely to happen just around the bend that no one else can see? Second, to make yourself relevant. To be enough of an academic that you don't have an axe to grind, that your advice is taken seriously and objectively. And yet to be skilled enough politically that you're not just a fifth wheel out there, throwing off academic fluff." Part of this, he says, is the ability "to make your alliances with the key people, understand the limits of a president's tolerance for divergence from his economic policy, and yet still maintain the respect of private economists and others in the political system for your economic honesty and credibility while still acting within the broad framework of administration policy. That's not an easy balance, but it has to be achieved."

But as Schultze makes clear, the chairman has, or should have, the distinct advantage of not having to pull punches. "You basically don't have any turf to protect. You don't have clients. You don't have the bankers or the farmers. You do have your professional colleagues. And, with some realism and common sense, bringing in that kind of professional advice is exactly what you're there to do."

Key Relationships

Within the Government

Reports to: President

Works closely with:

White House chief of staff
Director, Office of Management and Budget
Assistant to the president, economic and domestic policy
Members, Economic and Domestic Policy Councils
Assistant to the president, science and technology policy
Secretaries and senior economic officials, cabinet departments and certain
  agencies, especially the departments of the Treasury, Commerce, Energy,
  Labor and State, and the Environmental Protection Agency
U.S. Trade Representative

Outside the Government

Economists and economic faculties of the academic community; economic
research institutions; professional economic associations; senior economists
of corporations, banks, investment firms and securities brokers; industrial,
business and trade groups; Economic Policy Committee of the Organization
for Economic Cooperation and Development; occupants of equivalent
positions in other governments

Profile of Current Chairman, Council of Economic Advisers

Name: Michael J. Boskin

Assumed Position: 1989

Career Summary: Economics faculty member, Stanford University, 1970-89, including
  assistant professor,1970-75; associate professor, 1976-77;
  professor, 1978-87; and Wohlford professor, 1987-89
  Director, Center for Economic Policy Research, 1986-1989

Education: University of California at Berkeley, BA (highest honors), 1967; MA
  1968; PhD, 1971 (both in economics).

Chairmen, Council of Economic Advisors Since 1969

Administration	Name and Years Served	Present Position
Bush	Michael J. Boskin 1989 - present	Incumbent
Reagan	Beryl W. Sprinkel 1985 - 1988	Consulting Economist Olympia Fields, Ill.
Reagan	Martin Feldstein 1982 - 1984	National Bureau of Economic Research Cambridge, Mass.
Reagan	Murray L. Weidenbaum 1981 - 1982	Center for the Study of American Business Washington University St. Louis, Mo.
Carter	Charles Schultze 1977 - 1980	Director, Economic Studies The Brookings Institution Washington, D.C.
Ford	Alan Greenspan 1974 - 1977	Chairman Federal Reserve Board of Governors
Nixon	Herbert Stein 1972 - 1973	Senior Fellow American Enterprise Institute Washington, D.C.
Nixon	Paul W. McCracken 1969 - 1971	Edmund Ezra Day Distinguished University Professor Emeritus of Business Administration, Economics and Public Policy University of Michigan School of Business Ann Arbor, Mich.

5

COUNCIL ON ENVIRONMENTAL QUALITY

CHAIRMAN

Level IV - Presidential Appointment with Senate Confirmation

Major Responsibilities

- Advise and assist the president in developing long-term goals for federal environmental policy and the improvement of environmental quality. Keep federal departments and agencies focused on these objectives, mediating their differences to achieve the maximum possible integration and consistency of their environmental programs and actions. Assess scientific and economic factors affecting the national environment and recommend responsive policy adjustments and actions as necessary.

- Oversee the government-wide environmental impact statement process under provisions of the National Environmental Policy Act. Prepare the president's annual report on environmental quality.

- Maintain productive contacts with the private sector, scientific, and public interest communities whose collective activities and purposes are closely involved with the environment and the course of federal environmental policy.

Necessary Training, Experience, Skills

This job is involved to a significant degree with technical and scientific subjects--and debate surrounding many of them--which its occupant must be able to understand and fully participate in. They range from the infrared trapping capacity of gases in the atmosphere and the toxicity of chemicals measured in various ways, to energy and transportation policy and forest fires in national parks. "It's not a job for a literary humanist," a former chairman comments. Another veteran of the job recommends for the position a broad base of experience in environmental policy, acquired in government or in industry. Such an individual need not be a scientist by training, though that is preferable, but must be able call on such expertise within the CEQ staff, and understand what the staff is providing in response. Knowledge of government and of Washington, and a talent for managing different viewpoints, are also critical.

Insight

Propelled onto the federal stage in 1970, the Council on Environmental Quality (CEQ) was described by the president of the time as the environmental conscience of the nation. In its first ten years, the CEQ went on to compile an active and conspicuous record. Today the area of CEQ's mandate is attracting much more attention and debate, from a far more sophisticated public, than was the case at the dawn of America's environmental era. And there are at least some signs that this small White House office will regain and extend its impact.

In the meantime, since CEQ Chairman Michael R. Deland took over the agency in 1989, reconstruction has been a principal order of the day. In the 1980s, he says, "to charitably describe it, the council was allowed to wither on the vine, along with much else in the environmental arena." Now, with a different mind-set prevailing, he thinks the CEQ has begun "to reassert a major policy role." One encouraging indication has been that the president "is committed to the resuscitation of the council." Another was the decision to bring the chairman's office into the Old Executive Office Building adjacent to the White House, a move that boosted the council's prestige and increased the chairman's contact with other major figures in the presidential matrix.

More tangible evidence came in administration support for greater CEQ resources. That clearly helped Deland in the early task he describes as "trying to rebuild what was clearly a moribund entity." Much of his first two years went into work with the Congress in consecutive yearly attempts to increase the CEQ budget by 90 percent. From a figure of $861,000 in fiscal 1989, the Hill did approve a $1.5 million level in 1990 and moved to $1.8 million in 1991. At this writing, Senate and House panels had approved the CEQ's bid for $2.56 million in 1992.

Though this was clearly time worth investing, Deland would like to hold his involvement in day-to-day "fire fights" to a minimum. He knows that on substantive matters his and the council's job is to "think longer term and broader view," while the daily "cop-on-the-beat" responsibilities fall under the regulatory authority of the Environmental Protection Agency (EPA) and other agencies with environmental responsibilities. It is increasingly the CEQ's key mission to understand the country's constantly evolving environmental picture, and where that fits in a global context, and to try to focus the content and direction of an administration's policies and actions accordingly. In doing this, the council acts as a two-way channel supplying advice and coordination to the agencies while promoting promising ideas they generate.

The CEQ's three principal functions relate directly to that mission. First, the CEQ under the chairman's direction reviews federal government activity with environmental implications to be certain that it adheres to and promotes environmental policy objectives. The environmental impact statement (EIS) process and the annual environmental report to the Congress, described further on, are part of this responsibility. So is the preparation of quarterly assessments, for the president, cabinet and senior White House staff, of the environmental aspects of federal programs.

Second, the chairman is an essential arbitrator among the various departments when they differ on policy, helping to settle the differences before they rise to the presidential level. This puts the CEQ chief in the middle of debates on topics like wetlands, global climate change, and the move to make the EPA a cabinet department.

Third, the chairman operates as what Deland calls "an in-house environmental adviser to the president" who attends relevant meetings of the cabinet, the White House economic and domestic policy councils, and the National Security Council (NSC) This function includes, as former CEQ chairman James G. Speth (1977-81) describes it, the task of "putting environment into the energy picture, the transportation picture, the agricultural picture," and so on. It also entails, Deland says, serving as "the eyes and ears of the president with the environmental community in particular, but also increasingly with the industrial sector."

It is on the industrial/commercial front that Deland sees a primary opportunity in the area of pollution prevention: revising economic practices to stop pollution at the source. In his view, "we are really moving beyond the command-and-control, highly prescriptive regulatory structure that we've seen for the last 20 years. That approach has produced appreciable results "but often at great cost, without addressing many problems that are difficult to regulate. If we are to prevent pollution it will come, in my judgment, through the ingenuity and creativity of the private sector." A measure of success in this direction is already apparent, he contends, with "numbers of well-documented cases" demonstrating that "pollution prevention does indeed pay." As an example, he says, the Chevron company has reduced its corporate-wide toxic discharge by more than 60 percent and "saved ten million dollars in disposal costs."

To encourage this pattern, Deland says he has spent increasing amounts of time "reaching out" to the business, industrial and environmental sectors. At his suggestion, the White House set up a presidential commission on environmental quality to give additional institutional thrust to this effort; its members represent corporate leaders, environmentalists, and educators. In action designed to complement the commission's work, the CEQ manages a national competition for presidential recognition of innovative environmental and conservation programs.

Balancing protection against economic progress has, of course, long been a fundamental issue in the environment business. So enlisting the cooperation of the private sector is not exactly a new idea. But it is getting new attention. Russell E. Train, the first council chairman (1970-73), spells it out. In a foreword to the CEQ's 20th annual presidential report on environmental quality, he suggests that it is time for "fresh emphasis" on developing economic incentives to help attain environmental goals. A strong regulatory program will clearly continue to be "the foundation of environmental protection," he writes. But the existence of "literally millions of sources of pollutants" means there are "limits on the effectiveness of enforcement. It makes sense to try to engage market forces whenever practical."

In creating the CEQ, the National Environmental Policy Act gave it the responsibility to prepare the president's annual message to the congress on the state of the environment. "It was a very high-quality document," says Speth, and it took anywhere from a fifth to a third of the council's staff time to prepare. "But it was the CEQ's answer to the annual economic report by the president's council of economic advisers," even though "the quality and even the preparation of the report in the council's second decade became very sketchy." In an earlier day, Train writes, the responsibility for the annual message "put CEQ at the center of an ongoing interagency process that resulted in what I believe to have been the greatest outpouring of legislative and executive initiatives dealing with a single subject in our nation's history."

Among the executive actions Train lists in which the CEQ was a central contributor are the auto fuel economy testing program, the issuance of energy efficiency guidelines, and a ban on the use of DDT and regulation of off-road vehicles on public lands. The CEQ headed the U.S. team in negotiating an agreement with Canada on Great Lakes water quality. Elsewhere at the international level, Council thinking helped produce agreements on ocean dumping and on trade in endangered animal and plant species, as well as a U.S.-Soviet environmental pact. Council enterprise produced environmental cooperation with Germany and Japan, and it enlarged and animated the U.S. role in the environmental initiatives of NATO and the Organization for Economic Cooperation and Development.

Another CEQ assignment under the establishing legislation is to manage the process of environmental impact statements. Originally developed by the CEQ, the EIS guidelines introduced a significant new dimension into federal decision making and changed the outlook and habits of mind of an entire generation of government officials. An EIS is required of every federal agency which takes part in or authorizes a project with environmental implications in which there is federal funding or a federal permit (*de minimis* activities excepted). An agency must follow strict rules governing the timing of EIS preparation in relation to decision making about the project in question and, in general, must offer alternatives for public consideration. A draft EIS is a public document, available for public comment; for large projects, public hearings are usually scheduled. Revisions in a final EIS often reflect these inputs. During the 1980s, EIS implementation rules were eased to speed up the process and make it less likely to result in cancellations of projects. Though the CEQ cannot review all of the hundreds of statements written each year or supervise how each is carried out, it troubleshoots the entire process, counseling agencies on interpretation and application and, as mentioned earlier, resolving interagency differences.

The CEQ's founding statute also provides for a council composed of a chairman and two members. But in fact the two members' slots have remained unfilled, a situation that continues while the Congress ponders the recommendation of a blue-ribbon panel of environmentalists to eliminate them. The reasoning behind this proposed change, according to Deland, is two-fold. First, "in an era of financial austerity, resources were being devoted to positions that few chairmen in the past had figured out how to utilize effectively." Second, a "legal impediment" existed in the situation where, as a presidential adviser, the chairman was a party to decisions which then also had to be put to a CEQ vote.

The CEQ staff numbers about 30. "We're slim," Deland says, "and admittedly so on the scientific side. We are always looking for good talent." Meanwhile, he continues, the council works closely with scientists in the White House Office of Science and Technology Policy, the various departments and agencies, and outside groups. As an example he cites a recent CEQ report on biodiversity that, in addition to peer review within the government, received the scrutiny of experts at Harvard, the Smithsonian Institution, and the Missouri Botanical Garden. The council, Deland adds, also chairs interagency programs on assessment of acid rain precipitation, coastal pollution and habitat loss, and collection, analysis and reporting of environmental data.

Deland says the majority of his staff are "career professionals in law, international affairs, economics, and natural resources." A. Alan Hill, CEQ chairman in 1981-89, recalls that he had one person with scientific training in a total of 13 staff, all of whom he brought in from the outside. "Everybody had to do at least two jobs," Hill says. He was pleased with staff quality, but found it difficult to work with "extremely limited resources." In his day, he adds, the CEQ was sometimes used as a training ground for "OMB budget examiners with no appreciation for environmental concerns." Harvey Alter, manager of the Resources Policy Department of the U.S. Chamber of Commerce, thinks it important that CEQ staff "be able to interact closely with the entire scientific community. To do that, they have to have some peer respect. So they have to be pretty good." On senior staff appointments, Speth says, the chairman has always had a strong voice, and "it's up to the president how much trouble or help he wants to be. For the most part, these are positions that can be filled by the chairman."

While there is a close relationship between the CEQ and the EPA, Deland says, "I wouldn't characterize it as more extensive, in fact, than our relationship with Energy or Interior or Agriculture. We really deal across the board with all of the departments. It goes in cycles, depending on the issues of the moment." In the run-up to the Persian Gulf war of 1991, for example, most of his agency contact was at the departments of energy, defense, commerce and treasury. The chairman can expect to invest considerable time with the Congress in budget articulation and defense, as already noted; the CEQ's appropriations subcommittees in both houses are the panels on HUD, VA and independent agencies. On non-budget business, former chairman Hill says he testified often to the Congress on topics like whaling, ozone, acid rain and climate change. Deland has testified on global climate change, biodiversity, coastal programs, and the upcoming United Nations Conference on Environment and Development (UNCED).

On the subject of congressional relations, Speth raises the "tricky" question whether an agency in the president's executive office should rely on the White House's staff or do it itself. "We hired a congressional affairs director," he says. "I think it's very important to have good Hill intelligence." Deland has renewed that function.

What does the CEQ's agenda for the future look like? What should it look like? Hill thinks it is important for the government "to have an interdisciplinary approach to environmental problems," a view largely shared by Speth, who thinks environmental issues are getting "very multisectoral. It's no longer possible," he says, "to deal with these issues by putting them in an environmental cubby hole and treating them at

EPA, or in the case of land management, for example, at Interior." Every president is interested in the economy, he observes, but not always in the environment. Yet "so much of the job depends for success on a president who wants to use the council." The days of "being able to ignore the environment may have passed with the Reagan presidency," he suggests. But Alter, of the U.S. Chamber, questions the idea that presidency "was trying to kill" government's role in the environment, "as some people have charged." Instead, he thinks the administration was attempting to make good on a campaign pledge to slow down the regulatory process. "The CEQ does what the president wants it to do," he says. "That's different from what maybe it should do." In his view, the CEQ should be "an environmental conscience and philosopher to the country."

Speth believes the CEQ, as an agency in the executive office of the president, should use its energies today in a more concentrated way than in his time. The council, he says, should cut back on report writing (the council churned out about 20 major reports during his tenure, the best-known of which is *Global 2000*), and perhaps shift the annual state of the environment report to the EPA. Most of the CEQ's effort and attention could then go to making environmental policy in the White House, advising the president and developing policy initiatives and new ideas. It should have access to information across the government, and be able to synthesize it for the chief executive. "I would try to get some staff with real expertise on a range of environmental issues," Speth says, "and work closely with White House and other agencies to make certain the president is well served and develops a good environmental record." A sort of National Security Council of the environment? "Exactly," he replies.

Further, there is the UNCED conference, to be held in Brazil in 1992. The first such meeting, the U.N. Conference on the Human Environment, took place in 1972 and is regarded as a landmark in the development of internationalized attention to the environment. Deland says the CEQ plays "a major role" in the government's preparations for UNCED, including the function of liaison to nongovernmental organizations. These will include environmental, industrial, religious and other groups concerned with environmental affairs. The CEQ has also organized meetings around the country in connection with UNCED to gather public views and contributions. Deland emphasizes the importance of pollution prevention as "the key to environmentally-sustainable global economic development. We need to work with governments in eastern Europe and the developing countries as they begin to industrialize," he says. "We would like to try to ensure that they don't replicate some of the mistakes we've made in this country."

He sees U.S. environmental questions as "increasingly intertwined with other nations and international institutions." The links between the environment and food and water supplies, the phenomenon of environmental refugees, the general atmosphere of international cooperation or conflict--"all these things become matters of national security interest," he says, which is one reason he spends time with members of the NSC staff. A CEQ chairman must live with the reality that this country produces 22% of the world's total emissions of carbon dioxide, one of several "greenhouse" gases widely viewed as factors in climate warming. But Deland believes the United States is "an international leader in this arena," and suggests that some nations are "playing politics with the issue, publicly pledging to reduce emissions while avoiding specifics of implementation." Early in the next century, he says, this country will become a "statistically insignificant contributor of carbon dioxide as India, China and Brazil develop their resources" and U.S.-produced carbon dioxide drops as a percentage of the global total. "We have a real obligation, for example, to see that China uses the coal pile on which it sits in an environmentally sensible fashion." But, he concedes, the continuation of U.S. carbon dioxide emissions at the same level in absolute terms complicates an American leadership role on the problem.

The international environmental mission Deland describes "means transfer of technology, and it means dollars," he says. "It also means an opportunity for the private sector in this country to become much more actively and meaningfully involved in the developing world. And, particularly in eastern Europe, the Japanese and the Germans to a degree are beating us out of the starting blocks."

Thus, as has been the case from its beginning two decades ago, many of the issues the CEQ deals continue to be matters that don't stop at the water's edge. It's a point that Speth, like Deland, emphasizes. Developing countries, technology and trade, for example, are all international questions with environmental ramifications, he points out, that some entity, "just in raw governance terms," has to coordinate. "You're dealing with a new generation of issues which are going to require that. And you're dealing with a set of new approaches to old issues like pollution control that are going to require it. That's certainly the basic new role for the council as I see it," Speth says--"hammering out successful policies and coordinating interagency behavior." This has never been fully systematized, he notes. When a president, for instance, calls for an integrated policy "in some attractive, saleable package" to deal with global environmental issues--"taking into account that tropical deforestation contributes to global warming just as U.S. domestic energy policy does"-- the CEQ should be there to do it. "I don't know whom else you could turn to," he adds.

Key Relationships

Within the Government

Reports to: President

Works closely with:

Assistant to the President, Science and Technology Policy
Members, Committee on Earth and Environmental Sciences, Federal Coordinating
    Council for Science, Engineering and Technology
Domestic Policy Council
Economic Policy Council
National Security Council
Chairman, Council of Economic Advisers
Vice President's Council on Competitiveness
Administrator, Environmental Protection Agency
Secretaries of Agriculture, Commerce, Defense, Energy, Interior, State and
    Treasury

Outside the Government

Business and industrial executives; public interest organizations in the
environmental, energy, ecology, conservation, and agricultural fields; professional
environmental scientists; academic institutions; state environmental officials;
foreign environmental officials; international organizations

Profile of Current Chairman, Council on Environmental Quality

Name: Michael R. Deland

Assumed Position: 1989

Career Summary: New England Regional Administrator, Environmental Protection
                       Agency, 1983-89
                       Counsel, Environmental Research and Technology, Concord, MA,
                       1976-83
                       Various positions with EPA's New England Regional Office,
                       including Chief, Legal Review Section, and Chief, Enforcement
                       Branch, 1971-76

Education: Harvard University, BA, 1963
                       Boston College, JD, 1969

Chairmen, Council on Environmental Quality Since 1970*

Administration	Name and Years Served	Present Position
Bush	Michael R. Deland 1989 - present	Incumbent
Reagan	A. Alan Hill 1981 - 1989	Environmental Policy Consultant San Rafael, Cal.
Carter	James Gustave Speth 1979 - 1981	President World Resources Institute Washington, D.C.
Carter	Charles H. Warren 1977 - 1979	Not available
Carter	John A. Busterud 1977	Not available
Ford	Russell W. Peterson 1974 - 1976	President Emeritus National Audubon Society
Nixon	Russell E. Train 1970 - 1973	Chairman World Wildlife Fund Washington, D.C.

* The CEQ was established by the National Environmental Quality Act of 1969

6

OFFICE OF MANAGEMENT AND BUDGET

PROGRAM ASSOCIATE DIRECTORS
NATURAL RESOURCES, ENERGY AND SCIENCE
NATIONAL SECURITY AND INTERNATIONAL AFFAIRS

Senior Executive Service

(The associate director positions at OMB match closely in key responsibilities as well as necessary experience and skills, described below. Subsequent pages in this description provide individual perceptions and comment about each of the two positions under examination, and should be read together.)

Major Responsibilities

- Ensure that the actions and initiatives of executive branch components under the associate director's supervision conform to the policy and budgetary directions set by the president.

- Work with these assigned federal departments and agencies in preparation of their annual budget requests. Coordinate OMB's review of the submissions in development of the President's budget document. Supervise the agencies' development and presentation of corresponding legislative proposals and the pursuit of their objectives along prescribed policy and budget guidelines, and take a central role in mediating conflicting interests among them.

- Contribute to the formulation of administration policy in areas of the associate director's responsibility.

Necessary Training, Experience, Skills

"The people I've seen who have the toughest time in these OMB jobs," says a former associate director, "are those who have not had experience in government at the federal or state level. They lack a good feeling for what the chemistry is, what people's objectives tend to be on the Hill and in the executive branch. Experience in and knowledge of government is the most important."

That really says it all; we found no one who put a higher premium on any other single credential. The current and immediate past associate directors for natural resources, science, and energy had backgrounds of a decade or more in the executive or legislative areas, one of them in state as well as federal government. In the national security/international affairs area, the government experience of the present program associate director (or "PAD") is even longer. Work in such an environment usually provides practical exposure to the hard compromises in government between program objectives and financial realities, and to the development and execution of public policy. Direct experience with the Congress is immensely useful. "We're on the telephone continually with congressional staff people and sometimes with members," an incumbent PAD says. That two of his current three colleagues (at this writing) have served on the Hill may reflect how broadly the Congress figures in the accomplishment of PADS' tasks. While present and earlier PADs believe scientific or technical training is helpful, none of them feels it to be requisite. Analytical thinking, and communications and social skills, are important. So is stamina. As one former PAD warns, "you're not in a position to do favors and nice things for people. There's a tension between doing your job well and making friends. You can't have it both ways." On this note, another ex-PAD says the job needs "strength of character--the ability to tell people no, which is increasingly the OMB role--and innate courtesy, so they won't feel too badly when you do."

PROGRAM ASSOCIATE DIRECTOR
NATURAL RESOURCES, ENERGY AND SCIENCE

Insight

OMB's key marching orders flow from the mandate to shape an administration program that reflects both presidential policy objectives and the resources deemed to be available to reach them. It is the day-to-day mission of the agency's four PADs to see that this policy/budget prescription--as reviewed and adjusted by the Congress--works. Between them, they operate as chief point of contact and major conduit between the White House and the topmost managers of the executive branch.

PADs divide the components of the executive branch along generally functional lines into the four roughly equal jurisdictions which they oversee. The natural resources, energy, and science portfolio contains among others the departments of agriculture, interior, and energy, the Environmental Protection Agency (EPA), the National Aeronautics and Space Administration (NASA), the National Science Foundation (NSF), the Army Corps of Engineers and the Tennessee Valley Authority. For each of them, the PAD presides over successive stages of a yearly exercise whose end product is the president's budget document. Essentially, this begins with an agency's budget request and includes the review of this submission within OMB, its "passback" to the agency, and a period for appeals which sometimes rise to the highest levels of the West Wing. Thereafter, under the PAD's watchful tutelage, the agency prepares and presents to the Congress legislative proposals that frame its program within the revised budgetary guidelines. In the course of each year, as agencies and departments carry out their programs, PAD oversight aims to ensure that they don't--in word or deed--stray off the policy and budget reservation. Getting this job done, especially in an era of scarce resources, endows PADs with clout that some observers say comes close to cabinet-level power.

In managing the entire process, PADs cover a lot of ground. Sudden, overriding, urgent assignments--propelled by interest at the topmost levels of the White House--are imposed on top of the already frenetic routine, and are by no means unusual. Senior officials of the White House and the leadership of the assigned agencies and departments are part of the daily beat; consultation and negotiation with congressional members and staff are frequent, detailed and time-consuming.

One important issue for anyone interested in the effectiveness and productivity of the federal scientific community is its capacity to maintain its place in the sun. The question seems particularly appropriate for those at OMB who ride herd on budget and policy in the science sector. Does the community have the respect, even the esteem, of policy makers? Of those who vote and distribute the resources?

"Yes and no," says Robert E. Grady, the PAD for natural resources, energy and science since early 1989. He sees considerable regard at high administration levels and in the Congress for professional scientists in government, a factor which also shields them somewhat from political buffeting. But "they are systematically squeezed by the nature of the budget and by trends in the whole process of how government allocates its resources. They're under enormous pressure to fund their enterprise, as is the whole world of appropriations, because of simple arithmetic in the growth of entitlements." Taken literally, the logic of present trends, he says, is that interest on the national debt plus entitlements will eventually consume the federal budget entirely, leaving nothing for discretionary investment. "Even now, though a lot of our scientists are coming up with worthy projects and a lot of the individual investigators are greatly respected on the Hill, the system just can't deliver the money it would like to that group."

Some "enormously difficult choices" therefore lie just ahead; "if Congress keeps the size of the science pie constant, we won't be able at the same time to fund all individual investigator grants that are approved, fund the array of big-science projects currently on the drawing board, or adequately fund science and technology education. So we're going to have to think about how to build things smarter, cheaper, faster. And we have to find a way once again to make the process of approving individual investigator grants more competitive. Most importantly, we've got to invest more in the future--and the first and most important step is to bring mandatory spending under control."

On the merits, "science competes well" and obviously will get its fair share if more discretionary resources become available and--he repeats the view--entitlements are controlled. "But that's a big if," Grady warns. Without fundamental budget reform over the long term, he stresses, "I don't think the problem will be solved." He views a big part of his job as "trying to deliver funds for critical needs; one prerequisite of that is delivering a little less to not-so-critical needs." In the latter category, he cites an example--"areas where we're still giving two percent and at the most five percent direct loans to rural telephone cooperatives that are among the most profitable enterprises in the country. That to me doesn't make a heckuva lot of sense."

But Grady has no illusions about the political process. OMB has been stressing what he calls "the need to invest more in the future and less toward satisfying well-organized current constituencies." Yet "it's very less toward satisfying well-organized current constituencies." Yet "it's very hard to move resource allocations toward a more generalized notion of public interest or investing in the future when the narrow interests are so well organized, so well represented, so dominant in the electoral process--I mean, an unbreakable hold." Such situations constitute "the biggest single frustration" of his time in the job, a "one-trench-at-a-time struggle."

Each such struggle should answer the question, as Grady phrases it, "whether we are investing the marginal federal dollar in the area of greatest marginal return--for the health of the American people, or the environment, or whatever your interest is. In the environmental area, for example, there's a sense that the match between marginal risk and marginal investment isn't perfect. The same is true in public health questions. It's a useful debate for the president's science advisor to help frame and organize, along with the budget office and the other players."

The science adviser and Grady began working together for the fiscal 1991 budget year on what he calls "cross-cutting analyses of science budgets in general topic areas," using the interagency Federal Coordinating Council for Science, Engineering and Technology committees. They focused first on earth sciences. "I heard a lot of people in the scientific community outside government say this was a well-thought-out, well-organized way to approach the problem--to bring all the scientists from all the agencies involved into one meeting place, discuss the priorities and come up with a package that cuts across seven or eight agencies, then go to the Hill and ask for the package as a package." The same model was extended to other areas--science and math education, high-performance computing--in the 1992 budget. "We are enormously supportive of the mission of NSF," Grady adds. "We've stayed committed to its upward budget path and tried to begin addressing some of the new priorities they've outlined in education. We're struggling with how to address the question of academic research facilities. Direct appropriations subject to earmarking don't seem to be the best way to solve that complex, long-term problem, but we have recommended federal support for academic instrumentation. NSF is one of the favored agencies around here in the budget sense."

Though this program associate director does not need an explicit scientific background, "you obviously have to know enough to make educated judgments," says Robert K. Dawson, who had the position in 1987-89. "But I found my time better spent on policy, budget and management issues, because science is obviously something you can't fake when you're talking to a Nobel winner." Instead, he made certain his career subordinates--"outstanding certified scientists"--were kept informed and involved. "In all the areas, not just science, that made my job a lot easier. They knew it was their job to challenge the science that would be part of any decision."

three divisions whose chiefs are the PAD's key subordinates. Most of its PhD scientists work in the energy and science division and, specifically, in the nuclear energy and science and space branches. (Nearly all OMB professionals have a master's degree at minimum in their subject areas, or in public policy.) The unanimity of present and former PADs on the subject of staff competence is striking. Dawson calls them "superb technicians, unbelievably gifted. It's phenomenal the energy they expend."

But the PAD's relationship with the staff must be a thoughtful one. "They're back in the shadows," Dawson explains. "Not a lot of applause or recognition." He found it easy to cross the career/noncareer bridge. For one thing, "without daily reliance on the career people, budget directors and PADs just aren't going to know enough to do their jobs." To provide this kind of support, staff must be fully in the loop; this means "keeping them informed, just knowing that if they're going to be effective, to help you, you had better keep them up to speed." Failure to do so--and it happens far too often, Dawson says--can bring "devastating" embarrassment to a career OMB-er who "learns something from an agency under his or her charge that's happened with higher-ups at OMB."

"They are very serious people," Grady says. "They really do have the public interest in mind. It's an honor, a joy, to work with them. One of the fun things about OMB is that, both by tradition and current incarnation, it is a pure meritocracy. People are extremely unsentimental and not terribly concerned about hierarchy or organizational infighting. The way to be perceived well and get ahead is just to be smart."

Dawson offers some instructive thoughts about relationships with the components of government under the supervision of this position. "The agencies varied a lot," he remembers. "The good agency heads were those who sought you out, who stayed ahead of the curve, who looked at OMB as an ally. They would arrange monthly meetings at least, and there were always other discussions going on over testimony being cleared, or legislation, and day-to-day budgetary problems. One or two others didn't want to deal with OMB, didn't like the fact that somebody else had any role. There I found myself having almost to force a meeting; otherwise weeks or months would go by and the chances of a slugfest would go up. I used to tell secretaries of my departments that we were better off talking when neither of our shirt tails was on fire."

As to how this PAD's time divides among assigned agencies, Grady thinks that, overall, it is fairly evenly distributed between the major ones. He spent his first year mostly on environmental issues, including an "especially large amount of time on the Clean Air Act," helping to draft the administration's proposal and spending most of a month to negotiate it with senior senators. In 1990 came the farm bill, including a good deal of effort within the framework of that year's budget summit talks, and NASA appropriations issues. In the course of it all, Grady says somewhat dryly, he has gotten to know quite well the staffs of the House and Senate appropriations subcommittees with jurisdiction over the departments of housing and urban development, veterans affairs, and the independent agencies.

Among these independents are some of his key science and technology agencies, and the appropriation and allocation of resources for them presents what he calls "one of the biggest challenges in terms of funding science." This stems in part from the caprice of the congressional division of labor in appropriations responsibilities. This is how Grady explains it: "In one subcommittee--HUD/VA/independent agencies--you have funding for veterans' medical care which is enormously popular and very hard to resist; funding for housing and the homeless; for EPA and NASA; and for general science responsibilities including, for example, the NSF." Not only do agencies like NASA or NSF, with less popular or poignant agendas, tend to get badly squeezed in the funding process within the HUD/VA/independent agencies subcommittee, Grady says; the subcommittee itself usually ends up the loser in a larger and earlier pie-slicing game. This is the procedure by which the parent appropriations chairmen decide how to allocate to all of their subcommittees the annual domestic discretionary spending portion of the budget. And the HUD/VA/independent agencies subcommittee, Grady points out, "happens to be the one charged with funding many of the discretionary science programs."

As a result, OMB has in a sense found itself in league with the Senate and House subcommittee chairmen in lobbying for greater allocations "so that we could fund more of these science priorities." Grady credits them for good effort under "harrowing" circumstances. "We're sympathetic with their plight. That's the wall we hit every year at 60 mph."

Because of its role as an enforcer arm of the presidency and the increasing frequency with which it must say no, someone has called OMB the agency people love to hate. But in fact, Dawson reflects, "as long as I didn't personalize it with the agencies, as long as I tried to help them, people I dealt with basically understood what I had to do. Also, my willingness to go shoulder to shoulder with an agency head to the Hill, and fight their battle with them when they were right, diminished a lot of that."

Key Relationships

Within the Agency

Reports to:

Director
Deputy Director

Works closely with:

Assigned career staff

Outside the Agency

Assistant to the President for Science and Technology Policy
Assistant to the President for Economic and Domestic Policy
Assistant to the President for Cabinet Affairs
Heads of assigned agencies and departments and senior deputies
Economic Policy Council
Domestic Policy Council

Outside the Federal Government

A wide array of private and public sector groups concerned with the federal role in U.S. scientific and technical enterprise.

Profile of Current Associate Director
Natural Resources, Energy and Science

Name: Robert E. Grady

Assumed Position: 1989

Career Summary: Senior adviser, office of the president-elect, 1988-89
Senior adviser, speech writing and policy, Bush-Quayle campaign, 1988
Speech writer, office of the vice president, 1986
Director of communications, office of the governor of New Jersey, 1983-85
Administrative assistant, office of Rep. Millicent Fenwick, U.S. Congress, 1979-82

Education: Harvard University, BA cum laude, 1979
Stanford Graduate School of Business, MBA, 1988

Associate Directors for Natural Resources, Energy and Science Since 1969

Administration	Name and Years Served	Present Position
Bush	Robert E. Grady 1989 - present	Incumbent
Reagan	Robert K. Dawson 1987 - 1989	Vice President Cassidy and Assocs. Washington, D.C.
Reagan	Randall E. Davis 1985 - 1987	Partner Jones, Day, Reavis & Pogue Washington, D.C.
Reagan	Frederick N. Khedouri 1981 - 1985	Senior Managing Partner Bear, Stearns Washington, D.C.
Carter	Katherine Schirmer 1980 - 1981	Not available
Carter	Eliot R. Cutler 1977 - 1980	Partner Cutler and Stanfield Washington, D.C.
Ford	James L. Mitchell II 1975 - 1977	General Counsel and Exec. Vice President First Fidelity Bancorporation Newark, N.J.
Ford	Frank G. Zarb 1974 - 1975	President Smith Barney Inc. New York, N.Y.
Nixon	John C. Sawhill 1973 - 1974	President The Nature Conservancy Arlington, Va.
Nixon	William A. Morrill 1972 - 1973	President and CEO Mathtech Inc. Princeton, N.J.
Nixon	Donald B. Rice 1970 - 1972	Secretary Dept. of the Air Force
Nixon	Maurice Mann 1969 - 1970	Deceased

PROGRAM ASSOCIATE DIRECTOR
NATIONAL SECURITY AND INTERNATIONAL AFFAIRS

Insight

This PAD has budget and policy oversight for defense, foreign policy and intelligence activities. That responsibility covers, among others, the departments of defense and state, the government's intelligence community, and a number of agencies involved in international economic, trade and development matters--among others, the Office of the U.S. Trade Representative, the Export-Import Bank, the Overseas Private Investment Corporation, and U.S. participation in the World Bank and its sister international financial institutions.

With the dramatic revisions the world has witnessed since 1989 in national political systems and international relationships, how is this key job evolving? How should it evolve? Alton G. Keel Jr., who held the position in 1982-86, believes its objectives and priorities are changing radically, but not its functional responsibilities or the skills required.

"It's clear that the threat has changed, the world environment has changed, so defense priorities and needs have changed," Keel says. "The job now is to make sure that there is an orderly retrenchment of the defense budget, consistent with the president's own views and assessments. And that's an enormous difference. Same function but the objective is different."

Edwin L. Harper, an experienced former OMB and White House official, subscribes to the view that, in an era of diminishing resources, the political influence of PADs generally is increasing. In contrast to eras of defense buildup when OMB is "somewhat shackled," he says, the present period of constrained resources for national security should give OMB "much more leverage." Harper thinks it is therefore even more important to have an associate director in this sphere "who understands technology and its capabilities, and is able to wade into discussions on the merits of alternate defense technologies. The important role this associate director plays, along with the White House science and technology adviser, is interpreting technology for the president and others in OMB and educating the political leadership on the significance of the technologies we're dealing with--ours and those of other countries."

Further, with a number of countries trying to move from directed to free-market economies, Keel takes this view of the altered U.S. role: "Before, we were pointing out the weaknesses of centrally-planned economies. Now the world has come to recognize this. So our burden now is showing them how to make free markets work. Our advocacy has ended; their implementation is beginning. Our objective has changed. Part of the emphasis of this job now has to be on how we help them sustain the momentum, to make sure the transformation is successfully carried out and sustained."

But "whether you're building the defense budget up or down, the skills required are the same," he points out. "You ultimately must make sure the basic national priorities are being met. And in the case of the economic changes, where we have to turn exhortation into action plans, again I think the skills are very similar."

For now, the two main parts of the job demand attention in a proportion strikingly inverse to their budgets, as made clear by Robert Howard, the job's occupant since 1990. "National security is worth roughly $300 billion," he says. "The other piece, international affairs, is worth $20 billion, less than ten percent as much. In terms of my time, however, it's almost in reverse order, because there are so many details in international affairs that are of direct concern to OMB." It's an arena, he says, that needs continual OMB attention to little problems--"well, they're not so little. But they are politically tough problems that come up all the time: legislation, squabbles between agencies." Like his staff, Howard says, he spends significant time in the interagency/National Security Council process, and also with the office of the U.S. Trade Representative. And--even though the working relationship with the Pentagon is the closest and most interwoven of any at OMB--"it's the international affairs component that takes up the time."

Professional qualifications for this position? "I'll bet nobody who's ever had this job has felt altogether qualified for it," says Howard. His responsibility for Defense gets him involved from time to time in research and development programs, including the Strategic Defense Initiative (SDI); and the general international science area is part of the international affairs sector of his work. "Those issues sometimes have a research and development flavor," he says, "although the center of gravity is not technical." A physicist, he thinks technical training is useful, not essential. "It's good to have been in the government before," he counsels, "and good to know something about the Congress." He notes that three of his predecessors in the past ten years were congressional staff members. Howard himself has "been around OMB a long time," and worked previously at the old Bureau of Standards (now the National Institute of Standards and Technology).

Keel's views on this matter match Howard's. His is a deep science background--a bachelor's degree in aerospace engineering, a doctorate in engineering physics with a major in applied mathematics and aeronautical sciences, post-doctoral work in aeronautical sciences and mechanical engineering. "But I'd be the last one to argue that science issues in this job were a daily affair," he says. "These are really policy issues, strategic planning issues, budget issues. As much as anything else, your political instincts and your ability to think analytically and strategically, as well as legislative skills, were key for that position. I'd rate them higher than a pure science/technical background. Science and technology were not the focus."

"But did my background help? Absolutely." In fact, Keel says, his engineering and scientific training equipped him to ask the right questions of agencies seeking support for given proposals. This was important in determining whether an agency truly understood what it was advocating and was providing the correct rationale or justification. "It helped me make sure that what was being presented in seeking policy, budget or legislative support was valid." Projects on which his technical background proved especially relevant included the Stealth bomber, SDI, and technology transfer and strategic export control. "Even in terms of being able to put budget presentations together, and knowing and being comfortable with mathematics, it helped."

Precisely how widely a PAD ranges through the uppermost echelons of the White House depends on the management style and personal preferences of superiors at OMB and the executive office of the president. All of them, however, plug into an extensive network of hyperactivity within those circles that relates to their jobs. "I normally go along, either as the second guy or sometimes the first guy, to the deputies' meetings of the National Security Council (NSC)," Howard says. He is the OMB representative as well to a number of NSC program coordinating committees, "although I don't go to too many of them in person."

His closest associates in OMB are his fellow PADs and the other senior staff, the assistant director for budget review, the executive associate director for management, and the general counsel. He sees the director and deputy director "all the time." Howard regularly deals at the under secretary/assistant secretary level of the agencies he's responsible for; this extends to the secretary and deputy secretary of defense in the framework of such Pentagon gatherings as the Defense Program Review Committee; and he also sees "a fair amount of" the deputy secretary of state. With the smaller agencies, he normally talks with agency heads. But his contacts can range more broadly within an agency. "It depends on where the action is. Sometimes it's at a lower level--deputy assistant secretary, lower than that--we're not snobbish." At Defense, he also sees "assorted generals, assorted secretaries and assistant secretaries of the military departments."

In handling their agencies PADs encounter what Keel describes as inevitable bureaucratic resistance arising from the instinct to protect one's own constituents. Howard's phrase for it is "how people in agencies think, their special parochial way of thinking." The result, says Keel, is that agencies and departments argue for their own programs and priorities, "evolving their agenda instead of the president's. And the place where that comes into conflict with the president's policy objectives is OMB. You are literally the person who has to say no, and say it to cabinet members who come to you and make their pleas for their agency. And it does become 'their' agency after a period of time." Any administration can take office with its own set of objectives and designated department heads, he says. "But it's an extraordinary exception when ultimately those cabinet members don't become to one degree or another captives of their own bureaucracies and constituent interests."

Of course, many of those who lobby the Congress and the executive branch to protect and enhance the stakes of constituents and clients also seek a hearing at OMB. How frequent or broad is this dialogue, given the crowded, nonstop pace imposed on program associate directors? "You may not believe me," answers Howard, "but I'm not hard to see. Within reason, I'm pretty accessible." Keel operated with a similar philosophy. "I had an open-door policy for anyone who wanted to make their case to me," he says. For example, part of the job's oversight is foreign economic and security assistance, a fact that brought ambassadors and ministers in to plead their special needs--perhaps for debt forgiveness on foreign military sales or an enhanced shot at Economic Stabilization Fund money. Or the caller might be an American steel industry representative arguing for special protection under existing trade legislation. "Typically, it was on the basis of their wanting to see me," Keel notes. "I wouldn't solicit it, but would try not to refuse it, either. It was only fair to let them have a voice and let that be part of our analysis and conclusions."

A staff of about 60, all of them career service people, supports this PAD position. Were a vacancy to occur, Howard would have a strong voice in choosing his three division chiefs (each PAD office has a special studies unit in addition to those overseeing its assigned areas of government), and "would have some opinions" in the choice of branch chiefs. In principle, he thinks he has veto rights even on the examiner level, but has never exercised them. The staff includes some physicists and economists; "I want a certain number of those, a certain amount of that skill around," Howard says, so in hiring decisions "I might go after an economist, or someone who understands defense technology very well."

Keel echoes other present and former PADs in praising the caliber of staff. "Some of the best in government--good, talented, qualified people, objective, competent and loyal." But he sounds a cautionary note in tune with the comments of Robert Dawson earlier in this assessment. "It was clear that I was the representative in all my meetings, but I relied to a great degree on my staff to do the analysis. I would not have been able to be effective in the role I played without that work. If you try to work without them, I'm sure you'd have a staff morale problem. So, in work without them, I'm sure you'd have a staff morale problem. So, in part, how good the staff is and how good they feel about themselves depends on how they're used."

All the same, OMB staff analysts in the national security area find themselves greatly outnumbered in dealing with some of the agencies under their charge. Harper calls it "a David and Goliath" situation. OMB examiners face "tremendous armies of people at Defense and elsewhere who have the same kinds of skills that they have," he says. "From time to time, they just wear down the OMB professional staff. It's hard to come up with fresh ideas on issues that go on for years. Meanwhile, Defense has 10 or 20 times the number of people that OMB has." Harper thinks the PAD must often be the saver in these circumstances. "In some ways, it's the skill of the associate director that's critical to making or breaking the role OMB plays in the national security arena."

Key Relationships

Within the Agency

Reports to:

Director
Deputy Director

Works closely with:

Assigned career staff

Outside the Agency

Assistant to the President for Economic and Domestic Policy
Assistant to the President for Cabinet Affairs
Heads of assigned agencies and departments and senior deputies
Economic Policy Council

Outside the Federal Government

Broad sectors of the U.S. defense, aerospace and associated industries. Private sector groups concerned with U.S. foreign and defense policy, development and security assistance, and intelligence matters.

Profile of Current Associate Director

Name:	Robert Howard
Assumed Position:	1990
Career Summary:	Deputy associate director for national security, OMB, 1987-90 Deputy chief, National Security Division, OMB, 1981-87 Chief, Air Force branch, National Security Division, OMB, 1974-81 Budget examiner, National Security Division, OMB, 1969-74 Consultant in general science, Bureau of the Budget, 1968-69 Research physicist, National Bureau of Standards, 1960-67
Education:	Columbia University, BA with highest honors, distinction in physics, 1953 New College, Oxford, PhD, physics, 1957 Fulbright Fellow, National Physical Laboratory, New Delhi, 1966 Visiting research physicist, United Kingdom Atomic Energy Research Establishment, 1962 and summer, 1964 Post-doctoral fellow in physics, Carnegie-Mellon University, 1958-60

Associate Directors
National Security and International Affairs Since 1969

Administration	Names and Years Served	Present Position
Bush	Robert Howard 1990 - present	Incumbent
Reagan	L. Wayne Arny 1987 - 1989	President Wayne Arny Company Washington, D.C.
Reagan	Alton G. Keel Jr. 1982 - 1986	Deputy Chairman Riggs Bank Washington, D.C.
Reagan	William Schneider Jr. 1981 - 1982	President International Planning Arlington, Va.
Carter	Edward R. Jayne II 1977 - 1981	President McDonnell Douglas Missile Systems St. Louis, Mo.

Ford	Donald G. Ogilvie 1974 - 1977	Executive Vice President American Bankers Assoc. Washington, D.C.
Nixon	B.A. Bridgewater Jr. 1973 - 1974	President Brown Group Inc. Clayton, Mo.
Nixon	Kenneth W. Dam 1971 - 1973	Vice President IBM Corporation Washington, D.C.
Nixon	James R. Schlesinger 1969 - 1971	Senior Counselor Center for Strategic and International Studies Washington, D.C.

PART III

7

AGENCY FOR INTERNATIONAL DEVELOPMENT

ASSISTANT ADMINISTRATOR
SCIENCE AND TECHNOLOGY

Level IV - Presidential Appointment with Senate Confirmation

Major Responsibilities

- Increase the effective use of science and technology to assist the progress of developing countries. Formulate new approaches to the science of development assistance, to technology transfer and to research in the field of economic development.

- In support of this objective, oversee the Bureau of Science and Technology (S&T) responsible for all research activity of the Agency for International Development and for technical assistance programs administered overseas by the agency as part of U.S. foreign assistance.

- Work within the interagency process and with individual federal departments and White House officials to assist the agency's S&T mission. Establish and maintain coordinative relationships with international development assistance and health organizations and with the foreign assistance and development offices of the countries involved.

Necessary Training, Experience, Skills

Scientific or technical training is not essential, but running this job without it would be appreciably more difficult. The assistant administrator should feel comfortable in at least a few technical areas--bearing in mind that, as one of those who has held the position puts it, "we're not talking about superconductors here, we're talking about things like one-time syringes that prevent the spread of AIDS." Others place value on an understanding of the agency, on the ability to find support for S&T objectives in it and outside it, and on management skills and a feel for policy. A candidate with firsthand experience in the developing world-- "someone who has lived there, understands what it smells and feels like, and how people think"--obviously starts with a clear edge.

Insight

Since the second world war the United States has tried to help developing countries toward healthy economic growth and an improved and stable quality of life, not only in their own interest but to advance the goals of U.S. foreign policy. For most of the period, the Agency for International Development (AID) and its forebears have been the chief instrument of that intent. And within AID, the S&T bureau works to expand the role of technology and develop new applications for it in carrying out the agency's mission.

Out in the field, this objective finds expression in a number of specific activities in some 77 countries where experts on contract from the U.S. industrial, academic and nonprofit sectors work with S&T staff. For example, there is the transfer of technology into agriculture, reflecting the concern of developing countries with the security of their food supplies. Technology here means new hybrid seeds, fertilizers and uses of pesticides; it also means improved transportation and distribution systems. In the area of energy, which is crucial to economic growth, better use of technology can help both to expand the supply by greater reliance on, say, renewable sources, and to make energy consumption more efficient. On another front, S&T works to drive down high infant mortality rates through training and technology transfer in immunization, pre- and postnatal care and nutrition. Its family planning program is the bureau's largest, at about $100 million a year.

Backstopping this work in Washington is one of the two principal functions of S&T's 200-member staff. A key mechanism in this are the agency-wide groupings called sector councils. Each council brings together experts in a single discipline from the geographic and functional bureaus to address AID's scientific and technical efforts. Among its other impacts, this strategy produces a kind of synergy that strengthens the agency's ability to help developing countries take advantage of advances and innovations in technology.

The sector council approach took formal shape during the tenure of Nyle C. Brady, assistant administrator in 1981-89. "We tried to bring the technical staffs in Washington together to get them to focus on the subject matter itself," he recalls, "and not just on their particular administrative unit." Indeed, the need for such a cross-cutting structure had been apparent even earlier. "In these technical areas," says U.S. Congressman Sander Levin, who in 1978-80 headed S&T's predecessor bureau, "it really wasn't feasible for each of the regional bureaus to have a vital core of expertise. In everything from remote sensing satellites to post-harvest food loss problems, you really needed to concentrate that expertise in order for the agency to manage programs effectively and explore new ground."

The other primary responsibility assigned S&T at the time of its reorganization under the present title in 1981 is oversight of AID's research activities. "That covers all sectors" says Richard Bissell, a PhD social scientist who took over the bureau's leadership in 1990--"whether it's physical science like energy, agriculture or natural resources; or more human-focused sciences such as health, family planning, education or rural development." The agency's research budget is about $100 million a year which, with the bureau's support of technical assistance overseas, puts total annual S&T operating funds at about $400 million. That figure, Bissell says, has remained steady for five or six years, although it is augmented from time to time by "special cases," like the additional money provided in fiscal 1991 and directed at eastern Europe. In budget appearances before the Congress, however, Bissell defends a bigger figure than that of his own bureau, mirroring the sector approach to the agency's work. "Testimony on the Hill is not usually by bureau, but by subject matter, so I would, for example, testify on the health budget of the entire agency," he says.

With its own indigenous problems and those imposed by the long years of East-West rivalry, the developing world today poses a greater challenge than ever for development assistance. As testing or proving grounds for the ideologies and ambitions of the Cold War, some countries suffered unnatural distortion of their fledgling economies and politics that continues to plague them. As Cold War competition has dwindled, so have sources of support for developing societies. Political turmoil and civil war remain daunting obstacles to economic progress. They foster corruption and brutality, exacerbate the impact of famine, disease and natural disaster, and hamper the response. Even as science and technology advance the well-being of developed countries, the gap with the third world widens in some areas. For their part, the providers of assistance, faced with their own tightening resources, must shift gears and priorities.

Ironically, in this bleak picture, even the success stories have a problematic significance for the AID of the future. One element of this is what Nicholas Eberstadt, a visiting scholar at the American Enterprise Institute, calls the "negative selection phenomenon." Over the past 20 years, he says, S&T and AID in general have been dealing with countries that by and large are "economic problem cases." Those countries that have achieved self-sustaining economic growth, like Korea, Taiwan or Greece, "have graduated out of AID's responsibility." That leaves the rest--societies "where adverse economic policies and lawless, personalized administrations are the norm." In such countries, Eberstadt says, the prospects of progress are harder to measure by the economic criteria that aid donors like to use. "So probably the odds against success have increased" in the countries to which AID targets its efforts.

Another by-product of those successes abroad has been resentment at home of the role the agency has played in them. "Inevitably," Bissell says, "our attempts to encourage economic growth in developing countries through technology transfer may inadvertently have strengthened long-term competitors of the United States." Specific American agricultural sectors have complained, for instance, "that we've effectively helped competitors to grow and prosper." S&T touches another tender domestic nerve when changing priorities oblige it to trim or close out long-standing contractual relationships with U.S.-based institutions. "We have relationships with a lot of universities, particularly the land grant colleges," Bissell explains. "And having worked with us for over 30 years, they have come to associate specific AID programs and projects with their long-term planning."

Other, more political, sensitivities affect S&T activity in fields like environment and family planning. Pressures against the use of certain pesticides in the United States effectively prevent the agency from counseling their use anywhere else in the world, Bissell says, "even though they may still make some sense in certain areas abroad." As for family planning, he and Brady both mention strictures against "funding work that in any way relates to abortion," as Brady puts it. Research work deemed in any way to be detrimental to American industry or agriculture, Brady adds, "was frowned upon."

S&T's network of interagency relationships includes membership of several working groups within the structure of the Federal Coordinating Committee for Science, Engineering and Technology (FCCSET). On FCCSET's international side, the S&T assistant administrator chairs a subcommittee on science, technology and developing economies. The bureau also works in bilateral coordination with a number of individual agencies like the department of agriculture and the Environmental Protection Agency, using their various kinds of technical expertise in its own programs. "We tend to pick them up on detail, or in cooperative agreements, where we will buy the time of experts in those departments,"

Bissell says. There is considerable contact and work on joint projects with the National Academy of Sciences, and its National Research Council provides peer review for some S&T research projects. The bureau goes outside the government for help as well; its committee on renewable energy, for example, draws on the perspectives of members from industry and the universities.

Hearings and other dialogue with the Congress take a considerable part of Bissell's time. The most frequent ports of call are the foreign aid subcommittees, their parent foreign relations panels, and the appropriations committees of both houses. Brady and Levin report a good deal of travel when they had the job, inspecting specific projects and staying in touch with AID people on the scene; Bissell did not travel much in his first months, but acknowledges that this could change.

Virtually all members of the S&T professional staff have technical backgrounds. Again, the staff is organized along sector lines according to their specialties in agriculture, nutrition, health, family planning, education, energy, the environment and natural resources. During his stewardship, Brady thought "the technical background of the career people was not good because they weren't rewarded for being technical people. And nothing was done to help them try to stay up in their fields." Under the sector council set-up, Brady tried to change this by having the sector councils channel to him the names of S&T people in the field who seemed to merit special training. "I fought the battle to get them on the list," he says. "There may have been no more than three or four of them but at least they got that opportunity."

On the subject of staff in the field, Eberstadt believes, too many of them are "micromanaging" projects, partly because the Congress requires "fairly detailed reports" on numerous aspects of even very small projects. "It's not clear to me that that's the way to go," he says. "You need to have an awful lot of staff to respond to that sort of thing, and it takes staff attention away from making the project succeed." He levels another criticism at S&T itself. This is that the bureau, which he says was shaped mainly to develop and promote agricultural science and the dissemination of "green revolution" technology to low-income countries, is in some senses still fighting the last war. "In my own view," Eberstadt states, "there's a bit of too-little, too-late in that sort of structure." All the serious green revolution research, he says, was underway in the 1940s in the case of wheat and, for rice, in the early 1960s. "By the time AID got interested in this, the research and dissemination (of green revolution technology) were not terribly pressing."

But Eberstadt credits AID with establishing the S&T operation in recognition that "science and technology have a role to play in third world economic advance," and praises S&T's role in encouraging the development of "rural technology" and the involvement of American educational institutions in overseas technical assistance. To these should be added activities in other fields such as those cited by Brady and Levin: vaccine development, immunization, and oral rehydration therapy in the struggle against infant mortality, research that developed one-person "micro" enterprises, reforestation and solar-powered health clinics.

Then there is AIDS. In Levin's estimation it is S&T's biggest challenge. Though S&T is charged with addressing the international AIDS effort, "there's no handy precedent for dealing with it," Bissell says. "So one has to try to bring the best tools of American society to bear on a problem where all the scales of cost and resources and diagnosis are very different. There's a translation process there that involves science."

Within the agency itself, Brady says, "the biggest constraint is the establishment. You are trying to do science and technology in an establishment that doesn't have S&T very high on its agenda. So you're having to push upstream." Eberstadt puts this problem a bit differently. "Science and technology transfer programs are not on the list of projects that successive AID administrators have identified as successes," he asserts. "They may have overlooked them or misunderstood what was going on, but within AID's own apparatus the perception seems to be lacking that S&T projects have been identifiable successes for the organization."

"This job is very complex both in disciplinary and managerial terms," Bissell reflects. "Some of the challenges are very macro in scale." He sees a constituency for his bureau's work among what he calls "the informed public," interested in "whether we're making a difference." The best quality Americans bring to this effort, he adds, "is a strong sense of pragmatism about the use of science and technology. They've all read their biographies of Tom Edison and Cyrus McCormick. And they think, why not use technology so you can help change people's lives? It's nice to have that kind of support."

Key Relationships

Within the Agency

Reports to: Administrator

Works closely with:

Deputy Director
Other assistant administrators

Outside the Agency

Associate Director, International Affairs, White House Office of Science and
  Technology Policy
Members, Committee on International Science, Engineering and Technology,
  Federal Coordinating Committee for Science, Engineering and Technology
Assistant Secretary, Health, Department of Health and Human Services
Selected assistant secretaries and administrators, Departments of
  Agriculture, Energy, and Interior, and Environmental Protection Agency
Assistant Secretary, Oceans and International Environmental and Scientific
  Affairs, Department of State
Regional assistant secretaries, Department of State
Directors of component institutes, National Institutes of Health, Department
  of Health and Human Services
National Academy of Sciences
National Research Council, NAS

Outside the Government

Officials of the World Health Organization, the World Bank, and the Food
and Agricultural Organization and other international bodies within the UN
system concerned with the health, nutrition, population and economic growth
of developing countries; academic institutions; representatives of companies
in the food, energy, pharmaceutical and health care industries; private
voluntary organizations; development and foreign assistance officials of other
governments

Profile of Current Assistant Administrator
Science and Technology

Name: Richard E. Bissell

Assumed Position: 1990

Career Summary: Assistant administrator for policy and program coordination, AID,
                      1986-89
                      Director of program development, then director of research, U.S.
                      Information Agency, 1982-84
                      Executive editor, The Washington Quarterly (Center for Strategic
                      and International Studies), 1982-84
                      Managing editor, ORBIS (Foreign Policy Research Institute,
                      Philadelphia), 1975-81
                      Professor or lecturer, Georgetown University, 1984-86; Johns
                      Hopkins School of Advanced International Studies, 1982;
                      University of Pennsylvania, 1978-82; and Temple University,
                      1975-79

Education: Stanford University, BA, 1968
Fletcher School of Law and Diplomacy, Tufts University, MA,
1969; PhD, 1973

Assistant Administrators, Science and Technology Since 1969

Administration	Name and Years Served	Present Position
Bush	Richard E. Bissell 1990 - present	Incumbent
Reagan	Nyle C. Brady 1981 - 1989	Senior Consultant U.N. Development Program Washington, D.C.
Carter	Sander M. Levin* 1978 - 1980	Member, U.S. House of Representatives
Ford, Carter	Curtis Farrar** 1975 - 1977	Director, Admin. & Finance Intl. Food Policy & Research Inst. Washington, D.C.
Nixon	Joel Bernstein** 1970 - 1974	Deceased

* Held position as Assistant Administrator, Development Support Bureau
** Held position as Assistant Administrator, Technical Assistance Bureau

8

DEPARTMENT OF AGRICULTURE

ASSISTANT SECRETARY, SCIENCE AND EDUCATION

Level IV - Presidential Appointment with Senate Confirmation

Major Responsibilities

- Develop policy and plans in the areas of scientific and technological research, education and information to assist and improve the national output of agricultural products, and to protect the environment which supports the process.

- Manage department services designed to carry out these programs and to assist and collaborate with state agricultural research programs.

- Counsel the secretary of agriculture on science and education policies and operations. Work with other department organizations and federal agencies to promote and advance them. Represent the administration's policy and programs in this area to the Congress and to other governments.

Necessary Training, Experience, Skills

Some who know this position think it is best served by individuals at the doctorate level in a science, with exposure to agricultural research or extension service in or outside of government, or to work in a closely allied area. That kind of experience "establishes credibility and knowledge of the field," as one of them expresses it. Another view we heard, however, places greater value on the fresher thinking that a qualified candidate from outside that particular sphere might bring to the job. General agreement exists that knowledge of the legislative process at the state or federal level and demonstrated administrative skill, especially in an academic framework, are distinct assets.

Insight

As in many other areas of the federal science and technical community, biotechnology is a major focus of the thinking and effort that goes into this job. For example, Charles E. Hess, assistant secretary since May 1989, has spent considerable time developing a "scientific, risk-based definition" of those organisms released into the environment that need some degree of regulatory oversight. This is the transgenic plants and animals issue, he explains. In it, the concern is to provide sufficient public assurance about the safety of biotechnology products while not over restricting research or commercialization. Recombinant DNA is "a very precise and safe technology" and "we try not to single it out as being any riskier than conventional plant breeding," he says. He and his staff also invest time promoting biotechnology's benefits to society in the agricultural sector. Advantages like genetically increased resistance to pest-transmitted disease make it possible to reduce the use of pesticides; "designing" the production of meat to make it leaner "is good for diet and health."

Such techniques have led to problems with U.S. trading partners in Europe. They tend to feel, Hess says, that "the economic and social impacts" of technology should be considered just as much as efficacy, purity and safety in the regulation of products in international commerce. "We're totally opposed to that," he states. Social and economic impacts are valid considerations, "but you don't address them by a regulatory process that stops the technology because it may have those impacts. You do additional research to see what the impacts are, and if they're negative you work on mitigating them."

Given the importance of U.S. agricultural sales abroad to the country's overall trade picture, issues like these matter. They figure largely in the involvement of the Office of Science and Education (S&E) in the task of representing the United States in trade and agricultural circles overseas. As part of that effort, a task force on biotechnology research suggested by Hess was set up under the Federal Coordinating Council for Science, Engineering and Technology (FCCSET). A European counterpart group functions under the Commission of the European Economic Community.

The accent on biotechnology, and research in general, is hardly new to this position, or to the department of agriculture. During his service as assistant secretary (1983-89), Orville G. Bentley estimates that interagency coordination of the regulation of biotechnology and its products took 25 percent of his time. Late in his tenure, agricultural research gained significant momentum with a report by the National Academy of Sciences that called for an additional investment of $500 million annually in research "to strengthen the agricultural, food and environmental system." The report spawned the National Research Initiative (NRI), a department of agriculture-wide program managed by the assistant secretary for S&E. It directs new investigation in agricultural sciences to six areas--natural resources and environment, nutrition and food quality, plant and animal systems, developing new products, and markets and trade.

Fiscal 1991 was the NRI's first funded year; the 1992 budget asks for an increase of about 70 percent to $125 million, about a quarter of it destined for agencies under Hess's direct oversight. Assuming that NRI money remains free from congressional earmarking for special purposes, the administration plans to raise its request in ensuing years to achieve a $300 million level.

Kathleen Merrigan, a professional staff member of the Senate Committee on Agriculture, Nutrition and Forestry, welcomes the progress which the increased emphasis on research illustrates. But she believes it tends to obscure and perhaps weaken the original mission of the land grant colleges and the federal structure which has been built to support the U.S. farm system. Care should be taken, she feels, "that research projects help rural communities, family farms, the smaller as well as the bigger schools." For example, while the NRI includes water quality and sustainable agriculture--farming without excessive environmental damage-- among its concerns, she wonders about its adequacy to a situation where "we're facing incredible ground water contamination problems. As we start going into big science, biotech and all that, we seem to be separating more from that mission of trying to link to the communities." When the Senate took account of this concern in farm bill language listing "a broad set of priorities" for agricultural research, it created "a big issue between Congress and the administration" which Merrigan thinks will fuel continuing debate.

The S&E position was established, says Anson R. Bertrand, who held it in 1978-81, "to coordinate the nation's agricultural research and extension programs" in the department of agriculture as well as the land grant universities and state experimental stations and, further, "to interact with Congress and be a voice for the department in science and education matters." Four component agencies operate under the assistant secretary's authority to carry out that assignment. The biggest in terms of budget is the Agricultural Research Service, an in-house basic and applied research program with nearly 140 locations around the country including its national program staff headquarters in suburban Washington, and operations in several foreign countries. Among other areas, it concentrates on plant and animal science, soil and water conservation, commodity processing and nutrition. ARS also works to some extent with experiment stations in the states and with campuses, private-sector associates and other federal entities.

Next comes the Cooperative State Research Service, the main channel for federal support (under the 1887 Hatch Act) of agricultural and environmental research performed by the states. It is the link through which S&E financially supports and coordinates with experimental stations in all states and territories, and with the 1890 land grant colleges, Tuskegee University, and forestry and veterinary schools. Third is the Extension Service, acting as a national network for the transfer of technology, information and education to those who use it. In Hess's words, "it is designed to take information from the researchers and bring it to the users," as well as to act "a feedback system" to bring problems that need solving to the attention of researchers at the land grant college level. The Extension Service employs the skills of its own professional staff and those in the land grant colleges and in more than 3,000 county extension offices. Finally, the National Agricultural Library is the S&E information resource for the entire structure.

Budget authority requested for these operations for fiscal 1992 totaled $1.475 billion, compared with $1.434 billion in 1991. Running the assistant secretary's office adds about $550 million. Hess says about 47,000 people work under his general supervision, including those employed in universities. Their level of training varies from mostly PhDs in the two research agencies to master and PhD degrees in the extension service. He reports increasing difficulty in retaining research scientists, particularly those who work in-house, because of a barely competitive federal pay structure.

Meetings in the FCCSET interagency context and with the approximate two dozen advisory committees that serve this position occupy a substantial amount of time. Hess chairs FCCSET's Committee on Food, Agriculture and Forestry Research and is a member of each of the other six. This is one of the contexts enabling him to stay in touch with science and technology efforts on other fronts, such as the FCCSET-guided interagency study of global climate change, that affect his own responsibilities. The advisory groups have public and private members; they include such committees as those on agricultural biotechnology research, animal health science research, cooperative forestry research, national plant genetics resources, and policy for S&E competitive research grants. Hess follows a formidable speaking and panel discussion schedule across the country, and testifies regularly on the Hill.

Over the years, procedural issues seem to have presented as much challenge to this position as substantive questions. As the first to hold the job with its present parameters, Bentley had the task of defining it and, later, of "establishing recognition" within government as a whole of the department's elevated science and education responsibilities. Having put considerable effort into "coordinating planning groups at the highest levels to address some of the major issues," he believes that "one of the major jobs of the assistant secretary is to improve coordination and interagency cooperation in science and education." In Bertrand's view, the essence of the job is in fact partly procedural: "getting concurrence from the actors out in the research and agricultural communities, putting it together in a coherent package and presenting it logically within the administration and to Congress." Hess and Merrigan point to the congressional propensity to excessive earmarking of funds for physical facilities which remain underused for lack of staff and equipment. Elsewhere, Merrigan sees potential conflict of interest problems facing the assistant secretary where extension service agents also act as consultants for industry. She also calls for "more communication between divisions within agricultural science and between agricultural science and other sciences. We sometimes find that agricultural schools don't talk to medical schools in cases where they're both doing biotech. We're also finding that the agronomists aren't talking to entomologists who aren't talking to horticulturalists."

On a deeper level, Merrigan worries that lack of greater attention to the traditional but contemporary concerns recognized in the establishment of the present system will hurt it. "They really need to think about how to interact with the communities rather than trying to be ivory tower, top-of-the-hill scientists," she argues. Apart from programs like the National Research Initiative, she notes, "agricultural science and education has been level-funded for 20 years. If you look at a research and development chart by agencies, Agriculture doesn't even make the bar graph. There's still a lot of criticism of the land grant system, of the extension service." She says she gets regular inquiries from rural as well as urban members on the Hill about the savings that eliminating one or another of the system's components would generate.

Hess characterizes his task as "trying to achieve an agriculture which is economically viable, internationally competitive and environmentally sensitive." With respect to those goals, Merrigan believes that the "vote of confidence" embodied in increased congressional funding for research is both merited and encouraging. But it won't last, she says, without "some real change" responding to the "new sensitivities that rural America and the Congress are feeling." One of the job's major challenges, therefore, is "to convince the system as well as the funders that you are operating effectively" across the board "so you can move on into the new era."

Key Relationships

Within the Department

Reports to: Secretary of Agriculture

Works closely with:

Assistant Secretary, Economics
Assistant Secretary, Food and Consumer Services
Administrator, Foreign Agricultural Service
Assistant Secretary, Marketing and Inspection Services
Assistant Secretary, Natural Resources and Environment

Outside the Department

Assistant to the President, Science and Technology Policy
Members of seven principal committees, Federal Coordinating Council on
  Science, Engineering and Technology
President, National Academy of Sciences
Governing Board, National Research Council
Director, National Institutes of Health
Director, National Science Foundation
U.S. Trade Representative
Commissioner, Food and Drug Administration
Assistant Administrator, Pesticides and Toxic Substances,
  Environmental Protection Agency

Outside the Government

Professional societies and associations in the fields of agriculture, plant
physiology, livestock and poultry, chemistry and related areas; state
departments of agriculture; agricultural colleges and universities and their
associations; private members of science and education advisory committees
serving this position; technology and agricultural officials of the European
Economic Community

Profile of Current Assistant Secretary, Science and Education

Name: Charles E. Hess

Assumed Position: 1989

Career Summary:	Dean, College of Agricultural and Environmental Sciences, University of California at Davis, 1975-90; concurrently, associate director, California Agricultural Experiment Station, then director of programs, Division of Agriculture and Natural Resources, California Agricultural Experiment Station and Cooperative Extension Service Dean, Cook College, 1972-75, and director, New Jersey Agricultural Experiment Station, Rutgers University, 1971-75 Research professor and chair, department of horticulture and forestry, Rutgers University, 1966-71 Department of horticulture, Purdue University, 1958-66
Education:	Rutgers University, BSci, 1953 Cornell University, MSci, 1954; PhD, 1957

Assistant Secretaries, Science and Education Since 1969

Administration	Name and Years Served	Present Position
Bush	Charles E. Hess 1989 - present	Incumbent
Reagan	Orville G. Bentley 1983 - 1989	Emeritus, College of Agriculture University of Illinois Urbana, Ill.
Reagan	Terry B. Kinney (Acting) 1982	Retired York, S.C.
Carter	Anson R. Bertrand* 1977 - 1981	Retired Petersburg, Va.
Carter	M. Rupert Cutler (A)** 1977	President Defenders of Wildlife Washington, D.C.
Ford	Robert W. Long** 1973 - 1976	Not available
Nixon	Ned D. Bayley* 1968 - 1973	Retired

* Held position as Director, Science and Education Administration
** Held position as Assistant Secretary, Conservation, Research and Education

9

U.S. ARMS CONTROL AND DISARMAMENT AGENCY

ASSISTANT DIRECTOR, NONPROLIFERATION POLICY

Level IV - Presidential Appointment with Senate Confirmation

Major Responsibilities

- Advise the director of the U.S. Arms Control and Disarmament Agency (ACDA) in the development and application of U.S. policy to prevent the international proliferation of nuclear and other kinds of weapons of war. As part of this responsibility, evaluate on a continuing basis transfers of arms and arms manufacturing technology with implications for American policy. Direct the work of ACDA's Nonproliferation Policy Bureau. Oversee publication of an annual report on worldwide military arms transfers and expenditures.

- Track and assess compliance with the safeguards provisions required by the Treaty on the Nonproliferation of Nuclear Weapons (the NPT) governing the peaceful nuclear activities of individual member countries. Play a central role in U.S. participation in the NPT review process, and in the effort to extend NPT membership, broaden its impact, and promote its objectives, including eventual completion of a comprehensive test ban treaty.

- Work with other officials of the U.S. national security and foreign affairs community in the performance of these assignments. Maintain close liaison with the International Atomic Energy Agency, enforcer of peaceful nuclear safeguards and inspection provisions under the NPT, and with counterpart officials of other governments.

Necessary Training, Experience, Skills

The fundamental issues this job deals with are political issues, requiring political decisions. That requires experience in some policy context where those decisions are discussed, influenced and developed. That might be the arms control, intelligence or defense communities of government, or relevant work in a defense or foreign policy think tank, a national laboratory or a public interest organization. Since federal decision making is a group exercise, especially in matters of foreign and national security policy, this assistant director must also be resourceful, articulate and persuasive. At the same time, although the job has never been occupied by a "hard" scientist, it clearly needs an individual possessing substantial technical background, and one sufficiently comfortable with the technology and physics of weaponry. Such a person must be able to work with scientists, talk with them on their own ground, and speak the policy and technical language of the arms control business. In sum, the job requires high technical integrity exercised in a highly political environment.

Insight

This position covers the waterfront of worldwide arms manufactures and transfers--nuclear, chemical, biological and conventional. But its major attention goes to nuclear weapons. Specifically, this assistant director is part of the sustained international endeavor to confine the materials and technology employed in producing such weapons to safeguarded, peaceful uses. The extended furor over Iraq's nuclear facilities and weapons potential during the Persian Gulf war of 1991 and its aftermath has been a useful demonstration of the distance still to be traveled toward that goal. An understanding of the theory and practice of nonproliferation, and its strengths and weaknesses, is therefore important in this position.

As an international objective, nonproliferation was framed by U.S. foreign policy in the late 1940s and early 1950s, when it became evident that other nations were real or potential possessors of the necessary knowledge and skill to develop and test nuclear devices transformable into weapons capability. Nonproliferation became a key part of the ensuing general effort at arms control, which began in earnest after the cold war had become a way of life. That effort sent generations of U.S. and Soviet political leaders, their allies and their diplomats on a 40-year quest for ways to co-exist atop their respective arsenals. The ostensible aim was to control, reduce and ultimately eliminate production and deployment of nuclear arms and delivery systems, as well as other kinds of weapons and forces. Only in the 1989-91 period was this long effort capped by dramatic and genuine progress, events set in motion, of course, by the collapse of the Soviet bloc economy and military threat.

Within that broad context, nuclear nonproliferation has had its own measure of success. An early target was nuclear weapons testing. This is a necessary step for any country trying to develop a useable device, and is thus inimical to the goal of nonproliferation. Yet testing also continues to have its advocates among some of the established nuclear powers, including the United States. Years of impasse in negotiations to control or abolish testing finally led, in 1963, to the Limited Test Ban Treaty. That agreement, at least for its signatories, took testing out of the atmosphere, restrained the size of tests, and put them underground. Later, treaties on "threshold" testing and on nuclear explosions for peaceful purposes were also negotiated.

In 1968 the Treaty on the Nonproliferation of Nuclear Weapons (NPT) came into being. Under this pact, all non-nuclear states that are parties to it accept International Atomic Energy Agency (IAEA) "full-scope" safeguards--including IAEA inspection--on all of their peaceful nuclear activities. Further, countries supplying nuclear technology and materials to non-nuclear-weapon states must require IAEA safeguards on such exports and on nuclear materials they are used to produce. The NPT does not, however, cover exports to non-weapon countries who are not members of the treaty, and safeguards on the nuclear facilities of importing states are not required. Like many treaties, the NPT is vulnerable to willful, skillful violation, as Iraq proved in 1991.

The NPT provides for a review conference of member states every five years, an event at which the assistant director in charge of nonproliferation policy at ACDA is normally the U.S. representative. Kathleen C. Bailey, who led the Nonproliferation Policy Bureau (NPB) at ACDA in 1987-90, says the review session "is always a very big job," not only in the year it is held but in preparations during the year preceding. The review meeting held in 1990 provided a useful look at the ground the nonproliferation process has covered, and the ground it must still cover.

For one thing, the conference was unable to issue a closing declaration, basically because of a split on the issue of a comprehensive test ban treaty (CTBT). The limited test ban accord contained a commitment to pursue a comprehensive treaty; achieving one is generally seen as the best evidence that the nuclear weapons powers are complying with the key NPT requirement that all its adherent states work in good faith for an early end to the nuclear arms race. Only the United States and Britain oppose an early CTBT, arguing the need for continued testing of their own weapons. At the 1990 meeting, however, Mexico and some other NPT members proposed a link between progress towards a comprehensive treaty and the continuation of the NPT itself beyond 1995.

The dispute remained unresolved, and the final declaration failed as a result--even though the review meeting in 1995 is to take up the very question of how much longer the NPT will continue. This suggests that the leadership of the ACDA's nonproliferation bureau, among others, has vital work ahead in the run-up to 1995, both within the policy community in Washington and with other governments.

Other, more optimistic developments at the 1990 review session, though officially unrecorded because of the final document's demise, also helped lay out a work agenda for the years immediately following. These are tasks pursued through bilateral and other channels and in part, they fall to the NPB in Washington and counterpart offices and agencies in other capitals. For example, there was provisional agreement in the meeting to recommend--but only to recommend--that nuclear supplier countries require full-scope safeguards on their exports to any non-nuclear state, whether or not a member of the NPT. The United States strongly favors such a rule; several European countries do not. Second, a proposal surfaced in the review conference for more effective use of the IAEA's authority to request special inspections of facilities undeclared by a country and not included in the agency's normal scrutiny. Again, the example of Iraq (an NPT member) illustrated the usefulness of making such practice a more frequent reality. Third, France and China, both nuclear weapons powers but still (at the 1990 conference) not members of the NPT, showed at the meeting that they are moving further towards it and need continuing encouragement. Fourth, non-member South Africa apparently plans to adhere to the treaty. Fifth, Germany, still two states at the time, repeated the intention to refrain from weapons production of any kind and to continue adherence to the NPT. (China announced in August 1991 its decision "in principle" to sign the treaty.)

Around the world, several individual countries in addition to Iraq continue to present tough challenges to U.S. nonproliferation policy. Among them are Israel, a non-member of the NPT about whose nuclear weapons stock there is little doubt; and Pakistan, another non-member, still insisting on its commitment not to produce nuclear weapons in the face of widespread belief that it in fact has that capability.

In addressing these responsibilities and problems, and not only in the nuclear field, the head of the NPB needs scientific or technical knowledge to understand what is happening. For example, says Lewis A. Dunn, who held this position from 1983 to 1987, "in preventing a country from acquiring nuclear weapons you had to understand how close they were to getting them. Or you had to have a sense of whether particular items you were trying through export control procedures to keep them from obtaining would make a difference." In the area of safeguards, "there was a series of technical questions where basically you were trying to put into a peaceful nuclear facility a set of mechanisms and procedures to ensure that it wasn't being used for military purposes. That had to be grounded in a technical understanding of what was taking place."

Four divisions--International Nuclear Affairs, Nuclear Safeguards and Testing, Weapons and Technology Control, and Defense Programs Analysis--make up the Nonproliferation Policy Bureau's operating structure. The bureau has no duties in the development or defense of its budget. It employs about 60 staff members, about a quarter of whom are scientifically or technically oriented. Bailey says the technical proficiency of the few physical scientists and technicians in the bureau was excellent, but there were not enough of them. "One of the things I did was try to make sure that our job descriptions were written in a way that required some technical expertise," she says, "and we brought some people in with that kind of knowledge and background." Thus she recruited some staff from the IAEA (who arrived only after she had left the bureau due to the time required for security clearance). But Bailey says she ran into "constant problems" with the "politicization of what I wanted to build up as the science and technology positions." One of these jobs was used to "put somebody out to farm," she relates. "That's the kind of politicking that drives you crazy when you're trying to build the kind of science and technology base you need to make good decisions."

She felt "very comfortable" with the outside scientific community and relied on it "a great deal" to supplement her own knowledge. Her background was in nuclear nonproliferation studies in the Lawrence Livermore national laboratory and in intelligence, defense and national security affairs in the federal government. "Having come from that environment, I knew whom to call, and I did it frequently. I knew a lot of people in the technical community." She spent a fair amount of time keeping the White House science and technology policy office abreast of nonproliferation issues and technology transfer questions, and placed high value on that relationship.

The position entails a variety of continuing interaction with individuals and delegations from other countries, and periodic travel to conferences or bilateral meetings, and sometimes for public affairs purposes. ACDA General Counsel Thomas Graham thinks the individual in this position "probably has contact with a greater number of other governments than any other bureau chief in this agency." There is some, but not a lot, of contact with the Congress; Bailey says "State does most of the talking on the Hill." The foreign relations committees are the assistant director's main forums, with testimony perhaps four times a year, and there are some informal briefing chores. The Congress, according to Bailey, views ACDA as "kind of its own creation, so they're positive in their attitude toward it."

But within the executive branch, the current standing of ACDA as a whole gets low ratings. "It's clear," Dunn says, "that ACDA is kind of the stepchild of the process." Since its creation in 1961, for instance, "it has always been viewed by conservatives as a hotbed of fuzzy thinking." Moreover, its director by law reports both to the president and the secretary of state. "So whom does he report to?" Dunn asks. "The agency's relationship with the rest of the administration is affected by the fact that it doesn't have a lot of bureaucratic clout." As seen by Barry Blechman, who headed the bureau in 1978-79 as assistant director for weapons evaluation and control, the agency has been "clearly downgraded. It still plays in some of the testing issues, but not in START (the strategic arms reduction talks) or the conventional talks, or any of the central issues." He asserts that this perception is shared across the arms control and foreign affairs community. "It's widely understood," he says, "that the agency has been taken out of the loop." Bailey's view is that, "overall, ACDA is not that much of a respected agency in terms of political clout. If the president wants anything done on arms control, he calls on the secretary of state. So despite the director's charter responsibility as an advisor to the president, in reality it doesn't happen."

As for the nonproliferation policy job itself, there are other kinds of operating problems. Graham points out that the assistant director deals with three competing centers of policy making. Two are at the department of state. There, the role of U.S. negotiator on nuclear nonproliferation matters is filled by an ambassador at large who, according to Bailey, closely protected that assignment and was not a frequent interagency participant. Second is State's bureau of oceanic and international environmental and scientific affairs. Graham says, however, that the NPB "probably has 90 percent of the staff which works on nuclear nonproliferation issues." Third, the department of energy is also "a big player" in this field.

Another problem cited by Bailey lies in the interagency management of issues in other sectors for which this job has responsibility, like arms transfers or chemical weapons proliferation, or the missile technology export control regime. Where previously, these had been handled heavily out of the White House, she says, "it became more and more a unilateral process where the department of state acted alone and independently." In such circumstances, Dunn says, it helps if there is someone on the National Security Council staff who is following a particular set of issues closely. "That allows a kind of recourse, so that ACDA can make its case at State" with support from the White House. "It makes life easier."

What business the bureau did with the department of defense, Bailey recalls, was usually in the areas of arms transfers and nuclear nonproliferation, "and that's probably still the case." By law, she says, the ACDA director must advise the secretary of state when particular arms transfers are likely to increase the chances for an outbreak of conflict. "We dealt mostly with State but sometimes with Defense--where we had much less bureaucratic influence." In arms transfer matters, ACDA's main purpose at Defense was to "try to get a full hearing on the implications of a given transfer and occasionally to convince people that something made no sense whatever, like selling F-16s to a particular country when it didn't have long enough runways" she says. At least in the nuclear nonproliferation part of the job, "the rest of the government acknowledged that we knew a lot and had a right to play. But in the arms transfers field, they basically thought of us as something Congress had put into the process and they would be just as happy without us." Concerning nuclear nonproliferation, on the other hand, "the occasional job was to make sure that decisions weren't made at the deputy assistant secretary level--that if it was important enough, the decision had to be made at the White House. And there we had much more legitimacy."

Graham doesn't think the fundamental changes in the Soviet Union and in the U.S.-Soviet relationship have affected the work of the NPB director. Relations with the Soviets on nuclear nonproliferation policy have always been good, he notes. "They have had a great interest in stopping proliferation because most additional nuclear weapon states-- China, France and Britain--ended up pointing its weapons at them, not us. We and they have had very few differences on nuclear nonproliferation." In the Middle East it could be a different story for the NPB, he thinks. "If there is an initiative sponsored by the United Nations or the United States to negotiate a special regime for Iraq, not only for nuclear nonproliferation but for chemical and conventional weapons and missile technology, that could be an important adjunct to this individual's responsibilities."

Dunn makes an additional point on this theme. By focusing attention on nuclear and chemical weapons and missile technology control issues, he believes, the Persian Gulf war "makes it easier to deal with those issues. The job now operates in an environment more hospitable to controls than in the past. There is also greater recognition at the top of the administration that the spread of these weapons and technologies can come back to haunt us. The problem has more recognition than in my day."

Unlike the control and gradual elimination of the superarsenals of the superpowers, the problem of proliferating weapons of all varieties has an indefinite lease on life. All countries can play, including those once constrained to a degree by their client state status in the days of east-west confrontation, and the irresponsibility factor looms large. In this context, Bailey thinks the assistant director's position at the NPB will take one of two directions. "Either it will become increasingly important and get more resources and attention because of the concern over proliferation, not only nuclear weapons but chemical and biological weapons and missiles as well. Or other agencies will beef up their ability to deal with proliferation problems and suck away the authority and the activity that would be ACDA's. I think it's a function not so much of who is in this position itself, as of the director of the agency."

Key Relationships

Within the Agency

Reports to: Director

Works closely with:

Assistant Director, Multilateral Affairs
Assistant Director, Strategic and Nuclear Affairs
Assistant Director, Verification and Implementation

Outside the Agency

Assistant Director, National Security Affairs, White House Office of Science and Technology Policy
Ambassador at large, Nuclear Nonproliferation, Department of State
Deputy Assistant to the President/Senior Director, Defense Policy and Arms Control, National Security Council
Under Secretary, International Security Affairs, Department of State
Assistant Secretary, Oceans and International Environmental and Scientific Affairs, Department of State
Assistant Secretary, Politico-Military Affairs, Department of State
Deputy Assistant Secretary, Nuclear Forces and Arms Control Policy, Office of International Security Affairs, Department of Defense
Director, Arms Control, Office of Defense Programs, Department of Energy
Assistant Secretary, International Affairs and Energy Emergencies, Department of Energy
Directors, Los Alamos, Lawrence Livermore, and other national laboratories

Outside the Government

Arms control, nonproliferation and defense officials of other governments, especially those signatory to the Nuclear Nonproliferation Treaty; officials of the International Atomic Energy Agency; academic and policy research institutions, arms control groups and public service organization

Profile of Current Assistant Director, Nonproliferation Policy

Name: Bradley Gordon

Assumed Position: 1990

Career Summary: Legislative assistant, office of Sen. Rudy Boschwitz, U.S. Senate, 1987-89

Staff member, Committee on Foreign Relations, U.S. Senate, 1985-87

Political analyst, Central Intelligence Agency, 1979-85

Education: Brandeis University, BA (cum laude with honors in politics), 1971
University of Vermont, MA, political science, 1974
Columbia University, MPhil, 1978

Assistant Directors, Nonproliferation Policy Since 1969

Administration	Name and Years Served	Present Position
Bush	Bradley Gordon* 1990 - present	Incumbent
Reagan, Bush	Kathleen C. Bailey* 1987 - 1989	Senior Analyst National Security Research Fairfax, Va.
Reagan	Lewis A. Dunn* 1984 - 1986	Negotiation & Planning Manager Science Applications Intl. Corp. McLean, Va.
Reagan	Archelus Turrentine (Acting)* 1981 - 1983	Not available
Carter	George W. Ashworth** 1980	Not available
Carter	Barry M. Blechman** 1978 - 1979	President Defense Forecasts Washington, D.C.
Carter	Robert Behr*** 1977 - 1978	Not available
Ford, Carter	Thomas J. Hirschfeld (A)*** 1976 - 1977	Senior Staff Rand Corporation Santa Monica, Cal.
Ford	Thomas D. Davies*** 1974 - 1975	Deceased
Nixon	John M. Lee* 1970 - 1971	Retired

| Nixon | John J. Davis* | Not available |
| | 1967 - 1969 | |

* Held position as Assistant Director, Nuclear Weapons and Control
** Held position as Assistant Director, Weapons Evaluation and Control
*** Held position with the Nonproliferation and Advanced Technology Bureau

ASSISTANT DIRECTOR
VERIFICATION AND IMPLEMENTATION

Level IV - Presidential Appointment with Senate Confirmation

Major Responsibilities

- Ensure that international arms control and disarmament agreements to which the United States is party are sustained by an adequate capability to verify compliance and by measures to enforce fully their verification provisions.

- Supervise the work of the Verification and Implementation Bureau of the Arms Control and Disarmament Agency (ACDA) to that end. Staff U.S. negotiating delegations with bureau expertise in the fields of verification and implementation.

- In close consultations within the federal intelligence community and with U.S. on-site inspection teams and other federal agencies, analyze compliance with existing agreements, collaborating in efforts to improve and strengthen U.S. verification systems, techniques and skills. Draft an annual report to the Congress on compliance with verification provisions of existing agreements.

- Counsel and testify to the Senate committees on Intelligence and Foreign Relations in their scrutiny of proposed arms control agreements under advise and consent procedures.

Necessary Training, Experience, Skills

Individuals in this job must know how intelligence is analyzed, be able to design verification procedures to reveal what is desired, sift intelligence for what is significant and make balanced judgments about its meaning and the response required. An experienced ex-ACDA hand says verification "is very much a political animal," while recognizing the advantages a technical background confers in the job. An advanced science or technical degree brings added strength, and standing within the scientific community has value. This assistant director has to understand the U.S. intelligence community and function smoothly in congressional relationships. A non-scientist could do this work if solid technical advice were readily available and the other requisites mentioned were present.

Insight

One of the 20th century's hard lessons in international relations and military conflict has been that arms control cannot run only on trust, intent and belief. For it to be effective, all parties to agreements to limit or do away with the manufacture and deployment of weapons of war must be able to know--at every moment, and with a high degree of certainty-- that the agreements are being complied with. Increasingly in the age of nuclear weapons and ballistic missiles, verification came to be seen as an authentic and crucial element in the arms control process. Expert theorists and practitioners in the U.S. arms control community may differ between themselves on the who, what, how and how much of verification. But few have ever argued that it is not essential.

Illustrating this are the comments of Jack Mendelsohn, deputy director of the Arms Control Association, a Washington policy research organization. He notes that the V&I bureau in its present incarnation dates from the early 1980s, when the verification mission came into sharper focus. "It was not a benignly-designed change," he says; it coincided with the advent of "super enthusiasm" about the quality of compliance and non-compliance in arms control. At least part of the intent was to apply the "most narrow view of what verification is about," he says, and "in a sense, to give trouble to the policy process." He suggests that the position has been "a watchdog job, more than a creative policy job."

But Mendelsohn stresses that verification is also a highly important job. "We're entering a series of agreements with the most expansive, extensive, complicated verification provisions mankind has ever seen," he says. "It will make the INF treaty (on intermediate range nuclear forces) look like a school outing. We're going to be looking inside missiles to count warheads. All kinds of verification will be put in place under agreements on conventional forces in Europe, strategic arms reduction and confidence-building measures. You name it, we're going to have it."

Since the mid-1980s, spectacular events in the Soviet Union and improvement in U.S.-Soviet relations have indeed been generating a growing regime of international arms control agreements. Some have been or will be overtaken by events that remove the potential threats they were designed to control. Others, like the strategic nuclear arms pact signed in the summer of 1991, will continue to be relevant. One treaty, on conventional forces in Europe, is awaiting Senate ratification. Still other agreements lie in the future.

Verification is a complicated science and art. In Washington, a number of institutions share the task, not always felicitously. Drafting and getting agreement on the verification provisions of an arms control agreement are in the first instance the responsibility of the multi-agency U.S. team that negotiates it, guided by policy formulated at the White House with input from the state and defense departments, among others. Through its Select Committee on Intelligence and, ultimately, the Committee on Foreign Relations, the Senate has the duty to satisfy itself about the adequacy of treaty language, including verification conditions. For agreements in effect, the gathering of raw data about compliance has traditionally fallen to the intelligence community, which surveys the scene in a variety of ways, not least through direct observation by satellite. A striking new dimension of this process--on-site inspection of missile launch sites and associated activities--was added with the treaty on intermediate range nuclear forces that took effect in 1989; it is a mission of the defense department's on-site inspection agency. And at ACDA, the job of its assistant director for verification and implementation (V&I) is basically to see that the verification provisos of each agreement are sufficient and workable, that they are enforced and enforceable, and that U.S. verification skills improve.

The assistant director, however, has little real power to carry out these duties directly. Manfred Eimer, who has occupied the position since 1983, says "our job is to influence others." It is not easy. As he describes it, the resources required for verification functions belong to the intelligence community and the departments of defense and energy. For example, support for verification of compliance with the nuclear test ban treaties (the limited and threshold test bans and the agreement on peaceful nuclear explosions), must come out of department of energy funds. But one of Energy's responsibilities is the production and care of the U.S. nuclear arsenal; and Energy, Eimer says, "is not terribly interested in limiting testing." At Defense, he continues, "it's the same thing--we have an arms control agreement, and the on-site inspection agency is funded out of the Pentagon. They have to fund arms control which is really not their prime interest." On many occasions, though, Defense does lend support, he says, because it also "wants to hold the Soviets to high standards" of compliance. Yet the verification measures necessary to gain such compliance are less appealing because "it is not possible to add verification to a treaty without affecting your own freedom of action, and that is something the Pentagon and the Joint Chiefs don't like to lose."

In a real sense, therefore, this job is really one of a catalyst--urging, cajoling, persuading. It has small operating resources, and no budget defense duties. "My prime concern is really the budgets of other people," Eimer says, "to make sure, for instance that the intelligence community puts in the resources for verification. It's a constant battle. And with all the persuasion I can use, I can't get the Pentagon to put money into verification; that push has to come from somebody else. All I can get them to do is understand what it is that we need. But they aren't going to put it in on my say-so."

In this routine struggle, Eimer observes, "it's very hard for me to find allies." One ally he looks to is the Senate Intelligence Committee. It is there also that he does have "a few weapons I can use," and "the only way I get anything done is if people expect me to use them." By law, he says, "someone has to certify (to the Senate) that a treaty is effectively verifiable. The Senate in its review process has to concur with that." The relationships with the committee "are such that if someone like me goes up and tells the committee there is a problem with verification that needs to be resolved, they will take that seriously. If I say a treaty is not okay technically, they may take my word for it because they may not be able to second-guess the technical issues."

Situations like these can mean the committee's suspension of the advise-and-consent treaty ratification process while the difficulty is settled. Therein lie the weapons Eimer mentions. Halting the process can entail a major interruption. Eimer cites such an instance, when he told the committee about a "lack of clarity" in certain parts of a treaty text. "What they said was, you need to get back to the Soviets and we need an exchange of letters or other document that irons it out. In this case, it meant another session in Geneva and another agreement." When such a procedure is complete, the committee resumes work where it left off.

There is a "great concern" in the Congress, Eimer says, "that we not make mistakes on implementation now that we have an increasing number of treaties on the horizon. We've got people running all over the Soviet Union inspecting things, and there are reporting requirements, the reports have to be assessed, and so on. The other part of it, of course, is to provide assessments on how well the other side, especially the Soviet Union, has complied. It's kind of meaningless to have verification if there's no enforcement. Nothing works in verification unless the other side worries about detection."

The V&I bureau has a staff of 25, all based in Washington. During negotiating sessions overseas, usually in Geneva, there are always staffing problems at home because bureau personnel are assigned to U.S. delegations. "We are literally starving for people," Eimer says. With such a small group, he points out, "there really is a limitation on flexibility--on assigning someone to something other than his specialty, which is necessary from time to time." Most of his staff are career service. About half have technical backgrounds, and the rest are political scientists, Eimer says. He views the technical half as "adequately trained, with proper backgrounds." He is generally satisfied with the quality of their work, but is "sensitive to the shortcomings." He would like to leave a sound staff behind, and sometimes thinks of himself as a training officer.

In the course of his work, Eimer sees the ACDA director regularly, and reports good working relationships elsewhere in the agency. Outside it, his customary circuit includes the departments of defense and energy, the CIA and the Congress. The House of Representatives has no role in arms control treaties, Eimer says, but "we usually have to help the Senate convince the House to go along with these expenditures" on arms control.

Then there is the department of state. The director of ACDA has reporting responsibility to the secretary of state as well as the president, and many organization charts show a dotted-line relationship between the two organizations. Though ACDA is an independent agency, it sometimes operates more like a part of State (it is housed in the same building), and the degree of real influence it wields is usually a function of the relationship between the director and the secretary. Nominally, the negotiating processes in Geneva are under ACDA's control; in reality, State has the upper hand. Mendelsohn and others also make the point that some administrations have used ACDA as an outrider for advanced ideas about arms control, balancing more conservative bastions like the defense department and allowing principals like the secretary of state to take a middle position. It's a situation in which Eimer sees a need to underline his agency's statutory independence. As one of its most senior officials (a status which attaches to him, not to the position), he sometimes functions as acting director but does not attend the secretary of state's staff meetings. "We are not a part of State," he says. "To the extent we show up at staff meetings, it creates the impression that we are."

Most of the assistant director's influence is exerted at the senior interagency working level, Mendelsohn says. "That's where representatives from Defense, the intelligence community and the other agencies sit down and discuss the given issues. Once their ideas are batted around at that level, they go up to the principals and the decisions are made." The assistant director is a standing member of the policy coordinating committee on arms control of the National Security Council (Eimer usually sends his deputy to its meetings), as well as of the PCC on intelligence, which meets less often.

Eimer says his two biggest problems are "getting the treaties drafted properly, which is very hard, and getting the proper programs funded. A large amount of money is involved, and I don't underestimate the problem. The director of central intelligence fights it tooth and nail because if you spend the money for verification you don't have it for something else." In general, however, "all of us here to varying degrees think we were in part an agent that pushed the Soviets over the edge."

Though ACDA does not run the on-site inspection operation, Eimer says he "had the first team that went to the Soviet Union to look at a violation. It was in the fall of 1988, and even I could sense a change." He drafts the annual reports on Soviet compliance, and data produced by on-site inspection feed into it.

As real arms control increasingly becomes a fact of life, implementation will demand greater amounts of attention, energy and money, especially if chemical and biological weapons begin to pose larger technical challenges. "We're struggling to organize the implementation process," Eimer says. A "simple" treaty like INF requires substantial numbers of on-site inspectors. "The upcoming treaties have much more of it." The Congress "really worries about how we're going to implement all that, where the money is coming from, and the people, and how it will be organized. I need the data. My job is still to make sure the proper data are taken, that the Soviets stay within treaty bounds. There's a big management operation there. And people's roles change once a treaty gets signed. It's hard to get negotiators out and implementers in. They are different kinds of people."

Arms control is in little danger of becoming a victim of its own success, in Mendelsohn's view. But it will change. One indication is the recent alteration in the name of the bureau (from "verification and intelligence" to "verification and implementation"). If present arms control trends continue, he says, "you will have a lot of agreements that in effect provide for transparency--a classic bureaucratic term for openness. That is, we will want to remain certain that things are as good as they seem to be." That will mean the right of constant oversight of military activities and capabilities in Europe "to assure ourselves that what we put in place is still working." These are implementation tasks. As to what remains undone, Mendelsohn thinks "there will be pressure to seek even lower levels of forces than we'll get in the first round." He notes concern about short-range nuclear delivery systems that have not yet been covered, though they are next on the agenda, plus the questions of nuclear nonproliferation and chemical weapons.

"I don't think the arms control business is going to fold," Mendelsohn says. "Verification and implementation are going to expand. It's a growth industry."

Key Relationships

Within the Agency

Reports to: Director

Works closely with:

Deputy Director
Assistant Director, Strategic and Nuclear Affairs
Assistant Director, Multilateral Affairs

Outside the Agency

Director, Onsite Inspection Agency, Department of Defense
Under Secretary, International Security Affairs, Department of State
Director, Verification Policy, Office of International Security Policy,
    Department of Defense
Deputy Director, Intelligence, Central Intelligence Agency
Deputy Director, Science and Technology, Central Intelligence Agency
Deputy Director, Intelligence, Office of Defense Programs, Department of
    Energy
Policy coordinating committees on arms control and intelligence, National
    Security Council

Outside the Government

Arms control groups, defense contractors, professional science and
engineering organizations

Profile of Current Assistant Director, Verification and Implementation

Name: Manfred Eimer

Assumed Position: 1983

Career Summary: Various positions with the U.S. Arms Control and Disarmament
                       Agency, 1973-83, including acting assistant director, Bureau of
                       Verification and Intelligence; chief, Verification Division
                       Assistant director (intelligence) and assistant director (electronic
                       warfare and reconnaissance, Defense Research and Engineering,
                       Department of Defense, 1970-73
                       Vice president engineering), Space General Corporation, 1963-70
                       Deputy chief, division of the space sciences, Jet Propulsion
                       Laboratory, Caltech, 1953-63

Education: California Institute of Technology, BS,(engineering), 1947; MS, (aeronautical engineering), 1948; PhD, (aeronautics and engineering, cum laude), 1953

Assistant Directors, Verification and Implementation Since 1983*

Administration	Name and Years Served	Present Position
Bush, Reagan	Manfred Eimer 1983 - present	Incumbent

* Position created in 1983

10

CENTRAL INTELLIGENCE AGENCY

DEPUTY DIRECTOR, INTELLIGENCE

Senior Intelligence Service

Major Responsibilities

- Oversee the production of intelligence based on the analysis and interpretation of a continuous and broad inflow of information collected through CIA and other resources.

- Ensure the timely dissemination of these products in various formats for use by White House and other senior policy makers primarily in the defense, foreign policy, economic and commercial sectors.

- Consult and advise the director and deputy director, central intelligence on matters involving intelligence policy and the operations of the intelligence directorate. Represent the intelligence function in various White House-level interagency contexts, standing in as necessary for the deputy director at meetings of the deputies group of the National Security Council.

- Brief the intelligence committees of the Congress, as requested and appropriate.

Necessary Training, Experience, Skills

In principle, an individual without a CIA background could fill this job. As a practical matter, however, an outsider without the "apprenticeship" of previous agency work will begin with a significant disadvantage. As with other agency positions at this level, almost no other career experience provides adequate exposure to the rather special environment in which the position functions. While that may not be the immutable pattern for the future, the current deputy director and his three immediate predecessors are all agency careerists (the position does not require presidential appointment or Senate confirmation). Veterans of the job put a premium on analytical training and skill, and relatively little emphasis on the particular field of the deputy director's academic training. But it clearly helps to have some technical education and experience, and to know how engineers and scientists operate. The intelligence chief should be articulate, a prolific reader and familiar with Washington. But it isn't a political job in the sense that its occupant must network around town, an informed observer says. It's political because the deputy director must maintain objectivity both in the personal professional sense and in the quality of the intelligence directorate's products.

Insight

Six days a week this CIA directorate sends a daily intelligence brief to the president, and produces a lengthier report seen by selected senior decision makers throughout the executive branch. Each year, it issues about a hundred national intelligence estimates, plus an 18-wheeler truckload of major studies. These have ranged from the Soviet economic and military posture to Chinese university students, from offensive weapons capabilities in the Middle East to personalities in the foreign governments, from AIDS in Africa to environmental concerns in Brazil and narcotics in Burma.

Richard J. Kerr headed the intelligence directorate in 1986-89 before moving up to deputy director of central intelligence. In his estimate, the "major monographs" turned out annually under the supervision of the deputy director for intelligence (DDI) number between 750 and a thousand. "So you're talking about a couple per day that run from 25 to 100 pages on very complicated issues," he points out. The effort all this requires is "very much of a grind in the sense that this product keeps coming. It either overwhelms you or you let it go through you."

The job, says John L. Helgerson, DDI since early 1989, "covers a full range of analysis." There are several components to the directorate's role, he explains, but essentially its responsibility is to assess foreign technology developments, and existing and planned foreign weapons systems that pose real or potential threats to U.S. security. Hence science and technology is a principal focus. "Intelligence's responsibility is the protection of this country and the prevention of surprise in the strategic sense," Kerr adds. "No matter what else you do, the first priority is to provide information that will help the country defend itself." Areas like weapons and their deployment, the potential for technological surprise and arms proliferation "are major issues of concern and therefore become major issues for intelligence production. So it's not science in the abstract. It's science in terms of what difference it makes to the United States."

About half the directorate's activity continues to center on what has until now been known as Soviet affairs--a stance unlikely to change much in the near term, Helgerson predicts, although many in Washington and elsewhere argue for more change more quickly. The reason, he says, is that Russia and the other republics that have formed the Soviet Union, while less threatening than five years ago, are roiled by economic and political developments that attract just as much interest and require just as much work.

Across the breadth of his responsibilities, in Helgerson's view, "the greatest challenge is to decide what's worth doing and what isn't." In the technology area it takes "immensely skilled manpower and considerable collection (of data and other information) to assess the precise state of foreign capabilities." That, and the directorate's threat-oriented focus, are reasons he and his directorate don't undertake to assess all technology development everywhere in the world. "However interesting it may be," he says, "that's irrelevant to us for intelligence purposes." Instead, the directorate concentrates analytically on perhaps six to eight kinds of generic technologies with the potential to be security threats. Further, the aim is to follow those technologies "wherever they are being developed, rather than going after a specific country or organization," Helgerson says. Among the generic groups he lists are developments in advanced materials such as ceramics, composites and metals, advanced manufacturing techniques, data processing from microcomputers to supercomputers, avionics and propulsion systems, and remote sensing capabilities. Increasingly, this kind of tracking requires new analytic capabilities, including state-of-the-art information technology.

The intelligence directorate staff runs the gamut, as former DDI John McMahon (1980-82) broadly puts it, "from anthropologists to zoologists," among them physicians, psychologists, engineers, nuclear physicists and historians. He rates the staff of his day highly. "They were not only very capable people but spent a lot of time visiting high-tech laboratories and industry and really stayed current on what was happening technologically in the United States." He also values what he calls "ground truth" in an analyst--on-site, firsthand experience of some length in the country and region under examination. It was McMahon who laid out the substantive approach that the directorate uses today. Instead of trying to integrate the separate views of political, economic and military analysts, he brought them to examine a given subject together, so that the approach was regional or topical, rather than functional and, he thought, gained the added advantage of synergy.

Specifics about staff size continue to be classified, but the directorate represents roughly a quarter of the agency's work force including, according to Helgerson, "a significant number of very highly trained and qualified people in technical fields as well as others." At the same time, a fairly high proportion of the work is contracted to outside analysts. In house, academic training levels vary from BA to PhD, but there are more master's degrees than any other. "In most fields, particularly engineering, what we observe is that our people are typically a bit more qualified in academic background than their counterparts in the private sector," Helgerson says. Kerr thinks the attrition rate is "by far" the lowest in government, and much lower than in industry. The agency has some special hiring authority and various options about rewarding performance. As a result, he says, "we are pretty selective, but we don't have a problem getting people or keeping them. People come here for careers." There is, he observes, a certain "academic aspect" to the directorate, an "intellectual stimulus" that figures in the office's attraction. "There's a lot of debate here. People are not unwilling to come up and tell the boss he doesn't know what he's talking about, and argue about substantive issues. There's a lot of exchange."

"If it's not done well, this work is not worth doing," Helgerson says. He quotes his predecessor that the intelligence directorate is a service organization that "washes windows for the policy community," the secret being to wash the big windows and ignore the little ones. "And in technology," he observes, "what we have discovered is that, while we work for the defense department and the uniformed services, and Commerce and State and so on, the invitation is always there to get into ever-increasing numbers of things. The challenge is to do well in a few foundation technologies that govern advances in most others, develop real expertise in these, and not try to get into a lot of peripheral areas that would be tempting but very time-consuming, especially in manpower."

Since the early 1980s, when the directorate's budget grew appreciably, it has leveled off and declined somewhat (again, no figures available). The DDI doesn't defend the directorate's own budget to the Congress so much as that of intelligence community programs in which it is a primary player. On the Hill, the DDI's schedule is one of peaks and valleys. During budget season, personal appearances might average one per week, then drop away for two or three months. Testimony is mostly before the select intelligence committees of the House and Senate. Frequently, the DDI sees the armed services and appropriations subcommittees on defense of both houses, as well as the foreign affairs panels.

The directorate also delivers about a thousand briefings a year to the Congress on substantive issues. And demand is rising, to the point where, according to McMahon, "the Congress is now one of the leading customers for intelligence. Most members, when they take an overseas trip, now want a briefing." He thinks that is "all to the good." He also emphasizes the need to get intelligence to the policy maker early, in line with his belief that "once a policy maker decides something, all the intelligence in the world is not going to change it." That's why, he says, "we moved our national intelligence estimates from about 12 a year to more than a hundred. And we just fanned them out to the policy makers so they would have it before they realized they ought to be thinking about it. I think that should still be the emphasis today."

But if the audience for intelligence is a wide one, it is also characterized by deep differences of view on controversial issues, and the directorate often finds itself caught between them. Sometimes these lines of conflict divide the Congress and the White House, sometimes they split executive branch agencies, and sometimes they follow predictable party lines. It's a situation, says Kerr, "where what we say makes a difference and is going to be used by one side or the other." A recent example was the debate over economic sanctions against Iraq in the Persian Gulf war. Further back, at a given point in the cold war era, the directorate's calculation of Soviet military spending might not have fit with the defense department's view of the Soviet military threat and the budget it had developed in response. Or, say, with the views of congressional advocates or opponents of defense spending. "You have problems with somebody on every issue," Kerr says. In these circumstances, Kerr continues, "our only strength is a reasonable objectivity. The only thing we can live with is people having confidence that what we say, whether it is ultimately right or wrong, is our best judgment, independent of those forces."

Helgerson elaborates this point further. In writing its analyses, he says, the directorate tries to suit the needs of policy makers, whether it be a requirement for brevity, for length, for a high degree of generality, or for a volume of detail. "But what we insist on, in the end, is that we tell it like it is. And this has been one of our great advantages. Our credibility rests in large part on the fact that we don't have a policy axe to grind. So we're frequently called on as an honest broker among the many other agencies." These considerations take on added emphasis in light of criticism that the agency has sometimes departed from objectivity and shaped certain of its analyses to support the development of a particular line of policy.

The DDI spends considerable time, Helgerson says, talking to people in the substantive areas of the directorate about the heart of the work-- what issues are important, and how to address them. "It's primarily a management job," he reflects, "but management of substance." Much other time goes to the review process, in which the DDI looks at current intelligence every evening and sees nearly every product before it goes to publication. "So a lot of it is going back and forth with authors, people that are managing the process down below, gathering groups together to give some insight, talking to academics and other outsiders." His analysts attend 400-500 professional meetings each year, he adds, whether the subject is "electrical engineering or African politics." The directorate hosts about a hundred of these meetings, many of them in scientific and technical fields, and makes a point of seeking outside review of draft reports. The majority of these consultants are university faculty members and laboratory researchers. All of this, Helgerson says, is "to keep us from getting intellectually incestuous."

The CIA, of course, recognizes that it will need thoroughgoing overhaul to remain responsive to global developments. At the end of 1990, several CIA task forces were studying what its focus, capabilities and assets must be for the rest of the century and beyond. Peter Marino, an agency veteran who now heads Fairchild Industries, is among those who wonder whether the CIA, "which for years focused intently on the Soviet Union, will be able to absorb growing economic and technical intelligence requirements without a reevaluation of personnel." And some articulate observers are suggesting that, in addition to its space-age technical collection and processing systems, the agency needs to rely more on an old-fashioned but irreplaceble method of gathering information: human agents on the scene. However the CIA does transform itself, the DDI's role will remain key. "The problem," Kerr says, "is how you focus the resources you have on the right issues. That's an old problem, and it's not going to change."

McMahon suggests additional reasons why the position will continue to be central. "It has to be one of the key jobs in the agency," he asserts, "because it is a mirror through which the world sees the agency. The intelligence directorate never deals from a full deck, and never has all the information it needs, so it has to do a lot of extrapolating from bits and pieces. But if you are wrong with an intelligence estimate, everybody knows it. It's very critical the DDI do the job right, because so much of the U.S. machinery of government relies on it."

Helgerson sees the directorate's value reflected in the "many questions we get every day" from intelligence consumers like the president, the secretaries of state and defense, and the joint chiefs of staff. "We know they take seriously what we write for them," he says. "And as the one who oversees the production of this material, there's a kind of instant gratification to the process."

Key Relationships

Within the Agency

Reports to: Director, Central Intelligence

Works closely with:

Deputy Director, Central Intelligence
Deputy Director, Operations
Deputy Director, Science and Technology
Deputy Director, Administration

Outside the Agency

Director, Defense Intelligence Agency
Director, National Security Agency
Senior area directors, National Security Council
Under Secretary, Acquisition, Department of Defense
Director, Defense Research and Engineering, Department of Defense
Deputy Under Secretary, Security Policy, Department of Defense
Under Secretary, Political Affairs, Department of State
Assistant Secretary, Intelligence and Research, Department of State
Assistant to the President, Science and Technology Policy
Under Secretary/Administrator, Economic and Statistics Administration,
   Department of Commerce
Under Secretary, International Affairs, Department of the Treasury
Assistant Secretary, Defense Programs, Department of Energy

Outside the Government

Academic and industry professionals in a broad array of U.S. scientific and
engineering disciplines; defense and aerospace industry representatives;
intelligence officials of other governments

Profile of Current Deputy Director, Intelligence

Name: John L. Helgerson

Assumed Position: 1989

Career Summary: Career officer, CIA, including director, African and Latin
                  American analysis, and director, congressional affairs, 1971-89
                  Professor of political science, University of Cincinnati, 1970-71
                  Research affiliate, University of Zambia, Lukasa, 1968-69

Education: Saint Olaf College, BA, 1966
                  Duke University, MA, 1968; PhD (political science), 1970

Deputy Directors, Intelligence Since 1969

Administration	Name and Years Served	Present Position
Bush	John L. Helgerson 1989 - present	Incumbent
Reagan	Richard J. Kerr 1986 - 1988	Deputy Director, CIA
Reagan	Robert M. Gates 1982 - 1986	Deputy Assistant to the President National Security Council
Reagan	John McMahon 1980 - 1982	President & CEO Lockheed Missiles & Space Co. Sunnyvale, Cal.
Carter	Bruce Clarke 1978 - 1980	Not available
Carter	Robert Bowie 1977	Not available
Carter	Sayre Stevens 1976	Not available
Ford, Nixon	Edward Proctor 1971 - 1975	Not available
Nixon, Johnson	R. Jack Smith 1966 - 1972	Not available

DEPUTY DIRECTOR
SCIENCE AND TECHNOLOGY

Senior Intelligence Service

Major Responsibilities

- Support and improve the collection, processing, analysis and dissemination of intelligence through the development and application of technology.

- To that end, plan and oversee the work of the directorate of science and technology in researching new technologies and developing them for application to the intelligence process; and in collecting and processing information from various sources for use by the intelligence community.

- Function as science and technology adviser to the director of central intelligence.

Necessary Training, Experience, Skills

There are two principal points to keep in mind here. First, candidates for the position (it does not require presidential appointment or Senate confirmation) should have engineering or physical sciences training, or offer some area of expertise germane to the kinds of work the S&T directorate does. This is not only essential to running the directorate and providing it leadership; it is vital in conveying the content and import of the work to the mainly nontechnical management of the agency and other intelligence community users in terms they can understand. Further, solid credentials on the technical side are increasingly valuable as the CIA becomes more of a technical collection agency and less one that gathers information clandestinely. Second, like other colleagues heading other CIA directorates, this deputy director must know the nature of intelligence and its role in equipping government decision makers in the area of national security and foreign policy. That almost certainly means significant work experience, if not a prior career, in the CIA itself or possibly in a related area of government. Beyond these stipulations, the individual selected ought to have the standard executive skills--the ability to understand and manage people, to think strategically, to listen and to communicate up and down the chain of command.

Insight

Since the mid-1980s, the world has seen a quickening in the evolution of international relations, and a revolution in technology that has moved even faster. Together they have obliged the CIA, like its cousins in the foreign affairs community, to move toward change in both focus and operating style.

As a researcher in the delicate art of intelligence technology, as well as a gatherer of intelligence by technical methods, the directorate of science and technology (DS&T) is hardly immune to such change. At the same time, say current and former practitioners of these crafts, it must be careful change. "You can't just turn off some of the very complex systems that were developed over many years and aimed at the Soviet Union," in the view of R. Evans Hineman, deputy director from 1982 to 1989. For much of that tenure, he says, the primary intelligence objectives were the Soviet Union--a "very tough, advanced adversary"--and Eastern Europe. "We were driving at the cutting edge of every kind of engineering," he points out, "whether electrical engineering, signal processing or miniaturized electronic equipment that can operate in the field in the hands of nontechnical people." Now, Hineman says, "the rest of the world is at the top" of the intelligence agenda. But the growing requirement for information about other areas and other countries, he believes, doesn't alter the need to "keep an eye on the traditional target."

"There will be a residual interest in Soviet strategic military capability because they remain militarily a superpower," says James V. Hirsch, who has led the DS&T since the fall of 1989. The same situation exists for Eastern Europe, he adds. But "there is a definite shift of resources and systems that are allocated to those kinds of intelligence targets." The easiest such shifts, he says, are those where, for example, analysts in Washington are reoriented to different aspects of the same or a related subject. It takes longer to switch and adjust the monitoring of foreign radio broadcasts; longer still to refocus photography and imaging equipment in space. "Right now we are going through a period of hidden revolution, if you will," Hirsch says. "In terms of our thinking about and acting in the world, there's definite change."

The DS&T must manage these transitions in an era of virtually permanent budget austerity, when growth in resources struggles to match the general pace of inflation and the cost of research and development is rising far faster. "You have to do more with less and still work at the edges of the state of the art," says Peter Marino, president of Fairchild Industries and a former agency official. "More and more, the person in that job is going to have to have a certain vision about where intelligence collection should head, and make hard decisions." As Hirsch says, "technical collection is an expensive proposition. It's becoming less affordable in the sense that the time trend of costs for this kind of investment outstrips the growth of GNP." The same formula applies, he notes, to "big science" projects like the superconducting super collider, which "is on a cost curve that's steeper than the growth of the GNP," yet will prove more cost effective in electron volts per dollar invested than anything that preceded it. Similarly, Hirsch asserts, "if you talk about some of our major technical collection systems, we'll get more data per dollar than we've ever had before. So it's not as though we're facing a saturating curve. In terms of investment versus output, it's still a favorable ratio. It's just that national technical systems are very expensive." Coupled with the rapid progress of technology, this makes it "very difficult to decide which bets you ought to make, what you ought to invest in." But some of the advice the CIA is hearing these days is that, technical collection aside, the agency ought to make more and better use of its people on the ground--that there is no substitute in today's rapidly changing scene for the human factor in intelligence collection.

As one of four major elements of the CIA, the DS&T designs, develops and operates a wide variety of technical collection systems and equipment, including earth-orbiting satellites. These gather the raw material of intelligence from broadcasts, printed material, photographs and other imagery, and signals. The directorate processes what it collects and passes it along for analysis and use elsewhere in the agency. It thus provides much of the fuel on which the rest of the CIA runs, while serving also as the applied technology research arm of the entire U.S. intelligence community.

The directorate divides this work between seven divisions. These are the Foreign Broadcast Information Service (familiar to journalists and scholars to whom its products are also made available), the National Photographic Interpretation Center (a joint operation with the department of defense), and the offices of research and development, technical service, signals intelligence, development and engineering, and special projects. "We don't do very much in-house science and technology work," Hirsch says. That's because the various internal laboratories the directorate once operated could not match what the private sector was capable of. In integrated circuits, for example, "industry very quickly began to outstrip us, so we just closed them down."

Today, therefore, the DS&T contracts out most of its work, relying on industry for a large part of its R&D and to build the systems it uses, and on academic institutions for other R&D needs. "Most of the funds we spend on things," Hirsch says, "are spent in that way." But as Hineman emphasizes, "you need to have in-house the qualified people who can properly direct the work." One thing he insisted on: "we were not just passing money out the door to contractors and letting them do what they want. They were working for us as part of the team and we were directing the team." Moreover, Hirsch adds, "it's an essential ingredient of this job to keep attuned to what's going on in industry because you can very easily suffer from the green-door syndrome." This is the malady incurred by government managers who tend to stick with the same contractors year after year because of onerous and costly requirements to screen and/or clear companies and their facilities when classified work is involved. "You've got be careful to always be out pushing and looking for new ideas," Hirsch warns. If not, "it can really stultify your organization, because people get stale." The DS&T gets some insights in this regard through an advisory group called the Intelligence Research and Development Council, which helps the director of the agency stay abreast of developments in technology and R&D.

On the directorate staff, he says, "you'd find almost every brand of engineer and scientist we know of, broadly speaking." He is convinced that the directorate's success in attracting good people is the nature of the work. "No government job I know of, other than those requiring certain special-purpose talents, can command the same kinds of salaries that you can get in industry. I've seen both sides." The difference, he thinks, is that during the cold war intelligence was the name of the game-- "preventing Pearl Harbor from ever happening again. We were doing that every day, and supporting national strategic decisions. That's pretty heady stuff for the people who are doing the work."

Still, this appeal has its limits over time. "We were able to compete fairly well for, say, the first 15 years of an individual's career," Hineman recalls. "Then you run into some problems." These mainly concern income levels as children go off to college and outside offers beckon. "Nearly everyone that went out the door said, 'I really don't want to go, but I'm forced to,' " he says. "What can you do?" On this point, says Marino, "the CIA has a terrific record of growing people. But once they reach the point of successfully managing big systems, their attractiveness to outside industry is tremendous and it's hard to keep them."

Hirsch says he has the authority to choose his deputies and other senior people, "subject to the director's approval before they take office." In addition, at the director's request, a committee of agency deputy directors reviews the proposed filling of all senior posts, judging them from an agency--as opposed to individual directorate--point of view. In this exercise, at least one candidate from outside the directorate in question must figure among the group being considered for a given job.

Hineman tried to get "fresh blood" at every level of staff. "If you hire only at the bottom, you tend to put blinders on people and you'll grow them all the same way," he thinks. Other directorates may have reasons for doing that, he points out, "but with scientists and engineers and technicians, I think you can hire at various levels, being careful not to cut off the head room for the young people who are growing through." One other factor in the directorate's hiring grows out of the classified nature of much of the work. That prevents its scientists and technologists from communicating and commingling as effectively as they would like with colleagues in and outside of government. It prevents some of them from competing for prizes or receiving awards, and in many cases cuts them off from the benefits of peer review of their work and the return flow of information and comment that accompanies it.

Directorate officials past and present are somewhat constrained by the rules in what they can say on some subjects. One of these is the size of the DS&T staff. The closest approximation lies in the range of a few thousand. In the same way, no precise figures are available for operating resources; the figure can be said, however, to go beyond the "tens-of-millions" level, and to contain funding for certain projects from other agencies. Hirsch does say that a smaller percentage of the DS&T budget goes to personnel, and a greater part to R&D costs and investment in equipment, than in other directorates. "Each directorate put together its own budget," Hineman says, "and then we went and supported our portion of the agency's budget on the Hill." In his day, the DS&T budget trend was up, though its rate of increase dropped in the last year or two. "Nobody ever has enough money to do what they want," he reflects. "Did we have enough to do what we had to do? Yes. Could we have done a bit more and better if we had more money? Sure. But I never felt we were in bad, bad straits." In part, that was because he had the authority to halt one operation in favor of another of more urgency. "It's a game of trades, and you've got to prioritize the jobs and needs at hand, then draw the line where the money stops."

This deputy director doesn't visit the Hill as much his colleagues in the intelligence and operations directorates. "They're in the here and now, right up to their eyeballs," Hirsch says. "We provide support to both those organizations, so we're kind of indirect" where the Congress is concerned, "and unless it's an unusual circumstance, we're sort of behind the scenes." As Hineman says, "Congressmen are clearly more interested in what's happening today than what scientific and technical intelligence collection is going to look like in 1995." When the DS&T chief does visit the Hill, either for budget discussions or to testify on particular problems, he sees the House and Senate intelligence and armed services committees.

Beyond the challenges already mentioned for this position, those familiar with it also see a manpower problem. Hirsch cites a cumulative national shortage of science and engineering graduates. Yet, as Marino says, the CIA requires a strong staff of "unique technical people" for projects ranging from large systems development to analytical methodologies. "Some of the systems they build go out there and have to live by themselves forever, never being serviced. So the people running those programs have to be very strong technical managers."

Can the top DS&T job itself continue to attract people with adequate experience and perspective? "I think so," Hineman answers. Could someone from outside the agency do it? "You wouldn't want to take someone green to the CIA and put him in that job," he says. "It would be very difficult," Marino agrees. "The deputy director has a community responsibility having to do with support to the military, support to the community in general. And he has to communicate with that community and deal with the various organizations under his control. He needs to understand the vocabulary of all the sciences so he can at least talk intelligently to his customers and his peers."

Key Relationships

Within the Agency

Reports to: Director, Central Intelligence

Works closely with:

Deputy Director, Central Intelligence
Deputy Director, Intelligence
Deputy Director, Operations
Deputy Director, Administration

Outside the Agency

Deputy Director, Defense Intelligence Agency, Department of Defense
Deputy Director, National Security Agency
Deputy Director, Operations, NSA
Deputy Director, Research, NSA

Outside the Government

Contractor organizations for S&T directorate; informal consultants in scientific, academic and research communities

Profile of Current Deputy Director, Science and Technology

Name: James V. Hirsch

Assumed Position: 1989

Career Summary: Associate deputy director, science and technology, CIA, 1983-1989
President, Pathways Systems Inc., 1981-1983
Manager, strategic systems, Betac Corp., 1978-1981
Various research and analysis positions, CIA, 1968-1978
General Electric Corp., 1967-1968
Mitre Corp., 1959-1967

Education: Villanova University, BS, electrical engineering, 1957
Massachusetts Institute of Technology, MS, electrical engineering, 1959

Deputy Directors, Science and Technology Since 1969

Administration	Name and Years Served	Present Position
Bush	James V. Hirsch
1989 - present	Incumbent
Reagan	R. Evans Hineman
1982 - 1989	Vice President
The Analytical Sciences Corp.
Reston, Va.
Carter	Leslie C. Dirks
1976 - 1981	Hughes Aircraft
Los Angeles, Cal.
Ford, Nixon,
Johnson	Carl Duckett
1967 - 1975	Not available

11

DEPARTMENT OF COMMERCE

UNDER SECRETARY/ADMINISTRATOR
NATIONAL OCEANIC AND ATMOSPHERIC ADMINISTRATION

Level III - Presidential Appointment with Senate Confirmation

Major Responsibilities

- Administer a scientific agency of the department of commerce with a staff of 13,000 that observes, charts, analyzes and describes the planet's oceans and living resources; forecasts weather in the United States and its possessions; predicts conditions in the atmosphere and in the environments of ocean, sun and space; examines the impact of environmental changes over various time periods; and disseminates the information acquired to a wide array of public and private consumers.

- Participate in the development of policy shaping the federal role in environmental and marine resources management--for example, on the issue of global climate change. Oversee the government's management of the U.S. coastal zone, including wetlands and some aspects of offshore oil leasing; and its responsibilities in such areas as fisheries, whaling, marine mammal husbandry, and seafood quality.

- Advise and consult with the secretary of commerce on issues relevant to the mission of the National Oceanic and Atmospheric Administration (NOAA) and on policies and major decisions guiding its activity.

- Represent the United States in negotiations and discourse with other countries on topics ranging from fisheries to ocean management to global climate change.

Necessary Training, Experience, Skills

Nonscientists have run NOAA from time to time. But this job's current occupant and several predecessors concur that an accomplished advanced-degree scientist will handle it best. One of them characterized the requirement as "significant scientific credentials." These serve not just as the key to good leadership and full understanding of the agency's programs; not merely a way of knowing, as another put it, "whether somebody is schmoozling you or not." Such qualifications also ensure that the position will have the authoritative, comfortable association with qualified scientists in and out of government that is important to NOAA's work and reputation. High scientific qualifications strengthen this position's role and prestige at the international level; "the Soviets don't send anybody out who is less than academician-level," says a former occupant, "and we should do no less." And that's not all, he adds. It helps greatly if NOAA's chief has made a payroll, can understand a spread sheet, and knows how to run an organization with a $1 billion-plus budget. Finally, the individual must communicate effectively, internally and externally--"not just to read testimony before a congressional committee, but to be convincing."

Insight

In the beginning, says former under secretary/administrator William Evans (1988-89), young federal entities like the Environmental Protection Agency were created from whole earth: "the administration grabbed the clay, formed it together and said, this is an agency. Go forth and do this." NOAA, by contrast, emerged in 1970 as the sum of "bits and pieces and parts." Some of the parts were agencies with ancestral roots in the late 1700s. "They pulled them from wherever they were, called them a single agency and jammed it into the department of commerce. They said, 'this is what you are, guys.' And they called it NOAA."

In those days, Evans recalls, the fledgling organization's sole mission was to provide "the very best information we had--the best quality science"--to regulatory agencies like EPA. Then successive acts of Congress in half a dozen years brought NOAA to grips with marine mammal protection, coastal zone management, and endangered species and sanctuaries, in addition to fisheries. "It became a regulatory agency," says Evans, who had held other posts in NOAA. "The emphasis was not on science, it was on regulation. Then that changed and they slowly started to get back into science again."

And what is NOAA today? "An environmental agency, a very important one," affirms John A. Knauss, who took over as NOAA's chief in 1989. To be sure, he says, a "limited regulatory responsibility" does exist and he spends some time on it; these are matters like marine sanctuaries, the taking of shrimp, the preservation of turtles and the allocation of fishery quotas. As a further example, in making certain that coastal management really works, NOAA supervises each state's management program, a dose of regulation the states accept in return for federal funding of those programs.

Not surprisingly, some concern can be heard in the ocean-related business and industry sector about NOAA's regulatory activity. "They have changed," argues Charles Matthews of the National Ocean Industries Association, "from a basic scientific and technical organization designed to work closely with the academic, business and government communities to one that works with those three but has also taken on a very strong regulatory responsibility." He says the agency's main purpose now seems to be "regulating business offshore, instead of working with industry and business to develop the resources of the ocean." Matthews would like to see NOAA run by "a businessman with a scientific background," who would have "a business approach to solving problems."

But Knauss emphasizes that NOAA remains primarily responsible for monitoring the environment and predicting its future states, whether tomorrow's weather or the ecological response to something like Exxon Valdez. While others--the National Science Foundation, the universities, environmental scientists--share the expanding effort to understand how the environment works, NOAA has a key role, especially for monitoring. "We make most of the atmospheric observations and we and the Navy make most of the oceanic observations," Knauss says. A growing part of this work goes on in the context of studying global climate change. For years NOAA has launched and used geostationary satellites and polar orbiters for a variety of weather and other observations, many of them pertinent to studying climate change. The agency would like to supplement that with ground-based data-gathering, using technology like the radio acoustic sounding system that bounces ground radar off weather systems to detect changes close to earth that satellites miss.

How do those who have held this position perceive its mandate and priority objectives? When he took the job in 1988, Evans saw as his main task the consolidation of NOAA as "a whole, integrated agency," out of the "many-'splintered' thing" of its infancy. Further, NOAA is "a service agency. Our job was not just to provide the information so it went into reports and places where nobody could find it." Rather, it was to put it in the hands of decision makers in states and localities as well as at the federal level--"give them access to the most up-to-date information we had." He thinks the information still remains less accessible than it should. "NOAA's heading that way, but I think it's going to be a little while before they get there."

On this point, Knauss agrees, "people claim NOAA ran a black hole as a data management system, that you could send stuff in but you could never get it out. We have the largest number of environmental data sets in the world. They have been neglected and starved for reasons I partly understand: for most people, it's kind of a low priority step. But it's critically important and I've made it a very high priority to get our act together. We've set a goal that 90 percent of our data is going to be readily available within five years." Doing so is a question to some extent of new equipment and some new money, he adds, "but mostly it is just shaking the place up."

As for his top priority, Knauss inherited a program to modernize the weather service, involving new instrumentation, and felt it had to be the first focus of his attention. "It took a long time to develop. You don't start a program like that and then let it drag on." A third main focus for him is NOAA's and his own role in the process of assessing global climate change and developing policies and plans.

"In terms of dollars and clout," Knauss says that the Earth Observing System--the global climate change study program--currently represents the biggest interagency effort in which he personally takes part. At least half a dozen federal agencies are involved and the Office of Management and Budget (OMB) treats it and its budget as a whole instead of scrutinizing each agency's presentation separately. In this, Knauss faces not his usual budget examiners in OMB's government and economics office, but those who also look at other science and science-related agencies, among them NSF, NASA, Energy and EPA. Of the funds requested for global warming research in the president's fiscal 1992 budget message, NOAA's $66 million share would emphasize its major role in this issue.

Some people, including a former NOAA boss, suggest that the agency lives under the wrong roof. It's a question meriting some examination. John V. Byrne, administrator in 1981-84, saw NOAA as a science agency misplaced in a department primarily focused on commerce and international trade. Should it move elsewhere?

"There are advocates on both sides," Evans says. He doesn't entirely rule out the notion that NOAA might for some reasons and circumstances fare a bit better in an eventual department of the environment. But he questions the idea of NOAA as an independent agency lacking the authority and visibility that being part of a cabinet department can confer. "If you attend cabinet meetings (but don't sit at the table), unless you're a good networker you really have trouble getting decisions that are going to help you." He thinks NOAA is well enough off where it is "as long as you have a (secretary) who gives you a lot of autonomy and support within commerce." When he ran the agency, Evans says he got that kind of backing. "NOAA is the largest agency in Commerce and the secretary treated it that way." Still, he chafed at certain tasks. As U.S. commissioner to the International Whaling Commission (a collateral duty), he had a number of constituencies the law required him to be responsive to. "Some of the things we were supposed to do in the commission context ran very counter to the policies of the department of commerce. On one hand I worked for the secretary of commerce; on the other I was appointed by the president to the whaling commission. So who are you, whom do you address? I had some real problems with that."

Knauss points out that NOAA is "about 55 percent of the department in terms of people and money, and then there is the National Institute of Standards and Technology (formerly the Bureau of Standards), the patents and trademarks office, and the census bureau. I haven't done the numbers on it, but I suspect Commerce is misnamed. It's primarily a technical department."

Whatever its location, Evans thinks "there has to be a mechanism where NOAA has a stronger voice and can't be overruled by State or Commerce or others. You've got to be in a position where you have equal opportunity to debate the issues"--in short, somebody sitting at the cabinet table with NOAA's objectives in mind. To help produce this result in the current circumstances, Evans and Byrne believe that educating the secretary and the commerce department about NOAA is part of the job--"in language the secretary understands," Byrne adds.

Both Knauss and Evans report basic satisfaction with the scientific credentials and general performance of the NOAA work force, all but about 30 of whom are career employees. "I was very pleased with the upper management and with the bench scientists," Evans says. "I had a chief scientist and other high-quality scientists whom I wasn't going to second-guess." The agency's assistant administrator positions, he adds, should be designated career Senior Executive Service to minimize use of these mainly scientific jobs for the placement of unqualified individuals. Yet if general staff competence is not a pressing problem, Knauss says "it's been harder to get really good people to come in." At the same time, like other scientific and technical agencies, NOAA competes for talent with the private sector and the universities. "We just had one of our people leave and go to work at Princeton," he laments, "for a 40 percent increase in salary." In attracting able staff, Knauss favors bringing them in at various levels, not just at the bottom. "Once you get people in the federal government, unlike the university I came from, you don't have six years to decide whether they get tenure. They get it almost immediately. So ideally you bring in people who already have some kind of track record and you know they're going to be competent."

Evans remembers that "we didn't have trouble retaining staff, but in attracting them. NOAA is an old organization in terms of the average age of our scientists; 44 to 45 is average. We don't have the new bright guys coming in. They're going to Northrop or Lockheed."

Three key managers currently assist the under secretary/administrator. Two--the assistant secretary and the chief scientist--are presidentially appointed; the deputy under secretary is the third member of this troika. Between them they handle substantive matters and day-to-day operations, congressional relations, budget and administration. The extent to which NOAA chiefs have been able to choose these lieutenants and other subordinates seems to range from "having a voice" in the decisions to "complete control and autonomy."

In the 1980s, NOAA's budget managed only to keep pace with inflation. "In many ways," says Knauss, "the budget went down, because we took on some new responsibilities, including some satellites which eat up a lot of money." NOAA's fiscal 1990 budget, the first of the Bush era, was $1.586 billion, about a nine percent rise over the actual 1989 appropriation. As for fiscal 1991, "we're going in the right direction" ($1.855 billion). The agency's request to the Congress for 1992 was $1.949 billion.

NOAA, says Evans, also benefited in the late 1980s from what he calls budget serendipity. Just as military outlays were coming down, environmental issues took on new prominence and attitudes in the White House shifted in their direction. Cost problems with the satellites and with weather service modernization had been dogging NOAA, but "as soon as the global climate change issue came in, a lot of those things changed."

In budget allocation, the under secretary/administrator makes the key decisions on priorities and new initiatives. The budget is a principal consumer of time in this job; Knauss estimates it at 20-30 percent overall, "either working on or monitoring it," with peaks during periods of preparation and presentation.

Interagency groups and other federal bodies on which the head of NOAA sits include the Earth and Environmental Sciences Committee (part of the complex embraced by the Federal Coordinating Council for Science, Engineering and Technology), and its global climate change working group; the Marine Mammal Commission; and the Ocean Principals Committee, which groups the Navy oceanographer and the heads of NASA, the U.S. Geological Survey, and the National Science Foundation, among others. From time to time, NOAA's chief acts as a policy adviser to the secretary in meetings of the Domestic and Economic Policy Councils. Visits to NOAA installations and speeches and other public appearances require more travel within the country than Knauss thinks best. In his first year, he also visited western Europe, the Soviet Union and Japan on negotiating and conference missions; the job includes duties as U.S. delegate to UNESCO's International Oceanographic Commission.

Among Evans's working relationships outside Commerce, he attached great importance to that with OMB. "It's absolutely necessary to be able to sit down on a first-name basis with (the associate OMB director for economics and government) and discuss what the real issues are, the political implications, why you really need to do this or that, why it's important to the White House, what brownie points you get from it."

At the same time, says Evans, others at OMB can present problems. "Not necessarily the political appointees," but veteran staff further down the line who, in his view, had their own restrictive, unchanging ideas about the use of budget resources on which they constantly sought to persuade their superiors at the political level. When these notions prevail, Evans feels, the result for agencies like NOAA "is not good science." He also found some entrenchment within his own agency. It took the form of "little empires established out in the field" which did their own lobbying in the Congress and "tried to lace the budget with their own agendas." In this era of weather-data satellites, for instance, Evans thinks NOAA should eliminate small, remote weather stations--what he describes as "two or three people sitting on the side of a mountain in Muleshoe, Arkansas, where they've been running an anemometer for 45 years." Efforts to close them down, say Knauss and Evans, invariably bring strenuous complaints from Capitol Hill. This "works strongly against the effort to run an integrated agency," a situation, Evans asserts, that is also not good science. And such pockets of dug-in resistance "are still alive and well."

A more generalized problem arises, inevitably, on the resources front, even with a budget on a moderate uptrend. "You never have enough money to do what you'd really like to do," Knauss reflects. And what is that? "I think we have the programs in place," he says. "I'd just like to move them faster." Complicating the resources picture is what Evans in his time viewed as congressional micromanagement "in terms of making decisions on programs that should increase or decrease in funding based on agendas that had nothing to do with the value of a program, or the science, and having to sacrifice good programs for special interest projects like catfish farms in Arkansas or special laboratories in Hawaii." Projects like these "have nothing to do with NOAA's mission, and belong in the budgets of the department of agriculture and possibly the department of the interior," he says.

Another instance of budget difficulties flows from the vagaries of legislative drafting and the distribution of congressional committee seats. Congress has decreed that when ocean salmon swim upstream beyond the high tide mark, they are the responsibility chiefly of the department of the interior. Once the newly-spawned salmon head downstream and into the sea, they belong to Commerce and NOAA. Yet, Evans explains, Senators and House members from the important salmon states sit on the committees with jurisdiction over Commerce, not Interior. So, while millions of dollars in salmon hatchery money went into the Commerce budget for NOAA, "we never saw it. Whisk--right to the interior department. But it was listed as an item on our budget and a very significant one." As such, though NOAA does not get the use of the money, salmon fisheries take space in the agency's budget that presumably could supplement or fund other NOAA projects.

Despite such anomalies, Knauss feels fortunate that most legislators have genuine concern about the environment. "They do think it's important, for a lot of reasons for which science can provide only some of the answers. But I don't find myself patted on the head and told to go away, you're not dealing with the real problems. I think they do see environmental problems as real, and that science has to be part of the answer."

Key Relationships

Within the Department

Reports to: Secretary of Commerce

Works closely with:

Deputy Secretary
General Counsel
Assistant Secretary, Congressional and Intergovernmental Affairs

Outside the Department

Assistant to the President, Science and Technology Policy
Chairman, Council on Environmental Quality
Associate Administrator, Space Science and Applications, National
  Aeronautics and Space Administration
Naval Oceanographer
Assistant Director, Geosciences, National Science Foundation
Assistant Secretary of State, Oceans and International Environmental and
  Scientific Affairs
Director, Bureau of Land Management, Department of the Interior

Director, Fish and Wildlife Service, Department of the Interior
Director, U.S. Geological Survey, Department of the Interior

Outside the Federal Government

National Ocean Industries Association, National Fisheries Institute, Coastal
States Organization, Marine Mammal Coalition, National Fish and Seafood
Promotion Council

Profile of Current Undersecretary/Administrator
Oceans and Atmosphere

Name:	John A. Knauss
Assumed Position:	1989
Career Summary:	Professor of oceanography, and dean, Graduate School of Oceanography, University of Rhode Island, 1962-87 Provost for marine affairs, University of Rhode Island, 1969-82
Education:	Massachusetts Institute of Technology, BS, 1946 University of Michigan, MS, 1949 Scripps Institution of Oceanography, University of California, PhD, 1959

Undersecretaries/Administrators for Oceans and Atmosphere
Since 1969

Administration	Name and Years Served	Present Position
Bush	John A. Knauss 1989 - present	Incumbent
Reagan	William Evans 1988 - 1989	Dean, Maritime College Texas A&M University Galveston, Tex.
Reagan	Anthony J. Calio 1985 - 1987	Vice President Hughes Information Technology Reston, Va.
Reagan	John V. Byrne 1981 - 1984	President Oregon State University Corvallis, Ore.

Carter	Richard A. Frank 1977 - 1981	President Population Services Intl. Washington, D.C.
Ford, Nixon, Johnson	Robert M. White 1965 - 1977	President National Academy of Engineering Washington, D.C.

UNDER SECRETARY, TECHNOLOGY

Level III - Presidential Appointment with Senate Confirmation

Major Responsibilities

- Stimulate and coordinate the development of federal policies and programs to improve the competitiveness of American industry, especially in the applications of advanced technology and the building of new manufacturing and communications infrastructures.

- Act as a convenor and catalyst in assisting the private sector to formulate long-term technology strategies. Identify opportunities and regulatory and statutory obstacles in commercial innovation and technology transfer.

- Consult with the secretary of commerce and senior federal science and technology officials on the relationship of federally-supported research and development to these objectives, and on the direction of federal technology and trade policy in general.

- Oversee the line operations of the principal components of the Technology Administration--the Office of Technology Policy, the National Institute of Standards and Technology, and the National Technical Information Service.

Necessary Training, Experience, Skills

The position requires a professional engineer or scientist, preferably (though not imperatively) at the PhD level, with substantial experience in industry and the knowledge of what it takes to stay technologically current. This under secretary must understand the process of technology development and the problems associated with technology transfer. A sense of the public policy dimensions of the job's mission, gained through service in government or in an academic context, is a clear asset.

Insight

In its fiscal 1992 budget, the federal government requested about $76 billion for support of research and development, including R&D facilities. One third of one percent of that figure equals the projected 1992 budget of the only federal agency with the partial mission to assist U.S. industry in the technology development necessary to stay, or become, competitive. That agency is the National Institute of Standards and Technology, the major component of this under secretary's oversight responsibility.

The Senate committee staff member who makes that observation also points out that as of 1988 the Japanese government was devoting 4.8 percent of its R&D support to the same objective, and what was then the government of West Germany was earmarking fully 14.5 percent. To be sure, he adds, American industry does gain something technologically from other forms of federal spending. There are the technical advances that agencies like NASA or the defense department spin off now and again in the pursuit of their own responsibilities. And it's "inconceivable" that the U.S. agriculture or pharmaceutical industries would be where they are today without the department of agriculture or the National Institutes of Health. "But if you're looking at general manufacturing, general U.S. industry," he says, "the U.S. government has traditionally placed an incredibly low priority on it."

In this pattern, however, there are now some arrows that point upward. One was the administration's decision, announced in the fall of 1990, to give modest federal support to research during the precompetitive stage in the development of pivotal "generic" technologies. Another was development by the White House science and technology office of its related list of "critical" commercial technologies judged vital to maintaining and advancing U.S. economic and military strength--though it is unclear what government's part would be in helping bring them to full flower. A third encouraging sign is the role of the new Technology Administration (TA) at the department of commerce, established by legislation in 1989. Robert M. White, a physicist who took over TA as its first chief in the spring of 1990, views his key responsibility as "trying to improve the competitiveness of American industry." That general objective is finding expression in a number of specific initiatives by TA and the activities it oversees.

Among these is the Advanced Technologies Program, managed by the National Institute of Standards and Technology (NIST--examined elsewhere in this volume). The program provides a small amount of seed money in a competitive process to develop funding for industry-led R&D in the generic technologies that the White House is stressing. Created by the Omnibus Trade Act of 1988, the Advanced Technologies Program distributed $10 million among 11 winning R&D proposals in its first year. Last-minute maneuvering as the 101st Congress moved toward adjournment, however, cut fiscal 1991 funding for the program to $36 million from the higher figure TA had hoped for; reflecting that action, the 1992 budget document calls for the same amount, and labels it an "experimental" project whose results can't be predicted with certainty. "Congress has talked of making it $100 million in the future," White told us in the fall of 1990. "ATP's future growth will depend on its successfulness. If it stays very small I think there's some question as to its credibility and effectiveness."

In another program, NIST operates five manufacturing technology centers that assist small firms, chiefly by transferring to them advanced manufacturing technologies and methods developed in federal laboratories. The goal is two dozen such centers across the country, but the 1992 budget proposal cut funding for the centers by more than 13 percent. White also has a responsibility, exercised day-to-day through an assistant secretary for technology policy, to look for and help eliminate barriers to the commercialization of American science and technology where possible. In that capacity, TA talks with private sector executives about problems posed by federal regulations and tax and other policies to see where adjustments can be made that satisfy the requirements of law (and, of course, integrity). An example would be revising the time periods specified for amortizing the cost of certain production line equipment to align them more realistically with the true life of the equipment.

But perhaps the under secretary's most impactive function is to serve as what the Senate staff member calls a "catalyst" in getting companies together to think through their long-term technology needs. It's a matter, the staffer says, of "very quietly inviting people from industry to come in and saying to them, 'now what do you want to do in terms of technology and area X,' and getting those companies to think through what their options are in forming consortia or carrying out cooperative projects." This is not what anyone would call "industrial policy," he emphasizes. "It's not the government attempting to tell people what to do. It's the government trying to help industry people think through what industry people want to do." Again, the assistant secretary for technology policy has the line responsibility for making that happen.

Such efforts can extend beyond U.S. borders, as illustrated by Japanese proposals for international R&D in areas such as intelligent manufacturing systems. While most countries remain preoccupied by national research projects, the staffer says, the Japanese look ahead and see that "some things are just going to require international cooperation" because of very high costs or, perhaps, "just a need for coordination."

White sees his job as the position within government responsible for the competitive vitality of American industry from a technology standpoint. In his view, that is a steeply uphill assignment. "If you look today at any of the measures of where we stand in technological competitiveness, we're losing in all the technical areas," he comments. "Market shares, computers, semiconductors--everything is declining. My personal objective is to try either to slow that down, stop it, or turn it around; to try to awaken the country to the need to improve its ability to make things."

It's a familiar refrain: to be competitive these days is to be technologically proficient. But White is specific about what it takes to achieve that state of grace. Helping industry stay competitive, he thinks, means "improving the way in which we manage the whole technology innovation process," which he sees as one continuum--from concept to research and development and on to the manufacturing stage. And he believes the biggest challenge in that task is communication and coordination. "There is a tremendous amount of activity that goes on in the technology area," he says. "Getting that coordinated somehow--getting industry, government and academia to agree on an agenda and work together--is the answer." The country invests a huge amount in R&D, and "if we can get it focused, take advantage of it, I think we'll help ourselves a great deal."

The pursuit of these objectives brings the under secretary into frequent contact with a good many executive branch colleagues with related concerns and responsibilities. White works with the White House Office of Science and Technology Policy; sits on the Committee on Physical, Mathematical and Engineering Sciences of the Federal Coordinating Council for Science, Engineering and Technology (FCCSET); and chairs a sub-panel of the FCCSET Committee on Technology and Industry that is studying the 700-plus federal laboratories in connection with the technologies on the White House's critical list. He regularly sees senior research and engineering officials of the departments of Defense and Energy, the director of the National Science Foundation, and people at the Education and Labor departments; and is a member of the National Academy of Sciences' Government-University-Industry Research Roundtable. White has maintained his relationships with the outside scientific and technical community from which he came, and continues to write professionally in his field. On Capitol Hill he considers the Senate Commerce Committee his major stop. In the first year, his travel was mainly for speaking dates.

In addition to White's own tiny staff, NIST, and the Office of Technology Policy, the TA domain includes the National Technical Information Service, which among other activities acquires and markets an extensive range of R&D and engineering reports, and associated documentation and bibliography, on federally-funded projects in the

United States and overseas. Together, these components employ a staff of between 3,000 and 3,500, of whom 85 percent work for NIST. Their collective budget reflected in the fiscal 1992 request is almost $252 million. NIST, of course, accounts for something like 98 percent of TA funding. In addition to supervising the budget's development and supporting it at the Office of Management and Budget and to the Congress, White has a voice in Commerce's overall decisions on resource requests and uses where they affect the concept and functioning of his operations. "We are new, we're trying to become more effective," he says. "If we don't, we shouldn't be here."

But in absolute terms, says the Senate committee staffer, TA as a whole is underfunded, and is being loaded with increasing responsibilities by the Congress without getting the resources it needs. Part of what drives that, he says, is not only "the excitement of opportunity to really improve manufacturing" but an awareness "that our competitors are working on this kind of system, and in some cases and places already developing it."

Is a well-developed, firmly implemented technology policy enough by itself to turn the competitiveness corner? Not, it is suggested, when companies have the desire and the know-how but lack the facilities to fabricate a product. "You can't do advanced technology without the production capability," White points out. "Little companies, entrepreneurial companies go to a certain level, but to go on they need big amounts of money. That's the problem today." Our Senate committee source agrees. "When you see small hi-tech companies that can't afford to continue because of capital costs, you're seeing some of our best technology, in areas like semiconductors, go straight to Tokyo," he says.

That is one reason why government needs to move on a wide front to attack the competitiveness problem. "It's fine to talk about technology policy," the Senate staff member observes. "But if you don't also talk about trade policy, and the cost of capital, education and training, you run the risk--and it is very real right now--that we'll continue to develop great technology but American companies won't be able to afford to build the factories and make the products. And we'll end up once again handing most of it over to foreigners."

White put his finger on this problem in an article for the newspaper *Washington Technology*. "In the United States," he wrote, "using knowledge as an economic resource is both harder and easier. Easier because we build from a position of strength. Harder because strength obscures the need to change...Today the United States leads the world as a source of knowledge and technology in many fields. But we no longer lead in the use of that technology. Although history shows clearly how valuable technology is to economic growth, we have not found a way to factor that value into our economic analyses."

Thus, he told us, the importance of the contribution science and technology makes to national economic strength and well-being gets adequate recognition, for example, among the legislators he dialogues with in the Congress. But he does not think "that we as a nation have really come to grips with why we are losing market share in every hi-tech industry. I don't think we understand the problem and what it's really going to take to change it." Education is part of the answer, he believes, as well as "a commitment, a determination, to make things and not feel that it's okay to be only a service economy. We have to have high-tech industries. And we've got to get everybody in the country involved."

Key Relationships

Within the Department

Reports to: Secretary

Works closely with:

Deputy Secretary
Under Secretary, Export Administration
Under Secretary, International Trade

Outside the Department

Director, White House Office of Science and Technology Policy (OSTP)
Associate Director, Industrial Technology, OSTP
Committee on Technology and Industry, Federal Coordinating Council for
  Science, Engineering and Technology (FCCSET)
Committee on Physical, Mathematical and Engineering Sciences, FCCSET
Director, National Science Foundation
Director, Defense Research and Engineering, Department of Defense
Director, Defense Advanced Research Projects Agency
Director, Energy Research, Department of Energy
Assistant Secretary, Postsecondary Education, Department of Education
Assistant Secretary, Employment and Training, Department of Labor
Government-University-Industry Research Roundtable, National Academy
  of Sciences
National Academy of Engineering

Outside the Government

Manufacturing and foreign trade associations; senior officials of high-technology firms and consortia; the national professional scientific and technical community; state education, labor and industry agencies

Profile of Current Under Secretary, Technology

Name: Robert M. White

Assumed Position: 1990

Career Summary: Vice president, Microelectronics and Computer Technology
                       Corporation, 1989-90
                       Chief technical officer, vice president for research and engineering,
                       Control Data Corporation, 1984-89
                       Principal scientist, Xerox Palo Alto Research Center, 1971-84
                       Assistant professor, physics, Stanford University, 1966-70

Education: Massachusetts Institute of Technology, BS, physics, 1960
                       Stanford University, PhD, physics, 1964

Under Secretaries, Technology Since 1990*

Administration	Name and Years Served	Present Position
Bush	Robert M. White 1990 - present	Incumbent

* Position established by legislation in 1989.

ASSISTANT SECRETARY/ADMINISTRATOR NATIONAL TELECOMMUNICATIONS AND INFORMATION ADMINISTRATION

Level IV - Presidential Appointment with Senate Confirmation

Major Responsibilities

- Advise the president on domestic and international telecommunications matters, developing and recommending the substance and long-range direction of federal policy in this field.

- As manager of the National Telecommunications and Information Administration (NTIA), supervise the licensing and management of federal government use of its share of the radio frequency spectrum. With other federal agencies, formulate U.S. federal and private sector requirements for global spectrum share, and positions on related telecommunications issues, for presentation and negotiation at the international level.

- Oversee the research work of the agency's Institute for Telecommunications Sciences. Provide technical support to U.S. participation in trade negotiations.

- Administer a grants program supporting public television broadcasting.

Necessary Training, Experience, Skills

"The interplay between technology and policy is a very subtle one," says an observer familiar with the backgrounds of the last several occupants of this position. Accordingly, he believes there is no substitute for communications industry experience in making business and strategic decisions. For someone taking on the leadership of NTIA this provides some crucial perspective "on how technical standards are set--you can't just proclaim them--and how communications policy is made." The current assistant secretary thinks the job requires pertinent technical knowledge and economics training and, preferably, legal credentials. She and others also stress the importance of political skill, since "you really have to work at building informal coalitions."

Insight

Not much past a century ago, the potential uses of radio waves and the possibilities of voice communication powered through land lines by electrical impulse signaled the true start of the telecommunications age. A bit more than half a century ago, the Congress codified regulation of the new technology. The Communications Act of 1934 remains the determining legislation in the field today, even as science and commerce continue to multiply and extend telecommunications capabilities. Like a number of other building blocks of contemporary advanced societies, this technology is rapidly advancing into new ground.

"Just look at what's happened in recent years," says Henry Geller, NTIA's first chief from 1978 to 1980. "The most enormous changes you can imagine." They range from the video cassette recorder to high-definition television, from FM radio to fiber optics, from cable television to cellular telephones. They include the vibrations still loudly echoing through the telephone and other industries from the breakup of the Bell System monopoly in the early 1980s, and the new services and products it has spawned. Geller calls the 1934 legislation "outmoded, way out of line with reality," written at a time when much of the communications industry was a monopoly. "When you read the act, you'd never know that the whole concept today is competition."

He means primarily competition within the industry, but the word has a more universal sense where telecommunications is concerned. For the prime commodity of telecommunications is information conveyed in its various formats--in data, by voice, in the written word, by image, by coded instructions to computers. How available information is, its quality and quantity, how quickly it flows and by what means, how ready it is for use on arrival are increasingly key tests of a country's ability to manage its affairs, advance the health, education and well-being of its people, and remain competitive in the world.

Janice Obuchowski, a lawyer and former industry executive and Federal Communications Commission official, has headed NTIA since 1989. The most visible part of the job, she thinks, is "formulating administration policy in telecommunications" and functioning as its spokesperson. "The domestic component involves everything from trying to articulate a vision on where the nation's telecommunications infrastructure should go, to developing positions on concrete issues such as cable television reregulation, children's television, and AT&T

deregulation." David J. Markey, who led NTIA in 1983-85, also puts the policy component at the top of the list. "If your boss is going to be concerned about what you're doing, he's not going to call up and ask about the assignment of a couple of radio frequencies," he points out. "He's going to say 'what about this issue that Congress is legislating on, or the Cabinet Council is going to take up?' "

Note, however, that NTIA has a decision-making role only in the area of federal spectrum management. As pointed out by Michael C. Rau, senior vice president for science and technology at the National Association of Broadcasters, "there's no real power at NTIA to do anything in the private sector." That authority belongs to the Federal Communications Commission (FCC) and the Congress. NTIA's influence in this domain, Rau says, "extends to its ability to publish credible reports, make credible arguments and persuade, to whatever extent it can, the president or the Congress or the FCC." Recently, for example, the FCC has focused on low-power cellular communication for personal use and on high-definition television. The NTIA assists decision making on all such issues with recommended courses of action. "But they're just proposing," Geller says. "The FCC is disposing. I've always said NTIA is one of the least dangerous agencies in Washington because (its success) depends very largely on the cogency of its views."

Geller thinks the agency should always "be out there saying what is right and arguing for what is right. If you don't, you're missing a real opportunity because, believe me, the decision people will cut back from you. They give you two thirds or Congress gives you half. If you're not arguing for what's right, you're not starting from the right position." In Obuchowski's view, NTIA's biggest policy problems flow from "the fact that in this field the interests are so big, the money is so big--and yet they are fragmented, fighting one another. Cable is fighting telephone, the broadcasters are fighting both." The toughest challenge, she says, is to transform good ideas NTIA generates into national policy. Part of this involves getting off the books "archaic" laws that "preclude technology from being brought to market." It also means promoting as much new entry into the field as possible. But "all these old laws and regulations have their constituencies which are very entrenched and very well greased. The hardest thing is advancing an affirmative public policy perspective in such a contentious industry."

The assistant secretary runs NTIA through five deputies. Four of these--in charge of policy analysis and development, international affairs, federal spectrum management, and telecommunications applications--work in Washington. The fifth manages the Institute of Telecommunications Sciences (ITS), located with several other federal technical facilities in Boulder, Colorado. Obuchowski says the ITS lab, with about 120 mostly engineering and scientific employees, conducts two kinds of investigations.

One is "very advanced research" into radio wave behavior, especially frequencies high in the spectrum which have not yet been brought into commercial use. The other is in the area of broadband networks, "setting standards for video transmission and measuring video quality" and "trying to understand and organize standards by which broadband networks would be compatible." Like private sector laboratories in the communications industry, ITS is also in a good position to provide a forward look into telecommunications technology of the future.

The agency's federal spectrum responsibilities represent "the biggest chunk of our budget," according to Obuchowski. Using the spectrum does not deplete it. While it grows ever more crowded, it can be used and shared repeatedly, in changing mixes of applications. But efficient spectrum management is critical, as Geller explains, because it is a valuable and, in its own way, a scarce natural resource. Of the U.S. slice of the global spectrum, government entities, notably including the department of defense, use between 30 and 50 percent. The private sector has another 40 percent--where the FCC assigns the frequencies--and uses it in everything from broadcasting and telephone microwave links to police and taxi service and amateur radio communications. The rest of the spectrum is shared by both sectors. Obuchowski says NTIA's spectrum management, involving more than 100 people including a 40-person facility in Annapolis, Maryland, is highly computerized. "We license about 80,000 systems a year, all the way from air traffic control radars and military systems to the National Park Service, earth sensing satellites, and all the different spectrum-based technologies."

The task of allocating frequencies to federal agencies and specifying their use takes this assistant secretary to regular sessions of the Interdepartmental Radio Advisory Council. She also attends meetings of a White House-chaired telecommunications security advisory board whose other members include the heads of the FCC and the Federal Emergency Management Agency. The White House leads meetings on telecommunications issues related to economic policy that bring the NTIA chief together with representatives of the justice department, the Council of Economic Advisers, and the Office of Management and Budget. A policy group on international telecommunications policy issues, grouping NTIA, the FCC and the state department, convenes quarterly. Finally, the assistant secretary must oversee NTIA's part in hammering out U.S. policy positions on spectrum management and other issues with the FCC and the state department. And the job has a significant role in representing these positions at the World Administrative Radio Conference and other meetings under International Telecommunications Union auspices.

Of NTIA's 220 employees, three quarters are engineers and scientists; in the policy area, the staff is what Obuchowski calls "a mixture of lawyers, economists and technical people." Part of the strength of the spectrum staff in Washington is its component of people from the military establishment "who bring their training and knowledge of defense systems with them." She is pleased with present staff caliber. "This is a highly professional agency," in which "90 percent of the people have BAs or above and are highly motivated. You've got all the disadvantages of government, so you really have to develop a climate where some of its advantages persuade people to stay around." One of these, she says, is the facility at Boulder--"a real drawing card." Another helping factor: "Telecommunications is booming and the knowledge tends to be very marketable. People don't have a hard time moving in or out of different positions. We have a lot of great alumni." But she worries about adequately replacing valuable senior people as they retire.

The agency's budget divides chiefly into internal operations and grants to public broadcasting. For fiscal 1991, the total figure comes to about $42 million, Obuchowski says, of which grant funds are about $20 million. The internal operations segment has grown about 10 percent a year during her tenure, and the request for 1992 is $18.2 million. The 1992 budget does not formally state a grants figure, a seemingly dramatic cut. But the cut is apparent, not real. Due to a decision by the previous administration to eliminate support for public broadcasting, NTIA no longer asks for the money. This is done with the full expectation that the Congress, as it has done for some years, will appropriate it anyway (the estimated figure for 1992 is $24.5 million). In addition to channeling that money into public broadcast facilities, NTIA has also been funding the National Technical University, a satellite-operated advanced degree education program that links some 30 universities with large technology firms like IBM. A similar program, AGSAT, connects land grant agriculture schools with the offices of agribusinesses.

As for the future, Rau thinks that NTIA and the department of commerce do not take sufficient account of what he calls "the internationalization of the technical communications marketplace." In his view, while NTIA tends to focus on improvement and promotion of the American telecommunications industry, the state department takes a more pragmatic approach. State recognizes that "the U.S. is one player on a world stage and that in some cases the benefits to users and consumers are greater even if you do accept some foreign technology." Rau feels NTIA's leadership is increasingly attracted to "the political realm and non-technical issues." He believes it should concentrate instead on technical matters, like radio-wave propagation studies and interference analysis, that are "fundamental to the long-term health of communications. These issues may not be glorious things to work on, but they have a lot of merit, and all communications industries can benefit from NTIA technical analysis. Technical decisions have to be right when they're made. You can't go back a few years later and change things, because whole industries have meanwhile grown up around the technology. Technical issues are like one-way ratchets."

Markey agrees to the extent that "the more you know about technology, the better. But if you had the choice of being a brilliant scientist or a pretty good politician, you're probably better off being a good politician."

For her part, Obuchowski looks at her job as "not the most powerful communications job in Washington--that is the FCC chairman-- but the best. You get to cover the entire waterfront, everything from the political to the technical. There's a lot of process, we have the licensing and grants programs. But on the policy front both internationally and domestically, you really have the liberty to try to set and push an agenda. It's a soapbox job."

Key Relationships

Within the Department

Reports to: Secretary

Works closely with:

Deputy Secretary
Chief of Staff
General Counsel

Outside the Department

Chairman and commissioners, Federal Communications Commission
Assistant Attorney General, Anti-Trust Division, Department of Justice
Coordinator, International Communication and Information Policy,
   Department of State
Assistant Secretary, Command, Control, Communications and Intelligence,
   Office of the Secretary of Defense
Commander, Naval Computer and Telecommunications Command, U.S. Navy
Senior Director, Intelligence Programs, National Security Council

Outside the Government

Members and trade associations of the communications carrier industry and communications equipment manufacturers; the broadcasting industry; communications officials of state and local government; the International Telecommunications Union; counterpart representatives of other governments (among them Japan, Canada and Mexico)

Profile of Current Assistant Secretary/Administrator, NTIA

Name:	Janice Obuchowski
Assumed Position:	1989
Career Summary:	Executive director, international affairs, NYNEX, 1987-89 Senior adviser to the chairman, Federal Communications Commission, 1983-87 Chief, Common Carrier Bureau, FCC, 1982-83 Legal assistant to the chief, Common Carrier Bureau, FCC, 1981-82 Associate, Bergson, Borkland, Margolis and Adler, 1976-80
Education:	Wellesley College, BA, 1973 Georgetown University Law Center, JD, 1976

Assistant Secretaries/Administrators, NTIA Since 1969

Administration	Name and Years Served	Present Position
Bush	Janice Obuchowski	Incumbent
Reagan	Alfred C. Sikes 1986 - 1989	Chairman, Federal Communications Commission
Reagan	David J. Markey 1983 - 1985	Vice President Bell South Washington, D.C.
Reagan	Bernard J. Wunder 1981 - 1982	Senior Partner Wunder, Ryan, Cannon & Thelan Washington, D.C.
Carter	Henry Geller 1978 - 1980	Center for Public Policy Research Washington, D.C.
Ford, Nixon	John M. Richardson* 1973 - 1977	Not available
Nixon	Armig G. Kandoian* 1970 - 1972	Not available

* Held position as Director, Office of Telecommunications

DIRECTOR
BUREAU OF THE CENSUS

Level IV - Presidential Appointment with Senate Confirmation

Major Responsibilities

● Manage the Bureau of the Census, charged with the periodic counting and surveying of the country's population, housing, and much of its economic activity. This notably includes the decennial population and housing census and agricultural and economic surveys every five years. The bureau tabulates the data it collects and provides the results to a multiplicity of users throughout the public and private sectors.

● Direct similar projects by contract with other federal agencies and with state and local governments. Oversee the bureau's compilation of current statistics in such areas as U.S. trade, housing characteristics, and population trends, and its production of a variety of publications on particular features of the U.S. population and economy.

● Maintain the integrity of bureau operations and products. Represent the bureau and census policy and processes to the Congress and the public.

Necessary Training, Experience, Skills

Someone has observed that a technical background is probably sufficient in this job for directors serving in years ending with 4, 5 or 6. That's the middle period between decennial censuses. In decennial years and those closely surrounding them, however, the job has extra burdens of articulating, explaining and defending bureau policies and actions. Such a rule of thumb may indeed be an oversimplification. But the census bureau, an institution where integrity and detachment are watchwords, also provides information of enormous political and economic consequence. Almost inevitably, certain of its products spark controversy. Running it takes a combination of expertise and strong personal skills and character. A director needs training and experience in one or more such fields as survey research methodology, statistical analysis, or the practical applications of census products. As the focus of a close-knit government and national community of statisticians, demographers, and related groups, the position also requires a substantial professional reputation. The census chief should know something about the federal government, especially the Congress, be an able and agile communicator, and possess the personal toughness to run and defend the bureau with principled objectivity.

Insight

In July, 1991, two unenviable but critical choices faced the secretary of commerce concerning the disputed results of the 1990 decennial census.

One was to declare that the U.S. population figure, as measured by the census, would be statistically adjusted in light of a serious undercount. That would represent the first such revision in U.S. history and add a final, official echo to widespread criticism of census bureau methodology in the 1990 tabulation. The other, even more distasteful choice was to stick with the original 1990 figures, facing down the critics and adding fresh fuel to reproaches from cities, states and the Congress. Doing so, however, would ignore a stack of authoritative evidence that the 1990 figure was significantly out of line, some of that evidence provided by the census bureau itself. Whichever way it went, the secretary's decision would mean the loss or retention by certain states of several seats in the House of Representatives.

Every ten-year census of the U.S. population puts at stake billions of dollars in federal grants and assistance welfare payments, to say nothing of congressional seats and presidential electoral votes. Volatile almost by definition, these considerations took on an extra edge with accumulating indications that the 1990 census had missed many people and double-tallied many others. As reported by the General Accounting Office, 14 million such counting mistakes resulted in a net undercount of 9.7 million. In a post-census sampling (150,000 households) to provide a basis for deciding whether to adjust the 1990 totals, the census bureau reported among other findings that it had missed about two million African-Americans.

These were by no means the first undercounts in 200 years of U.S. census history. But the 14 million gross counting errors represented an increase in such errors of 50 percent over the 1980 census. The difference between undercounts for black and nonblack populations grew to more than 6 percent in 1990, from a bit over 5 percent ten years earlier. By some estimates, it was the first time in half a century that this undercount figure was greater than in the preceding decennial census. A transient and hard-to-locate population of minorities, low-income families, the homeless, and undocumented immigrants clearly complicated the Census Bureau's count. But even before the 1990 census, some populous cities and states had charged that previous censuses had miscounted their citizens and noncitizens. The department of commerce, parent agency of the bureau, settled their suit for redress by agreeing to consider readjustment. The bureau then conducted its post-census survey, setting the stage for the Commerce secretary's July 15 announcement.

The decision to stick with the original count surprised many. Cities and states who felt shorted by it announced plans to bring further suit, making it certain that the final decision would be up to the courts. The director and staff of the Census Bureau were reported to have recommended an adjustment. And the decision furnished a case study explanation of why the director must move skillfully in congressional relations and with the media, in addition to bringing technical proficiency to the job.

When Barbara Everitt Bryant took over direction of the census bureau (CB) in December 1989, all planning and preparation for the 1990 census was in place. "I could affect it to some degree operationally," she says, "but I couldn't make any alterations in the plan. I saw that a major impact I could make in my term would be early planning for the 2000 census and beyond." But she spent much of her first year with the Congress and the press, presenting and defending the 1990 census and its results.

While it would be hard to overestimate the significance of the decennial count, there is some suggestion that it overshadows, and detracts from, other vital CB activity. Terri Ann Lowenthal is staff director of the House Post Office and Civil Service subcommittee on census and population. She thinks the "intense focus" on the decennial-- "not just the one year but three years going in and a couple of years coming out"--is one factor that has made it hard for the CB "to attract attention, particularly in Congress, to its other programs." Another is the funding cuts of earlier years, which she says left measurements and statistical activities like current population estimates, the production of import and export data, and poverty surveys "dying on the vine." These are "basic surveys and samples" which, Lowenthal says, produce some of the most critical information the country needs. She takes note of efforts she sees underway to restore resources for activities like these. But she wonders whether the CB alone can manage the education task she thinks is necessary to "get out the message that it's not just the decennial census that's important."

Education will clearly help. Meanwhile, the current focus on the decennial census remains the inexorably logical product of its presently mandated role in the economic, and particularly the political, life of the country. Former director John G. Keane (1984-89) makes the point that "the timing of the census is driven by constitutional mandate. Congress can't stop it, and the president can't stop it."

Among the broad array of other services the CB performs are an agricultural census conducted every five years (years ending in 2 and 7), and another quinquennial survey of the manufacturing, minerals, construction and transportation industries, among others. There are monthly and quarterly studies on a variety of subjects, statistical compilations of commerce and housing data, population estimates, and a volume of other current reports and publications including the very important *Statistical Abstracts*. In all, the bureau runs 150 such surveys a year.

Varying in resources and staff, they act to fill in the picture framed by the decennial's concentration on people and housing. A great many of them use sampling techniques pioneered by the bureau, examining relatively small, carefully selected sections and cross sections of the national community. This permits extrapolation to the bigger picture in scores of areas ranging from income, industrial development, and foreign trade to agriculture and state and local government. Contracts from other federal agencies and states and localities fund about $100 million of annual bureau activity, like the 70,000 interviews it does every month for the Bureau of Labor Statistics to produce that office's monthly report on employment and unemployment.

Census Bureau products have a huge number of users of surprising variety; in Lowenthal's estimation, the CB is "the primary focus of the federal statistical system." Indeed, the bureau says it leads the federal government in statistical data collected, and employs the government's largest group of research statisticians and computer scientists. Its headquarters and field staff of nearly 9,600 includes about 3,160 core professionals in mathematical statistics, survey research methodology, programming, demographics, area specialties like the Soviet Union and China, management, economics, and the social sciences. There is a sprinkling of ethnographers, anthropologists, and psychologists. Census Bureau scholars, according to CB information, are also the largest federal source of papers on applied statistics and survey design.

"I liken the Census Bureau to a university without undergraduates or a football team," Bryant says. "It is a very research and academically-oriented place, with associate and full professors and even foreign graduate students." Before she took over, the bureau had already established a 21st century planning staff, a kind of "internal think tank." In the wake of the 1990 census, she says, "we are moving to an early-year research and development group," setting up a joint task force with other elements in Commerce to look at both policy and technical considerations for planning the 2000 census and census-related activities in the 2000-2009 period. It will have outside advisors "to broaden thinking about the census out to all the stakeholders."

On other fronts, Bryant has pushed the modernization of data collection with greater computer-assisted interviewing, and joined the bureau's efforts to a government-wide attempt to improve the quality of economic statistics. Funding for 1992 agricultural and economic censuses, she says, will "greatly enhance" coverage of the service industry, an area less well addressed up to now than the manufacturing sector. That, Lowenthal thinks, is one of the problems with data on the gross national product. "We have not quite caught up with measuring the service sector, the largest component of the U.S. economy," she says. "People don't realize that all these basic figures are way behind the times."

Lowenthal welcomes the renewed attention such situations are now getting after what she says were years of relative neglect, and points to a fundamental revision in the collection of U.S. export data as another example of improvement. Information about exports to Canada, the biggest U.S. trading partner, had been based on unreliable border counts of goods exiting the country. Now the CB gets much more accurate readings by simply using Canada's statistics on imports from the United States, which are taxed by Canadian customs and thus recorded. "Their import data become our export data, and vice versa," Bryant says. "It's done by electronic transfer." An addition for the 1990 census was the fourth generation of the CB's film optical scanning device for input into computers (FOSDIC), which fearlessly absorbs the contents of 1,350 census questionnaire pages a minute using laser technology. Perhaps the most notable innovation used in the 1990 decennial is the TIGER (topologically integrated geographic encoding and referencing) capability, developed with the U.S. Geographical Survey. It provides a computer-readable map and geographic data base for the entire country that, the CB claims, is spawning vast expansion of the geographic information systems industry.

"This is a very nonpolitical agency," Bryant says, pointing out that she and her aides for congressional relations and communications are the only three political appointees in the house. But the agency does have to navigate political tensions generated by the nature of its products and expressed in considerable and enduring pressure from city halls, statehouses, and the Congress. The results of the 1980 census brought scores of lawsuits. "Our data affect all of them so much that every political person feels he or she has a stake in the census and a right to be heard," Bryant comments. An earlier occupant of the job recalls pressures on the bureau from special interest groups and attempts to harass it because of "unpopular statistical programs."

In this contentious arena, Lowenthal believes the director's primary responsibility is to guard the bureau's integrity as a statistical agency. Keane agrees, stressing the need for absolute nonpartisanship "because the data have to be legitimate." Collecting data might be a mundane, routine activity, Lowenthal says, "and yet the product is such an industry and forms the basis for so much policy that it can be interpreted in many different ways." The director must "keep the bureau at a distance from the policy end" and focus it on maintaining the "highest standards" of expertise, professionalism, and objectivity. Significant to this goal is the proper distribution and decentralization of the bureau's effort.

The bureau, Bryant says, "has a two-pronged budget." Its basic component funds the year-by-year ongoing activity of surveys; its periodic component fluctuates broadly because of the decennial census and every-five-years economic and agricultural census. For fiscal 1992, "a fairly typical non-decennial year," the total budget figure is about $400 million, nearly $100 million of which is generated by contracts for surveys from other federal agencies. It includes some nominal spending on the decennial census, and will grow immensely as the next decennial year approaches. In 1990, for example, the total figure was more than $1.6 billion. The decennial is one area which normally presents no funding problems. "Everyone moans and groans" about its costs, Lowenthal remarks, "but they get the money."

The director defends the bureau's budget in Commerce's internal processes, then supports it at the Office of Management and Budget and before authorization and appropriations committees on the Hill. The oversight committees that hear most of Bryant's testimony (nine times in 1990) are the House Post Office and Civil Service subcommittee on census and population and the Senate Government Operations subcommittee on government information. Within the executive branch, the director attends a monthly meeting of statistical agency heads. Work the bureau performs for other agencies keeps her in regular touch with them. The Bureau of Labor Statistics is the biggest client, followed by the departments of housing and urban development, education, health and human services, agriculture and justice. She also co-chairs an interagency forum on the aging.

Bryant's comparison of her agency to a university campus includes its extensive connections with academic institutions. "We are very tied into the research community," she says, and notes the existence of four census advisory committees whose members represent professional economics, marketing, statistical and population associations. The bureau has research contracts with 40 colleges and universities. It encourages its own professionals to publish, attend conferences, and read widely in their disciplines. "I wouldn't be surprised," Bryant says, "if we don't have more links to the broad academic community than any other agency because so many people use census data."   There is a broad exchange with counterpart agencies in other countries and Lowenthal is struck by the extent of help the Soviet Union has asked for in measuring GNP. Through its international research center, the bureau furnishes technical expertise to developing countries, conducts training courses for them, and works with a number of other governments on the standardization of statistical methods and measurements.

With the beginning of her tenure, the commerce department made Bryant's position a part of the senior department staff. This was a useful boost, adding visibility to a job and bureau that are physically housed in a separate location.   More significant, Bryant says, was the improved opportunity for department seniors from the secretary on down, and including the budget managers, to "understand the importance of what we're doing." Besides her CB office, she has one in the department itself, and averages four visits a week. Release of the 1990 census results increased her invitations to speak and in the spring of 1991 she was appearing weekly.

When she took over the bureau, Bryant recalls, "I knew there was quality on the staff here. If not, I wouldn't have come. What surprised me was the depth of the talent. For example, the international center has outstanding Russian and Chinese speaking demographers and economists. The people who developed the TIGER system are somewhere near the genius level." But there is always the problem of attracting people on government salaries, even though recent executive-level hikes have made the bureau a little more competitive. Bryant thinks the bureau must bring people in at every level, not just at the bottom, to maintain links with the outside community and cross fertilization of ideas. "We are competing all the time in a couple of the hottest areas--mathematical statisticians and programmers," she says. "We actively recruit on a hundred campuses a year. You have to sell people on the idea that this is a more exciting place to be because you'll have the kind of data and information bases you'll never see anywhere else."

On this subject, Lowenthal notes the number of senior staff with many years of CB service. If the bureau is slow to change its ways, she says, that may be a factor. "They really take pride in what they do, and they should. But you get comfortable with the way you do things, and change is slow to come." She also believes the bureau, especially where the decennial census is concerned, is or should be on a threshold. As more people understand its importance, the stakes in the census grow. "The minority groups finally have a foothold, at least in politics, and they realize the census is it," she says, "and we don't have four million people as we did in 1790, we have 250 million speaking 20 or 25 different languages. I think there's a feeling that if we try to do it the same way we always have, the outcome--the level of accuracy--will simply not be acceptable." The addition of new technology to a highly scientific and technical operation will help turn this around. But beyond that, she points out, it is still early in the decade, with time "to fundamentally rebuild the structure of the census. Not tinker with basic design, but reexamine the whole design. If they don't grab that opportunity, they'll really regret it in nine years."

Bryant expresses similar thoughts on both counts. The bureau's technical thinking looks ahead, she says, "to what the leading edge for data capture and data processing is going to be in the year 2000, or a couple of years ahead of that when we have to lock in our technology." Moreover, she warns, "in the census bureau you have to watch against getting too ingrown. People come here, like it, and make a whole life here. It's better to have an infusion of new ideas. That's why I think our recruiting at the universities, our joint statistical agreements, being active in the professional associations, and listening to our advisers is a very important part of the ferment the bureau needs. You should do everything you can to shake up complacency."

Key Relationships

Within the Department

Reports to: Secretary

Works closely with:

Deputy Secretary
Under Secretary/Administrator, Economic and Statistics Administration
Director, Bureau of Economic Analysis

Outside the Bureau

Commissioner, Bureau of Labor Statistics, Department of Labor
Director, National Center for Health Statistics, Department of Health and
    Human Services
Commissioner, National Center for Education Statistics, Department of
    Education
Assistant Secretary, Policy Development and Research, Department of
    Housing and Urban Development
Director, Bureau of Justice Statistics, Department of Justice
Administrator, National Agricultural Statistics Service, Department of
    Agriculture
Chief, Statistical Policy, Office of Management and Budget
Commissioner, U.S. Customs Service

Outside the Government

Professional statistical, economic, and marketing associations; population organizations; mayors and governors associations, and individual state and local officials; the research and polling community; academic institutions; public service groups; minority, civil rights and civil liberties advocates; urban and regional planners; agricultural organizations

Profile of Current Director, Bureau of the Census

Name: Barbara E. Bryant

Assumed Position: 1989

Career Summary: Various positions at Market Opinion Research, 1970-89, including senior vice president and vice president for urban/education research
Adjunct professor of Marketing, Graduate School of Business Administration, University of Michigan, 1984-85
Public relations consulting business, 1965-70
Director of public relations, Oakland University, 1961-65
Free-lance writer/editor, 1950-61
Editorial assistant, University of Illinois, 1948-49
Art editor, Chemical Engineering Magazine, McGraw-Hill Publishing Co., 1947-48

Education: Cornell University, BA, physics, 1947
Michigan State University, MA, journalism, 1967; PhD, communication, 1970

Directors, Bureau of the Census Since 1969

Administration	Name and Years Served	Present Position
Bush	Barbara E. Bryant 1989 - present	Incumbent
Reagan	John G. Keane 1984 - 1989	Dean, Strategic Management University of Notre Dame South Bend, Ind.
Reagan	Bruce Chapman 1981 - 1983	Not available

Reagan, Carter	Daniel B. Levine (Acting)
	1980 - 1981
		Study Director, Committee for
		  Postsecondary Education &
		  Training for the Workplace,
		  National Academy of Sciences
		  Washington, D.C.

Carter	Vincent P. Barabba
	1979 - 1981
		Executive Director
		  Market Research and
		  Planning
		General Motors Corp.
		Detroit, Mich.

Carter	Manuel D. Plotkin 1977 - 1979	President M.D. Plotkin Research & Planning Company Chicago, Ill.

Ford	Vincent P. Barabba
	1973 - 1976
		Executive Director
		  Market Research and
		  Planning
		General Motors Corp.
		Detroit, Mich.

Nixon	George Hay Brown 1969 - 1973	Retired Sea Island, Ga.

DIRECTOR
NATIONAL INSTITUTE OF STANDARDS
AND TECHNOLOGY

Level IV - Presidential Appointment with Senate Confirmation

Major Responsibilities

● Manage the National Institute of Standards and Technology (NIST), the central federal laboratory engaged primarily in measurement technology and standards research to meet the needs of U.S. industry and boost its competitiveness around the world, and in providing services in support of improved public health and safety.

● As part of that mission, oversee external programs assisting small U.S. companies to acquire advanced technology; and awarding federal grants to private-sector initiatives that can speed the commercialization of new technology.

● Guide the institute in its contract services to other federal agencies. Maintain close relationships with federal and non-government scientific and technical offices, and with the U.S. industrial community, foreign technical laboratories, and the standards and measurements activities of international organizations.

Necessary Training, Experience, Skills

On the substantive level, running an agency of such intense technical focus takes an engineer or a scientist with an extensive background, not just at the research and development workbench but in managing R&D. Such experience also provides the professional credibility and reputation essential both to successful execution on the inside and to representing the agency's work on the outside. By preference, a director's previous career should have public as well as private sector dimensions; familiarity with government contributes to effective work with the Congress and the rest of the administration in maintaining and increasing support for the agency's programs. Integrity is important; a former director comments that "if NIST has one strength, it is the quality and impartiality of its work."

Insight

NIST was once NBS--the National Bureau of Standards, established in 1901. It is the oldest multi-program national laboratory in the country. And to John W. Lyons, its director since 1990, it is indeed a laboratory. "It's always been a place where people do technical work at the bench," he says. An even more fundamental observation he makes about NIST centers on its historical and exclusive role as "a lab responsible for working with industry." It carries out that role, as former director Ernest Ambler (1976-89) puts it, "not in an intrusive way of telling them what to do and how to do it, but in providing industry with the technical infrastructure it uses."

In 1988 that role took on added significance when the Congress, retitling NBS as NIST and revising its mandate, also gave it the management responsibility for two small new external programs of great potential benefit. They were born of the perception that the federal government must take a more substantial hand in accelerating the transformation of U.S. technological advancement into commercial reality. The idea was not only to contribute needed strength to the American economy but to help U.S. industry halt its loss of headway in the effort to remain globally competitive.

One of the new undertakings, the Advanced Technology Program (ATP), awards seed-money grants to private-sector consortia and other innovative and cooperative enterprises on a competitive basis. In fiscal 1990, its first year, ATP supplied almost $10 million in encouragement funds to 11 projects. They focus on areas like nonvolatile magnetoresistive semiconductors, advanced manufacturing technology for low-cost flat panel displays, advanced compensation techniques to improve the accuracy of machine tools, and precision optics for soft X-ray projection lithography.

"This has the potential for affecting the national economy in a big way--big developments, not small-niche special things," Lyons says of ATP. "It's something they've been doing in Japan, of course, for a long time. We've got a pilot program now. But if it's successful, there is talk of making it a very large program." Indeed, the Congress talked initially of pumping some $400 million into ATP in three years, raising it to an annual $100 million operating level. But eleventh-hour machinations at the close of the 101st Congress cut the 1991 appropriation from an expected $100 million to $36 million. That's still an increase from 1990, but the administration's 1992 budget proposal funds ATP at the same level.

The other new program set up manufacturing technology centers in five locations in the East and Midwest to improve the transfer of technology developed in federal laboratories to small manufacturing companies. While this activity also suffered a funding cut (of 13.5%) for fiscal 1992, Lyons expects it eventually to settle at a "steady-state $30-$40 million a year" and hopes to extend the network of these centers nationwide. The 1988 legislation also set in motion a third new concept, to help states develop technology extension agencies in a similar pattern to long-existing agricultural services. This initiative withered, however, in the wake of 1992 budget developments.

Innovative and potentially exciting as programs like ATP are, and whatever their eventual size and shape, the established, internal, continuing functions and services of NIST will remain equally crucial to U.S. industry and the general public. The institute runs research programs in physics, chemistry, radiation physics, and materials science. Among the many areas to which it gives attention are the standardization problems of computers; chemical, electrical and electronics engineering; automation in manufacturing; construction technology; the prevention, detection and control of fire; and earthquake resistant structures.

Measurement is a key NIST specialty. "Whether you're talking about the level of carbon dioxide in the atmosphere, auto emissions, sizes of things, or the fineness of a monointegrated circuit, all manner of measurements have to be made in a technological society," says Ambler. And the measurement services NIST is responsible for range very widely. It furnishes reference materials to environmentalists tracking trace quantities of substances in the environment, and instruments for upper atmosphere measurements. Typical of services NIST renders for a fee are its calibration of measuring equipment used in manufacturing, and its provision of well-characterized standard reference materials; manufacturers key their production processes to these to meet established national and international measurement norms. There are hundreds of other examples. What they add up to are standards governing the measurement and quality of countless common and uncommon items basic to life on the factory floor, in the home, and in many other contexts.

Structurally, NIST recently split its four basic laboratories into eight, each of which addresses an important area of technology. The labs specialize in electronics and electrical engineering, manufacturing engineering, chemical science and technology, physics, materials science and engineering, building and fire research, computer systems, and computing and applied mathematics.

NIST's distinction from virtually all other federal laboratories rests on more than its concentration on services in support of industry. In part, it is an historical difference. Older by a few years than its parent department of commerce, NIST was originally chartered, Lyons says, "to help just about everybody in society" in an era when no other federal labs existed. It continues to do so today, he points out, while "most other labs have a particular mission--in defense, energy, space, or whatever." Unlike most other laboratories, moreover, NIST gets its own annual appropriation directly, not through Commerce (though in the development stage its budget must clear the department). "We have our own appropriation measure and reauthorization," Lyons says, "which means there's an automatic statement of our mission. It is written down in the statute every year, and I can't really deviate from it. That's a little rigid, but it gives the force of law to our mission."

Another contrast can be seen in the status of the director. Among only a handful of other laboratory chiefs (all of them within the department of health and human services) Lyons is a presidential appointee. This has, he observes, advantages and disadvantages. It's good because "as a member of the team" he is more closely involved in policy discussions within Commerce's Technology Administration of which NIST is a part, and elsewhere in the department. It's bad because "these jobs"-- meaning presidential appointments--can "lie empty for fairly long stretches." He cites the gap between Senate-confirmed directors of the National Institutes of Health (NIH). In point of fact, however, the longevity of NIST's directors spared it that misfortune: Lyons is only the ninth individual to head it in 90 years.

In the view of Edward O. Pfrang, executive director of the American Society of Civil Engineers, one of the concerns of NIST's director in the coming period will be to continue moving gradually out of programs that are "getting tired--researched to the point where their benefit to the country is starting to diminish" and into less-explored new areas more relevant to rapidly increasing technological needs. Another is the requirement to "sell those exciting new programs to the Congress." A third is to maintain NIST's integrity, which makes it "the truly unique institution that it is." This is a point also emphasized by Ambler. "It has to be objective," he says. "It has nothing else going for it. It has no regulatory power; it doesn't assign blame or call anybody on the mat." That means, among other things, that a director must know and have the respect of the technical staff and the outside universe of scientists, technologists and industrial managers to which NIST relates. The same is true for communities to which some observers think NIST needs closer ties--trade groups and private-sector testing organizations.

Lyons talks about institutional issues that NIST must also deal with, one of them inherent in the Congress' 1988 restructuring. That is the operational and budgetary problem involving the coexistence of NIST's core internal activities in support of industry, the public and the scientific community, with its new external projects like ATP and the technology centers. External and internal programs can end up competing for resources, Lyons explains. Decisions on both are up to the same congressional budgeteers, "and they're going to be trading off for a fixed amount of money. That's a serious problem; we don't want to damage the laboratory with the demands of the outside programs." Since "everyone's aware of the potential mischief" in this, however, Lyons thinks things will work out. "But there's also a question whether you can really run two different sorts of programs in the same place, and a lot of people don't think you can." On the other hand, he adds, NIH does it very well. "So I think we can do it, with a little fast-stepping and a lot of support from the administration."

Next comes the question of resources itself. "Any federal manager who doesn't think manipulating the budget through the system is his first challenge is crazy," Lyons asserts. "All policy is really set in the budget process. So the question is, can we get a decent rate of growth in the institution to match the demand." The demand comes from the "high-tech side of industry" and is "growing by leaps and bounds." With the country well into the computer age and entering the information age, NIST customers grow more sophisticated and ask more support from NIST. "If we're going to remain relevant, we have to grow in some proportion to that demand," Lyons believes. "We don't have to match it exactly, but there has to be growth of some sort."

NIST operates on about $370 million a year, according to Lyons. Only part of that--in fiscal 1991, some $205 million--comes from appropriated funds. That portion of the budget has been in a flat pattern for some years, except for the nominal inflationary adjustment. (The 1992 budget requested $247 million in appropriated funds, including the rise in support for ATP.) Something in the neighborhood of $100 million flows in, mostly in small increments, from the contract services NIST provides to approximately 100 other federal agencies. Fees charged to the private sector add about $30 million. The balance comes from the value of salaries of private-sector professionals who work at NIST on loan from companies working with the institute on projects of mutual interest. There are 200 such individuals currently at NIST under these formal arrangements with outside organizations. The private-sector contribution to NIST operating resources has gone up "pretty strongly" over the last decade, Lyons reports, as has income from other agencies. Recognizing at the beginning of the 1980s that the U.S. military build-up would likely squeeze its appropriated funds, he says, NIST "went after industry participation and deliberately increased it very substantially."

Lyons spends "an inordinate amount of time" on the budget. "I steer the place by prioritizing the budget proposal. What I put first is likely to get funded; what I put eighth is unlikely to be." In addition to funding existing programs he has discretionary funds that go to starting new ones. "That also really steers things," he says, "because if those seeds grow, they may become big budget items later." In that sense--budget driving policy--he considers himself a policy maker. "There are a lot of folks who think they're making policy," he adds, "and find their budgets don't reflect it."

Are NIST's overall resources adequate to its tasks? Pfrang doesn't think so. "They had the same problem when they were the National Bureau of Standards," he recalls. "They always got new mandates but not the resources to go along with them. That is a clear-cut problem. I don't think they are being given the means they need to do the things they should be doing."

What about staff? When he worked at NIST, Pfrang recalls, some of his subordinates received "all sorts of offers" to take senior academic positions that would have paid a great deal more. But "they had so much freedom and opportunity to do intellectually stimulating things that they stayed on a lot longer than they would have at another agency." That experience may be one reason he views the staff retention problem as less severe at NIST than in other scientific and technical federal entities. He also believes a NIST staffer is likely to enjoy a higher grade level than would be the case elsewhere, the result of special legislation that took NIST employees out of the federal system. But the retention of competent work force is another of the institutional issues Lyons worries about--how to keep a "first-class staff" in the face of the disadvantages of government work that is "burdened these days by threats of furlough and by relatively noncompetitive pay for senior professionals." His answer is to "have an institution that's fun to work in, even with the disadvantages. And we've been successful. But you always worry that some last straw will come along and you suddenly start losing your best people." NIST has in fact lost some senior staff recently to the universities. "But when we lose them," Lyons says, "we lose them to full professorships. It's a little hard to get too upset when one of your people goes to a leading campus as a fully-tenured professor. I think we're competitive with the best labs in the country."

NIST employs a 3,000-strong, heavily scientific and technical staff, 2,500 of them at its attractive, contemporary suburban Washington headquarters. The rest work in NIST's laboratory in Boulder, Colorado; a handful based in Fort Collins, Colorado and in Hawaii transmit weather and time signals across both major oceans. "Because measurement is very pervasive, the skills resident in our agency are very broad," says Raymond Kammer, NIST deputy director who held the top post in an acting capacity in 1989. "There are few areas in physical science and engineering where you won't find experts here." Kammer calls the staff "world competitive," and other veterans of the NIST leadership offer equally high estimates.

Congressional authorization of NIST's appropriated funds rests with the Senate Commerce and the House Science, Space and Technology committees. "The authorization hearings are really budget-related," notes Ambler, "but they're also oversight." These and the relevant appropriations subcommittees are the director's chief stops, although specific issues can attract attention from other quarters, and general interaction with the Hill is fairly high. For example, when counterfeit bolts whose markings falsely indicated a high tensile strength were discovered in nuclear reactors, the Congress summoned NIST to testify on the subject. Legislators then decided that the institute should oversee accreditation of the many laboratories that test bolts, and asked it to develop legislation to that end.

Better than once a week, Lyons finds himself in meetings where policy matters are discussed. He is a member of the Committee on Technology and Industry of the Federal Coordinating Council for Science, Engineering and Technology, and of other groups working both on the interagency and international levels. "There is no industrialized country that doesn't have some form of NIST, at least in the area of metrology," Kammer says. Accordingly, the director figures prominently in a network of relationships with counterparts around the world, and in efforts at international standardization of measurements.

Early in his tenure Lyons scheduled many public appearances in the effort to increase public understanding of what NIST is trying to do. "We're going to do more of that," he says. But NIST has a problem, he adds, in "getting before the top executives of industry. We can get to the mid-management people, but it's hard to see the chief executive officers, and we're looking for opportunities to do that." At the same time, NIST has "very strong connections with the principal universities," Ambler says, and the connection is mainly scientist to scientist.

"For a long time," Pfrang reflects, "NIST has been able to stay free from partisan political pressures. The only reason is because of the enviable reputation that it has for impartiality and the thoroughness of the work it does." Yet, he continues, there were times in the institute's past when it would have benefited from some political sensitivity, not in partisan terms, but "in what the needs of our industry and society are." He suggests, therefore, that a director cannot afford to be "narrow or uni-disciplinary in his thinking." NIST's leader must understand and appreciate the value of work over a broad spectrum--on one hand, programs that are deeply involved in research "as fundamental as you'll find anywhere in the world" and, on the other, research programs that are more applied in nature.

Kammer underlines another consideration in managing this job effectively. "There is a lot of pressure to do the short term and no pressure to worry about the long term," he says. It's easy to disassemble a laboratory or a skill, "but it takes somewhere between five and ten years to establish a credible laboratory. And, in a difficult science, ten years to be competitive on a world basis." It requires great discipline to keep building in an area that will only be useful later on, he points out. "Striking some kind of balance between immediate and longer-term needs is uniquely the job of the director."

"We have a reputation here of being a bit slow, but never to get it wrong," Lyons says. "It's the old Bureau of Standards ethic." Most of the people at NIST came because of NIST, he notes, not because it is a federal agency. "In fact, most probably came in spite of the fact that it was federal, because they liked the reputation and the management. That's why I came here. It's a very high-class place."

Key Relationships

Within the Department

Reports to: Under Secretary, Technology

Works closely with:

Assistant Secretary, Technology Policy
Director, National Technical Information Service
Directors, Manufacturing Technology Centers

Outside the Department

Committee on Technology and Industry, Federal Coordinating Council for Science, Engineering and Technology (FCCSET)
Associate Director, Industrial Technology, White House Office of Science and Technology Policy
Committee on Federal Laboratories, FCCSET
Directors of federal laboratories nationwide
Senior officials of federal agencies which are contract clients for NIST services
Assistant Administrator, Research and Development, Environmental Protection Agency
National Academy of Engineering
National Academy of Sciences

Outside the Government

Extensive range of scientists and engineers in manufacturing firms and industrial research laboratories, on university campuses and in professional academies, associations, and advisory boards; manufacturing and industrial trade associations; heads of NIST counterpart organization in other countries; international scientific and technical organizations

Profile of Current Director, National Institute of Standards and Technology

Name:	John W. Lyons
Assumed Position:	1990
Career Summary:	Various positions at NIST (formerly National Bureau of Standards), 1973-90, including Director, Center for Fire Research; Director, National Engineering Laboratory; and Deputy Director (1983-90) Various positions with the Monsanto Company, 1955-73, including manager, research and commercial development activities
Education:	Harvard University, BA (chemistry), 1952 Washington University, MA, 1963; PhD, 1964 (both in physical chemistry)

Directors, National Institute of Standards and Technology Since 1969

Administration	Name and Years Served	Present Position
Bush	John W. Lyons 1990 - present	Incumbent
Bush	Raymond A. Kammer (Acting) 1989	Deputy Director National Institute of Standards and Technology
Reagan, Carter, Ford	Ernest Ambler* 1976 - 1989	Director Emeritus, NIST
Ford, Nixon	Richard W. Roberts* 1973 - 1975	Deceased
Nixon	Lawrence M. Kushner (A)* 1972	Retired Gaithersburg, MD
Nixon	Lewis M. Branscomb* 1970 -1971	Director, Science, Technology and Public Policy, Kennedy School of Government Cambridge, MA
Nixon, Johnson, Eisenhower, Truman	Allen V. Astin* 1951 - 1969	Deceased

* Held position as Director, National Bureau of Standards

12

CONSUMER PRODUCT SAFETY COMMISSION

CHAIRMAN

Level III - Presidential Appointment with Senate Confirmation

Major Responsibilities

- Oversee the development and application of standards, regulations and procedures by the Consumer Product Safety Commission (CPSC) to protect the public against injury from consumer products. Shape the agency's agenda and reach action decisions on specific product issues with the support of the other CPSC commissioners. Supervise administrative management of the agency.

- Ensure the effective research, collection and dissemination of facts about product hazards and preventive measures. Act as the federal spokesman on these subjects and on consumer protection policy.

- Coordinate the CPSC's work with that of other federal agencies with consumer product responsibilities. Represent the agency before the Congress.

Necessary Training, Experience, Skills

A majority of our interviewees favors training or experience in one of the fields CPSC makes use of--science, engineering or law, for example --fields that have also provided insights into the agency's broader concerns. The job involves daily contact with the agency's scientists, engineers, accountants and lawyers. "You can't be all those things," a former chairman recognizes, "but in order to render rational decisions, you must keep up with all of them." Another who has held the job says "it helps to be a lawyer who has defended federal agency administrative or regulatory decisions. You don't need specific scientific or technical knowledge. But the ability to analyze and integrate information from diverse disciplines of science and technology is very important." In addition, a long-time observer of the agency suggests the value of a background in injury prevention and an appreciation of consumer behavior.

Insight

With 500 employees, the CPSC by most counts has more than 15,000 consumer products to worry about. They range from crib toys to all-terrain vehicles, from infant cushions, balloons and erasers to fireworks, lawn mowers, water coolers and water beds--everything, in short, except food, drugs, boats and cars. To try to keep tabs on them, the agency has a variety of techniques to gather information. Among these are complaints called in by hot-line, the collection of incident data, the accumulation of injury statistics through surveys of hospital emergency rooms, and its own research. Depending on the nature of each real or apparent problem, CPSC handles it in one of three ways. It can order or negotiate the recall of a product from distribution, especially if a "substantial hazard" exists. It can develop standards for a product's manufacture and use and issue them as regulations with which compliance is mandatory; sometimes an outside group will petition CPSC for such action. Or, third, CPSC can communicate to and educate the consuming public about the potential dangers and suggested safe uses of a product. To help reach decisions about a product's safety and how best to ensure it, the agency employs statisticians, engineers, behavioral scientists, chemists, epidemiologists, physicists and other technical specialists who together make up a majority of the staff. CPSC operates a health sciences and engineering laboratory just outside the capital.

Jacqueline Jones-Smith has chaired CPSC since the end of 1989. She says the commissioners' key collective task is to "evaluate the data that's presented--medical, physiological, engineering, economic, human factors--analyze the risk, and make a policy decision on what is the best solution to take in addressing that risk." To that definition, former commissioner and acting chairman R. David Pittle (1981) adds some important perspective. "The chairman must make sure the commissioners operate as a cohesive unit," he says. "They don't have to agree on the issues but they must work together in a spirit that will try for quick resolution of the issues before them." Further, the chairman must see that commission decisions get "proper and professional" handling and that "the staff has the resources to carry out the commission's wishes."

Mary Ellen Fise of the Consumer Federation of America sketches two levels on which the chairman's job operates. The first is decision making. Here, like the other commissioners, the chairman has one vote on substantive policy matters like product recall, rule making or budget. Second is executive responsibility--running the agency day-to-day. That falls only to the chairman, and includes the hiring of top staff. The other commissioners may share in overseeing these senior people, "but the chairman has control. It's not collegial, it's really the chairman's choice."

Although the Consumer Product Safety Act calls for a commission of five members serving seven-year terms, CPSC has had only three since the mid-1980s. "What happened," says Fise, "is that the slots would open up and (the administration) wouldn't fill them. So then the appropriations committee said, 'okay, you're not going to appoint them, we're not appropriating for them.' And they cut the appropriation for the commissioners. Now, if the president wanted to go back to five, he'd have to ask Congress for the money." According to Terrence Scanlon, CPSC chairman in 1985 and again in 1986-89, "it was a budgetary decision" aimed at saving a quarter of a million dollars per commissioner by not filling vacancies. At first, Scanlon says, he thought it was a good move. "In retrospect," however, "I don't think it was. It was easier to reach decisions with five than with three. In reality, CPSC should be a single-administrator agency."

Meetings of the commission take place only if a quorum is present. They are open proceedings, announced ahead of time, and are tape recorded. Notice of any meeting of a commissioner with an outside party appears in advance on a public calendar. If the commission decides to consider a case for possible rule making, it must move through a three-stage process that can be canceled at any point.

Severe cuts in budget and personnel for most of the last decade have made an adequate focus on CPSC's responsibilities and goals nearly impossible. Frequent leadership changes in the same period have not helped; the agency swung between four chairmen and five acting chairmen in the eight years from 1981 to 1989, after an initial eight years with only three chairmen. CPSC's own fiscal 1992 budget request documents part of the problem. Since 1980, it reports, the commission has reduced its personnel by nearly 50 percent and its operating costs by almost 60 percent. One result is that "the commission has become more selective in its enforcement and regulatory actions and generally seeks voluntary solutions with industry first." Besides carrying the potential for "reducing the regulatory gains of the past," the report continues, the cuts "have introduced the serious possibility of delay into commission proceedings." In 1990 and 1991, for example, the commission could only partially fund its priority projects, "an important vehicle for fast tracking serious problems."

The CPSC budget requests sent to the Congress for fiscal years 1991 and 1992 have contained small to moderate increases after years of reduction--about $37.1 million and $39.2 million, respectively. But in inflation-adjusted figures used in the agency's budget presentation, the 1991 request was about 60 percent of the funds appropriated in 1980. Among other results, that left no money in 1991 for contracting for outside research, says Fise. "If some technical, complex problem comes up, they're stuck. Or it means they work on something for four or five years instead of a much more consolidated time. Budget is unquestionably their largest problem." A November 1990 article in *Government Executive* magazine suggested the irony of such situations. With no money for equipment to test emissions from kerosene heaters and unvented gas space heaters, the magazine said, CPSC in 1989 had to resort to using old gear being junked by another agency. It was so broken-down that the commission spent 350 hours during one month to fix it--at a price in staff time estimated to exceed what new equipment would have cost.

About 60 percent of the agency's staff works at its Washington offices or laboratory, the rest in regional and field offices in 35 states. Jones-Smith considers CPSC "lucky, because we don't have a high turnover overall." There is the usual competition for talent with the private sector. And because CPSC is a small organization, it sometimes loses people to bigger federal agencies "where there are higher Civil Service levels and more mobility." The chairman has a four-member personal staff including a legal assistant. Besides the commissioners, about half a dozen of the agency's senior staff posts have usually been politically appointed.

Jones-Smith says she has spent "a great deal of time" with the Congress, especially in the fall of 1990 when the Congress reauthorized CPSC for the first time since 1983. "You have to know the Hill process," Fise advises. "When the commission goes up to testify, generally the chairman presents the only statement. The committee may ask if other commissioners have statements, but when they want to ask questions and nail them down, they question the chairman." It helps, she adds, if the chairman is "politically astute," especially in fostering relations with committee chairmen and minority members. Both Jones-Smith and Scanlon report a lot of travel during their tenures, to visit field offices and handle the public affairs dimension of the job. "Travel to the field is important, and I've done a lot of it," Jones-Smith says. "While in the field, I set up meetings with relevant consumer, industry, safety and state and local organizations. Many of these organizations have tight budgets and can't come to us. There is a concerted effort to establish more cooperative interaction between CPSC and outside organizations."

Reflecting on the nature of a CPSC commissioner's work and its impact, Pittle takes an objective, realistic approach. He doesn't think "industry is evil or doesn't care" about product safety. What mostly happens instead, he says, is that healthy competition among manufacturers does not guarantee the elimination of unhealthy by-products like preventable illness, injury or death for consumers. The marketplace will always require a monitoring and regulating agency like CPSC, in his view. But "the regulators can't be extremists--in either direction." Rather, they should be balanced and schooled by education or experience in the areas they regulate, "because that tells the people who have to live with those regulations they are hearing even if they don't always like the outcome. They deserve a scale that's accurate. I think that's paramount." Jones-Smith takes the same position. "Very early on, in any substantive decision," she states, "you have to be up front and consistent in providing a rationale. People don't always like what you've decided, but they need to feel you've made a fair decision."

Similarly, Pittle believes that even a dedicated, competent staff will achieve little unless the agency's leadership sets a clear standard of objectivity. What a commissioner should be saying, in effect, is "if you bring me the data, I will enforce the law," Pittle argues. When he had to make a decision, for example, "it wasn't because I liked or disliked something. I had to make it based on the data itself--whether there were sufficient injuries to act." The chairman has to believe, and be seen by the product manufacturer to believe, that "CPSC has laws on the books and is going to enforce them," Fise adds. "And when there's a problem not enforced by law, CPSC is going to take action. And while the industry will have an opportunity to submit a voluntary standard, CPSC should make it clear that it is not waiting for manufacturers alone to address the problem."

Despite its budget and personnel constraints, Pittle believes CPSC continues to do good work, albeit on too small a scale, and must not be allowed to fade. "There is an unheralded benefit--the injuries that didn't happen," he says. "CPSC is in the business of removing negatives from the marketplace." But once a dangerous product is removed, "people don't relish how glad they are that it's not there anymore." Today, he notes, few people remember flammable children's pajamas, shatterable architectural glass in storm and patio doors, "chain saws that could kick back and hit you in the face," or when "kids used to drink drain cleaner" because the cans lacked child-resistant closures. There is no constituency for continuing to monitor something that is no longer a problem, "only for removing a problem that has manifested itself. I think the agency is a critical part of the marketplace because the health and safety components of products are externalities to our market system. You can get injured or killed, and it's very hard to leverage that experience onto the manufacturer so that he or she can change the product." That process doesn't work, Pittle says, "unless there is an independent, non-economically interested party like a federal agency that steps in and says this must change."

Jones-Smith is moderately optimistic about the future. "Product safety is an area where new attention is being focused." She thinks this may be fueled by growing attention to product liability considerations, the possibility of increased regulation at the state level, and "the desire for a more level playing field from a regulatory standpoint. This is one of the first times we've seen industry and consumer groups interested in a stronger CPSC."

Key Relationships

Within the Department

Reports to: The President

Works closely with:

Other CPSC commissioners

Outside the Department

Administrator, Environmental Protection Agency
Administrator, National Highway Traffic Safety Administration, Department of Transportation
Chairman, National Transportation Safety Board
Chairman, Federal Trade Commission
Commissioner, Food and Drug Administration, Department of Health and Human Services

Outside the Government

A broad spectrum of consumer and product liability groups; manufacturing, pharmaceutical and food industries; international business and standards organizations; and state and local health, transportation and product safety liaison officials

Profile of Current Chairman
Consumer Product Safety Commission

Name: Jacqueline Jones-Smith

Assumed Position: 1989

Career Summary: Maxima Corporation; attorney, County Attorney's Office, Montgomery County, Maryland; and Federal Election Commission

Education: Swarthmore College, BA, 1974
Syracuse University, MS, 1978
American University, LLD, 1984

Chairmen, CPSC Since 1973*

Administration	Name and Years Served	Present Position
Bush	Jacqueline Jones-Smith 1989 - present	Incumbent
Bush	Anne Graham 1989 (Acting)	Commissioner, CPSC
Reagan	Terrence Scanlon 1986 - 1988	Vice President Heritage Foundation Washington, D.C.
Reagan	Anne Graham 1986 (A)	Commissioner, CPSC
Reagan	Carol G. Dawson 1986 (A)	Vice Chairman, CPSC
Reagan	Terrence Scanlon 1985 (recess appointment)	Vice President Heritage Foundation Washington, D.C.
Reagan	Nancy H. Steorts 1981 - 1985	President Nancy H. Steorts & Associates Chevy Chase, Md.
Reagan	R. David Pittle 1981 (A)	Technical Director Consumers Union Mt. Vernon, N.Y.

Reagan	Stuart M. Statler 1981 (A)	Deputy Executive Director Association of Trial Lawyers of America Washington, D.C.
Carter	Susan B. King 1978 - 1981	President Steuben Glass Company New York, N.Y.
Ford, Carter	S. John Byington 1976 - 1978	Pillsbury, Madison & Sutro Washington, D.C.
Nixon, Ford	Richard O. Simpson 1973 - 1976	Not available

* The CPSC was created by the Consumer Product Safety Act of 1972

13

DEPARTMENT OF DEFENSE

ASSISTANT SECRETARY
COMMAND, CONTROL, COMMUNICATIONS AND
INTELLIGENCE

Level IV - Presidential Appointment with Senate Confirmation

Major Responsibilities

- Advise and assist the secretary of defense in matters of policy concerning the worldwide command, control, communications and intelligence (C3I) operations of the department, as well as the priorities, requirements and resources for those functions, including related warning and reconnaissance activities.

- Serve as chief advocate for national C3I systems that cut across service and agency lines. Supervise and coordinate the planning and actions of the military departments in the C3I area, emphasizing coherence in the use of systems and equipment. Provide budget guidance and management and technical oversight for all C3I systems acquired and used by the department. Manage counterintelligence oversight and the reinforcement of the protection of defense information. Act as C3I coordinator for the department with foreign governments and international organizations.

- Supervise the department's corporate information management (CIM) initiative, implementing the principles of this system throughout the department to improve the quality and consistency of the data it handles.

Necessary Training, Experience, Skills

This position operates in a strongly technical environment. Though none of its veterans suggests that it requires PhD-level training, they agree that the job's occupant needs solid technical or scientific background; this might be a degree in physics or electrical engineering buttressed by experience in communications and control systems in the military or industry sector. "When it comes to the nitty-gritty of the technical facets of a program," a former assistant secretary says, "you have to be able to interpret it and you need the background to make that kind of judgment." But candidates must also have some hands-on intelligence background which, since it is a rarer credential, is judged the more important qualification to focus on in filling the position. Its current occupant, though a bacteriologist by training, had a strong chemistry and physics background, and more than 20 years of exposure to C3 systems, their physics and their programmatics, including 12 years in the Congress as an intelligence committee staff member.

Insight

Duane P. Andrews, assistant secretary in this job since 1989, calls his operation "the sensory and nervous system of the department." And within that system, he says, "there are a number of separate sub-systems." These are not only the C3I functions of the job's title, but also counterintelligence, as well as the department's corporate information management (CIM) initiative. "These are all different information communities," Andrews notes, "and they are not yet fully integrated."

But he feels comfortable with the effort to do so. "The technologies have much in common, and their problems are really very similar. Taken together, these activities all relate to the use of defense information, and if you look at it in a broader context, you'll see that the job is really managing the information infrastructure for the department." He thinks it makes "a lot of sense" to combine the C3I functions that "generate, transport and use information" with CIM, which "increases effectiveness and efficiency through better use of information, and with counterintelligence and security countermeasures, which protect the department's information."

In combat, C3I provides military commanders with several vital perspectives and capabilities, all electronically or automatically assisted. It enables them to view the dispositions of the opposing forces and of their own; to receive intelligence about the movements of the adversary and the potential targets they present; to confer on battle plans; to issue orders and assign targets for attack by varying combinations of forces and weapons; to observe the results and the changing situation through a surveillance system; and to adjust plans and continue until the objective is achieved or the combat concludes.

Roughly speaking, military operations take place in either a strategic or a tactical environment. For C3I, each presents a different set of considerations, as pointed out by Thomas Quinn, who is the principal deputy assistant secretary in the C3I office, and has twice headed it in an acting capacity. With strategic systems and especially those used to deliver nuclear weapons--missiles, missile submarines, bombers--orders go out, action is taken, the situation is observed by sensors, commanders review the situation, new orders are issued. "The whole thing is a closed circuit and continues until the situation is over," Quinn says. "With tactical forces (troops, tanks and artillery on the ground, aircraft in localized combat, ships engaged at sea), it is more complicated, with a lot more direct reaction over a longer term, different dispersal of forces, more levels of command and control. There are more variables in a tactical situation, with local commanders having more authority. But basically, the C3I concept is the same."

The assistant secretary, Quinn says, is responsible for "both policy and oversight of all that goes on" in providing the "wherewithal to do C3I." For the command, control and communications part of the function, "wherewithal" covers a substantial terrain. It means choosing between technical options and making decisions on the architecture of systems. It requires clearing, supervising and coordinating the processes by which the department and its components acquire and operate everything from communications satellites, ground- and space-based radars and microwave relays to computer banks, data distribution systems, transponders, and hand-held cellular telephones. And it entails a good deal of budget guidance and review, and a deft hand with the Congress. The office is responsible for the systems to operate that third of the country's air traffic control network that is owned by the department of defense, and provides much of the support to the White House Communications Agency.

To make all this work, the office "tries to be certain that C3 resources, policy and intelligence are available to implement whatever the president's and secretary's policy is," Quinn says. While policy doesn't exhibit frequent change, he observes, intelligence runs "the whole gamut from how national intelligence is used by the strategic and tactical people to the actual organic intelligence capabilities of the military services, and some of the policy and acquisition that support that activity."

John A. Wickham, a retired Army general who is president of the Armed Forces Communications and Electronics Association, stresses the important task of this position in "building coherence among the budgets of the military services and agencies in C3I and automation systems across the board." What he has in mind is "oversight of the C3I dimensions of budgets, trying to see that adequate resources go to programs which the secretary of defense feels are joint in nature and which the services may not have emphasized enough. Can the programs proposed by the services be developed by industry, supported by the Congress, managed by the department?" The answers to such questions, he says, are part of the responsibility of this position.

Entwined with issues like those are resistant problems like redundancy, in which each of the military services develops its own equipment to serve a given purpose. In an earlier time, Quinn explains, there were military activities that one service could perform alone, or largely unassisted. That has changed, especially in the era of Grenada, Panama and the Persian Gulf war. Now, he says, "there are absolutely joint operations in which no service has the entire or even dominant responsibility. And the services have come to accept that." In joint operations, equipment like the C3I gear of each service must be "interoperable" with that of the others. "The services have now embraced interoperability," Quinn says. "But even though they interoperate, the hardware will be different. The Navy will build one kind, the Army or the Air Force some other kind. And they will give you all kinds of documentation and justification why it has to be different."

What about developing single systems that serve the needs of all the services? That is also a difficult proposition, Quinn replies. Interoperability is one thing; commonality is another. "The services are perfectly happy to use one basic piece of equipment--a radio, say--but each wants its radio to be the one adopted by the others." One answer to this, he says, is to form joint programs by canceling separate service efforts to build the same item (Quinn uses the example of a tactical data system), bringing their staffs together and trying to create one program from three separate ones. But what occurred in the example used was a "host-tenant arrangement in which the programs hadn't changed and were not actually meshed into one. They were each still doing their own thing." To create a genuine joint program, he thinks, the department must "start from scratch, wipe out the existing individual programs, create a new office, put new people in it, and start with the single program in mind. That might work."

"You have to understand how to get the military services to do things they might not want to do," Andrews points out. It can't be done through orders, since the C3I assistant secretary has no authority to compel the services to do anything. "I can develop instructions and issue directives," Andrews says, "but they don't respond to me in a chain of command sense." Leadership is therefore essential. He supports the view of the current secretary of defense that filling this job effectively means finding a candidate who has the hard-to-acquire intelligence background, plus an understanding of command, control and communications that can be expanded as the work proceeds. "I don't need to be an engineer on the programs," he says; "I've got people to tell me specifically whether that widget works. But I need to know enough about the technical details to decide whether they're leading me down the wrong path. And most important, I have to understand the risks involved and the particular options presented to me."

In Andrews' estimation, his office does "more policy and R&D management than engineering. Engineering is not our job. Our job is to provide the framework," he says. To provide C3I for the department "is really to provide the leadership, so that the system provides the details. The services are the producers. We have to tie them together in an architecture and supply leadership to move them in particular directions, or stop them when they're going too far in an area, or get them together when they don't want to be together--that sort of thing." The C3I area, in fact, is one where--unlike weapons systems that may never be used--the opportunity exists to find out what actually does work, because the equipment is frequently in operation.

The office of the assistant secretary for C3I has split lines of upward responsibility. For all matters except acquisition, it reports to the secretary. For acquisition questions, which Andrews says account for 30 percent of the office's work, the office goes through the under secretary for acquisition. Program development and budgeting--and the defense of both--are major parts of this position's duties. Though Andrews is constrained from providing the overall money figure for which he has responsibility, he says his unclassified budget is about $30 billion, not including intelligence. It has been his experience that senior Pentagon decision makers, when faced with budget cuts, will often opt to protect some of their C3I programs. "Generally, we probably do better than average, though in real terms our budget for C3I is going down, just like that of everybody else in Defense," he says. On Capitol Hill, most of this assistant secretary's business is with the armed services and select intelligence committees. There are, of course, also the appropriations committees to deal with, and the science subcommittees of both houses show regular interest.

Within the executive branch the amount of interagency and bilateral contact in the job is high. The assistant secretary chairs or sits on a number of interrelated groups in the telecommunications and communications security field, some at the White House level. The office avails itself of outside advisory help and guidance from research associations, and participates in symposia with other federal agencies. These activities and events often receive input from executives in the communications and data processing industries and from other sectors relevant to C3I work. An abundant flow of speaking requests comes in to the assistant secretary, and appearances average once a month.

Andrews' immediate office, within the Office of the Secretary of Defense, has a staff of about 200. Including the defense agencies and activities over which he has direction, control and authority and those where he has staff supervision, the number of people working in the information area, he says, goes into the "tens of thousands." The agencies in the latter category (staff supervision) include the National Security Agency/Central Security Service, the air force and navy special intelligence programs, the Electromagnetic Compatibility Analysis Center, and the Defense Courier Service. Among the units in the former category (direct control and authority) are the Defense Information Systems Agency, the Defense Intelligence Agency, and the Defense Communications Agency. Of the 200 on Andrews' own staff, most on the command, control and communications side are scientists and engineers. The intelligence staff is about evenly divided between engineers and career intelligence professionals. The CIM operation has attracted a significant number of computer scientists and information specialists. He says he is "delighted" with overall staff quality.

Wickham thinks the biggest challenge for this position in the future is "to find a balance between C3I requirements and the resources available for them. One is going up, the other down. Balancing the two is as crucial as determining some of the technical issues within programs." Andrews expresses a similar view: "How do you build down a defense budget? We're in one of the biggest build-downs we've ever had. The problem is to do it smartly."

Communications electronics, which is C3I's business, is in Andrews' view "one of the most technologically challenging areas in the department. We're constantly faced with questions of the appropriate places for technology insertion in the acquisitionary process. We're constantly looking at technical risk and risk management. We're constantly looking for opportunities to provide leadership that will help us in the future in those areas."

Both as a policy responsibility and in his capacity as head of the C3I functional component at Defense, he feels it incumbent on the leadership of the office "to encourage industry to maintain the production base for C3I systems, and to develop promising technologies that will assist us in our business." The computer industry has been "very helpful" in providing the tools to do the C3I job--a "technology push," as he calls it. "We're also having to pull it along in areas that may ultimately have a lot of commercial application but may start as defense applications. So I'd say that R&D management and technology insertion are the major challenges the job faces in the technical area."

Key Relationships

Within the Department

Reports to: Secretary
Under Secretary, Acquisition

Works closely with:

Director, Defense Research and Engineering
Deputy Under Secretary, Strategic and Theater Nuclear Forces
Deputy Under Secretary, Tactical Warfare Programs
Directors, command, control, communications and intelligence, military
departments
Assistant secretaries for acquisition/research, military departments
Assistant Secretary, Program Analysis and Evaluation, and directors of this
function in the military departments
Director, National Security Agency
Comptrollers and equivalent officials, military services
Deputy, Command, Control and Communications Systems, Joint Staff of Joint
Chiefs of Staff
Members, Defense Acquisition and Defense Resources boards

Outside the Department

Director, White House Office of Science and Technology Policy
Deputy Director, Science and Technology, Central Intelligence Agency
National Telecommunications and Information Systems Security Committee
(chair)
Emergency Communications Resources Board
Joint Telecommunications Resources Board

Outside the Government

National Security Telecommunications Advisory Committee;
telecommunications industry officials; communications engineers and
researchers in industry and academic institutions; professional electrical
engineering associations; command, control and communications officials of
NATO; counterparts in other governments

Profile, Current Assistant Secretary, C3I

Name: Duane P. Andrews

Assumed Position: December 1989

Career Summary: Professional staff member, Permanent Select Committee on
Intelligence, U.S. House of Representatives, 1977-89
Officer, U.S. Air Force, 1967-77

Education: University of Florida, BA, 1967
             Central Michigan University, MS, 1974

Assistant Secretaries for C3I Since 1969

Administration	Name and Years Served	Present Position
Bush	Duane P. Andrews 1989 - present	Incumbent
Reagan	Gordon A. Smith 1988 - 1989	Not available
Reagan	Thomas P. Quinn (Acting) 1987	Principal Deputy Assistant Secretary C3I
Reagan	Donald C. Latham* 1981 - 1987	Loral Corporation New York, N.Y.
Carter	Gerald P. Dinneen 1977 - 1980	Foreign Secretary National Academy of Engineering Washington, D.C.
Nixon, Ford	Albert C. Hall** 1971 - 1976	Not available
Ford	Richard H. Shriver*** 1976	Not available
Ford	Thomas C. Reed***	Not available
Nixon	David L. Solomon (A)**** 1974	Not available
Nixon	Eberhardt Rechtin**** 1972 - 1973	Retired Palos Verdes Estates, Cal.
Nixon	Louis A. deRosa***** 1970 - 1971	Not available

* Held position from 1981-84 as Deputy Under Secretary, C3I
Prior to 1977, the C3 and intelligence functions were separate positions. Listed are those who held each position.
** Held position as Assistant Secretary of Defense (Intelligence)
*** Held position as Director, Telecommunications & Command & Control Systems
**** Held position as Assistant Secretary of Defense (Telecommunications)
***** Held position as Assistant to the Secretary of Defense (Telecommunications)

ASSISTANT SECRETARY, HEALTH AFFAIRS

Level IV - Presidential Appointment with Senate Confirmation

Major Responsibilities

- Advise and make recommendations to the secretary of defense on the medical and health activities of the U.S. military establishment and the issues involved, and on their significance for the substance and direction of defense policy.

- Set policy for and manage these functions, including research, with the constant objective of maintaining the health and medical readiness of U.S. military personnel and the effectiveness of the medical staff and facilities supporting them.

- Guide and supervise the administration of health care to military retirees and to the civilian survivors and dependents of active duty uniformed personnel.

- Work closely with the surgeons general and other medical staff of the military services to assure the fair, balanced and consistent conduct of the department's health affairs. Maintain cooperative relationships with other federal agencies whose health or medical research responsibilities relate to those of the department of defense.

Necessary Training, Experience, Skills

Present and past occupants and observers put great emphasis on administrative experience and the large responsibility the position carries in that area with the management of programs worth $13 billion a year. But they believe a physician's credentials are even more important. "Some people believe that a first-class administrator can do it," a former assistant secretary says, "but that's where medicine has gotten itself into major trouble today--they're trying to organize medicine as if it were a factory producing nuts and bolts. I don't think a non-physician can do that job." The post requires an MD, says another, because most of the occupant's major working colleagues "are MD-oriented." Success or failure, he adds, "will depend on the ability to interact with MDs, nurses, podiatrists, pharmacists and the like. An individual who doesn't make it in the medical community is not going to make it in this position." In fact, a look at the modern history of this job shows that about 85 percent of its occupants over the last 20 years have been physicians. The current assistant secretary also values previous government experience that includes exposure to relationships with other agencies and the Congress.

Insight

As in all combat situations, the planning and administering of medical care to American armed forces fighting the Persian Gulf war of 1991 was the first preoccupation of the assistant secretary, health affairs. Medical readiness--the ability to provide expert care to troops in battle anywhere in the world as well as to those at home--is a 365-days-a-year proposition, and the premier responsibility of this position. It means the capacity to treat the health effects of any kind of combat--conventional, biological, nuclear, chemical. It requires the flexibility to adjust to changes of whatever degree in the deployment of U.S. forces in response to evolving defense and political relationships around the world. As things turned out, of course, the task of U.S. military medicine in the Gulf was far easier than feared.

With or without war and casualties, however, perhaps the toughest dilemma facing this position today lies in a parallel area of responsibility. That is the severe deficit being run by the medical care system for military families and retirees.The Civilian Health and Medical Program of the Uniformed Services (CHAMPUS) provides medical and health services to more than nine million individuals in the United States and abroad. They are the spouses and children of members of the armed forces on active duty, the survivors of deceased members, and retired members and their families. In the first instance, CHAMPUS aims to serve these people using the department of defense's (DOD's) own medical facilities and employees, those who also treat active duty uniformed personnel. This in-house system operates some 170 hospitals and about 800 medical and dental clinics around the world with a military and civilian staff of 200,000. Second, for those dependents and retirees who live further than a designated distance from such facilities--or who choose not to use them--CHAMPUS runs a medical insurance program that pays most of the cost of private care. In the last half decade, as dependents increasingly elected the private option, its cost more than doubled.

Overall, CHAMPUS is a $3 billion-plus operation whose deficit in fiscal 1990 was $700 million. In 1992 the figure could go to a billion dollars. While the shortfall also reflects the increasing cost of health care generally, it is further burdened by the reduction in available Pentagon medical staff created when war takes many of them out of the country and away from their usual locations. Dependents and retirees who would normally receive treatment from DOD doctors and hospitals must then get it privately, increasing the insurance claims levied on CHAMPUS. This has forced an increase in the share of physicians' bills and in deductibles paid by dependents, and a reduction in services covered.

Dr. Enrique Mendez Jr., assistant secretary since 1990, heads the present Pentagon effort to try to "marry" CHAMPUS more closely with DOD's direct-care system for uniformed personnel into what he calls "a coordinated care mode." For example, he is testing the potential of giving base medical commanders responsibility for their local or regional costs, with more power to decide the best mix of on-site and outside health care in their local areas and to contract locally for the outside portion. Another possibility involves requiring a greater part of beneficiary health care to take place in DOD facilities. Both these solutions, however, encounter problems in the current shortage of DOD medical staff to operate the facilities. Meanwhile, a private-sector contract to test the reform of CHAMPUS reportedly has saved 20 percent of what the program normally costs in two states where many of its beneficiaries live. This experimental initiative apparently will not go further, however, until the Pentagon can compare it with other cost-cutting experiments under way.

Dr. M. Roy Schwarz, executive vice president of the American Medical Association, thinks part of the test of effectiveness in this job is the ability "to work with people who have risen through the ranks of three different military establishments and with a politically-appointed, highly-visible secretary, and to satisfy everybody on the Hill." Even more taxing is the question of "how to assemble the resources to provide health care for the military plus their dependents and at the same time have enough personnel of the right kind. You've got to take care of colds, flu, pregnancies, venereal disease every day. And if suddenly some crazy man decides to cross a boundary with his tanks, you have to mobilize and go halfway around the world in a few hours. When you go into battle you need neurosurgeons, trauma experts, orthopedists, pathologists, radiologists, who are always in short supply. How do you get those? The fact is, you can't plan for a mobilization. It just happens. That's the most difficult long-term challenge. That and money."

These twin responsibilities for the care of civilian dependents and the medical readiness of the armed forces involve the assistant secretary in a wide range of specific concerns which feed into and support those goals. They include preventive medicine, drug and alcohol abuse, quality assurance, information systems, personnel and research. Mendez chairs the Defense Health Council, the coordinating body for DOD health affairs; and sits on the department's Medical Standardization and Medical Examination Review boards and several other Pentagon groups coordinating health promotion, epidemiology, medical readiness and reserve matters. Handling the position's congressional business is a regular and fairly frequent chore.

In addition to a principal deputy and a chief of staff, this job oversees five other deputy assistant secretaries in charge of budget, health services financing, health services operations, medical readiness and professional affairs. "In each of these main areas," says Dr. Robert N. Smith, assistant secretary in 1976-78, "there were problems in logistics, manpower and facilities, readiness--which included estimated casualties-- and environmental concerns."

A staff of about 500 serves the office of the assistant secretary, ranging from those in the headquarters office to some 400 others working in field activities that include information systems, construction of facilities, and the CHAMPUS office. "Training is very important to me," Mendez says, discussing the overall quality of DOD's far-flung health care forces. "We have maintained very fine residency programs in all three services that have allowed us to be able to retain people. We have a health care professions scholarship program which supports the basic U.S. medical school system." There is also the Pentagon's own medical school, the Uniformed Services University of the Health Sciences.

"By and large the quality of the staff and the support I had was just fine," says Dr. John H. Moxley III, who held the position in 1979-81. But keeping staff at the MD level is something else. "The situation then was that it was difficult to retain physicians, and that hasn't changed. There's no way you're going to be able to pay military physicians what they can earn in the private sector, at least in the foreseeable future." According to Mendez, the difficulty of attracting physicians varies by discipline, the hardest being surgical subspecialties like those in neurology, orthopedics and ophthalmology. It is easier in the case of doctors in pediatrics and internal medicine. As for career DOD medical support staff, "they are remarkably good," in Schwarz's view, "given the turnover, the disillusionment that can occur, and the fact that they are not very visible or applauded."

Does the so-called tradition of interservice rivalry extend into the medical sphere? "I think you always see that," Mendez answers. "Somebody always asks why one service has something which another doesn't. Rivalry isn't bad if it's healthy. If it's just invidious comparison, then it's unhealthy. But I don't mind people competing if the result could be excellence."

He advises future assistant secretaries to bear in mind that the health affairs responsibility "doesn't exist independently of the rest of American health care." Indeed, the Pentagon's ongoing experience in managing its medical and health programs, including the effort to bring the CHAMPUS deficits under control, represents in effect a laboratory for innovation and improvement with application elsewhere in public health administration and in the private sector. "It is part and parcel of what else goes on in the country," Mendez says. "Therefore it's necessary to know what's happening, to participate in an exchange of views, to play in those arenas with the other people in federal medicine. I feel that very strongly."

Key Relationships

Within the Department

Reports to: Secretary of Defense

Works closely with:

Deputy Secretary

Assistant Secretary, Force Management and Personnel

Director, Manpower and Personnel Directorate, Secretariat of Joint Chiefs of Staff

Assistant Secretaries of the Army and Navy, Manpower and Reserve Affairs

Assistant Secretary of the Air Force, Manpower, Reserve Affairs and the Environment

Surgeons General of the Military Services Director, National Institutes of Health

Directors, component institutes, NIH

Chief Medical Director, Department of Veterans Affairs

Directors and senior staff, Walter Reed Army Medical Center and other leading military medical facilities

Outside the Department

Assistant Secretary, Health, Department of Health and Human Services

Surgeon General, U.S. Public Health Service, Department of Health and Human Services

Secretary of Veterans Affairs

Chief Medical Director, Department of Veterans Affairs

Director, National Institutes of Health

Administrator, Alcohol, Drug Abuse and Mental Health Administration, Department of Health and Human Services

Outside the Government

American Medical Association, American College of Physicians, American Psychiatric Association, American Psychological Association, American Hospital Association, American Nurses Association and many other professional medical groups; National Military Family Association, veterans organizations, representatives of health insurance and health maintenance organizations

Profile of Current Assistant Secretary, Health Affairs

Name: Enrique Mendez Jr.

Assumed Position: 1990

Career Summary: Secretary of health, Commonwealth of Puerto Rico; medical
                       director, Damas Hospital, Ponce, Puerto Rico; dean, then dean
                       and president, Ponce, Puerto Rico School of Medicine, 1983-90
                       Career officer, U.S. Army Medical Corps, 1955-83, including
                       assignments as division surgeon; field hospital commander;
                       command surgeon, Southern European Task Force; surgeon
                       general of the Army; and Commanding General, Walter Reed
                       Army Medical Center

Education: University of Puerto Rico, BA, 1951
                       Loyola University School of Medicine, MD, 1954

Assistant Secretaries, Health Affairs Since 1970*

Administration	Name and Years Served	Present Position
Bush	Enrique Mendez Jr. 1990 - present	Incumbent
Bush	David Newhall III (Acting) 1989 - 1990	Consultant Bailey, Morris and Robinson Washington, D.C.
Reagan	William Mayer 1983 - 1989	Director California Department of Mental Health Sacramento, Cal.
Reagan	Vernon McKenzie (A) 1983	Retired
Reagan	John Beary (A) 1981 - 1983	Sr. Vice President, Science and Technology Pharmaceutical Manufacturers Assn. Washington, D.C.

Carter	John H. Moxley III 1979 - 1981	Korn/Ferry International Los Angeles, Cal.
Carter	Vernon McKenzie (A) 1978 - 1979	Retired
Carter, Ford	Robert N. Smith 1976 - 1978	Retired Toledo, Ohio
Ford	James R. Cowan** 1974 - 1976	Not available
Nixon	Richard S. Wilbur** 1971 - 1973	Vice President Council on Medical Specialties Lake Forest, Ill.
Nixon	Louis M. Rousselot** 1970 - 1971	Deceased

* Position was created in June 1970
** Held position as Assistant Secretary, Health and Environment

DIRECTOR
DEFENSE ADVANCED RESEARCH PROJECTS
AGENCY

Senior Executive Service

Major Responsibilities

- Administer an agency which identifies and supports the research and development of highly advanced technologies with primarily military applications.

- Work with the Office of the Secretary of Defense and the research and acquisition chiefs of the uniformed services to assess the priority high-technology needs of the military establishment. Determine how the agency will help meet these requirements through seed money and other support of research projects and ideas emerging in the private sector and the national laboratories. Direct the allocation of this support and monitor its use.

- For these purposes, maintain continual contact with the leadership of the engineering and scientific communities in industry and the universities, and of the national labs. Recommend the backing of additional advanced research in promising areas not otherwise addressed by the services.

Necessary Training, Experience, Skills

Leading the Defense Advanced Research Projects Agency (DARPA) in exploration of defense technology's outer edges and directing the support of research in that area requires training at the PhD level in a technical field or hard science. Just as important is substantial experience in managing technology--in industry, not just in a government or industrial laboratory; to quote the current occupant of this job, "managing is all you do." To these credentials the director should add an innovative, entrepreneurial approach, and a broad acquaintance in the industrial and research base on which the agency draws.

Insight

DARPA's basic task was and is to provide the U.S. military with the best competitive advanced technology available by seeking out and funding the research most likely to provide it. That mission echoes back to 1958, when the agency was born out of U.S. shock at the Soviet launching of Sputnik. Craig Fields, who ran the agency in 1989-90, says "the original notion was avoiding technological surprise. The main job of the agency now is not only avoiding surprise but trying to promote it--with our side on top."

The agency has done well enough that at times it finds itself the topic of a mostly theological debate about government's role in promoting U.S. commercial competitiveness. The same is true of NASA and other federal agencies developing, managing or deploying high technology. But given its success as a trail blazer in seeking out and supporting revolutionary technical and scientific research, DARPA's profile in the debate has seemed higher than most.

Certainly, that was true during much of the past decade, when government has categorically shunned support of high technology research and development aimed mainly at commercial applications. The reasoning runs along these general lines: If the commercial potential of a specific technology is promising enough, industry should exploit it without government investment that might end up favoring one industry or company over another. Such choices would amount to official "industrial policy" and are better left to the free market. If, however, government-funded development of a technology specifically for defense or other public-sector purposes happens also to spin off commercial benefits in the process, so much the better.

Critics of this philosophy have warned that it deprives American industry of an immense competitive advantage on a consistent basis. They call instead for deliberate, up-front, continuing government participation in the pursuit of advanced technology with public and private sector--dual-use--potential. Helping to make this case are a number of DARPA's past efforts that over the years have produced striking payoffs in both areas. Among them is the agency's key founding role and continued support of the Sematech computer chip consortium, one of several recent DARPA contributions to U.S leadership in computer science. The list also includes DARPA's funding of research into high-definition television, critical new materials such as ceramics, high-energy lasers, and artificial intelligence products and services.

To some, including not a few in high places, the debate over government's role is largely one of semantics. The White House, for example, says it recognizes government's responsibility to support research during the "pre-competitive" phase of critical new generic technologies, regardless of their intended application. And where DARPA is concerned, former director Fields thinks it has only accidentally been a focus of the argument. "DARPA, in trying to do its very straight-line mission for the department of defense, has a very strong impact on non-defense parts of the economy," he says.

The past 18 months have meanwhile seen modest but clear evidence of increasing federal attention to R&D with commercial as well as defense or other public sector applications. Typical of this is the proposed increase of $638 million in fiscal 1992 support for research and development in high-performance computing. DARPA would receive the biggest share (36 percent) of this increase. One of the program's components is the national research and education network, the so-called information superhighway. It would connect thousands of industries and campuses in an information exchange relationship many hundreds of times faster than today's data nets.

Victor H. Reis, DARPA's chief since 1990, says "it is really information technology where the big changes are taking place. Computer technology, microelectronics, networks, software. All the things that go with that. It's the main thrust of what we're working on."

Research projects funded by DARPA are largely born in the projected future requirements of the military services, formulated in constant dialogue between the agency and service acquisition chiefs, and with the under secretary for acquisition and other seniors in the Office of the Secretary of Defense. DARPA also has an open-ended mandate to come up with its own ideas, usually well out in front of the nearer-term needs which the services focus on most. There was little outside attempt to influence projects, recalls Robert S. Fossum, director of the agency in 1978-81. "But it did happen occasionally, most often when a project contractor would work through his members of Congress to have favorable specifications written into the authorizing legislation."

In fiscal 1991 DARPA operated on a budget of $1.2 billion, plus another $300 million in projects managed for other agencies. At any given moment, its four operating divisions have more than 2,000 research contracts out to about 300 contractors. Reis and Fields use the phrase "cultural change" to describe the desired impact of DARPA's work on the defense establishment's approach to radical new technologies. Such transitions are not easy for the military services. Before signing on to the production stage of a far-out design or concept, they like to see some functioning incarnation that proves it will really work. Yet if DARPA contributes resources to such demonstration models--the prototype of the Stealth bomber was an example--it has less to spend on the funding of cutting-edge research that is more properly its mission.

For its part, industry is attracted to DARPA's role as a flashlight illuminating unexplored terrain. A leading semiconductor executive told Reis, for example, that DARPA provides "a vision of where we are going in terms of the technology." Further, he said, "we like the fact that you act as a technological broker." His company benefited from the synergy produced when DARPA tied it into a group of small companies and universities whose collaboration the company had not been aware of. Finally, he said, his firm likes to compete for DARPA contracts because everything the agency does is competitive "and that sharpens us up."

DARPA's sustained record in spurring the march of defense technology has won wide and admiring recognition. The list is long. It ranges from the M-1 rifle and balloon-borne radar in the early 1960s (when the agency's acronym was ARPA), to infrared detection; from phased array and over-the-horizon radar and other ballistic missile defense systems that fed into the strategic defense initiative, to the Army's new battlefield simulation network. Smart bombs and much of the other space-age technical pizzazz that caught the world's attention in the 1991 Persian Gulf war trace directly to DARPA.

The director's job itself requires what Fields calls "good taste" on several levels. One of them is judging potential projects--"which ones are going to be big technical winners; which are going to have real impact on the military." Another is personnel--knowing "which of the right people to hire, who has real technical depth and who only seems to, who is entrepreneurial. And who has real management skills, because the job of running an enterprise operating in 50 states and several foreign countries is pretty challenging." Fossum underlines another function of the director--to protect the agency from a tendency to impose rules and regulations that reduce its effectiveness. "DARPA is a small agency that reflects the style of the director and should not be bureaucratic," he says. "The director's job is to provide a management environment that enables the agency to do its job." At the same time, Fossum adds, the agency's chief must see that channels of communication to high-level decision makers remain open and broad. That especially includes the under secretary for acquisition to whom the director reports.

Reis describes the agency's technical staff as mostly at the upper middle management and senior executive service levels. A third of them are middle to upper middle grade military officers, most with master's degrees or PhDs. Their presence helps DARPA in its relationships with the services. About 15 percent of the agency civilian staff are there under the Intergovernmental Personnel Act. It permits an inflow of people with needed skills from academic and nonprofit institutions; they retain their former salaries--usually higher than what they would earn as government employees--and their status with their former organizations, to which they return after DARPA tours of two to four years. The average service of agency staff, civilian or military, is three or four years. "It was always

designed for a fair flow of people in and out," Reis says. He would have
liked more flexibility in hiring, he adds, and in what he could pay.

Fields thinks personnel is the agency's number one problem--"so
large there is hardly a number two. How in the world are they going to
attract and retain the best people?" Jacques Gansler, a onetime Pentagon
official who is senior vice president of TASC, also thinks staff is DARPA's
primary worry. "Technology requires relatively young, smart, aggressive
people on the edge of the state of the art," he says. "You can't afford, at
the top or all the way through the organization, to have people about to
retire. DARPA should have a younger average staff age than the rest of
the department. And it should be able to draw on people with industrial
experience from the top down." Beyond that, Gansler is concerned with
DARPA's ability to retain budget in the battle with the services. Fields
agrees money is a big (and perennial) problem, "but not that big. The
agency could use 50 to 100 percent more than it now gets, but not much
more. You can only do so much." Reis agrees. "Could I do better if you
gave me more? Sure. Give DARPA the same amount, is it going to be
a disaster? No. Money is not the biggest problem it is facing."

And what is? Reis sees it as "maintaining the right kind of defense
industrial base--one that can build what we need at prices we can afford.
We don't have an arsenal state here. It's industry that provides the
equipment. If they don't, we're not going to do very well." Is this sort of
a reverse twist on the industrial policy issue? "In defense there's no such
thing as a free market," Gansler says. "It's one hundred percent
regulated--one buyer and one or two suppliers. Given that, government
as the only buyer has to come up with a technology strategy. Now you
don't have to call that industrial policy, but it clearly must consider both
demand and the supply side." Here he raises the point made by Fields
and cited earlier. "What kind of industrial structure do you want? Do
you want to buy all your electronics, engineering and production in
Taiwan, Singapore, Japan?"

The answer, Gansler believes, is "a world-class, domestically-based,
state of the art industry for national security as much as for other reasons.
And that means having dual-use requirements. If you say you're only
going to consider what Defense needs and not the commercial viability of
a product, then you come out with one answer. That's the way we do
business now. It's a change to consider also what the commercial viability
would be. And it's a shift I think has to be made." At the same time, as
Fields puts it, DARPA has to "look out five-ten-twenty years and see
what kind of national security environment we'll have to deal with, what
the technologies are that will enable us really to succeed. To do that is
difficult since you first have to determine who your competition
adversaries are."

With the Soviet Union no longer the preeminent potential U.S.

adversary, Fields perceives a "much greater fixation on being able to respond to regional crises in a timely manner." It can't be assumed, however, that the sophistication of the weapons used in such crises will be lower. At the same time, given the slight lessening of the overall threat, he foresees "tremendous pressure" to meet it at far lower cost. "To me that requires a technological as well as a management solution." Gansler thinks the world will remain "a dangerous place, with less rational actors in the third world." Even while cutting back on the size of armies and numbers of tanks and ships, "you want to keep your technology base." Since, in his view, the military services have not emphasized that, "DARPA has been getting more emphasis. It's the reason Congress is throwing more money at DARPA now. I would argue that DARPA will be getting more of a role."

Key Relationships

Within the Department

Reports to: Under Secretary, Acquisition

Works closely with:

Director, Defense Research and Engineering
Director, Operational Test and Evaluation
Director, Defense Intelligence Agency
Assistant Secretary, Acquisition, Department of the Air Force
Assistant Secretary, Research, Development and Acquisition, Department of the Army
Assistant Secretary, Research, Development and Acquisition, Department of the Navy

Outside the Department

Director, National Science Foundation
Assistant to the President, Science and Technology Policy
Secretary of Commerce
Under Secretary, Technology, Department of Commerce
Chief, National Security Agency
Deputy Director, Science and Technology, Central Intelligence Agency
Assistant Secretary, Research, Department of Energy

Outside the Government

Chief officers of technical academic institutions such as Caltech and MIT; heads of science and engineering departments on these and other campuses; defense and aerospace contractors; professional engineering and scientific associations; American Defense Preparedness Association, National Security Industrial Association, American Institute of Aeronautics and Astronautics, and similar groups

Profile of Current Director
Defense Advanced Research Projects Agency

Name: Victor H. Reis

Assumed Position: 1990

Career Summary: Acting director, DARPA, May - November, 1990
Deputy director, DARPA, 1989-90
Special assistant to the director, Lincoln Laboratory, Massachusetts Institute of Technology; senior vice president, Science Applications International Corporation; and other senior-level posts in government, industry, and higher education, 1963-89

Education: Rensselaer Polytechnic Institute, BME, 1957
Yale University, MEng, 1958
MA, PhD, mechanical engineering, Princeton University, 1962

Assistant Directors
Defense Advanced Research Projects Agency Since 1969

Administration	Name and Years Served	Present Position
Bush	Victor H. Reis 1990 - present	Incumbent
Bush	Craig I. Fields 1989 - 1990	President Chief Technical Officer, Microelectronics & ComputerTechnologyCorp., Austin, Tex.
Reagan	Raymond S. Colladay 1988 - 1989	Vice President, Research and Development Martin Marietta Bethesda, Md.
Reagan	Robert C. Duncan 1985 - 1987	Director, Operational Test & Evaluation DOD

Reagan	Robert S. Cooper 1982 - 1984	President Atlantic Aerospace Greenbelt, Md.
Carter	Robert S. Fossum 1978 - 1981	Prof., Electrical Engineering Southern Methodist University Dallas, Tex.
Carter, Ford	George H. Heilmeier 1975 - 1978	President and CEO Bellcore Livingston, N.J.
Nixon	Stephen J. Lukasik 1971 - 1974	Vice President, Technology TRW Space & Defense Sector Redondo Beach, Cal.
Nixon	Eberhart Rechtin 1969 - 1971	Professor of Engineering University of Southern Califonia Los Angeles, Cal.

DIRECTOR
DEFENSE RESEARCH AND ENGINEERING

Level IV - Presidential Appointment with Senate Confirmation

Major Responsibilities

● Shape direction and content for the research and development of defense technology central to weapons, weapons systems, communications, and associated support structures. Make the budget and other choices in these matters that best meet the future needs of the military services in an era of changing defense policy and objectives and decreasing resources, and that help preserve the national manufacturing and R&D base in defense technology.

● Develop policies, provide advice and recommendations and offer guidance for these efforts. Serve as the department's chief technologist, mediating among differing requirements and contending factions in and between the services and providing the leadership to bring them together. Seek where possible the development of generic technologies with multiple uses at reduced cost.

● Represent the department in interagency councils in the discussion of defense research and engineering projects and problems. Chair the Nuclear Weapons Council. Conduct effective liaison with the Congress, defending the research elements of the department budget and articulating and explaining the objectives of department research and engineering.

Necessary Training, Experience, Skills

Training in an engineering or scientific discipline, with an updated grasp of current technological advance, is the first requirement. The right candidate for the job will be well wired into the national science and technology communities, but also understand defense strategy in non-technical terms--history, economics, the relevance to foreign policy. Also essential is a familiarity with the defense department and its operating relationships with the White House and other agencies, and with the needs of the individual military services and their organizational imperatives. Finally, a sensitivity to the process of and stakes in political decision making serves this position well.

Insight

Two events of 1991 will serve to speed the evolution in U.S. defense policy and posture that has been in process since the mid-1980s. The short war in the Persian Gulf underlined again the continuing danger of regional crises that pose different problems of military response than those that U.S. military forces have long been principally geared for. And the seismic political transformations in the Soviet Union seem likely to lower the potential military threat from that quarter several substantial further notches, with consequent technology and budget implications in a wide range.

This changing international security picture will continue indefinitely to be a highly determining fact of life for the research and engineering function at the department of defense. Regional conflicts or potential conflicts and the possible need for relatively small-scale military intervention are now recognized as "the major concern," says Stephen Lukasik, a vice president of TRW Inc. who in 1971-74 directed the Defense Advanced Research Projects Agency (DARPA). "We're worried about the proliferation of advanced technology including aircraft technology, and of nuclear and chemical technology into third world countries." The goal of the director of defense research and engineering (DDR&E) is now to exert a significant leadership role--a technology as well as a requirements role, he says--"in converting our military forces into the kinds of forces required in the future."

For example, he continues, the war in the Gulf showed that theater ballistic missile defense is "a larger part of the equation than before," and that "precision munitions are very effective and make sense." The lesson he draws is that "regional conflicts make technology more important because we have to do things neatly and cleanly." Another discipline that proved its value anew in the Gulf, he adds, is the collection, processing and distribution of information. Again, stealth--"a technology just coming into the inventory"--worked effectively, and will require sophisticated management to bring it all the way. Finally, noting that arms control agreements with the Soviet Union have changed the strategic relationship, Lukasik says this means smaller numbers and changes in the kind of systems employed in U.S. strategic nuclear forces. All of these technologies, he states, "must be main items on the DDR&E's plate."

Essentially, the director of defense research and engineering tracks the quality of the defense department's technological muscle in a variety of fields in a continuous effort to assure that the military services are technically up to their assigned jobs--and will stay that way in the future. That means evaluating the services' own estimates of where they think they want to be at given points down the road and what they will need, reaching decisions on how to invest limited R&E resources to get them there, and then seeing that the work is done. Along the way, the director must negotiate familiar problems of interservice rivalries for R&D funds and their tendency to prefer competing, rather than complementary, systems.

Charles Herzfeld held the DDR&E position from early 1990 to mid-1991, and is now a consultant on science and technology and national security to the White House Office of Science and Technology Policy (OSTP) and the National Security Council; as of early September 1991 he had not yet been replaced.   Herzfeld views his former job as "the key place to make sure that the United States will continue to have technical superiority over any other power in the world and that this superiority is available in a form the military can use." The late Richard D. DeLauer, who held these responsibilities in 1981-84 as under secretary for defense research and engineering, called it "the top technology position in the department for research and analysis, international programs, tactical warfare, and space."

Herzfeld agrees that the basic issue affecting the work of the director is "the change in priorities, or in the direction from which one thinks military defense problems are coming." Since he has always believed that the "near-exclusive" U.S. focus on the Soviet Union was a mistake, Herzfeld says, "I'm quite comfortable intellectually with the way things look now." But he's not ready to say that the potential Soviet danger has disappeared. "It's still the only country that can destroy us in an hour, and still has and will continue to have by far the largest land army in Eurasia."

But if the road which this job must follow is generally evident, Herzfeld lists a number of complicating factors in traveling it. Resources is one. "The total technology package" the director is currently responsible for investing--in research and development of defense-related technology, in the development of weapons systems and in the strategic defense initiative (SDI)--is about $40 billion. It is decreasing, "as it should," Herzfeld says. "The biggest problem is how to make choices," he emphasizes, a problem inevitably worsened by competition between the services for funds amid a budget crunch. "It's really a zero-sum game now," Herzfeld notes, where if a new project starts, the resources "have to come from somebody's hide."

The second biggest problem, he says, is "how to organize" the DR&E effort across the department. "The in-house technology effort is not well-focused and is organizationally very fragmented. The system is now 40 years old, grew like Topsy, and pieces were added without anybody thinking hard about it." Thousands of people on the technical payroll are not doing technical work, he asserts, "but the bureaucracy finds it easier to cut programs than overhead and support functions, because programs are identified with line items in the budget, while indirect costs are much harder to find." Another consideration for the director of DR&E, it can be added, is the increased attention focused on accountability as the result of various procurement malfeasances that have buffeted the department over the past decade. Positions like this one that are associated with the procurement function are especially sensitive in this regard.

In the 1970s and early 1980s, when direction of the research and engineering functions of the department resided with an under secretary, that job's occupant reported directly to the deputy secretary. When the under secretary for acquisition position emerged in the mid-1980s as part of reform recommended by a commission headed by former deputy secretary David Packard, research and engineering lodged at the director level, reporting to the new under secretary. In Lukasik's view, removing the job's direct reporting line to the topmost reaches of the department is one of several changes that have made the job harder to do. Among the others, he says, the military services are "more independent" of oversight from the Office of the Secretary of Defense (OSD), and the SDI office and the assistant secretary for command, control, communications and intelligence have separate reporting relationships. All of these require coordination by the DDR&E from a science and technology standpoint, Lukasik says, yet each has a different reporting structure. To Herzfeld, "bureaucratic infighting" is currently "more prominent than one would like to see," no doubt exacerbated by years of declining resources, and "an enormous amount of time is spent addressing issues that would be easy to solve if people didn't dig in and say 'you have to make me do it.'"

The office of defense research and engineering divides structurally into four areas--research and advanced technology, test and evaluation, strategic and theater nuclear forces, and tactical warfare programs. A deputy to the DDR&E heads each of these; their collective staff totals about 175. The position also has authority over DARPA, with about 100 employees, the Defense Nuclear Agency, with some 2,000, and the Defense Science Board and the assistant to the secretary for atomic energy.

In addition to regular and frequent meetings within OSD and with research, development, acquisition, testing and budget managers of the military services, the DDR&E sits on the Defense Acquisition Board. This job also chairs the Nuclear Weapons Council, which works up decision memoranda for the president governing the manufacture and custody of the U.S. nuclear weapons stockpile. At the White House level, the director does business at the Office of Management and Budget, the National Security Council staff, and the director of OSTP. Herzfeld took particular satisfaction in the several cross-agency programs engineered by OSTP since 1989 to speed national progress in urgent science and technology areas. The most important for his purposes was the high-performance computing initiative, in which Defense and the Department of Energy are the major players. These projects operate under the general guidance of the Federal Coordinating Council for Science, Engineering and Technology (FCCSET), where the DDR&E is a member of the FCCSET committee on physical, mathematical and engineering sciences.

In assessing this position, Lukasik thinks it important to recognize that it operates in more than one context and that, beyond its formal duties, the job's mission has national significance. "It has both a narrow set of responsibilities as well as very broad connections," he says. For example, the choice, characteristics and development of weapons systems are "intimately related" to U.S. foreign policy, since in a real sense each is a function of the other.

Second, he believes, the defense establishment plays a major, if decreasing, part in national technology policy that goes back to the second world war, and has had considerable impact on manufacturing technology in matters like efficiency, quality, low cost, reliability, and standards. He cites Defense's continuing key role in the technology of information and computing and its link to national concerns about U.S. competitiveness. The defense industries with which the DDR&E deals "are companies with both international and defense business, and the health of those organizations and the kinds of science and technology issues the Pentagon assists with are therefore important. Where that really comes home is in the information sciences." Much of the current technology in computing, he says, "is still heavily influenced by Defense--integrated circuits, software engineering, artificial intelligence, optical processing, and computer networking."

One objective of the DDR&E should therefore be "to preserve the core technological capabilities the country will need in the future." The department, he asserts, has had considerable impact on U.S. manufacturing technology. "We've got a defense structure in government, industry and academia that has been heavily related to the defense business. As that decreases, this person has to see that essential capabilities, institutions and linkages are sustained. These are all issues that the DDR&E has to recognize and nurture."

Third, a good part of the U.S. national intelligence function is directly connected to the defense department, "because it is either military intelligence in the narrower sense, or because the staffing of operational intelligence functions requires a worldwide capability in terms of basing, communications and the like."

For reasons like these, Lukasik believes the central task of the DDR&E is to function "at the confluence of these considerations of foreign policy, technology policy and the operational management of the intelligence system." Is this too broad a mandate in today's circumstances? Lukasik doesn't think so. "The job has been that way since it was established. So you can argue that there is 30 years of evidence that the job is doable. It's very much of a coordinating and leadership job--making the best of a very difficult set of national security interactions."

Key Relationships

Within the Department

Reports to: Under Secretary, Acquisition

Works closely with:

Deputy Secretary
Members, Defense Science Board
Director, Defense Advanced Research Projects Agency
Director, Operational Test and Evaluation
Vice chairman, Joint Chiefs of Staff
Research, development and acquisition executives, military services
Command, control, communications, intelligence and automation executives, military services

Outside the Department

Director, White Office of Science and Technology Policy
Members, Committee on Physical, Mathematical and Engineering Sciences, Federal Coordinating Council for Science, Engineering and Technology
Assistant Secretary of Energy, Defense Programs
Senior Director, Defense Policy and Arms Control, National Security Council
Associate Administrators, Space Science and Applications, and Aeronautics Exploration and Technology, National Aeronautics and Space Administration

Outside the Government

Engineering and R&D departments of defense contractors; research and development, firms and general manufacturing and engineering companies; trade associations of defense and aerospace industries; university science and engineering departments; professional engineering societies; defense officials of other governments

Profile of Director, Defense Research and Engineering Until May, 1991

Note: As of September 1, 1991 this position had been vacant since May 1991. The biographic information that follows pertains to the individual who held the position up until that time, and who was interviewed for this book.

Name:	Charles M. Herzfeld
Held Position:	1990 - 1991
Career Summary:	Vice chairman, Aetna, Jacobs, Ramo Technology Ventures, 1985-90 Various research management positions with ITT Corporation, 1967-85, including vice president and director of research and technology Various positions with the Advanced Research Projects Agency, Department of Defense, 1961-67, including director Various positions with the National Bureau of Standards, Department of Commerce, 1955-61, including associate director Lecturer, University of Maryland, 1954-61
Education:	Catholic University of America, BS, chemical engineering (magna cum laude), 1945 University of Chicago, PhD, chemical physics, 1951

Directors, Defense Research and Engineering Since 1969

Administration	Name and Years Served	Present Position
Bush	(Vacant)	
Bush	Charles M. Herzfeld 1990 - 1991	Consultant, Assistants to the President for Science and Technology Policy and National Security Affairs
Reagan	Robert C. Duncan 1987 - 1989	Director, Operational Test & Evaluation, DOD
Reagan	Donald A. Hicks 1985 - 1986	Chairman Hicks & Associates McLean, Va.
Reagan	James P. Wade Jr. (Acting) 1984 - 1985	CEO Defense Group Inc. Arlington, Va.
Reagan	Richard D. DeLauer 1981 - 1984	Deceased

Carter	William J. Perry 1977 - 1981	Chairman Technology Strategies & Alliances Menlo Park, Cal.
Ford, Nixon	Malcolm R. Currie 1973 - 1977	Chairman and CEO Hughes Aircraft Co. Los Angeles, Cal.
Nixon, Johnson	John S. Foster Jr. 1965 - 1973	Consultant, TRW, Inc, Redondo Beach, Cal. Chairman, Defense Science Board, Department of Defense Washington, D.C.

DIRECTOR
OPERATIONAL TEST AND EVALUATION

Level IV - Presidential Appointment with Senate Confirmation

Major Responsibilities

- Advise and consult with the secretary of defense and senior assistants in setting policy and procedures within the defense department for the testing of new weapons, weapons support systems, equipment and munitions.

- Oversee the conduct of all such testing under realistic, operational conditions. Direct the analysis of test results to assure that product performance meets all requirements and standards. Report independently to the highest levels of the defense department and to the Congress on the conclusions reached in the operational testing of proposed major defense acquisitions.

- Work in close coordination with the research, development, acquisition, test and evaluation communities of the military services, and with the under secretary of defense for acquisition and other senior officials of the secretary's office and the secretariat of the Joint Chiefs of Staff.

- Report annually to the secretary and the Congress on all department test and evaluation actions in the preceding year, with comments and recommendations on the testing status of large weapons programs.

Necessary Training, Experience, Skills

The nature of this job virtually compels the combination of an engineering degree, research and development background, and operational experience. Its occupant should understand and be able to work with the science and sophisticated engineering and design involved in today's weapons, but also have first-hand knowledge of how they actually work in the field. Familiarity with the R&D/acquisition world at the Pentagon and with the Congress is very highly recommended. An aptitude for getting things done outside normal channels when necessary, a feel for the interplay of military service rivalries, and a capacity to withstand and work productively under pressure are all extremely helpful resources.

Insight

In the mid-1980s, with new and often expensive weapons flooding into the U.S. military establishment, the Congress established the requirement for a single, senior authority at the Defense Department to be certain that they worked.

The rationale driving the director of operational test and evaluation (OT&E) is not much more complicated than that, even if the work itself is. "One of the problems in defense acquisition is that doing the research and development and then producing the items is at times more important than what the items will accomplish," according to Rudy Deleon, staff director of the House Armed Services Committee. It is not clear, he says, that a weapon like the Patriot ground-to-air missile would have achieved its Persian Gulf war success if the requirement for full testing had not existed. "That is, not simply to test it while it's sitting in the laboratory, but when it is out on the desert with sand blowing into it" and the operator running the test is working under the same conditions as the soldier who later will actually use it in the field.

Robert C. Duncan, who has directed OT&E at Defense since 1989, elaborates further on the testing requirement. A weapon or system must pass the testing before it can go from what is called low-rate initial production--L-Rip in Pentagonese--to full production, he explains. "No system contractors can be involved. The tests must be manned by normal soldiers, sailors and airmen, not by the so-called 'golden crews' specially selected and trained. It must operate in conjunction with the other systems it would work with in wartime. Every test really creates a miniature war, if you will."

OT&E can be likened to the tight and narrow squeeze between two halves of an hourglass. On one side are the months or years of time, talent, planning and resources a defense contractor invests in bringing a tank, an attack aircraft, a communications system, or a submarine into readiness. On the other may lie the green fields of full production contracts, continuing profits from the project in question, esteem and new projects. In between is the sticky wicket of the testing process, which often unfolds in phases and can itself take large amounts of time. With so much at stake, serious pressures from varying directions surround OT&E, the gatekeeper. "You're trying to determine whether something in which an enormous investment has been made will do its job," Duncan says, "and whether it should be permitted to go into production with even more money spent to put it into the field." It's no surprise that a new weapon or system reaches the OT&E stage of its life accompanied by "a huge constituency build-up" embracing the engineering and manufacturing communities associated with it, the Congress, and elements within the Defense Department and the military services themselves.

Even before the end of the Cold War and related developments, the pace and volume of new weapons development was trending downward. But little suggests that this has lessened the intensity of the environment in which testing and evaluation take place. To protect the integrity of the process and provide some insulation for the OT&E director and staff, the establishing legislation requires that the selection of the director be a function of competence, not political affiliation. The president alone can appoint and remove directors and, in the latter case, must explain to the Congress. In reporting on a new weapon the director must state whether the testing and evaluation were adequate, and whether they confirm that the items or components actually tested are effective and suitable for combat. Identical reports go directly to the secretary of defense, the under secretary for acquisition, and to the armed services and appropriations subcommittees of the Congress; the secretary and under secretary may comment to the Congress on a report but they cannot change it. No full production contract can be signed until these procedures are complete.

But the testing process itself, says Deleon, "has not yet been self-enacting. There has had to be a series of initiatives where Congress has prescribed certain testing thresholds for systems before monies could be spent above a certain threshold." Ideally, he adds, "you'd want to see the system work so that those testing milestones would be accomplished without the Congress tying up the funds."

A mixed military and civilian staff of 40 assists the director of OT&E. Duncan has deputies in three main areas--strategic, conventional, and command, control, communications and intelligence. They are civilians in the Senior Executive Service. Reporting to them are action officers who oversee individual programs; these individuals are senior civilians or military officers at the colonel or Navy captain level. According to John E. Krings, director in 1985-1989, testing plans originate with the services but the director has final approval, which affords the vital opportunity to make certain that requirements are properly written, with adequate "checks and balances" throughout. It is the individual services which carry out and fund testing under OT&E supervision. A product designed to be used by all the services, perhaps in different versions, receives joint testing; such trials can extend over several years. The director also has responsibility for maintaining and supervising the operation of a dozen and a half major test ranges.

The only committee Duncan sits on, inside or outside the Pentagon, is the Defense Acquisition Board, chaired by the under secretary for acquisition. But his work takes him into countless meetings across the defense establishment concerned with a range of issues from technical problems to test plans and policy guidance and enforcement, as well as to the Hill in connection with specific programs. Since his office has only a relatively small administrative budget to manage beyond the budget for operating and improving the test ranges, no significant budget defense duties attach to the job.

Historically, the Defense Department's testing process has featured serious inadequacies and intense protectiveness among contractors and in the military services. Has the establishment of OT&E had the desired results? In Deleon's view, the office's annual report to the Congress "has turned out to be pretty good, and is getting better all the time." Essentially, he says, it identifies major weapons programs "and lists where the director thinks they are on that testing check list. Some get better grades than others. In the past we've used the list during budget mark-ups to decide where it's appropriate to cut funding." As for OT&E's effectiveness and clout within the defense community, "it's been a mixed result," he says. "You don't create a new organization in the Pentagon bureaucracy and expect it to be a power point overnight." But with "some pushing" from the Congress, he thinks the office is gaining impact.

He cites two considerations. "The first problem the director has to deal with is that he's there and reporting to the secretary of defense on the testing concerns and problem areas. If he's going to do his job, he needs to know what doesn't work and therefore needs more testing. His biggest problem right off the bat is that the services probably want to tell him as little as possible, or just enough to get by." This relates directly to what Deleon calls a line of demarcation in the Pentagon. It divides the "operators in the field who do the fighting and the flying" from the "program managers who basically want to get their programs through with the minimum amount of controversy." Collectively, this amounts to a departmental "schizophrenia" between wanting to make sure the technology works and wanting to make sure to meet the production schedule within cost. Of the three generally accepted measurements of the procurement process--cost, schedule and performance--the testers are really concerned with performance, the program managers with cost and schedule. Tests that reveal problems disrupt schedules and increase costs. "So it is not a natural instinct for the services to want to go to the chief tester and unload their problems."

In that context, it is worth noting the comments of Charles K. Watt, OT&E acting director in 1984. He stresses the importance for this position of "informal channels" that can function within the bureaucratic process to help get things done, and the establishment of personal relationships throughout the various Pentagon hierarchies. Trust and confidence among those involved in projects, and patience, are "essential ingredients," he says. But all decisions, he adds, must be backed by sound reasoning and facts.

A second problem in this job, Deleon says, has been getting the secretary of defense and his senior people to bring the director of operational testing into the life of weapons and systems in the early stages. When programs are discussed and critical decisions made, those involved should seek the tester's opinion and give it the proper weight, he believes. But this "was a change that took some getting used to."

Overall, Deleon suggests, the verdict on OT&E is still out. Because defense budgets are going down, the Pentagon has had to make "a lot of tough decisions on weapons," he says. But it has not yet had to make many tough decisions "on new weapons about to enter production and requiring decisions on whether their testing has been adequate. In that sense, I think that whether the Cheney Pentagon is fully utilizing the testing apparatus is an open question."

Key Relationships

Within the Department

Reports to: Secretary

Works closely with:

Deputy Secretary
Under Secretary, Acquisition
Director, Defense Research and Engineering
Research, development and acquisition officials in the office of   the
  secretary and within the military services
Defense Acquisition Board
Test range commanders
Directors, Air Force and other defense laboratories

Outside the Department

Members and staff, Senate and House armed services committees and
  defense appropriations subcommittees
Assistant Director, National Security Affairs, White House Office of Science
  and Technology Policy

Outside the Government

Professional scientific and engineering organizations and institutes; academic research and development staffs; test and evaluation officials of other governments and of the North Atlantic Treaty Organization

Profile of Current Director, Operational Test and Evaluation

Name:	Robert C. Duncan
Assumed Position:	1989
Career Summary:	Director, Defense Research and Engineering, 1987-89
	Assistant Secretary of Defense (Research and Technology), 1986-87
	Director, Defense Advanced Research Projects Agency, 1985-87
	Various positions at the Polaroid Corporation, 1968-85, including assistant vice president and program manager
	Various positions at NASA, 1964-68, including chief of the Guidance and Control Division and assistant director of the Electronics Research Center
	Special assistant to the Director, Defense Research and Engineering, 1961-63
	Chief of the Space Branch Programs, Office of the Chief of Naval Operations, 1961-63
	Naval officer and fighter pilot, 1945-60
Education:	U.S. Naval Academy, BS, 1945
	U.S. Naval Postgraduate School, BS, 1953
	Massachusetts Institute of Technology, MS, aeronautical engineering, 1954; PhD, aeronautical engineering, 1960

Directors, Operational Test and Evaluation Since 1983*

Administration	Name and Years Served	Present Position
Bush	Robert C. Duncan 1989 - present	Incumbent
Reagan	John E. Krings 1985 - 1989	Consultant Arlington, Va.
Reagan	Michael D. Hall (Acting) 1984 - 1985	Consultant Colorado Springs, Colo.

Reagan   Charles K. Watt (A)   President
                1984   Scientific Research Corp.
                                             Atlanta, Ga.

* The position was established in 1983 by the fiscal 1984 Defense Authorization Act

ASSISTANT SECRETARY, ACQUISITION
OFFICE OF THE SECRETARY OF THE AIR FORCE

Level IV - Presidential Appointment with Senate Confirmation

(The responsibilities and circumstances of these civilian positions in the Air Force, Army and Navy departments are similar. In chiefly addressing one of them, the profile that follows is nonetheless representative of the research, development and acquisition functions of all three.)

Major Responsibilities

- Direct the policy planning, timing and execution of all programs related to the research and development of weapons, weapons systems and support equipment, intelligence-related R&D, and to their acquisition. Ensure that they adhere to performance requirements and are delivered and handed over to the operating forces in functioning and supportable condition.

- See that the service's R&D and acquisition programs accord with policies and guidelines set by the office of the secretary of defense, coordinating in detailed fashion with the under secretary of defense for acquisition. Oversee the associated budget development, presentation and defense.

- Communicate effectively with the Congress on the concepts and goals involved in these activities. Establish and maintain close control of and accountability for the service's acquisition procedures.

Necessary Training, Experience, Skills

There are two mandatory credentials. The first is strong technical training, such as a PhD in an engineering field. Second is an extensive, production-floor background in industry. That should include a familiarity with systems and systems analysis, and a knowledge of presentation methods to ensure that proposals coming forward are properly prepared. It should also entail a thorough understanding of the transition between bench model and production phase, a veteran of one of the jobs says, "so that you have a feel for what industry is telling you in terms of credibility." Candidates who know the defense department, and have had exposure to research, development and acquisition processes in that context, have a clear advantage.

Insight

"We really only do two things here," says John J. Welch Jr., assistant secretary of the air force for acquisition since 1987. "We build the budget, and then we execute what Congress gives us." But under that modest description come $30-40 billion in annual weapons and weapons systems acquisitions and more than five million contractual actions a year. Welch's assignment involves, in his own words, "more jobs than you can shake a stick at."

Fundamentally, of course, he is the senior procurement executive of the air force, charged with "managing and ensuring an effective and efficient acquisition process." Acquisition, Welch notes, is a broad term that also covers science, technology, and logistics, especially the logistics support associated with weapons systems. But there are a number of collateral duties, among them U.S. representative to the NATO research and development group in Europe, and chairman of the executive committee for the F-16 multinational program.

In the acquisition area itself, Welch has two goals. One is to speed up the process. "It is taking longer and longer to get new systems from the time we think of them until our users get them, especially if they involve much R&D," he says. As these times stretch out, "you get into a loop where the technology is changing so fast that you want to get it to the field more quickly. And you find at the front end that you may be taking higher risks than you want because you don't know how long it's going to take." Objective: "shorten and simplify the cycle."

Second, Welch wants to strengthen communications to avoid "disconnects" between the people involved at various points along the acquisition track. At one end are users who know what they need in terms of the military capabilities of a given system. At the other are those who must "break that down and understand it in terms of its characteristics" in order to see what is available or can be developed in the universe of applied technology, and get it into the system and into production. "Many people are involved," Welch explains, "and you can get seams in the system. That is the potential for a disconnect," when for example components arrive before or after they are needed, or are not what they were expected to be, or cost more. "We're trying to work on that," Welch says. Further, he adds, investing time at the front end of the cycle, to understand not merely what the user wants by way of a weapon or a system but how it is to be employed, provides the opportunity to see how to solve problems and to "trade off" capabilities. He thinks that is "the highest-level investment we can make--getting everybody together and really talking it out," and not just getting "sort of a solution."

The progression from prototype to production is "where a lot of systems fall apart," in the view of Richard L. Rumpf, who in 1987 and 1989 was the navy's acting assistant secretary for research, engineering and systems, as it was then called. (The job's present title is research, development and acquisition--RDA--as is the army's equivalent position). Industry over promises, or the government underestimates, the transition capability of systems in the process of production, Rumpf says. That results "in many false starts, where major programs get way downstream and fall apart because industry couldn't make the shift from R&D to production because the R&D wasn't mature enough." He stresses the importance in these positions of a broad understanding of the art of defense acquisition that includes research, "getting one's hands dirty in the development phase of some kind of program, and understanding the transition aspects through some kind of industry background." The "real issue in this sort of job is sorting out the misrepresentations from the truth," he says, "and that takes somebody with experience. But if the person is only experienced on the production or sales side of industry and has never done any R&D, then there's really no appreciation for the length of time it takes in some cases to develop something, or test it, and so on." Can a career individual fill this job? "I'd say in some cases a career person would be better if there has been some previous outside hands-on experience in industry or a laboratory."

In addition to the effort at better communication within his air force domain, Welch discusses other ideas for improvement. Among these is development of "a more consolidated layer of management," one feature of which is to "take some brigadier and major generals with good program experience and cluster programs under them and give them more direct oversight. This is the Program Executive Officer system." He wants to "take a broader look at investment strategy" and get "a better insight" into the balance between "modernization for the future and what we're doing today." While there has been "a fair swing" in importance from strategic to conventional weapons, Welch thinks "we've still got to keep our strategic modernization going." He thinks better coordination is necessary between headquarters and air force laboratories around the country, and believes the big challenge in the laboratories "is not to work on things that are out in the commercial sector that we can go and buy," such as the better microprocessing systems produced commercially.

Rumpf touches on the same point. "We don't yet use enough commercial sector products, which would save money," he says. "Instead,

we concentrate on what we call mil-spec things, which are over-specified."
At the same time, he emphasizes, "we must be very careful--and here's
where the astuteness of the individual in this job comes in--that the
military is not fighting with commercial products that can't take the
environment; for example, computer disks that clog up with the fine dust
of Saudi Arabia."

The notion of balance also figures in Welch's comments on systems
design. "A lot of our science and technology really goes into trying to get
the right information infused at the right place--trying to make sure we
don't go too far. We've found that if you let people go all the way, they
forget there's a pilot in the airplane, or a missile officer at the console.
So we have to be certain that we're not reaching out to do things we don't
need to do, or increase the risk." At the same time, Defense R&D and
acquisition people hear a lot of advice about taking too much risk, he
comments. "Well, this is a risk business. We would be an absolute failure
if we weren't in it. Call it managing risk. We're looking for that edge,
that performance necessary to win."

Welch says further that there are "a lot of things we can learn from
business," such as recognizing that "there are priorities to things like
schedule, to performance, and to cost, and you ought to trade those things
off, not hang into just one." In the military services that's usually hard to
do "because for every mach number, every weight number, every bomb
load number, there's an advocate in this building."

In the air force acquisition office, programs divide into "major" and
"other-than-major" categories. There are 42 in the first group, says
Welch, defined "by the number of dollars we spend on the research,
development, testing, engineering and procurement that's committed to
us." The B-2 bomber is an example. Such projects collectively represent
50 percent of the acquisition money his operation spends and get most of
the publicity. Other-than-major programs number about 700 and "in
many cases our technical challenges are in the smaller programs" such as
the mission planning systems in individual aircraft. The navy's RDA
budget is currently around $35 billion; the army's, about $14.5 billion. In
Rumpf's time, the mainline responsibility was "to take a system from the
birth of a concept and nurture it to the point of full production, when we
handed it off." Now, he says, "the job entails not only that, but staying
with a system all the way through its life in the fleet."

The biggest recent change that has intervened for all of these
positions, however, involved making the acquisition assistant secretaries
of each military department responsible not only to their own service
secretaries but interactive directly with the under secretary of defense for
acquisition (USDA). Explaining this, Welch says the defense acquisition
community operates in "a different execution posture" in the wake of the
Packard Commission, the Goldwater-Nickles Act and the defense

management review (reorganization and reform efforts partly concerned with correcting Defense Department acquisition procedures that have bred scandal on more than one recent occasion). "There has been a very powerful move to associate accountability and responsibility very closely and identifiably, a lot of process control and improvement," he adds.

In relations with the Congress, Welch says, "I have never felt lonely." He describes one of his biggest single challenges as "trying to understand and work effectively with this word oversight." He puts the number of committees with some sort of oversight over his work at 54, says he testified 57 times in 1989, and that his office was involved in 2,000 briefings on Capitol Hill in 1990. But Welch doesn't object. "It's very much a part of this job, and even in the process of being confirmed you commit to being responsive, because that's what their job is." His list of other overseers and quasi-overseers is long: personal and committee staff, the General Accounting Office, special investigations, less formal groups, institutes around town doing studies, and the defense and air force inspectors general and general counsels.

Apart from the Hill, Welch spends considerable time visiting the contracting firms which are his suppliers, and sees their representatives in Washington frequently. He tries to visit all air force laboratories once a year. Air force acquisition offices in five European capitals maintain an information exchange on technology developments among NATO allies. "We are the science and technology spokespeople for the air force," Welch says, "we put out an annual policy statement, and we fund the laboratories through the Air Force Systems Command. I think the air force was really founded on science and technology."

Rumpf's activities as head of navy RDA followed a similar pattern. "If you're a champion of joint programs, you really have to interact very heavily with the other services," he points out. "You can't dictate; you have to build coalitions." Among the tasks that involved him as the principal deputy assistant secretary in the navy's RDA office was cross-fertilizing knowledge between the navy and its contractors about stealth characteristics for aircraft from a technical perspective. That led to the birth of other kinds of advanced projects and intelligence work, known as "compartmented" (i.e., highly classified) programs, which Rumpf can't discuss. He had charge of all R&D in these programs, a responsibility that now resides solely with the assistant secretary. "The assistant secretary has to have that responsibility across all platforms and all warfare areas," he says.

About 500 people work in Welch's office and, he relates, "you can be sure that whatever hours I spend here, they spend more." Their talents vary, he says; many are not scientists or technologists. He tries to keep a balance between the staff's military and civilian components. The military staff are a combination of "people who have been in science or technology a good part of their careers and people with operational background--right out of the cockpit. I think the mix is good." Among several current training programs, the air force acquisition office began offering in 1989 a nine-year program to attract qualified individuals with undergraduate degrees in which they obtain admission to graduate school, join the acquisition office, and alternate service as staff members with earning their doctoral degrees. Rumpf says the navy RDA office is able to attract technically qualified civilian staff, but retaining them is difficult amid competition with private-sector salaries. Typically, they come from national federal laboratories or from other military service contexts prior to which they had acquired industry experience. This recruiting and turnover pattern of may change with the decline of defense budgets.

What about the day-to-day problems of these jobs? "In some ways it's irritating because there are just too many agendas," Welch says. "I was in the aerospace industry all my life. It's very different to come here. In a corporate meeting, there might be differences of opinion and maybe even different ways suggested for doing things, but generally there was a common objective. Here, you go to a meeting without any idea of the agenda of half the people there." The instability of the resources picture is also a hampering factor. "Sixty percent of our budget line items are changed every year. When you remember that we're working about eight or nine years of budgets at any one time, spending out the last three and working on the next six, that's a lot of instability." Rumpf also found "a lot of frustration" in the job "because it's a pressure cooker" not designed for those who can't live with the tension. Adding to this are the restrictions that occupancy of positions like these puts on future civilian employment; they are a product of the effort to remove or alleviate perceived conflicts of interest inherent in the "revolving-door" syndrome linking the Defense Department and the defense contracting industry. But Rumpf says he "would take the job again, in a heartbeat." There is satisfaction, he says, "in working with disparate ideas and trying to pull things together, to make things happen. It's kind of like being a teacher."

As for issues the navy RDA office will have to deal with in the near future, Rumpf sees several that apply as well to the R&D/acquisition operations of the other military services. First is the obvious fact of the decreasing size of the services and of their budgets, which will force choices of priority. The navy is faced with that "in spades," he says. Second, the threat to U.S. security now comes less from a single large adversary than from many small ones. "We need to understand the nature and degree of sophistication" of these various potential sources of danger to enable the United States to maintain technical superiority. Next is the need, mentioned earlier, to increase the services' procurement of commercially-produced systems and equipment.

Finally, Rumpf believes, "with the opening up of eastern Europe and the emergence of a multipolar world, we need to understand how to work more with our allies, who have a lot of excellent technology that we keep at arm's length. Better electro-optics have been developed in France than in this country, for example." Occupants of the service acquisition positions, he says, "must consider how to draw in foreign involvement in ways that don't compromise the capability of a weapons system by being vulnerable to a potential enemy. We don't have the money to invest in the development of certain pieces of technology. If the allies have already done it, why not take advantage of that?"

Key Relationships

Within the Service

Reports to: Secretary of the service

Works closely with:

Under Secretary
Assistant secretaries with responsibilities in financial management, operational command, control, and communications; logistics; engineering; installations; and automation

Within the Department and Elsewhere in Government

Under Secretary, Acquisition, and staff
Director, Defense Research and Engineering
Counterparts in other military departments
Assistant Secretary, Program Analysis and Evaluation
Assistant Secretary, Command, Control, Communications and Intelligence
Comptroller
Inspector General

Outside the Government

Wide range of officials in a variety of defense contracting and related firms; corporate trade associations; military acquisition officials of allied countries; military and technology trade press

Profile of Current Assistant Secretary, Research, Development and Acquisition, Department of the Air Force

Name: John J. Welch Jr.

Assumed Position: 1987

Career Summary: Various positions with the Chance Vought Corporation (later Ling
                       Temco-Vought), 1951-1969 and 1970-1987, including vice
                       president for programs, corporate vice president, and senior vice
                       president
                       Chief scientist, department of the air force, 1969-70

Education: Massachusetts Institute of Technology, BS, engineering, 1951

DIRECTOR
INFORMATION SYSTEMS FOR COMMAND, CONTROL, COMMUNICATIONS AND COMPUTERS
OFFICE OF THE SECRETARY OF THE ARMY

(The Air Force, Army and Navy departments manage their complex communications and automated data systems for command and control in combat and for administrative services in similar, though not structurally identical, ways. This profile chiefly describes one of the positions in question. The counterpart Air Force functions reside with a deputy chief of systems for command, control, communications and computers; in the Navy, it is the director, space and electronic warfare in the office of the chief of naval operations. Career flag officers, usually at the three-star rank, fill these jobs, appointed from within their services. While the positions obviously differ in some important specifics, they have much in common in terms of scientific\technical content, mission, problems, and working relationships. The intention here is to convey a general sense of the function as it exists in all three military services.)

Major Responsibilities

- Plan, design, operate and maintain effective combat communications between field commanders and headquarters units at the tactical and strategic levels, using modernized battlefield command and control systems linked to automated data processing capabilities. Supervise the automation and standardization of data management for administrative functions--logistics, personnel, pay, and health care.

- Oversee the acquisition, operation and maintenance of equipment and systems to provide these services, including planning and budget development and defense.

- Work closely with the assistant secretary of defense for command, control, communications and intelligence, and with counterpart officials of the other military services. Maintain regular contact with military communications and information systems officers of other governments as appropriate, and of the staffs of formal military alliances in which the United States participates.

Necessary Training, Experience, Skills

A substantial background in communications and electronics, preferably with an engineering degree and an accent on systems orientation, heads the list. Almost as important is a deep understanding of the military service in question; in fact, these responsibilities are best served by senior career professionals with field combat and command experience. But stay away from "technocrats," one incumbent cautions. He sums up the right occupant as "someone who has commanded at all levels, knows the service, has a systems approach to things, and can handle technical matters with facility."

Insight

Like the Office of the Secretary of Defense (OSD) for the department as a whole, the military services assign the direction of their individual command, control, and communications ("C3") functions to a single office usually headed by a military official of flag rank. To those responsibilities, the Air Force and Army have added a fourth "C"-- management of automated information systems supporting both combat operations and administrative support activities. In the Navy, this job does not include the automation component--that is found in a separate office--but has a space warfare responsibility.

"Basically," says Lt. Gen. Jerome B. Hilmes, the Army's C4 chief since 1989, "I'm the Army's communicator and automater," a mission that "runs from cradle to grave." The responsibility includes, first, the "architecture"--the engineering of sophisticated, electronically or automatically assisted systems for both battlefield and management activities so that they interact, rather than interfere, with one another. Second, the C4 director must manage the acquisition of the hardware and technology that go into the systems. As Hilmes outlines it, "we plan, we program the monies on the Hill and do the budget fights with OSD and the Hill; we get the money to our acquisition people--the program managers and the procurement executive officers; we acquire the equipment, and we field it to the troops. Then we operate and maintain it."

In combat, the key objective of Army C4 is to realize the full potential of automated, linked communications and information systems put at the disposal of commanders at both the tactical and strategic levels. That means, for example, electronic maps in tactical operations centers on which Army field commanders can view what's happening in real time, issue orders, and see the results; as well as talk to each other, to higher authority behind the front, to combat theater commanders further back and, via satellite, to the highest command levels in Washington and elsewhere. It also means combat support in areas like logistics where automated data management, in Hilmes' words, "keeps track of your beans and bullets so you don't run out at a critical time."

The most recent example of Army C4 operations in a wartime environment is the Persian Gulf crisis of 1990-91. "Both communications and automation were big challenges," Hilmes says; and, at least in his description, the Army met them well. When the 82nd airborne division arrived in Saudi Arabia, it took only one communications soldier to set up immediate communications with Ft. Bragg, North Carolina, using a suitcase-sized tactical satellite receiver. "But the U.S. buildup was very rapid and very large," Hilmes goes on, "and it quickly became a matter of having enough band width on the satellites and enough tactical receivers down there, and then getting out of the single-channel and into a multichannel, high volume, big connectivity mode. So we got the bigger dishes over there." As the new headquarters rolled in, including the central command complex of General Schwarzkopf, "we were able to keep enough capability up there via satellite that we had all those headquarters connected not only among themselves within the theater, but back here to various base camps in the United States and to the Pentagon."

On the automation side, each unit deployed to the Gulf took with it the personnel, pay, and other records from in its normal garrison environment, loaded in a "ruggedized" computer usable in the field. That enabled the units to continue to maintain and work with their own data on the scene. "But very quickly, just as with the communications, as we got more and more units over there, we had an interconnectivity problem," Hilmes relates. "I now had 24 battalions of the XVIII Airborne Corps wanting, say, to talk with the corps paymaster." C4 had to build up a more "robust" automation network, carrying it eventually to the point where "you could pass all the pay data in that corps back to Ft. Benjamin Harrison in real time, over a satellite with high data volume rate capabilities." This did not develop as quickly as the communications "but the logistics systems, the pay, the personnel systems were all working."

In 1989, when Vice Admiral Jerry Tuttle took over the directorate in the office of the chief of naval operations (CNO) with responsibilities roughly equivalent to Hilmes', its title was space, command and control. Not long after, as the result of a study requested by the CNO, Tuttle's office acquired a new name--space and electronic warfare--and took its place alongside other established Navy warfare disciplines--anti-submarine, anti-surface unit, and anti-air. In the process of transforming the role and operations of the organization, one of Tuttle's early moves was to shift his telecommunications from narrative ("the wrong type of communications") and paper ("the wrong type of format") into data. "In ten years, 90 percent of our communications will be data," he says. He combined the office's telecommunications and data systems operations into the Computer and Telecommunications Command. A second principal division handles the standardization and interoperability of the Navy's C4 systems.

The third is the Navy Space Command. On that dimension of his job, Tuttle says, "we had space in our title before, but we were observers at best. No one in the CNO's office knew where to go for policy, guidance, and leadership in space. So we took that role. Not just communications, but navigation, weather satellites, intelligence sensors, anything in space resides here now. We're doing a better job, but we have a long way to go, and a lot to catch up with in space."

One important task was to develop the profile of a space and electronic warfare commander. This prototype ultimately emerged as a combination of skills from other areas of Navy expertise with care taken, says Tuttle, "that it wasn't dominated by a particular discipline, be it a cryptologist, an old electronic warfare aviator, a cruiser skipper or whatever." Commanders fitting the description would be able to ensure the operation of C4, disrupt an adversary's systems, exploit space and deny it to opponents, and locate and target an adversary while avoiding one's own detection and targeting. Today, Tuttle adds, "we have some bright young flag officers who are doing this pretty well."

Tuttle likes to describe his area of responsibility as ranging from transoceanic cables to the Voyager spacecraft, with an electromagnetic spectrum "between direct current and light." He wants the Navy "to recognize that if they have a telephone problem or a satellite communication problem, then it's my problem and they can come to me to resolve it." He reports "a beautiful working relationship with the systems commanders, the technical people who engineer. I build the architecture, they do the engineering."

Hilmes lists two major challenges in advancing the state of the Army's C4 art. One is making certain that battlefield functions like fire support, air defense, maneuver, intelligence and combat service support are "appropriately interconnected" with C4's automated battlefield systems "and come along in an integrated fashion." The communication links-- such as "area comm," a system analogous to civilian cellular telephone, the new combat net radio, and the Army Data Distribution Center--"are generally out front" compared to the automated battlefield functional systems, Hilmes says. "That's about $20 billion worth of stuff we're talking about. Bringing it all to fruition soon and in an integrated fashion is easily my biggest problem, and the one most directly related to the combat readiness of our units. If that comes about as we anticipate and commanders can truly have a common picture of the adversary and friendly situation at all levels of command, then we'll have really taken a giant step ahead in shortening our commanders' decision cycle, and putting them inside the cycle of any adversary."

The second challenge involves what Hilmes calls "the garrison, or business, side of the house" and its approximate 3,000 automated systems of the kind found throughout the private sector. His objective here is to eliminate duplication and "get the Army on one coherent architecture, using one set of standardized data elements--an Army data dictionary, if you will--so that we can fully share information in paying and training people, administering contracts, conducting audits" and other management functions. That would allow the Army, he thinks, to manage information at half its current cost. "We can probably save a billion dollars a year if we can get our business practices standardized and on open systems platforms instead of vendor-dependent platforms."

On the Navy side, Tuttle's current budget is $3.2 billion and, in line with general defense funding, has been in a pattern of decrease. "I'm taking big-time cuts," he says, "but I can tailor my investment strategy accordingly." His rule of thumb is that the electronic components of any item that won't be delivered for four years "will be dated. And what you buy in state of the art components is reliability." Since 1970, he asserts, that reliability has gone up by a factor of ten to the sixth power, permitting changes in maintenance and training strategies. "The way I live within my budget and still modernize the fleet is by closing schoolhouses that are teaching antiquity," he says. "If I can buy an electronic component that is not going to fail during the enlistment of a given individual, why teach him Ohm's law?"

Hilmes' budget is also declining overall from a fiscal 1991 level of $3.2 billion, due partly to recent completion of the acquisition phase of the multibillion dollar area comm system. He views his basic budget situation, however, as "holding where we are." The Army C4 operation employs 650 people, 150 at the Pentagon and the rest in three other locations in the Washington area and in New Jersey. Seventy percent of this staff is civilian, including seven "civilian generals" in the Senior Executive Service. Hilmes is pleased with the civilian-military mix. "You've got the civilians, who don't tend to move and who can be deeper experts in some of these very complex, high-tech areas. But you also have, for instance, the young major coming in from the field, fresh from field tactics and smart enough to get into the management issues at hand. He's got the civilian there to get him deeper into the technical aspects as well as for the institutional memory." The average division director is a full colonel, and "behind every colonel is a GM-15, which is about the same grade in the civil service. And that's not by accident. So I call it a really good marriage that gets the best of both worlds."

About 67 percent of Hilmes' professional staff have master's degrees. "And you can make the military system respond to you very well," he adds. "Maybe I need an officer with a master's or a background in spectrum management. I can get that officer. He's been out with the troops, but he's also had a tour in spectrum management and has a degree in that or a related area." This situation is tougher where the civilian staff is concerned. "I've got mostly good, dedicated civilians," Hilmes says, "but they tend to get captured by this rat race in the Pentagon and if they don't really work hard at it--there's so much going on that it's hard for them to make the time to do it--they get out of date fast in this technology. So it's a tough problem, but overall I feel pretty good about the staff." Faced with very complicated acquisitions, he notes, he can call in a team from a private-sector defense consulting organization "and get a second opinion, simply because when you launch a billion-dollar program you want to make sure you're approximately right."

For Tuttle, "the most difficult problem I'm confronted with is how to train the people that populate the complicated community of space and electronic warfare. Especially in automated data processing. ADP is basically doubling in speed and capacity every 18 months. You have to stay on the leading edge of the technology and get a generation of people that grew up on Pac Man and are better able to assimilate." Further, his command "has a tremendous void in satellite communications," one he thinks will take some time to fill. "What I inherited was people who knew the funding profiles of their programs but didn't know the programs. I'm more interested in people knowing their programs from a technological and requirements standpoint."

Hilmes says he typically has two sets of testimony to the Congress (armed services and appropriations subcommittees of both houses), one in early spring to defend the new budget request, and again later to answer questions and work out "snags." In the automation area, these appearances are usually in tandem with the assistant secretary of defense for C3 and intelligence. For the communications component of his budget, Hilmes testifies jointly with the Army assistant secretary for research, development and acquisition. "When he goes to present to the committees the Army's case for acquiring things, I go with him to speak to the C4 part of that picture." According to Hilmes, all the military services follow the same practice.

"Trying to bring a large bureaucracy like the U.S. Army into the information age in a really efficient way is a challenge of the first order," Hilmes feels. "There are so many pieces impacting everybody. That and the people you work with, in the building and in the private sector, in other countries and other armies, are a major reason I think most of us military professionals are still in the Army after 30 years and more. It's really personally satisfying, and right now we work at it 70 or 80 hours a week. You couldn't do that if you weren't having fun."

Key Relationships

Within the Service

Reports to: Secretary of the Army

Works closely with:

Under Secretary
Assistant secretaries for research, development and acquisition; installations and logistics; financial management; and manpower and reserve affairs
Deputy chiefs of staff, operations and intelligence

Within the Department and Elsewhere in Government

Assistant Secretary, Command, Control, Communications and Intelligence, Office of the Secretary of Defense
Director, Defense Research and Engineering
Counterparts in other military departments
Director, Defense Communications Agency
Director, National Security Agency
Chief Scientist, NSA
Deputy Director, Science and Technology, Central Intelligence Agency

Outside the Government

Communications, electronics and computer/data processing industries and their trade associations; professional groups such as the National Security Information Association and the Armed Forces Communications and Electronics Association; counterpart officials in the defense establishments of other countries and of military alliances and arrangements to which the United States is a party

Profile of Current Director, Information Systems for Command, Control, Communications and Computers, Office of the Secretary of the Army

Name: Lt. Gen. Jerome B. Hilmes

Assumed Position: 1989

Career Summary: Career officer, U.S. Army, 1959-present, including deputy assistant chief of engineers; commander, southwestern and north central divisions, Army Corps of Engineers; commander of Army systems testing and evaluation, Office of the chief of staff; and field commands in Europe and Vietnam

Education: U.S. Military Academy, BS, 1959

University of Iowa, MS, 1964 and PhD, 1965, both in civil
engineering
Completed U.S. Army Engineer School and Command and General
Staff College; and Naval War College

14

DEPARTMENT OF EDUCATION

ASSISTANT SECRETARY
EDUCATIONAL RESEARCH AND IMPROVEMENT

Level IV - Presidential Appointment with Senate Confirmation

Major Responsibilities

- Oversee the activities of a six-division agency engaged in education research, statistics, outreach, information dissemination and grant making. Coordinate and direct this work to equip the education community with better tools in understanding its tasks, improving its methods, and devising innovative and more effective solutions to problems. Work with other federal agencies with specialized responsibilities in these areas.

- Counsel the secretary of education in policy matters where knowledge and perceptions gained in these duties are relevant.

- Assist in representing the department's agenda and views to institutions, educators, parents and other constituencies throughout the country. Address broad areas of the government's education policies with general audiences in a public affairs context.

Necessary Training, Experience, Skills

Emphasis in this position goes more to practical skills and experience in the field than to formal credentials like a doctorate in education. Academic training or administrative background obviously helps to earn standing with the community this position focuses on. But credibility--which is important--can also come through work in the education-oriented business or nonprofit sectors. Either way, former assistant secretaries and observers of the job also value specifics like experience as an education researcher or in managing research; a commitment to research that can be used; and a sense of the nature and realities of the American school system. They stress an ability to work productively with diverse groups and viewpoints. As one of them puts it, "political skill with a small p is absolutely essential in the mine fields out there, in terms of the folks you have to deal with internally and externally." Scientific credentials are not prerequisite, but the job's occupant must be able to understand and evaluate the agency's scientists and their work.

Insight

Only in the last couple of years has this job enjoyed the combination of time, resolve, and resources to generate momentum and impact. During its first year, 1980, the primary concern was to assemble and make sense of the many disparate programs placed under the jurisdiction of the new Office of Educational Research and Improvement (OERI) and give them a conceptual framework and direction. The position then limped uncertainly through a period when the existence of the department itself came into serious early question and its programs under severe review. Today, encouraged by factors like the administration's support for increased funding for fiscal 1991 and 1992 (1992 request: $296 million), the agency is again attempting to do the kind of work envisaged by its early leaders. OERI was "a demoralized agency," says Gerald Sroufe of the American Educational Research Association, "but I think it's coming back."

F. James Rutherford was the position's first occupant in 1980. It emerged, he says, from a long period of "trying to invent the department of education and what its purposes would be," and the 40-plus separate program elements within the new OERI didn't connect with each other. He felt then, and still believes, that the department of education's best chance to help "reshape" American education "was for this particular unit to provide the intellectual pizazz, the sense of direction to move the department to be seen as something more than just a source of funds or of help in making up for some of the inequities in the system. We had to design the future and build up some public receptivity to a more innovative federal presence in education."

Trying to rake OERI's bits and pieces of programs together, he also thought the agency should focus on "how to get the kind of information and knowledge needed to help the vast education system improve itself -- not only what you need to collect, but how to shape it so that it comes to practitioners in a form they can use." He looked ahead to a new kind of relationship with the consumers of his office's products. In it, "the practitioners help to determine the kind of knowledge and insights and information they need, which drives your collection and research process." In turn, "the articulation of the research findings and the analysis reshapes the thinking of the practitioners, and you begin to build in a positive feedback, feed-forward spiral."

In the ensuing years, ideas like these lost headway. Dilemmas like the one cited by former Assistant Secretary Donald J. Senese (1981-85) clouded the scene. "At the same time that the Office of Management and Budget was recommending phasing out the library program," he recalls, "Congress was reauthorizing the program each year and increasing the money for it." He was thus administering money his own superiors didn't think was necessary. "And the difficulty was that if you were going to present positive accomplishments of the program, you had to do it in a way that didn't sound as if you needed the money for the next year."

Under Christopher T. Cross, assistant secretary from 1989 to mid-1991, OERI in fact began to move forward. But Cross saw his first task as restoring confidence and morale to the 450 people who staff OERI's six units---the National Center for Education Statistics; the offices of Research, Information Services, Library Programs, and Programs for the Improvement of Practice; and the Fund for the Improvement and Reform of Schools and Teaching (FIRST).

The next step, Cross says, "was to reform the agency to center it much more on helping the larger education community, to make it think from the level of the practitioner." The traditional posture of working only with the education research constituency, in his view, "got OERI nowhere. It hasn't helped the field any because just talking to yourself doesn't advance the state of change in the educational world at all." It's a world that reaches beyond schools and teachers; Cross tried also to "begin to be of service to parents, so that the data we produce will help better inform them in terms of their role as parents and of the education of their children."

He put early emphasis on two approaches to this. One was greater dissemination of the wide variety of information produced by the office's six divisions. "If it just sits here, published or not, it's not getting to people. So I tried to get it out, connect our work with people in the field, the policy community, the parents." As one example, OERI in 1990 published a book on helping children learn geography that was the second best-selling book put out by the government that year--10,000 copies in August alone, "incredible for a government publication."

Cross's second initial emphasis went to collaboration with other organizations. "The issues we're faced with in education don't especially lend themselves to being fixed within the bureaucratic boxes of an agency or subagency or any particular set of institutions," he says. "You really have to reach beyond that." Accordingly, the agency has collaborated extensively with the National Science Foundation (NSF), with the department of health and human services (HHS), labor department, the National Aeronautics and Space Administration, the arts and humanities endowments, and the energy department. The work with the NSF has included joint funding of projects managed by the American Association for the Advancement of Science (AAAS) and the Mathematics Science Education Board. It enables those bodies, says Cross, "to really develop better textbooks on mathematics and science, better curricula materials for kids to use in schools."

Activities like work with the President's science adviser and the National Space Council tend to give this position the quality of math and science czar at Education. The assistant secretary also chairs a subcommittee working group of the Federal Coordinating Council for Science, Engineering and Technology that is reviewing all federal education programs in science and mathematics. In his first year, Cross concentrated on such matters as OERI's funding for 35 research centers and laboratories. The job took him on four trips overseas in that period, and public affairs activity increased steadily. "The area is one that draws a lot of interest because we're the locus of a lot of things in the public arena," he says. "I represented the department during the development of the National Education Goals, a process that involved the White House and the National Governors Association." He spent an estimated 20 percent of his time in public appearances, and another 20 percent in the Congressional dimension of the job, including budget defense. The job's chief points of contact on the Hill are the Senate Labor and Human Resources Committee, the Senate and House Appropriations subcommittees for Labor, HHS and Education, and the House committees on Education and Labor, and Science, Space and Technology.

One of OERI's two principal scientific units, the National Center for Education Statistics (NCES), is now a $60-million operation that Cross predicts will exceed $100 million by 1995, comparable to the Bureau of Labor Statistics. The Office of Research, second, is the agency's educational research capability. Among these two divisions and in other aspects of his work, the assistant secretary manages or encounters a wide variety of scientists. In the NCES program, "he has to deal both with social scientists and psychometricians," says Sroufe. "And in the present concern with math and science, he has to deal with hi-tech people in Labor and Energy. Partly by default but partly because of his position, he's the one working with Energy, not anybody on the secretary of education's own staff, so he gets into the hard science aspects." Sroufe thinks a technical individual with skills broader than his or her own discipline might survive in the job, "but it would be extremely difficult for someone to go in there who was just a psychometrician and could not see the value of the social sciences, for example."

Yet the important credential, Rutherford believes, is not substantive scientific training, but an informed perception of the American school system. "You have to know it is a complex system, and that it doesn't always operate the way it claims to operate. The job requires somebody with a pretty sophisticated notion of the realities of the system, where and how decisions get made, and how it ramifies up and down--the schools, the districts, classrooms, the states, the federal role."

Because of OERI's importance within the education bureaucracy, Sroufe points out, this assistant secretary naturally has a close working relationship with the secretary. "Therefore he has a closer relationship with the White House than most of the other agencies at Education do, and that means he has to be sensitive. It creates both constraints and opportunities. They use him a lot, he stands in for the secretary, he's kind of the first among equals at the assistant secretary level. The kind of information he deals with makes him the logical person when the department has to come up with some policy. They're going to call the person who does research and improvement because he's got his hands into so many things." It's a much more visible position, Sroufe says, and requires the ability to move smoothly between the department, the administration and the education community.

Besides its chief, OERI has a number of other noncareer staff, including the deputy. Cross reports complete support from above in moving people in or out of those slots, even though "you obviously had issues to deal with" on politically-appointed jobs. The position also has exempted hiring authority and Cross brought in more than 30 people without going through the Civil Service system. Conversations with some who have headed or observed OERI give mixed reviews to the overall quality of the staff. "One thing that is moderately inhibiting," Sroufe observes, "is that the department and OERI still get must-hires from the White House. They tend to have skills that are not immediately useful." At the same time, he asserts, OERI as a whole "is understaffed. They have gained many programs but have hardly changed the staff at all." Rutherford, while stating that the agency "has always had some good people over there, people who don't get much attention from the outside world," also thinks the department generally is short of individuals knowledgeable about science and mathematics education. While the assistant secretary job itself does not need scientific training, Rutherford sees need for "a cadre of people, including senior people, who know the territory, who have a deep understanding of how science works, what the stakes are, how it relates to medicine and engineering."

At the same time, welcoming the renewed emphasis on "providing a sense of esprit within the agency," Sroufe also praises current efforts to get OERI into two areas he thinks the department itself has neglected. These are early childhood education, and more and improved use of technology. "In both," he says, "Cross has worked hard to reach a position where he can be a player, but it's certainly not part of the department. So it's important to have people in that job with a sense of what is going on and how to change the bureaucracy to address new needs."

Looking at the circular evolution in how the position has been conceived over the past decade, Rutherford thinks the loop is now complete. He sees "very hard efforts to build a really forward-looking, coherent purpose for OERI." The notion is back in favor, he says, "that one of the key parts of the job is to provide an intellectual conceptualization of the federal education role."

Key Relationships

Within the Department

Reports to: Secretary

Works closely with:

Under Secretary
Deputy Under Secretary, Planning, Budget and Evaluation
Assistant Secretary, Elementary and Secondary Education
Assistant Secretary, Special Education and Rehabilitative Services

Outside the Department

Associate Director (Education), White House Office of Science and
   Technology Policy
Assistant Director, Education and Human Resources, National Science
   Foundation
Assistant Secretary, Planning and Evaluation, Department of Health and
   Human Services
Staff, White House Office of Science and Technology Policy
Assistant Secretary, Employment and Training, Department of Labor
Chair, National Endowment for the Arts
Chair, National Endowment for the Humanities

Outside the Government

American Association for the Advancement of Science, American Educational Research Association, and numerous other organizations focused on various aspects of education, especially in the elementary-secondary sector

Profile of Current Assistant Secretary
Research and Improvement

Name: Diane S. Ravitch

Assumed Position: 1991

Career Summary: Adjunct professor, history and education, Teachers College,
                      Columbia University, 1975-91
                      Author, editor, lecturer on education topics, including principal
                      writer, California K-12 history-social science curriculum; chair,
                      Educational Excellence Network; chair, American Federation of
                      Teachers Education for Democracy project; and co-chair,
                      National Academy of Education task force on the Future of
                      Educational Research Priorities

Education: Wellesley College, BA, 1960
                      Columbia University, PhD , history, 1975

Assistant Secretaries, Educational Research and Improvement
Since 1980*

Administration	Name and Years Served	Present Position
Bush	Diane S. Ravitch 1991 - present	Incumbent
Bush	Christopher T. Cross 1989 - 1991	Executive Director, Education Initiative Business Roundtable Washington, D.C.
Bush	Patricia M. Hines (Acting) 1988 - 1989	Deputy Asst. Secretary Department of the Army
Reagan	Chester E. Finn Jr. 1985 - 1988	Director, Educational Excellence Network Vanderbilt University Washington, D.C.
Reagan	Donald J. Senese 1981 - 1985	Deputy Assistant Secretary Territorial & Intl. Affairs Department of the Interior

Carter	F. James Rutherford	Project Director
	1980	Education 2061,
		American Association for the
		Advancement of Science
		Washington, D.C.

* Position created by the Department of Education Organization Act, PL 96-88, October, 1979

15

DEPARTMENT OF ENERGY

ASSISTANT SECRETARY, DEFENSE PROGRAMS

Level IV - Presidential Appointment with Senate Confirmation

Major Responsibilities

- Direct the research, design, development, production and testing of nuclear weapons for national defense; their modernization as required; and the maintenance, surveillance and security of the weapons stockpile. Carry out this work in accordance with presidential directives, developed with the department of defense, that govern the size and characteristics of the nuclear weapons inventory.

- Through the Office of Defense Programs, manage the extensive complex of research laboratories, reactor sites, and production and testing facilities that constitutes the nuclear weapons program. Oversee the productive employment of a 100,000-plus nationwide work force, half of them contractor personnel, with a very substantial proportion of scientific and technical professionals.

- Assure the safe custody, control and ultimate disposal of facilities within the weapons complex that have been or will be closed for reasons of safety, obsolescence and surplus capacity. Take a central role in the related and expanding program of environmental clean-up and recovery required by the operations of the complex in the past. Help to coordinate this effort with other agencies in and outside of the department of energy.

- Supervise the imminent and fundamental restructuring of the complex, proposed in early 1991 by the secretary of energy and at this writing under congressional and public examination and debate.

Necessary Training, Experience, Skills

There is almost no question that this assistant secretary needs a very strong technical or scientific background. Some who know the job well say it needs a nuclear physicist or engineer. Others add specifically that its occupant should have a working knowledge of reactor operations, such as that gained in the weapons program itself or in the Navy nuclear program bequeathed by Hyman Rickover (where the job's current occupant spent two-thirds of his Navy career).

But there are other important, newer requirements dictated by the massive changes that for several years have been overtaking the nuclear weapons program. "Since James Watkins (became secretary of energy), the major responsibility in this job has been environmental cleanup," one observer points out, "and the person in that slot ideally should have good environmental credentials as well." A knowledgeable congressional committee staff member thinks competence in the health and safety requirements imposed by nuclear materials and reactor operations is also necessary, since safety of the production facilities will take "massive amounts" of the individual's time. This source also stresses an ability to communicate with and assure the public on these matters. And one former occupant of the job offers this comment: "We didn't worry 10 or 15 years ago whether something we planned had more Republican or Democratic support. We had a mission and we went and did it. Now you can't do that. You have to look at the political ramifications of everything you do. That's a major change. It means the guy running the place has to have political savvy as well as some background in the system. So, where historically it was scientists and engineers, you now need someone with a technical background plus a few street smarts."

Insight

Three factors combine to make this one of the most forbiddingly difficult assignments in town. The first is a legacy of past mistakes that has shut down reactors and production plants across the country and exposed them as threats to human safety and the environment. It has left behind a vast and dismayingly complicated set of cleanup, overhaul and restructuring tasks that stretch beyond the horizon. Second, these problems have crippled execution of what is still the job's formal mandate

--building and preserving the U.S. nuclear deterrent. By consequence, the energy department's Office of Defense Programs (DP) is unable today to fulfill the nuclear weapons requirements laid on it by the president. Third, the cost of renovating, consolidating and making the complex and its operations safe, and of training and retraining its work force, threatens to explode out of control. Some say it already has.

Future assistant secretaries managing the defense programs responsibility at the department of energy need to understand not only the two chief dimensions of this crisis, but what brought it on.

From a weapons-making standpoint, the dilemma revolves around key ingredients. Plutonium, a metal, and tritium, a gas, are lethal and difficult nuclear materials used to fuel and augment the power of thermonuclear explosions. Existing weapons stockpiles make further production of new plutonium unnecessary; the manufacture of new weapons draws on plutonium reprocessed from existing warheads retired from service. But the key and critical site of this operation, the department of energy (DOE) plant at Rocky Flats, Colorado, became over the years an environmental disaster. In mid-1989, investigators and inspectors from the FBI and the Environmental Protection Agency (EPA) descended on Rocky Flats on evidence of improper storage and disposal of dangerous waste materials. Several months later the plant closed, halting the only operation in the country capable of turning salvaged plutonium into weapons parts. The department prefers eventually to clean up the Rocky Flats site and get out. But in the interim it wants to reopen the plant to get the weapons assembly line moving again. A new "special recovery" facility at Savannah River, South Carolina, built over seven years for about $90 million, will retrieve plutonium from scrap. But it lacks the Rocky Flats capacity to fabricate it into weapons parts.

Tritium, too, is recoverable from existing weapons, and DOE is doing so. A General Accounting Office (GAO) report has asserted that the salvage of tritium can in fact meet the entire current need for it. For a number of reasons, however, among them tritium's decay rate of 5.5 percent a year, the department believes it needs new production. As an immediate step, it wants to restart one of three tritium reactors at Savannah River, all of which closed in 1988 for safety reasons. Since then the three plants have soaked up more than $2 billion in rehabilitation efforts, and DOE has closed one of them permanently after sinking $800 million into it. Another may be renovated and put on hold. As of late winter 1991, restart of the third reactor had been postponed several times, and in April the secretary of energy told a Senate committee that it can never run at more than half speed because of meltdown danger in the event of a coolant water accident. As a later step in the tritium game, DOE has plans for a new production reactor program to replace the Savannah River trio.

In the view of Robert DeGrasse, a member of the House Armed Services Committee staff, "the systemic problems in the Rocky Flats and Savannah River facilities are very challenging at this stage." Solutions at both sites will represent "dramatic changes in the culture of the DOE--the training of people, the modes of operation, and the openness with which the department operates."

So much for the problems on the weapons side of the defense programs job. They define the position's most immediate goal--to get weapons production back on track. Yet the other large and growing responsibility--to eliminate the festering facilities and dangerous practices produced by four unregulated decades of making, handling and disposing of radioactive and other perilous materials--is widely expected to dominate the department of energy from now on. Much of it looks increasingly like an environmental recovery and waste disposal agency; the department has set up a new operation separate from DP and responsible for cleanup and restoration. The work ahead is neither cheap nor quick: The GAO has estimated its cost over the next quarter century at $200 billion.

In January 1991 DOE proposed a massive long-term reconfiguration and modernization of the nuclear weapons complex. It would reduce the size of the complex, consolidate its sites and ensure their safety, permanently shutter old plants like Rocky Flats, assure proper handling of hazardous material, and clean up the environmental damage. Indeed, the "first priority" claimed by the proposal is "to protect the environment and provide for proper public and worker health and safety." As the plan made its way through congressional scrutiny and public debate, predictions about its ultimate shape were impossible. In about 1994, final decisions will have to be made. But even the first foothills of the mountainous restoration task have not been easy. DOE has missed some deadlines set out in numerous environmental cleanup agreements it has signed with state and other federal agencies. In one such case, it faced a $300,000 fine levied by the EPA.

Inability to perform its mission fully, environmental destruction: how did the nuclear weapons program get into this double-barreled briar patch? John Tuck, under secretary of the department, concurrently headed DP on an acting basis in 1989-90, and oversight of it remains one of his responsibilities as under secretary. He explains the problem in terms of "a big shield that operated to protect a particular way of handling things," allowing noncompliance with environmental rules, adding that "we frankly do things in Rocky Flats today that would not pass standard anywhere else." Richard A. Claytor, who took over the job in late 1990, says "it wasn't that we didn't obey the laws. We reached the conclusion they didn't apply to us. There were obviously incidents, some of which I think were exaggerated, but there's no question we didn't physically take care of our complex or train our people or do all the things we should have done." Environmentalists, of course, use harsher words about the situation. Senior scientist Thomas Cochran of the Natural Resources Defense Council says "the whole place is in one helluva mess because they mismanaged it from an environmental and safety standpoint for 40 years." Prior to about 1983, according to Cochran, DOE took the position that under the Atomic Energy Act, it "didn't have to comply with any of the environmental regulations," even though the EPA claimed the lead authority on such matters under the Act. "We won a lawsuit that overturned that (the DOE position)," he adds. "It was a combination of that lawsuit, the fallout from Chernobyl and some aggressive press reporting that has put this enormous pressure on the DOE to put safety and environmental issues up front." Another factor in the origins of the department's problem may have been a tendency to set goals without sufficient reliance on outside advice and counsel or adequate openness to public concerns.

It's not hard in any case to see why the assistant secretary position in DP has had 12 occupants in 13 years, seven of whom were in an acting status only. In taking it over, Claytor notes, he was the first "permanent" individual in the post in three years. DP's budget, the biggest in the department, stands at a requested $6.7 billion for fiscal 1992. The job supervises two dozen facilities in 12 states. They include a number of field operations offices and the national weapons laboratories at Sandia and Los Alamos, New Mexico and at Lawrence Livermore, California. The labs alone employ 24,000 people. Livermore and Los Alamos are run by the University of California, Sandia by the AT&T Corporation; they are what Claytor calls not-for-profit contractors. The rest of the complex is operated for profit by "management and operating" contractors like Westinghouse, General Electric and Martin Marietta.

"It's a huge job," says Troy E. Wade, a 30-year veteran of DP who ran it in 1987-88 as acting assistant secretary. "You have such a wide variety of things to worry about, from manufacturing plants to the national labs. The span of control is huge and complicated. It's like running a Fortune 20 corporation." Cochran uses almost identical language: "If it was a private company, it would be in the Fortune top 20. It's the key job in DOE."

By 1989, in fact, the burdens weighing on this job had grown to such proportions that several of its functions were stripped out and assigned elsewhere in DOE. Major among these was the establishment of the Office of Environmental Restoration and Waste Management, whose big job, in Claytor's words, "is cleaning up a lot of the facilities we used to run." It is getting a rising share of the DOE budget, "as it should," while DP's "tends to remain somewhat static." The DP job also lost some "peripheral responsibilities," he adds, "like the intelligence function. And the policy making role for writing procedures on safeguards and security can be handled by someone else, and that has been changed. That makes this job somewhat smaller, and that's fine." Still, it requires "about an 80-hour effort--12 hours a day, two hours work at home every night, and about eight hours over the weekend. There are hundreds of issues; at any point maybe 30 are extremely urgent, and many others have to be watched."

The position requires regular, often frequent, appearances on and dialogue with Capitol Hill. Claytor testified seven times in one three-week stretch in the spring of 1991. While Wade remembers tough sledding now and then with some of the authorizing committees--Energy and Commerce in the House, Armed Services in the Senate--Claytor reports satisfactory support from the armed services and appropriations committees of both houses, while acknowledging that a number of members "don't want any weapons made." Contrary to some advice he received, "if congressional staff people call, I'm available. Some are extremely good, and they are powerful and influential." His public affairs activity is limited by "the national security implications of the job; a lot of the work is classified." But his office gets many questions from the press and has a three-person public affairs staff. Considerable exchange takes place with the environmental community. "You've got two distinct groups," says Wade. "You have those who oppose you on really no other grounds than that they oppose anything connected with nuclear matters or war. And then you have groups who challenge what you do because they have concerns about the effect on the environment."

A major point of contact in the job is the Nuclear Weapons Council, on which the assistant secretary shares membership with senior officials of the department of defense (DOD) and the Joint Chiefs of Staff. Chaired by the Pentagon's director of Defense Research and Engineering, this body shapes the agenda for developing, managing and disposing of the U.S. nuclear weapons inventory. Once approved by the president, its decisions become nuclear stockpile memoranda--the DP assistant secretary's basic marching orders on the weapons-making side of the job. "DOD's objective is to get the weapons produced, and we have that obligation to them," Claytor says. "On the other hand, it's our obligation to do it safely and DOE has not in the past paid enough attention to that and to complying with environmental laws. So we're doing that and a great deal of money is going into that area. I think DOD understands it and is more sympathetic."

In addition to the Nuclear Weapons Council, the assistant secretary's working environment outside DOE includes contact with the White House Office of Science and Technology Policy and senior defense and arms control officials of the National Security Council. The position benefits from outside advice and counsel in one important sense--a large advisory board convened by the secretary to examine the future of the three weapons labs. Though the labs' core mission is decreasing, they employ "a marvelous wealth of talent," Claytor says. "The secretary is trying to see with this advisory board how to retain that talent, get it into other areas. We need to retain our weapons capabilities, but at the same time we need to know what we can do to keep the good people in positions where they contribute in other areas." Tuck stresses that "we don't think it's a good idea for those labs to be busted up simply because the nuclear deterrent business has been diminished. We particularly think it's important to keep the kinetic energy of those scientists."

Historically, this job's relationship with the laboratories and field offices it supervises has required strong management, confidence and a hands-on style to stay in control. Sylvester R. Foley Jr., assistant secretary in 1986-87, points out that many field managers had served years in the complex and were inclined to be "800-pound gorillas who didn't like a lot of interference." Others have warned about the danger that new assistant secretaries, struggling with a very steep learning curve, can end up as captives of the structure. Tuck views the lab directors as "incredibly powerful people" who "don't always pay attention to what the headquarters guidance is. That's not a criticism, it's just that they've been operating together a lot longer than the political leadership of the department, which changes frequently." It's unusual for that leadership to interest itself closely, as is currently the case, in matters which had long been the domain of the laboratory directors.

What that means for this position, Claytor explains, is that the secretary of energy has revised some of the DOE reporting structure. The field offices' vague, somewhat autonomous relationship to headquarters has given way to a system where, among other changes, four of the operations offices report directly to Claytor. "As far as I can see, headquarters had been more of an administrative operation that handled budgetary matters and pretty well let the field run things. That's changed. I now have line responsibility for everything that goes on--contract issues, safety, health, production."

Using seagoing command structure as an example, Tuck compares this and related changes in DOE to the repeater on a ship's bridge that confirms the execution of engine and rudder orders. "You have to establish systems to ensure that what you promulgate as policy and guidance actually gets followed up. Unless you do, it'll eat you alive. You'll look back in a month and try to figure out what happened and you'll never know." But Wade has doubts, not about the objectives of the changes, but the way in which they took place. "Watkins (a former Navy admiral) changed the ground rules appreciably by imposing Navy standards on a system that was ill prepared to deal with them. He chose to apply overnight a yardstick that those people had never seen before, and measure everything by it. If it didn't comply, he shut it down. Damn few things complied with his yardstick, and damn few things are running today. There's a lot of trauma in the system now." The situation would have produced, he adds, "a major collision course" between DOE and the Pentagon if not for the coincidence of far-reaching change in the Soviet Union and progress in arms control negotiations between the superpowers.

Why, in fact, is the defense programs complex a dominating part of DOE, and not in the defense department? The answer lies in DOE's ancestry: One of its grandparents was the Atomic Energy Commission, where the nuclear weapons responsibility first resided. DOE simply inherited it. "Through the years of convoluted law making," Wade says, "the weapons program was married to a bunch of other technologies in this thing called DOE, and it's just not a good fit. In fact, that's probably one of the toughest challenges this assistant secretary has--carrying the mail for an agency that frankly would prefer that the whole business was somewhere else."

Should DP move to the Pentagon? The Atomic Energy Act clearly distinguishes between military and civilian responsibilities in nuclear weapons making, with research, development, testing and production reserved to civilian control. "That's why the Atomic Energy Commission was born," notes Wade. Over the years, he continues, that premise has been tested and revalidated several times, and he was among those who supported it. "But I'm not sure it's true any longer. We may be at a point where it might be prudent to meld the weapons program into Defense, perhaps as a separate agency there. One of the most difficult parts of this job is to get its budget responsibilities in sync with the budget requirements of DOD."

While the original intent was to keep the weapons under civilian control, Cochran says, "in effect, the control and the policy have been turned over to DOD. And DOD, because they don't have to pay for the weapons, has no incentive to save money in this part of the budget. They just tell the DOE what to buy and what to build." Despite that, he says, "I'm not sure that hiding the weapons program in the Defense department is the solution."

On the question whether the technical training and competence of the complex's work force is adequate, Claytor says "we have some fine people." However, "we need to do a lot to bring in new staff and train those we have. There are not enough technically qualified people at headquarters and to some extent in the field." The problem worsened in the 1980s when, according to Tuck, "technical talent just jumped off the DOE rolls like rats leaving a sinking ship." But two recent changes in the rules allow the department to pay higher salaries in critical senior positions. One permits hiring from industry and elsewhere at salaries above the normal Senior Executive Service scale, up to cabinet level. That makes it possible, Claytor observes wryly, for him to hire someone who would earn more than he does. Under the other new rule change, DP can with special permission hire people retired from other civilian and military federal jobs and allow them to continue receiving their retirement pay. Yet DeGrasse, of the House Armed Services Committee, says he is "not sure that is going to solve the department's mid-level talent requirements. I would prefer to see them build at the ground level, with people who are coming out of school or have been out a few years."

"I'm trying to build career people in place who will have some tenure in all the subordinate positions," Claytor says. "My job will continue to be political, and that's fine. But we need a backup capability to have continuity." One snag he notes here is that the weapons research and development program must by law be managed by a military officer of flag rank. "That's good in that it brings in the outlook of the user of the weapons. But typically the assignment is for only two or three years. So you have a top guy coming in who runs the program, and then he's gone."

Taking some perspective on DP's future as a whole, Tuck says "we have to convince people that there's a multistage effort going on here, one that will get us to a record of decision in early fiscal 1994, when the secretary has to decide what the complex will look like in 2015. So there's a time from now to late fiscal 1993, a transition from then to complex 2015, and a complex from 2015 on. All of those different time lines reflect different demands for resources against different scenarios of activity."

And for how long does the United States need to manufacture nuclear weapons? Part of that debate, in Cochran's view, is "whether you need a new weapon every time you have a new launch vehicle." He argues that vehicles can be manufactured to fit the weapon, much as the capsule in a manned space shot is reconfigured to fit the environmental constraints of its occupants. "But there's been a tendency to redesign the criteria for new warheads so that, in effect, you're redesigning the warhead every time you need a new system." In any case, Cochran maintains that production of new warheads "is not really going to be the most important problem. It's the health of the people who live around these facilities that should be the major focus of their attention."

The "biggest challenge," Claytor sums up, "is to carry out the things we have to do within budget restraints. Upgrade the safety, the health, the environment, meet our mission, reconfigure the complex, get out of Rocky Flats and into other facilities. We have to spend a bunch of money. Everybody wants more money, but we have to preserve the deterrent. DOD has a bit more flexibility; they can cancel a bomber program or some huge weapons system. I don't know what I can cancel. I've got a program that is defined. I've got to produce the weapons that require these expensive facilities. We've got to make them right and make them safe. Big, big problem."

Key Relationships

Within the Department

Reports to: Secretary of Energy

Works closely with:

Under Secretary
Director, Office of Environmental Restoration and Waste Management
Assistant Secretary, Environmental Safety and Health
Directors, Los Alamos, Sandia, and Lawrence Livermore National
  Laboratories
Directors, Albuquerque and San Francisco Operations Offices
Director, Office of New Production Reactors
Assistant Secretary, Congressional and Intergovernmental Affairs

Outside the Department

Members and staff, Nuclear Weapons Council
Director, Defense Research and Engineering, Department of Defense
Vice Chairman, Joint Chiefs of Staff
Assistant to the Secretary, Atomic Energy, Department of Defense
Assistant to the President, Science and Technology Policy
Senior Director, Defense Policy and Arms Control, National Security Council
Assistant Administrator, Air and Radiation, Environmental Protection
  Agency
Chairman and Commissioners, Nuclear Regulatory Commission

Outside the Government

Heads of corporations managing field components of the nuclear weapons complex, such as General Electric, Westinghouse, and Martin Marietta; environmental organizations; and antinuclear weapons groups; aerospace and defense contracting firms

Profile of Current Assistant Secretary, Defense Programs

Name: Richard A. Claytor

Assumed Position: 1990

Career Summary:	Principal deputy assistant secretary, nuclear energy, department of energy, May-October, 1990
	Various positions, including vice president and director of project operations, Burns and Roe Enterprises Inc. (architect-engineering firm), 1973-89
	Captain (ret.), U.S. Navy, 1949-73
Education:	U.S. Naval Academy, BS, 1949
	Webb Institute of Naval Architecture,BS, Marine Engineering, MS, Naval Architecture, 1956

Assistant Secretaries, Defense Programs Since 1978*

Administration	Name and Years Served	Present Position
Bush	Richard A. Claytor 1990 - present	Incumbent
Bush	John C. Tuck (Acting) 1989-90	Under Secretary Department of Energy
Bush	John L. Meinhardt (A) 1989	Executive Assistant Sandia National Laborartory Albuquerque, N.M.
Reagan	Troy E. Wade (A) 1987 - 1988	President AWC Inc./Lockheed Las Vegas, Nev.
Reagan	Sylvester R. Foley Jr. 1986 - 1987	Vice President Raytheon Co. Arlington, Va.
Reagan	Don Ofte (A) 1985	Retired
Reagan	William W. Hoover 1984 - 1985	Executive Vice President Air Transport Association Washington, D.C.
Reagan	Robert L. Morgan (A) 1984	Not available
Reagan	Herman E. Roser 1981 - 1984	Deceased
Reagan	Robert L. Morgan (A) 1981	Not available

| Carter | Duane C. Sewell
1978 - 1981 | Not available |
| Carter | Donald M. Kerr Jr. (A)
1978 | President
EG&G Inc.
Wellesley, Mass. |

* The Department of Energy was established by the Department of Energy Organization Act of October, 1977

ASSISTANT SECRETARY, NUCLEAR ENERGY

Level IV - Presidential Appointment with Senate Confirmation

Major Responsibilities

● Direct research and development programs in the use of fission energy for electric power generation in commercial plants, for the propulsion of naval vessels and space vehicles, and for uranium enrichment and sales.

● Oversee the repair and restoration of sites of environmental damage, and the cleanup and neutralizing of radioactive waste materials, made necessary by operation of the department's nuclear weapons production complex.

● Advise the secretary, and act as a principal administration spokesman, on nuclear energy issues. Conduct the government's business in the nuclear energy area with other countries, and represent U.S. positions in international contexts.

Necessary Training, Experience, Skills

The current occupant of this position came to it with experience in the operation of nuclear reactors. He also had a background in the design and development of nuclear power plants, and in managing in the private sector that provided exposure to the federal government including the Congress. Technical literacy is a minimum qualification, one of his predecessors suggests, but "management, leadership and communications skills" are more important. A scientist without those attributes "would fail in the job." A private-sector expert familiar with the work thinks a specialized technical, legal or government background is "absolutely" necessary, and also stresses management ability. Overall effectiveness in the assignment is a function of the individual's "political sensitivity and understanding," this source says. "In the past, people looked on it as sort of a technical job, but the last thing you need is someone who is a technical program manager. That would not be effective. There are a lot of stakeholders to be sensitive to."

Insight

To some extent, the future shape of this job depends on whether the United States in the 1990s decides to turn more toward nuclear energy for its civilian electric power needs. Such a development would be what the industry likes to call the revival of the nuclear power option. Considerable support for such a move exists, and not only from the nuclear power industry itself. The Bush administration, in its energy policy message of early 1991, emphasized the option. It laid out the goal of increasing U.S. capacity for nuclear-powered electricity production and facilitating the licensing of plants. It might be said to have foreshadowed that intention with the appointment as assistant secretary in 1989 of William H. Young, a marine and nuclear engineer with a background in both public and private sector nuclear energy production. Young says his principal goal in taking the job was "to revitalize the nuclear energy option for the commercial generation of electricity." And those who favor the option offer economic, geopolitical and environmental arguments in support of it that respond to familiar national concerns.

But will it happen? In the last 15 years, two circumstances have weighed massively against further development of nuclear power in this country. One was the maze of lengthy federal and state licensing procedures that enormously expensive nuclear power plants must negotiate before they can go on-line. Complicated by a multiplicity of plant designs, this unpredictable approval process helped to sideline industry interest in building new plants. None has been ordered since the late 1970s. Only one was under construction in 1991. Power companies and financial investors were further staggered by defaulting nuclear utility investments in the Pacific Northwest and elsewhere.

The second factor, of course, has been enduring public anxiety about nuclear plant safety and waste disposal--a concern to which department planners need to be continuingly sensitive. It is a disquiet fed by the near miss at Three Mile Island and immeasurably deepened by the disaster at Chernobyl. Aggravating this is the seemingly intractable and still-unresolved problem of what to do with radioactive wastes piling up at the country's 110 or so existing nuclear plants. Although the public does not seem unalterably opposed to nuclear power as one major eventual answer to U.S. energy needs, most opinion polls continue to reflect widespread unease about its dangers. In most estimates, it is the loss of the national community's confidence in nuclear power that presents its advocates with their toughest challenge. There have been some important changes in individual Capitol Hill positions on the subject. Still, it hardly needs stating that without a significant, definitive shift in the public's attitude, the overall congressional stance is unlikely to change.

Some cite another element in this uncertain picture--the future course of the rate by which electricity demand increases. Overall, the direction of demand is up. But when the economy declines, the rate of increase drops. An electric utility association study in early 1991 documented the pattern from 1988, when the rate of increased demand was 4.9 percent, to 1989, when it stood at 2.4 percent, through 1990, when it had dropped to 1.6 percent. The rate also slows as the price of electric power rises.

According to Kenneth Bossong, director of the Critical Mass Energy Project, the nuclear power industry today generates 19 percent of the country's electricity. He believes far better alternatives to it exist in terms of safety, economics and environmental impacts. Which alternatives? "The cheapest is improved efficiency and conservation," he says. "There is nothing technically or economically to stop the United States from reducing its projected energy use by at least 50 percent in the next 20 years, if not sooner." It's Bossong's belief that, "beyond efficiency, most remaining supply needs can be met by renewable energy sources, which now provide about 10 percent of the overall energy (as opposed to electricity) supply. That's more than nuclear power. Those technologies are available now at less than the cost of nuclear power plants. So, in terms of marketplace considerations, renewables are far more attractive as an option than nuclear power."

All of this--the reality of the U.S. nuclear energy posture, and the debate on future courses--clearly has implications for the nature and tempo of the work in the Office of Nuclear Energy at DOE. And vice versa. "The department of energy has a number of important programs, the success of which will determine whether this country sees a revival of nuclear energy," says Edward M. Davis, president of the American Nuclear Energy Council. "So the assistant secretary's job is one of the key positions there."

Besides overseeing advanced research and development focused on designing new-generation commercial concepts like the modular high temperature gas and advanced liquid metal reactors, Young manages efforts to improve the light water reactor--the nuclear technology now used to generate electric power. The latter project, in cooperation with industry, aims at producing advanced light water reactor designs that utility operators could acquire in the current decade. The object is also to produce standardized, certified designs, in coordination with the Nuclear Regulatory Commission (NRC), that would simplify the licensing process. In addition, Young says, "improvements in this technology make it safer, and overall you end up with less risk of release of radiation and possible exposure of the public." At the same time, his office is part of a team working to improve the legislative climate in which these developments go forward. One proposal, for example, would alter the NRC's public hearing procedures to license a nuclear plant so that last-minute interventions could not prevent an already-built facility from going into operation.

"Nuclear energy has been under a cloud of concern and fear about the use of the technology," Young reflects. "I think that's changing. I've seen it change since I've been here." The chief obstacle, from his vantage point, "is budget. The job of this government is to enable the private sector to use this technology. We are developing the new designs that would be used, and we're doing that on a cost-shared basis. If there is a restraint, it's in terms of the amount of money that we can apply in this budget climate. And in Congress, it's a mixed bag. You have both strong supporters and strong opponents of nuclear energy."

In Young's domain at DOE, commercial nuclear energy matters are the responsibility of the Office of Civilian Reactor Development. Other units, each headed by a deputy assistant secretary or director, handle naval reactors, space and defense power systems, environmental restoration and waste management (which works closely with DOE's Office of Defense Programs) and uranium enrichment.

Shelby Brewer, who held this job in 1981-84, remembers the 1982 "crisis" in the uranium program "--about a $2 billion a year business that would be Fortune 500 in the private sector." The sale of excess European uranium inventories had cut into the U.S. market. "We took steps to correct that, not by erecting barriers but by cutting our production costs, reformulating all our contracts. We just slimmed down the operation, got into a competitive posture, and regained the market." But David Rossin, acting assistant secretary in 1986-87, describes the uranium program as a "major absorber of time" and says "we're still arguing about what to do with it." By 1986, he says, the Office of Management and Budget "was forcing DOE to hold enrichment prices at high levels, hoping to reduce the deficit. The competitive edge was lost, and even American utilities were shopping overseas." Davis thinks the program "must be restructured to compete. It was a major enterprise of the department that has been suffering losses. Its customer base is threatened. It has to be reestablished and redirected." Meanwhile, to replace an old enrichment technique known as diffusion, Young says, "we're developing a new one at the Livermore laboratory using lasers."

While the office continues to develop and refine nuclear power systems for the Navy submarine fleet and certain surface vessels, it is also working on sources of propulsion power in a different realm. It develops radio isotope thermoelectric generators for space exploration ventures that will include a mission to the sun, as well as for use by the Strategic Defense Initiative.

These programs add up to a budget of about $2.5 billion a year, and the office's basic budget pattern, Young says, is one of increase. He has "an extensive interface" with OMB on budget matters, in which "very little comes easily." He testifies ten to twelve times a year on the Hill. The most frequent stops are the Senate and House appropriations committees; and, on the authorizing and oversight side, committees in both houses concerned with science, energy, environment and regulation. Recalling his own relations with the Congress, Brewer says "I fared okay. There wasn't a lot of political support from the White House; they told me that going in--'Nuclear power is not popular, so you have to earn your own chits.' " He thinks he testified more in the first Reagan term than anybody except the secretary of defense. "The Hill had become enormously more complex than in the good old days of nuclear power, when there was only one committee and one stop--the Joint Committee on Atomic Energy. I had over a dozen committees to deal with, all with conflicting, overlapping jurisdictions."

On the international front, Young reports, the United States has cooperative agreements on nuclear power technology and information exchange with various countries. He describes one special initiative that resulted from the explosion of the Soviet reactor at Chernobyl. It had become clear that further such accidents would make things worse for other nations using nuclear power and, Young says, the current secretary of energy, James Watkins, offered the Soviets help to improve operational safety. Young visited Moscow and developed an agreement on U.S.-Soviet cooperation that includes the training of Soviet citizens in American nuclear power plants.

His staff numbers 300, with about 25 at DOE headquarters; the rest work in offices in the Maryland suburbs. Young estimates that 70 percent of his work force have technical backgrounds. Technically, he has no complaints about the quality of his staff, though he thinks "they are not accustomed as much as I would like to giving a very direct and focused answer." It is very difficult to recruit and retain people at the senior levels. "The only place we're successful in staffing is at the lower grades, bringing in younger people and building from that standpoint." Brewer thinks attracting and keeping staff has become a "big handicap" for the department as a whole. "The complexities of the issues have just overcome them for reasons beyond their control."

Summarizing from an outsider's vantage point the issues facing the assistant secretary in this job (in addition to overhaul of the uranium program), Davis thinks the difficulty in attracting experienced, qualified personnel from the private sector is high on the list. Next comes "interfacing with the NRC to develop standardized plant designs that are safer, more reliable and more economical." Related to that is resolving the "impasse" on nuclear waste disposal. Finally, "the R&D program under this position is an ad hoc collection spawned and protected through political constituencies. They don't make much sense in the 1990s; they're outdated. How you reprogram and redirect away from the past into something new that relates to where you want to go is extremely important." His view is that "the current administration is making great strides and progress in that direction."

Davis thinks the post in the last decade and a half has evolved from managing technical programs to managing the culture of the technology. "Where science skills were once vital, today it's political skills." The cause, he speculates, may be the decline of the budget in terms of new programs, and the decline of the technology component of the job along with it. In the same period, "two major reactor accidents changed the political landscape entirely"--a "sea change" also spurred by the evidence of global climate change. "It's that landscape that's still shifting that the person in this job has to manage. Basically, it's managing change."

In that context, Davis sees the atmosphere for a comeback of nuclear power as more encouraging than ever. "If it doesn't happen in the next five years, it probably won't." He asserts that the industry has learned from Three Mile Island, and cites other reasons why comeback prospects have improved--electricity shortages in the country, especially on the East Coast; U.S. overdependence on foreign oil, "a perception sharpened by the Gulf war;" the "substantial environmental benefits" of nuclear power in the era of the greenhouse effect; and a predicted increased use of electric vehicles that would hike the demand for electricity. In Rossin's view, "nothing the DOE does on nuclear is going to change things overnight. It is vital to keep the research programs going so that the NRC and the industry focus on getting standardized reactor designs licensed. But the advanced designs will take more than a decade to enter the marketplace." The sharp rise in oil prices at the beginning of the Gulf war brought many policy makers and members of Congress to feel that perhaps their constituents would be more open-minded about nuclear power, he thinks. "That's important for the long run. But for anything meaningful to happen by the end of the century, the changes have to start now."

"Success in this job really involves your vision," Young says. "Where are you taking this whole program? Civilian nuclear power, for example-- how do you see that the various elements needed to enable that technology to move again are being brought together? It's really strategic planning."

Key Relationships

Within the Department

Reports to: Secretary of Energy

Works closely with:

Deputy Secretary
Under Secretary
Assistant Secretary, Defense Programs
Director, Office of Civilian Radioactive Waste Management
Director, Office of Energy Research

Outside the Department

Chairman, Nuclear Regulatory Commission
Director, Strategic Defense Initiative Organization, Department of Defense
Associate Administrator, Aeronautics Exploration and Technology, National
   Aeronautics and Space Administration
Assistant to the President, Science and Technology Policy

Outside the Government

Officials, trade association representatives, and laboratory scientists of the
nuclear power industry; environmental organizations; manufacturers of power
plant equipment, reactors and associated equipment; professional science
groups and academics; counterpart officials of foreign governments

Profile of Current Assistant Secretary, Nuclear Energy

Name: William H. Young

Assumed Position: 1989

Career Summary: President, William H. Young & Associates Inc., 1985-89
Various positions with Burns & Roe Inc., 1971-85, including vice
   president, project operations and vice president, breeder reactor
   division
Various positions with division of naval reactors, U.S. Atomic
   Energy Commission, 1962-71, including associate director,
   submarines

Education: Webb Institute of Naval Architecture, BS, naval architecture and
   marine engineering, 1956
George Washington University, MS, engineering, 1961

Assistant Secretaries, Nuclear Energy Since 1978*

Administration	Name and Years Served	Present Position
Bush	William H. Young 1989 - present	Incumbent
Reagan	Mary Ann Novak (Acting) 1988	Vice President Parsons Brinckerhoff Washington, D.C.
Reagan	Theodore Garrish 1988	Senior Vice President American Nuclear Energy Council Washington, D.C.
Reagan	James W. Vaughn Jr. (A) 1987, 1985 - 1986	Senior Vice President NUS Corporation Gaithersburg, Md.
Reagan	A. David Rossin 1986 - 1987	President Rossin & Associates Los Altos Hills, CA
Reagan	Shelby T. Brewer 1981 - 1984	President ABB Combustion Engineering Nuclear Power Windsor, Conn.
Reagan	Mahlon E. Gates (A) 1981	Retired San Antonio, Tex.
Carter	George W. Cunningham 1980	Technical Director Defense Nuclear Facilities Safety Board Washington, D.C.
Carter	John M. Deutch (A)** 1979	Institute Professor Massachusetts Institute of Technology Cambridge, Mass.
Carter	Robert D. Thorne (A)** 1978	Retired

* The Department of Energy was established by the Department of Energy Organization Act of October, 1977
** Held position as Assistant Secretary, Energy Technology

DIRECTOR, OFFICE OF ENERGY RESEARCH

Level IV - Presidential Appointment with Senate Confirmation

Major Responsibilities

- Advise the secretary of energy on the department's energy research and development activities. Keep watch on the research and development programs of the department as a whole for gaps and overlaps and recommend corrective steps.

- Manage the department's $2 billion-plus research programs in basic energy sciences, high-energy and nuclear physics, magnetic fusion, and the health and environmental implications of energy technology. Oversee the operation and administration of national non-weapons research laboratories which conduct a significant part of this research.

- Administer the Office of Energy Research (OER).

Necessary Training, Experience, Skills

Those knowledgeable from service in or dealings with this job agree that it requires plenty of close exposure to scientific and technical matters. They would favor candidates with doctorates in, say, physics or chemistry, or electrical or chemical engineers. An academic or industrial background is important, together with established scientific or technical achievement. An observer of the position is quite precise about it: "We're talking about a scientist, somebody who's not bamboozled by the Hill or the military, somebody with some independent stature, and curious and open about energy sources other than what his or her own discipline would lead to." But if the job has traditionally gone to trained scientists and engineers, a non-member of those fraternities with the right other credentials might qualify. A former occupant says "I can imagine it being an unusually gifted lawyer with extensive experience in scientific and technical matters." Another source thinks it would be "interesting" to bring in "somebody from industry, very smart, task-oriented, who knew how to manage."

Insight

As part of the inheritance from its ancestral Atomic Energy Commission, the department of energy (DOE) funds most of the country's fundamental research in high-energy nuclear physics. For the foreseeable future, the centerpiece of this effort where the department is concerned is the Superconducting Super Collider (SSC), to be managed and run by the Office of Energy Research. This biggest and by far most powerful of accelerators is under construction 35 miles southeast of Forth Worth, Texas. Jamming beams of protons together at speeds approaching that of light, SSC will set off the release of titanic energies equivalent to those present at the universe's birth, a moment when particles like the instantly extinct Higgs boson theoretically existed. By reproducing such particles in SSC's collisions, scientists hope to push understanding of these matters well beyond its present advance and, just possibly, provide conclusive insights into the origin of matter. When the SSC office was established in OER in early 1989, the final cost of the SSC--to be completed in 1999-- was put at $4.3 billion. The fiscal 1992 federal budget request doubled SSC annual funding and put the final total cost estimate at $8.249 billion. In size, cost and objective, SSC is a prime exhibit in the enduring debate over the absolute and relative merits of big and little science. Like other big-science objects of that debate, such as the Freedom space station and the Earth Observing System, it must continue to face the scrutiny of increasingly hard-eyed congressional funders. It also tests this assistant secretary's skill in extensive negotiations with other countries for the global participation and hoped-for international cost-sharing that are significant elements of the project.

OER is also fully engaged in the widespread (but not yet fully coordinated) public and private sector effort to identify and increase concentration on "critical technologies" judged necessary to keep the United States competitive. Through the department's national laboratory network, OER two years ago began focusing on several such technologies including lasers, supercomputers, superconductors, materials synthesis, biotechnology and energy itself. Oversight of the non-weapons units in the department's 25 single- and multi-purpose national laboratory system is, in fact, one of the three major elements of this position. And it may be a reason why the Congress, in establishing the department of energy, designated the director's job and that of the secretary as its only two statutory offices. Grant P. Thompson, a Washington energy consultant, says "this grew partly, in my view, out of the way Congress thought about the department--they really saw it as driven by technology that would save us, and the director of energy research was conceived as the central figure in discovering technological solutions to our energy problems."

That in turn goes directly to two other responsibilities that, with the SSC, represent this job's main concerns. As science and technical advisor to the secretary, the director monitors the scientific health and welfare of DOE and proposes remedies to problems perceived. In some respects, says Alvin Trivelpiece, OER director in 1981-87, this amounts to a warrant to search for deficiencies and inefficiencies anywhere they exist; it can involve DOE's huge defense programs complex, not normally part of the director's province, or the department's efforts in energy efficiency and conservation, renewable energy sources, and solar and hydroelectric power. Such a "busybody's license," as Trivelpiece terms it, "can cause a tremendous number of problems if not exercised with care." With the sometimes reluctant agreement of those whose domains he examined, Trivelpiece recalls, he "went in and did technical analyses of programs and problems and tried to provide them with sound technical advice." In most cases, he adds, the assistant secretaries in charge of the programs did not have technical backgrounds.

The third major duty is management of the research programs (magnetic fusion, high energy and nuclear physics plus health and environment, and basic energy sciences) that are part of OER itself. Together, they represent one of the biggest basic research operations in the federal government. It is the energy sciences program which runs the department's newly-invigorated effort in critical technologies. Among the national laboratories which execute most of these programs and comprise part of the director's domain are such renowned names as Brookhaven, Fermi, Argonne and the Stanford Linear Accelerator Center. The programs embrace thousands of individual projects, many conducted in close collaboration with academic and corporate entities around the country. In addition, OER's support of university research puts it squarely in the business of trying to educate greater numbers of energy scientists and extend the range and muscle of scientific investigation on campus, particularly in areas of high priority.

Though SSC funding doubles in the fiscal 1992 budget request, James F. Decker, acting director in 1989-91, says OER was level-funded in 1990 and 1991, and his "major problem will be developing and carrying out the office's programs within budget constraints." At least half of the OER staff of 350 have scientific or technical training, he reports, but finding and keeping adequately skilled and trained staff is difficult.

John Deutch, a former provost at MIT who earlier held the OER director's position in 1977-78 before going on to more senior posts in DOE, points out that OER's roots are in the tradition of the old Atomic Energy Commission and Energy Research and Development Administration, another of the department's predecessors. In OER's earlier days, therefore, "there was a source of technical people from the laboratories, and a real history of involvement and what were then perceived to be effective programs," he says. But for the past ten years or so, technical staff quality in his view has suffered badly from government's inability to attract and retain qualified people. Trivelpiece adds another dimension to this point. "The rules, the strategies, the tactics have a strong connection back into the AEC. It was an administratively lean organization with well-trained technical people at most key managerial positions. As time passed and things changed, DOE became a large, traditional, bureaucratic cabinet agency. As a result there is less emphasis on the need for people with the appropriate technical training and the ability to recruit them has diminished. It's very hard to bring in people as interns and have them grow up in the job. You need people who have actually had to write proposals, do research, write papers, deal with people in peer review circumstances, and understand both the ethics and the requirements of doing advanced competitive research."

The OER director spends a significant amount of time with the congressional aspects of the job, much of it in budget presentation and defense before the Senate and House Appropriations subcommittees on Energy and Water Development. Oversight rests in the Senate Energy and Natural Resources Committee and the House panels on Science, Space and Technology and on Energy and Commerce.

Thompson thinks one of this job's challenges might be "trying to take the big chunk of DOE devoted to weapons production and weapons R&D and redirecting those resources into civilian purposes." He believes further that the country is moving in the near- and medium-term away from oil and towards natural gas, along with a continued decline of interest in nuclear power. "That trend provides a lot of opportunities for the national labs and the director of OER to redirect those talented technologists and analysts and turn them towards those complex issues." It should be noted in this context that the Bush Administration's energy strategy, announced in early 1991, includes new emphasis on nuclear power.

Does the OER director play a significant role in developing national energy policy for this country? The answer is a nominal yes, depending on whether the genuine will and intent at the upper political levels of government to implement such policy makes it a genuinely meaningful exercise. But prerequisites also exist at the departmental level. An OER director "can be critical to the formulation of any sensible, long-term energy strategy for the United States," Deutch says. "But there are two parts to that. First, the secretary of energy has to be interested in the subject, and second, the director has to have an excellent working relationship with him or her. That doesn't always hold in this job. If it doesn't, you might as well not be there."

Key Relationships

Within the Department

Reports to: Secretary of Energy

Works closely with:

Assistant Secretary, Nuclear Energy
Assistant Secretary, Fossil Energy
Assistant Secretary, Conservation and Renewable Energy

Outside the Department

Assistant to the President, Science and Technology Policy
Assistant to the President, Domestic Policy Council
Director, National Institutes of Health
Director, National Science Foundation
Director, Office of Technology Assessment
Executive Director, Commission on Physical Sciences, Math and
  Applications, National Academy of Sciences
Administrator, National Aeronautics and Space Administration
Assistant Secretary of State, Oceans and International Environmental and
  Scientific Affairs
Members of high-performance computing subcommittee, Committee on
  Physical, Mathematical and Engineering Sciences, FCCSET

Outside the Government

International Energy Agency and other multilateral and bilateral energy
forums in which the United States participates; advocacy groups, public
service organizations, and corporate and trade association representatives in
the fields of energy and environment

Profile of Current Director, Office of Energy Research

Name:	William Happer
Assumed Position:	1991
Career Summary:	Professor of Physics, Princeton University, 1980-91
	Various positions on the scientific faculty of Columbia University, 1964-79, including professor of physics, and director, Columbia Radiation Laboratory
Education:	BS, University of North Carolina, 1960
	PhD (physics), Princeton University, 1964

Directors, Office of Energy Research Since 1977*

Administration	Name and Years Served	Present Position
Bush	William Happer 1991 - Present	Incumbent
Bush	James F. Decker (Acting) 1989 - 1991	Deputy Director Office of Energy Research Department of Energy
Reagan	Robert O. Hunter 1988	Rancho Santa Fe, Cal.
Reagan	James F. Decker (A) 1987 - 1988	Deputy Director Office of Energy Research Department of Energy
Reagan	Alvin W. Trivelpiece 1981 - 1987	Director Oak Ridge National Laboratory Oak Ridge, Tenn.
Carter	Edward A. Frieman 1979 - 1980	Not available
Carter	John M. Deutch 1977 - 1978	Institute Professor M.I.T. Cambridge, Mass.

* Position created by the Department of Energy Organization Act, PL 95-91, October 1977

16

ENVIRONMENTAL
PROTECTION AGENCY

ASSISTANT ADMINISTRATOR, AIR AND RADIATION

Level IV - Presidential Appointment with Senate Confirmation

Major Responsibilities

- Direct the development, promulgation and enforcement of federal
  regulations and programs to control and prevent air pollution,
  principally through administration of the Clean Air Act of 1990
  (CAA). Set standards for air quality and for emissions from
  stationary and mobile sources of actual or potential pollution.
  Oversee federal radiation protection and radon mitigation programs.

- Seek legislation as necessary to define or redefine the objectives at
  which these efforts aim, and to strengthen the authority to carry out
  them out. Speak for federal air pollution control policy to the
  Congress, foreign governments and the public. Assist and provide
  guidance to state and local officials with substantial responsibility to
  enforce federal regulations and manage programs in the control of
  air pollution.

- Administer the Office of Air and Radiation and the work of its staff
  of 1,800 in support of all these activities, including adequate in-
  house research and testing.

Necessary Training, Experience, Skills

Though this position does not require substantial scientific training,
two former assistant administrators believe the lack of some technical

background or experience is a handicap. "You have to be able to make the technical arguments, craft them and manage the process," says one of them. But the job's current occupant has a somewhat different perspective. "I'm a lawyer, not an engineer or scientist," he says. "I don't think I have the technical expertise to judge a scientific issue, but there are plenty of people around here who do." He sees his role as motivating them, providing the resources, and listening to them and other parties involved. "Because this is such a far-reaching activity," he asserts, "one of the skills that's crucial is the ability to build a working consensus between the affected parties, other federal agencies, and state and local governments." Another former occupant values the talent for sorting out details of complex problems and comparing different approaches to solutions, because air pollution control issues "are fraught with uncertainty. It's helpful to have someone in this kind of job who enjoys digging into the issues."

Insight

One reason why people differ over the credentials this position needs may be the somewhat cyclical nature of its past and future agendas. The dominant features have been the 1977 and 1990 enactments of landmark clean air legislation, the second of which reauthorized and greatly expanded and strengthened the scope, objectives and impact of the first. Skippering such legislation through the hazardous political terrain it must cross even before reaching the climax of Congressional passage demands one mix of skills. A different blend is required by the subsequent task of figuring out precisely what the new law says, what policy should be and how to implement it. That is a trial-and-error period of setting standards, making and enforcing regulations, building consensus and resolving disputes.

In the view of William G. Rosenberg, a lawyer who took over the position in 1989, "it's a combination of an entrepreneurial, management and technical role. It's not one or the other. You go from the policy side where we were when (the 1990 legislation was in process) to setting the regulatory framework to actually applying it. So at different points, I suspect the assistant administrator will have different measures of policy, regulation and enforcement. Over time the mix will shift."

Richard E. Ayres, chairman of the Clean Air Coalition, has watched seven individuals function in the position. He is struck by "how different it is under different people." The job "is in the books as a technical job," he says. "It's a job that deals with a technical subject. But it's really a policy job. Experience in the policy process, facility in dealing with it--and that means with politics--is the crucial element. And enough familiarity and aptitude with technical issues to be conversant."

"When I was there," recalls J. Craig Potter, assistant administrator in 1986-88, "my responsibility was really to carry out existing policy in several areas and focus to a great extent on implementation. As opposed to the situation now, where you're seeing a change in policy and a lot of focus on where the policy ought to be and how you might change it in the context of the (new) Clean Air Act." Also, Potter adds, "in the wake of some of the problems the Environmental Protection Agency (EPA) had in the early 1980s, we had an unusually burdensome responsibility to make sure, from a process and substance point of view, that what we did was proper. There was real concern, not only at the political level but below, about what the EPA's role was."

Rosenberg spent his first two years developing legislation to reauthorize the CAA, shepherding it through the White House, defending it on the Hill and handling the negotiations. His key task was to provide "strategic and technical support" to EPA's administrator, acting as his chief advisor in developing "the political strategy and substance." Despite pressure on the White House and the Congress to weaken the administration's proposal, he says, "what came out was close to 90 percent of what we proposed. We're pretty buoyant at the moment, because we accomplished something big."

Since then, Rosenberg has been moving into implementation. He calls the CAA "a massive undertaking" involving "upwards of $25 billion per year of nongovernment expenditure, or 25 cents per day, per person" when fully implemented. "It will require a major reform of our procedures and efforts to take out of the air 56 billion pounds of pollution that's going in every year," he says, and it carries economic, health and ecological implications for every part of the country. The act involves "fundamental regulation" of the auto, oil, steel, chemical, bakery and newspaper industries, among others--"virtually all productive programs and consumers of energy." One of his goals is to develop clean air initiatives consistent with U.S. economic and energy objectives. "To implement a bill of the magnitude of this one, therefore, you have to be skilled in dealing with energy and economic policy."

David Hawkins, who held the job in 1977-80, points out that even a small change of detail in writing a regulation in the CAA context can impose millions, sometimes billions of dollars of yearly costs on an industry. Not surprisingly, most of those affected show intense, fierce interest in such rule making. "About three weeks into the job," Hawkins says, "it dawned on me that my principal function was to absorb pressure. One thing you couldn't delegate was being there, listening to people who had a problem with whatever we were doing, weren't doing, were about to do, or about not to do. For every day you had, you could fill up three days of calendars with demands for meetings with people outside."

In this respect, Potter remembers the "tremendous amount of effort that goes into any kind of rule making that surrounds a traditional air pollutant. We have five criteria pollutants that result in national ambient air quality standards, and they come up for review periodically." For example, the standard for sulfur dioxide--the major element in the acid-rain problem--"involved a review of something like 14,000 documents." He says rule making in the air program probably represents more than two-thirds of EPA's total. "It is truly the trial by fire kind of thing, where you are simply immersed in technical detail. It's not just the scientific information you have to absorb, it's rule making procedures and the voluminous nature of what goes into a regulatory proceeding that encompasses the kind of technical issues you find."

"This is not a place where people make friends, because whatever you propose will be viewed as not strict enough by the environmental side and economically restrictive by business and industry," Rosenberg says. "This is a regulatory function with a large political component; it involves very significant oversight by the Congress and the White House. My goal is to lay the foundation for the national agenda contained in the Clean Air Act amendments of 1990, particularly by encouraging regulatory reform and innovative compliance strategies through the use of market-based incentives."

But if the focus of the work has switched once again to implementation, Hawkins doesn't see any major qualitative changes in the issues. He thinks the bigger workload ahead partly represents the requirement "to catch up for all the work that wasn't done in the last decade." At the same time, the occupant of the job "is still going to be required, for example, to make judgments on what is the best technical level of control that has been demonstrated for certain source categories." He does think the new legislation's acid-rain provisions will require some new skills in this job or in its close subordinates. The air office, he notes, will be running a program which for the first time allows polluting sources to transfer control obligations back and forth. "A market is going to develop," he says, "and it will require writing regulations to document the existence of the things being traded."

The air office functions in headquarters locations in Washington; in a large laboratory in Ann Arbor, Michigan, where it specializes in vehicle and fuel testing; and in several complexes in Durham, North Carolina. Its staff works in all three, and in EPA's regional offices. "We have unique relationships with state and local enforcement people," Rosenberg says. "In many respects the states enforce the CAA under guidance from the federal government. We have a sort of holding company and each state has its own permitting program." But his office regulates the auto industry directly, and the reauthorized CAA added three major areas of direct federal responsibility--fuels, reduction of power plant pollution, and the phase-out of chlorofluorocarbons.

Rosenberg characterizes his staff as "an extraordinary group of able scientists, engineers, political scientists, economists and analysts of all types," and calls them "highly dedicated, aggressive, battle-tough individuals." Potter agrees that the technical competence is outstanding, but says EPA is plagued by "tremendous short-staffing and a shortage of resources," as well as "a certain amount of aggressive turf grabbing." He was constantly driven "by the desire to make things more concise, deal more effectively with issues. And I found you simply can't do that in an agency like EPA. Things take time. Rule making takes time." That leads EPA to "overpromise" what it can accomplish and "it ends up short in time and resources."

Potter believes such factors will cause the air office to miss some deadlines in setting standards under the new CAA in the time frames established. "We've tried to create a system now that avoids risk management in addressing air toxics. We're taking a technology-based approach. That's a monumental task, and we still have to deal with the question of residual risk from a health point of view." On personnel, Ayres says, "the biggest shortcoming is how few staff there are. The new law makes this worse. It's a big, big law to administer. It requires a lot of people to really deal with it. And there are never enough."

The air office currently operates on an annual budget of about $500 million. About a quarter of that goes in grants to the states. For fiscal 1992, EPA sought a 35 percent increase for the air office, including $117 million for implementation of the new CAA amendments--"to do many more things than we ever had to do in conformity to this act," Rosenberg says. "To some extent, it's a onetime requirement. It's not only our budget that's relevant. We're concerned with the other offices in EPA and how well they're funded, as well as with groups elsewhere in the government. Much of the scientific information we rely on is not part of the air office budget."

Even in the mid-1970s, Ayres reflects, this position was contending with "a whole series of new regulations." After enactment of the first CAA in 1977, "there were lots more. And there will be lots more now. At that point, it becomes a big management job--taking a too-small army and figuring out how to work your way through 50 or 60 regulations that are supposed to be put out in two years by an agency that was averaging about five a year for the last several years. Management is one of the key skills here."

The basic political reality of the job, in Potter's view, is its "interface between the political system and what is a nonpolitical agency, an agency that doesn't want to be tainted in any way with any kind of political contact or connection." On the Hill, he says, "you find exactly the opposite." Environmental politics is "a dominant fact of life; you're called to task in a political context every day." The Congress, he says, wants the public to believe that "whatever economic downside there is to what you do from a regulatory point of view can be absorbed and dealt with. I'm not saying that isn't true, just suggesting there is no real understanding in the legislative process of what that trade off is." "You really have the duty to look at both sides of these issues," Hawkins says. "And that creates a psychological tendency to gravitate to the middle as a comfortable place to be. The problem is that each person's perception of where the middle is comes from how many voices there are and how loud those voices are on each side of an issue."

Pressures and problems of the job aside, Rosenberg is glad he took it on, "though I wouldn't call it fun. It's a very hard job." Potter calls it "very intense under any circumstances," but rewarding; "it gives you a perspective that's essential to understand where we're going not only with environment but with regulation in general." "It's such a huge job, so much is done there, and interesting things happen," says Ayres. "It gives you a broad view of corporate America, the working of the government, the play of a major political issue."

Key Relationships

Within the Department

Reports to: Administrator, EPA

Works closely with:

General Counsel
Associate Administrators for Congressional and Legislative Affairs, Pesticides
   and Toxic Substances, Solid Waste and Emergency Response, and
   Research and Development

Outside the Department

Council of Economic Advisers
Assistant Secretaries for Fossil Energy, Nuclear Energy, Defense Programs,
   Department of Energy
Chairman, Federal Energy Regulatory Commission
Assistant Secretary, Office of Policy, Management and Budget, Department
   of the Interior

Outside the Government

State and local clean air enforcement officials, counterpart officials in foreign governments, a very wide range of manufacturing and service industries and trade associations, and of organizations and individuals in the environmental community

Profile of Current Assistant Administrator, Air and Radiation

Name:　　　　　William G. Rosenberg

Assumed Position:　1989

Career Summary:　Chairman, The Investment Group, 1982-89
President, Rosenberg, Freeman and Associates, 1977-82
Assistant administrator, energy resource development, Federal
　Energy Administration, 1975-77
Chairman, Michigan Public Service Commission, 1973-75
Executive director, Michigan State Housing Development
　Authority, 1969-73
Attorney, Honigman, Miller, Schwartz and Cohn, 1965-69

Education:　　　Syracuse University, BA, 1961
Columbia University, JD, MBA, 1965

Assistant Administrators, Air and Radiation Since 1972*

Administration	Name and Years Served	Present Position
Bush	William G. Rosenberg 1969 - present	Incumbent
Reagan	Don R. Clay (Acting) 1988	Asst. Admin., Solid Waste & Emergency Response EPA
Reagan	J. Craig Potter 1986 - 1987	Partner Oppenheimer, Wolff & Donnelly Washington, D.C.
Reagan	Charles L. Elkins (A) 1985	Senior Counsel, EPA
Reagan	Joseph A. Cannon 1984	President and CEO Geneva Steel Provo, Utah

Reagan	Charles L. Elkins (A)** 1983	Senior Counsel, EPA
Reagan	Kathleen M. Bennett** 1982	Managing Director Environmental Affairs James River Corporation Richmond, Va.
Reagan	Edward F. Tuerk (A)** 1981	Retired
Carter 1977 - 1980	David Hawkins*** Council	Natural Resources Defense Washington, D.C.
Carter	Edward F. Tuerk (A)*** 1977	Retired
Ford	Roger Strelow*** 1974 - 1976	Vice President Bechtel Environmental Inc. San Francisco, Cal.
Nixon	Robert L. Sansom**** 1972 - 1973	President Energy Ventures Analysis Inc. Arlington, Va.

*The EPA was created by Reorganization Plan 3 of 1970
**Held position as Assistant Administrator, Air, Noise and Radiation
***Held position as Assistant Administrator, Air and Water Management
****Held position as Assistant Administrator, Air and Water Programs

ASSISTANT ADMINISTRATOR
PESTICIDES AND TOXIC SUBSTANCES

Level IV - Presidential Appointment with Senate Confirmation

Major Responsibilities

- Ensure the effective testing and evaluation of pesticides in use in the United States. Oversee development of standards, regulations and procedures to control existing and new pesticides and toxics judged harmful to humans or the environment. Direct activities to enforce these rules.

- Manage the Office of Pesticides and Toxic Substances, which has responsibility for these activities. Collaborate with other federal agencies working in related areas.

- Act in a liaison capacity with state officials in the same field, and with other governments in the context of the Organization for Economic Cooperation and Development. Speak publicly for administration policy on pesticides and chemicals issues.

Necessary Training, Experience, Skills

A former assistant administrator thinks the ideal individual for this job "is a scientist who doesn't retreat into the narrowness of his or her specialty. I could have done a better job, primarily in managing the organization, if I'd known more science." Others who have held the position stop short of recommending a professional scientist, but strongly emphasize the value of familiarity with technical subject matter. One reason, according to an experienced observer of the job, is that "people make fewer mistaken assumptions if they have some degree of technical background." This source rejects the idea of a "general manager with no background on these issues," but suggests that a lawyer with years of work on the issues would be an adequate alternate candidate. The job's current occupant says "my life would be easier if I had a much stronger founding in science." She describes the judgments she has to make as "a balance of science and policy" that require an ability to understand their "general public policy ramifications." Another asset, in her view, is experience in managing a big organization.

Insight

Two statutes govern most of the work of the Office of Pesticides and Toxic Substances (OPTS). Under the Federal Insecticide, Fungicide and Rodenticide Act (FIFRA), the office regulates the content, use and tolerance level in food of substances designed to kill or reduce various kinds of insects, rodents and plants. The Toxic Substances Control Act (TSCA) gives the office similar jurisdiction and enforcement responsibilities for chemicals such as asbestos, PCBs and lead. This involves testing and analyzing, especially of new products, judging the extent of any hazards they present, and writing rules to control them. A third law administered by the office, the Community Right to Know Act, requires companies to submit inventories of their emissions of some 330 toxic chemicals.

In environmental law, TSCA and FIFRA occupy a distinctive place. "They're both product regulation laws as opposed to pollution control laws," according to Steven Jellinek, who was assistant administrator in 1978-80. That makes them harder to administer. In pollution control, for example, a typical decision might be to "clean up the stuff that's coming out of this pipe to X level, and we know it's going to cost so and so much, and we know the electricity rates will have to go up a penny." That's not easy, Jellinek agrees, "but it's a lot easier than to say, 'well, the risks of this product are such and such, but the benefits are such and such, so we're going to play God and weigh risks and benefits and decide whether we're going to allow the product to be used or take it off the market.' " To him, the essential challenge of the pesticides and toxics laws thus lies in the benefits/risks balance.

The two statutes have some real or potential overlaps that are worth noting. Some hazardous substances have both pesticidal and non-pesticidal applications and are thus open to regulation by either law depending on what the application is. Again, although pesticides are registered under FIFRA, regulators at OPTS set tolerances for pesticide levels in food under provisions of the Federal Food, Drug and Cosmetic Act. That legislation is really the basic directive for actions of the Food and Drug Administration.

Describing the pace of this job, Linda J. Fisher, assistant administrator since mid-1989, says "today I'm in back-to-back meetings all day long. It's hard to get phone calls in, and it's hard to get time to think. Evenings and weekends, driving to work, or running, that's when I can really think about the bigger-picture policy issues and how our decisions fit into them." Issues on her immediate agenda include a renewed emphasis on reviewing pesticides, implementation of the recent phase-out decision for asbestos, and lead in paint, soils and drinking water. She travels domestically and internationally, attends intergovernmental meetings, sees state environment officials and testifies frequently before the Congress. There is also "a decent amount" of media activity. "There is a lot of interest when we make a big chemical decision--such as in June (1990), when we took mercury out of paint," and such announcements are frequently followed up by morning and evening television appearances.

Further, Fisher sees "a change of philosophy" throughout the Environmental Protection Agency (EPA). "We're trying to target our programs to areas of highest environmental health risk and to get pollution prevention and market-oriented concepts in place and working, so that you have industry choosing not to pollute, rather than all of us rushing around trying to clean up what's been done." But John A. Moore, a toxicologist who held the assistant administrator post in 1983-88, thinks EPA's "command and control process" has to change. "It doesn't have the span of technical skills to be able to be prescriptive in exactly how a job is to be done. I think it has got to realize that it can identify what the issues are and the criteria for success, and then leave it to others to figure out a way. The private sector has a lot more innovative ways to achieve something once you tell it what it must do. Why not give them a chance to fail, rather than have the agency do it poorly and often not on time?"

Nobody, meanwhile, pretends that OPTS is adequately staffed in numbers of scientific/technical people. Fisher says "the pay scale and the government's tendency not to put people into the Senior Executive Service unless they're good managers as opposed to just good scientists, is posing us a lot of challenges" in hiring and keeping qualified people. Though pleased with overall staff quality, she warns that "I don't think we can just shrug our shoulders and say that's the way it is. We are making decisions important to society and we need to have the best technical minds. We are too small for what we do and the issues are absolutely critical, whether for industry or the public. That means there's a lot of pressure and a lot of tension in those decisions." Moore notes that "the motivation is very high, but OPTS does not have enough technically and scientifically trained staff to address the job." Karen Florini, an attorney with the Environmental Defense Fund, concurs that OPTS has "some people who are dedicated enough to stick it out," but "they need to attract and retain many more than they're able to do at present." She also notes that working conditions in parts of EPA "are among the worst, stuck off all by themselves in a crummy mall," and not convenient to mass transit.

OPTS employs a staff of 1,500. Eighty percent of them are in the office's headquarters in Washington, where most of the technical work takes place, the rest in EPA regional offices. Though Fisher says a "great proportion of our professionals are scientists or have science backgrounds," the office contracts out some of its evaluation work. In effect, the staff is thus a "combination of in-house and outside" scientists, she says.

Reflecting on the impact of the office's two key statutes, Florini thinks TSCA has far greater promise than the manner in which it has been wielded so far. She cites Section 6 of TSCA, "which basically lets EPA do pretty much whatever it needs to do, be it banning or limiting certain uses, or limiting certain disposal channels, imposing production restrictions, or anything in that area of activity." But in TSCA's 14 years, she finds it has been applied to only "a handful of small-scale, around-the-edges stuff," and to one big action on asbestos. That "took ten years to develop and had a seven-year phase-out schedule." Florini says OPTS is now focusing greater attention on TSCA, "trying to figure out how to use the tremendous potential of section 6."

Jellinek perceives a dislike for TSCA within the Senate Committee on Environment and Public Works, one of several committees in both houses with focused interest in OPTS. The Senate environment panel, he points out, wrote virtually every environmental law except TSCA (which was written by the Commerce Committee), and "thinks it is a weak act. It's not their kind of act. Their laws gave EPA specific instructions for how to regulate. But TSCA gives EPA the discretion to weigh and balance risks and benefits." This may be one reason why, as Florini points out, the statute has never been reauthorized. That makes it, she says, "just about unique among all the environmental statutes, all of which have undergone routine congressional scrutiny in several reauthorizations."

Resolution of the asbestos issue turned on interpretation of another TSCA provision, recalls Moore, this time in section 9. He refers to language in the statute that says, in his paraphrase, "once you identify a problem you think needs to be fixed, before you decide to use TSCA, you must defer to any other statute that might also be able to accomplish the same thing." On the particular question of asbestos, he and the then-EPA chief interpreted that language to permit writing of a new regulation, one that was later signed by EPA's current boss.

In his tenure, Moore thought the pesticides program deserved a major focus of his attention. "There was a feeling that it had lost its image of aloofness to the community it regulated," and "for many years had been in a full-time reactive mode." It had some very good technical people, he says, "but they were shell-shocked." He wanted to get them to the point of "not just sailing where people want to blow us." In his view, they needed confidence and "a clear direction as to what we were supposed to be doing, to get to our objectives, not just what somebody else wants to do." Pesticides, he says, are "emotionally sensitive both from a political and a public perception. You must succeed in managing the pesticides program if you're going to run OPTS."

Despite an increasing workload, the flat pattern of recent OPTS budgets, and continuing debate over where to draw the fine line between environmental and economic concerns, former occupants of this position think its nature is unlikely to change radically. "The issues haven't changed, and they're still very tough," Jellinek says. "In pesticides, for instance, what's more important? Abundant, relatively cheap fruits and vegetables, or virtually zero risk from poisoning? Where do you strike the balance?" His questions evoke the concepts of "relative risk reduction" and "worst risks first," ideas on which the EPA's priorities and the perceptions of the Congress and the public vary sharply. "Those are really difficult issues," Jellinek points out, "and they haven't changed."

At the same time, EPA as a whole is looking increasingly at the idea of risk-based priorities--the recognition that the agency cannot possibly do, simultaneously, everything that the Congress and the public expect it to. If that is true, the first task is to decide which environmental threats are most urgent by determining the risks of each, comparing them and establishing priorities. Second, the agency must communicate and explain those priorities to the Congress, the press and the public, showing which significant environmental problems demand more resources and which less significant problems demand less. But this "comparative risk assessment" is not easy. How, for example, does EPA compare the dangers of an airborne toxic substance that may cause a certain number of cancer deaths with the risks of filling in a given area of wetlands that might have ecological impacts?

Jellinek "loved the job, even though it was frustrating. It was the best job I've ever had. Every decision you make affects a real product. It affects the environment and people's livelihoods." The position offers the incumbent "a lot of discretion in making decisions. I would protect that discretion and use it creatively. The fun is using the discretion to find ways to make decisions that are in the public interest. Unlike many others, this job offers that opportunity."

Key Relationships

Within the Department

Reports to: Administrator, EPA

Works closely with:

General Counsel
Assistant Administrators, Solid Waste and Emergency Response, Air and
   Radiation, and Research and Development

Outside the Department

Commissioner, Food and Drug Administration, Department of Health and
   Human Services
Assistant Secretary, Food and Consumer Services, Department of
   Agriculture
Chairman, Consumer Product Safety Commission
Assistant Secretary, Occupational Safety and Health Administration,
   Department of Labor
Director, National Institute for Occupational Safety and Health
Director, National Science Foundation
Members, biotechnology subcommittee, Committee on Life Sciences and
   Health, FCCSET

Outside the Government

Counterpart officials of other governments, members of the committee on
pesticides and toxics, Organization for Economic Cooperation and
Development (Paris), representatives of environmental organizations, of
manufacturers and industry associations affected by the regulation of
pesticides and toxics, and of professional scientific associations

Profile of Current Assistant Administrator
Pesticides and Toxic Substances

Name: Linda J. Fisher

Assumed Position: 1989

Career Summary: Assistant administrator, Policy, Planning and Evaluation, EPA,
                1988-89
                Executive assistant to administrator, and chief of staff, EPA, 1985-
                88
                Special assistant to assistant administrator, Solid Waste and
                Emergency Response, EPA, 1983-85
                Associate staff member, House Appropriations Committee, U.S.
                Congress, 1979-80
                Legislative assistant, office of Rep. Ralph Regula, U.S. Congress,
                1976-78
                Legislative assistant, office of Rep. Clarence J. Brown, U.S.
                Congress, 1974-76

Education, Training: Miami University, Ohio, BA, 1974
George Washington University, MBA, 1978
Ohio State University College of Law, JD, 1982

Assistant Administrators
Pesticides and Toxic Substances Since 1972*

Administration	Name and Years Served	Present Position
Bush	Linda J. Fisher 1989 - present	Incumbent
Reagan	Victor A. Kimm (Acting) 1988 - 1989	Deputy Assistant Administrator OPTS, EPA
Reagan	John A. Moore 1983 - 1988	President Institute for Evaluating Health Risks Irvine, Cal.
Reagan	Don R. Clay (A) 1983	Assistant Administrator Solid Waste and Emergency Response, EPA
Reagan	John A. Todhunter (A) 1982	Toxicologist SRS International Washington, D.C.
Reagan	Edwin H. Clark (A) 1981	Not available
Carter	Steven Jellinek** 1977 - 1980	Environmental Consultant Jellinek, Schwartz, Connolly & Freshman Washington, D.C.
Carter	Kenneth Johnson (A)** 1977	Not available
Nixon, Ford	Glenn E. Schweitzer*** 1974 - 1976	Director, Scientific and Advisory Committee on USSR and Eastern Europe, National Research Council

* The EPA was created by Reorganization Plan 3 of 1970
** Held position as Assistant Administrator, Toxic Substances
*** Held position as Director, Office of Toxic Substances

ASSISTANT ADMINISTRATOR
RESEARCH AND DEVELOPMENT

Level IV - Presidential Appointment with Senate Confirmation

Major Responsibilities

● Manage the functions of the Environmental Protection Agency's Office of Research and Development. These support regulatory programs in each medium--air, water, toxics and pesticides, hazardous waste--for which EPA is responsible; and, in a long-term context, expand the base of scientific knowledge on which environmental protection rests. Supervise the work of the agency's national laboratories.

● Advise the EPA administrator on the science policy dimensions of agency programs and pollution abatement strategies, and on the regulatory and non-regulatory issues with which the agency deals.

● Represent the EPA on standing interagency coordinating committees. Ensure effective ties with other federal agencies and state agencies engaged in environmental monitoring and research efforts. Work and consult with environmental research officials of other governments and international organizations.

Necessary Training, Experience, Skills

Candidates for this position should offer a combination of scientific or technical training and proven management talent. EPA's research chief must have the discipline to handle sophisticated technical questions and enjoy the respect of science colleagues inside and outside of government, while running a large, rather structured organization with laboratories spread around the country. As a former assistant administrator says, "it's the wedding of the science and the management that's really key." The assistant administrator, moreover, should demonstrate the ability to understand and balance research requirements for programmatic support and for long-term improvement of the agency's scientific arsenal.

Insight

In a very real sense, directing research and development at EPA means working on an every-day basis with a fundamental tension between the two kinds of inquiry this position is responsible for. One is research designed to assist specific agency regulatory and enforcement programs in what are relatively short and finite periods of time. The other is pure research over a longer period, intended to increase the agency's grasp and store of environmental science in general.

It's easy to overstate this conflict, in operational if not in philosophical terms; and as in most such situations, the nominally separate kinds of research involved can overlap in practice. Anyone taking on the leadership of the Office of Research and Development (ORD), however, should understand this tension and its significance. Erich W. Bretthauer, ORD's chief since 1990, puts the issue this way: "The constant changing of priorities, of programmatic research, the new requirements of Congress to implement statutes, and a limitation of budget to do these things are often in conflict with managing the long-term fundamental research you need to address our problems in a more coherent way." Every assistant administrator has recognized this as a "fundamental" conflict, he adds, and "it has always been difficult to deal with."

Views of ORD research differ, of course, with one's relationship to it. The office does not seem to enjoy a lot of recognition from the outside environmental science community, which reportedly sees its research as too project-oriented, aimed more at bringing new regulations to bear than accumulating knowledge. But Steven Schatzow, a former EPA official, says he could have used more help from ORD "in terms of the kinds of pragmatic issues I had to deal with, where I needed technical or research support." He favors a stronger, more practical ORD role in helping EPA to do its daily regulatory job. Schatzow does credit ORD's basic research in the 1970s with developing "tools and concepts" that are in use today. "But that's an awfully long lead time," he points out, "and that's part of the problem I see."

The manner in which ORD functions, Bretthauer says, "is exceedingly complex." For one thing, most of the programmatic research ORD currently performs goes into projects of one to three years' duration to support EPA's greatly enlarged responsibilities under the 1990 reauthorization of the Clean Air Act. Yet ORD, whose requested fiscal 1992 budget authority shows a 12-13 percent rise (to $313 million), is expected to maintain its level of research effort in all of the other "media" that EPA is charged with protecting. The list is too long for detailed inclusion here. But on water, for example, it includes gathering scientific data on toxic pollutants, evaluating the impact of wastes dumped into the oceans, and supporting EPA's groundwater protection program. On toxic substances, it means, among other tasks, the development of scientific and technical methods to predict and control the movement of chemicals in commerce and the environment and measure their impact. On radiation, two key assignments are demonstrations of nonregulatory ways to reduce radon in homes and schools and the monitoring of department of energy nuclear weapons testing. Similar duties exist for hazardous waste management, drinking water and pesticides.

Another way to view ORD's work overall is to look at the functional areas in which, through its five component units, it studies the cause, effects and control of environmental pollution. These are research into pollution's effects on human health and on the ecology; the way it moves through ground and surface water, soils, and the atmosphere; how to identify and monitor it; and how to assess the risks it poses and reduce them. (Risk assessment of problems like environmental tobacco smoke and electromagnetic radiation have drawn considerable attention on Capitol Hill and in the media.) There are also a number of cross-media areas which ORD investigates, among them accidental releases, global climate change, technology transfer, biotechnology and wetlands.

Note, in addition, ORD's role in providing quality control for the agency as a whole. As former assistant administrator Stephen Gage (1977-80) points out, EPA in its development of regulations uses a great deal of data which originates in laboratories other than EPA's. ORD reviews that data, qualifies it where possible, and renders "an overall sense of the validity of the scientific basis used in preparing the regulations," he says. The office gets outside expert counsel in two ways. It uses EPA's 200-member science advisory board and its several standing committees for formal and informal program review. Bretthauer estimates that 70 percent of the board's work is directed to ORD. Second, the office seeks particular help for particular projects such as environmental monitoring and assessment, on particular aspects of which ORD turned to the American Statistical Association and the Board of Environmental Science and Technology of the National Academy of Sciences.

Because environmental concerns reach into many areas of government responsibility, ORD is involved in the work of most of the committees under the Federal Coordinating Council for Science, Engineering and Technology. It is fully engaged in multi-agency programs on high-performance computing, global climate change and educational improvement. Outside of government, the office has about 25 research agreements with corporations or private organizations which provide funding for projects comanaged with ORD. The office also supports environmental research in the academic community. Bretthauer places importance on good communications with the campuses and wants to improve ORD's relationship with them. Globally, he reports a "growing relationship" with the agency's international activities office, through which ORD supplies 60 to 70 percent of the technical support involved in 17 U.S. bilateral relationships with other countries in the environmental area. ORD plays a similar part in multilateral affiliations with the European Economic Community, the World Health Organization, and the Organization for Economic Cooperation and Development.

In its Washington headquarters, 12 national research laboratories, and a number of small field stations, the office employs a staff of more than 2,000 civil servants and 1,000 on-site contractors. About 70 percent have technical training. One problem hampering recruitment of staff, Bretthauer says, lies in the area of expectations. In the swirl of political and other winds that more or less constantly buffet EPA, priorities can shift suddenly as the Congress lays down yet another mandate or an administration revises a policy guideline. This can cut short the amount of research individual staffers might have expected and wanted to do in a specific area, and its prospect can discourage potential entrants. Until recently, the lack of a clear career path for ORD staff was another impediment to hiring. Previously, a bench scientist hoping eventually to move to the top of the career ladder usually had to switch into management duties to get there. Now, under a dual-track system instituted by Bretthauer, people who want to stay at the bench can do so and still attain Senior Executive Service salary levels.

"The need I would target most," Gage says about the office's work force, "is the need to have a well-qualified cadre." Even during his time in the post, when he says the office's budget increased by 40 percent, the staff level dropped from 1,900 to 1,700. "It was an extraordinary challenge," he comments, to carry on such a diverse research program with limited resources. Following his tenure, staff numbers fell further in what Gage calls the "massive" budget cuts of the early 1980s, and while a gradual buildup ensued, "many qualified people working in labs had left." Today "the rebound in some areas, like environmental engineering, has been fairly complete," he believes, but in others, such as health and ecological effects, it has been only partial.

Vaun A. Newill, who led ORD in 1986-88, thought most of the office's employees were "fairly good scientists, perfectly adequate to the jobs we had to do," and notes that "a tremendous amount of good research" takes place in government laboratories. "I think there are a number of good bench scientists in EPA laboratories," Schatzow agrees. But at agency headquarters, he suggests, R&D staff "tend to be people who are removed, and the question is how far removed, from the labs." He wonders how well such staff members can maintain their credentials and continue to speak as scientists.

Bretthauer thinks the office's current upward budget trend reflects "a significant recognition by the agency and the administration" that research must play a larger part in addressing the uncertainties encountered in environmental protection. He helps shepherd ORD's budget request through the agency and the Office of Management and Budget, and defends it on the Hill. "For the first time in eight years," Bretthauer says, "we have an active authorization committee on the Senate side (the Environment subcommittee on environmental protection) that is very interested in research." Both authorizing panels (on the House side it's the Science subcommittee on environment) seem more interested in an EPA research program assessing risk on a cross-media basis, he adds. Between 25 and 30 committees have some piece of the collective congressional jurisdiction of ORD.

Along with the ups and downs of its staff and budget history, the office has navigated an uneven road in other respects. In the first half of the 1970s, Gage recalls, "the science and engineering sometimes did not get done well because communications weren't clear, or there was no follow-up, or accountability wasn't established," and EPA science and technology did not have much of a reputation. Moving into that situation, the administrator under whom Gage served "tried to establish the scientific base for what we were doing," recognizing that regulations built on "clever legal arguments" would not stand up. According to Gage, "good, strong support for science and technology" characterized the period into the early 1980s. When he took over the job half a decade later, Newill remembers, "there had been no one (no appointed and confirmed assistant administrator) in the job for about two years and things were pretty much in disarray. People didn't have direction and were fighting each other instead of working. My major mission was to take the anger out of the system and get things back on track." He brought Bretthauer in as his deputy and "we really worked on turning the place around, getting it back to productive research. We weren't fighting big battles outside as much as fighting internal ones." Yet only since the advent of the present administration, in the view of another well-informed observer, has ORD begun to regain "respect within EPA" or has long-term research won real support. And only now, this source notes, is ORD's budget getting back to previous levels.

Gage thinks the reputation this job once had "has started to come back." But with the breadth of science and technology that EPA encompasses, "it's impossible for any one person to be exposed to all of it. My sense always was that, if you have some strengths in some areas, you don't try to function only in those areas; you step back and bring in qualified people around you to cover the areas you're going to be able to manage only most of the time." Schatzow has additional ideas about managing the job and about the directions it should take. More consideration must go, he believes, to science policy issues--"issues where, in a sense, whatever research you've got, you've got." That means that, regardless of where the research stands, "you've still got to cut on those issues; regulations based on science have to be made," he says. "When you're starting to talk about, say, how you deal with margins of safety, someone in the R&D office who can articulate the science policy aspects of it can become a very powerful player within the agency." Again, he thinks ORD has been a significant contributor in risk assessment where individual substances or situations are concerned. But on the question of comparative risk assessment--evaluating different kinds of risk against one another and developing the technique as a policy instrument--Schatzow thinks ORD has been less influential at EPA than the agency's office of policy.

In general, Schatzow sees the assistant secretary's role as more of a policy, coordinating and communications job, "playing a much bigger role in using what science we have to deal with public policy issues, as opposed to producing the hard science." When the solid waste office comes up with a new regulation, he says by way of example, it gets second-guessed by various agency offices on whether it makes sense, whether there is really a need for it, whether it is cost-effective. "It seems to me," he continues, "that what there hasn't been a great deal of, is second-guessing from a science point of view." That may be the role of ORD, Schatzow suggests: "to provide that kind of capability, that questioning, on the science side." That doesn't mean neglecting research. The ORD chief must manage research that is "very much tied into where you think the regulatory programs are going," and at the same time see to the advance of basic inquiry that doesn't support present programs but will do so years down the road. "That's the kind of predictive planning you need," he adds.

What about current proposals to establish an independent research institute, in which EPA would participate, to study such topics as the social cost of environmental policies, sustainable agriculture, climate change and restoring ecosystems? Bretthauer says "we are interested in exploring the concept of an institute" and that ORD has funded a panel to look into the proposals. It has also convened three public meetings to discuss the idea with representatives of the academic and other communities.

Backers of the institute concept assert that, for a variety of reasons, no existing entity adequately serves the needs to which it would respond. A better idea, Schatzow replies, would be to make ORD's programs more responsive to EPA's regulatory concerns. Others see little gain in creating another bureaucracy and depleting existing agencies of experience and expertise to do so. Still another school of thought argues that the proposals for an institute miss a more fundamental point. In this view, the issue is not whether to create a new entity or where it should be. It is whether research and knowledge, which by definition include uncertainty, are to be central to decision making and regulation or displaced by considerations of ideology and administration.

Key Relationships

Within the Agency

Reports to:Administrator

Works closely with:

Assistant Administrator, Air and Radiation
Assistant Administrator, Pesticides and Toxic Substances
Assistant Administrator, Water
Assistant Administrator, Solid Waste and Emergency Response
Assistant Administrator, International Activities

Outside the Agency

Members of seven standing committees of the Federal Coordinating Council for Science, Engineering and Technology
Associate Director, Environment, White House Office of Science and Technology Policy
Assistant Secretary, Health, Department of Health and Human Services
Director, National Institute for Standards and Technology
Assistant Secretary, Occupational Safety and Health, Department of Labor
Assistant Secretary, Health Affairs, Department of Defense
Director, Environmental Research Laboratories, National Oceanic and Atmospheric Administration, Department of Commerce
Assistant Secretary, Energy Research, Department of Energy
Assistant Secretary, Production and Logistics, Department of Defense
Director, National Institute of Environmental Health Sciences, National Institutes of Health

Outside the Government

Environmental research professionals in industry, academic institutions and public service organizations; environmental advocacy groups; state environmental and health officials; research officials of the World Health Organization, European Economic Community, and the Organization for Economic Cooperation and Development; environmental research offices of other governments

Profile of Current Assistant Administrator, Research and Development

Name:	Erich W. Bretthauer
Assumed Position:	1990
Career Summary:	Career official with EPA, 1962-89, including acting assistant administrator, ORD; director, environmental processes and effects program; and director, ORD Environmental Monitoring Systems Laboratory Professional staff, Committee on Environment and Public Works, U.S. Senate, 1981-82 (on congressional fellowship)
Education:	University of Nevada, Reno, BS, chemistry, 1960; MS, chemistry, 1962

Assistant Directors, Research and Development Since 1970*

Administration	Name and Years Served	Present Position
Bush, Reagan	Eric W. Bretthauer 1988 - present	Incumbent
Reagan	Vaun A. Newill 1986 - 1988	Washington, N.C.
Reagan	Donald J. Ehreth (Acting) 1986	Not available
Reagan	Bernard D. Goldstein 1984 - 1985	Professor and Chairman, University of Medicine & Dentistry of N.J. Piscataway, N.J.
Reagan	Courtney Riordan (A) 1982 - 1983	Director, Environmental Processes & Effects Research Office, EPA
Reagan	Andy Jovanovich (A) 1981	Not available
Reagan	Richard Dowd (A) 1981	Not available
Reagan	Courtney Riordan (A) 1981	Director, Environmental Processes & Effects Research Office, EPA

Carter	Stephen Gage 1977 - 1980	President Advanced Manufacturing Program Cleveland, Ohio
Ford	Wilson K. Talley 1975 - 1977	Not available
Nixon	Albert Trakowski (A) 1974	Not available
Nixon	Stanley M. Greenfield** 1971 - 1974	Not available

* The EPA was established by Reorganization Plan 3 of 1970
** In 1971-73, held position as Assistant Administrator for Research and Monitoring

17

DEPARTMENT OF HEALTH AND HUMAN SERVICES

ASSISTANT SECRETARY, HEALTH

Level IV - Presidential Appointment with Senate Confirmation (Incumbent is an officer in the Commissioned Corps of the Public Health Service)

Major Responsibilities

- Oversee the work of the Public Health Service (PHS), whose eight agencies are engaged in biomedical research, regulation, health care, protection and prevention with the collective task of maintaining and improving the health of the U.S. population. Act as spokesperson for these efforts to the American public and to business and industry, with emphasis on the role of public-private cooperation in promoting good health and preventing disease.

- Maintain effective liaison with other federal agencies sharing these or related responsibilities, including the health aspects of U.S. foreign assistance. Act as chief counsel to the secretary of health and human services on matters relating directly and indirectly to public health. Chair the Life Sciences and Health subcommittee of the Federal Coordinating Council for Science, Engineering and Technology.

- Represent the United States at international levels of effort and cooperation in public health affairs, with individual countries and in regional and worldwide organizations.

Necessary Training, Experience, Skills

Like the somewhat analogous health job at the department of defense, this position relies equally heavily on physician training and administrative experience in the health care or research fields. Clearly, the post requires a practiced physician. But its present occupant says a physician coming into it "without some experience in health promotion and disease prevention, in biomedical research, or in targeting services to minorities or the disadvantaged--someone without some concept of health beyond the purely medical model--would have trouble. The job is more than just how to take care of people who are sick."

Insight

Challenge: Tend the health of an industrialized, highly mobile, ethnically assorted and culturally vigorous community of a quarter billion people. Conditions: Do this in an era of breakthrough for medical and scientific discovery, amid a cornucopia of new products with health implications coming to market, but with a public sector perennially short of resources and a society which ranks astonishingly high in infant mortality. Warning: This goal is achievable only across a mine field of running public and political debate over medically-tinged ethical and social questions that range from AIDS to genetic engineering to animal rights in research.

As basic equipment for this undertaking, the assistant secretary, health (informally, the ASH) deploys the skills and experience of 40,000 scientists, physicians, technicians, managers and support staff in the several divisions comprising the U.S. Public Health Service:

- Biomedical and behavioral research is mostly the province of the National Institutes of Health (NIH), with an $8 billion budget and an extensive program of grants to universities.

- The Centers for Disease Control work to detect, identify and control or prevent chronic and infectious disease, as well as sickness and injury of other origins.

- In the Alcohol, Drug Abuse and Mental Health Administration, mental illness and addiction are the objects of intramural and funded extramural research aimed at better understanding of cause and therapy.

- The Food and Drug Administration (examined elsewhere in this book) regulates and enforces food, drug and cosmetic safety and labeling laws for more than half a trillion dollars worth of products each year.

- Health care delivery to underserved areas and to native Americans, and raising the level of patient care, are responsibilities shared by the Health Resources and Services Administration, the Indian Health Service, and the Agency for Health Care Policy and Research.

- Through updated profiles of harmful materials and the registry of exposure to or illness from them, the Agency for Toxic Substances and Disease Registry reduces or eliminates their impact on human health.

In addition to the heads of these organizations, the ASH gets planning and management help from the surgeon general of the PHS (also described elsewhere) and seven deputies.

Discussing some of the issues involved in this assignment, James O. Mason, assistant secretary since 1989, begins with biomedical research. "Whether we're talking about medicines, devices or knowledge that leads to treatment, cures and prevention, they really have their origins in biomedical research. But we've never decided as a nation if we're going to optimize what can be accomplished." As a result, "a lower percent of peer-reviewed, acceptable proposals are being funded today than 10 or 20 years ago. Where 45 percent of such research found funding in 1980, the current figure is 25 percent.

It's not that money levels available to federal grant-making agencies in research have dropped, Mason says. But two other factors absorb an increasing fraction. One is the indirect cost of research in the institutions where it is done--for administration, construction of facilities and maintenance. The other is the lengthened average life span of grants, up roughly from less than three to four years. While this is positive, adding stability and lessening the distraction of seeking renewals, it also reduces the total number of grants. Down the line, of course, lower grant funding levels augment an already worrisome tendency of the ablest college, high school and even grade school students to choose other, nonscience fields. One result, Mason asserts, is that "the United States is just not measuring up any more" in scholastic achievement in science.

A related problem Mason faces lies in the degree of "our national commitment to science education." For example, as part of the U.S. failure to adopt the metric system, young American scientists and engineers don't learn it in school and must adjust in their teens or later, hampering their competitiveness with peers in other countries. More generally, shortcomings in U.S. science education mean "we're working on a backlog of scientific illiteracy," Mason says. He cites such self-damaging consequences as Americans' rejection of foods irradiated to inactivate harmful bacteria and viruses. Such products are available in European stores, "and probably protect homes from salmonellosis and other diseases. But here people erroneously think that sterilization by radiation leaves the food radioactive."

Among the prominent crises and disputes which have marched across the path of this job in recent years are AIDS and its treatment, animal rights versus biomedical research, the use of human fetal tissue for similar purposes, the philosophic and medical implications of creating new organisms, and misconduct in the grant-making process. The ideological dimension of the fetal tissue debate, for example, was the chief reason for a vacancy of nearly two years (1989-91) in the leadership of the NIH. For Robert E. Windom, who held this position in 1986-89, AIDS was a major preoccupation. When he began, public awareness of the disease was still limited and clinical tests had proven the usefulness of the drug AZT. "When it became apparent that a drug was going to be available, we had more people wanting to be tested. Yet many lacked an understanding of the disease. The focus had to be education." AIDS alone took 25 percent of his total time; the animal rights issue and real or suspected scientific fraud were other big concerns. But many others required his "acute" attention. "You put out fires as they came along," he says. "You never knew from day to day what was going to be the feature attraction."

Mason calls himself an optimist about finding solutions to some of the problems confronting the management of public health. For example, "we're working with the Congress to see if we can't arrive at predictable, stable funding levels that biomedical scientists can depend on." Parenthetically he notes that "it's not as easy to get congressional support for biomedical science as it was in years past." To help the grant-funding process, he thinks the executive branch must demonstrate more leadership in bringing under control research's indirect cost to institutions. The research grant mechanism doesn't exist, he states, "to underwrite the day-to-day costs of American universities." Other sources of money must be found to reverse what Mason calls "the crumbling of our infrastructure"-- the obsolescence of clinics, research laboratories and equipment.

He also believes his office has an important role in encouraging a higher quality of public school science education. On animal rights, he says "we are taking the issue head on, rather than saying we'll let someone else fight that battle." This partly involves a public affairs effort "to let people know about the importance of animals in research." Another part of it involves the Congress, on which the ASH normally spends ten percent of his time. Mason thinks the Hill connection is "absolutely critical" in this job.

To seek outside scientific perspective and advice, the assistant secretary uses an established formal procedure. On the basis of a charter signed by the secretary, requests go out to prospective members of an advisory committee on the issue in question. The secretary must also okay the list of these invitees. Both professional and lay people--physicians and other health care providers, researchers, academics--can comprise such a panel. Normally, the group reports to the secretary and/or the Congress on completion of its work. Among the issues on which advisory committees have met in recent years are AIDS, child abuse, drugs, mental retardation and sleep disorders.

Windom, Mason and others who have held the ASH job believe strongly in the role and potential of prevention in health maintenance. "It was a great concern of mine," Windom says; his own medical practice had shown him the extent of avoidable problems brought on by lack of preemptive knowledge and action. As the ASH, he tried to "focus as much attention as possible" on prevention. In the late summer of 1990, Mason's office announced a program designating "300 measurable, realistic objectives" to boost health promotion and disease prevention in "22 priority areas" by the end of the century. He calls these "not government, but national goals;" they were defined over three years in a series of regional conferences in which some 300 public and private organizations took part. The program "is all doable," he says, encompassing not just how people take care of their own health but also clinical preventive services and data collection. "And the goals encompass the major killers and cripplers affecting society, including cancer, infant mortality, AIDS and drugs."

The PHS requested budget authority of $17.5 billion for fiscal 1992. Across the range of the service's responsibilities, changing priorities logically call for shifting patterns of resource use. But such flexibility has proved difficult in the face of advocacy groups which develop around each program and seek its perpetuation. Attracting qualified staff presents another administrative problem. Though some sacrifice salary opportunities on the outside in favor of service with the PHS, many good people are opting for private sector earnings 50 to 100 percent higher. Many of the best staff who have remained at PHS agencies are those who came in right out of school.

"You sort of have two staffs," according to Dr. M. Roy Schwarz, executive vice president of the American Medical Association. "Those who are older and have lived through it are either positive and have a good view of life and themselves; or they are sour, pessimistic and don't like themselves or their jobs. Then you've got the younger group. They don't know you're not supposed to be able to solve problems, and that's why they're there--they want to do something good." As they realize there are limitations, as their need for financial reward grows, "and they look at how long it takes to climb the ladder, they want to cycle out."

Given the extensive depth and breadth of the ASH job's domain, what might be done to strengthen and facilitate performance in it? Schwarz cites his group's official support for an independent department of health embracing the present structure, and possibly the Health Care Financing Administration, plus elevation of the assistant secretary. "As it is, the job is mid-level in the hierarchy and is often responsible and accountable for things over which it has very little control. And very little input because he or she is excluded from discussions where the decisions are made."

"It's an interesting question," Mason reflects. "I don't think we need organizational changing. You can straighten the deck chairs any way you want. But what it comes down to is whether people are willing to work together and sublimate individual interests for the good of the overall enterprise." To him, real enhancement of the job he holds will come from "building bridges" with other federal agencies, state and local governments, and the private sector.

This requires personal political skill, something Schwarz also emphasizes. "In many of these positions," he says, "although people have their own group or bureau, they don't have a lot of grounding in coalition skills --how you reach areas beyond your own expertise and concern and bring people who have resources and knowledge into a coalition to get to a point. As I watch Washington, it seems to me that's the secret: You have to understand how to push things through, which means you must understand who is in a position to push the buttons."

Key Relationships

Within the Department

Reports to: Secretary of Health and Human Services

Works closely with:

Under Secretary
Administrator, Health Care Financing Administration
Commissioner, Social Security Administration
Surgeon General, Public Health Service
Other assistant secretaries

Outside the Department

Assistant Secretary of Defense, Health Affairs
Assistant Administrator, Science and Technology, Agency for International Development
Assistant Secretary of Labor, Occupational Safety and Health Administration
Associate Director, Life Sciences, White House Office of Science and Technology Policy
Associate Director, Health and Environmental Research, Office of Energy Research, Department of Energy
Assistant Administrator, Solid Waste and Emergency Response, Environmental Protection Agency
Chairman, Federal Trade Commission
Assistant Secretary of Education, Elementary and Secondary Education

Outside the Government

Numerous medical professional, scientific and research associations; hospital and health care associations; state and local health agencies; individual firms in the health insurance and health care sector; pharmaceutical and medical appliance manufacturers; anti-disease volunteer organizations

Profile of Current Assistant Secretary, Health

Name: James O. Mason

Assumed Position: 1989

Career Summary: Director, Centers for Disease Control, and administrator, Agency for Toxic Substances and Disease Registry, Department of Health and Human Services, 1983-89
Executive director, Utah Department of Health, 1979-83
Associate professor and chairman, Division of Community Medicine, Department of Family and Community Medicine, University of Utah, 1978-79
Director of Church of Jesus Christ of Latter Day Saints health-care corporation, 1970-75

Education: University of Utah, BA, 1954; MD, 1958
Johns Hopkins Hospital, internship, 1958-59
Peter Bent Brigham Hospital, Harvard Medical Service, resident, 1961-62
Harvard School of Public Health, MPH, 1963; DPH, 1967

Assistant Secretaries, Health Since 1969

Administration	Name and Years Served	Present Position
Bush	James O. Mason 1989 - present	Incumbent
Reagan	Robert E. Windom 1986 - 1989	Health Care Consultant Sarasota, Fla.
Reagan	James O. Mason (Acting) 1985 - 1986	Incumbent
Reagan	Edward N. Brandt 1981 - 1984	Dean, College of Medicine University of Oklahoma Oklahoma City, Okla.
Carter	Julius B. Richmond 1977 - 1981	Professor Emeritus School of Medicine Harvard University
Carter	James F. Dickson III (A) 1977	Not available
Ford	Theodore Cooper 1975 - 1977	Chairman and CEO The Upjohn Company Kalamazoo, Mich.
Ford, Nixon	Charles C. Edwards 1973 - 1975	President Scripps Clinic & Research Fdn. LaJolla, Cal.
Nixon	Merlin K. DuVal 1971 - 1972	Retired Phoenix, Ariz.
Nixon	Roger O. Egeberg 1969 - 1971	Senior Scholar in Residence Institute of Medicine Washington, D.C.

SURGEON GENERAL
PUBLIC HEALTH SERVICE

Level IV - Presidential Appointment with Senate Confirmation
(Incumbent is an officer in the Commissioned Corps of the Public
Health Service)

Major Responsibilities

- Direct the activities of the commissioned officer corps of the Public Health Service (PHS). Assist the assistant secretary, health in planning, managing, and evaluating its programs and operations.

- Work to improve public awareness and acceptance of the goals of maintaining health and combating disease. Sustain and expand understanding of continuing developments in pharmacology, treatment and prevention that support those goals. Keep the U.S. population informed and instructed on health hazards originating in foods, drugs, dangerous substances, disease, harmful activities and neglect.

Necessary Training, Experience, Skills

Present and former surgeons general say this position requires a physician, and one whose career has not been limited to teaching or research. Candidates should have "worked at medicine," with experience in medical practice that will allow them to understand the clinical and public health dimensions of what the job involves. Beyond that, adds one who has held the post, the surgeon general must be "a diplomat, a people's person, and a listener;" another stresses the ability to communicate. A close observer of the job agrees: "There are certainly skills, gifts and abilities a surgeon general ought to have that he or she can't get in medical school."

Insight

Along with the Public Health Service itself, this position traces its roots back nearly 200 years, when the Congress set up hospitals to care for merchant seamen. With time, the job added the health care of native Americans and other groups to its responsibilities. Its modern history probably begins with the second world war, when the increase and growth of public health institutions across the country accelerated. In that process, the surgeon general position also took on the character of a federal counterpart to state and local departments of health. "That was probably the peak time for the PHS in that role," in the view of Dr. William McBeath, executive director of the American Public Health Association. "It was clearly looked to as the leader of the public health establishment, of the formal social institutions dealing with public health."

Though the surgeon general in the ensuing 25 years enjoyed distinction as the country's preeminent public health professional, McBeath believes several factors have since eroded the position's formal authority. First, the National Institutes of Health emerged as the most important locus of federally-assisted medical research, reinforced by special links to the Congress and the medical school establishment. Second, creation of what is now the department of health and human services (HHS) with an assistant secretary for health (ASH) diminished the surgeon general's significance and visibility in federal health responsibilities. It coincided with "an increasing desire of federal administrations for strong political control over federal agencies." Natural and expectable though this may have been, it put "an awful lot of pressure on the traditional, professional role of the surgeon general." Third, the birth of medicare and medicaid, and their placement in agencies largely removed from the surgeon general's control, produced a massive "tail that wags the dog" in federal health care financing. Fourth, the government closed down the PHS hospital system that had developed from the old merchant marine infirmaries.

Any judgment, however, that these circumstances have stripped the surgeon general position of the potential for renewed and permanent impact and influence may be premature. For example, the success with which former surgeon general C. Everett Koop (1981-89) directed national attention to the dangers of smoking and the seriousness of AIDS left an enduring imprint. "The only thing mandated by law is that the surgeon general inform the people of the country about those things they can do to prevent disease and those things they can do to promote good health," Koop points out. Most people, even those who opposed Koop's appointment to the job, agree that he gave it unprecedented effectiveness and influence in meeting that requirement. A combination of personal qualities and the circumstances of the day, McBeath reflects, enabled Koop to "seize the opportunity to become a far more publicly recognized figure and speak with greater authority" on a number of issues than any of his predecessors. "Koop didn't just tell kids not to smoke," McBeath points out. "He got up and said it's criminal for people to make their livings advertising tobacco products. That's what was unheard of."

For her part, Antonia C. Novello, surgeon general since early 1990, sees the job in terms of "ombudsman" and wants to extend its accessibility. As a "voice of the people," she is seeking to increase the surgeon general's function as a channel of outreach and dialogue for the health needs of all Americans. Specifically, she has chosen to focus her immediate efforts on health problems faced by women, children and families, such as immunization, childhood injuries and, of course, AIDS. "I listen to what people are telling me and then I bring those issues and concerns back to the policy makers," Novello says. "I don't make policy in itself, but there's no policy in health which I'm not a part of." She thinks AIDS and smoking will preoccupy the surgeon general indefinitely, but wants to pay more attention to women's health issues and to what she calls "the children's agenda," in which she lists the problem of underage drinking. She chairs an interagency task force on pediatrics and sits on or co-chairs several others addressing these issues.

Working with the secretary of HHS and the ASH on a "community-centered, family-based" comprehensive care model for AIDS has taken a considerable part of her time. Novello says she maintains an open-door policy for consultations with every other agency in HHS, works with other departments and the private sector on specifics like the labeling of alcoholic beverages, receives constant invitations for congressional testimony, and travels several times a month, in the course of which she tries to air the health problems of neglected or isolated communities and populations. She is usually met on such trips by a commissioned corps member of the PHS representing one of the country's four chief minorities.

The surgeon general oversees the general activities of the 5,700-strong commissioned corps and its personnel administration. To give a more tangible quality to her leadership, Novello says she tries to meets at least once a week with corps members, and says her involvement extends into many details of enlistment, assignments, retirement and awards. The office of the ASH provides the corps budget. Working out of offices at HHS headquarters and in suburban Maryland, the surgeon general has an immediate staff of 14 including a speech writer and a press assistant. She can also draw on the support services of the commissioned corps.

Like her, Koop has a high regard for the corps, which he terms "one of the most unsung stars in our crown; if we didn't have one, we'd have to go out and invent it because of the specific work it does" in a manifold range of public health programs throughout the country and abroad. Within the corps are chief officers for each of 11 disciplines--dentistry, hygienics and sanitary engineering are examples--and, says Koop, "each has a specific window" into private sector organizations in those fields.

Another major connection with the private medical and health care community is the SG's role as one of the "federal medical chiefs," a primarily military group of senior medical officers whose members sit in the House of Delegates of the American Medical Association.

These, and the job's links to the department of defense's health operations, were among the reasons Koop felt adequately in touch with the medical establishment in and outside of the federal government. But part of it, he adds, is the "previous reputation" of the position. Though the job has "neither power nor budget" (its funds are allocated by the ASH), Koop says "there was a day when it did, when the surgeon general was chief of the Public Health Service, and everybody answered to it. The aura of that post goes on. And even though I had no line authority with the National Institutes of Health or the Food and Drug Administration or any of the other PHS agencies, they all acted as though I did. They frequently came to me for advice or awaited my approval. Even though it wasn't necessary, it was a kind of deferential thing to the title." At a given moment, his daily routine might include discussing how to coordinate what he would say publicly, in a surgeon general's warning about aspirin and Reyes syndrome, with what the Food and Drug Administration would tell pharmaceutical manufacturers on the subject; or sorting out a problem between commissioned officers and civil servants; or responding to questions in a press interview or after a speech.

Koop considered his role as a central point in the PHS "around which both the commissioned corps and the civil servants rallied." Was this a bully pulpit? "I never thought of it that way. It was a real, honest-to-goodness pulpit, and a mandated one. It's all education and seeking new ways to communicate things that will change people's behavior." Thus, the onset of the AIDS epidemic, "and the failure of people to understand what we had already told them, made it essential that somebody talk, and nobody else was talking." The AIDS issue illustrated again the importance--at least in Koop's tenure--of media experience and skill in this job. On Capitol Hill, Koop felt he was expected not invariably to deliver "the administration's party line," and on some occasions made it clear he was speaking independently. The essence of his approach is that the surgeon general "should be a person of integrity to whom the public can look for absolutely straight answers," without the pressure of "a tobacco company, a pharmaceutical house, a special interest in the White House or the president himself."

In the wake of Koop's departure has come criticism that the position's independence has decreased and, inevitably, that it is less visible and more politicized. Novello says that, to make headway on the issues her office faces, "it is important that I be both a consensus builder and a diplomat. I meet with individuals and various health groups to listen to their concerns and, as surgeon general, that is what the position demands as the 'nation's doctor.' "

But if Koop, through public recognition and the pressure of circumstances was able to endow the surgeon general's job with authority that doesn't exist on paper, can it and should it retain that quality? Recalling struggles within earlier administrations about whether even to continue the SG position on the rolls, McBeath thinks it remains "very undefined, still with a lot of ambivalence and paradox." He admired what Koop was able to do, at the same time questioning whether it represents the only option for the job's future course. Was it, then, just an aberration, or the beginning of a new pattern? "The surgeon general's job declined in its powers over a period of time," McBeath says, "and Koop changed it dramatically by bringing in this new prominence to the public spokesperson role. I think we've got to wait and see what happens."

Key Relationships

Within the Department

Reports to: Assistant Secretary for Health

Works closely with:

Under Secretary
Directors and key staff, all Public Health Service agencies
Assistant secretaries for Human Development Services, Family Support Administration, Legislation, and Public Affairs
Commissioners for Children, Youth and Families and Administration for Native Americans
Administrator, Health Care Financing Administration

Outside the Department

Assistant Secretary of Defense, Health Affairs
Surgeons general of the uniformed military services
Chief Medical Director, Department of Veterans Affairs
Administrator, Food and Nutrition Service, Department of Agriculture
Assistant Administrator, Research and Development, Environmental Protection Agency
Dean, Uniformed Services University of the Health Sciences

Outside the Government

Public health organizations; professional medical, nursing and hospital associations; drug and medical manufacturers and their trade associations;

anti-disease volunteer organizations; officials of the World Health and Pan American Health organizations; health officials of other governments

Profile of Current Surgeon General

Name:	Antonia C. Novello
Assumed Position:	1990
Career Summary:	Various positions at the National Institutes of Health, 1978-90, including deputy director, National Institute of Child Health and Human Development, and legislative fellow to the chairman, Senate Committee on Labor and Human Resources Private practice of pediatrics and nephrology
Education:	University of Puerto Rico, BA, 1965; MD, 1970 Internship and residency, University of Michigan, 1970-73 Subspeciality training in pediatric nephrology, University of Michigan, 1974, and Georgetown University, 1975 Johns Hopkins University, MPH, 1982

Surgeons General Since 1969

Administration	Name and Years Served	Present Position
Bush	Antonia C. Novello 1990 - present	Incumbent
Reagan	C. Everett Koop 1981 - 1989	Chairman National Safe Kids Campaign Washington, D.C.
Carter	Julius B. Richmond 1977 - 1980	Professor Emeritus School of Medicine Harvard University
Ford	Theodore S. Cooper* 1975 - 1977	Chairman and CEO The Upjohn Company Kalamazoo, Mich.
Ford, Nixon	Charles C. Edwards* 1973 - 1975	President Scripps Clinic and Research Foundation La Jolla, Calif.
Nixon	Jesse L. Steinfeld** 1969 - 1973	Not available

Johnson   William H. Stewart   Not available
                       1965 - 1969

* Served simultaneously as Assistant Secretary, Health
** Functioned on an acting basis during period when position did not exist statutorily

DIRECTOR
NATIONAL INSTITUTES OF HEALTH

Level IV - Presidential Appointment with Senate Confirmation
(Incumbent is an officer in the Commissioner Corps of the Public Health Service)

Major Responsibilities

• Direct the country's leading biomedical research agency in the quest for the origin and cure of disease, functioning, in the words of a former director, as "the principal architect of biomedical research in the United States."

• Set priorities for the research, clinical and educative work of the institution in its own facilities, and for the extensive biomedical investigation it supports in academic and other centers around the world. Oversee preparation and defense of their budgets within the executive branch and before the Congress.

• Cooperate and communicate closely with other federal agencies and officials with responsibilities for medical research, the identification and control of disease, food and drug protection, and other aspects of health care relevant to the organization's work.

• Act as the principal voice of the agency within the federal government and to the national biomedical research community. Serve as a communications channel between all these points for the exchange of positions and views. In all such activity, promote and defend the value and purposes of biomedical research. Represent U.S. policy in this field to other governments.

Necessary Training, Experience, Skills

Only physicians should be considered for the leadership of the National Institutes of Health (NIH) and, of those, only individuals with a substantial record in administering a major medical research or health care facility. Whatever the administrative background, a candidate for this job should understand the methods, issues and stakes in biomedical research. The wider the connections with the community of professionals in medicine and medical research, especially its academic component, the more ably an NIH director will perform. Prior experience in or with the federal government is highly desirable. Considering the clear global leadership and visibility NIH continues to maintain in biomedical research, career achievement and reputation is vital in its top position. The same is true for skills in the human resources and communications areas, useful in relations with the Congress, the public, and the NIH staff.

Insight

In 1975, amid growing concern about the direction and control of the emerging new technology called genetic engineering, the scientific community decided to put a moratorium on its further development until rules could be developed. It asked the National Institutes of Health to take on the task. As NIH recognized, two considerations were involved. First, intense public anxiety had focused on the issue. But second, it was necessary to protect the freedom of continuing scientific inquiry in genetic engineering itself to establish the validity of the risks that had been hypothesized about it.

"What we decided," recalls former NIH director Donald S. Fredrickson (1975-81), "is that we must do it by voluntary guidelines, not by regulation." It was an "important decision," because guidelines would allow scientists a certain flexibility to enlarge knowledge and skill in this field, incorporating new information as it developed. By contrast, Fredrickson says, to regulate genetic engineering, as environmentalists and others preferred, would mean a more cumbersome and possibly counterproductive process--decision documents, impact statements, and the other implements of a regulatory regime. NIH secured the approval of the secretary of health, education and welfare (or HEW, as its parent department was then titled) to try a non-regulatory solution. With agreement from the other federal agencies involved that it would be the decision maker, and with public participation in its deliberations, NIH went the guidelines route.

By this time, there were something like a dozen bills in the Congress to regulate genetic engineering. NIH, however, was busy persuading industry to follow its guidelines and setting up a recombinant DNA advisory committee (now in its 16th year). In the end, not a single regulatory bill came off the Hill, Fredrickson notes, and as time passed, "we slowly learned that most of the feared hazards were not there at all. But NIH had to prove that, as a federal agency, it was capable of taking on this problem of great anxiety to many people."

This kind of exercise has helped build the international reputation NIH enjoys as what another former director, James B. Wyngaarden (1982-

89) calls "the number one research institution in the world." Even though the agency has in recent years run into some highly resistant problems, its 13 institutes continue to represent the leading U.S. center for the theory and practice of advanced medical science in dozens of critical disciplines. In addition to its in-house work, it funds almost all university life sciences research and as much as half the country's total biomedical research, which among other feats has produced new drugs to fight old and new diseases, significant clinical and research technology, and an expanding knowledge about the human body. NIH is a world leader in the effort to decipher the complex mystery of human genetics and its links to disease, including mapping the human genome, and in the attack on cancer and its prevention. Its work on cancer and accumulated expertise and insights in the fields of virology and immunology meant that NIH was ready with knowledge of the human immune system, unequaled anywhere else, when the AIDS virus began to make its deadly presence known.

From its beginning as a one-room laboratory in 1887, NIH has grown into an $8 billion, 300-acre complex in Bethesda, Maryland, just outside Washington. Linked closely to its scores of laboratories and offices are a 550-bed research hospital and clinic. Its National Library of Medicine contains the world's biggest store of biomedical information. The other major fixture on the NIH campus is the international center from which the agency manages its many funding and other relationships around the world. NIH has supported close to a hundred scientists who went on to become Nobel Prize winners; four of them were on the agency's intramural staff. "What we basically have," says Fredrickson (who remains associated with NIH through the National Library of Medicine) "is an agency responsible for determining the quality of research proposals, scientist by scientist, making a decision as to who gets funded, getting the money to the universities, and in a sense standing astride this system."

He notes another role NIH has developed, that of bringing into focus the facts about contentious and worrying public health issues. This began in the 1970s with alarms raised about the possible dangers of mammography examinations. The debate included a fierce and divisive discussion within NIH itself. The agency's solution was to convene a group of experts from every bias and under a certain format to decide precisely "what we knew and what we didn't know," Fredrickson says, "and lay it out for public so they would know." This was the first of the NIH "consensus conferences," a system which has covered such other issues as cholesterol and one that still operates today. To Fredrickson, NIH thus also is "a center of arbitration or distillation of what we really know scientifically. It's got this great collecting basin, where you not only hand somebody a textbook but a living discussion, an analysis of what we know right now. And all these things have to be worked out in the presence of the public."

Another aspect of this public dimension, to him, is the opportunity for the citizenry, through the Congress, to scrutinize and debate the course and objectives of NIH and the amount and allocation of the support it receives. "There is no substitute for federal support of basic research," Fredrickson emphasizes, "because there isn't any other source for it." Dollar for dollar in the federal budget, NIH budget defense each year takes more time than for any other agency, he says. The director spends about ten days with the House Appropriations Committee, and another two or three with its Senate counterpart. The hearings are the public's chance to question NIH's use of the money, Fredrickson says, and the answers "are NIH's responsibility as it interacts with the Congress."

That may not sound very different from any other agency's budget process. But the congressional connection has special meaning and importance for NIH. Consistently since the 1960s, and irrespective of the party controlling the White House or the Congress, legislators have increased funding for the agency over what the president has asked for. This is not only encouraging on its merits; it also helps achieve for NIH what NIH finds difficult to do for itself. As part of the Public Health Service, the director of NIH is a couple of levels removed from a position from which to help develop and promote the agency's budget at the top of the department of health and human services (HHS) or to argue it at the Office of Management and Budget. This may be one reason why support for basic science in the average non-defense science agency went up 12.2 percent in the president's fiscal 1990 budget, according to Wyngaarden, while NIH rose about 3.7 percent. But "Congress has rescued NIH every year," he says. The budget doubled during his eight years at the agency, "and that was chiefly because of congressional add-ons." He notes, however, that "the add-ons mostly come with a good deal of direction as to what to do with them." Such congressional earmarking, and the fact of separate budgets for each of NIH's individual institutes, tie the director's hands when it comes to moving money around. That's not the case, says Wyngaarden, with another big federal funder of scientific research, the National Science Foundation. There, "enormous flexibility" exists to direct funds to areas and opportunities that need attention.

As NIH has grown, the authority of its director has in fact diminished in several respects. Not only did the power to shape budget requests drift largely into other hands but, Wyngaarden says, the NIH director cannot alone decide on "a great many" of the key appointments at the senior scientist grade. While the director generally has a voice in these, "they all have to go up to the department level, and they may take six to nine months to come back." By that time, a nominee for a position may no longer be available. That doesn't make the job of attracting talent with government salaries any easier.

A more important constraining fact of life for the director's position, however, seems to be its and the agency's placement within the HHS hierarchy. There is some history here. NIH predates by years the creation of HEW in 1953. In those days, the surgeon general, the NIH director's only senior authority, gave NIH very broad operational latitude. "He was told to run the place as much as possible like a university within the confines of the federal establishment," Wyngaarden says. As HEW found its feet, developed its mission and established the position of assistant secretary of health, more and more authority at the NIH director level flowed upward. Where NIH directors once conferred with presidents from time to time, Wyngaarden says he never had a sit-down meeting in the oval office during his tenure at NIH. He thinks, moreover, that NIH's location within the Public Health Service's "stifling bureaucracy" cramps the essential qualities that made it a world-class institution. "It's not going to remain that way unless that situation is corrected," he warns.

A different perspective on NIH's relative autonomy comes from William McBeath, executive director of the American Public Health Association. "Although NIH is still a pro forma part of the Public Health Service," he says, "it is in my view completely independent of it." NIH has a special relationship with the Congress, he notes, and that connection is fairly well linked "to the medical schools and its own bureaucracy."

Yet another factor equally significant in reducing the director's clout over time is the job's evolution in relation to the component institutes it is supposed to oversee. "These powerful organizations are all moving centrifugally," Fredrickson observes. "They all want to go off in separate directions." While this tendency is healthy for the individual disciplines which the institutes address, "they have to be constrained to continue to move around the center," he says. In the compromise of the early 1970s which ended the National Cancer Institute's move to break away from NIH, Wyngaarden relates, "many of the authorities of the NIH director were delegated to the director of NCI." NCI was also accorded the special mechanism of a budget bypass to the White House (see the profile of the NCI director position elsewhere in this volume). In the years that followed, other institutes gained various degrees of independence from NIH central direction.

"Many aspects of their governance were different," Fredrickson remembers, but he and the then director of NCI came to amiable terms about it. "I told him that, if there was going to be a schism with two popes, I was not going to be the one in Avignon," he says, "and from that day we never had a problem." But in operational terms today, Wyngaarden asserts, "the real authority is at the individual institute level, and the director is sort of in the middle." Every institute director wants to "micromanage the system," he says, adding that it is "far too carefully managed now. Science doesn't thrive when it's excessively managed from the top down."

The one control the NIH director has on the system, Wyngaarden thinks, is in responding to the appropriations subcommittees about how the NIH would use additional resources if they were made available. The director has the chance at that point to "massage the budget request, and accept or reject certain components of it," he says, and every year he put "the maximum amount of money into individual research project grants." What the director really doesn't have, he points out, is an ability to control the flow of information between the department and the institutes, or between the congress and the institutes since each of them has its own legislative liaison. "I would hear about something only when it went dreadfully wrong," Wyngaarden says.

But the NIH director does have the ability "to represent the agency --and there's a lot of representational work with the department, the administration in general, and with the Congress. That's both to promote things we wanted to see accomplished and to intercede in the event something could be damaged." He probably spent more time on the latter than the former, Wyngaarden estimates, and grew fond of paraphrasing Yogi Berra that the director's job is "95 percent damage control and the other half is budget." And in that, he adds, "there's more truth than poetry."

For fiscal 1992, the administration requested budget authority of $8.8 billion for NIH. Of this, $6 billion will finance the grant support of basic research, an increase in this area of about a third of a billion dollars, and $851 million of it is designated for HIV-related research. Since about 1980, NIH total grants per year have risen to 20,000; they aid the work of some 50,000 scientists in this country and abroad. Total disbursements for research are at all-time highs. But in 1990, the agency funded only 25 percent of the new research proposals it received, a record low. The value of the average grant is greater, however, and its length has stretched, providing recipients more stable funding and saving time in renewal applications.

How far should NIH's mandate reach in supporting the competitiveness of U.S. industry in areas like biotechnology? The question goes to the enduring issue of basic versus applied research. The "struggle" between them "is a fundamental tension that is still as big today as it was in 1941," Fredrickson comments. Sheldon Wolff of the Tufts University School of Medicine and the New England Medical Center thinks that "biomedical research in this country has flourished because of the NIH, not because of industrial accomplishment or investment." One of this job's challenges, he says, is to remind the executive and legislative branches "that the NIH is a national treasure--that it supports basic research in the biomedical sciences and is one of the few places where that is done. It was those kinds of investments in the 1970s that made possible the explosion of information that's occurring today." A look at what Germany and Japan invest in biomedical research, he says, shows that they "spend about twice what we do, per capita. We spend more total dollars, but not as much as a percentage of GNP. That used not to be the case." The NIH, Fredrickson believes, must always go in two directions. It should remain a center of basic science "because it must stand for the science community and make it as effective and well equipped as possible." But the agency can never ignore the potential for "the movement or the translation" of its work into practical applications, even though that may bother some believers in pure science for its own sake. "It has to be the living proof that this is a whole continuum," he says.

NIH's relationship with the biotechnology industry has meanwhile been growing, putting it into the middle of a heated discussion about what the nature of such ties should be. Legislation enacted in 1986 promotes cooperation between NIH and industry and has spurred more than 400 cooperative research and development agreements between NIH-funded scientists and individual firms. The shortage of research money is, of course, what drives this trend; according to NIH figures, industry's share of the total bill for health R&D in the United States is approaching half, compared to less than a third a decade ago. Although the agency recognizes the implications of links that are too close and has moved to limit them, the situation worries some observers who think that NIH's basic posture may be altered. On another level, the NIH has been troubled by misconduct within the ranks of its intramural staff by individual scientists who improperly exploited their connections with industry. The problem has generated high-visibility congressional inquiry and led in 1990 to establishment at NIH of an Office of Scientific Integrity.

NIH's intramural staff numbers 15,500. Almost 5,000 are doctorate-level scientists, and a third of the total staff is foreign. The director is an officer in the commissioned corps of the Public Health Service, at a salary of $108,300 that Wolff terms "ridiculously" low. Wyngaarden discovered, shortly after he took over as director, that senior salaries of the defense department's Uniformed Services University of the Health Sciences, just across the street, were pegged to the average pay of equivalent positions at five medical schools in the area. "Their salary scale at the top is twice NIH's," he says. To ease this circumstance, NIH had earlier approved a carefully safeguarded policy of retention by senior staff of honoraria earned in speaking engagements. On his watch, Wyngaarden applied the same rules to consulting, and later the Federal Technology Transfer Act provided for the retention of patent royalties earned by NIH staff. As he points out, however, these three mechanisms benefit a mere hundred or so of NIH's doctorate-level staff. "And they're the same hundred," he says. "It doesn't get spread very widely. On the other hand, those are also the hundred we're most likely to lose. So it has been helpful."

Salary, and the limits on the NIH's director's authority described earlier, are only two of the reasons why no Senate-confirmed presidential appointee filled the job for two years between 1988 and 1991. A third major factor was what someone has labeled the "politicization" of biomedical research. This is the current official policy prohibiting federal funding of research using tissue from aborted human fetuses for transplant into humans (though, curiously, not into animals). All the evidence is that several of the early prospective nominees for the NIH leadership in the 1989-90 period rejected the job partly because of the so-called litmus-test question put to them ahead of time about their views on abortion.

In early 1991 Bernadine P. Healy, a physician and professor specializing in heart disease, became the agency's 13th director. She supports fetal tissue research. In accepting appointment, she said she would not change that personal view but, as a member of the administration, would support its position against such research. Notable among her early initiatives at NIH has been the organization of a large program focusing on women's health, including breast cancer and heart disease, the two biggest killers of American women. She is equally committed to minority health issues and to minority training.

Given its perceived structural problems, the harm being slowly done to senior staff quality by noncompetitive salaries, the erosion of authority and the other difficulties this position faces, can prescriptions for improvement be written? Since leaving NIH Wyngaarden has considered and discussed with the White House two frameworks to put the position on a new footing, but says only one is practicable. As a freestanding agency, and provided that it remained under the jurisdiction of the same congressional committees as at present, NIH might prosper, he says. But such a change is "politically unlikely" and, further, NIH does benefit from being perceived on the Hill as part of the "health enterprise." Wyngaarden, therefore, would take NIH out of the Public Health Service but not out of HHS, and make the director an under secretary, reporting to and representing the secretary on the science policy committees at the White House.

Absent a change in the status of NIH along such lines, he advises, "the most important thing a director can do about the situation is to establish a solid relationship with the Congress. There is no other country that involves science policy the way we do, or that funds its institutions the way we do. It's a kind of lengthy open hearing process." He looked on NIH's congressional hearings "as one of the highlights of the year," a period in which he would spend the better part of three weeks testifying on both sides of the Hill, and able as well to hear and comment on every component institute's testimony. It was also an opportunity to hear what representatives of the outside community had to say to legislators. He had "considerable input into the process," Wyngaarden says, and "I think that being able to do that is very important."

Key Relationships

Within the Department

Reports to: Assistant Secretary, Health

Works closely with:

Surgeon General
Directors, NIH component institutes
Commissioner, Food and Drug Administration
Director, Centers for Disease Control
Administrator, Alcohol, Drug Abuse and Mental Health Administration
Administrator, Health Research and Administrative Services
Commissioner, Food and Drug Administration
Director, National Institute for Occupational Safety and Health

Outside the Department

Director, National Science Foundation
President, Institute of Medicine, National Academy of Sciences
Assistant Director, Health and Life Science, Office of Technology Assessment, U.S. Congress
Assistant Secretary, Health Affairs, Department of Defense
Assistant Secretary, Research and Development, Environmental Protection Agency

Outside the Government

The national and world medical and health community--professionals in medicine, biomedical and disease research, clinical care, public health, disease prevention and teaching; university medical faculties and research departments; health care, hospital and nursing associations; voluntary health organizations; biotechnology industry; advocacy groups on medical and medical research issues

Profile of Current Director, National Institutes of Health

Name: Bernadine P. Healy

Assumed Position: 1991

Career Summary: Chairman, Research Institute, Cleveland Clinic Foundation, 1985-91

Deputy director, White House Office of Science and Technology Policy, 1984-85

Various positions with The Johns Hopkins University School of Medicine and Hospital, 1976-84, including director of the coronary care unit, professor of medicine and assistant dean

Education: Vassar College, BA, 1965
Harvard University Medical School, MD, 1970

Directors, National Institutes of Health Since 1969

Administration	Name and Years Served	Present Position
Bush	Bernadine P. Healy 1991 - present	Incumbent
Bush	William F. Raub (Acting) 1989 - 1991	Deputy Director NIH
Reagan	James B. Wyngaarden 1982 - 1989	Foreign Secretary National Academy of Sciences Washington, D.C.
Reagan	Thomas E. Malone (A) 1981 - 1982	Vice President American Association of Medical Colleges Washington, D.C.
Carter	Donald S. Fredrickson 1975 - 1981	President D.S. Fredrickson & Associates, Inc. Bethesda, Md.
Ford	Ronald Lamont-Havers (A) 1975	Deputy Director for General Affairs Massachusetts General Hospital Boston, Mass.
Nixon	Robert S. Stone 1973 - 1975	Director, Center for Health Systems & Technology Texas A&M University College Station, Tex.
Nixon, Johnson	Robert Q. Marston 1968 - 1973	President Emeritus University of Florida Gainesville, Fla.

DIRECTOR, NATIONAL CANCER INSTITUTE
NATIONAL INSTITUTES OF HEALTH

Presidential appointment with Senate Confirmation (incumbent is an officer in the Commissioned Corps of the Public Health Service)

Major Responsibilities

● Manage the National Cancer Institute (NCI), a $1.7 billion agency devoted to the prevention, diagnosis and cure of cancer. Direct and coordinate its major functions of basic research and clinical trials, grant making to fund the independent research of others, and core support of comprehensive centers throughout the country that work toward the same objectives.

● Work closely with the National Cancer Advisory Board and the director, National Institutes of Health (NIH) to shape, protect and enhance these activities. Maintain productive relationships with other components of NIH, and with the national medical research community, especially in the biomedical area.

● Act as spokesman for NCI's work and goals to the Congress and to national and international audiences and organizations.

Necessary Training, Experience, Skills

A trained scientist, probably a physician, will handle this position best. For example, its incumbent says the NCI director "should be intimately familiar with scholarly science issues as they apply to human beings. That doesn't necessarily mean an MD, but the job would not be a good idea for someone unfamiliar with the principles and importance of clinical trials and issues related to prevention, to early diagnosis and control of cancer, and the requirements of moving things from lab to bedside and vice versa." A previous director favors a physician in the post because "you're trained to make decisions quickly even though you don't have all the information, you're pressed, and there's a life at stake." In any case, candidates for this job need such qualities as distinction in research, good organization, an ability to set and maintain priorities, and articulacy. One of those who has held the position suggests further that

NCI's leadership requires different combinations of background and skill at different stages. "What matters is what era it is, what resources are available, and what the initiatives and issues are."

Insight

The National Cancer Institute has certain "special authorities" with respect to budget, reporting responsibility and the appointment of its director. These set it off from most of its fellow NIH organizations and in fact from most other executive branch entities. They flow from the 1971 National Cancer Act, which framed the congressional view of cancer as a top national health priority demanding the focus of a strengthened NCI with enhanced access to resources. The legislation, controversial then and now, made NCI's director a presidential appointee and established presidential review and ombudsman panels. It also permits NCI to express its real "professional needs" directly to the president in a "bypass" budget that parallels and supplements its conventional budget submission through the NIH and its parent department of health and human services (HHS).

Preventing and curing cancer is "probably among the most complex and difficult assignments in science today," says Dr. Samuel Broder, NCI director since early 1989. One million Americans, he said in early 1990, would learn they have cancer during that year, and about half would eventually die of it. The response must be "an intense effort to generate knowledge and apply it quickly." Moreover, he told a House Appropriations subcommittee, the product of NCI research belongs to people of every age, income, race, location and social status.

The thrust of this effort carries well beyond U.S. borders into bilateral research programs with a dozen countries including Japan, China and the Soviet Union. It involves multilateral cooperation within the World Health Organization, the Pan American Health Organization, and the International Association for Research on Cancer. And NCI is providing low-cost or no-cost flows of information to users in Poland, Hungary and Czechoslovakia, struggling back to the mainstream after 45 years in the shallows. "It's a flagship for efforts throughout the world," says Dr. Arthur C. Upton, who headed NCI in 1977-79.

NCI is both a principal player and the preeminent support system in the country's battle against cancer. It conducts research on its NIH campus outside Washington and at its Frederick, Maryland, research facility about 50 miles away, using its own full-time employees and contractors. It is also a major source for the funding of institutional and individual research nationwide. It further helps finance a network of 55 cancer centers around the country that compete for core NCI funding somewhat in the manner of research grantees. The centers provide an interdisciplinary focus on cancer at the local, regional and national levels. Mostly located in the technical environment of universities and medical schools, many of them mount a full-court press: basic research, a high level of clinical activity, heavy patient loads and active engagement in community cancer control programs. Coordinating all of this work enables NIH to develop knowledge about new drugs, therapies, and preventive procedures in a continuous process of discovery, refinement and application.

To give NCI the extra measure of independence and control judged necessary to sustain this mission, the 1971 legislation created two entities. One is the National Cancer Advisory Board (NCAB). Its approximate 18 members are appointed by the president and function, Broder says, like a board of trustees. For certain kinds of issues, this mechanism essentially gives the NCI director a line of accountability to the president separate from the day-to-day reporting responsibilities to the director of NIH. The legislation also established the three-member President's Cancer Panel. Its chairman has authority to convey to the president any matter the director feels is impeding the work of NCI. This gives the director of NCI what amounts to an appeals board linked directly to the president.

A third authority accorded to NCI by the Congress is the bypass budget, described by a recent NCI document as the funding necessary to take full advantage of "the scientific opportunities currently available." NCI and the NCAB develop the bypass budget and send it to the president independently of the Office of Management and Budget; at the same time, NCI shapes a conventional budget through the conventional channels. The bypass mechanism, Broder explains, "doesn't mean we can live on whatever budget we want. We have to live within the budget allocation Congress gives in the standard process. At the same time the special authorities are designed to optimize the mission of the NCI and take care of the special requirements cancer research has." They are not, he adds, a means to gain "special privileges."

NCI's current budgets represent about 23 percent of NIH's appropriated resources. For fiscal 1991, NCI's appropriated regular budget amounted to $1.720 billion; the 1992 request is for $1.815 billion. In 1989, about 85 percent of total resources went to research and research support, 10 percent to resource development, and 5 percent to cancer prevention and control.

Dr. Vincent T. DeVita, NCI director in 1980-88, remembers handing the bypass budget directly to the president on more than one occasion. He calls it "clearly a symbolic way of making a statement legally that otherwise was considered budget busting." The two budget documents, he says, "always differed by a considerable amount," leading sometimes to awkward questions from the Congress. "We've routinely gotten less than the bypass budget asked, but it has an impact, and an effect on planning," Broder says. "Some aspects of the budget, certain emphases, do get incorporated into policy." In the past few years, notes Alan Davis, a vice president of the American Cancer Society and a veteran observer of NCI, the bypass figure "has crawled further away from the actual," largely because of the demands put on NIH resources by the AIDS emergency.

AIDS research began at NCI because that's where most of the work on retrovirology had taken place. About 15 percent of the budget went to AIDS; the drug AZT was an eventual product. As time went on, funding increases for NCI were often earmarked for AIDS research. "With a finite pool of money and increasing support for AIDS, it was illogical to say that cancer research was still going to do just fine," DeVita says. "But it was hard to argue that publicly, because it sounded as if you were against AIDS research." This is more of a problem now, he adds, "and it's also been coupled with the budget crisis."

"There are always more good ideas to pursue than we have the resources for, and that requires a lot of intense prioritization," says Broder. In 1983, NCI funded nearly 29 percent of the new applications for research support recommended by its review process. That figure reached above 31 percent in two succeeding years, but in 1989 stood at just over 19 percent. While funding resources have risen, they have not kept pace with the number of applications. One of the issues in this squeeze is the value of basic research versus the demand for product, and the need to strike the right balance between them. Here Broder takes the view that while NCI is a scientific and scholarly organization, it must also ensure that the public has confidence in and is comfortable with how it uses its resources. "In that sense, we have to deliver a product, we have to deliver results. We can't simply say our job is to do basic research, without worrying about whether it has any meaning or application. We routinely have situations in which people of good will with strong merit on their side can look at the same facts and come to opposing conclusions." Hence, he explains, NCI must seek balance and a diversity of opinion and activity.

Another set of considerations involves the relative priorities placed on the prevention of cancer and on treatment of the disease. Reflecting on this, Upton notes the naturally strong desire to relieve suffering and the consequent powerful impetus toward treatment. Much more difficult, he thinks, is getting support for prevention, "especially when it may only benefit somebody ten or 20 years in the future." The U.S. medical community is not nearly as committed to prevention as to treatment, he asserts. Instead, "American medicine is more nearly crisis-oriented." Though efforts at prevention should equal those of treatment, the cancer program finds itself working through "a medical establishment that is not itself attuned to the same goals." But Broder says on this point that "we've made prevention activities a very high priority, which Congress has been interested in for a long time, and it is now becoming incorporated into everybody's thinking."

What about the charge that NCI grant making tends to favor the same old large institutional research operations over individual projects that have equal potential for significant advances? "I don't think it's fair to say that NCI doesn't listen to the small scientists," Upton responds. He points to the percentages of grant approvals by age. "The young scientists are doing better than the old ones. It's true that there are established investigators who somehow seem to get renewed year after year, but that reflects their ability, not the fact the NCI likes them. Because if the study sections don't think that what they're proposing when they go in for renewal makes sense and has scientific merit, they get disapproved."

A high percentage of NCI's 2,500-member staff are professional scientists, a group Davis calls "first-rate." One of the agency's strengths, Broder senses, lies in its provision of "exceptional opportunities for people at very early phases of their careers that normally would not be available. In part, that's because the place has a way of allowing careers to flourish." NCI has a retention problem not because of dissatisfaction but because employees "get a lot of early professional growth and then they get astonishingly lucrative and important and scientifically reaffirming job offers with a lot of responsibility." That is not all bad, he adds. "What it's doing is opening up new opportunities for people to be creative, to succeed and move to other positions, which brings credit to them and to the institution that generated them. It adds a certain dynamism and vitality you might not otherwise get."

In the view of some, NCI's unusual situation within NIH has earned it a few problems along with the advantages. Davis mentions the "envy" of other NIH institutes as one of the NCI director's problems. He suggests also that the agency's special authorities may be one reason for recent difficulty in finding qualified candidates for the NIH director's position. There seems no question that the agency's privileged position has created frictions between its director and the chief of NIH. "We often had differences of opinion," DeVita says, adding that he sometimes signaled them by using the bypass budget or the President's Cancer Panel as a vehicle. On this issue, Broder believes that NCI's special authority and special issues have benefited everything up the line--NIH, the Public Health Service, the department. "The commitment NCI was able to make to basic research in the 1970s produced the explosion in biomedical research and the revolution in bioengineering," he says. "Many issues relating to the U.S. lead in biotechnology are directly related to research NCI was able to do. Many of the programs we pilot or experiment with become adopted as NIH policy. NCI should be part of NIH; it's important for its unique, distinctive component role to be there."

Broder also thinks the NIH "experiment"--the idea of having research programs linked to categorical institutes--showed "enormous insight." Few taxpayers other than scientists would agree that public funds should support research project grants per se, he believes. "It's unlikely people would understand intuitively and clearly if you just asked for support for science in general." Instead, the NIH concept harnesses science to the attack on disease, with the public able to articulate the degree of concern it attaches to cancer, heart and lung disease, diabetes, and the rest. "That," Broder declares, "is a stroke of intense genius. Cancer was the first categorical institute in the 1930s and it set the model. I'm not sure people realized what they were doing when they did it, but it was an intuitive thing and very effective. I think it has been responsible in large part for the commitment of resources people have been willing to make to the medical system. We have to preserve that particular approach."

DeVita calls NIH "a fairly magical place," and thinks the leadership of NCI "may be the best on the NIH campus at that level. Like every job, it had things that were a pain in the neck, but there were also many exciting things." Upton uses some of the same words about the position. "I never questioned that I was doing something very important; I couldn't imagine anything more fulfilling." It didn't allow him to attend seminars, however, or visit libraries or read scientific literature, activities he believes are necessary to be effective. "But the fact I couldn't do it doesn't convince me that somebody else might not be able to," he emphasizes.

Broder feels the job's occupant needs sensitivity to what NCI can and cannot do, and the need to address "certain social forces." The role of poverty in cancer, for example, "is an important area to come to terms with. If you don't make that connection, you may not be serving people who have the worst cancer statistics. You have to push programs that make a difference in prevention, early diagnosis and treatment for all Americans, particularly individuals who are underserved." Though the position requires some understanding of budgets and resource allocation, he says, "it would be a mistake to have someone who is overly focused on those aspects. In this job you have to see the forest and the trees. The hyperanalytical, entirely budget-driven approach would not be fully useful for this job."

Key Relationships

Within the Department

Reports to: Director, National Institutes of Health

Works closely with:

National Cancer Advisory Board
President's Cancer Panel
Commissioner, Food and Drug Administration
Directors of other disease-related NIH Institutes
Administrator, Agency for Health Care Policy and Research

Outside the Department

Chairman, Nuclear Regulatory Commission
Assistant Secretary, Environment, Safety and Health, Department of Energy
Assistant Administrator, Research and Development, Environmental
   Protection Agency

Outside the Government

World Health Organization, American Cancer Society, American Association
for Cancer Research, American Association of Immunologists, Association
of Community Cancer Centers, American Society of Clinical Oncology, other
professional associations in cancer subspecialty areas, and directors of
counterpart agencies in 11 countries of western Europe, Japan and the Third
World

Profile of Current Director, National Cancer Institute

Name: Samuel Broder

Assumed Position: 1989

Career Summary: Associate director, Clinical Oncology Program, NCI, 1981-88
                     Senior investigator, Metabolism Branch, NCI, 1976-81
                     Investigator, Medicine Branch, NCI, 1976-76
                     Clinical associate, Metabolism Branch, NCI, 1982-75
                     Residency in medicine, Stanford University, 1971-72
                     Internship in medicine, Stanford University, 1970-71

Education: University of Michigan School of Medicine, MD cum laude, 1970
                     College of Literature, Science and the Arts, University of
                        Michigan, BS, 1966

Directors, National Cancer Institute Since 1969

Administration	Name and Years Served	Present Position
Bush	Samuel Broder 1989 - present	Incumbent
Carter, Reagan	Vincent T. DeVita Jr. 1980 - 1988	Physician in Chief Memorial Sloan Kettering Cancer Center New York, N.Y.
Carter	Arthur C. Upton 1977 - 1979	Ch., Dept. of Env. Medicine N.Y. Univ. School of Medicine New York, N.Y.
Ford	Guy Newell (Acting) 1976 - 1977	Not available
Nixon, Ford	Frank J. Rauscher 1972 - 1976	Retired
Nixon	Carl G. Baker 1970 - 1972	University of Maryland College Park, Md.
Kennedy, Johnson	Kenneth M. Endicott 1960 - 1969	Deceased

COMMISSIONER
FOOD AND DRUG ADMINISTRATION

Level IV - Presidential Appointment with Senate Confirmation

Major Responsibilities

• Direct the work of the Food and Drug Administration (FDA) in regulating the safety and reliability of the national food supply and of human and animal drugs, vaccines and other biological products, medical devices, radiological products and cosmetics manufactured in or imported to the United States. To this end, assure timely monitoring, inspection, evaluation and enforcement.

• Work with other elements of the department of health and human services (HHS) and with other federal agencies with related responsibilities. Consult the assistant secretary for health and other senior department officials on FDA policy and, as necessary, on specific issues the agency deals with. Represent U.S. food and drug policy to the Congress and to other governments and international institutions.

• Maintain liaison with health officials of states and localities, and with the professional nongovernment medical and biomedical research communities and the pharmaceutical, food, health care and other industries under FDA regulation.

• Serve as principal administration spokesman on food and drug matters.

Necessary Training, Experience, Skills

The optimal requirements to make an impact on this difficult assignment begin with a knowledge of food and drug law. Lack of it is a handicap in implementing the FDA statute and its revisions and amendments, and there is almost no time to learn these basics on the job. Next, the commissioner should almost certainly be a medical doctor, preferably one who has taken care of patients. Biomedical research training and experience, if not imperative, is a distinct asset here; the same is true in the area of pharmaceuticals. Third comes a close familiarity with the Washington political process, especially with the Congress, and a sense of how policy evolves. "I don't know how anyone could do this job who hasn't worked in this town before," says one of those who has held the post. Fourth is the ability to manage projects and people, coupled with an ability to think logically. Finally, but hardly least, is the skill of communication, a requisite in everything from interagency policy discussions to the Hill to the television studio. And a veteran of the position suggests one further resource that will serve the commissioner well: the hide of a rhinoceros.

Insight

The enormity of the tasks facing the FDA and the complexity of its problems defy attempts to draw comprehensive but concise conclusions. But the Committee on the FDA, an advisory group appointed in 1990 to study the troubled agency, came close. In a progress report during the course of its investigation, the committee said that "circumstances inside and outside the FDA are challenging the agency's ability to perform its appointed tasks." Not bad for understatement, either.

A brief outline of those circumstances, and the tasks assigned to the FDA, is a necessary exercise in understanding the challenges to the leadership of this overburdened, understaffed and under-equipped agency --even as it appears to be turning some sort of a corner:

- Food and drugs scarcely describe the reality of what the FDA tries to cover. It is supposed to regulate products worth half a trillion dollars a year. As it likes to point out, that's about 25 percent of everything American consumers spend their money on. To meet this responsibility, the agency in 1990 had a budget of only $600 million to operate with.

- Resources improved for fiscal 1991. But, as pointed out by David A. Kessler, FDA commissioner since late 1990, the 1991 budget ($654 million) equaled less than a sixth of the annual gross revenues of a major U.S. cosmetics company. It brought the FDA staff back only to its level of 11 years earlier. The proposed 1992 budget would rise to $770 million. But some $200 million of it would take the form of user fees on companies the FDA regulates--an idea the Congress has not found appealing.

- To monitor the manufacture, import, transport, storage and sale of the products it surveys, the FDA employs 1,100 inspectors and investigators. According to agency statistics, they visit just under 20,000 facilities each year of the 90,000 businesses the FDA regulates, collecting 70,000 samples of everything from cosmetics, wine, microwave ovens and the national blood supply to canned fruit, phenobarbital and prosthetic devices. As a result of these efforts, says the FDA, an annual 3,000 products are voluntarily withdrawn from the market or removed by FDA-instigated court order, and it detains a further 20,000 imported items at their ports of entry. Each year the agency approves nearly a thousand new drugs, including 20 to 30 in the breakthrough category.

• In 1988, four members of the FDA's generic drug division accepted bribes from manufacturing companies to speed up agency approval of their products. Several companies also provided false information to the agency. Eighteen convictions of individuals or firms resulted, along with a plunge in public confidence about the safety of generic and nongeneric products alike. In another case, a grand jury in April 1991 began looking into charges that FDA officials unlawfully passed along word about pending drug approvals to securities investors.

• The question of confidence is only part of a complicated tug of demands that trap the FDA between citizens, companies and the Congress. Since 1979, said the FDA committee report, the Congress has enacted 21 pieces of legislation "that add significant new tasks to the vast range of statutory demands" on the agency. But it has failed to add the necessary resources to do these jobs. Yet the Hill is quick to complain if FDA work lags or encounters trouble. For their part, consumers question why new drugs don't make it to market faster, while expecting the FDA to vet each one carefully. As for the manufacturers, they support a strong FDA that will generate consumer confidence in their products, but want it to give due consideration to the problems that robust regulation and enforcement causes their development and merchandising operations.

• One of the FDA's worst afflictions is the wide dispersal and deteriorated condition of its physical plant. "Abysmal," said the committee on the FDA succinctly. Much of the agency's scientific equipment is obsolete and its management of information needs extensive upgrading. The FDA works out of almost three dozen buildings scattered through 11 locations in the Washington area, and 40 laboratories in the capital and elsewhere. (It also operates in 157 regional and local offices around the country, and runs the National Center for Toxicological Research in Arkansas and the Engineering and Analytical Center in Massachusetts.) According to the *Washington Post*, the FDA's microbiological research takes place in a building whose walls can be seen through, whose floors heave, and whose cellar is vulnerable to snakes. A trailer houses veterinary research, and a termite-eaten cabin shelters agricultural research. The low point in Washington, the newspaper said, is a downtown building housing many laboratories and a thousand employees where, among other indignities, lab space is insufficient, the roof leaks, black ash floats into working space and parts of the ceiling come down on employees' heads.

- Every year the FDA must respond to public health emergencies. Most demand the personal and usually public participation of the commissioner. Cyanide in over-the-counter pain relievers, cocaine in malted beverages and benzene in soda water are recent examples. There were also the separate alarms about the quality and purity of prepared food for infants, described by Frank Young, commissioner in 1984-89, as "baby food in glass--and glass in baby food."

- The deregulation environment of the 1980s weakened the agency's capacity to handle the expanding expectations focused on it. Its clout with industry and credibility with the public and the Congress lost ground while new pharmaceuticals, biomedical products and food processing innovations poured onto the market. A significant part of the FDA's decision authority shifted to the secretary of the department. Its attempts to crack down on false or misleading claims about the fat, fiber and cholesterol content of foods ran aground at the Office of Management and Budget. Annual growth in its budget meanwhile averaged two percent in 1980-1990. Staff positions, which numbered above 8,000 at the end of the 1970s, totaled less than 7,000 five years later; today, with the most recent addition of 500 positions, the level of about 8,400 full-time equivalent positions is only back to what it was at the beginning of the 1980s. Inspections of products and of food and drug manufacturing dropped from 36,000 to 18,500 between 1980 and 1989. Seizures of contaminated food and tainted drugs fell by more than half in the same period. These shrinkages also took place at a time when advances in technology were beginning to confound the FDA's conventional divisions of labor by blurring distinctions between drugs and devices, foods and medications.

With this forbidding picture as backdrop, two developments dating from 1990 have helped launch the FDA on what seems to be a new course. First came an explosion of significant new legislation--especially the Nutrition Labeling and Education Act and the Safe Medical Devices Act--plus a $100 million appropriation for a new central FDA headquarters. Second, the advent of Kessler gave the beleaguered agency its first permanent, Senate-confirmed leadership in nearly two years.

Kessler thinks of the FDA as, quite simply, "the most important consumer protection agency in the world." He describes its mission in equally plain terms. The FDA should make it possible, he said shortly after taking over, for Americans to enter their pharmacies "without worrying about the potency or effectiveness of generic drugs;" for consumers "to be able to eat seafood with confidence;" and for management to know, when an agency investigator arrives at a factory, "that the FDA means business." Among the areas competing for his agency's attention, he listed as most urgent the AIDS epidemic, food labeling, blood safety, generic drugs, seafood, prescription drug advertising, regulation of medical devices, dietary supplements, a framework for regulating biotechnology, and international harmonization of regulatory standards.

One of the FDA's first steps under Kessler, early in 1991, was a strike at misleading food labeling. In well-publicized actions, the agency moved against orange juice advertised as fresh, mayonnaise billed as cholesterol-free, and claims in other areas from mouthwash to tomato sauce that the agency views as less than truthful. In a comment presaging changes to come, Kessler has said he doesn't understand "how much sodium and fat are too much" when he reads nutrition labels in their current format, adding that "I don't think in terms of grams" (widely used in content labeling). Not to be overlooked, either, is the point he makes that changes in labeling rules reflect more the need to assure fair competition than the historical FDA role as protector.

Another reformist sign at the agency is the revision of rules for getting new cancer drugs onto the market. By law, decisions on new drug applications are supposed to require only six months. In reality, it took up to two years in the 1960s and 1970s, and up to three years in the 1980s. Each year of delay costs a manufacturer millions of dollars. Now the FDA has eliminated a substantial amount of obstructive bureaucratic procedure, telescoping and accelerating the process. For example, lower-level officials can now approve applications without review by their seniors. In other moves, it doubled the staff which looks at the advertising of prescription drugs, and hired 100 additional investigators, many of them for a new Office of Seafood to bring fish and shellfish under mandatory federal scrutiny.

The FDA's new look has not, of course, pleased everyone. From some quarters have come doubts about the philosophy, targets and even the morality of what the agency is trying to do; from others, skepticism that it can make any appreciable dent. An energetic debate continues: should the FDA confine its activity to its inspector/policeman regulatory role? Or act more as a public health agency working with industry and the public, balancing pros and cons to develop more sophisticated judgments on the net societal benefit of the products it examines?

Given the FDA's condition and the pressures and counterpressures swirling around it, Kessler surprised no one by affirming that he assumed its leadership "with no illusions." In May 1991, not long after he took over, the Committee on the FDA (chaired by Charles C. Edwards, a former FDA commissioner) came in with its final report to the secretary of health and human services. Restoring the full credibility of the FDA, the conclusions of the report made clear, is the most compelling overall priority, requiring more staff, more money and greater enforcement muscle. In nearly 30 specific areas, it urged changes in the agency's mission, status, authority, enforcement capability, management and resources.

Most significant and controversial, perhaps, was the committee's belief that the FDA and the commissioner must have more autonomy and control. As a "third-tier" component of HHS, it said, the FDA has less independence in dealing with the Congress and the public than any other federal health and protection agency. While the commissioner's authority is expressed through published regulations, limitations on that authority and on managing the agency's internal affairs are "especially debilitating." In particular the Edwards committee focused on the decision in 1981 that "significant regulations" would henceforth require the approval of both the secretary of the department and the assistant secretary for health. These constraints, the panel said, have caused unacceptable delays in issuing regulations and, equally serious, contributed to lowered morale among agency professionals and to perceptions that the FDA is inadequate to its assignment. Removing these constraints requires nothing less than taking the FDA out of the Public Health Service, the committee said, allowing its chief to report directly to the secretary, and giving the commissioner "authority to issue regulations and manage the daily operations of the agency."

Kessler's views have a similar thrust. "It has been a difficult period for the agency," he says--"the generic drug scandal, erosion of resources over more than a decade, the inability to keep up with all the new demands. Basically, there's a sense that the FDA is incapable of carrying out its statutory mission. My job is to regain the agency's credibility." That objective heads his agenda. And as he emphasized from the beginning, public belief and confidence in the agency rests in large part on ensuring the integrity of its processes.

"There are thousands of decisions this agency makes, and things we do and products we get off the market, that we never tell anybody about," says James S. Benson, FDA deputy commissioner and acting head of the agency from 1989 to 1990. "We just do our job, and so often that fact gets overlooked. But for every thousand good things that get done, one bad thing is what gets the publicity." He thinks good public relations is one of the commissioner's major challenges, that the agency must do better at "keeping the public well-informed about how we do our job." The FDA is always in the middle of controversy, he says, "and that's what makes the job interesting--I'll put the 'interesting' in quotes. We have to keep balancing the people's concerns against the proper scientific or regulatory or legal decisions." Biotechnology, with growing impact in many directions, is one area where this comes up. "It goes to food, to drugs, to diagnostic tests," he points out. "It really covers the waterfront within the agency. We're constantly grappling with what is the right amount of evidence to justify a risk-benefit decision on a drug or a device approval."

Balancing risks against benefits is one factor governing the speed with which new products, especially drugs, move through FDA analysis to the market. The idea that moving good products to needful consumers quickly is just as vital as keeping bad products away can be a jarring concept to FDA traditional procedures. But it is a theme that shows up increasingly in the comments of informed observers. "They don't help anybody if a safe and effective drug is delayed for two years," says Gerald J. Mossinghoff, president of the Pharmaceutical Manufacturers Association. For understandable reasons, the industry has worked to help the FDA speed things up with loans of computer equipment and by cosponsoring with the agency a project on computer-assisted new drug applications. But it isn't only the pharmaceutical makers who support this cause. The Edwards committee report said the FDA must recognize that approval of useful and safe new products "can be as important to the public health" as preventing the marketing of harmful products. And institutions working to combat AIDS continue to underline what they see as insufficiently rapid access to new medicines that seem to have potential.

In the Congress, the FDA crosses paths, and sometimes swords, with many committees. Adding to its general operating problems is the anomaly that most legislation concerning it originates in the health committees, while budget oversight in both houses rests with the Appropriations subcommittees on Rural Development, Agriculture and Related Agencies. Among other committees in the House with interest in the FDA are the Energy and Commerce subcommittees on Oversight and Investigations; Health and the Environment; and Commerce, Consumer Protection and Competitiveness. In the Senate, it's the Labor and Human Resources subcommittees on Children, Family, Drugs and

Alcoholism. In both houses, the select or special committees on aging also look over the agency's shoulder.

Young, who says his workweek averaged 80 to 90 hours, believes he spent nearly a quarter of his time on the Hill. Benson comments that the FDA is "always under a congressional microscope" and frequently the subject of investigations by the General Accounting Office. Between 1985 and 1990 he counts 103 oversight and legislative hearings on the agency. Members of the Congress introduced about 50 bills in 1988-90 with direct effect on FDA authority, he says, and two or three times that many with indirect impact. For all that dialogue with the Hill, however, the Edwards committee pinpointed a long-neglected failing. Its report called on the FDA commissioner and the secretary of HHS to "exert stronger leadership with the Congress" to correct the gap between "the FDA's statutory responsibilities and its appropriated resources."

Approximately 2,100 members of the FDA staff are scientists, more than half of them chemists and microbiologists. "Job for job at the senior level," says Young, "I felt they would be at least equal to what I have seen in comparable university positions." FDA people, Kessler says, "really identify with the mission of the agency once you articulate that mission and let them do their jobs. You need to generate that kind of enthusiasm." The agency is bringing in a new management team, he adds, "people who are giving up very lucrative outside jobs. There's no shortage of people who want to come in and serve."

But at other levels at least, there is the usual problem of vying for competent employees with industry and the campuses. "We have a tremendous staff here," Benson says, "and they're very dedicated." He fears, however, that the speed of scientific and technological evolution will leave the FDA behind unless it can attract and compete. "We need to put much more energy into training and continuing education, giving people some opportunities. We do very little of that, simply because of the work load." Medical reviewers, for example, need some quality time in clinical practice to stay close to their specialties. The same principle applies to areas like veterinary medicine, biotechnology and food; and to special issues such as the biological compatibility of materials like artificial hearts and pacemakers.

The FDA's new legislation, new leadership and new look may or may not convince the many observers who foresee disaster if dramatic changes don't take place. Review committee chairman Edwards told the Senate the agency is "living on borrowed time" and predicted a "public health catastrophe" unless it gets more money and independence. Others call for more longevity in the top position, but worry that the pattern of six commissioners in 11 years will continue. "It is an undoable job," says M. Roy Schwarz, executive vice president of the American Medical Association, "one that will continue to turn over amid war and threats of war as it struggles along." That's because the position's mandate is unbelievably broad, the agency doesn't have the resources to carry it out, "and the position has chewed up good people." But Schwarz is "glad there are people willing to do this job. I admire them."

"I wouldn't have taken the job if I didn't think we could make strides," Kessler says. "I think there's a sense that people recognize what's at stake. The White House, Congress, HHS, OMB--everybody is lining up, supportive of reestablishing a strong agency." It's also worth noting that, as the first commissioner who under a recent statute required Senate confirmation, he was approved in eight days--without a hearing. "They had a hearing after they voted me in," Kessler points out. "I think that sends a signal that they're willing to allow us to get on with the work."

Key Relationships

Within the Department

Reports to: Assistant Secretary, Health

Works closely with:

>   Director, National Institutes of Health
>   Directors, NIH component institutes
>   Director, Centers for Disease Control
>   Administrator, Alcohol, Drug Abuse and Mental Health Administration
>   Administrator, Health Research and Administrative Services
>   National Cancer Advisory Board
>   Advisory Committee on Health Care Technology Assessment
>   Administrator, Health Care Financing Administration

Outside the Department

>   Administrator, Food Safety and Inspection Service, Department of Agriculture
>   Associate Director, Life Sciences, White House Office of Science and Technology Policy
>   Biotechnology subcommittee, Committee on Life Sciences and Health, Federal Coordinating Council for Science, Engineering and Technology (FCCSET)
>   Committee on Food, Agriculture and Forestry Research, FCCSET
>   President, Institute of Medicine, National Academy of Sciences
>   White House Council on Competitiveness
>   Assistant Secretary, Health Affairs, Department of Defense
>   Assistant Secretary, Oceans and International Environmental and Scientific Affairs, Department of State
>   Assistant Secretary, International Organization Affairs, Department of State

Assistant Director, National Science Foundation
Assistant Administrator, Pesticides and Toxic Substances, Environmental
  Protection Agency
Chairman, Nuclear Regulatory Commission

Outside the Government

American Medical Association, American Association of Academic Health
Centers, Association of American Medical Colleges, and other medical and
academic groups; an extensive range of pharmaceutical and medical device
manufacturers and their trade associations; grocer and food producer
associations; agribusinesses and farm groups; consumer organizations;
cancer, heart, diabetic and other organizations concerned with specific
diseases; international bodies such as the World Health Organization and the
biotechnology staff of the Organization for Economic Cooperation and
Development; state and local health officials

Profile of Current Commissioner
Food and Drug Administration

Name:	David A. Kessler
Assumed Position:	1990
Career Summary:	Medical director, Hospital of the Albert Einstein School of Medicine, 1984-89 Consultant to chairman, Committee on Labor and Human Relations, U.S. Senate, 1981-84
Education:	Amherst College, BA, magna cum laude, 1973 University of Chicago Law School, JD, 1978 Harvard University Medical School, MD, 1979 Internship and residency, Johns Hopkins University Hospital New York University Graduate School of Business Administration, advanced professional certificate, 1988

Commissioners, Food and Drug Administration Since 1969

Administration	Name and Years Served	Present Position
Bush	David A. Kessler 1990 - present	Incumbent
Bush	James S. Benson (Acting) 1989 - 1990	Deputy Commissioner, FDA

Reagan	Frank A. Young 1984 - 1989	Deputy Assistant Secretary Health, Science & Environment HHS
Reagan	Mark A. Novitch (A) 1983 - 1984	Vice Chairman The Upjohn Company Kalamazoo, Mich.
Reagan	Arthur Hull Hayes Jr. 1981 - 1983	President and CEO EM Pharmaceuticals Inc. Hawthorne, N.Y.
Carter	Jere E. Goyan 1979 - 1981	Dean, School of Pharmacy University of California San Francisco, Cal.
Carter	Donald Kennedy 1977 - 1979	President Stanford University Stanford, Cal.
Nixon, Ford	Alexander M. Schmidt 1973 - 1976	Deceased
Nixon	Sherwin Gardner (A) 1973	Vice President Grocery Manufacturers Assn. Washington, D.C.
Nixon	Charles C. Edwards 1970 - 1973	President Scripps Clinic & Research Fdn. LaJolla, Cal.
Johnson, Nixon	Herbert L. Ley Jr. 1968 - 1969	Consultant Rockville, Md.

18

DEPARTMENT OF HOUSING AND URBAN DEVELOPMENT

ASSISTANT SECRETARY
POLICY DEVELOPMENT AND RESEARCH

Level IV - Presidential Appointment with Senate Confirmation

Major Responsibilities

- Assist the development of housing and urban development policy through extensive evaluation and analysis of existing and proposed department programs and directions. As part of that process, conduct research, both in-house and on contract, to illuminate national housing conditions, needs and priorities.

- Monitor and evaluate programs designed to improve the operations and effectiveness of the department.

- Plan and manage the activities of the Office of Policy Development and Research to carry out these responsibilities.

Necessary Training, Experience, Skills

No engineer has filled this position since 1972, and no scientist since 1983; the last three occupants, including the incumbent, have been economists. The reasons for this seem clear enough. Training or practical experience in economics is more relevant to the job's chief current emphasis on policy development, whereas in an earlier, more munificent day, technology research played a relatively bigger role. But research, and the newly-assigned duty to monitor and assess efforts by the department of housing and urban development (HUD) to improve performance, remain an important co-responsibility. Technical or social science credentials are therefore a substantial resource in directing such activities and fully understanding their results and significance. The position also benefits from such other attributes as experience in local or state government, an understanding of the Congress, research and analytical skill, academic or think-tank background, and the ability to manage and communicate.

Insight

A glance at a HUD document tracing the history of this office shows that, since its beginnings a generation ago, the function now called Policy Development and Research has covered a lot of ground while undergoing a couple of basic changes of focus. It has also known peaks and valleys where resources are concerned, expanding in the first ten years to embrace milestone projects, then beginning a long decline which has only recently, and modestly, been reversed.

Among the office's first initiatives in the late 1960s were the investigation of urban technologies like the use of high-velocity water in earth tunneling, and "slippery" water to boost the throw of fire-fighting hoses. It also developed new construction technologies--such as the more efficient use of lumber and of prefabricated cores to upgrade old high rises--and big construction demonstration projects embodying new techniques. One of the latter projects used manufactured components in building hundreds of demonstration dwellings around the country.

But by the very early 1970s, the emphasis had switched from the technology of housing to its management, and the economic and social problems involved. The office undertook what is still the biggest project of its history: a ten-year housing allowance experiment that, according to a HUD document, created "the rationale for the current voucher program." A controlled trial conducted in several cities nationwide, this program cost $100 million. "Some called it the biggest piece of social science research ever conducted by the federal government," says Mary Nenno of the National Association of Housing and Redevelopment Officials. In the same period the office set up housing surveys and mortgage and market indicators to keep track of shifting housing patterns. In 1973, the present PD&R office was born in the merger of existing operations with a HUD policy analysis unit. Called on to assist in a wide-ranging review of scandal-plagued housing programs, the new operation acquired evaluation experience and added economists to its staff. These developments marked a second change of emphasis, as the serving of HUD's policy and research needs became central in PD&R operations.

Today, says the federal budget document, PD&R undertakes "programs of research, studies, testing and demonstrations related to the HUD mission." It does this work "internally and through contracts with industry, nonprofit organizations and educational institutions, and agreements with state and local agencies." But as made clear by the comments of current assistant secretary John C. Weicher (since 1989) and some others who have held or are familiar with the job, policy development is this job's dominant feature. It involves "fleshing out" the ideas of the secretary and other senior HUD officials, Weicher says, modifying or adding to them as necessary, and "shaping them into coherent policies that can then be turned into legislative proposals, or regulations or programs that don't need to go through that process. We have a very broad portfolio here and that's the heart of the job, the most important part of it." To Donna Shalala, the University of Wisconsin chancellor who headed PD&R in 1977-80, the job is "the chief policy position in the department" (at the subcabinet level). Yet the role is not to make policy, she explains, "but to organize the department for policy making in the science and technology area. It is the innovation center to try out new things." Among the national problems to which this function seems likely to apply in the coming decade is that of absent or deteriorating urban infrastructure.

In the 1981-83 period when he was assistant secretary, says E.S. Savas, it was the "PD" of PD&R that got the emphasis in the context of the Reagan administration's stress on basic policy changes. The office gained influence within the department, putting forth such new policies at the urban enterprise zone that Savas developed. Construction technology and lead paint abatement in housing were PD&R's principal science or technology-related programs in this period. "Lead paint was chemistry and housing construction was engineering, but my principal science and technology involvement was on the policy side, especially economic analysis," he says. He expresses pride in his role in the "transformation of housing policy from building more public projects to giving vouchers to eligible low-income households." This has turned out to be, he asserts, an "extremely successful approach, helping far more people for the same amount of money." But, he notes, it required a "sea change in policy, attitudes, legislation and the flow of funds." And the voucher system today retains a politically controversial edge.

During his first 18 months in the job, Weicher cites two major projects as examples of the policy development function, both of which PD&R developed as parts of housing authorization legislation. One was a group of initiatives under the "HOPE" project designed to broaden the number of families and individuals housed in their own homes. It included ownership for tenants of public housing, new programs for the homeless and elderly, and enterprise zones and related tax incentives. The other was reform of the single-family mutual mortgage insurance fund under the Federal Housing Administration, prompted by studies that concluded the fund was losing money. It was PD&R's job to develop policy that would turn that situation around, and get it into the housing bill. Still in the context of the bill, Weicher says, the office designed a formula for the allocation of funds for housing modernization. Instead of disbursing money on the basis of specific project application, funds under the new scheme are allotted according to need.

Another PD&R project relates to the national dilemma over bankrupt and foundering savings and loan institutions. Weicher notes that recent legislation gives the HUD secretary new day-to-day responsibility for regulating the government-sponsored Federal Home Loan Mortgage Corporation, together with its long-established assignment to regulate Fannie Mae. It places the secretary on the Oversight Board of the Resolution Trust Corporation (the treasury department entity charged with resolving the tangled affairs of ruined S&Ls, disposing of their properties and paying their depositors). "The secretary set up a financial institutions regulatory staff to advise him in these matters, and that activity is housed mainly within PD&R," Weicher adds.

On still another front, the office provides staff support for a commission dealing with state and local impediments to the building or rehabilitation of low-cost housing. And, in a brand-new role assigned it by the Congress in 1990, it is responsible for tracking and evaluating department-wide programs of reform, a commitment HUD undertook in the wake of the scandal and mismanagement of the 1980s. For PD&R, this has meant important additions to staff and budget.

From highs of 200 staff positions and a $65 million budget in fiscal 1976, PD&R dropped off to $20 million by 1982, and to a low of $16.2 million and about 125 positions in 1986. Because the funding cuts forced the office to reduce research it contracted to the outside and to compensate for that internally, its staff level fell less dramatically; by the fall of 1990, it had in fact risen to 137. For fiscal 1991, research budget outlays were estimated at $19 million. Two-thirds of the research money goes to data collection, funded mainly in PD&R's Office of Economic Affairs and spent mainly on contract with the Bureau of the Census to determine housing conditions and needs. Even though this American Housing Survey occurs only every other year, half as frequently as it once did, it remains a "major source of information outside the decennial census," Nenno says. The assistant secretary negotiates and oversees execution of the contract with Census and helps put together the final report. "A big responsibility," in Nenno's view. The remaining research funds, in the Office of Research, are directed to the other areas of PD&R concern. Again, some of these projects are contracted to the outside, as with a University of North Carolina study of HUD's low-income home ownership program.

As noted earlier, budget and staff figures began to grow in 1991 with the assignment in 1990 of new evaluation and monitoring tasks. The Congress added specific funding support of $8 million (PD&R had asked for $25 million) and 20 new positions for the purpose, pushing the office's estimated budget for fiscal 1992 to about $28 million.

Weicher thinks that more than half his staff can be described as "technical and professional by any reasonable definition." A third of them, including economists, are in the Office of Economic Affairs. "I tend to look for people with PhDs or equivalents," he says. "We have a lot of people in grades 12 to 15 with advanced degrees in economics, engineering and political science, and there is the occasional degree in history or international relations."

While Savas and Shalala report active to heavy interagency meeting schedules during their tenures, Weicher's is more modest. He sees the press from time to time, does some public speaking, mostly to realtor and home builder groups, and has "a fair amount" of congressional testifying to do, generally before the housing and appropriations committees. "Quite often," Nenno says, "the Hill authorizes and directs the department to do research studies and report back, and these have to be handled with considerable skill."

Despite congressional interest in reform at HUD, Nenno says support on the Hill is currently at "a low level." The amount of money available to HUD for research is "really minimal, in fact one of the smallest among all the departments," she observes. "But the need for research in so many HUD areas is like an open book." The reason she finds for this--what she terms "a certain lack of confidence" on the part of the Congress--lies primarily in "skepticism" about the "use of the department as a political instrument going back to the early 1980s."

There are other problems, some of them inherent in the nature of HUD's mission and hardly new. In her time, Shalala reflects, the job was "very tricky" in the sense that it was "a staff position rather than a line job," and powerful line positions at HUD objected to a department-wide policy-making process to which PD&R contributed. That was the main political fact on the inside, she recalls. Externally, reality took--and takes-- the form of "powerful housing constituencies, plus minority and community-based constituencies, beating on the department." In a different setting--the institution of the voucher system--Savas remembers "enormous opposition from vested interest groups, and the Congress, to changing the status quo."

Nenno thinks the formation of an outside advisory group around the assistant secretary--"academic community and research people in the various associations"--would be a useful step. In Shalala's day this need for outside perspective may have been met to some extent by the presence of as many as 25 visiting university faculty members at a time, supplementing staff resources for periods of a year. Nenno thinks an advisory panel of the kind she suggests today could offer advice on issues needing attention and help evaluate research results, and that institutionalizing such a group and scheduling regular meetings would increase its effectiveness. She also would like to see the development of a priority agenda for research, and greater recognition for the leadership position at PD&R as "the important, powerful role in the department." The job should function as "a very close advisor to the secretary," she says.

Weicher sees no need to change the mandate of the position. "The job is defined by what you bring to it and by what the secretary and deputy secretary want," he says, and its range is certainly broad enough. "I don't lack any of the responsibilities my predecessors had, and I have some they didn't have." The reward this work offers, in Shalala's view, is that "you learn a lot, and you learn how to transmit and explain it. You get a chance at very high-level policy making. You're right there in the middle, not out in the bureaucracy. It's a good job."

Key Relationships

Within the Department

Reports to: Secretary

Works closely with:

Deputy Secretary
General Counsel
Assistant Secretary, Housing/Federal Housing Commissioner
Assistant Secretary, Community Planning and Development
Assistant Secretary, Legislation and Congressional Relations
Assistant Secretary, Public and Indian Housing

Outside the Department

Associate Director, Demographic Programs, Bureau of the Census
Senior staff economists, President's Council of Economic Advisers
Officials of the Resolution Trust Corporation, Federal National Mortgage
Association and Federal Home Loan Mortgage Corporation

Outside the Government

State and local housing officials; National League of Cities, U.S. Conference of Mayors, National Association of Counties; National Association of Homebuilders, National Association of Realtors; Council of Large Public Housing Authorities; low-income housing advocacy groups; American Association for the Advancement of Science; housing and urban specialists on university faculties; officials of the Organization for Economic Cooperation and Development

Profile of Current Assistant Secretary
Policy Development and Research

Name: John C. Weicher

Assumed Position: 1989

Career Summary: Associate director, economic policy, Office of Management and Budget, 1987-89
F.K. Weyerhauser Scholar in Public Policy Research, American Enterprise Institute, 1981-87
Deputy staff director, President's Commission on Housing, 1981
Director, housing and financial markets program, Urban Institute, 1977-81
Assistant, then associate professor of economics, Ohio State University, 1967-77
Various positions with the department of housing and urban development, 1973-77, including deputy assistant secretary, economic development; and director, Division of Economic Policy
Assistant professor of economics, University of California at Irvine, 1965-67

Education: University of Michigan, BA, English, 1959
University of Chicago, PhD, economics, 1968

Assistant Secretaries for Policy Development and Research Since 1969

Administration	Name and Years Served	Present Position
Bush	John C. Weicher 1989 - present	Incumbent

Reagan	Kenneth J. Beirne 1988 - 1989	Vice President National Association of Realtors Washington, D.C.
Reagan	June Q. Koch 1984 - 1987	President Construction, Marketing & Trading Inc. Washington, D.C.
Reagan	E.S. Savas 1981 - 1983	Professor & Chairman Management Department Baruch College New York, N.Y.
Carter	Donna Shalala 1977 - 1980	Chancellor University of Wisconsin Madison, Wis.
Ford	Charles J. Orlebeke 1975 - 1976	Director Urban Planning & Policy University of Illinois Chicago, Ill.
Nixon, Ford	Michael H. Moskow* 1973 - 1975	Vice President Premark International Deerfield, Ill.
Nixon	Harold B. Finger* 1969 - 1972	Consultant Washington, D.C.

* Prior to 1974, held position as Assistant Secretary, Research and Technology

19

DEPARTMENT OF THE INTERIOR

ASSISTANT SECRETARY, WATER AND SCIENCE

Level IV - Presidential Appointment with Senate Confirmation

Major Responsibilities

- Supervise the programs and activities of the Bureau of Reclamation, the U.S. Geological Survey and the Bureau of Mines, three technical agencies comprising the Office of Water and Science. Through them, shape and execute policies to conserve and augment national water supplies and mineral resources and ensure their effective public and private development and management. Oversee geologic investigation, topographic and geographic mapping activities, and natural hazards research.

- Direct data collection and analysis to support these objectives. Assess the status of U.S. water, mineral and energy reserves. Provide advice on science matters to the secretary.

- Consult and cooperate with other federal agencies, and with state and municipal bodies, working in the same areas. Represent the department in interagency meetings and other official contexts dealing with water and minerals questions.

Necessary Training, Experience, Skills

Solid management experience and/or significant technical training in such areas as engineering, geology or water resources management are valuable in this job. A law background might suffice if it includes extensive experience in a field related to the jurisdictions of the position; the current assistant secretary practiced "water law" for many years, representing a federal reclamation project and working closely with civil engineers and hydrologists. Even so, he thinks it "wouldn't hurt to know a little more about physics or chemistry." Whatever combination a candidate for the position offers, a knowledgeable observer calls it "primarily a management job" that also requires some tough political skills, especially where the Congress is concerned.

Insight

Water is the preoccupying issue this position deals with, and it comes at the assistant secretary in several dimensions. First, the fundamental changeover of the Bureau of Reclamation from building dams and irrigation systems to managing them better, begun in 1988, has not finished. Second, a long, unresolved dispute continues over the philosophy of water allocation, especially in the western states. Shall it go predominantly to farmers, as reclamation law has traditionally prescribed, or do those who want more water for environmental purposes such as fish and wildlife have a legitimate claim? Third, the debate about who should have responsibility for research, management and regulation of ground water still simmers, driven partly by concern over the extent of ground water contamination. Fourth, turf battles within and between agencies and within the Congress over responsibility for flood control, navigation and dam safety have hampered progress in those areas.

The fiscal 1992 budget request of the Office of Water and Science stands at about $1.7 billion and, according to John M. Sayre, assistant secretary since the fall of 1989, "the overall trend has been a slow increase." He professes to be "well satisfied" with the knowledge and training of the scientists and technicians among his staff of 17,000 working in several offices in and around the capital and across the country.

In one observer's view, the U.S. Geological Survey (USGS) and the Bureau of Mines (BOM) are "the two really technical areas" under Sayre's supervision; they "largely run themselves" and require mainly budget support from the assistant secretary. USGS and BOM, staffed mostly by trained scientists, are primarily research and technical information-gathering organizations. USGS studies resources such as minerals and energy, geologic hazards like earthquakes, volcanoes and landslides, ground and surface water and water quality, and produces topographic maps for consumers around the world. The BOM's primary mission is an adequate national supply of non-fuel minerals through research on extraction technology, use and reprocessing. The Bureau of Reclamation is charged by statute with providing dry western states with adequate water supplies for year-round support of agriculture. It also furnishes water to municipalities and oversees hydroelectric power and flood control operations.

As described by Thomas F. Donnelly, executive vice president of the National Water Resources Association, the ground water argument turns in one respect on whether the states or the federal government should have jurisdiction in management and quality control. How to handle contamination is an inner element of that question. "In many areas of the country," Donnelly says, "ground water supplies are contaminated. Do we need to solve the problem by funding and technical assistance to the states, or does the federal government need to step in and impose very strict water quality standards on the states?" For now, he thinks, the states' position has won out. "I'm not going to tell you that's the right position, or if it will prevail in the coming years. All we need is another Love Canal, and the Congress will take over and the federal government will regulate our water supply nationwide." In any case, he sees the issue as one the water and science assistant secretary must take on, since both the USGS and the Bureau of Reclamation have a role.

The USGS, in fact, is proceeding with its recently-begun National Water Assessment Program which, next to earthquakes, is its biggest activity extending over the next decade. The assessment is looking at both ground and surface water. When ground water was a hot item in the late 1980s, Donnelly recalls, there was some pulling and tugging even within the federal government. "When it looks like Congress is going to pump additional money in, then all of a sudden federal agencies get interested," he says. "The Environmental Protection Agency wanted full jurisdiction over all aspects of ground water--research, regulation, everything, and the question became one of who was more qualified to do the research." To him the answer is clearly USGS. Again, "it is an area where the assistant secretary has to protect that role, rather than roll over and let EPA take over the program."

Sayre meanwhile reports "some wonderful cooperation" in the water assessment task from other federal agencies including EPA. "They're very excited at the fact we're working together," he says. "That's a very important one coming on." In addition to that and pushing reorientation of the Bureau of Reclamation, a number of other significant issues and projects fill his schedule. One is the congressionally-mandated study (in 1987) of the western reclamation program, which some critics portray as an abuse of federal subsidies by large farming enterprises (Donnelly calls this the biggest problem on the assistant secretary's agenda). Another is USGS's applied research and monitoring of real and potential earthquakes, a $50 million program with a worldwide network of 100 stations (Sayre attaches "major importance" to it). Third is the problem of drought. Many areas of the western United States experienced a fourth consecutive year of it in 1990. This unprecedented string is raising predictions in some quarters that drought will soon become the water and science office's biggest challenge as municipal and agricultural water supply systems fight over a dwindling supply.

Sayre estimates that 35 percent of his time goes into interagency meetings. He was co-chair of the former National Acid Precipitation panel, and currently sits on the Committee on International Science, Engineering and Technology, "looking at what we can do in the international field to help American trade in such areas as intellectual property." He represents the secretary on the Trade Policy Review Group and in interagency groups concerned with emergency mobilization preparedness and Antarctic policy, among others. Sayre says his office is substantially involved in the coordinated federal study of global climate change. His main points of contact on the Hill are the Senate Committee on Energy and Natural Resources, the House Interior Committee, and the relevant appropriations subcommittees of both houses. He travels frequently inside the country, and attends international meetings such as a conference in Egypt on water supplies for developing countries.

Although the directorships of his three sub-agencies were occupied when Sayre came on board, he expected to have a concurring voice in filling them as and when they came open. The White House personnel office, he says, "generally gets preliminary recommendations from the National Academy of Sciences" for position of director of the Geological Survey, and "they carry a lot of weight." His principal deputy is a PhD physicist whom Sayre finds "immensely helpful" and is also scientific advisor to the secretary of the department.

Joan Davenport, assistant secretary in 1977-81 under a different title (Energy and Minerals) and with somewhat different responsibilities, thinks a scientific or technical background is "essential" for the directors of USGS and BOM. The assistant secretary "should understand the sciences," she says, but also "must know how to manage and delegate. To do this successfully, you must have people you have confidence in."

She makes a second, perhaps even more important point. It is especially relevant to the assistant secretary's staff and line roles for the secretary as both science adviser and, essentially, science overseer within the department. "The person who is responsible for these bureaucracies has to have a vision of why the American public is supporting these groups and their science. What is expected? If there was one broad theme, it was where are we going and what are the benefits--for the nation, for the science itself, for these bureaucracies, for those constituencies--and what is the balance? Those questions recurred not only in various forms at the policy level. They recurred within the bureaus themselves in practical terms."

Key Relationships

Within the Department

Reports to: Secretary of the Interior

Works closely with:

Solicitor
Assistant Secretary, Budget and Program Resources Management
Chief of Staff
Assistant Secretary, Indian Affairs
Assistant Secretary, Fish and Wildlife and Parks

Outside the Department

Assistant Administrator, Water, Environmental Protection Agency
Assistant Secretary, Oceans and Atmosphere, National Oceanic and
   Atmospheric Administration, Department of Commerce
Assistant Secretary, Natural Resources and Environment, Department of
   Agriculture
Director, Civil Works, U.S. Army Corps of Engineers
Assistant Director, Geosciences, National Science Foundation
Members, Committee on International Science, Engineering and Technology,
   FCCSET

Outside the Government

National Water Resources Association, National Hydropower Association,
and other groups concerned with water use, protection, and conservation;
Association of Metropolitan Water Agencies, Interstate Water Pollution
Control Administrators, and other state and local water organizations and
officials; mining industry firms and associations such as the American Mining
Congress; and counterpart officials of other governments

Profile of Current Assistant Secretary, Water and Science

Name:	John M. Sayre
Assumed Position:	1989
Career Summary:	Partner, Davis, Graham and Stubbs, Denver, Colorado, 1966-89
	Private law practice, Boulder, Colorado, 1950-66
	Officer, U.S. Navy, 1943-46
Education:	University of Colorado, BA, 1943; JD, 1948

Assistant Secretaries, Water and Science Since 1969

Administration	Name and Years Served	Present Position
Bush	John Sayre 1989 - present	Incumbent
Reagan	James W. Ziglar 1987 - 1989	Managing Director Paine Webber Washington, D.C.
Reagan	Wayne N. Marchant (Acting) 1986 - 1987	Chief, Laboratory & Research Services Division Bureau of Reclamation Department of the Interior Denver, Colo.
Reagan	Robert N. Broadbent 1985 - 1986	Director of Aviation McCarran Intl. Airport Las Vegas, Nev.
Reagan	Daniel N. Miller Jr.* 1981 - 1983	Not available
Carter	Joan M. Davenport* 1977 - 1981	Congressional Review Specialist Congressional Research Service Library of Congress Washington, D.C.
Ford	William L. Fisher* 1976	Director, Bureau of Economic Geology, Univ. of Texas Austin, Tex.
Ford	Jack W. Carlson* 1975	Consultant Potomac, Md.
Nixon	Stephen A. Wakefield* 1973 - 1974	Partner Akin, Gump, Strauss, Hauer & Feld Washington, D.C.
Nixon	Hollis M. Dole* 1969 - 1972	Not available

* Held position as Assistant Secretary of Energy and Minerals. In 1983, the functions of the then-existing Assistant Secretary for Energy and Minerals and Assistant Secretary for Land and Water were separated and recombined into the positions of Assistant Secretary for Water and Science and Assistant Secretary for Land and Minerals.

DIRECTOR, U.S. GEOLOGICAL SURVEY

Level V - Presidential Appointment with Senate Confirmation

Major Responsibilities

- Manage a 10,000-employee agency responsible for assessing and reporting on national resources in energy, minerals, water and land, and for studying earthquakes, volcanoes and other natural hazards as well as the geology of planets and their satellites. Plan and supervise the collection and interpretation of geologic, hydrologic, chemical and physical data, mapping, research, and production of graphic and digital information and materials involved in this responsibility.

- Assure bilateral and multilateral coordination of the agency's work with that of other entities of the federal government, and its collaboration with state and local programs. Assist a number of foreign governments engaged in the same fields.

- Advise the administration and the Congress on technical issues in the area of the agency's competence that relate to policy and regulatory decisions.

- Through contact with state and local communities, academic institutions and industry, see that U.S. Geological Survey (USGS) programs reflect evolving national needs in such areas as resource development, land use, city planning and environmental protection.

Necessary Training, Experience, Skills

The chief of USGS must be a scientist and--equally important in the judgment of those knowledgeable about the job--an experienced and skillful manager. Of the agency's 11 directors over 112 years, all met the first requirement, and eight worked their way to the top through the USGS ranks, learning in the process the shape and feel of the organization and how it runs. But promotion to this position from within need not be an immutable pattern, says one observer. He thinks a scientist from private industry, a state agency, or an academic environment, such as the National Academy of Science, could handle it competently provided that management ability was a strong suit.

Insight

If anything, the history of USGS leadership overstates the case of those who argue for more relevant training and greater longevity in senior federal jobs. Since the founding of USGS in 1879, its directors have exclusively been geologists who averaged more than 10 years in the job. Dallas Peck, USGS chief since 1981, spent the preceding 30 years in scientific endeavor ranging from geology and volcanic studies to geothermal power and remote sensing. He was a member of the USGS staff during most of that period, but his work took him into laboratories, campuses, and advisory and professional groups all over the country, and to scientific missions and conferences abroad. Such memberships and associations have of course continued during his period as director.

While he remains a career U.S. civil servant, Peck is also a presidential appointee. Selection to the post, he says, draws on a slate nominated by the National Academy of Sciences--a practice, incidentally, that could benefit nominations to a greater number of senior federal science and engineering positions. "Traditionally it's been apolitical," he adds, "and since we're in the data business, we are very even-handed in working with Republicans or Democrats, the administration or the opposite party."

Peck describes USGS as "a research and technical information-gathering agency." The areas of its concerns--water, land and minerals-- are fundamental in supplying most of what this or any other country consumes. Preserving and in some cases enlarging these resources, and providing broader, more usable information and deeper insights on their safest, most productive use requires persistent research and technically effective methods of putting the knowledge gained at the disposal of the country.

USGS pursues this mission on a fiscal 1991 budget of about $768 million (the proposed figure for fiscal 1992 is $767.7 million). Just over a quarter of that flows from a thousand cooperative water resources projects which USGS runs with states and municipalities, from other federal agencies for services performed, and from other governments for technical assistance. State and local governments contribute about $60 million to the joint water projects and USGS matches that with federal money; together these funds represent half of the total USGS water program.

Water resources are one of the agency's three principal operations, and part of the reason why USGS operates in 200 national locations. The program keeps tabs on the amounts and qualities of ground and surface water and the systems that produce it, and surveys the impacts on these assets of water use and of events in nature. On land and offshore, the geologic division focuses in similar fashion on energy and mineral resources, and in addition studies natural hazards--earthquakes, volcanoes and landslides (USGS runs a worldwide network of 100 seismological stations). It produces geologic, geophysical and geochemical maps, and examines the geologic processes that continue to alter the earth with a range of consequences for its human inhabitants. The mapping division, using geographic and cartographic data from many sources including aerial photography and remote sensing, publishes topographic and a variety of other maps on a wide selection of scales. It also retains this data in digital format. Mapping division products help to guide enterprises such as land management, resource development and environmental protection. Mapping also furnishes information used by the federal intelligence community; USGS has secure facilities permitting the examination of classified material.

Peck says USGS has bilateral "coordination committees" with more than a dozen other federal agencies. There are also such other permanent activities as the correlation of water data, in which some 30 federal agencies take part under USGS chairmanship; and a new federal geographic data committee of 12-15 agencies that the Office of Management and Budget has asked USGS to organize and lead. According to Peck, this group will coordinate "not just maps but digital map data, and not only digital cartographic, but geodetic and geologic" and several other kinds of data. While overseeing his own agency's role in these various efforts, he also chairs the Committee on Earth and Environmental Sciences (CEES) within the Federal Coordinating Council for Science, Engineering and Technology, newly revitalized by the White House science advisor. A key CEES task is oversight of the multi-agency program to examine global climate change. "It's really broadened my experience," Peck says, "in terms of working across the whole federal scientific community." The experimental "cross-cutting" budget shared by the project's participating agencies gained a funding increase for the overall effort of about a third in fiscal 1991. As Peck notes, CEES "is now being used as an example for additional expanded and elevated federal councils."

Internationally, USGS plays a substantial role. Peck has several times visited Saudi Arabia, for example, where for 25 years the agency been studying the geology and mineral resources of non-petroleum areas of the country; the Saudis are funding all of this work. In Peru, Chile, Bolivia and Venezuela, as for other Latin American countries in the past, USGS has been developing geologic surveys and training staff to track mineral resources. It helps Indonesia assess volcanic activity and Pakistan to examine coal resources. There are cooperative programs with 60 other countries that include earthquake predictive projects with China and the Soviet Union.

Peck figures he spends "80 to 90 percent of my day in meetings." These include weekly sessions within Interior's Office of Water and Science, of which USGS is a part; and staff meetings of differing sizes with the secretary perhaps twice a week. The director averages four trips a week between his office southwest of the capital and downtown Washington 15 miles away. On Capitol Hill, the agency's funding oversight goes through the Interior and Insular Affairs Committee of the House and the Senate Energy and Natural Resources Committee; on the appropriations side, it's the Interior subcommittees of the appropriations committees of both houses. Oversight hearings occur on both general and specific matters in all these and other panels.

William L. Shafer of the House Interior Committee makes the point that "Congress is always more supportive of USGS than the administration." In the Congress and in industry, "they're viewed as an excellent science organization with well-qualified people. We usually authorize 10 to 30 percent more for them than the president." But he still thinks budget is one of the agency's crucial problems, considering "the many things people want them to do." In fiscal 1990, "they got by adequately. They didn't do everything they should or would like to do. Their budget isn't everything they want, but it's probably adequate for the program they have developed."

Fiscal 1991 did bring almost a 20 percent funding hike, and Peck doesn't feel USGS has been treated any worse than others. But he views current funding as insufficient for what he thinks USGS needs to do. "The line items in our budget," he says, "are, for example, earthquake hazard reduction, oil and gas resource studies, cooperative water investigations, map data handling. Over the last ten years those budgets have been pretty static; they certainly haven't increased at the rate of inflation. As a result, we've cut the level of study and hired very few people. We've decreased our staff maybe 10 to 20 percent over that ten years."

Shafer says the disparity between federal and private salaries--a problem mostly rooted in the budget and not confined to USGS--means that "young, bright scientists are not beating on the door of USGS to get in." As another reason for this he cites an absence of "opportunities for advancement--you could work there for a lifetime and never become more than a GS-13 or GS-15 geologist or engineer." Peck acknowledges some difficulties on the recruiting and retention front, young scientists included. For example, "because of the downturn in the oil industry a few years ago, very few people are going into earth sciences these days." When oil was booming, "we would lose some of our geologists. And right now we're losing some hydrologists because of the concern about water and water quality. The consulting business out there (California and other parts of the West) is very good."

At the same time, he says, "we're the big research and technical investigation outfit in the public sector in geology, hydrology and mapping. We work closely with the universities. We're able to attract people because it's an awfully good research environment. Out of 10,000 employees, more than a thousand are PhDs. We can compete with the best and by and large keep them." Most people, he adds, spend their careers with the agency because of the research ambience "and we try to take care of that." USGS also "works pretty hard" at sending its people back to school. Further, Peck notes, "we tend to have a fair exchange of people with the universities. Our people go for three months and teach, and university people come here for their sabbatical years."

Peck spends about a week of every month traveling. "Part of that is going to our field centers--to meet the people, see how things are going." He also accepts a certain number of invitations to speak. He has been an officer in the Geological Society of America, and tries to attend meetings of other professional societies "to stay alive as a geologist." At USGS he has a laboratory where he pursues personal research projects on Sierra Nevada granites, an old interest. This inevitably suffers from the size of the workload and the breadth of the schedule, however, and "every year I get a little less done."

Key Relationships

Within the Department

Reports to: Assistant Secretary, Water and Science

Works closely with:

> Director, Bureau of Mines
> Commissioner, Bureau of Reclamation
> Director, Bureau of Land Management
> Director, Fish and Wildlife Service

Outside the Department

> Members, Committee on Earth and Environmental Sciences, FCCSET (chairs committee)
> Under Secretary/Administrator, National Oceanic and Atmospheric Administration, Department of Commerce

Director, Bureau of the Census
Assistant Secretary, Defense Programs, Department of Energy
Assistant Director, Geosciences, National Science Foundation
Associate Administrator, Space Science and Applications, NASA
Deputy Director, Intelligence, CIA
Assistant Administrator, Solid Waste and Emergency Response,
    Environmental Protection Agency
Director, Defense Advanced Research Projects Agency, Department of
    Defense
Chiefs, Forest Service and Soil Conservation Service, Department of
    Agriculture
Chief, Corps of Engineers, U.S. Army
Director, Defense Mapping Agency, Department of Defense
Director, Federal Emergency Management Agency

Outside the Government

Representatives of energy extraction industries and hydroelectric utilities;
geology, hydrology and cartography associations; state and local water
officials and disaster and emergency offices; professional engineering groups;
foreign government officials in the fields of geology, earthquake preparedness
and vulcanology

Profile of Current Director, U.S. Geological Survey

Name: Dallas L. Peck

Assumed Position: 1981

Career Summary: Chief geologist, USGS, 1977-81
                        Geologist, USGS, 1954-77
                        Part-time geologic field assistant, USGS, 1951-53

Education: California Institute of Technology, BS, geology (honors), 1951; MS,
                           geology, 1953
                        Harvard University, PhD, geology, 1960

Directors, U.S. Geological Survey Since 1969

Administration	Name and Years Served	Present Position
Bush, Reagan	Dallas L. Peck 1981 - present	Incumbent
Carter	H. William Menard 1978 - 1980	Deceased

Ford, Nixon	Vincent E. McKelvey 1972 - 1977	Deceased
Nixon	William A. Radlinski (Acting) 1971	Retired
Nixon, Johnson	William T. Pecora 1965 - 1971	Deceased

20

DEPARTMENT OF LABOR

ASSISTANT SECRETARY
OCCUPATIONAL SAFETY AND HEALTH

Level IV - Presidential Appointment with Senate Confirmation

Major Responsibilities

● Supervise implementation of the Occupational Safety and Health Act protecting employees in more than six million U.S. work places. Manage the activities of the Occupational Safety and Health Administration (OSHA) to that end.

● Formulate and publish standards to reduce or eliminate hazards at public and private sector work sites, consulting with labor, management and other affected parties, and cooperating closely with other federal agencies. Develop regulations to enforce these rules and, through inspection, ensure compliance with them. Oversee grants to states where occupational safety and health programs operate, and work with the state agencies which manage them.

● Counsel the Secretary of Labor on OSHA policy and actions. Represent administration policy in these matters to the Congress.

Necessary Training, Experience, Skills

Whether or not the occupant of this job is a scientist or engineer by training, it requires substantial technical grounding. Even those who put administrative skills and integrity first think this assistant secretary must have practical technical or scientific knowledge, at the very least including a grasp of "the principles of proof and the hypothesis approach to problems." A management and/or technical background in an industry with substantial safety and health responsibilities, for example, would help to meet these requirements. At the same time, there should be some previous exposure to the mechanisms of government, and especially to the regulatory process. Individuals with good scientific/technical credentials but no understanding of how to apply rules to the workplace would, much of the time, be spinning their wheels.

Insight

For people who work, safety and health on the shop or factory floor can literally be a matter of life and death. For management, most of which generally accepts good working conditions as its proper responsibility, health and safety requirements also have important impacts on the bottom line. For OSHA, which must set the standards and shape the rules in this contentious arena according to the law, the main challenge is to apply them effectively and fairly in an often skeptical, recriminatory atmosphere. Thus, like other federal agencies and offices whose job is partly or wholly to regulate and enforce, OSHA and the assistant secretary who directs it live in something of a cross fire.

To be sure, things may not be quite as bad in this regard as they may have been at times in the past. Gerard F. Scannell, who has headed OSHA since 1989, quotes two U.S. senators recalling that the OSHA of the 1970s was the object of more hate than the Internal Revenue Service. "And I think it was because labor thought OSHA was working only for business," he says, "and at other times, business thought it was working only for labor." That atmosphere helped to make some of OSHA's leaders controversial figures.

But attempting to regulate the safety and health of six million work places remains "an incredibly tough job," in the view of J. Davitt McAteer, executive director of the Occupational Safety and Health Law Center. OSHA, as he describes it, has had an "enormously difficult time" trying to deal with its assigned tasks: to develop standards designed to minimize or eliminate work-related safety and health problems in a wide assortment of sizes and severities across the society; to carry out the educational role that these objectives imply; and, not least, to deal with employers who often don't like such interference in matters they think they know best.

Roughly 12,000 to 15,000 people a year die in the workplace, McAteer estimates, and about 150,000 are injured. "People are right to be critical of OSHA because it hasn't done a lot of things right, but I'm not sure the critics could divine a better scheme. The science and technology are inordinately difficult." Chemicals, for example. "Benzene is the best cleaner in the world," he says, "but the problem is that it kills the people who are using it." When OSHA raises such a problem, employers and plant operators are likely to object if the agency can't suggest a safe substitute. "All the products OSHA has had to address are those we use throughout our society," McAteer points out, "and all of a sudden along comes this upstart agency to tell the entire country to turn it around and stop using lead or benzene. It's right, it's absolutely critical, but it's hard."

It's no surprise then that Scannell decided that his principal goal would be "to involve all the partners." Before taking the post, he says, he had been struck "by the number of people who felt left out of the process." OSHA had worn various labels: "pro-labor, or pro-business, or pro-science, or no involvement. I thought it was important to embrace all of them--business, labor, academia, the professional scientific and engineering societies, and anyone else who has an interest in contributing to occupational safety and health." Some don't, he acknowledges; "some only want to throw hand grenades. But the goal is to get the people involved in the process." Has he been successful in this so far? "Would you expect me to say anything else?" he replies, adding more seriously that he thinks progress has been made and "people say at least I'm willing to listen to them."

Along similar lines, the AFL-CIO in early 1991 announced plans to support a stronger, mandated participation by labor in the dialogue. Marking the 20th anniversary of OSHA's founding statute, the union said it would push for major legislation requiring employers to set up labor-management committees on health and safety and give workers a new voice when management deals with OSHA to settle health and safety concerns and alleged violations. As of early summer, these proposals were still at the draft stage. For OSHA's part, Scannell says it supports the AFL-CIO's general goal in this regard, noting that his office currently keeps the labor side in a case advised on the status of the agency's negotiations with the employer in question, and asks for its comments. "Especially in the abatement area," he observes. "Abatement concerns hazards, and workers are well-qualified to provide valuable input."

If he stops short of endorsing a specifically mandated labor role in this enforcement end of the business, Scannell points at the same time to the inclusive nature of OSHA's procedures at the standards-writing stage. "There isn't a proposed standard that goes out of this agency any more until it has been discussed with all sides," he asserts. "To do otherwise would be impermissible." This approach has had one of its biggest impacts, he thinks, on workers in chemical and petrochemical plants. "We not only involved the unions in the plants, we involved the industry, the American Petroleum Institute, the states. 'Touch all the bases,' I said." The resulting OSHA standard drew "no sniping or anything like that, only fine tuning. And it wasn't a ho-hum standard, it was a major regulatory action." The point, Scannell believes, is that if OSHA succeeds in "embracing the players" in this way, it lessens the pressures from a Congress "inundated" by complaining constituents. "And that's the way it should be." To this basic operating philosophy, he does add the caution that, once in the rule-making phase, "you have to be more precise in reaching out because you might otherwise get into *ex parte* rule making, which is illegal."

Science and technology play a "very important role" at OSHA, Scannell says, and are particularly relevant for the offices of Health Standards and Safety Standards, two of OSHA's seven units. Further, the legislation which created OSHA also established the National Institute for Occupational Safety and Health. NIOSH, an independent body under the Centers for Disease Control of the Department of Health and Human Services, functions as OSHA's research arm. "When we have issues for which no private studies exist, or studies which have not been peer reviewed, we will ask NIOSH to do it," Scannell explains. In fact, OSHA depends on science and technology "for much of what we do." A two-way relationship evidently exists here. Scannell believes, for example, that OSHA actions often "drive the technology to develop better methods of analyzing samples of toxic substances or in testing for drugs. Five years ago," he says, "you might have had ten to fifteen percent false positives in drug testing. We don't have that today because the drug testing issue has driven companies to improve their technology."

OSHA operates on an annual budget authority of just over $300 million (the fiscal 1992 estimate) and the recent pattern, in Scannell's word, has been "steady." Between 20 and 25 percent of the budget figure takes the form of grants to states, about half of which operate their own occupational safety and health programs. Scannell supervises a staff of 2,500, the majority of whom have technical backgrounds, including "highly qualified scientists and engineers in our standards organizations," he says. About 15 percent of the staff works in Washington; the rest, including 1,200 compliance officers and 150 inspection supervisors, are based in about ten regional and a hundred local field offices. OSHA, McAteer says, has to hire its inspectors "not at top-of-the-line rates, but at government rates. They have to go into a variety of places, a different one every day, and enforce a set of rules that at last count was 3,000 pages long. So you get some college kid with an industrial hygiene or safety engineering degree and you tell that person to go out there and enforce this regulation. You've got an opponent in the plant operator, who isn't anxious to do that. It's a difficult job."

Opportunities for staff training, an important item on Scannell's agenda, diminish as budgets get cut. "I'd like compliance officers to be extremely professional, well-trained, and well-equipped. I'd like them to be diplomats. We are sometimes invasive in getting into the workplace, whether it's a Seven Eleven store or Exxon. I'm not saying they're not properly trained, but I think we owe them the opportunity to be as technically qualified as possible as health and safety professionals. Our training institute needs to be improved." OSHA could "always use some more compliance staff," he adds with tongue-in-cheek understatement. But, he says, "I always go back to the OSHA Act. It's not our place to make the workplace safe, it's the employer who has the responsibility. We have 30 percent more employees than when the act was written, but we're starting to get involved in economic inspections." That means, for example, that instead of the average 15 hours OSHA would spend in a petrochemical plant inspection, "we're now in there for a month or two months."

At the end of 1990, OSHA and the Environmental Protection Agency (EPA) overcame a significant barrier to effective enforcement in parallel, related areas of responsibility. The differences arose from their respective enabling statutes. Under them, OSHA worries about what goes on inside the workplace, EPA about protecting the environment and about dangers to public health everywhere else. In agreeing to exchange information, cross-train their inspectors and refer possible violations to one another, the two agencies ended an era in which consistent cooperation between them was rare. One notable difference between their enforcement powers remains, however: while EPA can seek criminal penalties for some injuries in the workplace, OSHA can ask only civil penalties for the violation of safety laws. It's an anomaly that some in the Congress are thinking of correcting.

In addition to its efforts with the EPA on this and other projects, OSHA has regular business in other parts of town. It is one of several regulatory agencies assembled by the White House Office of Science and Technology Policy to see what can be done to achieve uniformity in those core processes of all regulators--risk assessment and risk management. Part of its responsibility covers health and safety rules within federal agencies themselves and in this context, for example, the secretary of energy asked OSHA to do an extensive evaluation of that department's health and safety program. OSHA also works with the departments of Agriculture and Defense, and with other agencies.

A company disagreeing with a penalty proposed by OSHA after an inspection can contest it within 15 days. Such cases go to the three-member Occupational Safety and Health Review Commission, whose administrative law judges, after hearings, reach decisions which become final commission orders. A loser, however, can still resort to appellate court. OSHA's heavy workload so preoccupies its scientists that Scannell saw the need for a science advisory board. "There are so many standards and so many studies--are they good?" he asks. But making the decision to establish such a board and actually getting one "are a couple of different things," he notes. While his own department supports the idea, people elsewhere apparently don't.

OSHA and its chief have a more or less continuous colloquy with the Congress. Former assistant secretary John A. Pendergrass (1986-89) says he had no idea when he began of·the extent of legislators' influence on the agency's work. Most pressures from the Hill, says Scannell, "originate in the constituencies." OSHA, for instance, once proposed a standard for a blood-borne pathogen that was "misinterpreted by many dentists. We got inundated with letters from Congress. We had to address it, meet with dentist associations and other groups." That's another reason why "it's important that we do an exquisite job of communicating what we're doing to the regulated community."

How does OSHA decide which workplaces to inspect? In 1989, it looked at one in every eight general industrial facilities, while in meat packing, a high-hazard industry, the rate was one in four. Data from the Bureau of Labor Statistics helps OSHA to identify and concentrate on such industries. But OSHA is guided also by specific complaints to which the law obligates it to respond. Selection of which high-hazard sites to inspect, Scannell says, "is random." He does not apply pressure to get the inspection numbers up, though some pressure to do so exists. It would be easy enough, he reflects; regional administrators can be "creative." But "that wouldn't mean that quality inspections were being made, and I'm insisting on quality. To get the numbers up, I'd need more people. But I'm not sure that's the way to go. It's a fine balancing act."

McAteer argues that OSHA "has never done a good job on the data," among other reasons because "it doesn't collect and control its own data." Rather, collection is done by the Bureau of Labor Statistics. OSHA "doesn't establish the number of people killed, the number injured, and the number of industries we need to focus on," he says; all are tasks he considers vital. "We've made a national commitment to safe working places, and American industry has accepted the notion that this is a desirable goal," he comments. "People shouldn't have to get killed to make a living. We have to start finding out how many are being killed and in which industries, and then assess that and go after it." Additionally, "we need to take a serious look at the number of inspectors who get up every day and go out on an inspection"--648 by his count in 1989. "Six hundred and forty-eight, and there are five million workplaces. It'll take them a long time to get around."

OSHA should also emphasize its educational role, McAteer thinks, since "people err mostly because they don't understand and have failed to take account of the risk." Finally, in cases where employers "simply disregard the health of the worker," OSHA should "nail them"-- something he believes the agency has not pursued as vigorously as it could. Civil penalties "have to be high enough to make a significant difference," he says. "And we don't collect enough from them." He makes a comparison with motor vehicle speeding fines. "We know which states have better safety records by the amount of money they collect, and it works. If you raise the fines and you enforce, you keep people alive."

Yet as his comments cited earlier indicate, McAteer has few illusions about what OSHA is up against. "They have to grapple with extraordinarily difficult science problems and political problems. They haven't done as well as they ought to. But you have to understand the magnitude of the difficulty." This can go beyond just the practicalities into questions of philosophy and morality. On the health side of the OSHA mandate, for example, McAteer describes the question of trying to balance risk and benefit as suggested by the OSHA statute. Work contains inherent risks, which can be tolerated only as long as the benefits derived from a workplace activity outweigh them. When risks equal benefits, "it's time to make the cut." One of the questions this raises, however, is whether a cost can in effect be placed on human life. "To its credit," McAteer says, "actually to the credit of the scientists who raised it, OSHA rejected that notion." And the Supreme Court in a series of cases has ruled out such use of "cost-benefit analysis." But it was "one of the issues the assistant secretary had to struggle with, since the act and its legislative history were unclear."

That leaves the problem of pure risk assessment and management, an area where McActeer believes the agency has "failed over the years. We know, for example, that if we promulgate a regulation requiring lock out, tag out of electrical facilities we can save X number of lives. But changing the mechanics of electrical facilities is expensive." He asserts that, for the most part, OSHA has required actions of this kind only when forced to by political or other pressures from various sources.

In the view of Robert A. Rowland, assistant secretary in 1984-85, "OSHA is never going to be big enough to be a policeman." The system "is never going to work," he says, without voluntary compliance by employers, a goal that received major emphasis from the administration of his day. He does not think "overly harsh penalties" will do the job, either. He thinks the establishment of a cooperative environment could change this picture. Currently, he says, "OSHA has no procedure for helping employers comply; it's all penalties. An employer can't ask OSHA to come in and look at a situation because the agency will cite them and impose a penalty. This defeats cooperation."

Scannell has still other ideas. Prior experience in industry and now at OSHA has called his attention to the fact that "companies do audits of their health and safety programs, just as they do for the financial aspects of their businesses." Financial audits, however, result in reports to boards of directors or audit committees; health and safety audits do not. To try to change that, the department wrote to about 600 chief executive officers suggesting they treat health and safety audits with equal weight and get them before their boards of directors. He thinks this can have a "major impact" on corporate health and safety programs "that are good, but are sputtering because the issues brought up in these audits are not being addressed." It all gets back to his belief, Scannell says, that "the employers who have the responsibility can make it happen. OSHA and the government can't. We should not be in every workplace, only those where the employers are not doing it."

With its several layers of tough-nut problems and high exposure, is this job worth having? "I've enjoyed it," Scannell says. "We're all interested in preventing workers from dying and being injured. I haven't met anyone in business, labor, the universities or anywhere who has any other goal. Different agendas, but the same goal."

Key Relationships

Within the Department

Reports to: Secretary

Works closely with:

Solicitor
OSHA Review Commission
Commissioner, Bureau of Labor Statistics
Assistant Secretary, Mine Safety and Health Administration

Outside the Department

Assistant Administrator, Enforcement, Environmental Protection Agency
Director, National Institute for Occupational Safety and Health,
    Department of Health and Human Services
Assistant Director, Environmental Affairs, White House Office of Science
    and Technology Policy
Members, subgroup on risk assessment and risk management, Committee on
Life Sciences and Health, Federal Coordinating Council for Science,
    Engineering and Technology
Assistant Administrator, Research and Development,
    Environmental Protection Agency

Outside the Government

Labor unions; manufacturers associations; state and local employment health and safety officials; medical, nursing and hospital associations; industrial health and safety advocacy groups; National Safety Council, American Society of Safety Engineers and other professional and public service organizations

Profile of Current Assistant Secretary
Occupational Safety and Health

Name: Gerard F. Scannell

Assumed Position: 1989

Career Summary: Director, Corporate Safety/Fire/Environmental Affairs, Johnson & Johnson, 1979-89
Various positions at OSHA, 1971-79, including Director, Office of Federal Agency Safety and Health Programs; and Director, Office of Standards
Safety director, Rohm and Haas Co., 1965-71
Safety manager, Thiokol Chemical Corp., 1962-65
Supervisor, safety engineering department, Aetna Casualty and Surety Co., 1958-62

Education: Massachusetts Maritime Academy, BS, 1955

Assistant Secretaries, Occupational Safety and Health
Since 1971*

Administration	Name and Years Served	Present Position
Bush	Gerard F. Scannell 1989 - present	Incumbent
Bush	Alan McMillan (Acting) 1989	Deputy Assistant Secretary OSHA
Reagan	John A. Pendergrass 1986 - 1989	Pendergrass & Associates Falls Church, VA
Reagan	Patrick R. Tyson (A) 1985 - 1986	Constangy, Brooks & Smith Atlanta, GA
Reagan	Robert A. Rowland 1984 - 1985	Consultant Austin, TX
Reagan	Thorne G. Auchter 1981 - 1984	Thorne G. Auchter & Co. Ponte Vedra Beach, FL
Carter	Eula Bingham 1977 - 1981	Professor, Department of Environmental Health University of Cincinnati

Ford	Morton Corn 1975 - 1977	Professor, School of Hygiene and Public Health Johns Hopkins University Baltimore, MD
Ford, Nixon	John H. Stender 1973 - 1975	Not available
Nixon	George C. Guenther 1971 - 1973	President Talmage Tours, Inc. Philadelphia, PA

* The OSHA was established by the Occupational Safety and Health Act of 1970

COMMISSIONER
BUREAU OF LABOR STATISTICS

Senior Executive Service with Presidential Appointment

Major Responsibilities

- Direct the Bureau of Labor Statistics (BLS) in the continuous collection and analysis of national statistics on employment and unemployment, inflation, producer prices and other economic and social conditions.

- Develop monthly or quarterly indices and indicators as appropriate, based on these surveys. Report certain of these, such as price and employment data, to the White House at regular, fixed intervals for public announcement. Brief the secretary of labor and congressional and media audiences on the content and significance of the information. Ensure the nonpartisan nature of the work of the BLS, and the objectivity and factual character of its products.

- Work with other federal agencies with related responsibilities, particularly in the statistical area. Stay current with thinking and trends on the national economic scene through broad contact with labor and financial analysts, the university community, statistics professionals, and economists and other social scientists. Maintain links to counterpart organizations in other countries and to international economic institutions.

- Oversee the BLS in its function as the research arm of the department of labor, performing special surveys as required.

Necessary Training, Experience, Skills

Though academically trained in international economics, the present commissioner went back to school years later to acquire additional basic instruction in mathematics and statistics. There is no question about the job's demand for solid grounding in these fields. The chief of BLS has a good technical staff to rely on, but must have a highly developed feel for statistics, know what questions to ask, and be able to detect problem areas. Experience in running a statistical operation is a plus. Further, a commissioner should be able to deal firmly but diplomatically with a broad mix of users and audiences, including the Congress, with a strong sense of the BLS mission and the skill to project its importance to the national community. Finally, a veteran of this post thinks courage is crucial for the authority, independence and objectivity which are important to good performance.

Insight

Janet L. Norwood, chief of the Bureau of Labor Statistics since 1979, presides over one of the most consequential numbers-crunching operations in the country, if not in the world at large. One doesn't have to look far for the reason. "More and more," Norwood reflects, "the economy is being run by numbers." And a look at some of the BLS's work and its significance for what is still the world's biggest economy bears her out.

- Thousands of decision makers with a stake in or responsibility for U.S. economic performance focus on changes in the monthly Consumer Price Index. As the country's major inflation indicator, it is the best-known BLS product. CPI data play a role in economic activity in every sector, from judgments about stock prices and interest rates to the deliberations of the Federal Reserve Board, from the plans of corporate purchasing agents to the flow of international trade. The CPI informs the thinking of those who make policy on Capitol Hill and in the White House, and affects federal entitlement programs like social security, veterans' pensions, and school lunch payments. Millions of private sector pay checks are adjusted by cost-of-living premiums geared to the index. And, of course, the CPI assists Internal Revenue Service analysts in projecting federal income tax brackets. In sum, says Norwood, "we estimate that more than half the people in this country have income that is affected in some way by the CPI."

The BLS develops the index by sending its field collectors into retail establishments and other places of business every month to gather price data on thousands of goods and services bought by U.S. consumers. It processes the data and, within three weeks of the price reference date, releases the resulting CPI to the chairman of the president's Council of Economic Advisers--a crucial feat of speed and timeliness in which Norwood takes particular satisfaction.

Because fresh CPI information is sensitive, Norwood uses considerable care and precision in transmitting it to the White House at a predetermined moment each month, just prior to public announcement. Even the secretary of labor, Norwood's boss, doesn't get to see it first.

● Figures on employment and unemployment, also announced monthly, draw similar attention. Based on two BLS surveys, the Current Employment Statistics program (CES) and the Current Population Survey (CPS), these indicators are another important guide to the present and future state and direction of the national economy, with not only factual but psychological impact on expectations and decisions. The CPS, designed by Norwood's office and carried out under contract with the Bureau of the Census, looks into 60,000 households to see who is working, who is seeking work, and who is not. It produces, Norwood says, "a tremendous amount of demographic data used for all kinds of policy purposes." The CES adds to this picture in examining 300,000 business payrolls for information on numbers of jobs, hours and earnings. For this survey, the bureau contracts with each of the 50 states, retaining responsibility for what is collected and how, and for quality control.

● The importance of the BLS producer price program lies in what it often foreshadows for behavior of the CPI, as well as the monthly picture it provides of price movement at the wholesale level from raw material to finished product. In the fall of 1990, for example, this program provided a broad universe of observers with a blow-by-blow view of how the big spurt in oil costs at the start of the Persian Gulf war worked its way through the economy, from wellhead prices to wholesale figures for intermediate products used in the economy as a whole.

● For its quarterly employment cost index, the BLS samples occupations in business establishments. It learns what jobs in the selected companies earn, and what their fringe benefits cost. The result is the cost to employers of their work forces, and it has, Norwood says, become a "major economic indicator."

These programs, in her view, produce the most sensitive of all the statistical indicators. And precisely because they are sensitive, nonpartisanship is just as imperative as sound procedure. None of the protracted, difficult budget summit discussions in the fall of 1990 could have taken place, she says, without BLS data in projecting federal revenues and expenditures. "If people think that we are not objective, they won't believe what we say," Norwood explains. "It is important to be credible. The public has to have confidence that the agency is really operating objectively, and that means you have to run a very open agency." In political campaigns, as another example, opposing candidates frequently interpret the same set of BLS statistics differently. "And people come to us," she says. "Sometimes we're in the position of correcting people. We have to be sure we say it as it is."

Though the nonpartisan nature of this job is not framed by statute, it is pretty firmly fixed in practice. Norwood carries the rank of an assistant secretary and reports to the secretary of her department, but she is a commissioner to distinguish her position from those of policy-making officials. In addition, the position has a fixed term of four years, appointed by the president but not coterminous with an administration. Further still, Norwood notes, "I was appointed by a Democratic administration and reappointed twice by Republican administrations, and I don't think anything attests more than that to the nonpartisan character" of the position. She testifies on unemployment data each month to the bipartisan Joint Economic Committee of the Congress, "and that helps, too."

Along with this goes a clear measure of independence that is reflected in the dual cast of the BLS mission. As part of the Labor department, the bureau performs research for it and turns out a number of studies on topics like child care, drug testing in the work force, and training. But as a national statistical agency in its own right, the BLS functions independently. "At times that can be a little difficult," Norwood observes, but she has served with eight Labor secretaries "and we have worked things out quite well. Every secretary recognizes that there are certain things we have to do independently." These duties regularly involve the commissioner with the Federal Reserve Board, the Council of Economic Advisers, and statistical policy officials at the Office of Management and Budget. Norwood meets with the chiefs of other statistical agencies and offices, and represents the department in a group working under the chairman of the Council of Economic Advisers to improve the development of economic statistics.

About 98 percent of the BLS staff of 2,400 are quantitative economists, statisticians or computer support personnel--the bureau's three basic disciplines. Of the total, 1,500 work in four Washington locations, the rest in eight field offices. "The people we hire are in tremendous demand," Norwood says. "We only want the best." To that end, she maintains "a lot of contact with the heads of economics and statistics departments in many universities throughout the country." The bureau has little problem attracting competent younger staff because its statistical operations are challenging, its products have high public policy visibility, and certain of its data are attractive to researchers because they are confidential and not available elsewhere.

"That works well for a while," Norwood says of her younger staff. "But later people begin to realize the difference in pay is too great. We're getting to the point where we're not able to compete with the universities for the bright PhDs." The turnover is high, a condition she says is true of most scientific and technical agencies today. "All the federal agencies have had trouble in the last few years," says Barbara Bailar, executive director of the American Statistical Association. The problem for the BLS, she thinks, "is that the supply of people who are really knowledgeable about these kinds of issues is really small. You have to find people with education in certain statistical areas and do a lot of on-the-job training."

A deputy and six associates assist the commissioner to manage the agency. Besides its work in the areas of prices, employment, wages, salaries and fringes, the BLS operates a variety of other individual programs, including technology, living and working conditions, occupational projections for the future, and three kinds of productivity--labor, capital and multi-factor. "We have very good people here," Norwood says, and one result is that "someone is always trying to involve our staff in other kinds of analysis that get into policy issues. We have to be very resistant to that."

In its dealings, for example, with the Congress, for which the BLS does many special studies, "we get asked to do things that we prefer not to do," Norwood points out. In one case, testifying on an immigration bill, she had to resist an initiative which would have directed the bureau to determine labor shortages in individual localities as a basis for deciding who could enter the country. That, Norwood told the legislators, was not possible in a market economy where wages and working conditions make the necessary adjustments. Another bill would have put the BLS in the position of deciding the levels of locality pay for federal officials outside Washington. Objecting "strenuously" to that idea, Norwood stated that such decisions were policy matters, not a part of the BLS role. "We would provide the data, discuss it with them, work it through with them, but they had to make the determination."

Is there pressure on the BLS to produce information that follows a party line? "Definitely," Bailar says, "it's always been a problem." The BLS ran into it in the 1970s, she recalls, "when they were issuing the employment/unemployment stats, and the administration kind of stepped in and wanted to issue the numbers itself." It was at that point, she relates, that the commissioner was invited to give the monthly presentation to the Joint Economic Committee. "Pressure comes at different times," according to Bailar--"when the economy changes, during a recession, when times are good, when labor unions are feeling a pinch."

The BLS's estimated budget authority for fiscal 1991 was $255.1 million; for 1992, the request is for $308.9 million. The BLS has had to cut a number of programs over the years. "The most important thing," Norwood thinks, "is that sometimes we didn't have the funds to invest in the research we need to do. We're doing all right now, but we're not building for the future, and that's a very serious problem." Uncertain budget patterns also cost the bureau staff time and spirit. "We're always having to reestimate what we can do," Norwood comments. While various activities can be cut out or performed less often, "you have to redesign things completely and that costs people and time. So many such options are not open to you. It's hard to maintain morale in a period when people don't know what's going to happen."

Geoffrey Moore, commissioner in 1969-72, now directs the Center for International Business Cycle Research at Columbia University and, he says, uses BLS statistics "all the time." Statistical budgets "need to be kept replenished. The new advances are very important, and we can learn a lot from having new types of data that we didn't know how to construct before." Bailar makes a related observation. "This is an enormous scientific undertaking," she says. "One of the main problems is that few people in policy-level jobs, where the commissioner has to go to get the dollars to do her job, really understand why it costs so much money to do surveys. They don't grasp the technical necessity for doing it right. They don't see why a lot of money must go into redesigning these surveys."

But keeping up with the state of the art, Norwood asserts, is vital. In a statistical agency, a built-in bias exists against change, she says, "and that's a good thing in many ways, because you need continuity. But if the agency doesn't move forward, it moves backward." She believes it one of her most important tasks to insist on moving ahead. "And that can be difficult, especially in a period of declining budgets. The easiest thing to do is to shave a little here and a little there, but in the end you have reduced quality, and I've refused to do that." If the budget must be cut, the BLS drops a whole program rather than parts of it. "That's hard," Norwood acknowledges, "because any program you have has users. But I think it's necessary because otherwise you end up with a very poor statistical system."

In at least one state of the art, the BLS is evidently staying even. Rather than "go through the long, drawn-out process" of acquiring its own complete mainframe capability, the bureau adopted what Norwood calls a "two-computer-center policy." For its mainframe work, the bureau uses the computer facilities at the National Institutes of Health, and also contracts with the private sector. "Many people think of statisticians as people with green eyeshades who sit in the corner just mapping out numbers," Norwood says. "They don't realize that we use some of the most sophisticated computer systems there are."

The BLS has developed a network of international relationships. For ten years Norwood has chaired the working party on employment and unemployment statistics of the Organization for Economic Cooperation and Development. The bureau is heavily involved in Labor department technical assistance to Poland and Hungary. And while Norwood tries to hold down her international travel, she recently visited Moscow at the Soviet government's invitation to review its price statistics situation. The CPI, she notes, is "probably the best such index in the world. We're considered the experts in that area." The agency also maintains ties with government statistical organizations around the world; for example, it has a special relationship with Statistics Canada, which combines the Canadian versions of the BLS and the Census bureau, among others. This centralized statistical system is typical of many governments, and contrasts with the dispersed U.S. approach.

Bailar criticizes the decentralization of the federal statistical system. "It doesn't make sense to parcel these things out--labor surveys by the Labor department, educational surveys by Education, energy studies by the Energy Information Administration," she says. Such a piecemeal approach precludes a "clear picture of the resources needed" for the greater effectiveness of the entire federal system. She doesn't think Washington will pull its various statistical units into one operation any time soon, because "no agency wants to give up what it already has." But she sees some signs of change, such as the proposal to exchange data between statistical agencies that have no regulatory functions.

In the meantime, Bailar perceives changes coming in methodology. "The time of going out and knocking on doors for interviews has come to an end," she suggests. And while the BLS does collect data by telephone, the calls are still routinely assigned to interviewers who do them from home. "Most agencies are using central telephone data collection," Bailar continues. "That's going to become more and more powerful." Instead of notations on paper, data will be entered into lap-top or hand-held computers and down loaded directly into the agency's computer for tabulation. Bailar expects these sea changes to make the BLS much more efficient and "probably raise the quality. It may remove the need for intermediate operations, field offices and all that sort of thing. And that's a painful proposition. Very exciting technically, but very disrupting when you look at it from the organizational point of view."

Field offices, of course, are only part of the BLS collection system. Norwood calls the agency's cooperative program with the states the "best developed" in the statistical area, and one of the best in the country generally. The employment security agency in each state performs data collection both for the state and, on contract, for the BLS. "It means we don't have three or four thousand people on the payroll that we would otherwise have to employ," Norwood points out. "But more important is the fact that what we're doing stimulates and educates the states, and elevates their standards for statistical work."

All BLS data collection, Norwood reminds us, is done with the voluntary cooperation of respondents. "That means the respondents have to know who the Bureau of Labor Statistics is. They need to know something of our reputation, to understand why the data are important, why it's important for them to provide us with accurate information, and how they themselves might be able to use those data. So the public image of the bureau plays a big role. And I consider that a very important part of my job."

Key Relationships

Within the Department

Reports to: Secretary

Works closely with:

Deputy Secretary
Assistant Secretary, Employment Standards
Assistant Secretary, Pension and Welfare Benefits
Assistant Secretary, Occupational Health and Safety
Deputy Under Secretary, International Affairs

Outside the Department

Director, Bureau of the Census
Heads of other federal statistics agencies (National Center for Education Statistics, Energy Information Administration, etc.)
Chairman, White House Council of Economic Advisers
Chairman, Federal Reserve Board
Committee on National Statistics, National Academy of Sciences
Office of Statistical Policy, Office of Management and Budget
General Accounting Office

Outside the Government

American Statistical Association, International Statistical Institute, and other professional groups in that field; professional economic and research associations; statistical agencies of the states and of other governments; Organization for Economic Cooperation and Development, European Economic Community, and International Labor Organization; college and university faculty members; public administration organizations

Profile of Current Commissioner, Bureau of Labor Statistics

Name:	Janet L. Norwood
Assumed Position:	1979
Career Summary:	Career service, Bureau of Labor Statistics, 1963-79, including deputy commissioner, 1973-78; and acting commissioner, 1978-79 Research and teaching, Fletcher School of Law and Diplomacy, Tufts University; and Wellesley College
Education:	Douglas College, Rutgers University, BA, 1945 Fletcher School, Tufts University, MA, 1946; PhD, 1949

Commissioners, Bureau of Labor Statistics Since 1969

Administration	Name and Years Served	Present Position
Bush, Reagan, Carter	Janet L. Norwood 1979 - present	Incumbent
Carter, Ford, Nixon	Julius Shiskin 1973 - 1978	Deceased
Nixon	Geoffrey H. Moore 1968 - 1973	Center for Intl. Business Cycle Research Columbia University New York, N.Y.

NATIONAL AERONAUTICS
AND SPACE ADMINISTRATION

ADMINISTRATOR

Level II - Presidential Appointment with Senate Confirmation

Major Responsibilities

- Lead the U.S. effort to enlarge knowledge and understanding of the universe and the solar system, including the earth, through manned and unmanned missions to near and deep space. As a fundamental part of this mandate, oversee the careful planning and execution of extensive programs of space science research in many disciplines.

- Address the resources of the agency to the continuing challenges of space flight and the requirement for capable, cost-effective payloads, human and otherwise. Supervise the design, development, construction and launch of safe manned vehicles and of the earth satellites, observation platforms, planetary orbiters and distant space probes employed in NASA programs.

- Counsel the White House on the formulation of U.S. space policy. Take a central role in government-wide decision making about the use of American space assets and experience in the study of environmental problems, and the pursuit of technological progress and other national goals. Coordinate NASA's work closely with that of other federal agencies and of other governments.

- Articulate space policy and objectives to the Congress, and function as chief public spokesman on these subjects in this country and abroad; both cost-sharing and competition are significant features of NASA's international relationships, and of this job's responsibilities.

Necessary Training, Experience, Skills

NASA in the last half decade has navigated a stormy passage of such broad dimensions that talk about scientific and technical competence in its top job seems almost an afterthought. There is no question that a NASA administrator with that competence always has a clear edge. It is important for understanding what scientists and engineers are saying, for recruiting good technical management, and for penetrating bad information and advice. A science/technical background is arguably even more of an advantage at a time when the reliability of NASA instruments and equipment has been increasingly in question.

Note at the same time, however, that an early NASA leader, James E. Webb, widely recognized to have been one of its most effective, had no such background. It seems clear to informed observers, in fact, that putting the agency on a calmer, more productive course and keeping it there takes an unusual combination of leadership strengths in which technical expertise is only one useful resource. Proven management and communications skills, boldness, a receptivity to outside views, and commitment are others. Another highly important asset is political aptitude--the ability to relate to a wide variety of influential players, from presidents to Congressional staff members, from industrial heavy hitters to bench scientists. The trick is not just to survive the mine field which their collective pressure often represents, but to steer through it successfully and with vision, strengthening the agency and injecting it with confidence and purpose.

Insight

No present problem is likely to dim forever NASA's sparkling past achievements, the skill and belief of many of its scientists and engineers, or its continuing potential as a pioneer in technology's brightest era.

Yet of all the missions NASA currently flies, its most urgent lies close to hand, an earthbound mission. It is to develop an integrated, cohesive, long-term concept of the agency's purpose and objectives that finds wide national agreement and support--and then stick to it.

That imperative won't be found in any boilerplate inventory of the NASA administrator's duties. Yet in reality it tops the list. By all evidence, nothing less can correct the recent record of disabling equipment failures, delayed missions, backed-up schedules, and high and rising costs. It is a record that distresses the space and science community and is painfully visible to the world at large. But the task of redefining, reorienting and redirecting the agency is scarcely a job for a single individual in any case. It is one in which the administration, the Congress, the scientists, and the public must also join. There is implicit recognition of this in the view of Richard H. Truly, NASA administrator since 1989, who sees his role as "trying to help pull together the achievable options so that the president, during this national debate about the space program, can weave his way through and make the right policy decisions." Acknowledgement of the need to put NASA on a new footing is also evident in the establishment of the National Space Council, headed by the vice president.

Further along these lines was the late 1990 report of a White House fact-finding panel on NASA headed by Martin Marietta chairman and chief executive officer Norman Augustine. Its five-point recommendations suggested remedies to NASA problems that drew support from many quarters, including NASA itself. They included establishing science as NASA's priority and giving the main job of cargo lifting to an unmanned booster, with the problematic space shuttle in a back-up role. But the Augustine panel is only one in a string of eminent groups called together since 1985 to examine space policy and problems. The latest is a commission headed by former astronaut Thomas Stafford that turned in its report in June, 1991. Among its points was the conclusion that the United States should drop the earth-orbiting space station project as a means to acquire the experience and knowledge necessary for manned solar system exploration, and instead revive its lunar program for this purpose.

The Augustine and Stafford suggestions are only starting points; the tough part of this job is the implementation. And some, including some in the Congress, suggest that these latest prescriptions may get only lip service from a NASA still too inflexibly rooted in its own ways. Others wonder aloud or in print whether the agency, trying to cope with multiple and often conflicting constituencies, will ever be able, or allowed, to pull up its socks.

Well-founded or not, such speculations are themselves part of the continual cross fire the agency must cope with. They, too, illustrate the need for a durable, broad-based consensus about what NASA is supposed to do. As things now stand, says John Logsdon, director of George Washington University's Space Policy Institute, NASA lacks "sharp purpose, a politically-supported mission against which it can plan its programs. A measure of success in the administrator will be to create among those who pay careful attention to NASA--in industry, the universities, Congress, and the press--confidence that the agency has well-conceived programs that it can carry out." Yet, in Truly's description of the current scene, "everybody supports the space program, but no two of them are talking about the same space program."

It wasn't always that way. Conceived in the U.S. embarrassment over the 1957 flight of Sputnik, NASA took over the work in progress of the old National Advisory Committee for Aeronautics, dating from the 1920s. Though NASA's earliest years were rocky ones, studded with failed launches, the new agency enjoyed strong political support and the encouragement of an enthusiastic, if frequently disappointed, public. From the early 1960s, NASA accelerated rapidly--and for the most part brilliantly--into the space business, and the country cheered. Success followed success--space walks, long-duration earth orbiting missions, weather and communications satellites, the Apollo manned moon landings, deep space shots, and spectacular planetary mapping and photography. Significant scientific investigation accompanied each step, producing both pure discovery and applications in technology and commerce. And early in the 1980s the re-usable space shuttle seemed to herald a new stage of the agency's advance. NASA was literally and figuratively in orbit.

As with many objects in that situation, however, the agency's trajectory was already in slow decay. The Challenger shuttle disaster of 1986, traumatic as it was, seems only to have signalled underlying circumstances and patterns that some observers say had long been developing. Small but costly errors, as with the Hubble telescope, had begun to mar a record of huge accomplishment. The post-Challenger shuttle timetable bogged down in a swamp of technical problems. With the country's only weather satellite creaking along on dying batteries and expected to go out of service in early 1993, NASA in mid-1991 was encountering pointed suggestions from the Congress and elsewhere that it buy and put up a replacement of the same kind. That's because the next generation of improved weather birds that NASA builds for the Department of Commerce had been plagued by faulty construction and other delays and might not be ready in time, leaving the United States without space-based weather information. In short, while some of the brilliance remains, NASA's name these days is entangled more with repeated shuttle problems and the uncertain fate of the Freedom space station, the centerpiece of the present space program.

As originally planned, the station would serve as a 30-year orbiting home for scientists studying space and the earth, and for supporting such announced but distant ventures as a permanent base on the moon and manned exploration of Mars. But the station ran into nothing but problems. Initially understood to cost $8 billion and to fly by 1993, it is now pegged at $30 billion, plus operating costs, and under present plans its operational target date has slipped by half a dozen years. Rapid turnover has characterized the management of the program. Its current status evolved from many reconfigurations, including one ordered by the Congress late in 1990 when it was evident that costs were skyrocketing.

Those revisions deprived the space station of all but two scientific projects, fueling further doubts in the Congress and elsewhere about its ultimate value. They, and the delays they caused, have created permanently raised eyebrows and hackles among the Europeans, Canadians, and Japanese who are U.S. partners in the station and would contribute two laboratory modules and a robot arm to it. Assembling the station will require about 25 flights of the troubled shuttle vehicle, an additional reason for concerns about the reality of the planning.

In the spring of 1991, the House Appropriations Committee killed the space station. Crash lobbying by the administration then revived it in the full House. In July, the Senate followed, voting the full $2 billion the administration had asked for the project for fiscal 1992. The action, however, meant significant cuts for other NASA programs. And the eventual fate of the space station still remains deeply in question.

There are a number of reasons for the development of these kinds of program-specific situations, and for NASA's more generalized problems. Most of them are daily facts of life for the administrator and his chief lieutenants:

- Incentive. In the salad days of the 1960s, NASA's feats were fueled by perceived rivalry with the Soviet Union. John Kennedy set the tone early: catch up with the Soviets, pass them, land on the moon. And it was done. As history and economics slowly drew Moscow's fangs, however, the cold war faded and, with it, the urgency to compete. Gradually, NASA developed the cautious, layered habits of a bureaucracy, even while it continued to believe and say it could do everything assigned to it at the leading edge.

- The system. As the most expensive project NASA has ever attempted, the space station naturally draws Congressional fire in a budget-crisis era. So do many other NASA ventures. But if the agency has to fight even harder these days for its money than in the past 15 or 20 years, the paradoxical truth is that its budget authority has been climbing steadily. And what the agency does spend, and where, and how, are matters of keen and contentious interest for members of Congress whose corporate and individual constituents benefit (a situation NASA has long since known how to manipulate). It is no less important to scientific groups pushing to get their preferred projects into NASA missions, or to others in the scientific community who think expenditures like NASA's steal funding from "little" science projects they favor. A constituent group that foresees a decision from the administrator's office that it dislikes can often use political influence to try to head it off. "That's our process and it's the one you live in," says Alan M.

Lovelace, a former deputy administrator who also served in the top job in an acting capacity (1975-81). "If you aren't a pragmatist and a realist about how you get things done, you're going to be very frustrated." Thus, amid a wide and genuine debate on the merits of what the space agency can and should be doing, its interests bounce constantly between those durable Washington institutions, turf and pork.

• Appropriations. NASA lives with a curious Congressional funding structure. In its appropriation subcommittees of both houses, it must compete for resources each year with agencies responsible for big and/or urgent, well-known domestic needs--among them housing, the environment, and veterans. The comparison can be invidious.

• Authority. Much real power and most of the technical strength resides in NASA's seven space centers and laboratories. Some say too much power, and that these facilities tend sometimes to compete against one another to the detriment of general progress. Some have their own strong ties to Capitol Hill. Natural and understandable, these phenomena also create unusual problems of control.

• Habit. Though it is learning through bitter experience, the agency still shows a bent for some overoptimism about costs and underestimation of the time projects require. In part, this is a hangover from the can-do psychology of an earlier period, when money was less tight, things cost less, and other national priorities were not--or did not seem--so numerous. Further, NASA managers have reportedly preferred to pare down programs in times of restricted funds, rather than eliminate any of them.

• Work force. Though overall turnover is lower than at any time in the last eight years, in science and engineering personnel it is high. Since its beginning in 1984, the space station program has had five managers. In fiscal 1989 and 1990, according to NASA's own figures published by *Government Executive* magazine, the agency lost half of its mid-level staff in those areas. The average grade of those departing in 1990, the magazine said, was 2.5 grades higher than that of those hired in the same period. In the last three to four years, the growth of the work force has not matched that of the budget.

• Public attitudes. Someone has described popular belief in NASA as the proverbial mile wide and inch deep--still animated by the popular image of humans in space, but not very profound or thoughtful about what space means to the national interest or to them as individual citizens. Unmanned programs using sophisticated, automated instruments on vehicles that travel much farther may be far more productive and less expensive. But they are usually less visible, apt to attract less public support and more concern about cost.

"This is a very peculiar situation in a variety of ways," Logsdon says. On one hand, the administration firmly supports both the traditional NASA mission of scientific research and space exploration, and a new, central role in such efforts as the study of global climate change. It backs a continued rising curve in NASA funding. That adds up to "an unprecedented opportunity to put the NASA program on a sound, long-term footing," Logsdon believes. "On another hand, we're in the midst of overall economic problems. And on yet another hand, the agency's performance has not been very good." The Congress, while not halting the substantial net funding increases of the last several years, took a billion dollars or so off NASA's fiscal 1992 request and will continue to look hard at individual programs. The administrator, Logsdon sums up, "is between several hard places and a falling rock."

The 1992 NASA budget request, for spending authority of $15.7 billion, represented a 13.6 percent boost from 1991 (about eight percent in real growth). That would continue the rising pattern of funding that has brought NASA close to the lead among federal agencies in percentage increase. Space science is a leading priority, up a requested 21 percent in 1992. Though the Augustine report suggested real growth of 10 percent annually during the 1990s, it was unclear at this writing where the Congress was headed on the 1992 NASA budget, or what the pattern in the following few years might look like.

Figured into these increasing totals is another program--total cost $30 billion--that is the second main feature (with the space station) of NASA's current agenda. This is the earth observing system (EOS), a key NASA contribution to the multi-agency "mission to planet earth" on which work began in 1991. EOS will study the interrelationship between earth's oceans and land masses and the atmosphere, the effect of animal and plant life on climate, and other processes that are producing global climate change. Truly's direct involvement in this program is enlarged by his membership of the White House-run Federal Coordinating Council for Science, Engineering and Technology (FCCSET), which energized the U.S. climate change effort conceived in the White House of Science and Technology Policy. As now scheduled, the first EOS spacecraft will go up in 1998. When the system is operational, its remote sensors in polar orbit will over a 15-year period churn immense amounts of data into an advanced data and information system on the ground--so much data that doubts have arisen as to NASA's capacity to handle it.

EOS, too, has its share of problems and critics. Questions among NASA and other scientists about its scientific value and relevance led the House science committee in the spring of 1991 to request an investigation by the General Accounting Office. At around the same time, bidding was postponed for six months on a chief component of the data processing system. Serious questions about ultimate cost have been asked by those who wonder whether EOS can succeed and think existing equipment can do the job. During the summer of 1991 it began to seem possible that NASA, under pressure from critics of EOS, might have to cancel the project's large instrument platform and substitute three smaller vehicles. Further changes, like a substantial budget cut, would damage the EOS time table and threaten continuation of the project. Yet it probably enjoys the broadest support of any major NASA program.

NASA's experience with the space shuttle even since the Augustine report has lent new urgency to that group's assertion that the space program needs a more reliable, and probably larger, transport vehicle. Though the agency originally planned 50 or 60 shuttle missions a year, the total to date is nowhere near that figure, and the maximum number flown in any year stands at nine. Besides dependability, size has been a limiting factor. The dimensions of the Hubble telescope had to be shaped to fit the shuttle's cargo capacity; and the shuttle's altitude limitation meant a much lower, less productive orbit for Hubble. The agency could of course develop a new, heavy cargo lifter, but it would be 1997 at least before it could fly. "They really have to find some way to obtain a launching capability independent of the shuttle," says Burt Edelson, a former NASA associate administrator for space science and applications. "The shuttle is gobbling up all the money and limiting the programs. All the payloads that are lined up are getting pushed back. That leaves them with an impossible job with the space station."

Truly says his civil service work force numbers a little more than 24,000, augmented by 45,000 support-service contractors who provide such services as printing plant operation. The total effective work force thus comes to about 70,000. Between support-service personnel and the prime contracting companies which design and build the launchers and the space vehicles and systems, Truly says, "about 85 percent of our work goes out to contractors."

That situation is a cause of concern among NASA veterans and NASA-watchers. The agency's science operation, Logsdon points out, "is really an organization like other government science organizations which support work by the scientific community, mainly in universities. They need to be managers of the projects on which scientists put their payloads, and able to choose between alternative scientific proposals." Most of this is done at NASA headquarters, not in the field, "and so you need science managers." And, he adds, "I think they're good." But in the engineering department, he continues, "there is a sense that NASA has lost its technical edge, that there's too much contract management and not enough hands-on engineering throughout the organization. And so the ability to make sharp judgments on engineering projects has been lost over the last 10 or 15 years." Philip Culbertson, a former NASA associate administrator in charge of the space station, and Robert A. Frosch, NASA administrator in 1977-80, offer similar observations. "It may be," Frosch suggests "that the inside has been forced over the years to lean too heavily on a miscellany of contractors to do too much. The capability inside to deal with problems is not as strong as it used to be." Culbertson says the agency "has become more and more a manager of people in industry, and has lost some of its in-house capacity to do real systems engineering. They need more people directly involved in hands-on engineering."

A National Academy of Public Administration study published at the beginning of 1991 bears all of them out. It reported a survey of 2,000 mid-level NASA scientists and engineers in which less than 25 percent felt the agency's strength in their fields was as great as in the past. Further, almost 60 percent of them thought NASA should restrict the amount of technical work it contracts out. *Government Executive* reports that the agency has, in fact, started repatriating some of its technical jobs by bringing positions formerly filled on contract into its own civil service ranks.

But NASA, like just about every other federal scientific and technical agency, has trouble replacing staff who leave, an especially worrying problem at the senior technical levels. The Augustine recommendation in the personnel area was that NASA try to upgrade pay levels for all staff or exempt certain of them from the limits of the pay scale; or, if neither of those alternatives is realistic, to begin adapting NASA centers and laboratories to the model of its Jet Propulsion Laboratory in California. JPL is managed for NASA by the California Institute of Technology, does not operate under federal government personnel rules, and its salaries are private-sector level. Augustine himself has said that JPL is "the brightest spot in all of NASA."

Former administrator Robert A. Frosch (1977-80) emphasizes the value of a smooth collaboration between administrator and deputy administrator (who are, incidentally, the agency's only two presidential appointees). "It's a lean office, and they have to divide the load; neither can carry the other," he says. These two top officials, Lovelace adds, must also serve as "translators and interpreters to the public, to restore its belief and support." Further down the management line, Logsdon perceives a certain homogeneity of outlook, but thinks the agency has good depth. "They are all out of the manned space flight culture," he says, "and many of them are ex-astronauts or friends of astronauts. It's a '90s version of the right stuff--it's still 'leave us alone, we'll take care of it.' But in terms of technical integrity and management quality, the people who are third, fourth, fifth and sixth in line at the agency are the best that have been there in a long time."

That should facilitate the administrator in the "outside-oriented" role Logsdon thinks is as important as high-quality technical management on the inside. As a former NASA insider, Truly acknowledges, "I have to work hard at keeping my hands off the steering wheel." The job, however, requires him to cover many exterior bases. These range from senior interagency meetings in the context of FCCSET and the National Space Council to one-on-one consultation with the top people and their deputies at the departments of Defense, Commerce, Energy, Transportation, among others, the science and technology policy office at the White House, and the National Science Foundation. They include visits to NASA field centers, to academic institutions, to foreign space agencies and officials, to corporate headquarters around the country, and-- quite often--to Capitol Hill for testimony and other kinds of less formal fence-mending and tending. The administrator meets with in-house and outside advisory boards and councils, and sits on the Government-University-Industry Research Roundtable of the National Academy of Sciences. Truly has defended the NASA budget to the president, and can and does go to the Oval Office on policy matters when he thinks it necessary. But space policy is basically made in the National Space Council, chaired by the vice president.

As recently as 1989, the Voyager 2 spacecraft reminded the world of U.S. space achievement with pictures of Neptune from three billion miles away. Today, in the view of some of its critics, the agency despite the sweep of its future plans has become a bureaucracy in early middle age, with an instinct for survival mixed into the old pioneering spirit. In Truly's view, that is "a bum rap as a generalization for NASA. NASA is an organization of true excellence, and I believe we have retained that excellence." As with any 30-year-old entity, he thinks there are "places we need to improve," and that would be the case 30 years from now if NASA were torn down and a new organization were built in its place.

Truly thinks the space program is at "a turning point:" while it has been on a certain plateau for a long time, "now at least we have the opportunity to engage in a debate that could drastically change it by the end of the century." Meanwhile, he says, "we're living in a different world from the 1960s. We have to run our programs in today's environment, not a magic one, and it's far different."

Key Relationships

Within the Government

Reports to: President

Works closely with:

> Director, White House Office of Science and Technology Policy
> President, National Academy of Sciences
> Members, National Space Council
> Federal Coordinating Council for Science, Engineering, and Technology
> Deputy Secretary of Defense
> Secretary of Energy
> Deputy Secretary of Commerce
> Director, National Science Foundation
> Secretary of Transportation
> Administrator, Federal Aviation Administration
> Secretary of the Air Force
> Secretary of the Navy
> Members, Government-University-Industry Research Roundtable, National
> Academy of Sciences

Outside the Government

> NASA prime contracting firms in aerospace and engineering; aerospace
> industry trade associations; university research directors; professional
> science and engineering societies; aeronautics and astronautics groups;
> astronaut and test pilot associations; space, defense, science and diplomatic
> officials of foreign governments and international organizations

Profile of Current Administrator, NASA

Name: Richard H. Truly

Assumed Position: 1989

Career Summary: Associate Administrator, Space Flight, NASA, 1986-89
                Career U.S. naval officer, 1959-89 (service as a NASA astronaut,
                1969-89 including pilot, space shuttle Columbia, 1981, and
                commander, shuttle Challenger, 1983); retired as vice admiral

Education: Georgia Institute of Technology, BS (aeronautical engineering),
                1959

Administrators of NASA Since 1969

Administration	Name and Years Served	Present Position
Bush	Richard H. Truly 1989 - present	Incumbent
Bush	Dale D. Myers (Acting) 1989	Consultant San Diego, Cal.
Reagan	James C. Fletcher 1986 - 1988	Senior Fellow Institute for Technology & Strategic Research Washington, D.C.
Reagan	William R. Graham Jr. (A) 1986	Chairman and CEO Xsirius Inc. Arlington, Va.
Reagan	James M. Beggs 1982 - 1985	Chairman Spacehab Inc. Washington, D.C.
Reagan	Alan M. Lovelace (A) 1981	Corporate Vice President Commercial Launch Services General Dynamics Corp. San Diego, Cal.
Carter	Robert A. Frosch 1977 - 1980	Vice President, Research Laboratories General Motors Corporation Warren, Mich.
Ford, Nixon	James C. Fletcher 1971 - 1976	Senior Fellow Institute for Technology & Strategic Research Washington, D.C.
Nixon	Thomas O. Paine 1969 - 1970	Chairman Thomas Paine Associates San Diego, Cal.

ASSOCIATE ADMINISTRATOR, SPACE FLIGHT

Senior Executive Service

Major Responsibilities

- Manage the Office of Space Flight (OSF), responsible for the planning, integration and operation of all NASA missions into near and deep space, manned and unmanned, including the current space shuttle and projected space station programs and other civil launch activities. Oversee the development, acquisition and testing of launch vehicles, payloads and associated equipment.

- Administer the agency facilities whose work chiefly supports space flight operations (the Johnson, Kennedy and Stennis Space Centers and the Marshall Space Flight Center).

- Coordinate the activities of OSF as necessary with those of other federal agencies, and represent the office in negotiations and agreements with other governments, with international organizations, and with commercial users such as the communications satellite industry. Speak for the interests of NASA space flight within the executive branch and to the Congress. Act as spokesman on space flight issues to a variety of institutional, academic and public audiences in the United States and abroad.

Necessary Training, Experience, Skills

Though an advanced degree in some branch of aeronautical engineering or space science would clearly be an advantage, it is not imperative. Perhaps more important, says the current occupant of this job, is leadership--"the ability to direct, as opposed to manage"--and "technical and operational understanding." All these qualities need not be present in the same person if the "right deputy" is in place. For example, "a person with almost no technical background, but a really experienced manager who in industry has directed large-scale programs and understands strategic planning, how you build programs, could be excellent--but he'd have to have a strong chief engineer." One former associate administrator argues strongly that NASA tends to fill too many senior jobs like this one with competent insiders, and that it would benefit by the presence of some talented outsiders with different perspectives. Finally, this job lies at the center of a continuing, often stormy public discussion about NASA's role and direction and whether the agency justifies the money it spends. Its occupant needs the substantive and communications skill, and the personal poise, to take a leading and productive part in this debate.

Insight

Each of this job's main areas of responsibility represents a major problem or a continuing management challenge--or both. Take the space shuttle. Its past adversities have by no means been forgotten. But the chief technical issue today, according to William B. Lenoir, associate administrator since 1989, is "how do we get more operational?" The vehicle has several systems that don't work exactly as intended, or trouble-free, he says. "It's like a temperamental car--it does fine if you are a mechanic or the car spends a lot of time in the repair shop." In the transition from developmental to more operational status, the test is twofold: how to sever the link where possible between the shuttle's operators and the engineering expertise amassed during development; and how to maintain that same link where it's still necessary. And, Lenoir continues, the process must go forward safely, and without affecting productivity "so that we don't go too far and then find that instead of eight flights this year, we've got only four."

Or look at the Freedom space station, an earth-orbiting research laboratory with living quarters that was supposedly headed for launch in about 1999. Conceived in the 1970s, Freedom for several years was a key NASA project; at this writing, it must still be so considered, but it appears to be living on borrowed time. The station has encountered numberless obstacles, from multiple redesigns to funding slowdowns. Professional scientific organizations viewed its ever-rising cost as a threat to funding for basic research. And in March 1991 a National Research Council panel reported that the space station's latest, simpler design did not satisfy "the basic research requirements" it is supposed to serve. These developments have played out, moreover, to the disquiet of the project's several foreign participants.

Apart from these, one of Freedom's toughest problems may lie in the planned role of the space shuttle in the station's construction and maintenance. In December 1990 a White House panel on NASA headed by Martin Marietta chairman and CEO Norman Augustine viewed this task as so important that it merits a back-up transportation mode. It recommended shifting the shuttle's mission in building and supplying the space station largely to an unmanned heavy-lift vehicle. The shuttle would take the back-up role. But a heavy-lift launcher would meanwhile take several years to reach the pad at Cape Canaveral.

When we talked with him in late 1990, Robert O. Aller, a consultant who headed NASA's Office of Space Operations in 1983-89, already thought the space station, like the shuttle, was in "big trouble." The reason for "so much controversy over the configuration, the purpose, the long-range use of these programs, is that in space things have gotten totally out of hand in cost," he says. On this point, Lenoir suggests that "because of decisions made years ago, we have a space station that has more different pieces, managed by different organizations, and more complicated interfaces than you would prefer. It was done that way for a reason, but today we pay that price. The engineering integration across those interfaces, making sure we don't forget something or discover a problem later, is our number one challenge." On an even more fundamental level, he clearly agrees that the problem was one of "laying out a space station that we can afford within the congressional guidelines, that is worth doing when built and is a reasonable way to spend the country's money."

The administration's fiscal 1992 budget request for the space station asked only an eight percent increase. But in May 1991 the House appropriations subcommittee with jurisdiction for NASA canceled the space station. The full House restored almost all of the appropriation, however, and the Senate followed suit. But these decisions came at the expense of other NASA programs. Freedom's ultimate configuration, and its final destiny, remain unclear.

Then there is the heavy-lift vehicle itself, which NASA since the fall of 1990 has been exploring with the department of defense. OSF's task here is to mesh NASA requirements with those of the Pentagon, weighing at the same time the possible benefits to U.S. commercial competitiveness. "How ought we express a requirement that says we should be attentive to the global posture of American industry?" Lenoir asks. "What does that mean? How do we integrate those together, lay options up and pick an answer? It sounds like policy, but there's a lot of technical depth required to make the decision."

The space station, the shuttle, the heavy-lift vehicle and other planning-stage projects like the Earth Observing System (part of the government-wide global change study), a permanent moon base and manned missions to Mars fall into what Lenoir calls the "programmatic" area of his responsibilities. Managing the four space centers under his jurisdiction is the "institutional" part of the job. And it is no less demanding. Philip Culbertson is a NASA veteran and a former associate administrator in the mid-1980s, creating and heading the space station program when it was a separate operation (it was merged with OSF in

1989). "The real technical strength of NASA," he notes, "is at the centers. And NASA has rather deliberately cultured a certain degree of autonomy in them." Center directors feel, probably correctly, that they are as important to a program as any of the managers at headquarters, he says. "Because of the way NASA administrators operate, center directors know that, if they have a real problem, they can go directly to the administrator, no matter whom they formally report to." Even the formal reporting responsibility has swung back and forth over the years. The interest of congressional delegations from states whose districts include the centers complicates the situation further.

What it all means, Culbertson says, is that a manager's control over his programs at the centers runs "somewhere between 10 and 100 percent. It varies with the strength of the program director in Washington, the personalities at the centers, whether two centers are involved in a single program." The associate administrator must be "smart enough from a management standpoint to know how to get the technical problems brought to his attention and smart enough technically to know when to step in and make a decision." He also has to "know enough about the relationship between people, dollars, schedules and program requirements to defend the budget that goes to each center and the number of people NASA is willing to commit to the centers responsible for his program."

OSF, Lenoir estimates, "is roughly half of NASA--I think we've got about half the people and 60-65 percent of the budget." In fiscal 1991, the OSF appropriation was just short of $8 billion. The 1992 request stands at $8.88 billion. "We manage problems differently today than five years ago," he says. "We're undergoing more change. We're much more budget-conscious." Compromises, and economies of scale and quantity, play a greater role. "That leads you to a different set of management practices. If the money doesn't always turn out well, we'll make it take a little bit longer."

Culbertson's reflections on this job provide some idea of the turbulence that routinely swirls around it. First, those who build launch vehicles and those who use the payloads that go onto them are two distinct groups, he points out. For any given mission, they must reach a fine balance between desired payload and what weight the launcher can put into space. It is the boss of OSF who must draw the final line. And if launcher design is stretched to accommodate greater payload, schedule delays can result, causing OSF potential trouble with the user. Third, if the delay raises the mission's cost, the associate administrator must also answer to the NASA comptroller, and the two together must face the Congress.

Partly for reasons like these, Aller sees a problem with this position in its too-great span of responsibility. Another, in his view, is a more general NASA ailment--though he exempts the current OSF associate administrator from it. This is what he calls "too many NASA people running NASA." In any environment, whether it's the military, or NASA or industry, "the longer you're there, the more you view the world from that institution and that kind of dictates the way you do things," he says. In his view, the agency lacks sufficient management experience. "And that's what this job is: manage big programs, get the funding for big programs, make sure the centers are responsive to the needs." He thinks the agency would do well to bring in "some good outside industry experience." But current federal ethics regulations affecting both entry into and departure from federal service have made such solutions more difficult than they once were.

This job puts its occupant on the road frequently. There is also "a significant public affairs side to it," Lenoir adds. "You ought to be able to speak the English language, which isn't always the same as NASA language. You have to talk about the program. We owe the country an understanding of why we do it, and what it does for them. It helps to be able to give a speech on no notice on any topic you deal with."

OSF has many international technical and operational relationships. Germany, Italy and other foreign governments use the shuttle; so does the European Space Agency. The Japanese are paying OSF to fly a space laboratory mission. Lenoir calls these "essentially government-to-government contracts," which OSF negotiates and signs. The space station numbers Japan, Canada and the European Space Agency among its partners; here, OSF undertook both policy-level and working-level agreements. "The space station is an international movement and that's going to be a challenge," Lenoir says. "We've got a lot to learn."

Day to day, Lenoir deals with an immediate staff of eight, but a headquarters total of 200 comes under his wider supervision in Washington. If personnel at the four centers are added, a complex of about 10,000 people traces up through the associate administrator. OSF staff falls into three groups, Lenoir says. At one end are "a very few" people with long service but little growth in the job. At the other are a large number of recent college graduates "who are just among the very best." In the middle, "we've got a lot of good, experienced people." He doesn't think staff quality has decayed, but "our process isn't applying that expertise as well is it should. In an engineering sense, we don't always present analysis, the numbers, the black and white, to prove our case. I've been fairly brutal on this, by not accepting that, by making us do good analysis. That doesn't mean the individuals are incapable of it. But they've fallen out of practice."

If the agency can continue working on programs at the front of technological advance, Culbertson believes, it can get the technical talent it needs. Though salaries have improved, they won't appeal to people "if the jobs are not as much fun, not as challenging, or not as attractive. If

the space station is canceled, it's going to make a significant difference."
He adds that "the problems today don't seem to be a lack of good people,
but of people who are good because of the knowledge they have gained
through successes and failures they have already been through." NASA
needs "more people in technical management roles who have survived bad
decisions and, in so doing, learned how to make good ones."

Lenoir describes one of his goals as "a robust, long-range outlook
that's not upset by the continuing policy and budget shifts." Where the
flight systems are concerned, that means "redoing our planning,
particularly in the advanced programs, with more focus on a top-down
drive, looking five or ten years ahead, trying to keep our concept
development ahead so it will support our needs as they emerge." On the
institutional side, he wants "to beef up our engineering and project
management expertise."

Like numbers of other senior federal positions, this one can lead to
higher assignments in or outside of government. In any case, Lenoir
acknowledges, the private sector entails far less hassle than his present
environment. Sometimes he wonders how he was talked into leaving
industry and returning to government "at less pay, twice the work and ten
times the aggravation." But "on the satisfaction side, it's clearly a lot
more important to the nation. I would do it again. There are some
instances where you wish a particular event wasn't unfolding the way it is.
But the big picture is yeah, it's worthwhile, somebody has to do it."

Key Relationships

Within the Agency

Reports to: Administrator

Works closely with:

Deputy Administrator
Comptroller
Other associate and assistant administrators
Directors, Johnson, Kennedy, Marshall and Stennis Centers

Outside the Department

Director, Space Systems, U.S. Air Force
Director, Space Command, U.S. Army
Executive Secretary and staff, National Space Council
Assistant to the President, Science and Technology Policy

Outside the Government

Aerospace companies, certain other defense contractors and their trade associations; research and engineering firms; European Space Agency and space officials of individual countries including Japan, Canada, Germany and Italy; public and private institutions and audiences interested in space flight

Profile of Current Associate Administrator, Space Flight

Name: William B. Lenoir

Assumed Position: 1989

Career Summary: Director, program support for NASA Space Station; manager of several other systems engineering and analysis projects; vice president and member, board of directors, Booz, Allen and Hamilton Inc., 1984-89
Chief, mission development group in astronaut office, NASA Johnson Space Center; mission specialist on Shuttle Mission STS-5, November 1982; spaceborne launch director for first shuttle-based communications satellite deployment, 1967-84
Assistant professor, electrical engineering, MIT, 1965-67

Education: BS, electrical engineering, MIT, 1961
MS, electrical engineering, MIT, 1962
PhD, electrical engineering, MIT, 1965
Post-doctoral Ford Foundation fellowship, MIT

Associate Administrators, Space Flight Since 1969

Administration	Name and Years Served	Present Position
Bush	William B. Lenoir 1989 - present	Incumbent
Reagan	Richard H. Truly 1986 - 1989	Administrator, NASA
Reagan	Jesse W. Moore 1984 - 1986	President, Space Systems Div. Ball Corp. Boulder, Colo.
Reagan	James A. Abrahamson 1982 - 1984	Executive Vice President Hughes Aircraft Co. Los Angeles, Cal.

Carter, Ford	John F. Yardley 1974 - 1981	Retired St. Louis, Mo.
Nixon	Dale D. Myers 1970 - 1974	Consultant San Diego, Cal.
Johnson, Kennedy	George E. Mueller 1963 - 1969	President George E. Mueller Corp. Santa Barbara, Cal.

ASSOCIATE ADMINISTRATOR
SPACE SCIENCE AND APPLICATIONS

Senior Executive Service

Major Responsibilities

- Develop NASA policy and plans for scientific research in space. Direct the Office of Space Science and Applications (OSSA) in carrying them out through multi-disciplinary programs aimed at investigating and understanding the structure and evolution of the universe, solar system and earth; their impact on living organisms, including humans; and the uses of various manufacturing and commercial technologies in space. Supervise the work of the Goddard Space Flight Center and the Jet Propulsion Laboratory.

- Oversee the design, development and construction of NASA space payloads used in these efforts, and the funding of extensive academic research to support OSSA programs. Take a major role in senior-level interagency consultation on a wide variety of projects, such as the study of global climate change, in which NASA science figures centrally.

- Function as a key spokesman, especially to the Congress, in support and defense of NASA objectives in space science and its applications. Identify and establish effective relationships with congressional committees, members and staff with responsibility for space research and for NASA generally. Maintain productive working contacts with counterpart agencies and officials abroad, and with the space science elements of international organizations.

Necessary Training, Experience, Skills

There is almost no question that this position requires a trained scientist at the PhD level--and, preferably, a space scientist. Four of the six individuals who have filled the post in the past 20 years had done previous service at NASA. (The agency's only two presidential appointees are its administrator and deputy administrator.) One former occupant of this post warns that an associate administrator without such a background will face "an enormous learning curve." But, as with many other leadership jobs in federal science and technology, this one also demands substantial administrative experience, leadership talent, and small-p political skills. The ability to work with the Congress, defending OSSA programs and enlarging support for them, falls into this category. So does familiarity with planning techniques and resources management: budget is a major exercise in this position. Previous academic associations are useful.

Insight

Like most other scientific research enterprises, NASA's space science office works with laboratories, staff and equipment shaped into a structure that reflects the tasks assigned to it. The contrast with those other operations is in how OSSA must wield the tools of its trade. Essentially, these are sophisticated instruments that measure, sense, and record, backed by advanced systems that store, retrieve, and communicate. Made on earth, they must function accurately and reliably at what are often vast distances from it, sometimes for years and remote from human control. The OSSA scientists who set these payloads in motion must first design and get them built and launched. Then they have to manipulate them from afar with the dexterity and precision of earth-bound equipment, but with greatly reduced chances for adjustment, repair and replacement.

At ground level another, more down-to-earth difference distinguishes OSSA--and NASA--from most other government scientific and technical offices. This is the extra-strength public and congressional visibility of NASA's plans and visions, successes and failures. More than other leading-edge ventures, the achievements of a Voyager reconnoitering the solar system make the front pages, just as do the problems of the Hubble telescope or doubts about the satellite program at the heart of the proposed earth observing system. When exciting good news comes along, it helps NASA preserve some of the underlying prestige it has traditionally enjoyed on the Hill. For the moment, that remains one of the factors helping to sustain support for an increasing NASA budget even as many other national needs, including those of science and technology, vie for scarce resources. But there is also bad news from NASA, in varying doses. Two recent examples are the repeated mechanical failures and postponements in the shuttle program, and the still-looming possibility that serious flaws in the next generation of NASA-produced weather satellites will leave the country without any space-based weather data by early 1993. Tidings like these tend to threaten the prospects for other specific NASA projects with high price tags.

Thus the $30 billion space station, which the Congress had ordered redesigned in 1990, nearly went to the scrap heap anyway in 1991. Now reduced to carrying only two elements of the earlier research program designed in part by OSSA, the station remains the center focus for NASA critics who see the agency as inflexible, middle-aged, and in need of drastic overhaul.

OSSA runs all of NASA science, from astrophysics, space plasma physics, and planetary exploration to microgravity materials research, life science, communications research, and earth science. Definitionally, its work divides into "science," such as the origins of life, the effect of weightlessness on animals, plant growth, the health and safety of astronauts, and the search for extraterrestrial intelligence; and "applications," like the building of U.S. weather and communications satellites and the study of practical engineering problems. OSSA does not operate NASA's space missions, but builds all the payloads the agency flies, and funds just about all the space science research in the country.

Overall, OSSA's current activity encompasses the construction of about three dozen space projects, the management of a large program using balloons, rockets, and aircraft, and the support of work by 8,000 scientists in 250 universities and federal laboratories. Prominent on its agenda are the four long-life observatory platforms planned by the astrophysics program--the impaired Hubble, already aloft, the gamma ray observatory, and the X-ray and space infrared telescopes--each with higher resolution and sensitivity. "Basically," says Lennard A. Fisk, a physicist and onetime NASA scientist who has headed OSSA since 1987, "we're moving the pursuit of astronomy into space." Again, to pursue its probing of the solar system in the post-Voyager era, OSSA aims at putting orbiters around each planet. The Magellan and Galileo vehicles have already been dispatched to Venus and Jupiter; OSSA is building a Mars orbiter; and plans are underway for Saturn and comet orbiters.

While each of the office's seven disciplines is managed by a separate division with its own director, strategy and time line, Fisk explains that "we have also amalgamated each of them into a general plan for space science. You can't do everything that each discipline wants, all at once. You have to mix and match among the programs within the budget realities we face. So we have a plan that does that." In what NASA calls the "new start process," a program at its inception begins with very small funding, then builds as it follows its development curve. "Implicit in these plans is the assumption of a growing budget," Fisk says. "The NASA program underway today has to grow at about 20% a year, and the space science program is very similar." The question he asks is, "how do you do that in the context of a major budget deficit and plans now to limit the growth of spending to something closer to the inflation rate?" The "budget reality" he mentions is thus what he considers his principal challenge: "Executing a long-range program whose individual projects take decades sometimes to complete, when the budget is uncertain on a scale of days in this town." Another angle on this comes from Robert A. Frosch, a former NASA administrator (1977-80) who now manages the research laboratories of General Motors. While growth is of course the better alternative, he says, "a viable program could be run on a constant budget, with inflation adjustment."

Seen in perspective, what is the essential task of this position? To Frosch, the space science chief is the individual "who's got to reach out to the scientific community and extract from it some reasonable consensus about the key problems to be attacked, and how. And then to decide with their help, and the help of others at headquarters and the laboratories, what the program ought to be--what instruments have to be built and flown, what data are required, what it's going to cost, when it can be done. Then somehow cram that into a program and a budget that makes some sense in the NASA context, while fending off all the other claimants." In sum, "to take the whole collection of things scientists want a mission to do in space and beat that down into a real program in which there are some things you can do in a sensible order and a sensible way."

En route to assembling these rational scientific expeditions, as Fisk points out, "you get a lot of advice and a lot of help from different constituents." While NASA laboratories are key in executing the agency's programs, most of the research supporting space science takes place through the 3,000 grants a year that OSSA funds at universities. "So we have a large and vocal external community," he says. "The good part about that is that those people are very supportive of the programs. The flip side is that they are very independent," and thus "very impassioned in their opinions about how the programs should be run and what the priorities should be. A lot of that gets funneled in through the academy and advisory committee structure." He likes to joke, Fisk says, that OSSA gets the counsel of 100 advisory committees. In reality, "they don't all advise me--it's up and down the hierarchy here, and there's some duplication. But there are probably a thousand people advising us on how to do business."

"We had numerous groups," agrees Noel W. Hinners, associate administrator in 1974-79, such as an in-house physical science advisory panel that consisted mostly of university scientists plus two from NASA. Another prime source of input, he says, was the Space Science Board at the National Academy of Sciences. "There's probably more advice than you want or need," he recalls. A good deal of advice is sought "for political reasons" of keeping the outside community happy as much as for genuine reasons of getting sound guidance, he suggests. "It's a balancing act." The administration and the National Space Council, of course, also look over the agency's shoulder continuously. And then, Fisk says, there is the congressional dimension. "Our committees are supportive--and they're interested. They have very definite opinions on how NASA and space science ought to run." In times of unlimited funding, "it would be easy to make everyone happy," he comments. "In times of very constrained funding, you get advice at cross currents."

Given the extent and complexity of the space science function, it's not surprising that the work of the individual in charge ranges widely across the government and beyond. In addition to the Congress and the Office of Management and Budget, for example, the associate administrator is in frequent contact with officials at the National Oceanic and Atmospheric Administration, which uses the weather satellites OSSA builds, and at the National Science Foundation, with which OSSA cooperates in joint research activities. There is a close working relationship with the Office of Science and Technology Policy at the White House. Besides regular trips to NASA centers and consultation with academic scientists around the country, there is travel for public speaking purposes--a pursuit judged vital in gaining and keeping public attention and support. Contacts with OSSA's industrial contractors are frequent. Because the United States has led the development of space technology and systems, says Burt Edelson, OSSA chief from 1982 to 1987, he played a part in setting up "a number of international cooperative organizations." Today, the space science leader at NASA talks often with representatives of foreign space organizations, some of which are U.S. space station partners.

Within the executive branch, participation in the work of the Federal Coordinating Council for Science, Engineering, and Technology (FCCSET) is probably the most important element of the associate administrator's role outside NASA itself. It centers in the FCCSET Committee on Earth and Environmental Sciences. Representing about a dozen federal agencies, this group has established a set of integrated studies of the probable causes of global climate change. Critical to its work is space-based observation, popularly known as the mission to planet earth, or MTPE (OSSA also plays a fundamental part in the parallel effort called mission from planet earth). And basic to MTPE is the Earth Observing System (EOS), a planned $30 billion matrix of remote sensing platforms in orbit and ground-based supercomputers. For 15 years, beginning in the late 1990s, EOS is to collect data on a variety of earth processes, like the interaction of oceans, atmosphere and polar ice caps, at the rate of 30 or 40 trillion bits of information a day and make it available to legions of researchers and analysts.

Like the space station, however, EOS has encountered turbulence from critics who deem it too expensive, think its chances of success are uncertain, and claim its job can be done with existing technology at less cost. In addition to members of Congress, some of these opponents reportedly are scientists within NASA. In August 1991 it appeared possible that pressures from these various quarters, including a White House review committee, might force NASA in its fiscal 1993 budget request to drop the project's large instrument vehicle, known as EOS-A, and put the instruments into three smaller platforms instead.

Fisk estimates his testifying appearances in the Congress at ten times yearly. Normally, appropriations committee hearings take a couple of days, but the authorization committees--the Senate Commerce subcommittee on science, technology and space and the House Science subcommittee on space--"hold frequent hearings on specific targeted subjects," he says. A substantial and constant amount of informal interchange with members and staff adds to the dialogue. "They are smart people," Fisk notes, "not generally scientists or engineers, but they've been around long enough that discussions can be very detailed and technical."

OSSA's own staff numbers 225 at headquarters, plus the NASA center personnel, and the contractor work forces over which the associate administrator has indirect authority. Most of the office's professional staff are engineers or scientists. The quality of their technical training is good, Fisk thinks, "but there are some gaps--positions we have not been able to fill simply because government salaries are not competitive."

During his time in the job, Edelson says, a NASA job carried prestige. "The people on my staff and at the centers were really top flight--and dedicated, hardworking. They came in early, worked late and on weekends" and traveled frequently, often at their own expense, to attend conferences. Hinners also remembers a staff that was "quite competent." But he saw a problem in allowing its members to remain too long away from the field--from NASA centers or the university community. "I don't think people should make a career out of headquarters operations," he says. "They get too far away from knowing how the job really gets done." He says some individuals who worked with him 15 years ago are still there, "and they've gone stale. They're not incompetent, they just need reinvigorating."

With a fiscal 1992 budget request of nearly $4.1 billion (a 21 percent increase from 1991), OSSA spends one of every five NASA dollars and is among the biggest science organizations in the federal government. About 20% of the budget is committed to EOS, and more than half of it is spent in industry. OSSA builds some of its smaller spacecraft in NASA centers, but the bigger, more complex ones are constructed by contractors like TRW and Lockheed. "You're managing huge, important programs," says Edelson, who was there during the "engineering phase" of the Hubble telescope, a $1.5 billion project that "spent as much as $100 million a year." Notwithstanding Hubble's troubles after its launch, the problem at the outset, in Edelson's words, was "to design, develop and construct the finest, most complex optical instrument ever built for use in space. And at the same time, you had a thousand or so little research tasks at the University of New Mexico or MIT that ran $50,000 or $100,000 a year." On the subject of Hubble, Fisk wonders if he'll ever see an article that doesn't say "Hubble took a wonderful picture in spite of its serious mirror problems." In fact, he says, the telescope has worked better than expected after its flaw became evident, and is transmitting "some serious pictures."

"I used to joke," Fisk reflects, "that there was nothing wrong with space science that another billion dollars couldn't cure. Now I have the billion but I still have some problems." A key question that OSSA will have to answer in the next few years, he thinks, concerns the funding of EOS. His present $2.5 billion budget "will have to grow to four billion to execute that program. It is one that I and many others think is essential. We're talking about the future of the planet, and understanding what human beings are doing to it so that policy can be made." He doesn't think EOS is optional "if you live here and your children are going to live here." But given its high cost, "it would be a high-risk adventure to try, learn only a few things, and then try to make decisions." Correct execution of the program, he emphasizes, will take substantial growth of funding. "And the budget deficit is still there, the constraints are still there."

How will these problems, and NASA's in general, affect outlook and performance in this job in the coming period? "It's going to be tough," Frosch answers. "It's hard to ask people to take that responsibility, to walk into a situation where you know it's paved with terrible problems and you're not sure what you can do about it." The nature of the problems hasn't changed, in Hinners' view, but "they're tougher now because of what's happened historically," and the budget situation is worse. "So there's more pressure to produce. The job is viewed much more now as a sacrifice than something good to do."

For a future head of OSSA, Frosch says, the "absolute first thing to do" in these circumstances would be "to spend a lot of time trying to find out what the hell is really going on. And that might take a fair amount of time." He doesn't favor "hitting the deck running and reorganizing everything before you find out what's inside the box." As for Fisk, his advice depends on where a new chief of NASA space science is coming from. "If it's a card-carrying scientist I would say, first of all, execute the program and be enthusiastic about it. People like good news. If not, the first thing is to go out and learn the community out there. The sensitivities of the community are very real issues in this office. And we are very much a product here of the community we support."

Key Relationships

Within the Department

Reports to: Administrator

Works closely with:

Administrator
Deputy Administrator
Other associate and assistant administrators
Directors, Jet Propulsion Laboratory and Goddard Space Flight Center

Outside the Department

Associate Director, Physical Sciences, White Office of Science and
Technology Policy
Committee on Earth and Environmental Sciences (Vice Chair), Federal
Coordinating Council for Science, Engineering, and Technology (FCCSET)
Members, FCCSET working groups with space science or general NASA
relevance
National Academy of Sciences
National Academy of Engineering
Assistant Administrator, National Environmental Satellite Data and
Information Service, National Oceanic and Atmospheric Administration
Assistant Directors, Mathematical and Physical Sciences, and Geosciences,
National Science Foundation
Director, U.S. Geological Survey

Outside the Government

College and university science faculties; space vehicle design, aerospace and
engineering companies; research organizations; aeronautical and
astronautical associations; European and Japanese space agencies;
international organizations with space responsibilities and interests

Profile of Current Associate Administrator,
Space Science and Applications

Name:	Lennard A. Fisk
Assumed Position:	1987
Career Summary:	Various positions at the University of New Hampshire, 1976-87, including professor of physics; vice president for research and financial affairs; space science center director; and project director, solar terrestrial theory group

Visiting associate in theoretical physics, California Institute of
Technology, 1974
Astrophysicist, Goddard Space Flight Center, NASA, 1971-77

Education: Cornell University, BA (physics), 1965
University of California, San Diego, PhD (applied physics), 1969

Associate Administrators, Space Science and Applications Since 1969

Administration	Name and Years Served	Present Position
Bush, Reagan	Lennard A. Fisk 1987 - present	Incumbent
Reagan	Burt I. Edelson 1982 - 1987	Johns Hopkins Foreign Policy Institute Washington, D.C.
Reagan	Andrew Stofan (Acting)* 1981	Not available
Carter	Thomas A. Mutch* 1979 - 1980	Deceased
Carter, Ford	Noel W. Hinners 1974 - 1979	Vice President Martin Marietta Bethesda, Md.
Nixon	John E. Naugle 1969 - 1974	Not available

* Held position as Associate Administrator, Space Science

NATIONAL SCIENCE FOUNDATION

DIRECTOR

Level II - Presidential Appointment with Senate Confirmation

Major Responsibilities

- Direct an independent agency currently managing more than $2.5 billion annually in federal funding grants to maintain and advance academic research in science and engineering; to improve science,mathematics, and technology education; and to promote U.S. scientific and technological cooperation with other countries. Emphasize the transfer of technology generated in foundation-supported research into commercial productivity that strengthens the country's position in global economic competition.

- Keep the foundation abreast of events. Ensure that management of its resources effectively and efficiently reflects the rapid evolution of scientific and technological endeavor and consistently supports projects and inquiries with the greatest potential benefits to American society. Establish constructive working relationships with the president's science adviser and budget director and their staffs to coordinate major elements of foundation strategy with the development of national science policy and the work of other agencies.

- Address the foundation's program and defend its budget before its authorizing and appropriations committees in the Congress. Represent the foundation and articulate its goals to the national and international science and engineering communities. Serve as an advocate and symbol to these audiences of high-quality U.S. achievement in science and technology.

Necessary Training, Experience, Skills

Those who have held or observed this position and know it well stress three requisites. First, prospective directors must have science and/or engineering training to at least the master's degree level and, second, an eminence among science and technology peers that goes well beyond ordinary individual achievement. Third, as with other federal positions that manage science and technology projects and budgets, candidates for this one need demonstrated experience in running an organization. "A Nobel laureate who has spent a lifetime in the lab" would be an ill-advised choice, says a closely-informed outsider. By the same token, familiarity with political Washington and the federal science and engineering world goes a very long way in handling this tough job productively.

Insight

Several features distinguish the National Science Foundation from most other federal executive agencies, including those with significant science and technology roles.

First, the foundation is almost unique in terms of how it is run. Its birth pains in the late 1940s were attended by a debate over the initial recommendation that it be an independent, nongovernment foundation, though governed by a presidentially-appointed board and run on federal money. President Truman is said to have insisted that if the new organization was to operate with federal funds, it could not be completely independent; it would have to be an agency of government. In what was termed a compromise, the Congress established the National Science Foundation (NSF) in 1950 as an independent federal agency, governed by a director and a National Science Board of 24 part-time members appointed to six-year terms by the White House from the scientific, engineering, academic and industrial communities. The legislation assigns policy making to the board, and administration of the foundation to the director, a presidential appointee who serves a six-year term.

Second, and more important, are the differences in orientation that mark out the NSF from most other agencies. Unlike the departments of Defense and Energy, for example, which also support a great deal of basic research, the foundation is not primarily a "mission" agency. "We don't generally dictate or specify the kinds of research we will support," explains Walter E. Massey, the physicist and science educator who took over as NSF director in March 1991. "We respond to research ideas that are generated by and large by the research community itself." Most of the research the NSF funds takes place in universities. It can and does support it elsewhere, Massey adds, but in point of fact, except for a very few companies, most basic research in this country is carried out in universities and federal laboratories. And "we generally do not support research in other agencies' labs."

Third, the NSF differs in the way it evaluates the approximate 30,000 applications for funding that it receives each year. "We rely very much on the community itself," Massey points out. "We probably use over 50,000 scientists, engineers and educators involved every year in our various review groups and advisory committees." The foundation sends proposals out to individuals for review, he says, or brings groups of them together in panels. "They rate the proposals, give us advice, and our program officers then make recommendations based on them." Among federal agencies, only the National Institutes of Health (NIH) employs this kind of extensive exterior review for its research proposals. The rest use their own staffs.

Of the total current federal research and development budget of $76 billion, the NSF administers only a fragment--about 3.5 percent. How much of a force can the foundation be in this overall picture? "A great force," replies Erich Bloch, who led the NSF in 1984-90. He is credited with doubling its budget, enlarging the network of NSF-supported centers for research in engineering and in science and technology as well as for other centers for university/industry cooperative research; and greatly boosting NSF attention to emerging engineering and industrial technologies with more direct application to U.S. economic strength and global competitiveness. "The foundation is really only responsible for the mathematical and physical sciences, social and behavioral sciences, and engineering," Bloch says. (Medical science is almost all at NIH.) "So you might say it has a limited portfolio. But within that is a big area, a key to basic research that's being done in the country. What doesn't get funded by the NSF doesn't necessarily get done."

Obviously, Bloch says, the foundation doesn't fund a hundred percent of basic research. Rather, "it sets a direction, a policy. It can focus on areas that are very difficult for others to focus on. It can look at different approaches to things. So it's a very potent kind of force." The NSF's own figures show its support ranging from a sixth to a third of the total federal investment in investigative areas like global climate change, education and human resources, manufacturing and materials, and other pivotal sectors.

Elaborating on what he sees as the primary components of his mission, Massey says one of the NSF's "major" issues is "to make sure our support is adequate to maintain the strengths we have built up in our research institutions in the areas we support." That's increasingly hard to do because the foundation's budget, while it has grown, hasn't grown enough, and there are many more institutions to support. In another main area--education in science, mathematics and engineering--the foundation's targets are several. Among them are making a high-quality science education available to every school child; helping those who embark on science or engineering careers to get the best professional teaching; seeing that the system produces scientists, engineers and mathematicians in sufficient numbers to meet the needs of the U.S. economy; making certain that nonspecialists have opportunities to expand their science backgrounds; and helping science and engineering students to build helpful personal and institutional relationships. With science education taking on new urgency in most informed judgments, NSF resources to support research in this field have zoomed upward, from nearly zero in the 1980s to about $430 million today. "It's a fifth of our budget in terms of what we fund," Massey remarks, "but it's an area where the NSF plays a very significant role, probably much greater than most people realize. In terms of science, math and technical education at all levels, we have more programs and activities than any other agency." A third key issue in Massey's view is how the foundation can assist the "translation of research into economic productivity, and what we can do here to move research from the labs into the commercial markets."

To be effective, an NSF director must pursue these and other objectives in a "very complex environment," says Roland W. Schmitt, president of Rensselaer Polytechnic Institute and a former chairman of the National Science Board. This goes well beyond the fact of National Science Board oversight that puts the foundation in a different operating mode than other agencies. For one thing, he says, the NSF has in the academic community a rather special kind of constituency. It is a "natural constituency," and also one that "isn't very powerful politically." It regards the foundation as a "premier institution in how it does its job," with a highly important role to play. That doesn't imply, Schmitt adds, "that they're always pleased with exactly how the NSF does things. But the agency is an extremely critical one for them, kind of a flagship government agency in the support of academic science."

Then there is the budget relationship with the Congress. Here, the foundation runs into the curious logic also encountered by certain other science and technical (S&T) agencies, where its requests for resources must ultimately contend with those of unrelated and highly needful causes with much broader constituencies. "However orderly the fashion in which the administration may put together an S&T budget across all the agencies," Schmitt comments, "the Congress scrutinizes it in a dozen different ways, and the NSF budget, for example, is lumped into the same appropriations subcommittees with Veterans Affairs and housing." That's one reason why work with the Congress is important to this position and requires a substantial investment of time. In addition to the appropriations subcommittees on Veterans, HUD and Independent Agencies of both Houses, the NSF does most of its business on the authorization and oversight side with the Senate committees on Commerce, Science and Transportation and Labor and Human Resources, and the House Committee on Science, Space and Technology. "We have a great deal of support on the Hill from the committees and from individual members," Massey says.

Another factor in the director's complicated world, Schmitt notes, is the need to keep NSF plans and actions generally aligned with the philosophy and purposes of the administration. This connects to what he believes must be a close working relationship with the president's science adviser, who also heads the White House Office of Science and Technology Policy (OSTP). While that individual has no formal jurisdiction over the NSF chief, Schmitt says, to the extent that the science adviser has the ear of the president, the director of the Office of Management and Budget (OMB) and others at that level, the adviser "can have great influence" where the NSF is concerned.

"Our access to the president and the White House is mostly through the science adviser," Massey confirms, and the relationship "works very well." It is helpful from an organizational standpoint, he says, because of the reactivation of the Federal Coordinating Council for Science, Engineering and Technology (FCCSET) by the current science adviser, D. Allan Bromley. Through FCCSET, in Massey's words, "various agencies dealing with research can work together, bring issues forward and resolve those that require interagency discussion." On a personal level, Massey says, Bromley is an old friend and is "one of the reasons I took the job." While the NSF does not work through Bromley's office on specific issues, "I think it's safe to say that on major policy concerns I coordinate with OSTP." A further point to note: in the past, during interregnums or weakness in the leadership of OSTP, the voice of U.S. science and technology in government has, de facto, usually been that of the NSF director.

In fiscal 1990 (the last year for which final figures were available at this writing) the NSF took in 29,000 new proposals for funding research. It issued 8,900 new awards for a "success rate" of 31 percent; and 6,000 continuing awards. Some proposals the foundation receives are in response to its own solicitation. This is dictated, Bloch says, by the foundation's perception of "what the infrastructure of the country needs, what the foundation thinks and sees as important. It's a response to some of the problems of the country. It's concerned with what you think science and engineering can contribute, where you think the big breaks might occur." Some areas of science, Bloch notes, attract more interest and work than others. "So you have to stimulate some fields because people are not going into them. There are fads in science just as there are fads in clothing."

Is the much-debated issue of big versus little science significant in the NSF picture? "I think it's an overworked issue," Bloch replies. His definition of big science is based on what he has observed, namely that for people in science, "it is always something that's bigger than your own grant." The country needs certain projects, like the superconducting super collider, he says. "We should have big projects because we need big projects. We don't need them all by 1995. But you can't study astronomy unless you look through a telescope. The issue is one of priorities, not whether there should be big projects."

The NSF's first budget, in 1951, was $150,000. For fiscal 1992, it requested $2.7 billion. Some of that steep historical curve upward was fashioned in the second half of the 1980s, with overall annual increases of about nine percent impelled by the perceived need to bring the NSF more into line with the country's industrial and economic needs. In 1988 came an administration pledge to double NSF's budget in five years. But while the Congress continued to go along with healthy boosts for math and science education, it held down the rate of increase elsewhere. The 1991 budget message bravely repeated the goal of doubling the foundation's annual resources, this time by 1993, and asked for an 18 percent increase in support of basic research, to a total of about $2 billion. Out of the budget summit of 1990, however, the foundation ended up with only $1.7 billion in basic research for 1991, behind the inflation curve. As for administrative funds to operate the foundation, the figure requested for 1992 was originally set at $127 million. In all likelihood, the agency will get less. The administrative budget hasn't been growing much, Massey says, and it isn't adequate to running the NSF. "The number of proposals we've funded has doubled in ten years," he notes, "but the operating budget has gone along at the same level in real terms."

Schmitt finds "a curious phenomenon" in the contrast between the steady, if modest, growth in NSF research support in constant dollars per capita and the unhappiness obvious among the research and teaching community over the recent pattern of reduced grant size and fewer grant acceptances. "The natural reaction of people out in the academic community is that the problem is one of a severe lack of money," he says. "And yet if you look at the objective facts, nothing tells you that is the case." One of the big challenges for the director, he thinks, is "to figure out what's going on there and what changes are necessary in policy and the way the money is used to fix that." "We've given birth to so many basic researchers," says H. Guyford Stever, a former NSF director (1972-76) who served simultaneously for part of that time as acting science adviser to the president. "There's been an expansionism in the field of science at the state universities and elsewhere" that has greatly increased the number of applicants for foundation funding. Or, as Massey says, "one facet of our success is also part of our problem." And, like the NIH and other federal funders of scientific research, the NSF must ensure that it can identify and deal with instances of misconduct and fraud in the grant awards that it administers.

Another issue for the NSF director is the sensitive question of federal money for the facilities--laboratories and equipment--used in the research government supports. "The pressure," Stever says, "has been to spend most of the money on the researchers themselves. And squeeze the equipment and facilities. That's a very bad thing in some places." Schmitt asserts that "neither the NSF or any other federal agency has addressed the facilities problem." He recalls a report some years ago, authored among others by Bromley, which "called attention to the deteriorating state of academic facilities around the country. And some things were done about it." These included a small program NSF began in the late 1980s under congressional pressure to fund laboratories for certain campuses; this was replaced for 1992 with a request in the budget for resources to purchase equipment. The facilities problem remains a tough puzzle that needs, most observers agree, an urgent solution. In any case, Massey thinks it exceeds the reach of the NSF alone and that a broader-based attack is necessary. Schmitt also doubts the NSF can resolve the facilities matter alone, but says "it ought to be working on it, pushing it with other federal agencies, and I don't think that has happened." But of the several principal areas of responsibility discussed earlier, Massey in fact gives priority to support of the research infrastructure. "It's going to be a much more serious issue because of the many constraints and pressures the universities are now facing," he says. "We haven't been complacent about it, but we haven't foreseen the kinds of pressures we're now seeing."

As for the NSF staff, Bloch points to "a major kind of problem." It stems, first, from the familiar inability of federal pay to compete with that offered by the private sector and the universities. "We had counted on more academic people coming in than from industry," he says, but over the last few years of his term the gap also widened between salaries at the level of the former federal pay cap and those in the universities. Second, and probably more important, is the disruption a tour in government means for talented scientists in their early or middle careers--the kind of individuals most valuable to the NSF in its extensive practice of recruiting some staff for periods of two to four years to provide a constant influx of new faces and ideas. Something between 25 and 35 percent of the work force comes to the NSF on this rotational basis. Bloch says the NSF ideally needs to recruit younger, not older, people for this purpose. But the career and family interruption this entails for them are severe obstacles.

"I haven't encountered any fundamental problems in terms of staff quality," Massey says. His early collective impressions have been quite favorable, generally matching those of his predecessors. If maintaining an influx of temporary and capable people is a problem, it also seems singularly healthy for the foundation. "We depend a great deal on them, and it's a great strength of the agency that we can hire people for two or three years and rotate them," Massey observes. "We do much more of that than any other agency." The flow of fresh faces also occurs in senior positions, "so that every two or three years you're changing managers and leaders. This is great because it gives our programs credibility and visibility, and we get new ideas." The NSF staff numbers 1,300. The director and deputy director are presidentially appointed. Below them, six assistant directors preside over operational divisions in the geosciences; behavioral, biological and social sciences; mathematical and physical sciences; engineering; education and human resources; and scientific, technological and international affairs.

Schmitt sees a substantial problem concerning the foundation's human resources. Difficult as it is to maintain an effective rotation of temporary staff through the agency, he says, it is even harder to find people for leadership positions like those of the assistant directors. Coming into such a job from, say, a provost's or dean's position at a university typically means a pay cut, and academic institutions are often reluctant to allow leaves of absence running up to three years. At the same time, it is his view that "unless you spend at least that amount of time at the foundation, you really can't get much done."

Within the government, the director's schedule embraces innumerable meetings, both at the NSF itself and with interagency groups and senior individuals across the federal executive and within the FCCSET framework. At the White House, besides regular contact with the science adviser and budget director and their staffs, these include sessions of the Economic and Domestic Policy Councils. The director is a member of the Government-University-Industry Research Roundtable of the National Research Council and of the Council on Competitiveness. Bloch says he made "hundreds" of speeches while in the job, most of them to science and technology and education audiences. Visits to universities and laboratories are frequent. "You want to go out and see what goes on," he says. "You have this or that large amount of money being spent, you'd better understand what's happening out there."

International interaction is high. The NSF is involved in bilateral agreements with some 30 countries, basically providing for mutual access to scientific and engineering research, which also entails frequent contact with the department of state. Looking ahead, Schmitt thinks "the international aspects of running the NSF" may be a subject requiring increasing attention. With a growing number of S&T projects demanding major international cooperation and coordination within fast-evolving political relationships, for instance, the NSF must see to the adequacy of opportunities for contact between U.S. scientists and engineers and their colleagues abroad.

Stever believes the NSF can and must continue to be "a good player in the White House science complex. The FCCSET is a powerful tool, and the foundation plays a solid role there, and it should. The NSF can be a friend, really, of the other science agencies--talk over mutual problems, see who is covering what--and it has done that reasonably well." Finally, the director of the NSF in Schmitt's perception "has got to make sure to keep the foundation relevant to national purposes and producing good results for those purposes. What are the new and emerging areas of science and technology that you ought to be moving resources into, and which are those that are perhaps not as productive as they once were? In other words, the strategy of shifting funding from the sunset regions into the sunrise regions. That's a generic problem."

For all such reasons, Schmitt warns, "it isn't adequate simply to make NSF constituents happy. There has to be vision and purpose that transcends that."

Key Relationships

Reports to: President

Works closely with:

Within the Foundation

Members, National Science Board
Deputy director
Assistant directors

Outside the Foundation

Director, White House Office of Science and Technology Policy
Secretary of Energy
Secretary of Education
Deputy Secretary, Department of Commerce
Under Secretary, Technology Administration, Department of Commerce
Director, Defense Advanced Research Projects Agency
Director, National Institutes of Health, Department of Health and Human Services
Director, National Institute of Standards, Department of Commerce
Heads of other departments and agencies with significant research and development budgets
Vice President's Council on Competitiveness

Outside the Government

Technology campuses; science and engineering faculties at other colleges and universities; state education officials; National Academies of Science and Engineering and other professional associations; research and development staffs in business and industry; members of NSF review and advisory panels; science and technology officials and communities of other countries

Profile of Current Director, National Science Foundation

Name: Walter E. Massey

Assumed Position: 1991

Career Summary: University of Chicago, vice president, research, 1982-91
Argonne National Laboratory, director, 1984-91; professor of physics, 1979-82; staff physicist, 1966-68
Assistant professor, physics, University of Illinois, 1968-70
Brown University, dean, 1975-82; professor, 1970-75

Education: Morehouse College, BS, physics and mathematics, 1958
Washington University, MS, PhD, physics, 1966

Directors, National Science Foundation Since 1969

Administration	Name and Years Served	Present Position
Bush	Walter E. Massey 1991 - present	Incumbent
Reagan	Erich Bloch 1984 - 1990	Distinguished Fellow Council on Competitiveness Washington, D.C.
Reagan	Edward A. Knapp 1983 - 1984	Director Los Alamos Meson Physics Facility Los Alamos, N.M.
Reagan	John Slaughter 1980 - 1982	President Occidental College Los Angeles, Cal.
Carter	Richard C. Atkinson 1976 - 1980	Chancellor University of California San Diego, Cal.

Ford, Nixon	H. Guyford Stever 1972 - 1976	Commissioner Carnegie Commission on Science, Technology, and Government Washington, D.C.
Nixon	William D. McElroy 1970 - 1971	Emeritus Professor, Biology University of California San Diego, Cal.
Nixon, Johnson 1963 - 1969	Leland J. Haworth	Deceased

DEPUTY DIRECTOR

Level III - Presidential Appointment with Senate Confirmation

Major Responsibilities

- Assist the substantive direction of an agency which annually funds more than $2 billion of basic research in science, engineering and mathematics, and in science education. Handle internal management and oversight tasks and special projects as designated.

- Support the director in every aspect of the foundation's activity, taking on major executive responsibilities that may be assigned. Remain at all times prepared to function as acting director. Represent the foundation in interagency contexts as necessary.

- Maintain broad associations with academic research and teaching faculties in science and technology, and with scientists, engineers, and managers in business and industry. Stay current with developments in the investigative fields supported by the foundation. Develop and sustain close familiarity with the science and technology programs of federal departments and agencies.

Necessary Training, Experience, Skills

A former deputy director points out that every individual who has held one of the top two jobs at the National Science Foundation has had strong credentials in a science or technology field. There is no question that they are necessary; in fact, with virtually no exceptions, the presidential appointments process over the years has honored the deputy director slot as a position that must be primarily science-based. In addition to degree-level training, the deputy must know and understand the world of academic research in science and technology, typically through experience on a campus, in industry, in government--or all three.

Insight

There is no standard model or realistic job description for the deputy director of the NSF. In establishing the agency in 1950, the Congress wrote nothing about the position beyond mandating its existence. Like many other second-in-command posts across the federal executive, the activity and range of responsibility in this one basically reflect the abilities, interests and objectives of the director.

There are some guidelines, however, useful both for those who occupy the position and those who appoint them. Foremost is the idea that an NSF deputy must be able to act for the chief of the agency in any sector of its endeavors, and on short notice. The range of those endeavors is broad. It begins with support of academic research in science and technology (S&T) and in mathematics and science education. It includes strengthening and sharpening the connection between that support and the country's economic and commercial vitality in an age of rapid advance in S&T along a wide front. It extends to the conduct of important substantive and policy relationships both inside and outside the federal government. And it encompasses the production of such publications as *Statistical and Engineering Indicators*, the bible of the federal S&T enterprise.

All of this means that the deputy should have, or acquire, the same levels of knowledge and expertise as the director about the foundation's work and the national professional and political environment in which it operates. Not every deputy will operate in this way on a regular basis. But every deputy should be able to.

Two other considerations are important in the choice of a deputy director. First, the individual selected should be personally compatible with the director. Second, the deputy's professional background ideally will complement the director's, rather than supplement or duplicate it. As an example, a director lacking substantial familiarity with Washington and the federal government is probably better off with a deputy who has that experience--and vice versa. This formula is even more critical, of course, as it applies to the respective scientific and technological expertises of each individual. Whether or not the director intends to deploy the deputy's skills and experience broadly across the foundation's activity, such complementarity adds strength to the NSF leadership.

"Different directors use their deputies in different ways," says Donald N. Langenberg, deputy director of the NSF in 1980-82. "My director (John Slaughter) and I thought of ourselves as partners. We generally took the view that we ought to be functionally interchangeable with respect to most things." Following a pattern seen in many federal agencies, the director in Langenberg's time handled external relationships --with the Congress, the rest of the executive branch, and the nongovernment community--and Langenberg saw to internal management of the foundation. But, he emphasizes again, "the division of responsibilities was not sharp. We felt that, should the need arise, either of us ought to be able to step in and do whatever the other was in the middle of doing."

One of the most important factors, according to Frederick M. Bernthal, deputy director since 1990, "is that the deputy be someone the director can trust on whatever the issue might be, whether it's personnel management, or a congressional issue, or the budget. You're pulled into almost everything the director does, and you obviously stand in whenever the director can't be there." While a good deal of in-house management and supervision usually falls to the deputy, even that depends on the director's inclinations, he adds.

Philip Smith, executive officer of the National Research Council of the National Academy of Sciences, notes that "all directors have used the deputy as a counselor. That has been fairly consistent going back to the very early days of the NSF." And from those days to these, he adds, directors have tended to assign to their deputies various kinds of special projects. In the early 1970s, for instance, the position had charge of creating, developing, organizing and running a program of applied energy research that ran for five years. John H. Moore, an economist and chemical engineer who held the deputy director job in 1985-89, ran the agency's international program--science and technology cooperation and international exchanges. This and other tasks regularly took him outside the NSF. During his tenure, he was a member of two subcommittees under the Federal Coordinating Council for Science, Engineering and Technology, and worked closely with the National Institutes of Health, the Food and Drug Administration, and the Department of Agriculture, and fairly regularly with the Defense Department. He sat on two working groups under the Economic Policy Council at the White House, and often had contact with nonscience departments like Treasury.

But from his personal knowledge of NSF directors and deputies since the agency's beginning, Smith offers the observation that almost every deputy at some point has been "frustrated" by the ambiguity of the job's duties. This can be all the more disturbing because the assistant directors of the foundation's operating divisions "are the real action officers." It's therefore important, Smith believes, for the deputy to come to early terms with this lack of job definition. Normally, he says, the deputy arrives at the NSF from a science or engineering discipline, generally in an academic background, and finds an organization with a broad mandate in which the new job's formal duty is to stand by for the director, or act in the director's absence. Negotiation between deputy and director about what the actual framework of their relationship will be is therefore critical. "If you don't have a clear understanding about that, you're going to be unhappy that you are seemingly in a very important job, but one without the clear assignment or mandate that some of the other equivalent positions around government have."

Would codifying the role and functions of the NSF deputy solve or alleviate this situation? "I would leave it exactly the way it is," Smith replies. "It's beneficial to have flexibility" that can respond to changes in the role or agenda of the foundation, or to special problems as they arise.

Given the requirement that the deputy director be able to run the NSF when necessary and handle a variety of specific external and internal assignments meanwhile, the foundation's mission and problems are just as much the primary fabric of this position as of the director's. The budget, for example. While the NSF's mission, as Bernthal says, is expanding rapidly, the resources to match are lagging. Moore points out that "we were able to persuade the administration in 1986 to commit to a doubling of the NSF budget in five years." But this has not developed even though, as he notes, the budget in this period rose by eight to ten percent, "which in these times is terrific." The October 1990 budget summit, however, was a setback, producing only a 2.5 percent increase for support of basic research in fiscal 1991, less than the inflation rate. Since 1986, in fact, support for individual researchers has grown only two percent. Still, the Bush administration has renewed the budget-doubling pledge for the NSF with a target date of 1993, and its fiscal 1992 request came in at $2.7 billion.

Meanwhile the NSF budget for supporting education in mathematics and science has been jumping by better than 20 percent a year, reflecting new concerns about education generally at both ends of Pennsylvania Avenue. The disparity between the rates of increase here and in academic research, Moore says, has resulted from the congressional approach to the NSF budget. "The administration would submit a budget with substantial increases for research and also for education. But the Congress would always reduce the increase in research and increase the increase in education."

In any event, Bernthal says, science and math education represents a "major new thrust" for the NSF. Related to it, he continues, is the broader question of "what's happening to the demographics of this country," which in turn goes to "the human resources sector that we've recently combined with education. Again, we're being asked to undertake what by any definition will be new initiatives." Among these is an improvement in the numbers of minorities and women that have entered science and engineering. "The statistics on this over the last 20 years are not terribly impressive," Bernthal says. "We have to do something different."

He also mentions "new pressure" from the Congress as well as in the country generally to derive more tangible results from research supported by NSF grants. The view is, he says, "that whatever the federal government funds in S&T research should meet national needs with respect to the competitive standing of the United States. It's the feeling that, while the Japanese think they aren't doing basic research very well and everybody looks to the U.S. model and the tremendous success we've had, that we haven't done very well in taking the fruits of that effort into the marketplace."

The development of views along these lines of course began well over a decade ago, and at the NSF, their apostle was Erich Bloch, director in 1984-90. In the latter half of the 1980s, Moore says, "the real change was in the perception of the importance of S&T, and of the importance to S&T of academic research. The NSF had to adapt to that change. So we reemphasized certain areas like engineering, for example, and we created a new director in computational and informational sciences." Education surged up on the priority list, as did the question of human resources mentioned by Bernthal. And the NSF expanded and injected strong new energy into its national and regional science and technology centers for cooperative research, in some cases between industry and university scientists and engineers, in areas like materials, supercomputing, atmospheric sciences and astronomy.

As the centers took on increasing weight, they engendered controversy. Some see them, Moore says, "as a shift away from the basic research mission of the foundation toward applications." Others, especially among academic researchers whose preference is for individual investigation in smaller facilities, object to working in large groups on projects whose object, at least in part, is commercial benefit. And this debate continues. "We've been hearing a fair amount of concern and discontent," Bernthal reports. It comes from "the individual researchers in the core disciplines"--fundamental chemistry, physics, biology, math, and the fundamental engineering sciences. These professionals watch the NSF budget continue to grow, and its mandate grow even faster, he says, while support for "pure" science research has barely been meeting inflation. (But neither has it shown any net decline, while the number of those competing for it has grown steadily.) Bernthal clearly shares in supporting the strong NSF move in the direction of producing some market return on its investments. But the complaints about support for basic research, he says, do indicate "a problem we can't afford to ignore. Make no mistake. I believe fervently in the principle that, if you don't support core research disciplines, pretty soon you won't have anything to develop and you won't have anything to put into the marketplace. And then you won't have to worry much longer about the NSF."

The deputy director and director are the only two presidentially-appointed positions in the foundation, but there once were five or six. Among them was a handful of assistant director jobs. It was a situation that Richard C. Atkinson, deputy director in 1976 (and director in 1976-

80), found cumbersome. "I really had more flexibility in recruiting people when I didn't have to go through the White House," he says. "Most people didn't care, anyway, that the position was appointed by the president. It was being recruited for the job and really feeling they had an important role to play." Just before he left, the White House accepted his recommendation that the number of appointees be cut to two.

On the whole, Moore was "very impressed" with the quality of the NSF staff (the current complement is 1,300). "It's a very capable, very knowledgeable, very experienced group of people. I think they try seriously to keep up with their fields." Langenberg, too, thought technical staff quality in his day was generally quite high. "I often said that if you replaced the faculties of most universities in this country with the staff at the NSF, you would improve the university," he recalls. It is NSF policy to recruit some of its staff on a short-term basis--two to four years--from the campuses and industry and rotate them through the agency. Such individuals comprise between a quarter and a third of the staff. "We thought that was very important because it keeps the place fresh," Moore points out. But since federal salaries don't compete with those on the outside, "the foundation has to recruit people who are more and more junior. For an NSF program responsible for several million dollars worth of research a year," he says, "it just doesn't make sense to have a really junior person in charge." Langenberg's own salary experience provides some idea of the dramatic comparative change that has occurred in compensation levels at the NSF and in work outside government. He arrived at the NSF as deputy with a "significant" increase in pay over his previous position on a university faculty. On returning to a university position two and half years later, it was, again, at a comparable increase in salary.

The comments of those who have held this position suggest that the issues haven't changed much in basic substance over the last 15 years. From his time in the position, for example, Atkinson recalls questions that continue to occupy center stage--science education, the role of applied research, and the related issue of "individual grants versus grants to the centers." The last-named topic is one Moore thinks will be at the top of the NSF agenda--"support for small-scale science, for individual investigators. It's critical. There is no doubt that individual investigators need relief." On another front, Atkinson believes the U.S. government was "really very poor in terms of international science activities. The State Department showed little interest, so it fell heavily in the domain of the NSF to ensure cooperative efforts between and among countries."

On this subject, Bernthal predicts, "we will inevitably be drawn more and more into the international arena, as will every agency in this city." This is an evolution fueled not only by the soaring costs of so-called "big science" projects like the space station that, other things being equal, make international collaboration financially advantageous. It is also, he says, because "corporate America is rapidly becoming internationalized. I have to think that the foundation more and more will have to take an international perspective. We are doing this already, in the sense that some of our domestic programs are being driven by international competition." The global approach also touches the policy arena in such matters as the effort to study global climate change. There, an assistant NSF director is involved in the attempt to coordinate the international effort so as to avoid duplication and carry out joint projects where appropriate.

"As you look across the NSF," Bernthal says, "you see a budget that's been going well in the last few years, especially compared to what could have happened. So we have been very fortunate." With the rise in what the foundation is expected to do and absent the development of alternative mechanisms for accomplishing it, he sees no reason why, "almost by default," the NSF won't continue to grow. "And we're beginning to feel the pains of that growth."

Key Relationships

Within the Foundation

Reports to: Director

Works closely with:

Assistant Directors
General Counsel
Inspector General

Outside the Foundation

Director, White House Office of Science and Technology Policy
Members, Committee on Physical, Mathematical and Engineering Sciences,
   Federal Coordinating Council for Science, Engineering and Technology
Senior executives of departments and agencies with major responsibilities in
   science, technology and education
Directors, national federal laboratories
Director, Office of Technology Assessment, U.S. Congress

Outside the Government

National Academies of Science and Engineering; national and international
science and technology communities and associations; college and university
science and engineering faculties; industrial research staffs; business and
industry executives; state education officials; national education associations

Profile of Current Deputy Director, National Science Foundation

Name: Frederick M. Bernthal

Assumed Position: 1990

Career Summary: Assistant secretary, Oceans and International Environmental and
                       Scientific Affairs, Department of State, 1988-90
                 Member, U.S. Nuclear Regulatory Commission, 1983-88
                 Chief legislative assistant to Senate majority leader, 1980-83
                 Congressional science fellow, American Physical Society; and
                       member, Senate professional staff, 1978
                 Professor, chemistry and physics, Michigan State University, 1970-
                       78
                 NATO senior science fellow, 1977

Education: Valparaiso University, BS (chemistry, with distinction), 1964
                 University of California, Berkeley, PhD (nuclear chemistry), 1969
                 Postdoctoral research staff scientist, Yale University, 1969-70

Deputy Directors, National Science Foundation Since 1969

Administration	Name and Years Served	Present Position
Bush	Frederick M. Bernthal
1990 - present	Incumbent
Reagan	John H. Moore
1985 - 1989	Director, International Institute
George Mason University
Arlington, Va.
Reagan	Donald N. Langenberg
1980 - 1982	Chancellor
University of Maryland
Adelphi, Md.
Carter	George C. Pimentel
1977 - 1979	Deceased
Ford	Richard C. Atkinson
1976	Chancellor
University of California
San Diego, Calif.
Ford	Lowell J. Paige (Acting)
1975	Not available

| Nixon | Raymond L. Blisplinghoff 1971 - 1974 | Deceased |
| Johnson, Nixon | Robert Ward Johnston* 1966 - 1969 | Not available |

* Held position under title of executive assistant

NUCLEAR REGULATORY COMMISSION

CHAIRMAN

Level II - Presidential Appointment with Senate Confirmation

Major Responsibilities

● Chair a five-member, policy-making commission with the mandate to protect human health and safety, and the environment, through the licensing, inspection and regulation of the civilian nuclear power industry.

● Oversee research in the areas of safety and environmental analysis and the development of standards and guidelines forming the basis of NRC regulations.

● Act as spokesman for the commission. Represent NRC policy within the federal government as necessary, and to the Congress. Speak for U.S. nuclear regulatory positions to international organizations and individual foreign governments.

● Provide administrative supervision of the NRC.

Necessary Training, Experience, Skills

An NRC chairman need not be a nuclear or mechanical engineer or a physicist, according to one earlier occupant of the position. What's necessary is "to be bright enough and inclined enough to understand and trace through technical arguments and lines of reasoning," he says, adding that "it's probably undesirable to be a great independent thinker. An eminent nuclear technology researcher would not only be unhappy but not be a specially good commissioner." That said, he agrees with others to whom we talked that technical background is important. "You wouldn't want to come in here totally ignorant of anything nuclear," one of them says. Going further, an outside observer stresses a working knowledge of the nuclear power industry or the nuclear Navy. "Many of the most knowledgeable people come from those backgrounds," he notes, "but at the same time those are not the only sources. You need someone with more objectivity who can see the flaws of nuclear power as well as some of the benefits." Given the continual requirement to develop consensus on often sensitive issues among five individuals representing both political parties, the job also needs managerial and negotiating talent and a sense of timing.

Insight

With the nuclear power industry and the Bush administration pushing for a rekindling of the "nuclear option" as a major energy source for the 1990s and beyond, attention has fastened for most of the last two years on the role of the Nuclear Regulatory Commission (NRC) in that effort. In particular, the NRC has been involved in attempted solutions to two of the many problems that since the mid-1970s have smothered the expansion of nuclear-powered generation of electricity for commercial use in the United States.

First, the NRC has been working with the department of energy and with the industry itself to standardize and improve the design of reactors. One goal is to modify the light water reactor designs now in use to make them safer and more economical. More critical for the future is development of an entirely new generation of reactors--among them the advanced liquid metal and modular high temperature gas variety--that would move the industry onto a new level of safety and reliability.

Second, and more controversial, is the NRC's desire to shorten and simplify the exasperatingly complex and protracted licensing ordeal that faces every new nuclear power plant. The NRC had proposed to do this by virtually eliminating the second of two public hearings it currently holds before a new plant can begin operation. The first hearing is part of the commission's determination whether to permit a plant to be built. The second takes place after construction but before the plant is allowed to go on-line; it has been, the industry complains, one of the vehicles employed by antinuclear groups to delay operation of new plants already built at high cost.

But groups who for various reasons oppose nuclear power say the second public hearing provides the opportunity for another look at a new plant in the light of information not available before it was built. In early 1989, the NRC tried to settle this debate with a plan to merge the construction and operating licenses into a single credential. It would be based, among other criteria, on the operator's choice of pre-approved plant location and reactor design. The NRC proposal provided for only one full public hearing plus, after construction, a severely-restricted second opportunity for further public comment. In 1990, a three-judge federal appeals court panel refused to permit curtailment of the second hearing, and the NRC then asked the full court to review the decision. That's where matters stood at this writing.

Kenneth M. Carr, who left the chairman's post in June 1991 at the end of his five-year appointment, thinks the NRC is encumbered by the system it was created under. "You've got to go through adjudicatory hearings for licensing cases and a structured, at times lengthy, process for issuing rules," he says. "Just the mechanics of the thing makes it very hard to get something done." That may be one reason why Carr believes that "youth is not something this agency needs in a commissioner's slot. You need maturity and judgment." And "if you're going to be chairman of this operation you've got to be a manager and be able to push things through to the finish."

The main arena where a chairman must accomplish that, of course, is within the five-member commission. "As chair, your responsibility is to see that the NRC accomplishes in some fashion at least a reasonable fraction of the work the statute assigns it," says Joseph M. Hendrie, chairman in 1977-79 and again in 1981. "You've got commissioners running off in all directions, often determined not to allow decisions to be made because they think they won't go the way they would like. To get a working majority on a given point and force the issue to the point where that majority can carry and the commission can actually take action is no mean feat." So a chairman must "cajole, threaten and influence others in any way possible so the work can be done. This is sometimes easy and pleasant and at other times terrifically difficult." Sunshine laws preventing the chairman from talking with more than one commissioner at a time in private "immensely complicates" the commission's work, Hendrie charges. The rule has good aspects as well as bad, "but it means bodies like the NRC must operate with one decision-making hand tied behind their backs."

Lando Zech, NRC chairman in 1986-89, agrees on the nature of the job's challenge at the policy level: "How to get things done with a five-headed body." He saw the chairman as the first among equals--the "senior judge." The chairman, he says, can vote first or last on an issue. "Voting first allows you to show the way, and most of the time I felt it was important for the chairman to take the lead. But if the commission is divided and you want to be successful on an issue, you might want to hold back." Hendrie takes the view that in bodies like the NRC, "about 70 percent of the time, generally speaking, any decision is better than no decision. If you're a real genius, you can figure out which 70 percent that is, because for the other 30 percent of the time, no decision is better than the wrong decision."

By law the NRC is an independent regulatory body. The president appoints its five members. No more than three can represent one political party at any time. A commissioner's five-year term does not run concurrently either with those of his NRC colleagues or with that of an administration. Chairmen sometimes come from among commissioners already on the board, as was the case with Carr, and sometimes directly from the outside, as with current chairman Ivan Selin, who succeeded him.

The chairman, Zech says, "has all the principal administration, budget and personnel problems, and all the day-to-day operational business of the commission. He runs the agenda and the schedule. He is the spokesman for the agency, and represents it to the Congress. Though all the commissioners generally accompany the chairman to the Hill, the chairman makes the commission's statement and leads the way." Kenneth Bossong, who heads the Critical Mass Energy Project, compares the job to the chief justice of the Supreme Court. "It sets the tone, and has a great deal of influence over administrative policy decisions in terms of what guidelines are given to the staff. The chairman is the most influential person in selecting top staff." Carr thinks that, "if you're going to be on the commission, there is some advantage in being chairman. You can move it in the direction you want it to go." Commission decisions are carried out through the executive director for operations and the principal statutory officers. "We set the policy," he says, "and he and the staff carry it out."

Some in the Congress and others outside have called for replacing the NRC's five commissioners with a single administrator. Zech strongly backs such a change, saying "it's really difficult to run anything by committee." He believes in "concentration of authority, responsibility and accountability. You've got to wrap it up in one person; you can't run anything efficiently with five heads--or three. Somebody has to be in charge." Carr, though, thinks the commission structure is better "because no one person has all the expertise you need to make policy for this organization." With a single administrator whose appointment was co-terminus with the president's, he adds, the regulatory function would zig and zag with each administration. "The way it is now, at least we change gradually, we don't make a right-angle turn." Most support for a single administrator, he says, came from industry sources critical of the way the NRC was operating. In Carr's perception, that was because the agency lacked strong leadership at the top: "If you merely try to achieve consensus among these five commissioners, you're never going to get anything done."

On the operating level, Carr describes several kinds of technical issues for the NRC. He lists extension of current operating licenses for the country's 110 or so existing nuclear power plants first. The commission grants licenses for 40 years, and the first of them, Carr points out, expires in the year 2000. "Putting in place the necessary rules and regulations to extend those licenses so we don't have to cut off any of the country's electrical generating power" was his top priority. Materials, control systems and advanced designs are other high-priority concerns. "Everybody wants an inherently safe reactor," he says. "I don't think we'll ever design one because the things are not inherently safe. I think we can get designs that are safer than the ones we've got out there, which I consider safe if they're properly operated and maintained." One goal for the new designs being worked on "is to get more time for an operator to take action to keep a plant safe--days, rather than hours."

Meanwhile, Bossong says, all reactors in the country are getting older. The average plant age is 12 years, he notes, and cites NRC data suggesting that "at age 15, safety problems begin to crop up." He predicts an "explosion" of such problems. Another danger, in his view, is that "most plants are running out of space to store high-level and low-level wastes." What to do with wastes may, in fact, be the most difficult obstacle in the path of a possible comeback for nuclear power in United States. Large amounts of time and money have gone into a permanent main waste burial site at Yucca Mountain in Nevada, for example; but doubts about its long-term safety have produced congressional pressure on the department to restudy the project, and it has agreed. Meanwhile, Yucca Mountain remains the only feasible nuclear waste storage site in the country. The NRC is attempting to deal with extremely low-level waste under a policy called "below regulatory concern;" according to Bossong, wastes in the BRC category--estimated at about 30 percent of the nuclear industry total under NRC guidelines--"can be dumped without regulation." He predicts that BRC will be blocked by lawsuits and by congressional action to reverse it, and says half a dozen states have taken legal action to prohibit it.

NRC operates with a $475 million budget and a staff of 3,200. A little more than 2,000 are spread through five buildings in Washington's Maryland suburbs; 900 others work in five regional NRC offices. There are also 200 NRC inspectors who live and work on-site at nuclear power plants. The agency contracts out its research, worth about $150 million of the budget total. Though the research share of the budget is "pretty good," Carr says it is only half of what it used to be. In real dollars, he points out, the NRC has been level-funded since it became a separate agency in 1974. "We have gone from analyzing designs and granting licenses to monitoring operating reactors. As we've done that we've had to shift budget priorities." As the budget held steady and the NRC added more responsibilities on the oversight and monitoring side, the research budget was the only source of the extra funding needed. "Somewhere there is a level budget we can operate on and keep up our work," Carr says. "And we're not there. It's somewhere around $500-525 million and between 3,200 and 3,500 people. We need to get there and then we can live with a level budget. But we have to get more money into research and get some of the backlog work done."

Rather than require the NRC to defend its annual budget request, the Office of Management and Budget (OMB) gives the agency guidelines. Sending the budget through OMB on its way to the Congress is the closest the NRC came to contact with the top of the administration during his tenure, Carr notes. Neither as a commissioner nor as chairman did he receive a call from the White House "ever, about anything," and he never felt pressure from that quarter on how to run the NRC. But as Hendrie points out, the Hill is another matter. "Assorted committees claim jurisdiction," he says. "A multicolored array. Some think nuclear technology is a good idea, some think it's not. A lot who don't know and don't care take up the cries of some of the folks in their constituencies."

If the NRC has little connection with the White House, it transacts a lot of business with other executive branch agencies. These include the Environmental Protection Agency on radiation standards; the Food and Drug Administration on irradiation of foods; the department of justice on hearings, investigations and penalties; the department of agriculture on the use of nuclear residues as fertilizer; the department of transportation on the movement of hazardous nuclear material; the department of energy on R&D funding and the future development of nuclear power capacity; and the department of state as the approving authority for the commercial export of radioactive materials. The NRC also attends to 30 or 40 U.S. cooperative agreements with other countries on the safe uses of nuclear power and information exchange. Carr journeyed overseas periodically. Inside this country he tried to travel twice a month on visits to nuclear power plants. Hospitals using radioactive medicines under NRC license are also on the chairman's itinerary; so are officials of the 29 states that act for the NRC in the materials licensing area.

Two advisory panels assist the commission. They are the Advisory Committee on Reactor Safeguards, created by the Congress, and the Advisory Committee on Nuclear Waste, established by the NRC itself. The committees choose their own membership from the scientific and technical communities and the NRC appoints the individuals selected to four-year terms.

Carr praises the NRC staff--"highly technical people, stable, they know exactly what they're doing, they've been doing it a long time." But he worries about "the input that keeps this expertise going," as people get older and universities close or reduce training programs because students see no future in it. The NRC staff contains many naturalized citizens who were trained in other countries. Low staff turnover means "a kind of stagnant operation," Carr says, hampering the entry of young technical people at lower levels. Although the agency manages the research it contracts out, "to manage research you have to have done some somewhere and we can't pay salaries to attract that kind of people." Hendrie thinks the technical training of the staff is adequate. "But regulatory work is not what the best minds gravitate to. As regulatory agencies go, the NRC staff is one of the best in terms of knowledge and competence in its own area. It's getting harder and harder to maintain this, however."

Where the training of nuclear plant operating staff goes, the NRC has a working agreement with the Institute of Nuclear Power Operations (INPO), a self-policing organization set up by utility companies after the incident at Three Mile Island. "They recognized the need to discipline themselves," says Hendrie. INPO established a training program complete with an accreditation board to examine individual utilities and hold them to agreed training standards. Carr believes the NRC-INPO agreement has worked well. The pact was challenged in court, however, on grounds that by the language of the law a training program must be conducted "by regulation or guidance." The NRC argued that guidance for the INPO program existed. While the court agreed, it told the NRC to write a regulation anyway. As of this writing, that remained to be done.

What philosophy should guide the NRC's managers? Zech thinks the role of the regulator should be--"and is, according to the law"--to "protect the public health and safety" but also "not to stop the peaceful benefits of nuclear energy. Regulators should encourage excellence in nuclear plant operations, cooperate with the industry when safety will be enhanced, shut the plants down if they're not safe, but authorize them to operate if they are. Regulators should demand compliance with the regulations, and bang those that don't comply."

Bossong agrees that "the job should be done the way the 1954 (Atomic Energy) Act envisioned--regulate nuclear power giving top priority to public health and safety." But "nothing beyond that. The NRC should not be a promoter of nuclear power. It should have no formal ties to the industry. It should simply be a group of five commissioners who in open, collegial decision making regulate the safety of nuclear power and aggressively enforce the regulations." At present, he asserts, commission decision making is open, but he suggests that the actual decisions are made "behind closed doors."

Zech characterizes the chairman's job as "one of the toughest, most lonely jobs in the federal government. You have great authority and a huge responsibility, and you work with a staff of competent professionals. Don't expect any reward except personal satisfaction."

"You don't get any well-dones from the White House or the Hill," Carr says. "You have zero friends. Nobody comes around and says 'hey, you're doing a great job.' But when you take the job, you know that's how it will be."

Key Relationships

Within the Commission

Reports to: (No reporting relationship to a superior; the NRC is an independent regulatory body)

Works closely with:

Other commissioners
Executive Director, Operations

Outside the Commission

Secretary of Energy
Assistant Secretary, Nuclear Energy, Department of Energy
Senior officials of other federal departments and agencies concerned with environmental and natural resources protection, food safety, export and transportation of radioactive and hazardous materials, and enforcement

Outside the Government

Nuclear energy industry and its trade associations; state officials responsible for materials and medicines licensing; officials and staffs of nuclear power plants; staffs of hospitals, including veterinary hospitals; nuclear regulatory officials of other governments; counterpart officials of international energy and nuclear regulatory bodies; public interest organizations

Profile of Current Chairman

Name: Ivan Selin

Assumed Position: 1991

Career Summary: Under secretary of state for management, 1989-91
Chairman and founder, American Management Systems, Inc., 1970-89

	Office of the assistant secretary of defense (systems analysis), 1965-70
	Research engineer, RAND Corporation, 1960-65
Education:	Yale University, BE, electrical engineering, 1957; MS, electrical engineering, 1958; PhD, electrical engineering (with distinction), 1960
	University of Paris, Dr. es Sciences, mathematics (highest honors), 1962

Chairmen, Nuclear Regulatory Commission Since 1974*

Administration	Name and Years Served	Present Position
Bush	Ivan Selin 1991 - present	Incumbent
Bush	Kenneth M. Carr 1989 - 1991	Vice Admiral (ret.) U.S. Navy
Bush, Reagan	Lando W. Zech Jr. 1986 - 1989	Retired Falls Church, Va.
Reagan	Nunzio J. Palladino 1981 - 1985	Retired State College, Pa.
Reagan, Carter	Joseph M. Hendrie 1981; 1977 - 1979	Brookhaven Natl. Laboratory Upton, N.Y.
Carter	John F. Ahearne 1979 - 1980	Executive Director, Sigma Xi Research Triangle Park, N.C.
Ford	Webster B. Todd Jr. 1976	Not available
Ford	Marcus A. Rowden 1975	Partner Fried Frank Harris Shriver & Jacobson Washington, D.C.
Ford	William A. Anders 1975	CEO, General Dynamics St. Louis, Mo.

* The NRC was created by the Energy Reorganization Act, signed into law in October 1974

24

DEPARTMENT OF STATE

UNDER SECRETARY
ECONOMIC AND AGRICULTURAL AFFAIRS

Level III - Presidential Appointment with Senate Confirmation

Major Responsibilities

- Provide the secretary of state with broad perspective on the development and implementation of U.S. foreign economic policy; and on the various individual issues and decisions with which it is concerned, among them international trade, monetary affairs, investment, debt, the environment, transportation and energy.

- Assert the department's views in the high councils of international economic policy making--at the White House, the treasury, commerce, and agriculture departments, the Office of the U.S. Trade Representative (USTR), and the National Security Council.

- Represent the United States in ministerial-level meetings of multilateral organizations concerned with international economic affairs, such as the World Bank, the International Monetary Fund, and the Organization for Economic Cooperation and Development; and in the periodic cooperative consultations conducted under bilateral agreements with a number of countries.

- Act as chief overseer (the "sherpa") for U.S. participation in the seven-nation annual economic summit meetings, including formulation of goals and agenda, assignment of key tasks, position papers and similar preparations, and coordination with other summit countries.

Necessary Training, Experience, Skills

As will be seen below, recent administrations have varied in their approach to this position, and opinion differs widely on its utility and potential. Whatever its configuration of the moment, however, those who have held the job over the last 15 years remain convinced of what still seems obvious--that it requires sound training in economics, preferably in the international arena, and experience in practical applications. One informed observer thinks the best candidates are "political economists," as opposed to what he says the job's occupants have tended to be: "pure economists, or someone who dabbles in economics but is basically a political scientist." Conversations about the position also suggest strongly that the individual selected needs some eminence as an economics professional, based on talent and achievement. Further, this under secretary must be able and willing to hang tough in the sometimes abrasive give-and-take of policy debate and negotiation within the U.S. government and with foreign counterparts.

Insight

Three decades of periodic restructuring and shifting management styles at the top have left this job without the permanently defined authority and scope that some of the State Department's other under secretary slots nonetheless achieved. It first emerged in the 1950s, disappeared some years later, then reappeared at the deputy under secretary level. At its present rank, the position has existed continuously since the late Nixon administration, functioning in a sometimes enigmatic relationship with the assistant secretary for economic and business affairs.

Since the early 1970s, the successive strategies, preoccupations and preferences of those in power have defined sharply contrasting parameters for this job. For part of the period, under secretaries nominally charged with advising on and helping to develop international economic policy operated on a relatively short leash, for secretaries of state who tended to run their own shows or gave economic matters only a secondary emphasis. At another time, the role was one of substantial range and contribution as sub-cabinet seniors in the responsible agencies shaped much policy and sought to minimize the number of decisions raised to the White House level. In short, says C. William Maynes, a former senior official at State who edits the quarterly *Foreign Policy*, the position is "important in some administrations and almost insignificant in others."

"When I went into it," recalls Richard N. Cooper, under secretary in 1977-80, "I decided there were three radically different ways one could conceive of that job, because it didn't have a natural definition except in terms of subject matter." Of the three--dealing with the substance of foreign economic policy making; a heavy congressional testifying role; or giving it heavy public affairs and spokesman responsibilities--Cooper chose the first. He thinks the job actually combines all three concepts, "so the question is really one of principal emphasis. It's a matter of what the secretary wants. The first of these roles is what I would call scientific. Not in the sense that you have to know Newtonian mechanics, but you really have to know some economics to do it. If you think of it as a policy job--essentially being the economic voice of the secretary on anything having an economic bearing--then it really is a scientific job requiring some formal economic training."

Finding his new office suffering a "relative vacuum" in the area of analysis, Cooper brought in two academically trained economists. One, a specialist in quantitative technique, helped beef up an existing unit called the Economic Analysis Staff. "There was also a strong economic unit in CIA looking around for a client," he says. "I became a welcome consumer and we got a lot of global macroeconomics going. We tied in with the Wharton global economic model, still in a relatively primitive state then, but we ran our simulations." These were used both in preparing economic summit meetings and in estimating outcomes of possible financial and commodity moves: "If we do this with monetary or fiscal policy, and Germany does this and Japan does that, what happens? If OPEC raises oil prices by 15 percent, what are the consequences? These were formal quantitative simulations. Then we massaged them to make them intelligible and used both those sets of analyses routinely, not just episodically. We used them as talking points for ambassadors in OPEC countries, for instance."

The same techniques helped to assess individual world commodity markets--for example, "the technical possibilities for limiting price movements and then what would be required by way of buffer stocks. Today's sole surviving commodity agreement--rubber--came out of that analysis." But the under secretary's involvement in scientific and technical matters does not stop there. W. Allen Wallis, who held the position in 1982-89, cites issues from acid rain to whales and including ozone, the space station project, AIDS, the superconducting super collider, semiconductors, cooperation with Japan in cancer research, and telecommunications. Each such topic requires overview from State in the international economic policy context.

Some of Cooper's comments suggest that, at the sub-cabinet level, the interagency process enjoyed in that period an unusual degree of latitude in coming to closure on key elements of foreign economic policy. Those taking part worked in collegial style, with considerable autonomy.

The terrain was large, and the composition of their regularly-scheduled meetings varied: State, Treasury, the White House and later, USTR; or State, Commerce and Defense; or State, Energy and the White House. Cooper says the strategy was "co-option, not confrontation. If somebody wanted to make it a presidential issue, it would go to the White House. But we tried to work things out without doing it that way. I think, on the whole, we succeeded."

The under secretary post since then has operated with less license, and less apparent impact, even with the strong interest in economic matters shown by one secretary of state during the period. Cooper points out, though, that the issues in the job are broadly the same. "There is trade policy, there is international financial policy, and--not quite the same but closely related--international macroeconomic policy." There are also the many "cats and dogs" of export control, sanctions, aviation and maritime policy, "lots of detailed decisions: does this count? Do you make an exception for that? The basic agenda remains; the details all change."

On the structural level, however, one significant change has intervened, in Cooper's view, about which he expresses mixed feelings. As he explains it, the under secretary job used to be that of a senior, seventh-floor principal, but not a line position. The assistant secretary heading the Bureau of Economic and Business Affairs (EB), which was and is a line job, reported to the under secretary but also had direct access to the secretary of state. This arrangement was by explicit decision of the secretary, not only to enhance the status of the department's assistant secretaries, but to allow under secretaries to focus on major problems without disrupting the normal flow of activity. Now, as Cooper views it, all bureaus are grouped under one or another under secretary; access to the top for assistant secretaries is greatly reduced; and this has brought the under secretary jobs themselves onto the line in fact if not on paper. "It means the character of the job has changed to the extent that more of the routine things have to go through it," he says. Pertinent to that observation may be the comment of a more recent under secretary, Richard T. McCormack (1989-91). "If you become totally immersed in the microeconomic issues," he says, "you can destroy your ability to sit back and look at broad policy and provide a broad policy context in which they should be moving." A further wrinkle in the current jurisdictional picture relates to the newly-broadened job of under secretary for international security affairs (ISA); in certain matters, like restrictions on the export of dual-use technology, EB has been reporting not to its own under secretary, but to ISA.

Another notable variable in this job has been its working relationship with the assistant secretary running EB. While the under secretary has a staff of five, EB numbers 250 or more; it is involved day-to-day in the detailed subsets of economic affairs and, with other bureaus, produces much of the analysis that goes into policy making. "If you're going to be a significant force as under secretary," Maynes notes, "you have to have special analytical skills or you just get outshined and outpowered by your assistant secretary, who's got all of the battalions." But the under secretary also has the responsibility to bring the assistant secretary into joint efforts to produce between them the best possible analysis. Other circumstances tend to confuse the responsibilities of the two positions, or to create uncertainty about which is the more important. "There's always an inherent tension" between them, McCormack observes, and personality and temperament can play a role. "If both want to be in charge of economic policy at State," says Cooper, "you're going to have them tangling all the time."

The best arrangement, in fact, seems to have been one in which each individual managed to complement, not duplicate, the efforts of the other; and where the assistant secretary, with access to the top of the department, was able and ready to sit in when the under secretary was away. Moreover, Cooper says, "if you have an analytically and bureaucratically strong assistant secretary, there's some scope for giving the under secretary more of a public relations job, particularly with the American business community." Maynes argues along similar lines. He thinks the under secretary job would gain strength as "a voice for bringing a different perspective" to economic policy issues. "To the degree you believe that is part of the department's role, then the under secretary should be very active on the Hill and have a public voice in the community," he says.

In the early Reagan years, the assignment of chief "sherpa" for economic summit preparation and management migrated from the National Security Council, where the Carter administration had lodged it, to State. (The function originated as an outside consultancy in the Ford era.) The department's under secretary for economic affairs (the title at the time), who had been a junior sherpa for these annual events, became the U.S. team leader. McCormack calls the summit "one of the most important decision-forcing mechanisms in the world of international economic policy...the level where the top technical people interface with the top political people in all the governments." Others differ on the significance of the summits, but they continue to demand an important part of the under secretary's attention and travel. Because of the long lead time required, the run-up to a summit meeting, held in the late spring or early summer, normally begins sometime in the preceding autumn or early winter. If there is a mid-year intergovernmental review of the previous summit, this fits into and augments the workload. Complicating the preparations to some extent is the rotation of the host role and meeting site each year. Noting what he terms the increasingly political cast and agenda of summit meetings, Maynes thinks others, inside or outside of State, could eventually challenge this under secretary for the chief sherpa role. It might go to Treasury, he speculates, or back to the NSC.

Further, Mikhail Gorbachev's presence during the 1991 summit in London was an important specific signal of western, and particularly U.S., concern about preventing a Soviet slide into economic and political chaos. That concern translates into a significant new emphasis on Soviet economic problems for this under secretary, and one not limited to the summit context.

Summit and other duties put the under secretary on a regular round of meetings and travel. The occupant usually speaks for State on the White House's Economic Policy Council (the secretary is titular representative), works with most of the department's people at and just below his level, and currently attends a periodic early-morning meeting with the secretaries of State and Treasury, the president's national security assistant, and the Treasury's under secretary for international affairs. Among other recurring contacts are meetings with the president's science advisor on topics like global climate change; and with other officials in the federal technology and development assistance communities. Then there are, in McCormack's words, "meetings that don't have names, groups that don't have titles." As for travel, Cooper remembers "a tremendous amount" of it in this job; he calculates that "nights away from Washington averaged 101 days a year." The missions of these trips swung between strategy sessions with counterparts in the governments of the other G-5 leading industrial powers, strictly representational activities, and "diplomatic persuading functions."

In staffing both the under secretary's office and the EB bureau, Cooper sees a critical requirement for State to be "literate enough that it can't be snowed" by faulty analysis coming either from other governments or other agencies of the U.S. government. "In that sense, there has to be scientific knowledge and background," not necessarily in the under secretary's office but at reasonably senior levels which allow the department to contribute constructively to policy discussion and debate.

Among career professional foreign service officers, Wallis thinks the economists "tend to be more realistic about economics and more analytical." He has a high regard for some of the foreign service officers who worked for him or in the EB and regional bureaus, and notes mistakes by the political leadership "that never in the world would have been made if they were talking to an experienced FSO." At the same time, Cooper worries about maintaining the technical training and caliber of the department's economics cadre. When he first served there in the 1960s, he worried that State would lose out to other government agencies if it couldn't keep up technically. Then, he says, the Foreign Service

Institute established a strong economics program and when Cooper came back 12 years later as under secretary, "the difference was visible." Now, he thinks, "that has decayed a lot because of the budget cuts. I think it's a big mistake."

Maynes sounds the same warning. Without more substantial training and grooming of talented career people from the inside, he believes, departments will lose more positions to appointments of outsiders. "As diplomacy gets more and more into these specialized fields, it's going to take greater investment in personnel than these institutions are used to making," he says. "If you want the department to play a role, say, in the nuclear field, you're going to have to do more than hope you get a very bright person who on weekends is reading *Scientific American* and trying to learn the language. You're going to have to give him maybe a couple of years at MIT so that you've created a specialist of real competitive merit. It's all very expensive--and the argument of the department will be, if we give them that degree of training, we'll just lose them (to jobs on the outside). But that's a risk they have to take."

Key Relationships

Within the Department

Reports to: Secretary of State

Works closely with:

Deputy Secretary
Assistant Secretary, Economic and Business Affairs
Under Secretary, International Security Affairs
Regional assistant secretaries
Assistant Secretary, Oceans and International Environmental and Scientific
Affairs

Outside the Department

Chairman, President's Council of Economic Advisers
Assistant to the President, Science and Technology Policy
Under Secretary of the Treasury, International Affairs
Under Secretaries of Commerce, International Trade and Export
Administration
Under Secretary of Agriculture, International Affairs and Commodity
Programs
Administrator, Agency for International Development
Senior officials, Office of the U.S. Trade Representative
Members of the White House Economic Policy Council
Cabinet-level contacts during economic summit meeting preparations

Director, Defense Technology Security Administration, Department of
Defense

Outside the Government

Counterparts in other industrially advanced countries; officials of
international financial institutions;representatives of manufacturing,
communications, energy, airline, and foreign-trade businesses and
associations; domestic banking organizations; and other private and nonprofit
groups oriented to foreign policy and trade

Profile of Current Under Secretary
Economic and Agricultural Affairs

Name:	Robert B. Zoellick
Assumed Position:	1991
Career Summary:	Counselor, Department of State, 1989-91
	Issues director, Bush presidential campaign, 1988
	Various positions, department of the treasury, 1985-88, including counselor to the secretary; executive secretary, deputy assistant secretary, financial institutions policy; and special assistant to the deputy secretary
	Vice president and assistant to the chairman and CEO, Fannie Mae, 1983-85
	Clerk, U.S. Court of Appeals for the D.C. Circuit, 1982-83
	Special assistant to the head of the Criminal Division, Department of Justice, 1978-79
	Council on Wage and Price Stability, 1979-80
Education:	Swarthmore College, BA, 1975
	Kennedy School of Government, Harvard University, MPP, 1981
	Harvard University Law School, JD, 1981

Under Secretaries for Economic and Agricultural Affairs
Since 1969

Administration	Name and Years Served	Present Position
Bush	Robert B. Zoellick 1991 - present	Incumbent

Bush	Richard T. McCormack 1989 - 1991	Guest Scholar Woodrow Wilson Center for International Scholars Washington, D.C.
Reagan	W. Allen Wallis 1982 - 1989	Resident Scholar American Enterprise Institute Washington, D.C.
Reagan	Myer Rashish* 1981	Economic Consultant Washington, D.C.
Carter	Richard N. Cooper* 1977 - 1980	Maurits C. Boas Professor of International Economics Harvard University Cambridge, Mass.
Ford	William D. Rogers* 1976	Senior Partner Arnold and Porter Washington, D.C.
Ford	Charles W. Robinson* 1975	Chairman and President Charles Robinson Associates Santa Fe, N.M.
Nixon	William J. Casey* 1973	Deceased
Nixon	Nathaniel Samuels** 1969 - 1972	Not available

* Held position as Under Secretary for Economic Affairs
**Held position as Deputy Under Secretary for Economic Affairs

UNDER SECRETARY
INTERNATIONAL SECURITY AFFAIRS

Level III - Presidential Appointment with Senate Confirmation

Major Responsibilities

- Oversee and coordinate the department of state role and responsibilities in the areas of arms control, foreign military assistance, arms transfers, international nuclear energy safeguards and nonproliferation of weapons, strategic trade controls and export licensing, and international science and technology cooperation.

- Advise the secretary of state on developments in these fields and how they should be reflected in the development of U.S. foreign policy. Speak for the department in high-level coordination of the work of the federal agencies involved.

- Represent U.S. views and policy on these matters in regular dialogue with counterparts or officials concerned in other governments, and articulate them to the Congress.

Necessary Training, Experience, Skills

The individual in this position must bring to it a solid grasp of the impact of arms transfers on U.S. scientific and industrial potential, of U.S. international objectives, and of the federal interagency policy process. Substantial familiarity with the shaping and carrying out of U.S. foreign policy is also imperative: without it, an under secretary will work under a severe operational handicap and, more important, will be unable to bring to bear the wisdom and international affairs perspective that is the job's primary mission. Scientific or technical literacy is a distinct advantage. Though adequate expert assistance is available, the under secretary should be able to understand the significance of the technology of specific issues for the decisions and policy choices to be made.

Insight

In the spring of 1990 this wide-ranging position underwent a bit of remodeling. It lost oversight of a function or two, such as international communication and information policy, but gained one of greater breadth --arms control coordination within the department. Its oversight within State was clarified to some degree with the decision that bureaus with line responsibility would channel their reporting through one (or more) of the department's under secretaries. The job even shed its cumbersome, not very descriptive title in favor of one that, though more concise, still doesn't cover its full scope. Coincident with these revisions and exterior to the department itself, the changes in national politics and international relationships of the last three years have altered emphases across the broad terrain under this position's supervision.

"Government responsibility for science activities is dispersed among many agencies," notes William Schneider Jr., under secretary in 1982-86, "but the international face of the government in that respect coalesces in the department of state." So the under secretary manages the coordinating function. Inside the department that means oversight of perhaps half the work of the Bureau of Oceans and International Environmental and Scientific Affairs and, to lesser degrees, specific activities of regional bureaus like European and Near Eastern and South Asian Affairs and functional offices like Economic and Business Affairs. Outside State, the coordinating role involves extensive interagency consultation at senior levels--from individual departments and agencies to the National Security Council and the White House.

Two of the under secretary's stops on this circuit are the chairmanship of the Committee on International Science, Engineering and Technology (CISET), a subgroup under the White House's Federal Coordinating Council for Science, Engineering and Technology; and membership on the National Space Council chaired by the vice president. Reginald Bartholomew, the current under secretary whose tenure dates from the job's 1990 restructuring, says CISET's task is to make certain that independent international activities of federal agencies in the science/technology field "are not running on different tracks at cross purposes" and to generate logical and productive cooperative projects between them.

"Let me put it this way," says Bartholomew about the oversight and coordination that are the key to this job. "I go to a fair number of interagency meetings. It's an important factor in my time." Some of the groups he sits down with are permanent bodies; others are ad hoc. In the context of the Persian Gulf war, Bartholomew set up a special oversight committee to handle arms transfers. "I signed a memo saying I was creating it," he recalls, "but you wouldn't find it on a government organization chart."

Arms control leads the portfolio of this job. The under secretary for international security affairs (ISA) is mandated to pull together the various strands of effort in this field inside the department itself, principally by the Bureau of Politico-Military Affairs and some of the regional offices. With arms control taking on significant reality, Schneider thinks this function has taken on greater importance; he adds that the under secretary was put in charge of in-house arms control policy to "adjudicate the wars between different factions" at State so the department would have a "single voice" on this subject in the higher councils of government. In fact, Bartholomew is the State member of the deputies committee on arms control chaired by the deputy director of the National Security Council. At the time we talked with him, he was preparing to visit Moscow for arms control talks with the Soviet deputy foreign minister.

Next comes security assistance--a euphemism for U.S. support to allies and friends abroad primarily to build and sustain military readiness and self-defense in contemporary war. Security assistance mainly comprises foreign military sales grants and economic support funds, under the respective operating authority of the department of defense and the Agency for International Development. The annual development of its budget and its implementation (estimated at $7.76 billion in fiscal 1991, and at $7.4 billion in 1992) probably consume as much time in this job as any other areas. "And with that," says Bartholomew, "goes a general brief for managing the whole process of decisions on arms transfers-- commercial as well as government sales." He thinks tight resources represent a major problem for his security assistance brief, putting him often in a position not just of robbing Peter to pay Paul but of robbing both.

Today, with U.S.- Soviet rivalry no longer staring defense planners in the face, security assistance is viewed as less important as a cutting-edge implement of American foreign policy. So is the urgency of the need to maneuver difficult, often controversial decisions on assistance between the Congress and its various recipients overseas. But for the under secretary, the responsibility continues to entail close oversight within the department (the Bureau of Politico-Military Affairs) and regular consultation outside it (the department of defense). It also involves often tough testimony on the Hill (as on Middle East arms sales policy in the spring of 1991).

Much of the science and technology content of the job flows from its role in international science cooperation. But the under secretary's need for scientific and technical literacy extends well beyond. For example, "there are all kinds of obvious scientific or technical dimensions to arms control," Bartholomew points out. "I spend a lot of time on fairly technical things about weapons systems, or fiber optics and telecommunications, or arguing with somebody over heat treating the casings of rocket motors. I do need to be able to understand some of the technical choices involved." Schneider voices similar thoughts. In this post, he says, scientific literacy "doesn't obtain only with respect to international cooperation." The under secretary "has to come to grips to some degree with the significance of data rates, for instance--do you want to cut off the export of microwave relay systems at the 500 megabytes rate, or 200 or 100? You don't have to be an electrical engineer, but you have to be comfortable with it."

But beyond this, Bartholomew makes the fundamental point that what the person in his position must be able to contribute is "policy sense, a knowledge of foreign policy and how the science fits in. That is the value added that I bring to an international scientific decision, not being able to design a better rocket motor."

International science cooperation involves not only the tending of the many U.S. bilateral agreements with other countries, but what Bartholomew calls "international megascience cooperative projects" like the superconducting super collider or the Freedom space station. The job does not take an interest in all scientific projects per se, he makes clear, but of those that fit into U.S. foreign policy objectives or have a part to play in "the kinds of relationships we're trying to maintain with different countries."

A case in point, albeit a somewhat negative one, is the space station. Surrounded by question marks about mission and funding, the station is an increasing enigma to the several foreign countries who are U.S. partners in the project and who need to be kept informed and on board. The problem nicely illustrates the combination of policy skill and familiarity with the technical side that this job requires. For instance, the vagaries of the space station's funding outlook has impact on such aspects of the project as its design. A potential redesign can in turn affect the role and investment of the station's foreign participants. "There are trade-offs between their voice in the program, their weight and the need to keep them with us and, on the other side, the range of technical options for adjustment of the program that makes sense," Bartholomew says. To balance these considerations, he must understand the options enough to see what does, in fact, make sense.

Schneider recognized science cooperation with the United States as a "valued commodity among friendly governments," and saw its utility in advancing American foreign policy objectives. As he describes it, the problem was that while science cooperation is mostly framed in official agreements between governments, "the primary engine of scientific development is the private sector," and the two were out of sync. He thought the answer was greater private sector involvement in the government's international science dialogue and a reduced dependence on bilateral agreements, "which were in fact the tail of the dog as far as science activities were concerned."

One step in that direction, Schneider felt, would be the recruitment of U.S. embassy science attaches from outside environments like the universities, rather than from the ranks of foreign service officers. They would serve tours of two to four years as government employees. But the 1980 Foreign Service Act had made this more difficult than previously. Result: while the U.S. Information Agency, for example, could bring in cultural affairs officers from the outside on this temporary basis, "at State it was still a bridge too far." Yet, Schneider says today, the situation "is recognized as a problem in the way we deliver science cooperation."

"A line I keep pushing," Bartholomew says on this subject, "is that international science and technology cooperation is going to become a bigger and weightier factor in our key relationships than it has ever been in the past. It's not a simple hydraulic theory of international politics where, as the military component of your relationship, say, with the Soviet Union goes down, it forces something else up." The nature of science and the amounts of money involved in "megascience," he asserts, make science a particularly important area for the department and for foreign policy. "So I have this sense that international science and technology cooperation is going to have to be built into the department's synapses, its way of doing business, much more directly and intimately."

Two other major assignments in this job's bundle of functions concern the nonproliferation of weapons of any kind, a somewhat paradoxical pursuit for an official also responsible for arms sales under the security assistance rubric; and the licensing of arms exports and trade in dual-use technology. In the licensing area, one segment of the under secretary's authority connects to the work of the Coordinating Committee on Multilateral Export Controls; this is an informal group of 17 western countries that for years has collectively decided strategy for controlling the export of strategic items in trade with the Soviet Union and Eastern Europe. Another part of it derives from the Arms Control Export Act. "And then," says Bartholomew, "I also get into licensing because of the export controls associated with missile technology" under a 1980s agreement called the Missile Technology Control Regime. Here again, the perceived danger in selling strategic technology to the Soviets and their former allies, though hardly eliminated, has receded. Thus Schneider views the export control function today as moving toward "a more amorphous control of exports to third world countries."

Bartholomew has a personal staff of eight, and augments its expertise by taking advantage of the young talent available for a year of government work through the American Association for the Advancement of Science. But he also relies on support "from our own, in-house expertise and that of other agencies," he says, to provide "main-line backup, to walk me through it." And, he continues, "I get very much what I need. In terms of state department resources, they're pretty good in these high-tech, megascience areas."

But Schneider doesn't find much recognition yet in State's recruitment policy of the fact that "science and technology are increasingly embedded in important public policy issues--trade, export controls, arms transfers, telecommunications." Instead, he believes recruitment is basically passive, driven by the fact of 18,000 yearly applications for only 200 available places. "Most of those 18,000 are people interested in foreign cultures and languages, which is definitely an asset for State's main activities." Meanwhile, "the need for scientific literacy is there, and there's a problem addressing it."

Key Relationships

Within the Department

Reports to: Secretary

Works closely with:

Deputy Secretary
Under Secretary, Political Affairs
Under Secretary, Economic Affairs
Assistant Secretary, Oceans and International Environmental and Scientific
  Affairs
Assistant Secretary, Politico-Military Affairs
Assistant Secretary, Economic and Business Affairs
Assistant secretaries of regional bureaus and intelligence and research

Outside the Department

Assistant to the President, White House Office of Science and Technology
  Policy
Associate Director, International Affairs, White House Office of Science and
  Technology Policy
Members, deputies committee, National Security Council
Members, Committee on International Science, Engineering and Technology
  of the Federal Coordinating Council for Science, Engineering and
  Technology
Director, National Science Foundation
Director, Defense Security Assistance Agency
Under Secretary, Export Administration, Department of Commerce
Assistant Secretary, International Security Policy, Department of Defense
Under Secretary, Department of Energy

Assistant Director, Scientific, Technological, and International Affairs,
National Science Foundation
Assistant Administrator, Science and Technology, Agency for International
Development
Chairman, Nuclear Regulatory Commission
Deputy Director, Intelligence, Central Intelligence Agency

Outside the Government

Manufacturers of nuclear materials and equipment, weapons and munitions,
and high-technology computing, electronics, telecommunications and other
related products; diplomats and senior officials of other governments; U.S.
professional science and technology communities; officials of international
organizations

Profile of Current Under Secretary
International Security Affairs

Name: Reginald Bartholomew

Assumed Position: 1990

Career Summary: Career foreign service officer, Department of State, 1974-1989,
including Ambassador to Spain, 1986-89, and Lebanon, 1983-86;
special negotiator for defense and economic cooperation with
Greece, 1982-83; and director, Bureau of Politico- Military
Affairs, 1979-81
Career civil service, Department of Defense, 1968-74, including
director, Policy Planning Staff, Office of International Security
Affairs
Lecturer in government, Wesleyan University, 1964-68
Teacher, social sciences, University of Chicago, 1963-64

Education: Dartmouth College, BA, 1958
University of Chicago, MA, international relations, 1960

Under Secretaries of State, International Security Affairs
Since 1973*

Administration	Name and Years Served	Present Position
Bush	Reginald Bartholomew 1989 - present	Incumbent
Reagan	Edward J. Derwinski** 1987 - 1988	Secretary Department of Veterans Affairs

Reagan	William Schneider Jr.** 1982 - 1986	President International Planning Arlington, Va.
Reagan	James L. Buckley** 1981	Circuit Judge U.S. Court of Appeals Washington, D.C.
Carter	Matthew Nimitz** 1980	Partner Paul, Weiss, Rifkind, Wharton & Garrison New York, N.Y.
Carter	Lucy Wilson Benson** 1977 - 1979	President Benson & Associates Washington, D.C.
Ford	Carlyle E. Maw** 1974 - 1976	Deceased
Nixon	Curtis W. Tarr** 1973	Chairman, Europe Intermet Corporation Atlanta, Ga.

* Position established in 1973
** Held position as Under Secretary, Security Assistance, Science and Technology

ASSISTANT SECRETARY
OCEANS AND INTERNATIONAL ENVIRONMENTAL
AND SCIENTIFIC AFFAIRS

Level IV - Presidential Appointment with Senate Confirmation

Major Responsibilities

- Assist the secretary of state in developing the science and technology components of U.S. foreign policy. Direct a department of state bureau coordinating a diverse range of corresponding U.S. international programs in support of that policy. Consult regularly with senior department political and economic managers.

- Take a leading part in interagency management of environmental, oceanic, energy, nuclear non-proliferation and other scientific and technical issues as they relate to foreign policy. Assure effective U.S. representation in international negotiations on issues in the bureau's areas of responsibility, taking a personal role as necessary.

- Oversee the activities of science counselors and attaches assigned to U.S. diplomatic posts overseas. See that U.S. participation in its various international science and technology relationships is apt and productive. Maintain similar connections with the relevant American professional communities.

Necessary Training, Experience, Skills

Veterans and observers of this post make two main points about filling it with the right individual. First, look at the issues likely to dominate the agenda of the job during the period of the appointment and select the candidate who offers the most relevant combination of training, experience and skill. Where law of the sea matters were prominent in the early 1980s, for example, most observers point out that international environmental, technology and trade concerns lead the list today and for the visible future. Second, the position requires an understanding of international relations and science and technology policy, and some grasp of the negotiating process and of the Washington environment. Therefore, don't choose a bench scientist without at least some of those attributes. "You have to have a general knowledge of science," a former assistant secretary emphasizes, "but you must be much broader in the overview of policy and how you make the mechanism work."

Insight

Coordination is the main name of the game in handling the disparate threads of responsibility that converge in the Bureau of Oceans and International Environmental and Scientific Affairs (OES). The diversity is enormous, according to Frederick M. Bernthal, who held the post in 1988-90, and the "crosscutting theme" is science and technology. One of the toughest assignments the job imposes is "convincing the department of state establishment that this is the theme that will run through 21st century foreign policy issues like environment and competitiveness."

"A tall order--and at the same time, the bureau doesn't have any money," he adds. "They don't really have a lot of the expertise, either. You don't expect to have credentialed nuclear physicists or space scientists over there, though they do have a couple. You rely on other departments for that specialized expertise. Your job is a coordinating job." His comments suggest that OES would gain if it were led by a senior scientist.

"Fascinating, all-consuming, controversial, contentious and enjoyable" are the descriptives offered by James L. Malone, assistant secretary from 1981 to 1985. "A very broad-ranging responsibility-- everything the U.S. is concerned with in international science and oceanic, environmental and scientific matters." In his first two years Malone spent about 50 percent of the time in his role as U.S. negotiator for the third United Nations Law of the Sea conference which, as he notes, is the longest, most extensive multilateral negotiation in which the United States has been involved.

Today law of the sea, and other areas of earlier focus like the Freedom space station with its foreign participation, have moved into the background of this job. In their places stand environmental concerns-- specifically global climate change, the thinning of the ozone layer and, to a lesser extent, acid rain. The U.S. effort on climate change alone, shepherded by the White House science policy office, involves State and a dozen other federal departments and agencies in a multifaceted program of data collection, analysis and policy development under the Federal Coordinating Council for Science, Engineering and Technology (FCCSET). Bernthal calls it "the most difficult science policy issue we've ever had--where all the issues of science, environment, politics and foreign policy tangle." The multilateral cooperation and policy aspects of this problem have an obvious international dimension. Current negotiations with Canada on climate change and Antarctica among other issues, and a UN conference on environment and development in 1992, are further evidence of the environment's widening demands on this assistant secretary. OES is also heavily involved in the work of another FCCSET committee, on international science and engineering.

Within OES, these matters are the working-level responsibility of one of this job's four deputies, who covers environment, health and natural resources and supervises a separate unit working on global change. Charles Higginson, executive director of the Council on Ocean Law, thinks this office faces the bureau's primary challenges. For example, he says, the rest of the world is trying to push the United States into setting agreed goals for cutting chlorofluorocarbons, and the Canadians are pressing very hard on acid rain. A U.S. lack of responsiveness on this, Higginson thinks, could endanger the U.S.-Canada free trade agreement. Comparable problems--or worse--must be considered in negotiations for a free-trade pact with Mexico. He also suggests that, while environmental credentials should be imperative in filling the assistant secretary post, a predilection with environmental issues must not overly divert its occupant from other duties. For example, according to Higginson, "admittedly successful negotiations under the Antarctic Treaty have taken up months of OES's and the assistant secretary's time. Is this the most important issue to the United States generally for OES to give that much attention to?" His point dramatizes the tug on OES to negotiate abroad rather than coordinate policies at home.

The bureau's other three main units handle science and technology affairs, oceans and fisheries matters, and nuclear energy and energy technology. The first of these is concerned to a large degree with managing U.S. bilateral and multilateral agreements with other countries. "We were the coordinating and balancing agency that brought the foreign affairs component into the picture and made certain that science and technology policy dovetailed into it properly," Malone says. As he explains it, the core of international cooperation in science and technology is work done privately, university to university, scientist to scientist. As these arrangements broaden and gain government support, agency-to-agency relationships emerge, and as the process continues, umbrella-type agreements develop between the governments themselves. "Our specific function," he says, "was to give it policy direction, management and coordination." This involved "intimate contact" over an entire range of issues with science agencies in Washington, as well as with counterpart agencies or ministries in other countries with important science and technology establishments.

Safeguarding the civilian uses of nuclear power around the world--in the jargon, nuclear non-proliferation (NNP)--remains an important objective for OES in the area of nuclear energy and nuclear technology. It requires careful, often sensitive attention to technical data and other sources of information and intelligence. It also demands equally careful diplomacy, conducted both with individual nations--over the years Pakistan is the most discussed, but not the only, example--and through the International Atomic Energy Agency (IAEA). Much of this work takes place within the framework of the Nuclear Nonproliferation Treaty and the international safeguards programs of the IAEA. OES has a hand in decisions on what this country will and won't export by way of nuclear materials and equipment destined for peaceful uses. And certain treaties still to be concluded in these areas have relevance for OES even though others have the lead. Note further that NNP is also the responsibility of the department's only remaining ambassador at large, who is staffed and supported by OES personnel.

In oceans and fisheries, the spotlight used to be on issues in commercial fishing and conflicting claims to ocean fishing grounds. OES continues to follow this area, reporting on it through the under secretary for economic affairs. At the same time, however, environmental/ecological problems like drift-net fishing and the Antarctic have moved toward the center. The bureau plays a role in the activities of the International Fisheries Commissions of which the United States is a member, in negotiations relating to the Arctic and Antarctic, and in whaling matters, marine research and the protection of marine mammals.

Helping OES to perform in this broad universe of responsibilities are about 35 science counselors and attaches assigned to U.S. embassies abroad and to several international organizations. Under the oversight of the assistant secretary, they bring an on-site focus to U.S. science and technology diplomacy, tend the operation of U.S. cooperation agreements, and provide factual reporting and analysis to the department on events, trends and evidence of scientific innovation in their areas. Additional, part-time support comes from a hundred or more political and economic officers at diplomatic posts around the world.

"OES is a unique place in that its constituency is all over the map," Bernthal says. "You're involved in everything, but don't have final responsibility for anything." He amends that slightly, because "the department does have final, lead responsibility on oceans and Antarctic policy." The bureau's work is also complicated, in Higginson's view, by the problem of overlapping jurisdiction. "It's quite clear," he says, "that this assistant secretary is responsible for U.S. oceans policy." However, the Bureau of Economic and Business Affairs (EB) has responsibility for seabed mining affairs. "And oceans policy is now basically tied to seabed mining, so that EB is really as important in this area, within State, as OES is." The situation, he notes, has in the past provoked "serious arguments" between assistant secretaries heading the two bureaus. There is also a lack of clarity about which under secretary--for political, economic or international security affairs--OES reports to. All three have jurisdictional mandates for pieces of the action in OES.

In general, Malone says, the level of OES staff training and background was satisfactory during his tenure. Counting the science counselors overseas, the bureau has about 140 employees, and operates on an annual budget of about $15 million. The big drawback where staff is concerned is the orientation of career service people at the department of state to those specialties--political and economic affairs--that have the best opportunities for advancement. They tend to resist service in OES, viewing it as an obstacle on the career path. "Can they," as Higginson asks, "afford to spend a year learning about the peaceful uses of nuclear energy when their next assignment may be as economic counselor in Buenos Aires?" Another angle of this situation, Malone says, is that most people drawn to foreign service careers do not have science or technology backgrounds. "Yet in many cases, the science and technology component of U.S. relations with other countries and international organizations depends very much" on people with just such backgrounds. The traditional solution, he says, has been to borrow staff temporarily from other agencies to fill the gap. Malone sees problems if State fails to develop its own cadre of science and technology career officers. "But it may never overcome the problem completely," he adds; "it's the nature of the foreign service."

This position entails considerable activity on or with the Hill. Committees with the greatest interest in OES areas of responsibility are the foreign affairs panels of both houses, the House Committee on Merchant Marine and Fisheries, and the Senate Commerce and House Science committees. In addition to the global climate change effort, the assistant secretary's schedule includes significant work in other interagency contexts; Malone chaired National Security Council groups working on oceans policy, population policy and nuclear nonproliferation. Travel is also involved, taking what Bernthal estimates was the equivalent of three months of his time in 1989. But that is down from the time that Malone says he spent on travel, mostly on law of the sea business.

Across the bureau's range of activity, Higginson finds one or two areas that, in his view, need more emphasis. One of them is nuclear power. "Years ago, one of the chief functions of OES was the peaceful uses of nuclear energy," he says. "I have seen less attention to that of late. And certainly nuclear nonproliferation is of great importance within the U.S. government." He thinks the U.S. is "falling behind" in both areas.

Though everyone agrees that the environment has become this job's biggest challenge, Higginson thinks the U.S. position on international environmental problems remains "not very responsive." As the principal state department officer responsible for the environment, he says, "the assistant secretary gets the flack even if there isn't a heckuva lot he can do about it." But, Higginson reflects, "I think we said at the beginning that maybe this is an impossible job..."

Key Relationships

Within the Department

Reports to: Secretary

Works closely with:

Under Secretary, Economic and Agricultural Affairs
Under Secretary, Political Affairs
Under Secretary, International Security Affairs
Assistant Secretary, Economic and Business Affairs

Outside the Department

Associate Director, International Affairs, White House Office of Science and Technology Policy
Assistant Secretary, International Affairs and Energy Emergencies, Department of Energy
Assistant Administrator, International Activities, Environmental Protection Agency
Associate Administrator, Space Flight, National Aeronautics and Space Administration
Assistant Director, Scientific, Technological, and International Affairs, National Science Foundation
Committees on International Science and Engineering, and Earth and Environmental Sciences, Federal Coordinating Council for Science, Engineering and Technology
Assistant Director, Nonproliferation Policy, U.S. Arms Control and Disarmament Agency
Assistant Administrator, Science and Technology, Agency for International Development
Director, Governmental and Public Affairs, Nuclear Regulatory Commission
Assistant Administrators, National Ocean Service and National Environmental Satellite Data and Information Service, National Oceanic and Atmospheric Administration

Outside the Government

Representatives of public policy and research organizations, scientific associations, academic institutions and professional groups interested in the fields of this position's responsibility; ocean industries and trade associations; relevant officials of other governments and international bodies such as the

Organization for Economic Cooperation and Development, the International
Atomic Energy Agency European Space Agency

Profile of Current Assistant Secretary, OES

Name: E.U. Curtis Bohlen

Assumed Position: 1990

Career Summary: Senior vice president, World Wildlife Fund, 1981-90
                           Vice president, Eastern Environmental Controls Inc., 1979-81
                           Consultant, Committee on Merchant Marine and Fisheries, U.S.
                             House of Representatives, 1977-78
                           Various positions with the department of the interior, 1969-77,
                             including deputy assistant secretary, fish and wildlife and parks
                           Various foreign service positions, department of state, 1955-69,
                             including political analyst for East African affairs, desk officer
                             for Afghanistan affairs, economic officer for the American
                             embassy in Kabul, Afghanistan

Education: Harvard University, BA, 1951

Assistant Secretaries, OES Since 1974*

Administration	Name and Years Served	Present Position
Bush	E.U. Curtis Bohlen 1990 - present	Incumbent
Bush/Reagan	Frederick M. Bernthal 1988 - 1990	Deputy Director National Science Foundation Washington, D.C.
Reagan	John D. Negroponte 1985 - 1987	U.S. Ambassador to Mexico
Reagan	James L. Malone 1981 - 1984	Partner Ernst & Malone Salinas, Cal.
Carter	Thomas R. Pickering 1978 - 1980	U.S. Ambassador to the United Nations
Carter	Patsy Mink 1977	Member, U.S. House of Representatives

Ford	Frederick Irving 1976	Not available
Ford	Dixy Lee Ray 1974 - 1975	Retired Fox Island, Wash.

* Bureau created in 1974 by the Department of State Appropriations Authorization Act of 1973

25

TENNESSEE VALLEY AUTHORITY

CHAIRMAN

Level III - Presidential Appointment with Senate Confirmation

Major Responsibilities

- Chair the board of a government-owned corporation with commercial sales of $5.5 billion, providing electric power to customers in seven states of the Tennessee River system and its major tributaries, and maintaining flood control and navigability of the main channel of the Tennessee River.

- Manage TVA programs of resource improvement and economic growth in that area that include fish and wildlife, forestry, watershed protection, research on fertilizers, and the promotion of tourism, industrial development and waste management.

- Represent the TVA to the Congress as necessary, especially with respect to the agency's federally-funded operations.

Necessary Training, Experience, Skills

TVA's present chairman was an automotive executive for 45 years with a bachelor of science degree. His two immediate predecessors were engineers, one of them with a legal background as well. Given the availability of counsel and guidance from engineers and technicians on the TVA senior staff, none of the three thinks this position requires scientific/technical training or background. One does acknowledge that his own training helped in "understanding the language," and it's clear that this background aids in the right choice of subordinates. Another emphasizes the policy-making dimension of the job and the broader knowledge that calls for. A close observer of the post thinks the credentials should to some extent vary with the agency's needs of the moment. When one of the big considerations is handling TVA debt, as now, he says, the job needs financial background. When the emphasis is on building or reopening nuclear power plants, the lack of a "full technical understanding" could be a recipe for trouble.

Insight

Its history and structure make the Tennessee Valley Authority a rare bird even among the diverse fraternity of federal and quasi-federal entities to which it belongs (it is a government-owned corporation). Born in 1933 in the first weeks of the Roosevelt Administration, TVA grew into something of a legend in its own time, and beyond. It promised a new era for the flood-ridden rural poor of the Tennessee River system, and symbolized the bold slashes at depression's stranglehold that were to follow on a national scale. And by almost any measure, it worked. Dam construction and other engineering began to tame the rivers, the Tennessee became navigable for 650 miles, and economic benefits, including new fertilizers developed by TVA, flowed. The agency drew wide acclaim, and a generation of school textbooks revered it as a model of benevolent government's good works.

But what had started as a controversial experiment in flood control, river navigation and economic development gave birth at the same time to another dimension--the generation of electric power. Over the years TVA acquired wholesale and retail power customers, among them municipal systems, cooperatives and investor-owned utilities, in seven states. Since 1959, its power program--coal-fired, hydroelectric and nuclear--has been financially self-supporting. Its electric power business is the biggest in the United States and one of the largest in the world. Among the Bonneville and other U.S. federal power administrations, TVA is also the biggest "federal utility," and just about unique because of its other responsibilities.

There are also problems. The TVA system serves 160 electric power distributors and 45 individual industries from a network of 33 hydroelectric plants, 11 coal-burning facilities and four nuclear reactors. It entered the nuclear power ranks almost 25 years ago, ordering 17 reactors between 1968 and 1974. "That turned out to be a bigger bite than anybody could chew," says Charles H. Dean Jr., who chaired TVA from 1981 to 1987 and stayed on as a member of its three-man board until 1990. His words probably understate the case. When the oil embargo of the mid-1970s hit, it drove up the price of coal. That in turn forced TVA to raise the rates it charged for electric power, a pattern that continued through the decade. Interest rates also went up. By that time, TVA had borrowed "billions," according to Dean, to build its nuclear reactors. When he took over as chairman, construction of the nuclear plants was behind schedule and far over budget. Power had meanwhile become costly enough that consumers had learned to do with less of it, and demand was thus less than earlier projections.

So TVA canceled almost half of its reactors--four in 1982, four more in 1984, at a cost of $4.6 billion. It laid off 20,000 people. Even so, the agency had nine reactors left, operating or under construction, and in 1984, five were operating. Then, as Dean puts it, "all hell broke loose. We were getting into a lot of problems; all the regulations were not being followed and we were losing top managers because of inadequate pay." TVA shut down all reactor plants. "So we had and still have about $14 billion borrowed and sunk into reactors, and only two were running as of 1990."

Yet today the reactor operating situation looks more hopeful. TVA's management of its reactors once earned a reprimand from the federal Nuclear Regulatory Commission and criticism from elsewhere in the industry on the grounds of safety. By contrast, the two-reactor Sequoyah complex--shut down for three years in the 1980s--ranked second in the United States and eighth in the world for safety and production level in 1989. Marvin Runyon, TVA chairman since 1988, plans to have nine reactors operating by 1999. TVA is also thinking about power needs into the 21st century and whether they should be met with further nuclear reactors. Runyon personally leans in that direction and favors a national energy policy "that will help people come to that conclusion." He notes that provisions of the strengthened Clean Air Act could ultimately make the use of coal for power generation more expensive than nuclear reactors. This country, he says, "must get our nuclear house in order to the point where plants can be built and licensed in as little as five years, as they do in France and Japan. When you take 17 years to get a nuclear plant started, the cost of money is tremendous."

Only three nuclear power facilities are currently under construction in this country, and no new plant has been ordered since 1978. Will TVA be the first to break the pattern? There are people who think so, according to Barry Worthington, executive director of the U.S. Energy Association, "partly because of their strong nuclear history. I guess 20-25 percent of their capacity is now nuclear. There are utilities who have more reactors percentage-wise, but few have TVA's overall nuclear capacity." He thinks TVA might be first almost by default: "Not so much a conscious decision to do it as because no one else would be willing to. If the CEO of an investor-owned utility decided to step up and order a new reactor, his board would probably commit him to an institution. It takes a lot to make that decision." While TVA "won't necessarily set the agenda" for the rest of the industry, Worthington says, "they'll be looked to. Whatever TVA does, you can be sure others are going to be paying attention to it."

In answering the question of what kinds of new plants it might want to build, TVA and every other electric utility must stare down an unknown that could sabotage whatever it decides. "No one knows what the future demand for electricity will be," Worthington warns. "Are we going to plod along at a two percent annual growth, as we are now, or go to a higher or lower curve? We're betting a lot on expectations of two percent; if it goes above that, we have some really serious problems in this country. And TVA is as good an example of that as any." He says TVA has adequate generating capacity to the year 2000 to meet a 2.5 percent annual growth in demand. If it escalates to three percent or a bit higher, "which is very possible," the agency would face a much more urgent decision. Further, he points out, it is increasingly difficult to add hydroelectric facilities or--because of environmental legislation--to build a coal plant. Yet TVA is such a large system that, if it adds capacity, it would have to build plants at the thousand-megawatt level. "Plants that size have to be either coal or nuclear, and those options are tough. The other option is to be a bit bolder and wait for developing technologies. At the top, the need for scientific and technical competence is going to increase."

Not surprisingly, questions of plant capacity and consumer demand are inextricably entwined with those of costs, finance, debt and competition. Rates play a significant role. "Power rates in the Tennessee Valley had gone up by 10.4 percent a year," Runyon says, and had reached the point where TVA was no longer competitive with surrounding utilities. "What that means is those utilities could take our customers. With the debt structure and facilities we have in place, overhead costs and loss of revenues, rates would just go up more. A death spiral. We got in and started figuring how to cut costs." Early in Runyon's tenure, the TVA board set the objective not to raise its rates for three years. Later, that commitment was extended for another year. Sales of electricity finance operation of the power side of TVA, since "we have to charge the lowest feasible rates consistent with our costs," Runyon says. Accordingly, by 1990, TVA had among other moves cut 11,000 of its work force, mainly on the power side. It also reduced overhead costs by 30 percent across all of its operations. By the end of fiscal 1991, accumulated cost savings were expected to total about $1.7 billion. In addition to the debt incurred on reactor orders, TVA has since 1959 been repaying about $100 million a year to the federal government for dams and plants built up to then. Until 1959 the power program was federally financed, but it had done well enough at that point that the Congress stopped funding it and required TVA to repay the federal investment. It is still doing so.

The agency's non-power, resource development side continues to be run with appropriated funds. The fiscal 1992 level was $119 million; $135 million was requested for 1992. TVA's board approves both the power and appropriated budgets; the appropriated side goes through the regular process of defense at the Office of Management and Budget and presentation and defense on the Hill. The chairman thus encounters the authorization and appropriations committees of both houses.

If flood control and river navigation are mostly achieved, TVA's assignment to improve the quality of life in its region is "a very ongoing responsibility," Runyon emphasizes. Damming water and holding it in reservoirs requires careful monitoring for environmental impact in such areas as oxygen content of the water and the levels at which reservoirs are held. And reservoirs have become "a source of income for the people around them--they build businesses and take advantage of the fact that the water's there." The reservoirs have also spawned and helped nourish tourism. TVA's research center at Muscle Shoals, Runyon says, developed 75 percent of the technology used in fertilizers around the world today. "One of our goals is to address environmental concerns associated with fertilizer use," he continues. "Fertilizers migrate from land to water. We're working to reduce fertilizer runoff and preserve the quality of groundwater."

The three directors of TVA's board, appointed by the president, operate as a collective chief executive officer. No special powers accrue to the chairman, who can be outvoted by the other two directors. But he is the agency's chief executive officer, literally involved, Worthington says, "in setting policy and directing operations, not on a daily basis but in terms of setting the focus." Directors serve nine-year terms that do not run concurrently; a new director is appointed every three years and, says Dean, members of the Congress from TVA's regions are usually in on the recommendations. The president selects the chairman, normally from among sitting directors, and can change that choice at any point. The Hill can remove a director by majority vote of both houses. Split decisions by the board must be by two out of three, but in practice Runyon recalls only unanimous votes. All meetings of the board, headquartered in Knoxville, Tennessee, are public.

Most of TVA's work with such executive branch bodies as the Environmental Protection Agency and the department of energy takes place at the staff, rather than the board, level. An exception is the Nuclear Regulatory Commission. Runyon says he tries to visit its members every six months, one at a time, "to discuss things in general, what we're doing, what our plans are." He travels constantly in the region TVA serves.

Twenty-six thousand people work for TVA, many of them engineers and scientists in a number of disciplines. The legislation that established the agency keeps directors' salaries just below what Congressmen earn, and the TVA act forbids any staff member from earning more than a director. That makes it hard to keep competent younger engineers, including those with management ambitions. The pay cap has resisted attempts to lift it, and has led some to joke that TVA's brain drain shows the agency is paying the going price for nuclear reactors but cannot afford the price of the people to run them. Runyon acknowledges the pay cap's impact, but points out TVA's ability to compensate to some degree with bonuses and retirement benefits. The recent congressional decision to raise House of Representatives and federal executive salaries has eased the problem to some degree. When Dean had the job, TVA hired a retired Navy admiral and other managers on contract to fix its nuclear programs because it could pay contract personnel more than the pay cap otherwise permitted. Though TVA took criticism for the $360,000 salary the admiral earned, the comparable job at a private-sector utility reportedly paid half a million. Runyon judges his scientific and technical staff adequately trained and qualified for their work. Dean adds that he "knew and depended on top executives at TVA to tell me what was going on, and I don't think they ever deliberately buried anything--but I don't think they always knew what was going on." That was one reason "we got in big trouble with our nuclear program and had to bring in so many outsiders."

Dissenting views exist about the direction and future of TVA. For example, S. David Freeman, chairman in 1979-80, feels it has lost its way. "It's sad that the investor-owned companies are ahead of TVA in the very initiatives that we were ahead on," he says. He thinks the agency is "letting the momentum of the religion of nuclear power" dominate, and doesn't feel there is "any rational basis for the federal government continuing to own and subsidize it unless it's helping to solve national problems." TVA should be an innovative influence, "and it's not. It's a wonderful example of what happens when the original mission of an agency is accomplished and the ongoing mission is not quite as dramatic. This need not be the case." In the late 1970s and early 1980s, he believes, "the problems we were trying to solve were just as important. Reconciling electric power production and air pollution is one of the central problems the country faces, and TVA was making a contribution."

Worthington finds TVA's nature "interesting and unique." While it operates as a business, he says, "it also has a whole other array of explicit and implied obligations that in today's culture it can't avoid." By these he means the external world, human rights, employment practices-- "all the environmental and social attributes which other organizations are also responsible for." Plus, he says, the fact that it provides service in so many different jurisdictions and must attune to several levels of political authority: governors, members of the Congress and the administration. "And because TVA is unique, I think they feel it a bit more."

Worthington predicts a recurrence of the question whether TVA should be privatized. "It's not high on the agenda today. But I think the pressure (that already exists from those who generally favor privatization) is going to become interesting." Much of the world, he asserts, is privatizing its power industries, and he cites Eastern Europe, Mexico and "much of South America" as examples. He believes the trend will grow. "Five or ten years from now, if you're seeing privatized systems even in the Soviet Union, the pressure will become enormous and the question will be, 'Why are we still doing it this way?'" In addition to crucial decisions on what kind of power plants to add to the system, "if you look a decade down the road, privatization is going to be the second big issue."

Key Relationships

Within the Agency

Reports to: The President

Works closely with:

Other TVA directors
Executive vice president and chief operating officer
Senior vice president and chief financial officer
Vice president and general counsel
Senior executive officer

Outside the Department

Chairman and commissioners, Nuclear Regulatory Commission

Outside the Government

Institute of Nuclear Power Operations; heads of TVA customer utility companies; electric power consumer organizations; energy and regulatory officials of states served by TVA; Electric Power Research Institute, Edison Electric Institute, U.S. Energy Association

Profile of Current Chairman, TVA

Name: Marvin T. Runyon

Assumed Position: 1988

Career Summary: President and CEO, Nissan Motor Manufacturing Corporation,
USA, 1980-88
Various positions with Ford Motor Company, 1943-80, including
vice president, body and assembly operations

Education: Texas A&M University, BS, 1948

Chairmen, TVA Since 1969

Administration	Name and Years Served	Present Position
Bush, Reagan	Marvin T. Runyon 1988 - present	Incumbent
Reagan	Charles H. Dean Jr. 1981 - 1987	Department of Nuclear Engineering University of Tennessee Knoxville, Tenn.
Carter	S. David Freeman 1979 - 1980	General Manager Municipal Utility District Sacramento, Cal.
Ford, Nixon, Johnson, Kennedy	Aubrey J. Wagner 1961 - 1977	Retired Knoxville, Tenn.

26

DEPARTMENT OF TRANSPORTATION

ADMINISTRATOR
FEDERAL AVIATION ADMINISTRATION

Level II - Presidential Appointment with Senate Confirmation

Major Responsibilities

- Direct the activities of the Federal Aviation Administration (FAA). Provide for and regulate the safe use of navigable U.S. airspace by civilian and military aircraft through operation of the nationwide air traffic control system. Oversee the issuance and enforcement of safety and performance rules governing the manufacture, upkeep and operation of aircraft using the system. Set and apply minimum standards for the rating and certification of aircraft and of air traffic control and airport personnel.

- Ensure adequate and effective research, development, design, procurement and testing of equipment, and the training of personnel, in support of these requirements. Allocate resources for airport and air route development. Revise and develop techniques to reduce adverse environmental impacts of U.S. aviation.

- Speak for U.S. aviation policy to the American public and represent it at the international level in multilateral organizations and with individual counterparts of other governments. Assist other federal agencies combatting the importation of illegal narcotics.

Necessary Training, Experience, Skills

Some combination of technical background and success in managing and motivating a large work force is critical if not indispensable. Most veterans of the job have had substantial exposure to aviation and/or the aviation industry--though they disagree whether it also demands personal experience as a pilot. It is clear, as one veteran of the job expressed it, that the FAA chief must know "how to communicate with the technologists, and be able to work with, understand and give direction to the technology side of this agency's functions." While running an agency of 50,000 employees, managing people and hardware in a technically complex operation, the individual in this position also needs the versatility to handle a high level of congressional and press inquiry, and operate frequently and comfortably in the public spotlight.

Insight

The FAA functions in several interlocking realms. It carries heavy regulatory responsibilities for aircraft in the air, under construction and in maintenance. As an operational agency, it directs an ever-increasing flow of civil and military air traffic all over the country and, to some extent, in foreign countries. As a technical agency, it is a designer, developer, tester and manager of complicated equipment and systems that control routes and navigation in the air and assist the movement of aircraft on the ground. FAA trains the people who operate its traffic control systems and inspect the airplanes, and it certifies their pilots. It calibrates U.S. military air navigation aids overseas (including operations before and during the 1991 Gulf war) and supports efforts to prevent illicit drug traffic at home (most cocaine smuggling occurs on light general-aviation aircraft). It is an important player in aviation security and counterterrorism. The prime theme for just about everything FAA does is safety, a buzzword that stirs the constant attention of the public and the Congress.

Trying to carry out this mandate involves FAA in scores of specific programs and interactions on many levels. These range from manning control towers to maintaining communications networks, from shielding local communities against air traffic noise to allocating grant money for airport improvement. "We don't do a lot of initial research and development," says James B. Busey, FAA administrator since mid-1989. "Our technologists work with the NASA labs and we provide R&D money to them, use their facilities for things like advanced airfoil work, flow dynamics." The ultimate beneficiaries of such work are the commercial aviation industry and other federal departments like Defense. But FAA also runs its own technical research center (in Atlantic City, N.J.). There the efforts of 600 scientists and technicians have given the agency the lead in such areas as explosive detection technology and the design of damage-resistant materials and techniques to protect commercial aircraft. The current FAA budget runs about $8 billion a year, and its trend over the past four years has been up by 12 to 15 percent a year. For fiscal 1992, the agency's budget request is $9.267 billion.

Since the deregulation of U.S. airlines in 1978, commercial air traffic has doubled. Half a billion passengers traveled by commercial air in 1990; Busey expects that figure to double by 2010. "That means more planes, more people, more noise, more use of the air space, more runways," he warns. In turn, that requires continual modernizing of the air traffic control (ATC) system and the prodding of local aviation authorities to improve and extend ground facilities. "Part of my job is to work closely with state aviation directors and make them more active in the evolution of their airports," Busey says. At the same time, "we have to walk that fine line between federalism and states' rights when it comes to the interface of the air space and the airport." The upgrading and growth of an airport is a local community responsibility, he points out. "We don't build airports and we don't run them." But for a plane two inches off the ground--"that's my bag," he says. Another of his responsibilities is to "support and promote aviation" with various audiences--"travelers and companies across the spectrum, from 300,000 general aviation operators to aircraft owners and the business and air taxi and large commercial sectors."

While traffic growth has soared, safety has improved. Langhorne M. Bond, FAA administrator in 1977-81, points out that the annual fatalities figure for air carrier crashes has probably stabilized at 150. "Not small-plane crashes but air carrier crashes, which is the big national preoccupation," he says. "That's something like a quarter of the homicides every year in the District of Columbia." His tenure included the only year--1980--without an air carrier fatality since the 1930s. Yet he recalls being riled, at the end of the year, by the cover of a national news magazine. "It was two air travelers flying strapped only to their seats in the midst of the clouds. The article inside talked about a crisis in air travel, claiming people were more and more afraid of it. It was completely inexplicable in light of all the scientific and statistical evidence." For Bond, the cover piece exemplified what he sees as a serious built-in ordeal for any FAA administrator. "The preoccupation with death in air carrier safety is immense, the Congress and the networks jump all over it. The results in terms of the overall safety record and the progress you might make are routinely disregarded as criteria for success for the agency." He thinks the "strain, the investigations by Congress, the lawsuits and the heavy media criticism" surrounding the air safety issue distract an administrator from other important work. "You can do a job, but in a sense, you can't win this battle," he reflects. "You will never get to the point where the airplanes don't hit the ground at some point."

The late 1980s saw sentiment gaining headway for an FAA independent of the department of transportation (DOT)--in 1988 the congressionally-established Aviation Safety Commission specifically recommended such a move; and alternatively, for breaking the air traffic control system out of the agency. These ideas drew support from some quarters of FAA itself and at certain points legislation was pending in both houses of Congress. Advocacy of it fed partly on the feeling that inexpert department staff were micromanaging FAA's operational responsibilities at the expense of the ATC system's level of safety. Now, Busey thinks opposition to this move has pretty well carried the day, and says the Congress doesn't intend to pursue it. He, for one, prefers it that way, explaining that "I would rather have that cabinet officer helping me fight my battles over in the White House and on the Hill, as a teammate and partner, than fight them myself." He believes in any case that an independent FAA would get more micromanagement from the Congress than it ever received from the department.

Phillip D. Brady, a former DOT general counsel, agrees. He notes that FAA began life as an independent agency and that some of that status still lingers in the attitudes of some long-time staffers. While there continue to be occasional accusations of "micromanagement," he thinks the problem has "cooled down" considerably, balanced by general recognition of the advantages of being part of a cabinet-level department. Bond says, "if you make a list of the things that are troubling the FAA, the independence issue would be pretty far down."

Busey spends an estimated 20-25 percent of his time dealing with the Congress. This rises during budget hearings--what Busey labels as "the slow dance on the killing grounds." FAA's primary oversight panel is the Senate Commerce subcommittee on aviation. "We're constantly testifying on noise, scientific and technical matters, budget, aviation education, you name it," he says. One continual FAA effort is to educate congressional staff in the intricacies of its work "and when possible, the Senators and Congressmen concerned." Not a day passes, he says, without telephone calls from members "concerning some aviation installation in their districts. Everyone's got their own little airport; they all want runway extensions, new taxiways, new navigation systems." FAA is supposed to respond to airport requirements on a priority scale governed by airport use, but "Congress finds a way to micromanage our budget and put in line-item requirements for these installations at their home fields. It's an emotional, highly visible issue because a lot of general aviation operators are major supporters of members." He regards the Congress as "a fact of life." FAA gets "thousands of letters a year from Congress asking about matters concerning constituents. And whenever there's an accident, an incident involving the way employees are treated, the size of the controller work force, Congress is involved."

The number of air traffic controllers, Bond asserts, is an issue FAA often contends with. "There's a myth out there that there aren't enough controllers. In fact, that isn't true. In the ATC discipline, the shortage is in the heavily-used facilities--Chicago, New York." Controllers shun such places in preference to lower-cost, easier-living areas, Bond says; he thinks differential pay will help solve the problem. But the nature of air traffic control itself, he adds, creates other difficulties. The work is well-paid and the fringe benefits unusually good. But the people attracted to it--"all type-A activists"--find it "quite routine and even boring." Their expectations and energy "naturally burst out beyond the routine of what is, after all, shift work." He sees no real solution to this situation, even though controllers work under excellent conditions and the equipment they deal with "gets better each year." Note, however, that the agency's fiscal 1992 budget proposed to add 450 controllers.

Busey points to what he thinks is another misconception about FAA's work. "Some say the skies are too crowded now," he says. "They're not. We just need to sectorize the system continuously to maximize the efficient use of the system." This issue of space has another dimension: "the ground side. How do we improve the capacity of the airports we now have? How do we encourage local communities to build new ones?" Underscoring the enormity of this task is Brady's reminder that despite the deregulation of 1978 and the huge expansion in air traffic, the last major new airport project was completed in 1974 (Dallas-Ft. Worth).

Among other major FAA problems Busey lists, aircraft noise is "a broad, continuing issue." It requires phasing out the older equipment, assisting the development of quieter planes, and then preserving their economic operation until technology provides the next generation of even quieter craft. Meanwhile, FAA spends $150 million a year in grants to communities near airports to assist in protection from the impact of noise. A third difficult issue Brady mentions involves aviation security. "FAA spends a substantial amount of time on it; it's a very high priority and can involve some very sensitive issues," he says. Other governments assert their sovereignty in deciding whether special U.S. security measures affecting them are in fact appropriate for their countries. On the other side of this coin, U.S. carriers argue that they are disadvantaged by having to implement security measures not imposed on their foreign competitors.

Inside FAA itself, Busey views administering the work force as a fourth key problem. In civilian manpower, he says, FAA represents more than 80 percent of the DOT total (and over half its budget). Personnel management demands substantial attention, he explains, because "we, the Social Security Administration and the Internal Revenue Service are the only three operating agencies with predominantly civilian work forces that provide direct customer service on a daily basis." In his view, that puts an extra premium on skill in internal communications, sensitivity to employees' problems, and experience in civil service rules and equal employment opportunity situations.

Concerning the caliber of staff, Bond thinks the level of merit varies from sector to sector within FAA. The agency isn't motivated "by the old spirit that NASA had in its best days," he says. "The aeronautical technical work force is good--solid, though not brilliant. The quality of the product that comes out the door in the way of regulations and surveillance is plenty good." But the air traffic control area is another matter. "The weakest part of the FAA is unquestionably its research and development and the technical management of the ATC system," he states. The agency "does not attract and hold the best people. They aren't coming into the agency."

Like other federal managers, Busey acknowledges "a lot of difficulty" keeping technical employees who can earn far more on the outside. But he detects some easing of this competition as defense contracting shrinks and its job opportunities dry up. He also realizes that "getting young engineers in the door is one thing; it takes years to build a solid body of scientific knowledge" in fields like fracture mechanics or air and fluid dynamics. In the meantime, he says, "we recognize that we can't grow this kind of talent, nor can we hire them from the outside and expect them to become career civil servants." As a partial solution, FAA brings in small numbers of people from the private sector on short-term hire; their salaries are supplemented by the industries from which they come. "As long as you're judicious, the civil service allows you a lot of flexibility," Busey says. In general, he is satisfied with the quality of a work force that he calls "very senior in terms of salary, because in order to keep the force stable, we've been able to get these positions upgraded."

Travel and public affairs activities take 30-35 percent of Busey's time, and the international side of the job is growing. He meets his counterparts in Canada, Britain and France once a year, and is improving relationships with those in Germany and Japan. Contacts "are evolving" with aviation authorities in the Soviet Union and eastern Europe. World aviation will continue growing, he says, and "it's in our interest that their systems of air space management, certification and rule making coincide with ours." He also invests time with U.S. aviation interest groups. Aggressive though they may be, they are "a very important part of the process. If we don't expose them to our thinking and get their ideas, we're liable to make dumb rules that are not enforceable." Under the

Advisory Councils Act, FAA has set up several groups to provide such input.

Busey grants that a company or association belonging to an FAA advisory panel might use that status to enhance its lobbying objectives with the agency. But as part of an advisory panel, he points out, that company will "hear everybody else's concerns and quickly learn that their parochial interest may have an undesirable impact on somebody else. All the rules we make are ultimately a consensus, a compromise, so they impact on everyone equally, if possible. When it's not possible, we just have to draw the line, say this is the way it's gonna be, and take the heat."

Key Relationships

Within the Department

Reports to: Secretary of Transportation

Works closely with:

General Counsel
Assistant Secretary, Policy and International Affairs
Assistant Secretary, Governmental Affairs
Assistant Secretary, Budget and Programs
Assistant Secretary, Administration

Outside the Department

Deputy Secretary of Defense
Director, Defense Research and Engineering, Department of Defense
Director, Federal Bureau of Investigation
Commissioner, U.S. Customs Service
Administrator, Drug Enforcement Administration
Coordinator for Counter-Terrorism, Department of State

Outside the Government

International Air Transport Association, Aerospace Industries Association of America, Aircraft Owners and Pilots Association, General Aviation Manufacturers Association, Airline Pilots Association International, National Association of State Aviation Officials, individual state and local aviation and other officials

Profile of Current Administrator, FAA

Name: James B. Busey IV (Admiral, U.S. Navy, retired)

Assumed Position: 1989

Career Summary: Commander in chief, U.S. naval forces in Europe and commander
in chief, Allied forces in southern Europe, 1987-89
Vice chief of naval operations, 1985-87
Commander, Naval Air Systems Command, 1983-85
Other assignments, U.S. Navy, 1952-83, including Vietnam, 1967-68

Education: Naval Aviation Cadet Program, commissioned, 1954
University of Illinois and Naval Postgraduate School, BA, MA,
management

Administrators, Federal Aviation Administration
Since 1969

Administration	Name and Years Served	Present Position
Bush	James B. Busey 1989 - present	Incumbent
Bush	Robert E. Whittington (Acting) 1989	Retired
Reagan	T. Allan McArtor 1987 - 1988	Senior Vice President Federal Express Corp. Memphis, Tenn.
Reagan	Donald D. Engen 1984 - 1987	President Air Safety Foundation Frederick, Md.
Reagan	J. Lynn Helms 1981 - 1984	President Consultants International Bridgeport, Conn.
Carter	Langhorne M. Bond 1977 - 1981	Of Counsel Santarelli, Smith & Carroccio Washington, D.C.
Ford	John L. McLucas 1975 - 1977	Retired

| Nixon | Alexander P. Butterfield
1973 - 1975 | Chairman and CEO
Armistead & Alexander Inc.
Los Angeles, Cal. |
| Nixon | John H. Shaffer
1969 - 1973 | Not available |

DIRECTOR, TRANSPORTATION SYSTEMS CENTER

Senior Executive Service

Major Responsibilities

- Plan and supervise research activities of the Volpe National Transportation Systems Center (henceforth, TSC), an agency working to advance the performance and help resolve the technical and engineering problems of the national transportation system. Manage the administrative tasks of the agency.

- Develop and carry out research requested by the department of transportation and other elements of the federal community. Maintain close contact with these departments and agencies to identify additional research opportunities of promise, and propose programs in response.

- As part of that effort, monitor national and international transportation issues, developments and trends with implications for federal responsibilities and needs in the transportation field. Carry out programs of technology transfer with the private sector to expedite the introduction of new technology into the national transportation infrastructure.

Necessary Training, Experience, Skills

It takes both technical and management skills to run the TSC. The center director should have science or engineering training at least at the master's degree level, and working research experience in either industry or government. Leadership of this agency has two key components. It requires the ability to administer an agency geographically removed from Washington, in every detail from personnel management to snow removal. More important, the director must keep TSC closely attuned to and ahead of evolving research requirements in the transportation field and see to the continually productive employment of its resources.

Insight

One distinctive characteristic of the TSC is its role as a sort of consulting firm within the federal government, literally earning its living on research contracts with the operating administrations of the department of transportation (DOT) and with other federal agencies. There is an element of free lance in this that has relevance for the kind of leadership TSC needs. "We are really a market-driven organization," says Richard R. John, director of the center since 1989. "Our charter permits us essentially to go out and market our services, both to the department of transportation and to other government agencies." James Costantino, TSC director in 1976-83, likens the organization to "a private business, in that it makes contracts for the kinds of work it will do, what it will deliver and how much it will cost."

Another unusual TSC feature is its lack of a budget of its own. It does not even appear as a line item in the federal budget, John notes. Instead, it is industrially funded by the department of transportation and other federal agencies. Since 1982, its obligational authority has increased by about 20 percent a year; operating resources stand at about $280 million annually. The director is accordingly not subject to the conventional budget cycle exercise with the Office of Management and Budget (OMB) and the Congress. At the same time, says Costantino, TSC's chief, when asked, will testify on the Hill in defense of those parts of "other people's budgets" which fund work performed at TSC.

The agency, John explains further, does appear "as a number of billets" in the DOT budget under the Research and Special Programs Administration of which TSC is a part. When OMB and the Hill look at TSC, he says, "they're primarily concerned with the number of billets we have. I've got no problem attracting people, because of the nature of the work we do" and TSC's location in Cambridge, Massachusetts, amid one of the country's top academic complexes. His main problem has been to get the ceiling governing the number of TSC billets raised, and in 1990 "for the first time OMB was sympathetic to this." John, a career official who has been at TSC since 1970, contrasts that attitude with the 1980s, when a "great interest" in whether the center could be privatized clouded any discussion of staff expansion. "This administration is much more concerned with maintaining a top-flight federal work force and pride in public service careers," he says. "As such, the center is seen as a national resource and a means to introduce new technology into the transportation system."

Still, TSC suffers somewhat "from feeling that it's the lost stepchild that nobody has on his scope," according to Amy K. Dunbar, an informed TSC watcher who is now director of government affairs for the National

Association of Bond Lawyers. A chief reason for that continues to be that "when budget-cutting time comes, people say 'well, you know we've got that facility up there in Cambridge; let's get rid of it.' Or, 'why not sell it off, turn it private? Since it acts like a private sector function, why not make it private?' " But Dunbar thinks "it is important that it stay public because it has achieved that nice mix of being a little more aggressive than a traditional government organization would be." TSC may not have the "protection" that conventional federal agencies enjoy, but that also "makes it more flexible, more responsive, less entrenched."

Capitalizing on those qualities is the key to effectiveness in this job, Dunbar feels. Assuring the continued funding of existing research programs for DOT and others is important. But the director must combine that with "a vision about the place" so as to know "if the research dollars are moving, and where," and to what extent TSC should move with them. That requires "a sense of where government is going, what the Congress is interested in." The director must then "figure out how to play all that back into the particular skills of TSC people" and how they can best fit into the changing mandates of other government organizations. Along those lines, John emphasizes, "what I'm trying to do is make the center much more proactive. We are reacting to existing needs as well as anticipating those in the future."

Precisely what kinds of work does the center do? "The major thrust in transportation these days," John responds, "is to apply information processing, storage and technology transfer to the transportation system. What we're really trying to do is couple the communication and information infrastructure to the transportation infrastructure." Information systems analysis and engineering are probably the chief areas of TSC work. John describes "the big technical issue" as "whether our system is going to remain world class, so that we can send our goods and people around the world as easily as others can send theirs to us. It's the tie-in between transportation and our economic position in the world."

The span of projects at TSC has been very broad. Among them are work on air traffic control and aging aircraft (just under half of the center's current effort supports the Federal Aviation Agency); examining high-speed rail links and the technique of magnetic levitation; locating flaws in rails and ensuring proper rail alignment; assessing transportation logistics for the defense department, especially in the 1991 Persian Gulf war; studying highway safety, vehicle crashworthiness, bomb detection, the operation of airport pass-through gates and the safety of children's car seats; accumulating figures used by North Atlantic air travel operators and ports and seaway managers; and keeping statistics on urban mass transit that provide the basis for DOT grants to cities and states.

"We contract out a lot," John says. "But it's very important to understand that we do the strategic planning and thinking and the program guidance here. We don't contract out the front-end work. When it comes to developing software, we would send that out."

TSC does part of its work on request, for DOT and other agencies, Costantino says. "It might be the outgrowth of legislative or budget hearings that produced the demand for a certain kind of report on something like magnetic levitation. Where is it going? What are the recommendations on what we should be doing?" In other cases, "like all good researchers, those people at TSC can spot things that need doing" and will approach DOT or another potential government agency sponsor with recommendations. "There's a big marketing component to research," he notes. "If you keep your research and your capabilities and your thoughts under a bushel barrel you'll never do anything, nobody will know what you do. They need your thoughts as much as you need their money."

Built in the mid-1960s, the TSC facility functioned until 1970 as an electronics research center for the National Aeronautics and Space Administration. When NASA closed it down, the center became part of DOT mainly through the efforts of former Massachusetts governor and then DOT secretary John Volpe, for whom TSC is named. In the 1980s, it tripled its obligational authority and kept growing. Today its six divisions employ 500 civil service staff, plus about 550 contractor personnel on site and almost that many more in the Cambridge area and elsewhere in the country. Many, perhaps most, of the approximate thousand people under John's direct or indirect supervision work in computer sciences, information processing and civil, mechanical, electrical and aeronautical engineering. "They do amazing systems analysis work," Dunbar says. "And the fact that they're sitting across the street from MIT and down the road from Harvard just makes it a place that can draw really talented people who go back and forth. It's a community that provides a lot of intellectual stimulation." Further, Louis W. Roberts, who directed TSC in 1984-89, recalls sponsoring a series of seminars several times a year as a sort of advisory process. "We invited people prominent in both academia and industry and through that mechanism we maintained and continue to maintain close relationships with what's going on outside."

Concerning the center's relationship with DOT and the rest of Washington, however, does the Cambridge location present a significant advantage or disadvantage? Roberts recalls "being badgered daily" from the capital, but thinks he and his staff also got more work done than would have been the case otherwise. Costantino estimates he and his deputies spent 20 percent of their time in Washington. They would touch bases "with all the key people--we used to call it running the traps--to be sure we were doing what we were supposed to be doing and had the latest information on what was going on." "They do have the ability to come down and communicate," Dunbar says. But "they could get killed if their travel budget was cut severely and they couldn't promote the work they do to the other agencies. If they were cut off in that fashion it would be a problem."

John thinks one of the biggest difficulties DOT and other agencies face is that "there just were not many people hired in the 1980s." The result for TSC is "a big, big gap" between its senior ranks and its more junior staff. As staff members at the leadership level depart, he worries about how to replace them. "The management team at the top needs to be strong" and know how to keep the center going, Dunbar says. "If you have a deadweight at the top, a lot of capable people would go elsewhere." Here again, TSC's key asset is its capacity to move in whatever direction research needs to go. "Instead of being more like the National Institutes of Health, with a specific, directed mission, they have a broad mission and can respond to the changes," Dunbar points out.

The key advice John offers along these lines is to "keep looking out to make sure that you are aware in Washington terms of where the levers are in the department. Make sure these people know the center exists and how helpful it can be. It is not sufficient just to react and do a good job. You have to move out and tell people who you are, what you've done and what you can do for them."

Key Relationships

Within the Department

Reports to: Administrator, Research and Special Programs Administration

Works closely with:

> Secretary of Transportation
> Administrators and deputy administrators of modal transportation agencies within the department
> Director, Research and Technology
> Assistant Secretary, Policy and International Affairs

Outside the Department

> Members, Transportation Research Board, National Academy of Sciences
> Assistant to the President, Science and Technology Policy
> Assistant Secretary of Defense, Production and Logistics
> Transportation and logistics officials of the military services
> Officials of other agencies served by the Transportation Systems Center

474 /THE PRUNE BOOK

Outside the Government

Engineering and science officials of transportation industry firms; scientific
and technical communities of Boston-area academic institutions

Profile of Current Director, Transportation Systems Center

Name: Richard R. John

Assumed Position: 1989

Career Summary: Various positions in the TSC, 1970-89, including leadership of key
programs in urban and intercity transportation; and a major role
in developing TSC capability in automotive research and analysis
Various positions in the AVCO Corporation, 1957-70, including
director, Applied Research Laboratory

Education: Princeton University, BS, 1951; MS, 1952

Directors, Transportation Systems Center Since 1970*

Administration	Name and Years Served	Present Position
Bush	Richard R. John 1990 - present	Incumbent
Bush	Richard R. John (Acting) 1989	Incumbent
Reagan	Louis W. Roberts 1984 - 1989	Retired Wakefield, Mass.
Reagan, Carter	James Costantino 1976 - 1983	Executive Director IVHS America Washington, D.C.
Ford	Robert K. Whitford (A) 1975	Prof. of Transportation Engineering Purdue University West Lafayette, Ind.
Nixon	James C. Elms 1970 - 1974	Retired Newport Beach, Cal.

* The Transportation Systems Center was established in 1970

PART IV

27

COMMITTEE ON COMMERCE, SCIENCE AND TRANSPORTATION U.S. SENATE

CHIEF COUNSEL AND STAFF DIRECTOR

Major Responsibilities

- Coordinate the collective work of the committee staff on legislation and other projects in areas ranging from aviation, advertising and competitiveness to science, space, technology and transportation.

- Provide policy counsel to the chairman on all aspects of the committee's activity, consulting closely on its legislative and oversight objectives. Maintain close consultative contact with the ranking minority member of the committee and with other members. Handle the committee's budget and hearings schedule, and assure the timely reporting to the Senate floor of legislation under committee jurisdiction.

- Build effective working relationships with counterparts on the Committee on Appropriations and other committees of the Senate and House with jurisdiction and interest in these fields.

- Direct the substantive efforts of the professional and clerical staff for the majority side of the committee, and manage it administratively.

Necessary Training, Experience, Skills

While science and technology are recurring elements across the broad range of this committee's work, they are not its major focus. Expertise in these areas is therefore useful but by no means essential. Hiring a technician or scientist, asserts a trade association representative who sees the chief counsel regularly, would be a mistake. The real need is for political, organizational, negotiating and public skills. "Here, the staff is choosing broad policy options to present to committee members, and doing political analysis to see if you have the votes to achieve them," the current occupant of the post says. "You need technical background to select those options, but not so much to make those political cuts."

Insight

"It's important to understand," says Allen Moore, who held this job in 1985-86, that its occupant "deals with all the items and subjects of jurisdiction of the Commerce committee. The science world is a relatively small piece of what the committee looks at, and therefore a relatively small piece of what the chief counsel ends up spending time on."

That's not to say that science and technology issues have not periodically preempted center stage in the committee over recent years. Problems like the blowup of the Challenger space shuttle in 1986 or, today, issues like the future of the overall space program or the federal role in technology development, are good examples. And a few of them represent not momentary bursts of concern but long-range questions that remain in the mainstream of the committee's attention.

Such matters, in the first instance, are mostly the concern of the science, technology and space subcommittee (S&T for short), one of eight which divide up the full committee's extensive domain. The other seven cover aviation, communications, foreign commerce and tourism, consumer affairs, the merchant marine, transportation and ocean policy. Orchestrating the efforts of their staffs in support of the committee's major responsibilities is one of the chief counsel's main tasks.

Thomas J. Donohue, president of the American Trucking Associations and familiar with the committee's work, sees the chief counsel as a sort of broker among a number of constituencies that can conflict sharply. Among them he counts the committee members themselves; their personal and committee staffers; the rigorous framework of the Senate's rules and processes; the administration in power and the executive branch agencies for which the committee has oversight; and the throng of private sector and academic entities with a close interest in what the committee does. With hard work, a good staff, and some discipline, Donohue says, one can handle these elements in "an orderly fashion." When they clash, as happens maybe half a dozen times a session during "closure on important business," the chief counsel becomes "very much a manager, a general, the master of the campaign. So you need somebody who builds good, long-term relationships, who has personal credibility, is very good at negotiations, and knows how to use power in a positive way." A general counsel without those attributes becomes "irrelevant" and "everyone walks around the counsel and makes deals with individual senators, the White House, and all kinds of other people."

To manage the committee's scientific and technical agenda within this environment, in the view of current chief counsel Kevin G. Curtin, "what you're really trying to do is understand what the policy options are. Why is it better to go to a high-speed computing network that connects universities, than to something else?" In the communications and consumer subcommittees, "all we have is lawyers. Because there, you need to do statutory, legal interpretation"--for example, "what does 'reasonableness' or 'effective competition' mean? Those are legal terms with obvious ramifications." In the S&T subcommittee, by comparison, "what you're really trying to do is understand how technology is promoted, what the choices are for the space program, and the like."

S&T consequently has "two PhDs and no lawyers," says Curtin, who has held his position since 1989. These staff members do the day-to-day analysis and "discuss policy options with me before the members get them." At that point, the policy areas are usually broad enough that "I'm not choosing among gigabits; they've already done that." Curtin's task is then to decide whether the options in hand really constitute ways to reach the particular objective in question, and what the trade-offs are--"not unlike any other subcommittee where you're choosing among options," he adds. In the initial stages of this process, subcommittee staffers are apt to see more than Curtin does of executive branch officials whose projects and budgets are at stake. What the agencies are more likely to talk to him about, he says, "are whether the votes are there to pursue an orbiting space platform or whatever the project may be. But you must have technically trained people to do the winnowing and preparatory process along the way, because they have the necessary expertise."

"One thing I learned over the years was how to assemble a good staff," says Ralph B. Everett, chief counsel in 1987-89. He believes the Commerce committee has the broadest jurisdiction of any in the Senate, and "you will not find a chief counsel who will be knowledgeable in each one of those areas." So he installed a "senior counsel system" in which each subcommittee staff was led by an expert in the particular area under its charge.

A major scientific and technical issue for the committee in his day was the intensifying concern about global climate change. Aviation safety and cable television were some of the others. But the major question for the committee in this area was probably the loss of Challenger and "how to put the space program together again." And the space program--more precisely, its future--clearly remains the committee's big issue on the scientific and technical front. It has oversight of the National Aeronautical and Space Administration (NASA), and the space agency's budget is the biggest the committee presides over. So it greeted with unusual interest the 1990 report on NASA's condition and capability by the White House-appointed Advisory Committee on the Future of the U.S. Space Program, led by Martin Marietta chairman and CEO Norman R. Augustine. With the report in hand, Curtin warns, a lot of basic policy decisions lie ahead. "First, how are we going to spend the money on space, and where is it coming from?" He thinks the premise has to be reestablished that space is a national goal and is important to the country. "Then, how will the money be spent? How careful is NASA with the money?" The expendability of launch vehicles and the commercialization and/or privatization of the U.S. space effort are other matters requiring urgent examination, Curtin says. They arise amid increasingly skeptical congressional and other views of the cost and viability of core NASA projects like the Freedom space station and the space-based Earth Observing System.

Other questions and concepts Curtin thinks will occupy his committee's attention in the period ahead are the environment, and "the competitiveness theme that emerges on every single scientific issue." Equally important, and linked to competitiveness, is "this notion of some kind of cooperative government/industry effort on technology--that neither can do it alone, and that we need some closer coordination." In fact, says Moore, while debate continues over how much the federal government should invest in research and development, "the main action at this point is through the tax code." The R&D tax credit--"part of the tax code, but always a temporary part"--is up for renewal, he notes. And he makes the seldom-observed point that "whether it should be extended or made permanent tends to be a larger congressional issue than the pure level of funding." He believes that federal funding of very large, pure research projects too expensive for other sectors of society is legitimate, with government then "looking for ways to share the knowledge" that is gained.

Curtin offers several reasons why science and technology budgets have fared as well as they have in the Commerce committee. First, some member senators have an abiding interest in scientific\technical areas: for example, South Carolina's Hollings in regional technical centers to assist small business, and Tennessee's Gore in global climate change, the Antarctic, and the high-speed computer network (Gore chairs the S&T subcommittee). Curtin thinks the comparatively congenial environment for science results at least partly from "the members' interest that through the lean years has sustained a certain level of funding." Second is the "growing awareness of the international marketplace and the need for America to compete or get further left out." Third, the present administration has shown some support for science and technology.

Although majority and minority members of the committee inevitably take different positions on certain issues, neither Everett nor Moore found a high level of partisanship during their tenures. Party-line votes were relatively few and tended to be, Moore says, "on the rare philosophical or budgetary issue." "Our major executive branch departments were Commerce and Transportation," Everett recalls, "and even under Reagan they did a good job of trying to work closely with the committee and let us know what they were doing. We had a fairly decent relationship." Further, Moore adds, it is "not uncommon for a minority staffer to be the dominant player on a given set of issues." During Republican control of the Senate in the early 1980s, he relates, the committee's leading expert on NASA and space shuttle problems was a Democratic staff member to whom the Republican majority looked for "a lot of the intellectual input." He remained "clearly a force to be reckoned with." Similarly, after the Democrats gained control of the Senate in 1986, a Republican staff member continued to play the main role on oceans and fisheries matters because he worked well with the majority members and staff "and everyone looked to him for the ideas, the consensus-building, and the leadership." It is important, Moore says, to recognize that the key person may or may not be the person who the organization chart says is in charge. "Sometimes a person has been there longer, knows the issues, has developed knowledge of the key players in town, and can be the key person on the staff regardless of who works for the majority or the minority."

With an annual budget of about $2 million, the chief counsel correlates the work of the 75-member committee staff as a whole, and provides substantive and administrative direction to its majority staff component of 50. "As with any committee," Curtin says, "you can attract people to come and do a period of public service. How long they stay is in part a function of their personal situation; salaries are lower than those in the private sector. It honestly is their sense of the excitement of the job and the notion of public service that keeps staff here. This is a unique opportunity to help determine the shape of the issues before the country."

As with other congressional entities the S&T subcommittee, according to Everett, has been able to draw on the services of individuals detailed or borrowed from executive branch departments to work on specific projects for periods of a few months. For outside counsel, the committee has "a cadre of people we call on informally," Curtin says. He can also turn to former staff members. And, of course, there is the expertise of the Congress' own professional agencies--the Office of Technology Assessment, the General Accounting Office and the Congressional Research Service.

To the already-mentioned questions that will engage this committee's science and technology responsibility, Moore would add another: "How much should science spending be subject to pork barrel politics?" The extent to which the Congress designates "winners and losers" in the race for federal funding for science-related research "is a dicey issue that really pits the elite research universities against everybody else," he says. The "everybody else" at one end of this tug of war has more votes than, at the other end, the senators and representatives of the states with the best research schools. In the middle are many legislators "who are concerned that scarce federal dollars ought to go to the very best places and fund the smartest people," but who also "don't want to have to vote against schools in their home districts who might stand to gain something."

The answer, in Moore's view, "is not to spread that money around but to focus it on those areas where we truly have the best and brightest minds. That issue is not going to go away. It will continue to fester, and divide interests in the Congress."

Key Relationships

Within the Committee

Reports to: Chairman

Works closely with:

Ranking minority committee member
Subcommittee chairmen
Other committee members
Minority Chief Counsel and Staff Director
Deputy Staff Director
Senior staff members of subcommittees
General Counsel
Press Secretary

Outside the Committee

In the Congress:

Staff Director, Senate Appropriations Committee
Staff Director, Senate Energy and Natural Resources Committee
Staff Director, Senate Committee on Environment and Public Works

       Staff Director/Chief Counsel, Senate Labor and Human Resources
          Committee
       Congressional Research Service
       Office of Technology Assessment
       General Accounting Office

In the Executive Branch:

       Assistant to the President, Science and Technology Policy
       Associate directors, Office of Management and Budget
       Senior officials of departments and agencies within jurisdiction of the
          committee

Outside the Government

       Representatives of a very broad range of companies, especially multilateral
       and trading firms, in manufacturing, defense, high technology, electronics,
       communications, transportation, and ocean products and fishing; trade
       associations; professional associations, including those in the scientific and
       engineering fields; consumer organizations; education groups

Profile of Current Chief Counsel/Staff Director
Senate Commerce Committee

Name: Kevin G. Curtin

Assumed Position: 1989

Career Summary: Senior counsel, Consumer subcommittee, Senate Committee on
                   Commerce, Science, and Transportation, 1987-89
               Legislative counsel, Senate Committee on Commerce, Science, and
                   Transportation, 1976-87

Education, Training: Fairfield University, BA (cum laude), 1973
               George Washington University, MA, 1977
               Georgetown University, JD, 1982

Chief Counsels/Staff Directors, Senate Commerce Committee
Since 1969

Name and Years Served	Present Position
Kevin G. Curtin 1989 - present	Incumbent

Ralph B. Everett
1987 - 1989

Partner
Paul, Hastings, Janofsky and
  Walker
Washington, D.C.

W. Allen Moore
1985 - 1986
Management Assoc.

President
National Solid Waste

Washington, D.C.

Gerald J. Kovach
1984

Vice President
MCI Telecommunications Corp.
Washington, D.C.

William Diefenderfer*

Wunder, Ryan, Cannon and
1981 - 1983 Thelen
Washington, D.C.

Anne G. Cantrel**
1981 - 1983

Chevy Chase, Md.

Aubrey L. Sarvis
1978 - 1980

Vice President
Bell Atlantic
Washington, D.C.

S. Lynn Sutcliffe
1977

President & CEO
SYCOM Enterprises
Bethesda, Md.

Edward A. Merlis**
1977

Vice President
Air Transport Assoc.
Washington, D.C.

Michael Pertshuk*
1968 - 1976

Codirector
The Advocacy Institute
Washington, D.C.

Frederick J. Lordan**
1969 - 1975

Deceased

* As Chief Counsel
** As Staff Director

28

COMMITTEE ON SCIENCE, SPACE AND TECHNOLOGY U.S. HOUSE OF REPRESENTATIVES

CHIEF OF STAFF

Major Responsibilities

- Oversee and coordinate staff work on the science, technology and space policy agenda of the committee and its six subcommittees. Manage the committee's budget, hearing schedule and other activities.

- Assist the chairman in shaping substantive policy concepts into specific legislative and oversight goals that are consistent with each other and with the interests of the country. Consult closely and continuously with the chairman on the nature, course and schedule of the committee's work. Coordinate these matters also with the ranking minority member, the minority staff director, and other members of the committee and their personal staffs.

- Establish and maintain productive contact with the staff leadership of other congressional committees with similar concerns. Provide substantive and administrative management of the committee's majority staff.

Necessary Training, Experience, Skills

Of the last four chiefs of staff--their combined terms span the last 12 years--two have been physicists, one a computer scientist, one a lawyer. Those we talked to about the position favor, at minimum, some scientific or technical background. One of them thinks the staff leadership of the committee should be equipped with both scientific/technical and legal credentials, whether in the chief of staff alone, or in tandem with the chief counsel. Whatever the case, he says, "real technical expertise about the issues" is a must. Additionally, one of those who has held the job values management experience; the chairman of an academic department or director of a moderately big research program are the examples he gives.

Insight

In early 1991 the start of the 102nd Congress brought a new chairman and a new look to the House Committee on Science, Space and Technology. The essence of these changes is reflected in the words of Radford Byerly Jr., who took over as committee chief of staff at almost the same time. "Chairman Brown," he says (George Brown, D-Cal.), "feels that science and technology should play a really major part in the affairs of the country, and that they haven't been playing that part as effectively as they could have."

What that has meant, besides Byerly's own appointment, is a realigned and leaner committee structure. Its subcommittees were trimmed from seven to six, reshuffled and renamed to clarify identities and jurisdictions, and brought into closer correlation with the committee's major issues. At least two subcommittee chairmen are on record with intentions to exercise more aggressive oversight and investigative responsibility. And chairman Brown has made little secret of his views on the substance of what needs to be done--for example, that government's role in assisting technology development must be far more assertive if the country is to compete around the world.

Stephen Nelson, program director for science, technology and government of the American Association for the Advancement of Science (AAAS), calls Brown "a real pro, a veteran, and an intelligent, thoughtful guy. I think the things he wants to do are really encouraging."

Byerly sees his own job "as helping make that happen"--assisting the chairman in tailoring his vision into precise objectives that advance his goals "and are also doable. They have to be achievable in the congressional arena, though they don't all have to be legislation." A series of hearings, for instance, can provide a "bully pulpit" and illuminate an issue without requiring legislation. "So I get into the policy, the substance of the goals, and how a piece of legislation or other action might achieve them." Then, he says, there is "the business of managing the committee's resources," principally including the staff. Here Byerly is conscious of the need not to get bogged down in particulars, and to "back away and see the forest;" he paraphrases T.S. Eliot's warning about details that come and go and can prevent work on the important big problems that are always present. Chief among other administrative tasks the chief of staff handles are the hearing schedule and the committee budget (about $5 million in fiscal 1991). "We have a limitation on our travel," Byerly says, "but we need to get outside Washington and see things instead of just relying on people coming here with an axe to grind."

Harold P. Hanson, chief of staff in 1980-82 and again in 1984-89, likens the structure of the 51-member committee to a college or university. The dean is the individual at the top, and "the subcommittees are like departments. That's where the real operation goes on, the making of legislation. I used to tell my academic friends that if they could figure out what a dean does, that's what I did as chief of staff."

The House science committee has five main concerns, each reflected in the focus of one of its subcommittees. During 1991, for example, the subcommittee on energy looked closely at the Bush administration's national energy strategy, especially at the balance between renewable energy sources and conservation as against nonrenewable sources like fossil fuels. One problem the subcommittee anticipated finding was the need to shift that balance a bit toward the renewable side.

Global climate change is a principal question for the environment subcommittee. While Byerly praises the administration for "very credible and creditworthy efforts" on the research side of this phenomenon, "we want to examine the bigger picture. Maybe there are things beyond the physical and natural science research--some social science research, for instance--that ought to be looked at." He also suggests the committee's recognition of a possible need for more "scope and balance" in the research effort, since its program relies largely on the space-based remote sensing project known as Earth Observing System (EOS). The environment subpanel also has some responsibility for energy matters, while the space subcommittee (see just below) obviously exerts authority in the environmental area because of EOS. Part of the chief of staff's job is to make the subcommittees work together, against a natural tendency not to. Coordination is necessary to produce a unified full committee position.

Biggest of the subcommittees is the space panel, responsible for the full committee's largest authorization. Its key concern is the future of the civilian space program. Byerly calls the 1990 Augustine Commission recommendations for the National Aeronautical and Space Administration

(NASA) "good common sense." But he wonders whether NASA, beneath the surface of its affirmative responses to the Augustine suggestions, is actually moving, or "doing a slow roll and not really making the recommended changes." The space subcommittee must therefore answer the questions "What's going on?" and "Do we agree with the Augustine recommendations?" One of the Augustine group's ideas was that scientific research and investigation should be NASA's first priority. Though Byerly agrees personally with that, he is not sure the American people do. In his view NASA's real priority from the beginning has been human space flight and that "is what people have responded positively to." He is not sure the response would be as supportive for a science-driven NASA. "On the other hand, some people think the manned space program is really a circus, and that we need to put that behind us and get down to serious business. I'm not sure we're there yet. So it's an issue we have to deal with." Central in such considerations is the earth-orbiting, and controversial, space station scheduled for operation late in the decade. In June 1991, the House Appropriations subcommittee with responsibility for NASA killed all funding for the space station, already authorized by the science committee. Led by Brown's committee, the full House later restored the money--but froze all NASA funding at its 1991 level. At this writing, the Senate had not acted.

Another Augustine suggestion that needs examining, Byerly thinks, is that each of NASA's space centers should become "a center of excellence," specializing in only one area to avoid overlap or duplication. "But there's also such a thing as a wasteful monopoly," he argues. "If only Marshall (space center in Huntsville, Alabama) does rockets, you have only one alternative rocket design coming up through the system and no competition between alternatives." Since competition is basic to U.S. practice, he asks, "doesn't it make sense in the space program?" He speculates whether the problems of the Freedom space station project have their roots partly in the lack of alternatives as it developed. "It was take it or leave it. Maybe we should have a different intellectual structure there--how do we achieve that?"

A new subcommittee on technology and competitiveness emerged from the realignment and redistribution of responsibilities arranged by chairman Brown. It acquired part of the former science, research and technology subcommittee and added the competitiveness dimension. Science now has its own subcommittee. In this separation of functions, Nelson says, "you can see that there is going to be a dual focus that sort of got masked under the single subcommittee before." On the competitiveness theme, Byerly notes the growing emphasis on the technology component, and finds "everyone running around with solutions." But he asks whether these "necessarily align with the real, underlying problems. We have a tendency to see a symptom and match it with a solution, but that may not really fix it. We're going to have to spend a fair amount of time making sure we really understand what we're trying to deal with. Some of these things may be cultural." He believes ideas like those in a recent book by James Fallows--that the United States should renew its reliance on old strengths like diversity and competition--are worth significant consideration.

With the subcommittee on investigations and oversight, the aim is to correct what is seen as insufficient exertion of authority in its areas in the past. It is conducting a series of hearings to bring closer scrutiny to how federal agencies under its charge are following congressional directives and spending their money. But this subcommittee won't be looking for surface symptoms as much as searching for root causes and considering corrective measures. Early candidates for this more stringent inquiry are the Environmental Protection Agency, NASA, the department of energy, and the National Science Foundation (NSF).

With respect to science, Byerly believes the big issue is "the health of the U.S. science establishment." To some degree, this turns on the question of federal support for basic scientific research. In 1987 the Reagan administration set a goal of doubling the budget of the NSF, the principal source of such funding. Progress towards that objective has been slow; the fiscal 1992 NSF request is for $2.722 billion, an increase of 18 percent, but achievement of the five-year goal is now envisioned in 1994. The science subcommittee has meanwhile aimed at reauthorizing the NSF well before expiration of its current term, but also at judging federally-supported basic research partly by its effectiveness in strengthening American competitiveness. These developments are playing out against a lively debate over perceptions that research money is increasingly scarce and complaints that too much federal money is going to "big science" projects like the space station. But prominent scientists, as well as university officials, science writers, and congressional technology and budget experts, challenge those views. And Robert C. Ketcham, science committee chief of staff in 1990-91 and a former committee general counsel, says "these are the times to ask hard questions. Many who are trained in science don't understand that they do not have a God-given right to the federal dollar." For his part, Byerly says "we know that giving them more money is not the answer. That's almost all they're asking for. So again, our job is to go behind that, see what the problem is and how we can fix it in a way that science can be effective in addressing the nation's problems."

What about the attitudes and approaches of committee members themselves on this subject, and on the role and importance of science and technology themselves? "Civilian science and technology policy are not matters that in the main have been in the frontal lobes" of the Congress as a whole, in Ketcham's experience. "They've understood they were important. The space station and some of the more dramatic things have been viewed for their nationalistic mileage and political opportunities to show that the U.S. is technically advanced. But day-to-day decisions on whether to spend money on a new relativistic heavy ion accelerator are not something that has achieved the same level of attention." At the same time, however, Hanson asserts that the science committee, more than any other entity, was responsible in the 1980s for blocking Reagan administration plans "to cut out the department of energy and the education component of the NSF." He says committee members are "basically pro-science," even while differing over issues like big versus little science, or acid rain--which split the committee geographically, not politically.

Within the committee, in Hanson's opinion, science is not especially vulnerable to political considerations. There were Republicans who favored research in a scientific area beyond what their administration was willing to support, for example, and fiscally conservative Democrats asking where the money was coming from. "That was a split on ideological, not political, grounds," he adds, perhaps with some tongue in cheek. Hanson agrees, however, that within the full Congress, science is "about the third or fourth most important thing" when hard choices must be made. It should be noted, even so, that overall funding for science is consistently rising. Compared with the pre-Sputnik days, Hanson says, "it's just fantastic."

Among congressional committees, with their majority and minority staff components, practice varies when it comes to managing them and organizing the committee's work. Within the House science committee, the chief of staff and the minority staff director exert substantive and administrative authority over majority and minority staff, respectively, and coordinate to assure that the work gets done. When he was chief of staff, Ketcham tried to see that the committee staff had a sizeable cadre of scientifically and technically trained individuals. He felt the level had "declined a little," something Byerly also suggests in pointing out that the chairman has called for improvements. "We have a lot of good people-- and one thing we will do is make better use of the people we do have," he says. Hanson calls the professionals who worked for him "outstanding. Not geniuses, but competent and hardworking." With no civil service or tenure to protect them, he notes, congressional staff have to produce. "And they were all trying to show how good they were and how much they could accomplish." As of early 1991, committee staff totaled about 77, of whom 35 were professionals. Most of these have advanced degrees, and there are a handful of engineers. The majority had prior experience in the executive branch or the private sector. Byerly has not encountered problems in retaining staff. "The pay and the work are good. These jobs require considerable political skill as well as the ability to take technical material and synthesize and explain it, understand what it means and why it's relevant to what we're doing." In addition to its own resources, the committee is a prime user of the four congressional support agencies--the Office of Technology Assessment, the General Accounting Office, the Congressional Research Service and the Congressional Budget Office (all profiled elsewhere in this volume).

The AAAS's Nelson has been "very favorably impressed" with committee personnel "from top to bottom." He runs the AAAS Congressional Science and Engineering Fellowship program, an umbrella operation for the various scientific and engineering societies that sponsor individuals to serve in staff positions on the Hill--about 25 each year. Over the years, dozens have become permanent staff in members' offices or on various committees. About 30 of them currently occupy such positions. This provides Nelson with a point of contact and is one reason, he says, for AAAS's good relationships. "It sort of goes both ways: they like to have our fellows, and we like to keep abreast and get the background of what's going on."

Ketcham thinks the work of the science committee has taken on an increasingly international aspect. Even before the changes in Eastern Europe and the Soviet Union, "it was clear that the change in western Europe would make a big difference in the way we do business here--and there," he says. The committee advocated more open arrangements in scientific cooperation and bilateral agreements, and "thought we should be working in cooperation with the Europeans on a space station, for example, rather than dictating to them what piece of the action they could have."

As Ketcham did, Byerly will do some traveling and public speaking "and some quieter, off-the-record speaking" as well. Does he seek outside advice and opinion to assist the committee's work? Far from having to look for it, he says, "it's targeted in on you. But often, it presents a certain point of view." The chairman of the committee wants to establish an advisory group of "wise people" without special interests to advance, "people who would at least try to answer questions for his benefit alone." Byerly has also talked with the White House Office of Science and Technology Policy about having "quasi-regular meetings" between their staffs, and thinks "we'll probably do the same thing with the National Academy of Sciences."

Nelson expects the committee, under Brown, to move more effectively through its decision-making processes and to be more timely in getting legislation onto the House floor and into law. He also believes the panel "will relate in a more constructive fashion with the other key players on the Hill on science issues." In light of evolution in the budget process and "Congress-wide developments over the past decade or two," he thinks the authorization committees "have generally lost a bit of influence over affairs. Mr. Brown's agenda clearly is to reassert whatever degree of authority he can for the committee. That's going to be tricky, and he's probably got the right person in the job to do that."

The chief of staff post, Ketcham says, offers "a precious opportunity to view the broad picture of what is important for U.S. science and technology." Its key task is to provide the chairman with that broader perspective: "for example, why it's important that we legislate about how to do things in the Arctic, and how that compares pro and con with building space-based telescopes."

"It's an interesting job," Byerly reflects, "in that it spans the minutiae of administering this committee, developing a salary structure and getting the right people in the right places, up to thinking about some of the grand issues of where the nation ought to be going in science and technology--or how science and technology can help it achieve other goals."

Key Relationships

Within the Committee

Reports to: Chairman

Works closely with:

Ranking minority committee member
Subcommittee chairmen
Other committee members
Minority staff director
Deputy chief of staff
Staff directors of subcommittees
Chief counsel

Outside the Committee

In the Congress:

Staff director, House Energy and Commerce Committee
Staff director, House Appropriations Committee
Office of Technology Assessment
General Accounting Office
Congressional Research Service
Congressional Budget Office

In the Executive Branch:

Assistant to the President, Science and Technology Policy
Associate Directors, Office of Management and Budget
Senior officials of agencies and departments within the committee's
  jurisdiction
President, National Academy of Sciences
President, National Academy of Engineering
Chairman, National Science Board

Outside the Government

Companies involved in research, development and manufacturing in the
areas of defense, aerospace, and a broad range of high technology and other
science-based activities; academic institutions; policy research groups;
professional scientific and engineering associations; environmental
organizations

Profile of Current Chief of Staff, House Science Committee

Name: Radford Byerly Jr.

Assumed Position: 1991

Career Summary: Director, Center for Space and Geophysics, University of
                    Colorado, 1987-90
                    Staff director, Subcommittee on Space Science and Applications,
                    Committee on Science, Space and Technology, U.S. House of
                    Representatives, 1975-87
                    Physicist, director of air programs, National Bureau of Standards,
                    1969-75

Education: Williams College, BA, 1958; MA, 1960
                    Rice University, PhD, 1967
                    Post-doctoral fellow, Joint Institute for Laboratory Astrophysics,
                    1967-69

Chiefs of Staff, House Science Committee Since 1969

Name and Years Served	Present Position
Radford Byerly Jr. 1991 - present	Incumbent
Robert C. Ketcham 1990 - 1991	Consultant Washington, D.C.

Harold P. Hanson*
1984 - 1990

Department of Physics
University of Florida
Gainesville, Fla.

J. H. Poore*
1983

Department of Computer
Science
University of Tennessee
Knoxville, Tenn.

Harold P. Hanson*
1980 - 1982

Department of Physics
University of Florida
Gainesville, Fla.

Harold A. Gould*
1979

Deceased

Charles A. Mosher*
1978

Deceased

John L. Swigert Jr.**
1973 - 1977

Deceased

Charles F. Ducander**
1969 - 1972

Deceased

* Held position as Executive Director
** Held position under former Committee on Science and Astronautics

29

CONGRESSIONAL
BUDGET OFFICE

ASSISTANT DIRECTOR
NATIONAL SECURITY DIVISION

(This position was selected as representative of other CBO posts at the same level with science and technology involvement, such as the assistant director for natural resources and commerce, responsible for all nondefense science and technology budget analysis.)

Major Responsibilities

- Direct a small staff of economists, statisticians and analysts developing timely, high-quality analysis to the Congress on the budget implications of its decisions in the area of national defense. Place particular emphasis on the balance of the division's analyses, ensuring that they include budget evaluation on all options available on a given question.

- Confer regularly with the senior staff of congressional committees that focus on defense and budget matters and generate the bulk of the National Security Division's work.

- In performance of this work, maintain a substantial range of informal personal and staff consultative relationships with department of defense and other executive branch officials in defense-related and foreign policy positions. Conduct similar contacts with the nongovernment community specialized in defense, budget and related issues.

Necessary Training, Experience, Skills

This position needs, first, a strong analytic background, preferably in economics. It supervises a staff that is mostly oriented to quantitative analysis; budget numbers are their raw material, and budget choices, in the framework of defense objectives, are what this division of the CBO tries to define. A PhD in math is unnecessary, but the job needs someone who is comfortable with figures. Next, the assistant director should understand national security issues and how the defense department and the Congress deal with them--and with each other. Third, technical training and experience in defense research and development is highly desirable. But in the view of one veteran of the job, the work requires "the mind set of the trade-off," something he thinks some scientists and engineers have difficulty with. Lawyers wouldn't do well, either, he adds, but are preferable to scientists because "at least a lawyer would be experienced at making a case for both sides." Be that as it may, the defense budget is what a former occupant calls the "bread and butter" of this post. And as the current tenant puts it, this assistant director has to be "a budget junkie."

Insight

One notable project of the CBO's National Security Division in the last two years concerned the effect on U.S. defense outlays of the virtual collapse of the threat posed by Soviet military power. When the Berlin Wall came down at the end of 1989, underlining dramatic political changes already underway, talk intensified in the United States about the "peace dividend" that would surely result. "Everybody was interested in how far you could cut the defense budget," recalls Robert F. Hale, who has led the division since 1981.

The study his staff undertook on this subject began with some rather "arbitrary" budget-cutting numbers sketched out by the congressional requesters, he says, and "we set out to try to give some examples of what those cuts would lead to." They consulted not only the Pentagon but experts elsewhere, including think tanks of various persuasions. The study embraced an entire range of alternatives in which interest had been expressed, from minimal measures to far-reaching change that seemed reasonable in a five-year period. Within those demarcations, it took up everything from the size of severance pay to which weapons systems might be eliminated.

"We came up with five options," Hale says, "costed them out using some models we have here, and also tried to analyze them in terms of their effects on our capabilities, comparing the forces we would have left to those the Soviets would have after the various treaties." As it does with about half of the 20 or so products it turns out each year (six to eight of them major efforts), the CBO published this one, and testified on it several times. It is one of the broadest studies the division has done. And despite subsequent developments like the Persian Gulf war of 1991 and the political zigs and zags and generally confused leadership picture in Moscow, Hale doesn't think that long-term interest in extensive defense budget cuts has flagged much.

As an example of a more focused analysis, Hale cites his division's study of the defense department's medical care system for military families and retirees; as these beneficiaries increasingly elect the system's private health care option, its costs and deficits have soared. In contrast to the wider distribution of the defense budget analysis, the division sent its report in this instance only to the requesting committee, and might add "half a dozen other staffers who are interested in it," Hale says. In a year, he testifies on average five to eight times in connection with his office's reports.

To casual observers, it may sometimes appear that the CBO's role in life is to gainsay the executive branch's version of what government costs by consistently publishing figures at variance with those issued by the administration. But the important words at the CBO are "choices" and "options." The agency's job, says David S. Chu, assistant director in 1978-80, "was to illuminate choices. The reports were always carefully down the middle." He remembers the joke T-shirt once sold at the CBO. On its front appeared a hand with its thumb up and the words "On the one hand..." On the back of the shirt, the thumb was down, with the words "On the other hand..." "The reports were like that," Chu says. "Sometimes it made for dreadfully dull writing because you had to be absolutely fair. We would work hard, bend over backward, to make sure that options which we thought were weak, but which had important constituencies, got a fair hearing. We would struggle with the weaker ones to try to strengthen them in order to avoid in any way taking a position on the issue."

The agency is supposed to be "nonpartisan," Hale says, "and we try to live up to that." But in his view, that adds to the interest of the job. Where people in the Pentagon must always support whatever decision is adopted after due debate, "we're not constrained to one option. We have the luxury of laying out a wide range of them, and within that range is something each of the analysts can believe in with fervor. I think that makes the job fun. Plus we get to look at a variety of topics that are of major interest in the defense debate, and often of major public interest."

In some of the congressional tasking, however, Chu sees an additional, if sometimes only implied, need--and a corresponding obligation for the CBO. As an example, he recalls a study in his day on the increased "prepositioning" of American military materiel in warehouses in Europe, a measure taken to heighten preparedness and gain time in the event of war. In its report, Chu says, the CBO tried to stress the significance of that decision in committing the United States to a "much bigger and earlier reinforcement of Western Europe by American forces" if an attack came. It was a "major policy decision," he points out. As a result, his division's report went beyond its immediate and nominal assignment of assessing how well the program was meeting its policy goals from a budget standpoint. "It raised the question, even if only implicitly, of what the policy goals were, and if they had changed." Part of what the CBO had really been asked in this case, he believes, "was to elucidate what was going on--to see if perhaps this was more than met the eye in terms of the specific proposal in front of us."

In the formal sense the CBO's work originates in congressional requests by letter, signed by committee chairmen or ranking minority members. But like two of the other three congressional investigative and research agencies, the CBO conducts a dialogue with committee staffs that in fact allows it to put a bee in the congressional bonnet. Indeed, the situation was hardly a case of "letter requests arriving blind," says Chu in describing these interchanges with the committees. He saw it as a mark of "managerial failure" if a letter from a major committee arrived "and we had no idea it was coming." Developing the expertise to respond to requests is not an overnight exercise, he says. "You want to take months, if not years, to build up the necessary data, modeling capabilities, staff and knowledge. So you have to be looking forward, in the best situation, a couple of years down the road to know what issues they're going to be concerned with." If everyone does his job well, that amounts to "a quiet, unofficial planning exercise" well before the formal request for a study arrives.

Asked to compare briefly the CBO and its sister agencies--the General Accounting Office, the Office of Technology Assessment, and the Congressional Research Service--Hale contrasts them in terms of focus. While overlaps exist between all four, he says, the CRS looks "at what the literature says" on a given subject and functions as a summarizer of existing information. The OTA's work concentrates primarily on science and technology issues, Hale points out, while the GAO "tends to be retrospective in its work," seeking to know if a program has worked, and what has happened in it to date. By contrast the CBO, in its preoccupation with the budget, "is almost entirely prospective." Its main role does not lie in telling the Congress that a given program has or has not worked. Rather, it is to show that "if you go ahead with this program, it's going to cost this. If you don't, it'll cost this. Here are your options within that range."

The National Security Division, one of four operational divisions, employs 20 people, including support staff. Professionally, the agency as a whole is heavily weighted toward economists, a third of them at the doctoral level, but Hale's group also includes a PhD chemist and a political scientist. Its members come from military backgrounds, civilian experience in the Pentagon, congressional staffs, think tanks, university public policy institutions and graduate schools. "We did not in general see our role as a training ground for other organizations," Chu says. "We tried to appoint people who were on average relatively experienced." Hale describes the agency as "quantitative in our orientation; we deal with budgets." That's what knits the CBO together, he thinks. His professional staff is "quite stable," averaging about five years in length of service. He enjoys broad independence in hiring and firing, though the director has a hand in the most senior appointments. "But that's more a question of whether an individual will fit into the corporate culture," he adds, "leaving it to me to know whether they're going to be good defense analysts."

Is the training of CBO people adequate for the work the agency performs? "You can always do better, but I think it's a very good staff," says Alice Rivlin, a former director of the CBO who is a senior fellow in economics at the Brookings Institution. For Hale's position itself, she underlines the importance of a "highly qualified and flexible" individual at a time of far-reaching changes in national security concerns.

In the normal routine of the job, Hale reports a good deal of contact for himself and staff with the executive branch of government, "because people here have expertise that's useful." The CBO staff does not, of course, participate in interagency deliberations on the executive side, a role that would in any case be excluded by the rule of careful impartiality on the issues. But "we're sometimes involved as guests or ad hoc members." He also stays in regular, but not frequent, touch with other individuals and organizations that have relevance to his work, such as the National Academy of Sciences and the Council for Economic Development, which asked him to sit in on a defense study. Others he lists are the Brookings Institution, the Center for Naval Analysis, and the Rand Corporation "because they do a lot of analysis that we use." Again, however, there are "no ongoing relationships, aside from the fact that we know the people, largely because we feel the need to be perceived as independent." There is also "a lot of informal contact" with the press. "They are frequently confused by the numbers that are thrown at them and find us helpful sources of information on that. That's true for some of the think tanks as well."

Travel is clearly a part of the assistant director's schedule, as well as for the staff of the division. Hale speaks regularly, and some of those appearances take him out of town, perhaps most often to locales like the

Air Force War Colleges in Alabama or the Naval War College in Rhode Island. He enjoys addressing military audiences and explains further that, since his office "depends on the Pentagon for data, I think I can return that favor and create a good image for ourselves." On staff travel, Chu says one of his policies "was to be sure that people went to see what they were writing about. There is something to be said for the tactile sense of knowing what something looks like. Those who came to the agency from military careers or service in the Pentagon, of course, didn't usually have to go back and look at something again. But for those who had not, we made a point: if you're going to write a report on it, go look at it." It's helpful, Hale agrees, to be able to say "well, I drove it." He tries particularly to get his junior staff out to see the items they are dealing with. And "we like our analysts to mix with people and keep our reputation up."

For the future, it's clear that continuing change in national political climates and international relationships will provide considerable food for thought among defense analysts everywhere, including the budgeteers in this division of the CBO. So will, in the jargon of the trade, the "changed nature of the threat." As the Congress delves further into these riddles it will, Chu thinks, put increasing pressure on the CBO to recommend the right answers. But "it would be a mistake to drop the nonpartisan, down-the-middle approach," he warns. "I think that may be the biggest problem the CBO is going to face."

Key Relationships

Within the CBO

Reports to: Director

Works closely with:

Deputy Director
Other assistant directors
General Counsel

Outside the CBO

Congressional committee staff members, chiefly of the armed services and budget committees and the appropriations subcommittees of the Senate and House of Representatives
Deputy Comptroller, Program and Budget, Office of the Secretary of Defense
Chief budget and financial management officers of the military services

Assistant Comptroller General, National Security and International Affairs,
General Accounting Office
Assistant Director, Energy Materials and International Security, Office of
Technology Assessment
Chief, Foreign Affairs and National Defense Division, Congressional
Research Service
Chief, Science Policy Research Division, CRS

Outside the Government

Research organizations and other groups and individuals, including
journalists, with professional interest in federal budget developments;
academic institutions

Profile of Current Assistant Director
National Security Division

Name: Robert F. Hale

Assumed Position: 1981

Career Summary: Other positions in the National Security Division, CBO, 1975-81,
including deputy assistant director, principal analyst and assistant
analyst
Study director and analyst, Center for Naval Analyses, 1971-75

Education: Stanford University, BS, statistics (with honors), 1968; MS,
operations research, 1969
The George Washington University, MBA, 1976

Assistant Directors, National Security Division Since 1974*

Name and Years Served	Present Position
Robert F. Hale 1981 - present	Incumbent
Davis S. Chu 1978 - 1980	Assistant Secretary Program and Analysis Department of Defense
John E. Koehler 1974 - 1977	Vice President Hughes Aircraft Company Los Angeles, Calif.

* The CBO was established by the Congressional Budget Act of 1974

30

CONGRESSIONAL RESEARCH SERVICE LIBRARY OF CONGRESS

CHIEF, SCIENCE POLICY RESEARCH DIVISION

Major Responsibilities

- Manage the work of the Science Policy Research Division (SPRD) in responding in short periods of time to specific congressional needs for information and analysis in the fields of science and technology. Ensure that division products are accurate and free from bias.

- Stay in regular contact with the staffs of individual members and committees of the Congress. Use these exchanges to develop and improve the division's ability to respond to existing requests and those anticipated for the future, and to initiate unrequested research as judged necessary or useful.

- In support of these responsibilities, follow closely the shaping of science policy by the executive and legislative branches. See that division staff remain attuned to scientific/technological trends and developments around the world and in touch with the national professional science and technology communities.

Necessary Training, Experience, Skills

Views differ a bit on whether scientific or technical training is imperative for this position, or merely valuable. But it's clear that an individual who lacks such background will labor under a severe handicap with repercussions inside and outside the office. That is especially true at a time when the expertise of congressional committee staff in these areas-- and that of some of the members they serve--has sharply risen. Candidates with experience in a "hard" science and in technology development and transfer are deemed preferable to social scientists. It is essential to understand the range of issues and the stakes involved in the development of science policy. In addition, the leader of this division needs to know congressional processes, and be ready to bring a firmly nonpartisan approach to the work.

Insight

The eight topical divisions of the Congressional Research Service (CRS) are essentially quick-response operations. Most informational and analytic work in response to specific requests from the Hill takes the form of short memos or telephone replies. By comparison to its three sister congressional agencies, CRS--an agency within an agency--deals in a much shorter time frame and much more narrowly. Where the Office of Technology Assessment (OTA) produces broad studies taking months and sometimes years, CRS ranges from answers for simple questions to fairly complex reports that require up to three months. Where the OTA and the General Accounting Office perform on-site assessment that normally generates new information, CRS has no field staff and bases its several thousand reports a year largely on research and analysis of information that already exists.

But CRS is a significant influence on the congressional and Washington scenes. And the differences between the congressional agencies, of course, are not accidental. Each agency has its own specialization; CRS's, says Richard Rowberg, the chief of the Science Policy Research Division since 1985, "is to be on call on a day-to-day, week-to-week basis." The work of his division requires not only a base of knowledge in science and technology, but of national policy in those areas as it exists, and of the directions in which it is evolving. "This is the research function which adds to our reference services," Rowberg notes. Before any research product goes to the Congress, the director's office looks at it for accuracy, professionalism and impartiality--considerations in which CRS shares common ground with the other agencies.

Does CRS wait for congressional requests or perform research on its own? "We have the option to do both," Rowberg says. He estimates that 70 percent of the work originates with a committee or individual legislator. The rest of what the SPRD does, it initiates. That includes all of its "issue briefs," continually updated papers of about 15 pages on matters which the division recognizes have broad interest--"topics, like high-temperature superconductors, on which we are sure to get a lot of requests," Rowberg explains. Issues which the division currently addresses form a long list--space, global climate change, technology transfer, biomedical research, AIDS, drugs, U.S. versus Japanese policy on supporting basic research, transportation safety, alcohol fuels, transportation technology, energy conservation, military research and development, and "the whole question of technology policy." Chief among the questions the SPRD expects to be adding over the next two or three years are Eastern Europe's capacity to develop and use information and transportation technology, the proposed U.S. national research and education network, science and math education, and the increasing role of technology in health care.

The division has neither mailing lists nor a press office, and distribution of a new report is rather informal. A requesting member of Congress may wish copies sent to colleagues; other members may ask for it; and the SPRD sends it to still others outside the Congress who it knows are interested, or who request it. If a member wishes that a report not be distributed, it remains confidential for as long as desired.

James M. McCullough, who headed this division from 1979 to 1985, perceives a "major change" over the past five or six years in the kind of work it does. Its primary cause, he thinks, is the development of science policy analysis capability in many other institutions and agencies, including the OTA. "With its resources focused the way they are," he says, "the OTA began to produce the types of studies the SPRD used to do," and could have continued to do with an expansion of its own resources. The SPRD no longer performs the "in-depth, critical analyses of science policy" it turned out before the advent of the OTA's "multi-year, million dollar contract studies," McCullough says. While he notes at least one exception to this--the study of U.S. and Soviet space policy, now extended to China and France--he finds the division's product less comprehensive than it once was. "The one place the division was very strong in was science policy," he recalls. "What I think has happened is that resources in general have expanded within all the agencies. Areas that were once just black holes until the SPRD produced documents on them are now being addressed by so many agencies that the SPRD is no longer as unique in these fields as it used to be." The level of sophistication on the Hill, in terms of staffing by scientists on the science committees, has simply reached a point no one could have foreseen a generation ago, he says, and the SPRD has felt the impact.

Today, in McCullough's view, the division's work is not long-range and anticipatory, but "shorter-term and more reactive." The SPRD has moved back toward what it used to be, "into the provision of what can be classified more accurately as information integration, rather than tertiary analysis leading to research and suggestions." The division continues to look ahead enough to be useful to the Congress in "planning the next appropriations," but not sufficiently far to reach the long-term policy category.

Those we talked to about this job raise a number of operational issues with which the division chief, and in some respects all CRS division chiefs, must contend. One of them is resources. As a single grouping, the SPRD and the other mainly scientific division, Environment and Natural Resources Policy, together draw only about $6.4 million of the annual CRS budget of $51.8 million. The two divisions' professional work force numbers 70 out of a CRS total of some 800. Rowberg speaks of the Congress's "almost unlimited appetite for information," a demand that steadily rises against a budget that has only grown slowly in recent years. In attempting to be responsive to the Congress, there are "some holes it would be nice to fill," he says. The "biggest disappointment" is the inability to do more than descriptive work in some areas. But he adds that more money would not always be the answer. "There are just a lot of things you'd like to do, some of which would take more resources, others of which require using resources you have in a better way." It is most important, he adds, "to be sure you use your resources as well as possible to supply the Congress with the information they are most in need of."

Christopher T. Hill, formerly a senior specialist in science and technology in CRS and now executive director of the Manufacturing Forum of the National Academy of Sciences, reflects on problems he observed on the personnel side of the SPRD chief's administrative responsibilities. The agency, he points out, essentially operates with civil service rules and procedures. "It's a difficult management job in the sense that the chief has a span of control over roughly 40 professionals and seven or eight support people, but almost no rewards or punishments, no incentives he can use to motivate people." Further, while CRS hiring procedures are "remarkably free" of pressure from the Hill because of "extraordinarily formalized and rigid" hiring regulations, Hill thinks those same rules frustrate division chiefs in identifying and recruiting the people they want. "If the chief needs somebody to work in, say, biotechnology and would really like to get a first-class person well trained in that area, it's very difficult to ensure that the recruitment and preliminary selection process will actually yield candidates relevant to the task he needs to get done."

Overlap, real or apparent, between division responsibilities appears to be another source of difficulty. John J. Schanz, who led the SPRD in 1985 and worked for six previous years as a CRS senior specialist, feels the SPRD suffered unduly at that time from a sense that other divisions enjoyed an "absolute right of review." But the nontechnical divisions did not feel similarly restrained when they incorporated scientific matters into their own work. "As a consequence SPRD found itself free to dispense benign, routine information about science and technology to Congress without interservice challenge," he says. "But if any other dimension was present in a report, e.g., legal, economic, foreign affairs, national defense, the other divisions involved would feel that these were their areas and that they should have oversight authority and final approval of the report. It seemed to me that SPRD, instead of being an equal partner in policy analysis, quite often ended up being merely a purveyor of scientific and technical information to be used in other division's reports on important and interesting issues."

There are two other concerns. The first involves a chief's control of the assignments his division takes on. "For the more mainstream kinds of issues," Hill says, it's usually no problem "to find someone (in the Congress) who's interested in a subject" and to stimulate the request for a study. This is an exercise in which the staff can also engage, of course, and "the chief is the victim. He may decide he wants a staff member to work this year on the problems of acid rain. But if that person has arranged with a committee to work on automobile air pollution, the chief cannot reject this assignment, because under CRS rules every request gets a response. A difficult situation," Hill says. Second is the way in which CRS as a whole perceives the SPRD. "As a scientific or technical person, the chief is working for an organization that doesn't understand him," Hill suggests. By its nature, he says, CRS focuses on public administration, economics, law--"the typical things government is involved with and the Congress is concerned with. So the senior management of the organization is always going to have little or no real empathy with what the science policy people do." Hill sees one proof of this in how CRS describes its mission to members of the Congress. "You hear them say 'The economics division does this, foreign affairs does this, and government affairs does this. And then we have the science policy division and they kind of do science.' "

About 60 percent of the SPRD's professional staff have formal scientific training, according to Rowberg. The division has nine PhDs, seven of which are in science or engineering. In the last three or four years, nine or ten staffers have left for better salaries, some at think tanks or public policy organizations, but others "because they have career plans they want to follow and find other good opportunities," he says. "I haven't been able to hire a lot of people because of the budget constraints, only about five people in the five years I've been here." The staff level is down about 20 percent from its ceiling.

"They haven't been able to hire many new staff," adds Hill, "except through the CRS graduate recruit program." But he thinks that program is damaging CRS over the long term. "Basically, it means all the people brought in are right out of school. They may be bright, and this isn't a knock on those people. Good people have been brought in, no question. The fact is that they usually have had little or no prior experience in state or federal government executive agencies, in industry, in environmental organizations or in universities doing research. And they're just green." Keeping up with the field and its developments and its meaning is a "very tough job," Hill says. He likes the way SPRD is currently encouraging its staff to go out on detail to other organizations, go to school, and seek other ways of broadening horizons. But he thinks the division needs many more staff education and travel resources to maintain a leading-edge capability.

Because of congressionally limited travel budgets, "we don't have a lot of money for our own forays outside Washington," Rowberg observes. "So a lot is dependent on invitations paid for by others, or visits by others to us, or people we can see here in town." To some extent, these connections rest with the initiative of SPRD analysts. CRS is, however, successful in drawing experts to workshops and seminars, even though it has limited funds, because the service is well regarded. It has "good book buying and journal subscription budgets." He says his division has "reasonably good contacts" with officials in federal agencies. "We call them often for help and information, we're on their mailing lists, and we attend many of the same meetings."

For Rowberg, working for the Congress "gives you a certain amount of detachment. That's one of the nice things about it. The separation between the two branches is really strong; you can really be on the outside looking in." At the same time, there is the need to maintain good relations with the executive branch and to do it with a high degree of political sensitivity. "But you can be a critic here, and that's part of our role. If you do it well and fairly, you'll get a lot of help, because the agencies have their problems, too."

Key Relationships

Within the Agency

Reports to: Director

Works closely with:

Deputy Director
Chiefs of other CRS divisions, especially the Natural Resources Policy
  Division
Assistant Director, Policy

Outside the Agency

Staff of individual members of the Congress and of congressional committees
Executive branch agencies with science responsibilities
Assistant directors, Office of Technology Assessment
National Academy of Sciences
National Academy of Engineering

Outside the Government

Scientists and technologists in industry and industrial laboratories, the universities, and professional organizations

Profile of Current Chief
Science Policy Research Division, CRS

Name: Richard Rowberg

Assumed Position: 1985

Career Summary: Manager and deputy manager, energy and materials program, Office of Technology Assessment, 1975-85
Technical and economic analyst, Federal Power Commission, 1974-75
Researcher and instructor, University of Texas at Austin, Department of Electrical Engineering, 1969-74

Education: University of California, Los Angeles, BA, physics, 1961; MS, physics, 1963; PhD, physics, 1968

Chiefs, Science Policy Research Division, CRS Since 1969

Name and Years Served	Present Position
Richard Rowberg 1985 - present	Incumbent
John J. Schanz 1985	Retired Fort Collins, Colo.
James M. McCullough 1979 - 1984	Retired Springfield, Va.
Charles S. Sheldon II 1966 - 1979	Deceased

31

GENERAL ACCOUNTING OFFICE U.S. CONGRESS

ASSISTANT COMPTROLLER GENERAL INFORMATION MANAGEMENT AND TECHNOLOGY

Major Responsibilities

- Direct a staff of 335 in evaluating the effectiveness of information management systems used or contemplated by federal departments and agencies. Report to the Congress the conclusions of these analyses, and recommendations based on them, improving legislators' ability to make informed decisions on the modernization of federal automated data processing (ADP) technology.

- Consult closely with Senate and House authorization and appropriations committee members and staff, among other congressional panels, about the extent, direction, and specific targets and objectives of this work.

- Maintain similar relationships with information systems managers and administrative officials of executive branch agencies. Work with the leadership of these organizations in explaining and smoothing the adaptation of personnel and processes to the necessary updating of their information technology.

Necessary Training, Experience, Skills

The ideal educational equipment, says the present occupant of this position, is a technical degree and an MBA. On a practical basis, since that combination is not easy to find, the assistant comptroller general needs a technical background in information management systems and ADP, some knowledge of federal agency structure and operation, and wide contact with people and organizations in the information technology field. An individual without significant previous exposure to such technology might make it in this job, but would require close support from competent and skillful senior technologists. Entrepreneurial talent and innovative skill are important.

Insight

In the mid-1960s, resources like computers and data bases were still foreign to most federal workers. Few agencies had by then gotten far down the path of installing automated information and communications systems. They were on their own when it came to deciding what to buy and how to integrate it into their operations. IBM was the dominant vendor and most ADP procurements were awarded on a noncompetitive basis. Naturally enough, many agencies opposed legislation, ultimately enacted, that brought procurement authority for all federal automated data processing equipment, and oversight of its operation, under one roof.

The law was the Brooks Act of 1965 (Public Law 89-306), and the roof in question was that of the General Services Administration. For some years thereafter, things went smoothly enough. The government procurement arena became much more competitive and cost effective. Federal agencies found it relatively easy to automate exclusively administrative functions like finance and accounting. Government outlays for computerization grew sharply, but there were also savings in time, operating costs and salaries.

A different picture emerged, however, with the bigger, more complicated information systems designed for the management side of government. Clerical and other support staff ran into difficulties trying to double as competent operators of advanced systems. Desk-top terminals were still a decade away, and the big existing computers were an expensive and, as later proved, impractical substitute. General Services Administration oversight was falling short, systems were not working and a lot of money was being wasted.

By 1983, with government's ability to function heavily dependent on its ADP systems, the Congress decided to call in its own evaluator--the General Accounting Office (GAO)--to help solve the problem. To that point, GAO involvement in the situation had been sporadic. But Congressman Jack Brooks, author of the 1965 legislation and then chairman of the House Committee on Government Operations, believed the seriousness of the situation called for establishment of a new unit within the agency. It would consolidate GAO's ADP expertise into a single office. There was considerable support for the idea from others as well. With that impetus, the Information Management and Technology Division--IMTEC for short--came into being.

A parallel and relevant evolution was taking place in the executive branch, also impelled by sentiment on the Hill. This was the establishment by law of the senior information resource management post, a new technical specialty in the federal career service. These officials are among those in each federal agency with whom the head of IMTEC and staff stay in closest touch. For IMTEC sees them as partners in the complex task of enabling the federal establishment to stay even with its information technology needs, in an era when the country is in the middle of a rapid evolution and multiplication of information's uses and formats.

That role is integral to the concept of the division's mission outlined by Ralph V. Carlone, who has led it since 1987. "We look at some very big systems," he says. "Over the years we've issued many reports to the effect that this or that agency isn't ready to go forward with building a multibillion dollar system. You have to ask yourself what impact you're having on government if you have to keep saying they're not ready." The important answer, in his view, is that IMTEC should function in a catalytic consultant role, not merely evaluating but advising, lending expertise laced with encouragement and support. "There's a very fine line between going in and being critical, on one hand, and on the other, getting agencies to change," Carlone argues. To achieve the latter, "you have to be in there, up front, talking to the right people and helping them understand the kind of criteria you're going to be using and the things that are important in successfully building that system."

Warren Reed, IMTEC's first director in 1983-86, divides the problems the division deals with into two groups. Agency-specific issues relate to how individual federal organizations use information technology-- computer systems, for example, or telecommunications networks--and the cost overruns, schedule slippages and other stumbling blocks they run into. Government-wide issues reveal themselves in areas like standardization. "The less of it there was," he says, "the more costs skyrocketed. Many agencies were spending money to do the same thing, developing different components. With standards, a commonality of purpose can be established, and one agency can take responsibility for developing a particular piece of technology to be applied across government."

The projects IMTEC works on also fall into two categories. As Carlone outlines them, "administrative-type operations" like the Social Security Administration and the Internal Revenue Service typically exhibit problems of skill levels, political sensitivities and rapid turnover at the top.

"The key is that no vision has been articulated at an agency level or, if it has, it changes with the tenures of these folks," he says. There is also the "big-brother syndrome"--fear of the implications of computerizing detailed personal information into some vast network of government information systems. In the second category, which includes defense agencies, Carlone cites the example of the North American Air Defense command headquarters. A three-year IMTEC inquiry of its information management systems revealed "a lot of things that technically did not work." His staff compiled a list of 80 technical points to be resolved, "and we are still involved in looking at how they're fixing it."

IMTEC is only eight years old. Are federal agencies in fact sufficiently receptive to the purposes it is supposed to serve? For Reed, the answer is no--but there is headway. He sees IMTEC's main objective as providing a credible method of determining whether "the government is getting the right kind of return on its investment." But this is "a difficult row to hoe--the idea of inserting into the power structure of those hard-core bureaucracies a new element that is foreign to the traditions of most of them. It's a very complex undertaking, a lot of brick walls they're still trying to get through." Part of the problem, he thinks, is that the information resource managers have not yet established firm enough footings within their agencies. "Although they've made much progress," he says, "they need to work with GAO in sensitizing agencies to the 'return on investment' question."

Much of the division's work reflects a high level of congressional interest in information management, either in requests to look at a particular system, or through mandates contained in enacted legislation specifying, for example, that an agency's information systems must pass muster before it can continue operating. The remainder of the workload flows from the division's goal of making more fundamental changes in the government's management of information technology. In all, IMTEC works on about 150 projects a year. One of its biggest recent assignments concerned the composite health care system at the department of defense. It had, says Carlone, "a number of sensitivities." One of these, from a political and ethical standpoint, was that in order to evaluate whether the department should proceed with a particular system, "we found ourselves in a position of knowing who the vendor of that system was going to be, 30 to 60 days before it was to be announced. We were sitting with some very sensitive information."

IMTEC's current annual budget stands at just under $21 million. A little more than 200 of its multidisciplinary staff of evaluators, engineers and computer personnel are headquartered in Washington; another 130 work out of field offices around the country. They have "impressive credentials in both management-related and technical fields," Carlone says. The division provides on-the-job instruction, as well as more formal training through attendance at conferences and participation in seminars. It also supports academic education, running a program in cooperation with George Washington University. In this, IMTEC pays a staff member's costs for seven to eight graduate courses leading to an associate degree in information technology or computer science. If the staff member is encouraged to go further, IMTEC will contribute to three or four additional courses.

Reed remembers that "we were not as successful as I would have liked" in recruiting the best talent off college and university campuses. He ascribes that not so much to salary levels as to what he terms the relative lack of opportunity within the GAO for "doing, versus evaluating the doing of others." He believes the diversity and quality of work in the private sector has more appeal. Carlone reports, however, that the division has done well in entry-level recruiting, and is currently having success at the upper levels as well. "The GAO is the most challenging organization to work for in terms of independence," he says. Some 50-60 percent of staff who leave the agency for other jobs, he adds, end up coming back.

Aside from more or less continuous working-level and informal contact with members of Congress and staff about the work of the division, Carlone occasionally appears in formal testimony. But his five deputies do the bulk of the hearings work within their own areas of specialty. The division's interests are sometimes also represented in testimony by other assistant comptrollers general, or by the comptroller general in addressing a broader subject, such as the savings and loan crisis, in which IMTEC has involvement. Public affairs activity has taken about 20 percent of the time in this job during the last two or three years.

The position involves some foreign travel, for such purposes as responding to the interest of other governments in how the U.S. government handles its own systems and problems. Officials of both developed and developing countries are looking for criteria, methodology, lessons learned and training ideas.

Carlone would like to build a skilled organization which has credibility with the Congress, the exccecutive agencies and the public, and which "doesn't miss a beat when I leave. If I can say we really had an impact on half a dozen agencies, did something to make them better, that to me is challenging." He likes the job because "it isn't black or white, and there is controversy." In working with programs and organizations like the Strategic Defense Initiative or the Federal Aviation Agency, "it's not like some other areas where you sign a report and it just fades away and is not heard of for years. Here, you know you'll have to defend a report. The intellectual thing you experience when you know it's a controversial position is exciting."

An informed congressional source says IMTEC is establishing a name for itself and increasing its influence in the federal automated data processing area. In the last eight years, meanwhile, there have been many lost opportunities, he adds. New "tensions" have developed, for example, between big centralized ADP systems in agencies and the arrival of personal computers on hundreds of individual desks. This offers a good opening for some decisive intervention by the GAO that could help determine future directions for automated data processing in government. In the view of this observer, IMTEC is more necessary than ever, and its director can be a "central, dynamic figure" in the federal ADP arena.

Key Relationships

Within the GAO

Reports to: Comptroller General

Works closely with:

Other Assistant Comptrollers General
General Counsel

Outside the GAO

Congressional committee chairmen, members and staff, especially the
government affairs/operations committees
Senior information resource managers of federal agencies and departments
Office of Technology Assessment
Congressional Budget Office

Outside the Government

Designers and manufacturers of automated data processing systems and equipment; professional data and information processing associations; counterparts in governments of other countries

Profile of Current Assistant Comptroller General Information Management and Technology

Name: Ralph V. Carlone

Assumed Position: 1987

Career Summary: Various positions with GAO, 1964-1987, including associate director, Energy and Minerals Division and deputy director for operations, Information Management and Technology Division

Education: Bloomsburg State College, BS, 1964

Assistant Comptrollers General
Information Management and Technology Since 1983*

Name and Years Served	Present Position
Ralph V. Carlone 1987 - present	Incumbent
Warren Reed 1983 - 1987	Senior Vice President BDM Corporation McLean, Va.

* The Information Management and Technology Division was established in 1983 organization works. The present occupant of this position is a 33-year GAO veteran.

Insight

"A lot of pretty complicated things are put before the Congress for its disposition," says Frank C. Conahan, who has run the Division of National Security and International Affairs since 1981. In the defense area, which gives the division most of its work, that means everything from weapons systems and force structures to foreign military assistance. Much of the subject matter has significant scientific and technical content. In weapons, Conahan explains, "you're talking not only about the envelope of an airplane or the body of a wheeled or tracked vehicle, but about all the avionics, instrumentation and composites that go into these things."

It takes an expert, experienced staff to digest and analyze this kind of information in raw detail and package it in a form that legislators can understand and use. "We do that on a daily basis," Conahan says. He recalls once informing a prominent member of the House Armed Services Committee that the defensive avionics in the B-1 bomber "didn't work." Surprised and irritated, the Congressman asked why. Conahan gave him "a fairly technical explanation." "That's not good enough," the Congressman rejoined, noting that a recent Air Force demonstration had convinced him the B-1 was the best bomber ever built. But, relates Conahan, "we were then able to translate further the plane's very technical deficiencies into a presentation the Congressman could understand."

That is fairly typical of what his division--like other components of the GAO--specializes in: Identifying the areas in which the Congress will be called on for decisions, doing the research and analysis, and providing what we consider objective and unbiased information." That's a mandate considerably enlarged from the GAO's earlier traditional role for the Congress as primarily an accounting agency. The end of the second world war marked the beginning of the change. As the U.S.'s own role in the world expanded and government grew, the GAO became a useful instrument for auditing and evaluating not just finances, but behavior, purpose and viability. The organization's staff diversified as its accountants were joined by economists as well as several kinds of engineers and scientists. In the middle to late 1980s, most of the bachelor degrees of the division's older staff were in accounting and business, reflecting the GAO's former business orientation. The 50 percent of the overall staff who also had master's degrees, however, had increasingly earned them in nonbusiness fields, with emphasis on quantitative and

ASSISTANT COMPTROLLER GENERAL
NATIONAL SECURITY AND INTERNATIONAL AFF

Major Responsibilities

- Plan and direct the audit and evaluation of federal executive
  programs in the areas of defense and foreign policy to a
  Congress in its oversight, authorization and appro
  responsibilities. Transmit the conclusions to the Congress b
  report or testimony.

- Manage the 1,000-strong staff of the Division of Nationa
  and International Affairs in this work. Consult frequ
  extensively with congressional committees and memb
  requests generate most of it.

- In support of these efforts, maintain close contact w
  defense and foreign policy agencies to assess the direct
  programs and their projected needs, and draw on the e
  broad range of other sources. Beyond analyse
  congressional behest, initiate additional lines of i
  potential value toward the same objectives.

Necessary Training, Experience, Skills

Training and experience in accounting, engineering,
business are all excellent backgrounds for heading this divi
must go to the use of the word "background" here, since
in the job pretty clearly needs several other quite specific c
is knowledge of the department of defense, with some
command, control and intelligence functions and still-tar
structure and procedures. Previous exposure to the work
affairs and defense-related federal agencies is a useful
familiarity with the Congress, as well as the political inst
effective relationships and outcomes there. One plac
qualifications, it's worth noting, is the General Account
itself, where one also gains a third and very impo
understanding of the GAO's rather special mandate a

technical skills; the same was true of the 30-odd PhDs on the staff. Since then, almost every new staff member has brought at least a master's degree.

At any one time, the division--with a current annual budget of $34.8 million--has about 350 individual projects underway, most of which will produce some sort of report or testimony to a Congressional committee or individual member, usually with recommendations for improvement. "We slice our area of responsibility up," Conahan says--Air Force issues, Army issues, Navy issues; research, development and acquisition; command, control, communications and intelligence (C3I); space, logistics, manpower and international issues. He describes "a continuing strategic planning process" in which staff days are apportioned among projects in swatches that run anywhere from a handful to a thousand. "That's after an awful lot of contact with an awful lot of the people (in the executive branch) who are administering these programs," he adds. Conahan runs this dialogue at one level, his staff at various others. Among his partners in these exchanges are all three military service secretaries, the assistant secretaries for C3I, "all the acquisition people," and the secretary of defense. He and his staff converse regularly with people in the Congress, seeking to know "where they think they want to be from their point of view in a few years' time."

In laying out the work it will do, the division puts together several kinds of plans--strategic plans designating all issues in a given area needing attention over two to four years; an annual list of all individual projects it will attempt; and plans detailing each of those projects. "We don't do 100 percent of them," Conahan says, "but a fair portion." He decides what he will personally follow up on. What governs his choices? "The stuff that's not routine, the stuff that's sensitive, the stuff that powerful members on the Hill are interested in, the stuff I know is not only sensitive but complicated and tough to do." That's the implementation side. Conahan invests a great deal of time in reporting the results. He "thoroughly reviews" and signs most of the division's reports and sees the texts of all congressional testimony by division staff. When we talked with him, he predicted about 55 pieces of testimony during 1990, a dozen of which he would do himself.

An important factor in understanding the division's workload is knowing where it originates, and why. As recently as six to eight years ago, an estimated 35 percent of the work took place at the direction or request of the Congress, a committee chairman, or an individual senator or representative. Today, according to Conahan, "close to 90 percent of what we do" is congressionally assigned. The remaining work is "self-initiated," and he hopes things will stay that way. Having what he calls this "time to ourselves" permits the division to maintain a base of intelligence and do some necessary "forward thinking." That involves reflecting on future needs and trends, researching them, testing ideas with competent and experienced sources, and performing analysis and evaluation on topics the Congress may need to become expert in--even before it knows it needs to.

A sometimes thin distinction separates work requested by the Congress on its own initiative from work which the GAO has suggested to the Congress that it assign. On another level, some have charged that the GAO encourages one or another private sector or other outside group to lobby the Congress for specific requests to the agency. Others suggest that the agency adjusts its reporting ahead of time to suit or accommodate various congressional viewpoints, that it has become in some ways an extension of congressional staffs. There is no question that the GAO works under continuous pressure. Derek VanderSchaaf, deputy inspector general at the defense department and a former House Appropriations Committee staff member, remembers the gauntlet the GAO sometimes runs on the Hill. "They would get whipsawed when two or more committees wanted different outcomes on the same or very similar issues," he says. "They were putting pressure on the GAO to come up with two differing answers." Further, Conahan says, "defense contractors spend an awful lot of time in this building because they're directly impacted by what we do." The day before he was to testify on a certain aircraft, he recalls, the CEO of the company that manufactures it stopped in to let it be known that the plane was "imperative to our national survival." He cites other stories to the same effect.

Lorraine Carpenter, director for GAO reports analysis in the Office of the Inspector General, department of defense, says it is not so much that the GAO "slants the reports as that the congressional requesters are much more specific in defining what they want them to do." On this point, says Conahan, "what is happening a little bit, and is disturbing to us, is that the nature of the request gets a little more narrow and constituent-oriented." Whatever the definition of constituent--an individual out in the district, an individual firm, a segment of industry-- "we're seeing a lot of that these days, and we have to be very, very careful." He expresses confidence that "we know where we're coming from" in such matters, and explains it this way: "We see things come in here which raise a question that wants a given answer. And if we were to do that job as asked, they would be likely to get that answer. What we need to do, and we spend an awful lot of time doing it, is work with that (requesting) principal and his staff to get that question asked in such a way that we can give a full and objective treatment of whatever that transaction is. And that's tough stuff."

"He's walking a very tough line in that area," Carpenter agrees. "They get some very difficult assignments as well as a lot of specific direction. They have less control over their work. They also are given some really political minefields, for instance the base closure thing." One episode of that problem, as Conahan tells it, took place as the result of a request to the GAO from 16 Congressmen listing about 40 bases on which the agency's evaluation was requested. The Congressmen believed, Conahan says, that in this work, had the GAO performed it, "a large number of those bases would have suggested themselves for closure." All 16 of those who requested the evaluation were members of the same party, and all but one of the bases in question were in districts of members of the other party. The GAO decided not to do the work. "The final decision, signed off by the comptroller general, was that we were not going to do that job." It fell to Conahan to impart this news to the 16. "So I got as many of them as I could in a room and went through the drill with them, explained we can't do this. And in the final analysis, they understood we weren't going to do it."

Recruiting staff presents little problem for this division. In 1989, it had 225 openings and 8,000 applicants. The GAO has a national recruiting program, with people constantly in touch asking what the agency's needs are and trying to help fill them. While the GAO does recruit at various upper levels if it needs a particular expertise, it brings in most staff at the entry level and trains them from there. Staff turnover is moderate; many of those who leave go to the private sector or to the inspector general offices of federal agencies.

Staff value is high because of the knowledge their work has given them. In a typical evaluation of an Air Force project, for example, division staff spend significant time in the program office of the project and have access to the contractor. They look at all of the concept formulation and its evolution, the research and development history, and all the early or mid-stage production. They talk to many levels of Air Force staff involved in the project. "By the time we complete one of these projects," Conahan says, "our people frequently know more about the program than many in the service program office." The GAO also employs the help of a large cadre of outside counselors from the ranks of retired military officers and other sectors.

Among its future tasks, Conahan's division will continue to assist congressional decision making on the restructuring of the U.S. worldwide military posture in the wake of far-reaching political, economic and social changes. "They're going to be doing major work in Europe in terms of drawdowns that have to be done," Carpenter says, and notes that the Congress has requested evaluation of various approaches to former Warsaw Pact nations, of what the future look and work of the North Atlantic Treaty Organization should be, and of the lessons learned in the Persian Gulf war. In a 1990 report addressing changing East-West security and economic relationships, Conahan wrote that "difficult choices must be made that will affect the future of military and civilian personnel, local economies both in the United States and Europe, and the defense industry...new East-West trade opportunities will lead U.S. business to enter these newly liberalized markets. The United States must weigh how it can best advance U.S. economic interests in ways that will also serve its security and political interests."

But as his division continues to dig into these questions, it must also maintain its high level of inquiry into the ever-increasing range and complexity of other congressional concerns in defense and foreign policy-- in an era of unyielding budget austerity. That will remain, down on the ground, a matter of "pulling plans together, dotting i's and crossing t's and deciding on a daily basis which jobs needs to get done," as he describes his routine. "We always have 20 jobs that have to get started tomorrow morning and only staff enough to do ten of them."

Key Relationships

Within the GAO

> Reports to: Comptroller General

> Works closely with:

>> Other Assistant Comptrollers General
>> General Counsel

Outside the GAO

> Chairmen, members and staffs of congressional committees, especially the armed services committees
> Senior officials of federal departments and agencies in the defense and foreign affairs communities, including inspectors general
> Office of Technology Assessment
> Congressional Budget Office
> Congressional Research Service

Outside the Government

> Defense and aerospace manufacturers and trade associations; professional accounting associations; defense, foreign policy, accounting and auditing officials of other governments

Profile, Current Assistant Comptroller General
National Security and International Affairs

Name: Frank C. Conahan

Assumed Position: 1983

Career Summary: Various positions within the GAO, 1958-83, including director,
                     European Branch (1974-76) and director, International Division
                     (1981-83)
                     U.S. Navy, 1956-58
                     Division of Audits, GAO, 1955-56

Education: King's College, BS (accounting), 1955
                     Executive Development Program, University of Michigan Graduate
                     School of Business Administration, 1968
                     Senior seminar in foreign policy, Foreign Service Institute, 1972-73
                     Advanced study program, Brookings Institution, 1978
                     Executive program in national and international security, Kennedy
                     School of Government, Harvard University, 1980

Assistant Comptrollers General
National Security and International Affairs Since 1976

Name and Years Served	Present Position
Frank C. Conahan 1983 - present	Incumbent
Frank C. Conahan* 1981 - 1983	Incumbent
J. Kenneth Fasich* 1976 - 1980	Not available

* Held position as Director, International Division

32

OFFICE OF TECHNOLOGY ASSESSMENT U.S. CONGRESS

DIRECTOR

Major Responsibilities

- Direct the activities of a nonpartisan agency providing the Congress with independent, authoritative, comprehensive analysis of technical and scientific questions involved in the making of national policy.

- Develop the content and objectives of this work through discussion with members of both houses of the Congress in their roles as committee chairmen and members, and as individual legislators, and with senior committee staff.

- Consult also on these matters with the chairman and members of the Technology Assessment Board, the agency's congressional oversight body. Secure board approval for all major projects, and keep it informed about agency operations in general.

- Ensure close staff communication and contact with the agency's expert counseling group, the Technology Assessment Advisory Council, about work in progress and conclusions reached. Develop the broadest possible associations within the national technology and science community on which the office draws extensively for the review of each of its studies.

Necessary Training, Experience, Skills

Beyond training in a scientific or technical discipline, the director of the Office of Technology Assessment (OTA) needs several kinds of experience and skill. Most important among them is probably familiarity with the processes of government, and specifically the political, economic and social environment in which the Congress acquires knowledge, judges issues and, with the executive branch, attempts to set policy. An OTA director should also understand how scientific knowledge becomes technology that can be applied to advance progress and solve problems-- and what kinds of problems technology itself can generate. The job requires some diplomatic aptitude. In short, the OTA chief must be what one former director calls a "professional generalist, more than just a good technologist."

Insight

As OTA director John H. Gibbons outlines it, the idea of OTA took root in the late 1960s when the Congress began to chafe at its lack of proficiency in the quickening world of science and technology. "The executive branch was able to marshal enormous resources and come in with arguments for or against specific projects," he relates. "Congress would hear many experts--and in any debate there was always at least one expert who would take the opposite opinion from some other." Increasingly, legislators felt confused, even overpowered by administration advocacy and by expertise that went beyond their then-existing resources. "They saw themselves on the short end of the stick in analytical capability," Gibbons says.

The Congress was also hearing authoritative criticism, as in studies it had requested of the National Academy of Sciences, that technology assessment of the day was "critically deficient" and "failed to provide early warning." Support on Capitol Hill grew for "institutionalized capabilities for science and technology," recalls Emilio Q. Daddario, OTA's first director (1973-77). Indeed Daddario himself, a Congressman from Connecticut at the time, remembers speaking publicly about the need for the Congress to develop a technology assessment board.

Specifically, continues Gibbons (who has led the OTA since 1979), the Congress knew it had to have experts of its own "not necessarily to tell Congress what to do, but whether there can be a consensus, how you can focus the debate, stipulate some of the things, so you can zero in on the elements that must be adjudicated in the political process. And thus elevate the debate." The eventual product of these perceived requirements was the OTA, born in the Technology Assessment Act of 1972.

Today, of course, the purposes the OTA was originally designed to serve remain valid. Yet the relentless advance of science and technology not only raises specific questions that legislators need to understand and, often, to answer; some of those questions are often important elements of larger national issues that rise to the highest levels of federal decision making. One need look no further than the revolution in the technology of information to see a challenge of major dimensions for national policy. The truth of the old cliche--information is power--has long been reflected in the way industrial and other countries live and handle their affairs. But information technology continues to test the capacity of its users and beneficiaries to rationalize and regulate it. Lawmakers therefore need to know and understand developments in this field and, further, how such developments can affect fundamental tenets of a constitutional, democratic society. It is that kind of need which frames the OTA's true contemporary mission and gives its director national and world prestige in science and technology matters.

"We're charged by the Act not just to kick tires," Gibbons says, "but to consider ramifications of the applications of technology, even in ethical terms." To do this kind of work, the OTA organizes its diverse staff not so much by specialty as around enduring problems like health, national defense or natural resources. That translates into nine program areas, divided equally among three assistant directors; they manage the operating divisions of Energy, Materials, and International Security; Science, Information and Natural Resources; and Health and Life Science (described elsewhere in this volume).

The director reports to the chairman of the Technology Assessment Board (TAB), whose 12 congressional members equally represent both houses of the Congress and both political parties. This group also includes the director, as well as the heads of the Congressional Research Service and the General Accounting Office. The board appoints the director to a renewable term of six years--rare in federal science and technology--exerts general oversight of the OTA, and approves the undertaking of OTA studies costing more than $50,000. But it is the director's intellectual and administrative authority and personal leadership, and the TAB's hands-off attitude, that determine the agency's ultimate impact.

At the expert level, the OTA gets two kinds of outside support. Broad, quality-control perspective and advice come from its ten-member Technology Assessment Advisory Council, a permanent (though revolving) body of leading scientists and technologists appointed by the director from the outside professional community. It meets about four times a year. Second, for specific study projects, the agency goes to considerable lengths to assemble review panels containing specialists in those disciplines a study has embraced, plus all viewpoints on the political, ethical and other kinds of issues it raises. The panels do not approve the resulting reports, but make certain that all data are considered.

The objective in each case is a balanced, fair, comprehensive and meticulous product, for which the full-time staff takes personal responsibility. In part, this practice is a legacy from the agency's early days, when most of the Congressional members of the oversight board had an OTA staff member assigned to them. Ridding the OTA of this partisan environment was "the most important thing I did there," says Russell W. Peterson, OTA director in 1978. His intention to do so had initially run headlong into the objections of two senators on the board; they threatened to cut the OTA budget in half if he persisted. "I told them I'd rather have half the budget and a credible organization than twice the budget and nobody paying any attention to us," he recalls. After a "knock-down, drag-out battle," Peterson says, the board voted 11 to 1 to authorize him "to clean house," and the agency has followed that path ever since.

By statute, committees of the Congress, not individual members, may ask for OTA studies. Requests can, of course, be informally stimulated by the OTA but in fact only a small minority originates by that route. It reflects, in Gibbons' view, the sophistication of congressional committee staffs. "It's increasingly rare," he adds, "that we think there's an area they should be worried about that they aren't already thinking about." The OTA conducts a more or less continuous exchange at the working level with staffs on the Hill. This helps develop "a sense of each other's capabilities, needs and timing," Gibbons says. "And we hope, before any major project is proposed by a committee, that it will have been preceded by a fair amount of dialogue between the senior technical staff of the committee and our own people."

Wherever a request begins, he explains, the OTA has to consider who the other congressional stakeholders are and if bipartisan interest exists. Further, it must "ferret out that interest across both houses, and meld a single research plan that all agree is a reasonable thing for us to be doing. And that's OTA acting as a sort of catalytic mechanism to see if all agree what the problems are." Work then proceeds, and "we may be delivering to six different committees" when it is complete. In connection with OTA studies, legislators often indicate they would like recommendations on what action to take, not just options; these are occasions for reminders by the OTA that this is not its role.

In undertaking a study an OTA division, under the director's supervision, must for its part make some specific determinations. What will the project's parameters and goals be? What are the important questions, and how much ground can be covered with available resources? The available knowledge on the subject must be examined and expert resources ascertained. There is the outside review panel to convene and decisions to be made on portions of the project that will go to outside contractors. And "once we undertake a piece of work," Gibbons notes, "the process is in motion and nothing stops it except my decision about its quality or the board's decision on whether we followed good practice and whether the report is fair."

The timing of a report's release is "somewhat dependent" on the requesting committee, but "they can't stop it." That's why some committees have been reticent about requesting certain studies; they want the knowledge but not necessarily the potential problems of making it public. Except for a small amount of classified work, OTA reports go to all members of the Congress and to the public simultaneously with their delivery to the requesting panel. On the Hill and off, OTA studies find a wide audience and OTA findings frequently make news stories. "The only measure I can give is that I get everything they produce," says Charles N. Kimball, president emeritus of the Midwest Research Institute and a former member of the Technology Assessment Advisory Council. "We've got people on our scientific staff who can't wait to get anything they turn out." Kimball adds that he also has close connections with some teaching hospitals, and "on medical issues, they just gobble it up. I think it's cutting edge."

In a typical year, the OTA responds to requests from 75 to 80 committees and subcommittees. Over time, Gibbons reports, the agency's work has gotten it into "some fire fights." One of the biggest stemmed from its "criticism, over several years and several reports," of the Strategic Defense Initiative, including the view that SDI represented too great a diversion of defense department R&D money into a single area. Another arose from its examination of U.S. manufacturing technologies and competitive stance, and government's role in helping small industries modernize, in moving ideas through the marketplace and into production, and in helping people to train and become more versatile. Among other results, this involved the OTA in the "industrial policy" debate and the role of such government entities as the Defense Advanced Research Projects Agency.

The OTA has to keep a sharp eye both on developments in technology's multifold universes and on their political and public effects. When Gibbons arrived in 1979, for instance, the phenomenon of global climate change had already been a topic of discussion for several years. "People and the Congress were getting more and more interested," he recounts, and wanted the OTA to study "the whole issue of the global atmosphere." That was impossible, the agency decided; "the data weren't there, they were still scientifically too uncertain." It adopted instead a step-by-step approach to the problem--acid rain, then the ozone layer and the stratosphere--continuing to fend off meanwhile requests for a major study. But when the impact of chlorofluorocarbons over the Antarctic emerged, "we knew the models and data were beginning to firm and it was time to come to grips with the issue in terms of public policy implications."

Again, tipped by the "science grapevine" to significant developments in high-temperature superconductors, the OTA informed the appropriate committee "and in six months we were doing a study," Gibbons says. On cold fusion, "I had lots of calls." His advice to the Hill was to "sit back and let science do its job first; see if you're dealing with an artifact or whether it's something actually to worry about." There is also the request which may not itself be appropriate but raises important other issues. A southern senator asked the OTA to look into the potential of tobacco as a food protein. The question was too focused for the OTA. But the agency did have an interest in the overall concept of plant utilization through technology like biological engineering. It performed a study along those lines which took care of the tobacco question, but also, as Gibbons puts it, "enabled us to put a foresight message in front of Congress about the ability to manipulate the properties of plants to mankind's benefit."

The relationship with sister congressional agencies--the General Accounting Office, the Congressional Budget Office and the Congressional Research Service--is close and regular. Each has its own mandate, and there is some useful overlap as well. "I think they reinforce each other very well," Peterson says. He points out, however, that while "all have great utility," the only one, with rare exception, that "really looks at these long-term problems holistically is the OTA." The GAO, for example, might assess the department of energy on how well it handles its programs; the OTA's interest would be in seeing whether those programs make sense in the framework of a national energy strategy. "We cross-notify whenever we take something on," Gibbons says. If two or more agencies are working in the same arena--and that's certain to be the case on important issues--they consult to ensure that their efforts are complementary and that "only an appropriate amount of gray area" exists between them. "That takes a bi-monthly meeting of senior people, an annual luncheon of the four agency heads and a daily communication link."

Currently the OTA has 143 permanent staff positions. Half of the 100 or so professionals on board have engineering, medical or scientific training; the other half come from a variety of other backgrounds that include the political and social sciences, law, economics and ethics. There are 40 support personnel. Gibbons calls the staff "richer in professional background" than any other agency of government. Beyond its in-house resources, the agency is able to bring in a selection of temporary staff--detailed from the other congressional agencies, loaned by the executive branch, brought in on sabbatical or post-doctoral visits, or hired only for the life of a project that might last from a few months to a couple of years. "All this gives us the equivalent of an extra 50 people, all professionals," Gibbons says, "a movement of people and ideas, and the ability to move our expertise up and down, left and right, to match the particular work Congress is seeking."

He sees the agency as a gathering place, too small to do the work itself, and needing all the help it can get. Nearly 1,500 people from the outside assist its efforts every year. It gets "extraordinarily fine critiques" of its papers and profits by "having our papers torn up, especially in the early drafts." OTA staff have come to understand this is a source of strength: "our success literally depends on staying constantly networked outside this institution. We spend a lot of time on the road. The last part of the budget I would cut would be travel, because you can make some awful mistakes by thinking you understand the world outside and not leaving Washington."

Gibbons makes individual hiring decisions only for senior staff. But he expects his deputies to review candidates for other positions thoroughly, and passes on every job offer before it is tendered. "I consider the person, the resume and the salary we want to offer. It's nice to be small enough to be able to do that." The OTA tries to stay as competitive for good staff as possible within the government community, but can't compete with industry or the universities. "So we make this a challenging place to work, where people find excitement in what they're doing and reward in being pretty sure that what they do will at least go before people who can make decisions with it."

He tries to compensate in other ways: "about once a year I close down the place and tell everybody to go home because it's a beautiful winter day or something. I know they'll end up working weekends, and one way to keep them involved and committed is to know this place admires and respects their capabilities." The agency gets many inquiries from leading academic institutions about placement for their graduates. "A pool of promising and capable people is not our problem," Gibbons believes. "The pool is there. We're simply limited by resources. We're eating people here, and I'd rather be growing people."

The OTA annual budget runs about $20 million. Though the Congress for about the last five years has tried to keep the agency level, some ground has been lost. It has tried to offset this by raising productivity. Inevitably, however--and with important consequences for its services and impact--the OTA has had to reduce the number of requests it accepts. "We are being hard-nosed about what kind of work we take on," says Gibbons. "We turn down more and more." He would like to do "a more thorough job than we're doing." While the budget has remained level or decreased slightly, the workload has doubled over five to seven years--"and more and more in extremely tricky areas where you can't afford to make mistakes. I think we're on a ragged edge. But we always try to reoptimize with whatever resources we have." He would like to upgrade OTA capital facilities, such as its computers, to maintain productivity; get a "modest" increase in its level of outside contracting, down to about 20 percent of the agency's work from 30-40 percent previously; and hire seven additional staff.

Despite these circumstances, Peterson thinks the OTA continues to be "a very effective organization" in the products it turns out. The major problem he sees is that "too few members of the Congress pay much attention to the OTA. I believe that's because most members of Congress, like most other decision makers in society, are more concerned with the present than the future. And most OTA studies deal with long-term factors." But Peterson finds other impacts that redress this situation. "Many, many people outside the Congress, and many staff people inside it, do pay attention to OTA. And from them, OTA's message gets back to the Congress." Likewise, "the technical community highly respects OTA and uses its reports, and key people serve on its advisory committees. They then take the message back through other channels" to the Congress and executive branch agencies.

At bottom, Gibbons thinks his agency's true value to the Congress is its ability to give legislators "access to highly specialized national wisdom on issues that constantly force their way onto public agendas." And to do it in a way that the elected representatives can trust, understand the process--so they know where the information is coming from and can apply their own political judgments to it." If democracy is to function, he says, "you've got to provide these kinds of mechanisms" so that elected representatives can "have the power that knowledge gives."

Key Relationships

Within the OTA

Reports to: Chairman, Technology Assessment Board

Works closely with:

Members, Technology Assessment Board
Technology Assessment Advisory Council
Assistant Directors
Chief Counsel

Outside the OTA

Congressional committee chairmen, members, and senior staff
Senior officials of executive branch agencies, especially those with significant
scientific/technological responsibilities

> Comptroller General, General Accounting Office
> Director, Congressional Research Service
> Director, Congressional Budget Office
> National Academy of Sciences
> National Academy of Engineering

Outside the Government

> The national technology, science and social science community in industry, colleges and universities, research institutions, and think tanks; professional societies and associations; corporate officials in the manufacturing, transportation, health care, pharmaceutical, food, energy and communications industries; counterparts of many of these organizations in other countries

Profile of Current Director, Office of Technology Assessment

Name:	John H. Gibbons
Assumed Position:	1979
Career Summary:	Director, Energy, Environment and Resources Center, and professor of physics, University of Tennessee, 1974-79 Director, Office of Energy Conservation, Federal Energy Administration, 1973-74 Director, environmental program, Oak Ridge National Laboratory, 1969-73 Physicist and group leader, nuclear geophysics, Oak Ridge National Laboratory, 1954-69
Education:	Randolph-Macon College, BS, mathematics and chemistry, 1949 Duke University, PhD, physics, 1954 Randolph-Macon College, ScD (honorary), 1977

Directors, Office of Technology Assessment Since 1974*

Name and Years Served	Present Position
John H. Gibbons 1979 - present	Incumbent
Russell Peterson 1978	President Emeritus National Audubon Society New York, N.Y.

OFFICE OF TECHNOLOGY ASSESSMENT /531

Daniel V. DeSimone (Acting)
1977

Consultant
The Innovation Group
Washington, D.C.

Emilio Q. Daddario
1973 - 1977

Attorney
Washington, D.C.

* The Office of Technology Assessment was established by the Congress in 1972 and began operation in 1974

ASSISTANT DIRECTOR
HEALTH AND LIFE SCIENCE

(There are three associate director positions in this agency. Each has equally demanding and challenging responsibilities in different areas of science and technology. That should be kept in mind in reading the profile below, intended among other objectives to characterize the kinds of work, issues and problems common to all three.)

Major Responsibilities

- Direct a multidisciplinary scientific staff of 65-plus in a broad array of studies requested by the Congress on developments and issues in the areas of health and life science. Organize representative, balanced advisory panels of outside experts in these and related fields to guide and support each of these efforts.

- Provide comprehensive, factual reports and fair, impartial statements of legislative options on the matters under study, assisting the Congress to understand their economic/political/social significance and to place them in the wider context of national policy choices.

- Through a high level of personal and staff contact with the professional scientific and health affairs community, ensure that the Division of Health and Life Sciences stays fully abreast of events in its area of specialty.

- Consult with the director of the Office of Technology Assessment (OTA) about the division's work in progress. Develop and manage its budget, and oversee personnel and other administrative matters.

Necessary Training, Experience, Skills

At a given moment, effective performance in this job might call for a background in medicine, training as a policy researcher, experience with lawyers and the law, or exposure to Washington's political proving grounds, primarily the Congress. Of these attributes, the medical credential is just about indispensable, particularly if the division's health program is not itself headed by an MD (the situation in recent years). Since 1983, the division has been led by a physician who had earlier directed the health department of a large state after serving as one of its public health commissioners, taught at two medical schools, occupied a senior post at a leading private cancer center, and worked as a U.S. Navy doctor.

Insight

"The problem," says Dr. Roger C. Herdman, assistant director since 1983, "is that science and technology are enormously important to policy makers of the Congress, and that the Congress is made up largely of people who for the most part don't understand science and technology." Members of the legislature usually don't have educational backgrounds in these fields, and their staffs don't have the time to research them, he explains. Yet they are the targets of all kinds of advocacy for special interests by people who do have the background. "That includes the executive branch, obviously, because any administration has a policy position on the major scientific and technical issues."

To fill this gap and help it to understand the implications of developments in a fast-moving but complex area, the Congress established the Office of Technology Assessment in 1972 (it began operating in early 1974). Writing in 1989 on the subject, Herdman put the purpose of the new agency in a nutshell. The OTA, he wrote, "is asked to evaluate science and technology as they relate to national policy." Or, as he put it to us, the agency "provides the Congress a series of options which are reasonable and from which they can select or ignore, so that they have a foundation on which to base their policy decisions." The OTA's first report to the Congress dealt with the bioequivalence of drugs, and was the product of OTA's then-existing health staff. This early focus on health was to evolve shortly into a formal health division which in 1978 became the core of the current Division of Health and Life Science.

Today the division handles assignments from the Congress in three areas. The health program covers health care, the practice of medicine, health technology, health financing and economics, pharmaceuticals, medical devices, and environmental and occupational health. In a typical recent project, it examined Oregon's experiment with prioritizing or rationing medicaid services, an effort fueled by the state's very tight resources. The second of the division's programs, biological applications, works in what Herdman calls "cutting edge genetics." This means studying and explaining the state of advance of the several technologies created by biological science, their future applications and the ethical considerations they raise. Reproductive biology and human aging are the other chief concerns of this unit. In the third area, food and renewable resources, the division looks into U.S. agriculture, the food industry, replenishable assets like ground water and soil nutrients, and such other matters of congressional interest as the import of plants and animals.

Division studies cover an extensive territory. A 1990 update on some of its current or completed efforts in the health program alone listed nearly 70 papers in 25 areas of inquiry. They ranged from AIDS-related issues (example: "AIDS and Health Insurance") to preventive health services under medicare ("Cholesterol Screening in the Elderly"); from biotechnology ("Transgenic Animals") to adolescent health care ("Indian Adolescent Mental Health"). Other projects singled out by Herdman were an examination of the research and development costs of pharmaceuticals as a factor in their price, a four-year scrutiny of unconventional treatments of cancer, and a four-part neuroscience series that, in part, entailed a study of neural grafts of fetal tissue. That required "a lot of time analyzing the ethical issues," Herdman recalls, "because it gets tied up with abortion."

What lends the products of these investigations a significant extra measure of authority is the OTA's elaborate review procedure, in which the agency vets the reports and conclusions of its own staff with project-specific advisory committees. These panels of outside expertise represent all of the national constituencies of the issues under examination and include specialists from applicable sectors and regions of the country. For example, in a study on the use of animals in research, Herdman says, "you get the animal rights people and the guys that do the LD-50s (toxicity tests) at the chemical companies and you make sure they're all on the same panel." Drafts of a major study can reach as many as 75 individuals for review. The agency believes that going to such lengths is basic to comprehensive, unbiased and accurate analyses.

Avoiding bias, in fact, is a principle embedded in the OTA's structure, at the top. In setting up the agency, the Congress sought to ensure its immunity from political influence and partisanship by establishing an oversight body to which it reports. The Technology Assessment Board embraces 12 members of the Congress, evenly balanced between each house and each political party, plus the nonvoting director of OTA. While it does not run the agency, the board sets policy, appoints the director and approves all projects exceeding $50,000 in cost. Its leadership alternates between Senate and House with each Congress. A second body, the Technology Assessment Advisory Council, advises the OTA and the board. Its ten public members, prominent scientists and technologists in their own right, are appointed by the director; the U.S. Comptroller General and the director of the Congressional Research Service are also members.

But in the agency's early years, nonpartisanship did not prevail within the staff. At that level, the OTA was likened to a congressional committee because everybody on it worked for one of the members of the board. "The real charge at that point was to make it less political, more scientific and objective," and to bring in staff less tied to the board, says Joyce Lashof, who ran the division in 1978-81. It took some effort by the second director of OTA to gain sufficient autonomy--Lashof calls it a "mandate"--to bring in professionals and keep the staff independent of political and partisan influence. That pattern continues to the present.

Strictly speaking, only committees of the Congress can request OTA studies, not individual members. This rule bends in certain circumstances, for instance when several (often influential) members express individual interest that a committee chairman might then formalize in a committee request. As outlined by Herdman, several factors generate congressional requests to OTA. Public views expressed with sufficient strength--on the use of animals in medical research, say--will produce proposed legislation. Committees with jurisdiction or interest in the matter then need to know how the banning of animals in cancer research would affect the costs of the research, the safety of its products, and progress toward better treatment. Or the Congress, planning ahead, must know how well programs like the Indian health service are currently working, or what it would take to move a program like medicare physician compensation towards certain objectives. Or, again, perhaps legislators want to peer into the future and assess the potential of new technologies in diagnosing mutational events in humans caused by occupational hazards or toxic exposure. OTA studies can also originate with the Technology Assessment Board, or with the director of the agency in consultation with the board.

Normally, study requests from the Congress take the form of detailed letters signed by a committee's chairman and ranking minority member. The division's first response is to get a feel for what is really being asked by consulting not only with the originating committee but with others, and with members of both parties and both houses. This dialogue helps, Herdman says, in sorting out the content of a request because "there's a lot more they are interested in than we can possibly do. So we refine it--this is the wrong question, that's the right one, this is what we can do, this is what we can't, this is what we should do."

Next, the division looks at the existing literature on the subject and reviews its inventory of experts to see what resources are available, and to develop the project's scope. It talks with other congressional agencies--the General Accounting Office, the Congressional Research Service and the Congressional Budget Office--to be certain the work won't duplicate their efforts. Then it assembles the review panel of outside advisors; these groups will usually have ten to 20 members and meet three to four times during the life of a study. Back-up help for them is available from the three other congressional agencies, liaison staff from committees on the Hill, and executive branch agencies. Herdman notes that OTA studies benefit significantly from the readiness of these agencies to provide data and invest time in helping investigative efforts.

In the final preparatory step, the division decides what parts of a project will be done by consultants and contractors outside of the OTA staff, and which of these experts are the best choices for the work. Though more than half of each project's budget goes to this work, the OTA staff writes the "vast bulk" of a study report. The OTA provides its reports to the Congress, but also makes them available to just about any other interested individual or group. Further dissemination comes from press conferences by members of Congress, staff testimony at congressional hearings, and staff-written articles based on the original study that appear in a variety of general and scientific publications.

The division's 66 staff members are mostly doctorate-level people, many of them technical--MDs and PhDs, the latter in such fields as molecular biology, ecology, anthropology or health economics--and JDs. Staff members tend to stay; many have served for ten years or more. Lashof found the staff to be "amazingly stable." Much of the staff who were there when Lashof came, as well as those she recruited, are still there. "It's a good work environment," she says. Herdman stresses the importance of the agency's small size. "OTA is about 200 people; it is very cozy, collegial, and in my opinion, has enormously high quality. It has never made a serious mistake. To have all those things, you have to stay smart, fast on your feet and flexible. So we have to stay small."

That's one of the reasons, he continues, why the OTA is not continually pressing for "tons of money." Where it used to spend two-thirds of its money on in-house and contract personnel, the figure has now dropped by about 20 percent. The OTA's three operating divisions (the others are Energy, Materials and International Security; and Science, Information and Natural Resources) share equally in the agency's budget. In 1991, Herdman's annual budget was $4.2 million. Two means exist for supplementing the budget when necessary. On rare occasions, when a congressional committee wants a study badly but resources for it are not available, a division director can ask the committee for them. Second, the OTA can sometimes get help from outside sources like the National Science Foundation, with which it cooperated on certain projects. The help can come either in cash or in the form of staff detailed from another organization.

The division has "an enormous interface" with federal agencies, according to Herdman. His own numerous contacts with executive branch officials take place not so much in that context, however, as because he "gets around" and because of such activities as his membership of a national health forum steering committee with representatives from several agencies and departments. He does not travel much; the rare exceptions have been a few foreign trips with congressional delegations. His staff travels frequently--"they actually go to the company that makes the product, the clinic that does the treatment, the university where it's being researched."

Naturally, the division runs into problems, some beyond the OTA's direct control. Among these are the obstacles it sometimes encounters in trying to do quality work in a timely fashion, says Dr. Philip Lee, director of the Institute for Health Policy Studies at the University of California, San Francisco. The study of drug labeling and promotion in underdeveloped countries is an example. "They couldn't get into Brazil and they couldn't get into Panama," Lee says; attempting to resolve this took months of negotiations that ultimately broke down. On the positive side, "one of the things they've done is pick very, very good people to do background papers. So when they take an area like technology assessment, they comb the country and manage with really limited resources to get very good people to do syntheses for them. They use different approaches to different problems." He thinks "that kind of flexibility"--not having a large bureaucratic organization--gives Herdman "more credibility" and means that "people are very willing to work with him."

Asked about major issues he sees ahead, Herdman points first to energy policy. Here, the OTA has dusted off data on coal, clean coal, oil, gas and nuclear energy that it developed in the past and has suggested to the Congress studies in various areas that would be relevant to an energy policy overhaul. A second area he mentions in this regard is agricultural economics. "We've been trying to help" by easing the impact of chemical fertilizers--"shifting the use of inputs to get good output without poisoning the country." Half of the country's ground water is bad, and getting worse, he says. "Once it's in the ground water, you can't get it back out. There are ways of dealing with that, it doesn't have to be that way."

In addition to matters like these, Lee thinks "the issues around technology and R&D and international competitiveness are going to become more complicated" in the future. The division will also face a challenge, he believes, in looking at the balance between the regulation of prescription drugs by federal agencies like the Food and Drug Administration and the National Institutes of Health. "I think we're under investigating that, and meanwhile we're pushing a lot of costs on to industry which is passing them on to the customer." Among more "politicized" questions with which he thinks the division will continue to be concerned is that of AIDS-infected health professionals.

At a deeper level, what do these concerns add up to? "My group thinks that the risk analysis and risk management the federal government uses is inconsistent and fragmented," Herdman says. "The economic implications of decisions to ban this, ban that are enormous. You make a decision on an environmental toxin that costs a zillion dollars to implement, and at the same time you won't spend what it takes to save a life by screening for breast cancer." He would like to see fewer contradictory actions by individual agencies and greater consistency in decision making. "I don't want to overstate it, but I think it's a problem-- whether a giant problem and a disaster, or simply something that needs to be fine tuned. We need to see if we are doing the job right, because it's costing a lot of money. Not only government money, but in the private economy."

On a personal level, however, "almost nothing bugs me about this job," Herdman says. "By and large it's a great place to work. And wonderful, really, to have the best and the brightest. You feel you're really making a contribution."

Key Relationships

Within the OTA

Reports to: Director

Works closely with:

Other Assistant Directors
General Counsel

Outside the OTA

Chairmen, members and staff of congressional committees, notably including the Senate Finance, Commerce and Agriculture committees, the House Ways and Means and Energy and Commerce committees, and the Veterans Affairs committees of both houses
Officials of executive branch agencies with responsibilities in health and life sciences
General Accounting Office
Congressional Research Service
Congressional Budget Office

Outside the Government

A very broad range of private sector companies, academic institutions, professional societies, nonprofit organizations, labor unions, advocacy groups, and individuals engaged in health issues, health care, biomedical research, health technology, medical practice, energy and agriculture.

Profile of Current Assistant Director
Health and Life Science, OTA

Name: Roger C. Herdman

Assumed Position: 1983

Career Summary: Vice president, Memorial Sloan-Kettering Institute, 1979-83
Director of public health, state of New York, 1977-79
Deputy commissioner, Department of Health, state of New York,
1969-77; concurrently, assistant professor and professor of
pediatrics, respectively, University of Minnesota and Albany
Medical College, 1966-79
Physician, U.S. Navy, 1959-61

Education: Yale University, BA (magna cum laude), 1955; Yale School of
Medicine, MD, 1958

Assistant Directors, Health and Life Science, OTA
Since 1978*

Name and Years Served	Present Position
Roger C. Herdman 1983 - present	Incumbent
David Banta 1982	Amsterdam, The Netherlands
Joyce Lashof 1978 - 1981	Dean, School of Public Health University of California Berkeley, Cal.

* The Health and Life Science Division of the OTA was established in its present form
in 1978

INDEX OF NAMES